THE MITCHELL BEAZLEY

LONDON
PROPERTY
GUIDE

'89

The London Property Guide

From reviews in the national Press and professional journals:

'The London Property Guide is well thought out and superbly put together . . . it is thickly packed with information – and all of it is to the point. Carrie Segrave gives a clear insight into how the property scene works.'

The Daily Telegraph

'Its main strength is an area-by-area analysis of the local property markets in a vast central slice of Greater London that follows closely the familiar area-codes of the A-Z London Street Atlas. The London Property Guide helps de-mystify a bemusingly complex city.'

The Financial Times

'. . . masses of useful facts, solid information and a leavening of sturdy and well-argued opinion by the editor and others. Although there are over 600 pages, they are well-written, designed and illustrated: an extremely valuable addition to anybody's bookshelf.'

London Portrait

'There is an enormous amount of information for London home-buyers and sellers in this new guide which looks set to become a regular annual publication.'

Estates Gazette

'For purchasers lost in the maze that comprises London's streets, Mitchell Beazley has produced the London Property Guide, the most objective and comprehensive handbook yet on the capital's housing market. Full of information such as turn-of-the-year prices, maps, details of schools and estate agents, it profiles each of London's areas in turn.'

The Independent

'London-based estate agents and developers should find plenty of excellent information in the new London Property Guide.'

Chartered Surveyor Weekly

'If you are searching for a house in London, or simply want to keep up to date with house prices in your area, you should reach for this informative annual.

The Sunday Times

'The London Property Guide is the book for those who own, or want to own, in London. It covers the area district by district giving prices, local features, agents, schools and transport. There are excellent articles on topics like investment and planning.'

The Daily Mail

'The London Property Guide details streets to watch in warts-and-all reports. The book's 600 pages are stuffed with facts, charts and maps.'

The Daily Express

'Assiduous reading will enable the buyer to find where the bargains are.'

The Times

THE MITCHELL BEAZLEY

LONDON PROPERTY GUIDE

'89

FOR BUYERS, SELLERS AND OWNERS OF HOMES IN LONDON

EDITED BY

CARRIE SEGRAVE

The Mitchell Beazley London Property Guide 1989
Edited and designed by Mitchell Beazley International Ltd, Artists
House, 14–15 Manette Street, London W1V 5LB

ISBN 0 85533 744 3

The author and the publishers will be grateful for any information
which will assist them in keeping future editions up to date.
Although all reasonable care has been taken in the preparation of
this book neither the publishers nor the author can accept any
liability for any consequences arising from the use thereof or from
the information contained herein.

Typeset by Bookworm Typesetting, Manchester
Reproduction by M & E Repro, Maldon
Printed and bound in Great Britain by William Clowes Ltd., Beccles

Editor and chief writer Carrie Segrave
Editorial Assistant Alessandra Perotto

Designed by Stephen Bull Associates

Production Controller Ted Timberlake

Computer Consultant Alexandra Boyle

Advertising sales: Carmen Compton (01-439 7211)

Senior Executive Editor Chris Foulkes
Senior Executive Art Editor Roger Walton

Maps Lynn Chadwick (Garden Studios)
Vignettes Tony Meadows (Garden Studios)
Architectural styles Arthur Baker

Contributors to 1988 edition

David Allison, Lucy Ash, Robert Ashton, Sue Balding, Rowena Chapman, Mary Comerford, Eljay Crompton, Keren David, Ruth Elliott, Katie Frankel, Naomi Fulop, Eddie Gershon, Sandra Grant, Elizabeth Hammond, Alison Higgins, Stephen Irving, Donu Kogbara, Mark Langlands, Mark Leslie, Matthew Lewin, Sue Mallia, Kay Marles, Debbie Martyr, Juliet Moss, Grant Prior, Karen Robinson, Gerard Sagar, Andrea Sangster, Shelagh Shone, John Smith, Max Velody, Roger Walton, Caroline Wilkins, Howard Willows, Helen Wood.

Additional contributors to the 1989 edition

Cornelius Alexander, Robyn Bechelet, Diana Durant, Sarah Griffin, Anthony Griffin, Simon Hopper, Rose Lloyd, Sarah Paget, Sarah Polden, Caroline Proud, Ruth Rothenberg, Simon Ryder, Philip Stiles.

Specialist writers and consultants

John Brennan, Peter Camp, Shirley Green, David Spittles, Daniel Taub, Susan Ware, Peter Wilby.

With thanks to:

Joanna Alexandroff, Linda Beaney, Richard Bernstein, Tony Botham, Martin Carleton-Smith, Zena Clayton, Alan Collett, Nigel Conradi, Margaret Cox, Audrey Druce, Lee Epstein, David Foster, Aviva Gershuny-Roth, Elaine Godwin-Brown, Suzanne Goldklang, Dominic Grace, Catherine Hassler, Tony Halstead, Giles Harbottle, Sheila Hyams, Julia Hesselberg, Valerie Hopkins, Judy Jackson, Tim Jackson-Stops, Julia Kaye, Anthony Lassman, Stuart Lawson, Sheila Lesser, Desmond Low, Jennifer Love, Helen Mars, Margaret McKenzie, Victoria Mitchell, Peter Morley, Alessandra Perotto, Alison Pilpel, Mark Pitman, Prudential Property Services for data for price trends graphs, Lis Rolls, Hope Samuel, Savills Docklands for Docklands research data, Bob Saxton, Alan Selby, Nina Shaw, Juliet Stait, Suzy Stone, Louise Sylvester, Ray Taylor, John Thorogood, Elizabeth Toppin, Edward Tufton, Adam & Susan Winton, John Wilcox, Vanessa Wood, and all the people in estate agents' offices and the property business who gave up their time to help our contributors.

Contents

Introduction

This Guide reports each year on London as a city to live in: not tourists' London, or historic London, but the place where millions of people have their homes. It is for house- and flat-hunters, for those selling a property and those investing. It is also, if you like, an annual report for everyone who owns a London home: an appraisal of the city that they have a stake in.

This is a new sort of survey of London: an attempt primarily to chart its different areas and their residential streets and neighbourhoods, and secondly to include within one book the facts about the current market in homes, the nuts and bolts of the property business, the changes that will affect the various districts over the next 12 months.

The heart of the book is an area-by-area description of London's residential neighbourhoods from 'A' for Acton to 'W' for Wimbledon. And you will also find chapters covering mortgages, choosing and instructing an estate agent, the legal steps in a sale. And – of particular importance this year – information on factors about to affect the value of every home in the capital: the new Community Charge ('poll tax'), the new Housing Act, the changes to London's education, and the plans for new road, rail and underground links. Plus guidance on how to approach 1989's market for homes.

The Guide has been completely updated for 1989. Every area has been re-researched, and we include the details of hundreds of new developments, from penthouses in the West End to six thousand new homes for Greenwich. Prices have been updated in January this year, thus giving a 'freeze-frame' picture of the start of the 1989 market.

Transport is the biggest talking point for 1989, as London comes close to a total halt. Government plans to invest billions in both roads and public transport could make a radical difference to the shape of London. Although it should be stressed that these are just proposals they must be watched – especially if your home, or one you consider buying, is in the path of one of the schemes. You could either find your fortune made or your house knocked down. Some areas could find themselves 15 minutes closer to the centre of town – with a consequent boost to property values.

The boroughs come into greater prominence this year as a factor in deciding where to live. Rates have always varied, sometimes dramatically, from borough to borough. But since the replacement Community Charge is to be paid per adult, not per home, large families thinking of moving may well think twice about the spending record of the council they will be taxed by. Similar thoughts will attend those moving with a school-aged family. With the abolition next year of the Inner London Education Authority, each borough will be responsible for its own schools. This not only has financial implications – some boroughs have far more children than others, and the cost will, again, show up in the poll tax – but the education policies they each adopt will vary widely. The 'Boroughs' and 'Education' chapters in this Guide form a briefing on the poll tax and schools debates.

As for the fate of the property market this year, there are already signs as we go to press of a spring awakening after the long, quiet winter in which prices finally took a breather from their seemingly inexorable upwards spiral. 'The market is no more a cast-iron money-spinner than any other form of

Winkworth

YOUR FIRST CALL
01-351 7465

Why not make Winkworth your first call? With over
40 offices, each one handling an extensive range of
properties from the smallest studio to the largest
family house, Winkworth offers unrivalled coverage
of London both north and south of the river. Each office
can offer you specialist local knowledge, and our total
understanding of the business was recently recognised
when we were judged 'Best Estate Agent' by
What House Magazine.

So, if you want to know about property in London, from
Catford to Palmers Green, from Bow to Knightsbridge or
from Notting Hill to Fulham,
make Winkworth your first call.

investment: what goes up can come down', we said in the introduction to the first edition last year. The London market was overdue for a slow-down: there was in early 1988 no longer any particular reason why property prices should race ahead of inflation, and we predicted a peaceful year with prices going up just ahead of the cost of living. No-one, however, legislated for the Lawson Factor: the Chancellor's Budget prolonged the buy-at-any-price fever; and then his autumn action to control inflation by forcing an increase of interest (and therefore mortgage) rates brought the market to a startled halt.

Both acts were, to say the least, unfortunate. Not for the market as a whole: prices, despite the more lurid headlines, are unlikely in the extreme to 'plummet through the floor'. The underlying strength is there, and so are the funds; for a full analysis, see 'The Property Market in 1989' and the 'Investment in Property' chapters. But to encourage the spread of home ownership, as this government has done, and to create an artificial boost as did the Budget by announcing the imminent ending of multiple mortgage relief – and then to slam on the brakes via interest rates, is hardly subtle stuff.

The effect is to damage precisely those people who had just struggled onto the bottom rung of the property ladder. Prices overall did not 'plummet'. People do not accept less than they believe their home is worth: unless they really have to sell, they sit tight until things improve. But those forced by increased mortgages to sell homes they had bought only months earlier at the very top of the market were left in a very dangerous position. Quite a few hapless first-time buyers learnt the hard way last winter that mortgage rates can go up very fast – and that sometimes it's tough to sell a house quickly, at least if you do not want to take a loss.

A major reason why the prices of homes are unlikely to drop steeply is the abundant supply of funds. Mortgages may be pricey, but they are plentiful. The days of mortgage famine are gone, and not only building societies but banks and foreign financiers are anxious to lend on the security of bricks and mortar in England's capital. Because of this competition among lenders, rules have been relaxed. Lenders are prepared to advance a much larger percentage of the overall price of a home than they used to. And they are also happy to base the loan on much more generous multiples of people's earnings. This, then, is the trap: somebody borrowing 90 per cent or more of the cost of a home, against an inadequate or insecure income, may well then be forced to sell when interest rates soar. At that point they may, unless they bought very wisely, find themselves able to sell for only, say, 80 per cent of what they paid. They can thus end up in debt. This bludgeoning of ordinary peoples' pockets and expectations is no way to control the wider economy.

First-time buyers should be aware of this possible trap and calculate whether they can afford a higher monthly repayment than that which is current when they buy. Government ministers should be aware of the undoubted loss of votes if they jeopardise people's hard-won homes. and perhaps the City and the building societies can find a way to slow the abrupt swings in mortgage interest rates. For a 25-year loan to fluctuate like the price of a penny share seems unnecessary, even ridiculous.

But first-time buyers are not the whole market: there are plenty of people moving who do not rely on mortgage finance. All this augurs, then, for the mark-time period in 1989 that was expected in '88. There will be homes around at good, sensible prices – and some downright bargains. This will be a great market for cash buyers. But buyers will find it pays not to count on them, and not to delay deciding on a house they like in the hopes of a rash of cut-price properties round the corner. In a quiet market, anything of real quality will sell; if thing stay somnolent, good new homes will not be offered for sale, and the choice will get smaller and less interesting. This is the effect of a stagnant market: buyers looking for types of homes that are just not for sale, and a help of mediocre homes, wearily chasing buyers.

The casualties of such a quiet period are estate agents. This is something of a historical first. The explosion of agencies in recent years could only be sustained by an everlasting boom. As soon as the excitement subsided, we saw signs of second thoughts. Already the first building society-owned estate agent has begun to close large numbers of offices. This is hardly surprising, since the reason behind the great buy-up of agencies by the societies and others was primarily to give themselves ready-made additional shopfronts from which to sell mortgages, insurance and the like, rather than to cash in on the agency profits. This business fell away as people stopped buying last winter. To be profitable, agencies don't need ever-rising prices; but they do need a good, brisk turnover of sales. It's questionable whether the insurance companies will stay loyal to their new acquisitions when they fail to show up well in the accounts.

In a perfect world, the quieter conditions would shake out, even more than such lumbering chains, the incompetent and the frankly dubious agencies who have come crowding in, in the last few years. In last year's introduction I drew attention to this situation,and predicted that it was something we would be hearing much more about. I suggested that 'the game had changed; the rules must catch up – fast.' After considerable further publicity, there is better news on this front. In the middle of last year, the government, not keen on any suggestion of a closed shop, declined to implement the missing clause of the 1979 Estate Agents Act that would force agents to meet set standards of competence. Instead, ministers urged the property business to put its own house in order and bring in self-regulation. The professional bodies, who seemed oblivious of the problems facing their industry – cowboy estate agents, gazumping, a rapid decline in public esteem – at last got their act together. A joint committee is working on ways to tidy things up. Meanwhile, two North London 'estate agents' are serving prison terms for deception, the publicity over which acted as a useful spur to their respectable brethren.

However it is necessary to reiterate my call in last year's Guide for trained and qualified estate agents. At the very least, offices should be supervised by those who are qualified. One of the professional bodies observed recently that the property business is polarising. The qualified professionals are moving out of hands-on house agency into the development and consultancy side, leaving you and I to buy and sell homes via untrained youngsters at best enthusiastic and at worst incompetent. Perhaps estate agents could use the quieter times of 1989 to train their junior staff.

· · · · ·

This book is the product of not only the expertise but the immense hard work and enthusiasm of a great – in both senses of the word – team of people. They are recorded on pages 4 and 5, but I would like here to add my personal thanks and acknowledge my debt to all the contributors from all over London, to my lynch-pin assistant Ali Perotto, and most of all to Jack Tresidder of Mitchell Beazley whose brainchild it was and to Chris Foulkes who made it happen.
Carrie Segrave

London, January 1989

SAVILLS

ATTENTION TO DETAIL

Choosing the right agent to handle your property matters is as important as your choice of Bank Manager, Solicitor or Accountant.

You expect:—

- Efficient and thoughtful service.

- Specialist knowledge and sound advice.

Savills work particularly hard to ensure that every client, from the initial introduction, receives excellent service and considerate personal attention.

We offer a wide range of top quality London houses and flats, and comprehensive Rentals, Professional and Investment, and Marketing Services.

How to use this book

The core of this book is an alphabetical directory of London's residential areas, from 'A' for Acton to 'W' for Wimbledon. Each area is profiled, with descriptions of the neighbourhoods it is made up of.

Supporting chapters introduce this core of information. These cover the state of the property market in 1989, the prospects for London this year, new transport plans, the new education and poll tax systems – all the detail you need to decide where to live in London.

To find out about an **area**, look for it in the A-Z section which starts on page 143. The initial letter of the area covered is printed in the margin of each right-hand page to aid speedy reference. A list of the areas covered is on page 145.

There is also a full index of streets and neighbourhoods at the back of the book.

Postal districts are listed on pages 54–58, each with a description of the areas it covers. Start with this list if you only know the postcode you are looking for.

Boroughs are profiled in a section starting on page 59. A map on page 60 shows their boundaries – as does the Area Key Map on pages 146–7.

Maps are provided at the start of each area chapter. A key to the symbols used in these is on page 145. See opposite for how to make the best use of the maps and the information pages which accompany them. These pages are for quick reference to the key facts about an area.

Prices: as an annual, this book is not intended as a price guide. It does, however, gather together average prices for different sizes of property in each of the areas, and thus provides a 'freeze-frame' picture taken at the start of the 1989 selling season. This gives you a basis for comparison throughout the year. For prices in a given area see the relevant Area Information Page (see opposite). See also the main price charts on pages 28–31 where you can search across London by price or flat/house size.

Future editions: this book is as accurate as the combined efforts of a large number of people could make it. This is the second edition, there will be a new one every year: we would be grateful to receive news from readers about changes to areas and any other comments and (constructive!) criticism. Thank you to those who took the time to do so last year.

The Area Information Pages

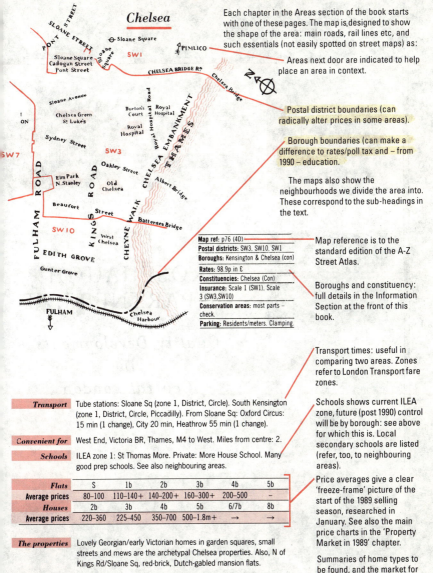

Chelsea

Each chapter in the Areas section of the book starts with one of these pages. The map is designed to show the shape of the area: main roads, rail lines etc, and such essentials (not easily spotted on street maps) as:

Areas next door are indicated to help place an area in context.

Postal district boundaries (can radically alter prices in some areas).

Borough boundaries (can make a difference to rates/poll tax and – from 1990 – education.

The maps also show the neighbourhoods we divide the area into. These correspond to the sub-headings in the text.

Map ref: p76 (4D)	
Postal districts: SW3, SW10, SW1	
Boroughs: Kensington & Chelsea (con)	
Rates: 98.9p in £	
Constituencies: Chelsea (Con)	
Insurance: Scale 1 (SW1). Scale 3 (SW3,SW10)	
Conservation areas: most parts – check.	
Parking: Residents/meters. Clamping.	

Map reference is to the standard edition of the A-Z Street Atlas.

Boroughs and constituency: full details in the Information Section at the front of this book.

Transport times: useful in comparing two areas. Zones refer to London Transport fare zones.

Transport — Tube stations: Sloane Sq (zone 1, District, Circle). South Kensington (zone 1, District, Circle, Piccadilly). From Sloane Sq: Oxford Circus: 15 min (1 change), City 20 min, Heathrow 55 min (1 change).

Convenient for — West End, Victoria BR, Thames, M4 to West. Miles from centre: 2.

Schools — ILEA zone 1: St Thomas More. Private: More House School. Many good prep schools. See also neighbouring areas.

Schools shows current ILEA zone, future (post 1990) control will be by borough: see above for which this is. Local secondary schools are listed (refer, too, to neighbouring areas).

Flats	S	1b	2b	3b	4b	5b
Average prices	80–100	110–140+	140–200+	160–300+	200–500	–
Houses	2b	3b	4b	5b	6/7b	8b
Average prices	220–360	225–450	350–700	500–1.8m+	→	→

Price averages give a clear 'freeze-frame' picture of the start of the 1989 selling season, researched in January. See also the main price charts in the 'Property Market in 1989' chapter.

The properties — Lovely Georgian/early Victorian homes in garden squares, small streets and mews are the archetypal Chelsea properties. Also, N of Kings Rd/Sloane Sq, red-brick, Dutch-gabled mansion flats.

Summaries of home types to be found, and the market for them, encapsulate the chapter for quick reference.

The market — Five years ago there were still scruffy streets in Chelsea. Now prices reflect the depth of the facelift, the length of the lease. Exceptional properties go well over the mainstream averages above. Local searches: 7 days.

Search times can vary from days to months between boroughs – often the downfall of a sale.

Highfields Grove, Highgate, N6

7-10 Connaught Place, W2

84 Cadogan Square / 1a Clabon Mews, SW1

Alexandra Court, 5 Moscow Road, W2

ROSEHAUGH
COPARTNERSHIP
DEVELOPMENTS LIMITED

Quality Developments
in
Central London

Entrance to Pencombe Mews, Denbigh Road, W11

53-55 QUEEN ANNE STREET, LONDON W1M 0LJ

13-23 Evelyn Gardens, SW7

2 Hyde Park Street, W2

Trinity Court, Gloucester Terrace, W2

Crown Court, 123 Park Road, NW8

11, 12 & 13 Kent Terrace, NW1

51/52 Hans Place, SW1

Rosehaugh Copartnership is the residential development subsidiary of Rosehaugh plc, which has specialised in the provision of high quality accommodation within the Central London area since 1980. From Highgate to Regent's Park, Hyde Park to Kensington, Tower Bridge to Canary Wharf.

The care and attention to detail we put into all our projects, whether it be the conversion of a terrace of period houses or the building of luxury new properties, has earned us an enviable reputation and one which we are determined to maintain.

Working with many of the major landowners, and on our own sites, we have had the opportunity to bring our skills and expertise to bear on complicated development situations which offer their own special challenge. That in turn has enabled us to gauge successfully the sort of new houses and apartments in which people prefer to live.

The Millbank Terraces, SW1

TELEPHONE 01-486 7100, TELEX 28167, FAX 01-935 0277

Pencombe Mews, Denbigh Road, W11

New Mill Wharf, Mill Street, SE1

New Caledonian Wharf, Odessa Street, SE16

The Anchorage, Cuba Street, E14

London

in

1989

What a house or flat is like to live in, and how much it costs to buy and is worth when you sell, depends upon a compex matrix of factors. These can be as mundane as the postcode and as esoteric as the architectural style. Decisions made by civil servants on new roads and tube lines, or by the local Town Hall on schools or the new poll tax, can and will affect your peace, your well-being – and, because your home's value is involved, your wealth.

This first section of the Guide aims to inform Londoners on what is happening to their city in 1989, to assemble in one place those hard-to-find facts on transport, schools, rates and local politics. It begins with an analysis of the property market in 1989, with unique charts showing the January price range for every size of home in 80 areas, plus an indication of their relative abundance or scarcity. Next, the field widens to assess the prospects for London as a going concern in 1989 with a briefing on the key issues – poll tax, planning, population – and a check-list of points to watch in 1989. London's creaking transport systems are at a turning point, and a chapter is devoted to the exciting plans for their future. These plans will, if they come about, change the way we look at large areas of London – and will have a dramatic effect on individuals and their homes. And next year the whole of London's school system gets a shake-up, with far-reaching consequences for our children and, as areas' reputations rise and fall, for property values.

Taken together, these chapters are an annual report for Londoners on the progress of their biggest single investment. Through our homes, we are all shareholders in the city.

Backing up the analysis are chapters decoding the arcane London post codes and listing the areas they cover, the boroughs with key facts and policies, the MPs who represent London, and the domestic architecture of the city and where the different kinds of home can be found.

The Property Market in 1989

The real action on house prices in 1988 was not in the capital but in the previously moribund Midlands and North, where rises of up to 50 per cent were recorded. London, for once, fell behind in the percentage rise race, evidence of a recurring pattern in homes market cycles: London moves first and stops first. But this year there was a particular reason for the sudden jamming on of the brakes:

The Year of the Chancellor

There were well-based expectations that in 1988 the London property market would return to equilibrium. The 1987 stock market crash had put a stop to speculation in property 'futures', and, in January '88, all the predictions were for quiet times. No bust, but after five years of steeply rising prices, no boom either. As it turned out, the boom had another seven months to run, thanks to an unexpected influence from outside the property world: the Lawson Factor.

1988 was, in property at least, the Year of the Chancellor. His Budget measures, and their sequel, affected the homes market in three ways. First, the tax cuts put substantial sums into the pockets of many Londoners. Second, the ending of multiple mortgage tax relief on one property created a deadline. Anyone wanting to take advantage of this valuable tax break had to have a deal done by August 1. The giddy upward spiral, which had faltered after Black Monday, was on again. Third, the sudden turn-around in interest rate policy lifted the cost of mortgages from the lowest in this decade to close to the highest. The net result of all three: from a frenetic July, everyone had to adjust to a very quiet October.

The unexpected abolition of all the higher-rate tax bands made quite a few Londoners several thousand pounds a year better off. These predominantly middle-aged people were the natural buyers of family homes. Lower down the market, every unmarried couple and group of friends who had talked about buying a flat but done nothing were given a deadline by the Budget. Estate agents were besieged by anxious buyers and the price of every two-bedroomed flat in London shot up.

This market was fuelled by virtually unlimited mortgage funds. The building societies, flush with funds from investors disillusioned with the stock market, had ample cash to lend. And they were joined by banks of every sort. In December '87 the building societies (who provide over half the mortgage funds in this country) committed to lend £2.9 billion. By July they were lending £5.4 billion per month. And by November the figure was down to £3.4 billion and indications were that the January '89 figure would be back under £3 billion.

People who borrowed at 9.5 or 10 per cent in the summer were badly stung by the rapid rise to around 13 per cent by Christmas – by which time it was plain that there was worse to come in the New Year. First-time buyers were especially hard-hit, with the added discomfort of having to face static, or even falling, prices, which meant that even selling up and going home to mother could mean a financial penalty. Despite this, mortgage defaults dropped during the course of the year.

By late in the year, newspapers which had been breathlessly reporting rocketing prices in the summer were gleefully talking of falling markets and 'desperate sellers'. Property professionals, eager with a bullish quote in buoyant times, were indignant when the press turned on them. In truth, up to the turn of the year, very few distress sales were happening. Asking prices had indeed fallen from the often wildly optimistic levels of the summer and were in many cases back to where they started the year. The stock market was too.

But unfortunately for bargain hunters, buyers found on close inspection that the tales of plunging prices related to few and specific cases only. Across the board the reaction of homeowners to prices which had certainly stopped rising was sullen inactivity. Only those who absolutely had to sell were prepared to take reductions on what they imagined their homes were worth. The few who did so comprised, first and foremost, not private homeowners so much as developers. Some, especially the smaller ones, needed to turn their stock into cash quickly. Some owner-occupiers had to move for job or family reasons. Others, but not many, found themselves over-stretched, having borrowed heavily, and traded down to smaller homes to reduce their outgoings.

The great majority of homeowners, however, simply stayed put. Which was a good thing since the number of buyers, especially first-timers, dropped even more than is customary over the winter. Much as in the weeks after Black Monday in 1987, estate agents' offices were empty and (in one instance) the staff were discovered playing Trivial Pursuits. The Chancellor breathed an audible sigh of relief, as taking the steam out of the housing market was a crucial plank in his policy of slowing down the economy.

The above generalisations have more to do with first-time buyers and the lower half of the market – which relies the most on borrowing funds – generally. Throughout the autumn agents were able to point to good, indeed, sometimes record, sales in the upper half of the market. This points to two truths: first, that the homes market in London is now highly fragmented and second, that even in a quiet market quality sells. There are still many people whose house-buying capacity was neither depleted by the stock market crash, nor reliant on cheap mortgage funds. They will continue to chase the best properties in whichever bracket they are looking.

All this has to be set in the context of the revolution in the London property market which has taken place throughout the '80s. (This was fully described in last year's Guide). One point worth stressing is the dramatic rise in the number of new homes being built in London. About half the action is in Docklands, but anyone who looks around will see new homes appearing in every corner of town. A decade ago the choice of a new home rather than a 'second-hand' one was just not available. And competition from new homes has forced developers to greatly improve the standard of conversions of period homes into flats.

The picture in 1989

So what will happen this year? Within the property market there are strong reasons why home prices will not rise dramatically. And equally strong ones why they will not gratify doom merchants by crashing through the floor. Before we discuss them, though there is one big caveat – and that is what happens in the wider world.

A recession in the world economy is by many calculations overdue. Such a calamity would have effects on property as on every other kind of market. There are fears that some of the world's banks are not as firmly based as they should be. And a recession could lead to some of the more exotic ones suddenly disappearing from the UK mortgage market. This could quickly tighten the supply of funds. Set against this is the confidence international finance has in London property, where you can lend at 13 per cent on the security of bricks and mortar. World confidence in the British government is also high. What is more, recession could equally well mean lower interest rates, which could be a positive factor for the property market. Much depends on how the London financial services businesses weather the storm: 23 per cent of the South-East's gross 'national' product comes from financial services.

Given no recession, however, these are the points which will shape this year's property market:

● Buyers are having to spend a historically high percentage of their income on mortgage payments. Across the country, the average for first-time buyers late last year was 25.7 per cent of net income going on repayments. In London, the figure was 33 per cent. And the figures were taken before the January hike in mortgage payments. They are higher than any recorded in the 1980s or 1970s. They back up another vital figure:

● The ratio between house prices and earnings is at its highest ever level. The national peak of 4.56 reached in the third quarter of 1988 was well in excess of previous peaks in years such as 1973 and 1979 – after both of which the market slumped. And the figure for London is well over 5. The normal ratio is, the graphs tell us, about 3 to 3.6 times annual income.

● The last two years saw many middle-class Londoners getting windfall sums from the sale of businesses, buy-outs, golden 'hellos' and handshakes. These seem to have fallen away and the unexpected bonanza, with its consequent decision to trade up, will be less in evidence in 1989.

Inference from these points: prices are not going to shoot up during 1989. But will they fall?

● There is no shortage of funds for mortgages. And it would take some outside cataclysm (recession? Chancellor?) to turn off the flow. This makes the fundamental difference between the situation now and that in 1974 or in 1981-2. It is lack of funds that really stops a market in its tracks. Moreover, fewer and fewer buyers are wholly reliant on borrowing.

● Wealth is far greater and more widely-spread than in earlier periods of gloom. Inheritance from home-owning parents and grandparents has recently emerged as a new and significant factor. Inheritance is putting billions each year into the bank accounts of quite ordinary people, who then are able to trade up in the housing market and (crucially) to help their sons and daughters onto the ladder. It is fair to say that without inheritance and loans from family there would be far fewer young buyers of London property.

● Salaries of managers and directors went up sharply in 1988, as did company profits. The woes of a relatively few sacked City whizz-kids caught the headlines, but most London businesses are doing well and rewarding their people. This means more money spent on homes.

- Most Londoners have little choice but to buy a home as soon as they can and thereafter stay as owner-occupiers. The choice enjoyed by their Continental cousins, of moving into the rented sector when property doesn't look like a good investment, is denied them. Changes in the rental scene will make a difference to the chronic lack of reasonable homes to rent – but not yet.

The homes market is thus illiquid. In bad times, owners refuse to take less money than they think their homes are worth – and stay put.

- People who last year might have moved out of town altogether are more likely to stay in the London market this year: the ripple effect has lessened the disparity between London prices and the rest of the country, and threats from British Rail of large increases for the long-distance commuter will also cause second thoughts.

- Forecasts of the demand for housing in London keep inexorably ahead of likely supply: see 'Prospects for London'.

Inference from these: home prices across the board are most unlikely to plunge, but things could well stay quiet, with mediocre homes hanging on the market and perhaps, paradoxically, a shortage of good ones for sale as their owners decide to wait for better times.

The year of the good deal

Buyers – particularly those with ready funds – will be courted this year. Firstly, there will be no shortage of choice of new homes – particularly flats – as builders and developers find themselves marketing the schemes begun in heady '87 in the quieter times of '89. The developers will be offering incentives to smooth the path of buyers – particularly of the valuable first-timer with no home of his own to dispose of before he can buy. These incentives can include paying solicitors' fees, stamp duty, moving costs as well as reductions for quick sales. Subsidised mortgages for the first year or so are also appearing. Another trend is to market property on the basis of what it costs the buyer per week or month, allowing a quick comparison with renting.

In slow times, developers, agents and even the private vendor have to work hard to capture the shy buyer. The big builders and developers are not afraid to spend considerable amounts on this, and you as a valued customer can benefit. But don't buy a second-rate property just because it's got a first-rate package wrapped around it. You, too, will have to sell the place sometime – and without the benefit of all that marketing muscle.

In the market for second-hand homes there will certainly be a few bargains to be had as speculators who bought the wrong home at the wrong price (wrong that is, for quick-buck purposes) cut their losses. Some longer-term investors whose properties have already appreciated may well decide that there are now more lucrative havens for their money and also decide to sell. (See also the Investing in Property chapter). Certainly asking prices will look more reasonable as last year's wild optimists stop trying to fool buyers into paying £20,000 over the odds.

The key this year will be to buy a home in which you will be happy to settle down for several years. This particularly applies in areas where much new development has been taking place. Not only are you unlikely to see a large leap in the value of your home in the short term, but any place is more difficult to sell – let alone sell well – while there are attractive brand-new homes with all the developers' packages attached also on the market.

A year of financial prudence

The advice to gear yourself to the hilt, to borrow as much as possible to buy the best home you can, got some of those who followed it into trouble last winter. Most households can, with some belt-tightening, survive a period of higher mortgage repayments. What can cause trouble for some is borrowing too large a percentage of the price of a home. If – for whatever reason – such a highly-geared borrower finds it necessary to sell in a stagnant period having borrowed, say 90 per cent of the cost, then he/she is in trouble if they can only get 80 per cent of what they paid. These are the real casualties; the vast majority of Londoners will scrape up the mortgage money until interest rates are allowed to fall and salaries rise to close the wage/house price gap – and prices in the pressured London market start rising again.

We move fast so you can.

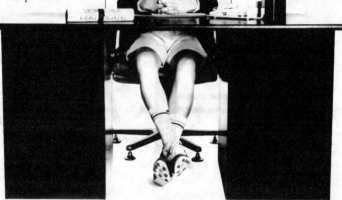

Finding the right home can take months. Losing it can take no time at all.

At Lloyds Bank, we pride ourselves on our turn of speed.

Once you've settled in your new home, we offer personal loans to help you improve and furnish it.

Even before you start searching, we can give you a certificate confirming your mortgage.

When you do hit home, the money will be yours fast and without much formality.

We offer endowment, pension-linked and repayment mortgages all at our competitive Mort-gage Rate.

If you are a first time buyer we offer advances of up to 95%.

For old hands 90% is our usual maximum.

Our usual maximum related to salary is three times your gross basic annual income, though joint borrowers can apply for a rather larger sum.

As well as a Cashflow Account to help you run it.

We also offer home and contents insurance.

For full details on our services to home buyers call in at any one of our branches.

We'll act immediately.

 **Lloyds Bank**

THE THOROUGHBRED BANK.

Ham

Where your London property tour starts...

PTONS

and finishes.

Whether you are looking for a London home or an investment
we offer the definitive guide to the finest property — from new
developments alongside the Royal Parks, Hampstead Heath
and the River Thames to a wide range of houses and
apartments of individual character.

All with international experience, our service departments
specialise in marketing, furnished letting, management,
valuations, surveys and finance.

Assembly Points:

Head Office: 01-493 8222. Barnes: 01-741 1063. Battersea: 01-585 1915. Barnet: 01-441 6776.
Catford: 01-698 2232. Chelsea: 01-835 1444. Crofton Park: 01-691 1111. Docklands: 01-790 3311.
East Sheen: 01-876 0115. Forest Hill: 01-699 1181. Fulham: 01-736 8211. Hampstead: 01-794 8222.
Islington: 01-226 4688. Lewisham: 01-463 0911. Norbury: 01-764 9499. Putney: 01-788 0034.
St. Johns Wood: 01-586 5999. Southfields: 01-789 7007. Streatham: 01-677 7677.
Sydenham: 01-778 5173. Upper Norwood: 01-761 6424. Wimbledon: 01-946 0081.

Price band indicator

This chart consolidates the data in the area surveys in this book, showing in broad terms what certain kinds of homes cost in each of the areas covered. This gives you a freeze-frame picture across London at the start of the 1989 selling season; a basis for comparison throughout the year.

   The prices given are for typical examples of the type of home. Where a range of figures is shown, this reflects price variations within the area: some streets command higher prices than others. Thus the range is also an indicator of the scope of the properties in the area: if the figures for, say, a 2-bed flat are 65-75 it is likely to be a fairly homogenous area; between £65,000 and £75,000 should give you a choice of such flats here. If 65-115, it becomes clear that

FLATS

Key					
65-75: range in £1000s	→ price carries over – too few for price average		◀ supply decreasing ▶ supply increasing		▮ scarce ▮ plentiful

	Studio	1 bedroom	2 bedroom	3 bedroom	4 bedroom	5 bedroom +
Acton	52-60	65-72	77-100	90-120	–	
Balham and Tooting	50-60	65-80	75-100+	88-120		
Barnes and Mortlake	58-70	70-85	80-120	110-170	200+	
Battersea	55-65	70-90	85-110+	95-130	150-200	
Bayswater	65-85	80-140	115-285	145-400	300-600	400-1m
Bedford Park	65-75	70-120	85-150	85-190	–	
Belgravia	–	150-300+	250-550+	450-900+	500-1m+	→2m+
Bethnal Green	55-65▶	55-78▶	60-110▶	65-110	–	–
Bloomsbury and King's Cross	55-80	77-140	95-175	125-230	–	–
Bow	48-65▶	55-75▶	60-105▶	70-100	–	
Brixton	46-59	55-72▶	68-85▶	75-95	90-125	
Camberwell	45-50	55-80▶	70-85▶	75-120	–	
Camden Town	60-75	65-95▶	85-150▶	100-170	–	
Chelsea	80-100	110-140+	140-200+	160-300+	200-500	–
Chiswick	60-70	70-100	85-150	100-160	→	
City and fringes	75-95	85-170	110-260	160-300	280-600+	–
Clapham	50-60	65-85	75-110	90-130	130+	
Clerkenwell	55-75	65-100+	90-130+	135+	–	
Cricklewood	45-65	58-75	70-95	80-100+	–	–
Crouch End and Stroud Green	60	63-77	70-130	90+	→	
Crystal Palace	45-55▶	49-65▶	65-85▶	68-77	–	
Dollis Hill and Neasden	52-55	60-70▶	65-80▶	80-90+	–	–
Dulwich	48-60	55-75	70-100+	80-120+	–	
Ealing	61-66	68-83▶	75-110▶	90-125	–	
Earlsfield and Southfields	58-63	68-75	75-90	87-100	–	
Finchley	58-65	65-80	75-160+	85-200+	125-300+	–
Forest Hill	46-53	55-66	65-80	75-85	–	–
Fulham	60-75	80-95	90-130	110-175	150-220+	–
Golders Green	60-70	75-100	80-125+	100-150+	–	–
Greenwich and Blackheath	52-65	60-90	80-130	95-200	–	
Hackney	45-55	50-65	60-80	70-95+	–	–
Hammersmith	70-75	75-90	90-135	115-160+	150+	170+
Hampstead	70-80	90-140	125-250+▶	175-350▶	275-650	350+
Hampstead Garden Suburb	–	70-90	80-130	100-200+	→	–

either there are some neighbourhoods which warrant a good premium, or perhaps there is a good supply of recently-developed, more luxurious flats: see the text for details. In all brackets, you will likely find cheaper (for example, unimproved) examples and/or exceptional ones at the other end of the scale: a plus sign is used where we have not included the prices for a small number of examples which would distort the averages.

Some areas have few of a certain size or type of home. Such scarcity is indicated. Places where certain properties are in good supply are also shown, as are increases/decreases in supply. Conversions and new building can change the balance of supply in an area. A blue arrow showing a decrease in large houses generally indicates that these are being split into flats.

HOUSES

Key					
80-100: range in £1000s	→ price carries over − too few for price average	◄ supply decreasing ► supply increasing		scarce plentiful	

	2 bedroom	3 bedroom	4 bedroom	5 bedroom	6/7 bedroom	8 bedroom
Acton	90-125	110-170	145-225	190-250	→350	300+
Balham and Tooting	90-120	110-160	130-190	150-220	240-300+	275-350
Barnes and Mortlake	125-155	150-220	190-280+	280-360+	350-550+	750-900
Battersea	120-140	135-175	175-200	190-300	250+	–
Bayswater	180-340	240-450	330-500	400-600+	500-1.2m	→
Bedford Park	130-200	160-250	190-375	250-500+	300-800	–
Belgravia	360+	425+	500+	550-2.5m+	→	→7m
Bethnal Green	90-135►	→►	100-150	–	–	–
Bloomsbury and King's Cross	125-250	150-260+	→	→450	–	–
Bow	90-140	100-180	110-200+	◄150-250	–	–
Brixton	85-120	95-135	105-160+	115-180+	◄130+	◄→
Camberwell	80-100	90-150►	100-200+►	120-200+	110-300+	250+
Camden Town	120-180	140-200	190-400+	200-450+	◄→	◄→
Chelsea	220-360	225-450	350-700	500-1.8m+	→	→
Chiswick	120-180	135-300	160-400+	200-650+	350+	–
City and fringes	180-260	200-470	→	–	–	–
Clapham	95-140	120-170+	140-220	155-300+	→	–
Clerkenwell	150-200+	210-350+	→	→	–	–
Cricklewood	80-95	90-125	130-250	185-250+	→	→
Crouch End and Stroud Green	90-110	120-165	140-250	180+	→	
Crystal Palace	76-90	79-135	◄110-200	◄150-200+	◄→300	
Dollis Hill and Neasden	80-90	95-150	125-160+	–	–	
Dulwich	80-140	95-160+	120-200+	165-300+	190-400+	200-500+
Ealing	95-130	110-165	→325	185-375+	–	–
Earlsfield and Southfields	90-125	115-160	165-210	225-350	–	
Finchley	90-120	110-200+	135-250+	150-400	225-400+	300+
Forest Hill	75-85	80-150	100-190	◄130-200+	150-250	
Fulham	150-180	150-220	200-350+	260-400	◄400+	
Golders Green	115+	140-170+	160-300	260-325+	375-500+	
Greenwich and Blackheath	95-150	130-200	190-400+	230-600+	300-1m+	
Hackney	75-100	80-130	90-160	◄110-250		
Hammersmith	130	140-200	180-275+	230-350+	350+	–
Hampstead	200-300	300-400	400-600+	500+	500-1.5m	500-2m+
Hampstead Garden Suburb	120-180	180-350	200-450+	350-750+	→	900+

FLATS

Key					
65-75: range in £1000s	→ price carries over	◀ supply decreasing		scarce	
	– too few for price average	▶ supply increasing		plentiful	

	Studio	1 bedroom	2 bedroom	3 bedroom	4 bedroom	5 bedroom +
Hendon and Mill Hill	55-65	65-85	75-150	80-200+	–	
Highgate	60-65	70-90	90-150	100-200	145-300+	–
Holland Park	60-90	90-125▶	135-250▶	250+▶	350+	→
Islington and Highbury	55-75	66-95	90-160	100-160+	–	
Kennington, Vauxhall and Stockwell	53-60	65-75	72-95+	80-115	110+	
Kensington	80-100+	90-175▶	130-250▶	180-400+	300+	→
Kentish Town and Tufnell Park	55-65	70-95	80-120	120-150+	150+	
Kew and Sheen	58-75	70-95	85-125	115-145	–	–
Kilburn and Kensal Rise	–	68-80	80-120▶	100+		
Knightsbridge	100+	175-230	250-350+	315-600+	500+	850-1m+
Lewisham	46-55	55-65▶	62-75▶	70-80	–	
Leyton and Walthamstow	50-60	57-60	60-70	68-72	–	
Maida Vale	70-80	80-125	100-250	120-250+	200-300+	
Marylebone, Lisson Grove, Fitzrovia	60-90	85-200	130-300+	160-400+	200-600	
Mayfair	70-120	100-200	200-350	275-450	450-1m+	→
Morden, Mitcham, Colliers Wood		60-70	63-80	67-85	–	
Muswell Hill	55-62	65-75	80-100+	100-130	–	
New Cross and Deptford	45-52	53-65	57-75	75-85	–	
Newham	50	53	58	67	–	–
Norwood, Norbury and Gipsy Hill	53-55	55-70▶	65-80▶	→	–	
Notting Hill and North Kensington	70-80	80-120	90-180	140-300+	180-400+	→
Peckham	48-52	55-63	65-75	75-82	–	
Pimlico and Westminster	60-100	95-145▶	125-240▶	180-270	300-400+	–
Poplar	50-60	50-70	55-90+	75-100	–	
Putney	60-70	75-85	90-120+	125-150+	150-175+	180+
Regents Park	–	150-300	250-450+	325-650	600-1m	→
Richmond and Twickenham	60-90	70-120+	80-165+◀	90-220+▶	140+	
Shepherd's Bush	57-65	70-85	85-125	100-140	–	–
Soho and Covent Garden	80-100	115-150	180-225+	250-300	–	
South Kensington, Earl's Court, West Brompton	80-110	100-175▶	130-275+	180-400+▶	325-450+	
Southgate and Palmers Green	58-62	63-72	70-80+	80+	90+	–
St John's Wood	70-85	90-125+	150-200+	225-500	375-500	430+
Stepney, Whitechapel	50-65▶	55-75▶	55-95▶	100+	–	
Stoke Newington	–	55-70	70-85	83-95	100+	–
Streatham	45-60	55-70	65-85	75-95	–	–
Tottenham and Finsbury Park	51-58	56-68▶	65-80▶	70-90+	–	–
Totteridge and Whetstone	55-65	60-70	70-95	75-150	–	–
Wandsworth	60	65-80▶	80-120▶	100-125	–	
Waterloo to Bermondsey	55-65	60-75	75-95	80-100	–	
West Hampstead	60-80	75-95	95-125	140+	170+	
Willesden and Brondesbury Park	55-68	60-80	68-120	80-130+	100+	
Wimbledon, Raynes Park, Merton Park	60-80	65-100	75-150+	90-220+	200+	–

HOUSES

Key
80-100: range in £1000s

→ price carries over
– too few for price average

◄ supply decreasing
► supply increasing

■ scarce
■ plentiful

	2 bedroom	3 bedroom	4 bedroom	5 bedroom	6/7 bedroom	8 bedroom+
Hendon and Mill Hill	100-140	115-250	150-360	200-450	500+	–
Highgate	125-175	155-260+	195-350+	250-400+	350-500+	450-1.2m
Holland Park	200-275	250-350+	375-500+	600-850+	1-2m	→3m+
Islington and Highbury	130-220	160-300+	200-400+	220-450+	450+	–
Kennington, Vauxhall and Stockwell	89-130	125-195	150-235+	200-320+	→	–
Kensington	250-300+	300-375+	360-575+	500-1m	800-1m+	→
Kentish Town and Tufnell Park	130-180	130-190	190-275+	280+	300+	–
Kew and Sheen	125-160	150-275+	185-400+	250-600	400-850	→
Kilburn and Kensal Rise	110-130	140-220	180-280+	180-300+	→	–
Knightsbridge	350	350-500+	500+	750-1.5m+	→	→
Lewisham	70-80	80-110	95-125+	◄120-165	160-240	–
Leyton and Walthamstow	73-80	80-110	90-115	110-125	135-150	–
Maida Vale	125-200	190-300	225-500	350-800	→	→1.2m+
Marylebone, Lisson Grove, Fitzrovia	170-300	200-400	250-450+	350-600+	→	–
Mayfair	275-350	350-550	550-1m	650+	850+	2m+
Morden, Mitcham, Colliers Wood	78-100	85-160	110-200	140-225	–	–
Muswell Hill	100-125	110-165	170-220+	220-260+	◄→	–
New Cross and Deptford	80	75-95+	88-110	110-150	140-170	–
Newham	70	73-85	85-95	110-180+	–	–
Norwood, Norbury and Gipsy Hill	70-90+	80-150	120-170+	140+	150+	200+
Notting Hill and North Kensington	150-200	160-300+	175-400+	350-750	500-800+	1m+
Peckham	80-95	85-115	95-145	110-180+	–	–
Pimlico and Westminster	195-250	280-400	300-500	◄375-600+	◄→	–
Poplar	90-110	100-140	125-160+	→200	–	–
Putney	140-160	170-190	180-270+	250-500+	350-700+	–
Regents Park	250-400	→	400-500+	950-1m+	1.3m+	9m
Richmond and Twickenham	90-190	105-225	165-400+	230-400+	300-800+	→
Shepherd's Bush	115-140	140-180	170-250	200-270+	300-350	–
Soho and Covent Garden	–	500+	→	–	–	–
South Kensington, Earl's Court, West Brompton	200-325+	250-500+	300-500+	◄500+	◄700-1m+	800-1m+
Southgate and Palmers Green	80-125	110-200	125-300+	145-500	160-500+	→
St John's Wood	200+	250-400	400-500	500-1m	900+	1.5m+
Stepney, Whitechapel	95-130	100-160	130-200+	→250	→	–
Stoke Newington	85-100	100-130	100-140+	120-160	130-160+	–
Streatham	80-95	85-150	120-170	140-180+	190-250	200-300+
Tottenham and Finsbury Park	65-90	70-125	90-155	120-170	140-190	
Totteridge and Whetstone	95-125	125-250+	200-400+	250-650+	→	→2m
Wandsworth	95-140	130-170	170-200+	200-225+	300+	–
Waterloo to Bermondsey	80-140+	95-160	110-190	120-200+	250+	–
West Hampstead	120-150	175-210	210-250	280-450+	→	–
Willesden and Brondesbury Park	80-100	90-160	100-200+	185-500+	230-700+	→
Wimbledon, Raynes Park, Merton Park	95-200	120-215	160-400	250-700	400+	500-900

London's most exciting development

Prospects for London

The property market does not exist in a vacuum. Good property professionals and smart homeowners take a wide view of the economy and politics of London, the country and even the world. Local decisions on roads, rates and planning can make or break a deal, and this is true for a flat in West Hampstead as much as for the building of Canary Wharf. This chapter is about the wider context in 1989 and about what might happen next in London.

Running London

For a heady couple of years, London managed very well without a central authority. The GLC having been assassinated by the Government, the job of running the city was split between the boroughs, Whitehall and various ad-hoc committees set up by groups of boroughs. Town halls seemed rather to enjoy having no Big Brother in County Hall to interfere – or steal the limelight. But all was not plain sailing. Councils which had taken on the jobs of running the administration of the ad-hoc committees complained that doing so distracted them from their real job. Even Tory Westminster, darling of the Tory Party for its innovative ways and free-market style, began to question whether a London-wide body was not a good thing after all.

Some aspects of London life are run by city-wide bodies. Transport, health, the police, redevelopment of the great swathe of Docklands, are all run by non-democratic (or only marginally democratic) boards. But as a group of academics who studied London's government concluded: 'these single-minded agencies have evident attractions but one cannot help being uneasy at their proliferation in London, and at the prospect of still further powers and resources being allocated to central government's nominees in the forthcoming reforms of housing and education. London's local government is being diminished.' (Michael Hebbert and Tony Travers, *The London Government Handbook*, Cassell 1988). The authors list almost 100 bodies concerned in some way with running London, from the Seaside and Country Homes Board (staff: nil) to the Inner London Education Authority (staff: 64,500). Maps in their book make the point: there are nearly 30 different ways of dividing up London for various specialised purposes. And nearly every one has a different set of boundaries.

Pressure grows for a London-wide forum to discuss and decide on transport, economic planning and other aspects of life that inconveniently cross boundaries. However the present Government is unsympathetic and little seems likely to happen. The nearest thing to a London planning authority is the London Planning Advisory Committee, created against Government wishes (a House of Lords amendment was responsible) as a forum for London-wide long-term planning. LPAC last winter delivered a draft report to the Government on the long-term future of such topics as housing, the environment, the economy and urban planning of London. Hebbert and Havers comment 'LPAC exemplifies quite clearly the general unsuitability of joint voluntary committees for policy-making or even policy advice'. Some boroughs refuse to take part, LPAC's job overlaps with several other bodies', and to add the final note of confusion it is based in Romford, about as far from Whitehall as you can get and, as Hebbert and Havers point out, separated by 38 stops on the Underground from Richmond, the council which provides the Committee's chairman.

Poll tax 1989

The great imponderable this year is poll tax. From April next (1990) London's residents will pay the new 'community charge' instead of the existing rates or property tax. This will inevitably have a marked (possibly dramatic) effect not only on house prices, but on the relative desirability of the various boroughs as places in which to live.

The tax will be levied on each person over the age of 18. This obviously benefits single people living alone, and penalises large households. The implications are slowly being worked out: and not all of them seem to have much to do with the government's avowed aim of making local government more accountable to its clients. For instance, rates bills on large, opulent London homes will be slashed dramatically when poll tax comes in. A favourite example is Mrs Thatcher's retirement home in Dulwich: current rates around £3,000 a year, likely poll tax bill for two inhabitants £1,000. A modestly-off family of four in a council house in East Dulwich will pay £2,000, whereas their current rate bill is under £500.

The poorer districts will be doubly hard hit: there, families are typically larger, rateable values lower. Thus for instance Asian and other minority groups living as they tend to in large family groups will be very much worse off when they have to pay the poll tax per head, rather than splitting a low rates bill among the household. Similarly, groups of sharers will have to find the full amount each. The key point to remember when looking at the figures is that under the new system each person pays the tax. With rates, each household pays.

The government has been carrying on a spirited war of words with the town halls over how much individuals will pay. Whitehall estimates produce the somewhat specious figure of £202 per head as a national benchmark charge. This is the amount a council is supposed to need from each citizen in order to provide a 'standard level of service'. According to Whitehall, all the Inner London boroughs are 'overspending' on that per-head rate to an extent ranging from £171 in Westminster to a bizarre £9,009 in the City. The point the government is trying to make is that each council will make a decision on how much it spends, and that the public will be able to see how expensive that decision is by comparing their local bill with the 'average' of £202. 'The extent to which the community charge may exceed £202 is simply a measure of the overspending by the authorities in that area. Likewise a full community charge of less than £202 is a measure of the economy of the authorities concerned.' So says Mr Ridley, Secretary of State for the Environment. He further added that the 'overspending' in Inner London was boosted by £218 per head due to the laxity of the Inner London Education Authority, to which the boroughs at present contribute.

What worries the Town Halls is the fact that after 1990 they will have to pay for education themselves. They see little scope in cutting the schools bill on their own, despite the legendary profligacy of ILEA. It will pay you to live in a borough with few children: they will need fewer and cheaper schools. Tower Hamlets and Greenwich, with a high proportion of children, will have to raise more money to pay for their schooling than Westminster with relatively few. (For more details see the 'Education' chapter.)

The minister produced figures which show what people would pay in the London boroughs if the poll tax was in force now. These are:

Poll Tax estimates

	Average rate bill per household	'Overspending' in each Borough	Full community charge per head	First year safety netted community charge
City of London	£688	£9009	£476	£488
Camden	£790	£437	£639	£438
Greenwich	£513	£387	£589	£277
Hackney	£623	£376	£578	£347
Hammersmith and Fulham	£457	£271	£473	£267
Islington	£597	£278	£480	£326
Kensington and Chelsea	£582	£138	£340	£384
Lambeth	£474	£288	£490	£277
Lewisham	£575	£375	£577	£320
Southwark	£452	£313	£515	£269
Tower Hamlets	£558	£414	£616	£312
Wandsworth	£370	£195	£397	£205
Westminster	£793	£171	£373	£448
Barnet	£673	£28	£230	£305
Brent	£720	£105	£307	£348
Bromley	£438	−£23	£179	£222
Croydon	£513	−£5	£197	£258
Ealing	£528	£32	£234	£249
Enfield	£566	£51	£253	£278
Haringey	£541	£89	£291	£302
Hounslow	£522	£41	£243	£277
Kingston-upon-Thames	£522	£26	£228	£267
Merton	£411	−£35	£167	£218
Newham	£490	£82	£284	£269
Richmond-upon-Thames	£604	£57	£259	£325
Waltham Forest	£485	£67	£269	£260

It should be noted that many boroughs (in particular those with Labour councils opposed to spending cuts) reckon that the true figure will be much higher. The unpredictable cost of education after the abolition of the Inner London Education Authority will be added to boroughs' spending, and thus to poll tax bills. This is just one of the imponderables keeping borough treasurers awake at night.

Last year saw a tale of confusion about exactly when poll tax would arrive in London. The original plan, as reported in last year's Guide, was for the new tax to be phased in over 4 years. After complaints from the boroughs, the government decided that all London is to get the poll tax in one go. Rates will end in April 1990.

The safety net

Rate rebates reduce the bill to a minimum of 20% of the cost for those people who are unemployed or on low incomes. Similarly, rebates will be available for the poll tax. And in the first year of the new system, a 'safety net grant' will ensure that poll tax in any one council is not dramatically higher than the old rates. This contribution is limited to £75 per adult. The table above shows the effect of this: in most Inner London boroughs, bills in 1990-91 will be lower than they should be. But take care: Outer London boroughs will pay more in the first year, and the Inner London ones will rise to the 'true' poll tax level in 1991-92.

Councils now face the task of actually collecting the money. This has led the government into more trouble from an unexpected source: local government treasurers. This hitherto unremarkable body of men surfaced to complain that the administration of poll tax would cost a fortune. £500m, to be precise, to hire new staff, rent new buildings and install new computers. The town halls pointed out that people in London keep moving around, and that tracking down who owes what is a year-round task. Waltham Forest, for instance, reckons to spend £6m – Whitehall has budgeted £1.3m for the borough to pay for imposing the new tax.

The worry about the cost of poll tax is exercising both Labour and Tory-controlled councils. Even true-blue Westminster is concerned and says that the Government did not realise what collecting the money and administration will cost.

The mechanics of Poll Tax

A sign of spring this year will be the sighting of poll tax canvassers on the streets of London. These hapless people will have to call at every home in the city with a form. The 'head of the household' will be responsible for filling in the names of everyone over the age of 18. Refusing to register is an offence punishable by a fine. By October, each council will have a draft register which will come into force the following April.

There is great debate about how many Londoners will contrive to evade the tax. Estimates range up to about 20%. Young people, ranging from down-and-outs to Kensington nannies, will be likely evaders. It is in the interests of students (and nannies) living in London to stay registered at their parental address outside the city, for London poll tax is going to be high. But canvassers will be on the lookout for such backsliders.

Non-payers can have their poll tax deducted from their pay under a court order. The self-employed may find the bailiffs on the doorstep. The ultimate sanction for hardened non-payers is prison.

The new Business Rate

Poll tax is not the only change next year. Rates on business premises will stay after domestic rates are abolished. But instead of being set by each borough, the business rate will be uniform across the country. Rateable values will still vary, depending on the valuation of a property set by the Inland Revenue. But the amount per pound will be the same. The Department of the Environment has calculated the percentages by which rate poundage will rise under the new system:

Business Rate estimates

	Change to national poundage		Change to national poundage
City of London	47.0%	Barnet	15.1%
		Brent	−14.3%
Camden	4.1%	Bromley	39.7%
Greenwich	−3.9%	Croydon	43.0%
Hackney	−3.4%	Ealing	21.2%
Hammersmith and Fulham	−2.8%	Enfield	10.6%
Islington	18.1%	Haringey	−2.4%
Kensington and Chelsea	104.0%	Hounslow	−4.8%
Lambeth	16.6%	Kingston-upon-Thames	19.8%
Lewisham	−2.2%	Merton	31.9%
Southwark	11.8%	Newham	−17.5%
Tower Hamlets	1.3%	Richmond-upon-Thames	13.7%
Wandsworth	60.4%	Waltham Forest	4.2%
Westminster	45.9%		

The implications are major. No longer will it be automatically cheaper to have your business premises in a low-spending borough (Wandsworth, for instance, or Kensington) rather than next-door and high-spending Lambeth or Brent. Thus we could see some well-placed but run-down corners, deserted by shops and businesses for lower-rated regions, revive as if by magic in the next few years.

Poll Tax and house prices

With rates, the bigger and more opulent your home the more you pay. With poll tax, everyone is equal. What they live in is irrelevant. If every resident in, say, Camden pays the same poll tax, be they inhabitants of a St Pancras bedsit or a Hampstead Heath mansion, the actual amount paid by the Hampstead-dweller will be a lot lower under poll tax than under the old rates system, whereas the bedsitter will pay more. It is a fair guess therefore that the price of large houses will rise yet further, because it will be cheaper than before to live in them. This will be seen to greatest effect outside London, where prices are lower. The rates on a country house are at present a bigger slice of the total cost of living there (mortgage, rates, bills) than in London. With poll tax, there will be no difference between two homes within any given council area.

So forget the worry about whether the rates on your new house will be too expensive. But remember to check which borough it is in. The difference between them will be less than at present, but still significant. See the table above.

According to a study by an Edinburgh professor of economics poll tax will cause windfall gains for home owners at the expense of those who rent. As Prof Gordon Hughes points out, you have to pay the poll tax, at the same rate, whether you buy or rent. This means the demand for owner-occupation will increase and drive up prices. Prof Hughes reckons on a 17% increase. Other calculations, by the Woolwich Building Society's Dr Steven Martin, put the figure at 12-15%.

Inner London prices will be boosted by the equalisation effect of the tax, but may be simultaneously hit by the very high levels of poll tax set by the London boroughs. If Mr and Mrs T, on retirement, moved to Surrey instead of Dulwich, they could well be paying £600 a year less.

Planning

Residents and councils in London's more salubrious areas are becoming alarmed about the way Whitehall is ready to overrule refusals of planning permission. A developer who gets turned down by the local planning committee can confidently expect a sympathetic hearing at the Department of the Environment, and the appeal route is increasingly routine. Town halls complain that the presumption at the DoE is that development is a Good Thing unless there are strong reasons to think otherwise.

Similar fears are voiced on the fringes of London where builders have their eye on Green Belt land, for 40 years sacrosanct. Both inner and outer London will see more in-fill and larger-scale developments as councils are overruled. Do not, therefore, take the local structure plan, or the council's assurances about what will happen on a given site, as gospel. A developer may have other ideas – and the odds are that Whitehall will back him.

Another planning change which is influencing London's living patterns is the move by a number of councils, alarmed at the rate which family sized homes are being turned into small flats, to limit this trend. One effect of hitherto uncontrolled conversions can be seen in Fulham, where a 15ft house frontage gives insufficient space for the two or three cars its inhabitants own between them. So now would-be developers can find that, for example, they will have to provide at least one home in each building which will sleep four and include the garden level. This can rule out conversions altogether for smaller terraces. Check carefully if you are buying with an eye to converting.

Changing the pattern

The stress on the eastern half of London, commented on in this chapter of last year's Guide, continues. The Government has appointed consultants to look at five large tracts of land in east London which could, it is calculated, provide as many as 20,000 new homes. These homes will be for middle and lower income groups, said the Housing Minister. The sites are the Greenwich Peninsula (6,000-home scheme already announced – see Greenwich chapter), the lower Lea Valley (Rosehaugh and Tower Hamlets council already talking – see Bow chapter), the Stratford Railway Yards, the Beckton Gas Works site just east of the Royal Docks, and, largest of all, riverside land at Barking Reach.

To these areas must be added the next stage of Docklands, the Royal Docks. The Docklands chapter gives details, and the Transport chapter pays particular attention to road and rail plans on this side of town.

Another factor in the rise of the eastern half of London could be the Channel Tunnel. When it is complete in 1993, businesses and individuals will want untrammeled access to the Tunnel and to its rail termini. The biggest of these is to be at King's Cross, an area of London in for some of the most ambitious changes over the next decade.

Planning policies favour expansion of industry and large-scale retail developments east of rather than west of London. Given this, the five large sites and the Docklands impetus, it seems a fair bet that most of London's new homes will be built on the east side of the city.

Counting people

Housing planners have to check birth-rates and add a couple of decades. Lots of babies were born in Britain in the early 1960s, and they are now young people looking for a home. The number of householders in the South-East, London included, will rise by 100,000 a year each year until 2001, say planners. But the biggest rise comes soon, with a decline in the rate in the second half of the '90s. In London, 150,000 extra households are projected by 2001. This could be an underestimate if the number of single- and two-person households goes on growing. Another unpredictable factor is migration. Nearly 20,000 Europeans moved into London in 1986: economic trends could easily boost this number. And people change their habits far faster than homes can get built.

A lot depends, too, on whose figures you believe. Those above came from the Government – but their credibility was dented when in late 1987 they were revised sharply upwards. This had the effect of raising the predicted number of extra households in London from 100,000 to 150,000. Then last year Bank of England researchers devised a mathematical model to predict household formation. Out of the bank's computer came a figure for 2001 of 871,000 more households than Whitehall predicts. And about a third of these extra households would be in London and the South-East.

The statistics obstinately show a surplus of homes over households in London of over 100,000. But delve further and you find 131,000 empty homes, awaiting sale or renovation or just empty for bureaucratic or private reasons. And you will find a pent-up demand of 255,000 people on the council waiting lists. With only 9,000 homes built in Greater London in 1986 – half the 1981 figure – pressure on available housing looks set to increase.

The invention of work homes

Countless futurologists have predicted the demise of the office as technology – computers, fax machines and the like – makes it possible for people to work where they live. In London, the predictions are starting to come about. Tower Hamlets has been in the lead in this, with an enlightened planning regime that is letting developers build 'units' that are part home, part office or workshop. Several hundred people in this fast-changing borough are now living above the office, carrying on trades and professions ranging from running a nursery school through journalism and surveying to marine engineering. Many of them serve the booming world of Docklands a mile or so to the south. At the other end of London, the new Plantation Wharf scheme in Battersea has smart 4-bed houses with a workshop/office at the back.

Strict planning laws attempt to deter buyers who fancy a large playroom or somewhere to store the boat. And the tax benefits, while considerable – split the space and you can claim part against your business, part as mortgage tax relief – do have implications when you come to sell. Developers are also rethinking the layout of schemes to allow efficient working: roads must be wide enough to allow lorries to get in, noise insulation must be good.

The workhome trend offers attractive options to the self-employed. And taking a larger view it may boost the conversion of decayed inner-city buildings into smart new 'units'. A sizeable workhome complex will have an effect on the surrounding streets, bringing in spending power and boosting the value of nearby properties.

Points to watch in 1989

1 Progress of road, rail and underground improvements detailed below in the 'Transport' chapter. They could make a radical difference to the property 'shape' of London. And the ambitious schemes could equally make – or blight – a home by their presence.

2 Net level of emigration from London. Two possible sources: owner-occupiers taking the profit from their home and relocating somewhere cheaper. And ex-council tenants who did well out of Right to Buy doing the same thing. Emigration frees homes for sale, but too much lowers housing demand and could reduce the investment potential of London homes. A contrary factor: rising long-distance rail fares and provincial house prices.

3 Level of inward movement, especially from Europe. The 1992 changes mean that increasing numbers of companies want a base in London.

4 Japanese buying of both homes and commercial property. They see London as a business springboard into Europe (every Japanese speaks some English, few speak French or German). Their presence will be felt in homes (Ealing and Acton, where there's a Japanese school, along with Richmond and Golders Green) and as investors/occupiers of leisure and office developments. Looking from Tokyo, *anything* in London looks cheap.

5 Watch out for more precise figures on Poll Tax – local quirks are inevitable. Some boroughs will be cheaper to live in than others.

6 Watch too the education plans of the boroughs now they will run schools. See 'Education' and 'Boroughs' chapters. A borough with a good name will attract homebuying parents.

7 Privatisation: water and electricity are already selling land; more will be sold.

8 Council property – develop an eye for a good tower block or well-designed maisonette. Ex-council homes, sold on by right-to-buying tenants, are some of the best inexpensive first homes seen for years. And a down-at-heel estate can become a smart enclave as tenants become owners. Houses are finding a ready market in some areas; flats can provide marvellous space for their cost, but won't rise in value as fast – look for high percentage of owner-occupiers.

9 Department of the Environment decisions on land use policy and the laxity/rigidity of planning controls. The pressure for building land is growing and ministers may decide to allow construction where the assumption now is that it is not possible – like your neighbours' back garden.

Transport

and its effects on London's areas and their homes

For the first time in 15 years, it seems possible that serious sums will be spent on new lines and new methods of transport for the capital. London's transport system started to hit the headlines last winter in a way not seen since the great Motorway Box battles of the early 1970s. Sadly, recent disasters on the existing system have overshadowed the exciting prospect of major investment in new ways of getting around. They also underlined the need for them.

1989 will be a watershed year. A whole range of plans have been drawn up – not all having much connection with each other it is true – and now the politicians must decide on priorities, allocate cash and generally face up to an increasingly immobile city. For the first time, it seems that the political will to spend the money is there. This possibility is precariously dependent upon the health of the economy and thus on external events. Planners ruefully recall that the last time big projects were about to begin, in 1974, the oil crisis came out of the blue and everything was shelved. Some schemes, such as the Heathrow express, have been given the go-ahead in the last 12 months, but plenty more are in the planning stage.

This chapter sums up the main plans and intentions of the transport bosses. Anyone buying or thinking or selling should study them carefully and also contact the local Town Hall. Some are setting up hot-lines (see 'Boroughs' chapter) to answer queries. New transport is a two-edged sword: depending on its proximity, a proposed scheme will improve your communications, affect your peace – or threaten to demolish your home.

As last year's *Guide* reported, the first total traffic snarl-up paralysed the City and West End in December '87. 1988 saw several more, with one complete halt caused by a student/police fracas on Westminster Bridge; another day of chaos stemming from a gas leak in Wandsworth and an unexplained (and thus even more worrying) jam one November evening when traffic took three hours to get from Shepherds Bush to Hyde Park Corner. Small events, or nothing at all, have become capable of stopping London. And contrary to the evidence of our congested streets, fewer people are commuting in by car. There are just more people making more journeys in more cars and trucks.

The same is true of public transport, nearly every part of which is running at or near physical capacity after years of gentle decline.

Prosperity is the cause. It says something about the underlying mood of Whitehall and the London Transport planners that the upswing in London's fortunes in the Eighties, and the resulting increase in passengers, took them completely by surprise. British Rail brings 500,000 people into London each working day, a total not seen since 1971. Across the country, and especially on express lines into London, rail travel is at its highest since 1961. The Underground adds 400,000 to the daily total entering Central London: indeed London Transport is under even heavier seige than BR. Tube traffic is up by over 60% since 1982. Sheer weight of numbers is forcing spending on projects like doubling the size of Angel station on the Northern Line, where the narrow central platform and slow lifts have made overcrowding positively dangerous.

Underlying the annoyance, confusion and sheer danger is the awareness, steadily growing, that London has to have decent transport if it is to go on functioning as a world city. A constant stream of natives and foreigners are reporting back from trips abroad with tales of the RER super-metro in Paris and

Frankfurt's well-integrated suburban trains and trams. And comparisons with London's creaking chaos are embarrassing the government, which is balancing an instinctive hatred of public spending with the knowledge that business is very mobile these days, and will move elsewhere if London does not modernise.

Studies and plans

A much-leaked report, the Inner London Rail Study, was due to be published by the Department of Transport as we went to press. It was compiled by civil servants and people from British Rail and London Regional Transport (LRT).

Debate about various plans went on throughout the second half of last year, with newspaper stories under 'London down the tube' headlines. Transport secretary Paul Channon responded with spirit, saying that the only reason the press were taking notice was that they had all been moved from their cosy dens in Fleet St and scattered all over London, thereby finding out what everyone else had known for years.

The leaks were unanimous that a key proposal in the Study was for up to three cross-town rail tunnels, similar to the deep-level RER metro in Paris. These would have a limited number of stops and would link BR lines on either side of the capital. For example, a new E-W link would run from Liverpool St across to Paddington, with a stop in the City and another in the West End.

These plans are in response to evidence that the Central Line eastwards is the most overloaded line at present, followed by the Victoria Line, especially N of Victoria, the District/Piccadilly W of Earls Court, and the Metropolitan Line NW. By the end of the century (only 11 years away) a modest 20% increase in traffic would mean that all these would become overloaded, with the resulting need to restrict passengers. That means, translated into English, stop people using the tube. That could be done by pricing them off it (and onto what?) or by letting congestion become acute and hoping businesses will go away. But whereas moving the office out of London once meant a choice between Milton Keynes and Swindon, it is now more likely to be Brussels or Lyons.

The 20% increase projected is challenged by the Central London Study itself, which (say leaks) forecasts 30% higher peak-hour demand by 2001.

Leaks say that of the major proposals in the Study, the E-W cross-town link is most likely, followed in descending order of probability by the duplicating of the Victoria Line between King's Cross and Victoria, and a new Chelsea-Hackney tube. This is back on the agenda after being abandoned at least once before: it would use the Wimbledon branch of the District Line, then a new tunnel through Chelsea and across to the City, then existing BR routes out to Hackney.

One disappointment for South Londoners is the playing down of plans for extensions to existing tube lines. LRT point out quite fairly that there is no point in encouraging more people to use the tubes when the central sections are at overloading point already. So much-mooted new lines out to places like Camberwell look like staying mooted, rather than actual, for some time yet. More hope is offered by integration of light rail technology and BR lines with tubes, as for example with the proposed links with Docklands into Southeast London (see below). This is not to say plans do not exist – LRT has learnt the Docklands lesson and is hoping to use the 'site enhancement' route, getting developers to pay for the new line from the profits made on land made more valuable by the improved access. But, says LRT, extensions must be the second stage after the capacity of the existing network has been stretched to the limit.

This takes the form of unspectacular but expensive jobs like realigning curves, bringing in new carriages, updating signalling, all with the aim of running trains faster and more frequently. LRT also have a pressing need to relieve congestion at stations: 25 central tube stations have a serious problem. The bill for sorting these out comes at present prices to £420m.

One scheme that will happen is a fast rail link between Heathrow Airport and Paddington (which had none at all before), allowing journey times of 17 minutes rather than the hour the tube takes. This line is being financed by the airport authority and should open in 1993. This is the year to buy a home within reach of Paddington, before everyone realises this.

Down in Kent, the Channel Tunnel is inching its way towards France. And experts fear that trains from the Chunnel to London will travel at about the same pace unless something is done. The lines to Dover through SE London are already packed, especially at rush-hour. Channel Tunnel co-chairman Alastair Morton described the South-East's rail system as a 'congealing mess'. Attempts to lobby British Rail into building a new high speed line in time for the tunnel opening have failed: BR say their forecasts indicate it won't be needed until the late 90s (the Chunnel will open in '93). So private interests are bidding to build and run the line. BR asked for proposals by this January.

London will obviously gain economically from a fast rail link, but homes in several areas of SE London could be affected by the new lines. Unlike in Kent, where completely new alignments have been proposed, the London lines would follow existing railways. But the construction of extra track, and the bridges and other works involved, taken with the overhead electric cables to be used, would blight many homes. A confidential BR study, leaked in December, identifies 6,500 homes affected, of which 350 would be demolished.

The Chunnel trains will, under present plans, terminate at Waterloo and King's Cross, with possible freight stations at White City and Stratford. Areas affected by the various routes from Kent to the central stations include Dulwich, Brixton, Peckham and Nunhead. Other areas will be affected by greatly increased traffic, running at higher speeds. Lines to be used include the West London link running from Clapham through Battersea, across the Thames to Chelsea Harbour and then between Chelsea and Fulham.

The train renaissance

British Rail's confidence was badly dented by the Clapham Junction disaster last December. It was ironic that the apparent cause was re-signalling work, itself part of BR's big investment in upgrading the network. This investment can only increase: BR like the tube is getting busier and busier. The new Thameslink cross-town line (you can now get from Herne Hill and Peckham Rye to Farringdon and King's Cross) is already running at capacity within a year of opening: BR are asking Whitehall for cash to spend on track works to allow better links with other lines.

There is a general attempt to 'beef up' the schedules to places in inner South London to attract people out of reach of a tube, or who could be weaned from the chaotic Northern Line. BR's research has convinced them that too few people know about their local train services: expect more local advertising. The integrated ticketing introduced in January means that commuters from inner London BR stations will get a better deal: it will now be as cheap to commute via train and tube as by tube alone. House prices should rise in such areas.

The great roads row

Almost unnoticed, major road schemes have crept back onto the London agenda. Since 1984, teams of independent planners and engineers have been working for the Department of Transport (DTp) on a consultancy basis, looking into four areas around London. In mid-1988 they published thick reports replete with maps showing possible new roads intended to relieve the bottlenecks they had spent the previous four years discovering. These reports are 'Stage 2A' of the studies. Stage 2b is under way with a report giving detailed plans to be published in the summer of this year (1989). It must be stressed that even at Stage 2b, these proposals will be just that: proposals. The report will be to the DTp, and what actually gets done is a political/economic decision. Watch out in the autumn of this year for the Cabinet decisions on 1990 capital spending: by then the Rail Study and the roads studies will be far enough advanced to have price tags.

At a local level, the Stage 2A documents have caused considerable mayhem. 3,000 people packed a meeting in Barnes after it was learned that the Southwest London assessment study included a proposal for a new road across Barnes Common. Local MPs, Tory and Opposition, announced their abhorrence of the schemes. Wandsworth Council, uncomfortably placed at the meeting point of three study areas, only decided against a public meeting when it was realised no hall in the borough was big enough to hold it. House prices have been hit in roads which are affected by the proposals. Some homes have proved unsaleable.

What must be stressed is that the options outlined in the four studies are alternatives. Not all (if any) of the plans will come to fruition. There is strong doubt among Whitehall-watchers whether the political will exists to carve new roads through gentrified suburbs: protests, legal actions, lengthy inquiries, people lying down in front of bulldozers – all are memories from past rows to haunt the nightmares of ministers. So the brief outline of the proposals which follows must be seen in its economic and political context. Remember the Ringway/Motorway Box saga of the early 70s: hardly any of the roads actually got built. And the terms of reference of the studies include public transport as well as road; traffic management and other low-key options as well as new motorways. The proposals for new tube, BR and light rail lines seem, however, to have been dreamed up by the constultants without much consultation with BR and LRT, who are really responsible. BR at least pour scorn on some of the consultants' plans. All four reports seem more confident with roads and traffic management than with public transport.

The South Circular

The South Circular study area is from Clapham Common east as far as Eltham. Nine packages of measures have been drawn up by the consultants for progress to Stage 2B. The first few involve limited improvements to the existing South Circular, involving some 'land take' (jargon for using land not now part of the road: could mean loss of gardens, even some demolition). Option D starts to get serious: a new road along the South London Line railway corridor, from Clapham High St through Brixton, Peckham and Lewisham. The road could be a toll route. About 800 properties would go, the cost would be £250m. Another scheme envisages rebuilding the South Circular on its present route to dual-carriageway standard, with flyovers and tunnels. 600 homes would go, cost: £300m. A proposal to create a new road to the south, with a tunnel from Sydenham to West Norwood, a new road through central Streatham, another through Tooting and the upgrading of Trinity Rd on Wandsworth Common, would cost 800 properties and £400m. A yet more radical scheme would take a major new road still further south, running north of Bromley and Croydon and south of Mitcham and Merton. 1,000 homes would go and the cost would be £1,000m.

South London

The second study deals with the southern approaches to London along the A23 from Gatwick and Brighton. Junction improvements along the A23 from Brixton Hill southward figure early on in the ascending list of options. The Merton relief road, running from the Purley Way NW to Merton, is already planned and is assumed by the consultants to be a certainty. The first major new road plan in the study is a bypass to the west of Streatham across Tooting Bec Common as far as the South Circular at Clapham. The number of properties affected is not shown in the study, but the road cost is put at £200m. More radical options involve a new road up the Wandle Valley and then along the BR line to Clapham Junction. The most extreme envisages a 'strategic highway' from Clapham, south to Tooting Common and on to Mitcham, to be built at 4-lane width and with tunnels beneath residential areas. An east-west road of similar standard on a line south of the South Circular would also be built.

West London

Perhaps the biggest road row of all can be predicted for this area, taking in the South Circular from Clapham to Kew Bridge and the north-south route from the Thames through Earls Court to Shepherds Bush. It is in this zone that the loudest protests have already been heard, perhaps because the most serene and expensive of suburbs – Chelsea, Fulham, Barnes, Putney – are affected.

One key route is at a more advanced stage than the others. This is WEIR, the Western Environmental Improvement Route (note that bland 'environmental'!). Plans for WEIR are quite advanced: it will run from the Shepherds Bush roundabout south along the railway 'corridor' between Fulham and Chelsea. What it does at the Thames is open to debate: at present, plans show a split, with one road running west to Wandsworth Bridge, another east onto Chelsea Embankment. It is here that the road is most controversial: damage to the Thames-side environment could be great.

The assessment study includes WEIR in several of its options, with an extension across the river via a new bridge at Chelsea Harbour, then a tunnel under Battersea to the NW corner of Clapham Common. 400 homes would be lost. Extended Weir is an option favoured by the consultants, who see it as useful not only for its easing of the Earls Court/South Circular problems, but also because it links up with the improved South Circular from Clapham eastward.

The South Circular is more intractable, there being no spacious railway 'corridor' to provide a route for a relief road. The consultants propose one solution which would use the existing Putney-Chiswick-Kew rail route but would probably mean closing the line. It would also mean an elevated road though Barnes, severe impact on the centre of Putney, and the loss of part of Barnes Common. About 600 homes would go at a cost of up to £500m. The option of forcing a dual carriageway along the existing South Circular route has not been recommended.

Other proposals are for an upgraded Roehampton Lane leading to a tunnel beneath Wimbledon Common, emerging at Trinity Rd (300 homes would go). Then comes the real shocker: a tunnel right along the bed of the Thames from the Hogarth Roundabout to Chelsea Bridge. All these have gone forward to Stage 2B.

East London

This study, which looks at the area north and east of King's Cross, out to the Lea Valley and up to Highgate and Tottenham, deals with one of the most complex areas. This, too, rejects the idea of upgrading long stretches of existing roads, concluding that the demolition of property would not be balanced by the gains. The proposals again make much use of railway 'corridors', with the interesting addition of an ex-railway: the much-loved belt of green along a former line from Highgate Wood east through Crouch End to Finsbury Park. Bypasses round the centres of Stoke Newington (to the E) and Hackney (to the W) feature in proposals. A proposed new Thames crossing just east of Tower Bridge would have interesting implications for some very expensive Docklands property in Wapping and St Saviours. Another new road could tunnel under Victoria Park and run along Hackney Road. In sum, the 'new road corridors' option for this area would mean the loss of up to 3,000 homes.

Freelance proposals

The general atmosphere of new ideas, plus some unsubtle Government prompting, has led the construction industry to come up with some ideas of its own. The most radical is for a grid of six toll tunnels across London, with massive car parks and interchanges with the tube. This is costed at £5.5bn, but would, say the proposers, be self-supporting 'and no more difficult to build than the Channel Tunnel'. A Thames-bed tunnel, which appears as a West London study option, has also been put forward by a private firm. With one private venture now going ahead – the new Dartford bridge on the M25 – do not rule out the private road – at least as long as this Government stays in power.

Transport in Docklands

If London as a whole faces transport thrombosis in 1989, Docklands faces complete paralysis. Already the LDDC (London Docklands Development Corporation) switchboard has to cope with irate motorists ringing up on their car-phones to complain about traffic jams. And the quantum leap in construction traffic caused by the various schemes now starting will make things worse. No-one expected Docklands to develop so fast, and consequently transport has not kept up.

By about 1995 things should be much improved, but between now and then congestion will grow worse before it gets better. The road snarl-ups will be complemented by overloading of the public transport system. Canary Wharf developers Olympia & York, accustomed to planning ahead, have taken to the water in a bid to get round the jams. Barges will be used to bring 85% of the building materials to the site from a transhipment point east of London. And the company has charted a riverbus from Thamesline to get executives to and from the development. So, too, has the City Airport.

Recent Docklands developments

1988 saw the opening of the North Circular extension road from the M11 to the eastern end of the Royal Docks. This provides a fast route out to the M25. Eventually, the road will extend south, forming the approach to ELRIC, the East London River Crossing, a giant new bridge across the Thames. ELRIC will give Docklands fast access to the M2 to Dover, and radically alter communications with southeast London. But not until 1994.

Last year also saw the start of the Thamesline riverbus service, with piers at Cuba Street (Isle of Dogs), Cherry Garden Pier (Rotherhithe) and Greenland Passage (Surrey Docks). The river boats connect Docklands (and its airport) to the City, the West End and South Bank and that other waterside development, Chelsea Harbour.

Docklands plans – confirmed

Roads get major work during 1989. The notorious 'red brick road' in the Isle of Dogs Enterprise Zone will be upgraded at a cost of £5m. This 2-lane road, which cost £1 a brick to build 5 years ago, has never been adequate. Now the LDDC are having to buy land from adjoining developments to relieve congestion. The biggest current road scheme is West Ferry Circus, at the NW corner of the Isle of Dogs, which will be the main route into Canary Wharf. This double-decker roundabout is being built and paid for by Olympia & York as an essential part of their giant scheme. Complete early 1990. West Ferry Rd N and S of the new Circus is being widened for completion late this year. A new 4-to 6-lane road is being built across the top of the Isle of Dogs, linking West India Dock Rd in the W with Preston's Rd in the E. From a big new flyover junction at the E end a new road will form the eastern entrance to Canary Wharf. The Poplar Link, as the E-W road is known, will be finished by the end of 1990, the Canary Wharf link by mid-1990. The Poplar Link will be continued eastward with a part tunnel link to the A13 at the Canning Town Flyover. There will also be a new bridge over the mouth of the River Lea. Progressive completion of this lot is scheduled in stages up to 1992.

The most ambitious new road is a tunnel linking the new West Ferry Circus with The Highway to the W. Most of the Limehouse Link will be in a tunnel passing beneath Limehouse, the building of which involves demolishing quite a few homes. Completion end 1992.

Over in the Royal Docks lessons have been learnt and major new roads are being built before, rather than after, the new developments. Schemes under way, all due for completion by mid-1990, include a link at the eastern end with the A13-North Circular junction, a new E-W spine road along the N side of the Albert Dock, and a new N-S road called Connaught Crossing which bridges the docks at the meeting of the Victoria and Albert Docks on a new swing bridge.

Public transport is no less active: Docklands Light Railway is being extended W into the heart of the City at Bank, again with Olympia &·York money. A single-track shuttle service should be running by the end of 1990, with the full service by 1991. The existing DLR is being upgraded, with longer platforms for longer trains, to raise capacity to 15,000 passengers per hour in each direction. A great improvement on the 4,000 currently possible, but the mismatch between the DLR's abilities and the 100,000 people who may need to get to Canary Wharf in the rush-hour is awe-inspiring. Presumably the LDDC hopes a lot of them will come from the E, for the DLR is being extended into the Royals and Beckton, with a northerly kink in the original planned route linking Canning Town into the network. Completion late 1992.

British Rail's North London Link is gaining renewed prominence as the Royal Docks move into the development frame. The line links Stratford, Hackney and other points in N London with Woolwich, with numerous interchanges with the underground en route. The 3-an-hour service currently carries only 500 people an hour through the Docklands section, but the LDDC and BR hope to change that. £10m is being spent in 1989 and 1990 on more frequent trains, new rolling stock, a new interchange station with the DLR extension and a new station at Silvertown to improve access to the City Airport. The East London tube line, the only public transport link between the Surrey Docks and the rest of Docklands, is being tidied up with LDDC money.

Buses are important in Docklands – in large areas they are the only form of public transport. The Isle of Dogs wll be the scene of an interesting experiment involving privately-run minibuses, not linked to the existing London Transport bus network. The Thames Transit service, if it materialises, will not accept Travelcard tickets but will be available for hailing in the street – like a cross between a bus and a taxi.

Future Docklands plans – on paper

Proposals for Docklands range from the likely through the wishful to the ridiculous. In order of likelihood are the following:

Though not in the LDDC zone, the Greenwich Peninsula scheme (see Greenwich chapter) is as big as anything that is: 6,000 homes are planned. It is certain, say inside sources, that a transport link of some sort – public or privately funded – will be built between the peninsula and the NE corner of the Isle of Dogs. This could be a branch of the Docklands Light Railway, or an eastward extension of the proposed new Canary Wharf tube. This proposal is for a £400m new tube line from Waterloo along the South Bank to the Surrey Docks, then under the river to Canary Wharf. It could then run on SE to the Greenwich Peninsula and/or NE to Blackwall. Olympia & York are, say London Regional Transport sources 'very keen to see further enhancement of rail access' to their mega-scheme. There was pressure to put an enabling Bill into Parliament in the 1988-89 session, but LRT did not think they were ready with all the details. What Olympia & York want they tend to get (partly because they are willing to pay a large share of the cost) so this link looks very likely. But the earliest feasible completion date is 1994.

The Docklands Light Railway, which ends a foot tunnel short of Greenwich, may well be extended across the river via the Deptford Creek area to Greenwich and Lewisham. This would tie in with a major plan to redevelop Dartford Creek itself. A detailed study into the DLR extension is under way and should report this year. A bill could be submitted in the 1989-90 session.

A southward extension of the East London tube line is also being studied, with a route running SW from Surrey Docks to Peckham Rye and East Dulwich. A northern extension, using a redundant BR viaduct through Dalston, is possible. An upgrade to the Shadwell station, where the East London Line meets the DLR, is a virtual certainty.

On the river, the slow build-up of Thamesline services should continue, with more piers coming into service as developments are completed and people (ie passengers) move in. Masthouse Pier, close to Burrells Wharf at the SW end of the Isle of Dogs, is ready. The big gap is a pier in Wapping, but this should come. And the existing Cuba St stop will move a few hundred yards N to become Canary Wharf's pier at West Ferry Circus. Eventually the service should extend E to Greenwich and the Royals.

Eastward extensions are also contemplated for the DLR, with lines on maps extending out to Barking and N to East Ham. But the Beckton link is not finished yet, so further additions must wait.

London City Airport, in the Royal Docks, struggled through 1988 after a setback in the early months when flights were suspended. Now Brymon, one of the two airlines, is planning Paris flights on the hour, every hour, in 1989. The City Airport looks certain to get permission this year to use BA 146 jets, which have a range of 900 miles compared to the current plane's 400, thus bringing most of Europe within reach. Road and rail plans detailed above will make the airport (already served by a well-organised riverbus link) easier to get to.

Conclusions

In this exciting but increasingly uncertain transport environment, homebuyers need to keep their wits about them:

● Take special care with searches if a home you propose to buy is within one of the current transport study areas. Your local council will have details of schemes.

● Take especial care if a property is close to an existing railway: rail corridors figure largely in all study plans. A quiet branch line now may be partnered soon by a four-lane road. And in SE London beware the high-speed Channel trains.

● Watch out for knock-on effects: a new road often merely moves the traffic jam to its ends.

● Do not assume unlimited private car mobility: another government (or even this one) may prefer, or be forced into, some form of road licensing.

● Do expect considerable public transport investment under this or any other government, unless the economy nose-dives. Therefore buy with an eye to plans and proposals (which will be updated every year in this Guide). But do not expect immediate results: new lines take years to build.

● Remember that compensation is paid if your home has to be demolished, but you get less if you are merely affected by noise, dirt or other side-effects. Losing a view is worth nothing. You can fight compensation cases: use a solicitor experienced in this work (ask the Law Society).

● Expect traffic from the south and east to grow faster than from other areas as the Channel Tunnel and Euro-liberalisation boost business in that direction.

● Watch Docklands: it is a big economic force now, but unpredictable. Major transport upgrades are planned, but it will be hard for the planners to keep up if the place really takes off. Conversely, gloom in Docklands could mean lots of nice empty roads for others to use.

● Take another look at British Rail services in inner London, especially south of the river. They are getting better and more convenient, especially with the amalgamation of the LRT and BR day-tickets.

Area Assessment Studies

South Circular Assessment Study,
Travers Morgan,
136 Long Acre,
London WC2E 9AE
Tel.: 01-836 5474

South London Assessment Study,
Mott, Hay & Anderson,
20-26 Wellesley Road,
Croydon CR9 2UL
Tel.: 01-686 5041

West London Assessment Study
Sir William Halcrow & Partners Ltd.,
Vineyard House,
44 Brook Green,
London W6 7BY
Tel.: 01-602 7282

East London Assessment Study
Over Arup & Partners
13 Fitzroy St,
London W1P 6BQ
Tel.: 01-636 1531

Copies of the stage 2 working papers are available from each of the consultants, price £20. Summaries are available free from the consultants or from borough councils.

Educating London

by Peter Wilby

Because of the Education Reform Act, which completed its passage through Parliament in summer 1988, schools throughout the country face big changes over the next few years. London schools face particularly dramatic changes.

The Act abolishes the Inner London Education Authority from 1 April 1990. Schools and colleges will be handed over to the 13 inner London boroughs, which will join the 20 outer boroughs as education authorities in their own right. Nobody can forecast what the long-term effects will be. The Government argued that ILEA had spent too much money for inadequate results; critics accused it of wanting to abolish the ILEA for no better reason than it was controlled by the Labour Party.

Teachers will transfer automatically to the boroughs, so theoretically, the disruption to individual schools should be minimised. But many London schools already have serious staffing problems created by the high cost of living in the capital. In inner areas, particularly, there are shortages of primary teachers and of secondary specialists, such as those teaching maths, science and technology. Southwark, Tower Hamlets, Newham and Ealing are among the worst hit areas; suburban boroughs, such as Croydon, have fewer problems.

The annual turnover of teachers in inner London has been increasing for several years and approached 25 per cent in 1988. The ILEA, in its dying years, has been told to spend less by the Government and many staff are leaving in anticipation of cuts. And it is likely that there will be further cuts in some parts of Inner London, after its abolition, as some boroughs try to reduce costs. So teachers, mindful of diminished promotion prospects (compulsory redundancies are unlikely), will probably continue to leave. Fears that pupils may suffer from lack of continuity in teaching thus have some justification.

There is less need for concern on another score. The switch to 13 separate inner London education authorities should not restrict parents' choice of schools. Under the 1980 Education Act, parents are entitled to send their child to any suitable school, provided there are spare places. There is nothing to prevent you from sending your child to a school in a neighbouring borough or, for that matter, to one on the other side of London. Far from reducing choice, the 1988 Act reinforces these rights. In the past, local authorities were allowed to set an 'admissions limit' to each school. This was not necessarily the same as a school's physical capacity. It was often set artificially low to ensure that, in a period of falling rolls, every school had its fair share of pupils. Now, authorities' rights to set such limits for schools have been abolished; from autumn 1990, the secondary schools will admit children until they are physically full. (No date has been set for the extension of 'open enrolment' to primary schools.) There will still be an appeals procedure for dissatisfied parents.

Nevertheless, it is still important, if you have children, to live reasonably close to a good school. If a school is over-subscribed, those children living nearest often have preference. (It is worth remembering that brothers and sisters may also have preference. So, once you have one child in the school, you will have a better chance of gaining admittance for the younger ones, even if you later move house.) Another consideration is that, particularly for primary education, a school nearby is more convenient. Remember that, if your child travels several miles to school, it is not just a matter of a morning and evening car run. Friends will also be widely scattered, requiring further journeys through busy London streets to collect your offspring from parties or tea invitations. Many teachers agree that neighbourhood schools allow more stable friendships among pupils and closer home-school links.

The way schools are organised varies widely between the London boroughs. Most, including the ILEA, have wholly comprehensive systems. Most inner London boroughs are likely to stay comprehensive after the changeover. Westminster and Wandsworth, however, may introduce some 'magnet' schools, specialising in particular subject areas such as science or languages.

Barnet, Bexley, Bromley, Enfield, Kingston, Redbridge and Sutton still have grammar schools. But most only have one or two and it is left to parents to decide whether or not to apply for places. Other schools in these boroughs are usually described as comprehensive and often have a reasonable number of bright children. Only Kingston has a fully selective system which sets out to cream off the brightest 10 or 15 per cent of the boroughs' children into grammars.

In most areas, children attend primary school from 5 to 11, and then switch to a comprehensive until they leave school. But some boroughs have rather confusing 'middle school' systems. In Ealing, for example, children attend a first school from 5 to 8, a middle school from 8 to 12 and then switch to comprehensives. Harrow has the same system but with the extra complication that children switch to a tertiary college at 16.

A tertiary college combines the work of a technical college with that of a school sixth-form; pupils can take anything from A-levels to basic building or carpentry courses. Richmond is another borough that has a tertiary college, while Merton is planning one. A few other boroughs have sixth-form colleges. However, there are doubts that many more will come on stream. The Education Reform Act allows schools to apply to opt out of local authority control if they are aggrieved in any way. So schools threatened with the loss of their sixth-forms can hit back by trying to get direct funding from the Department of Education and Science.

This means that the rather unsatisfactory situation in inner London is likely to continue. Because of falling rolls, many schools have too few sixth-formers to offer a reasonable choice of A-level options. The ILEA tried to get round this by grouping schools into 'consortia' so that pupils could take A-levels in two or three different schools. It is generally agreed that this has proved unsatisfactory with pupils spending far too much time travelling. Sixth-form centres, like that in Islington, have proved more satisfactory. These operate in much the same way as sixth-form colleges, except that pupils and teachers remain nominally on the rolls of neighbouring secondary schools. Further education colleges, such as Kingsway-Princeton and City and East, provide another option for inner Londoners. Many of them are rather like tertiary colleges, offering a full range of courses, including A-levels.

As well as schools wholly maintained by the local authority control, some parents will want to consider voluntary-aided schools. These are largely financed from public funds but have some freedom from local authority control, particularly in selecting pupils. Many are church schools, and while you may not have to be a practicing Roman Catholic or Anglican to get a place, church-going parents do get preference.

Many parents, of course, will also consider independent fee-paying schools, of which there is a wide selection in inner London. Fees vary widely, as do the academic qualities. The top schools are highly competitive in entry as well as very expensive and it may be necessary to get your child into a high-powered private preparatory school if he or she is to pass the entry exams. Some schools take part in the Government's assisted places scheme. This offers help with fees for bright children selected by the independent schools themselves. The extent of the help depends on a parental means test but, if your earnings are below average, you may qualify for full remission of fees. Some schools have their own bursary schemes for needy pupils.

Further information:
Inner London boroughs: some town halls have hotlines – or ask for Education Department (see 'Boroughs' chapter).
Outer London borough town halls.
Independent Schools Information Service, 56 Buckingham Gate,
London SW1E 6AG (tel: 630-8793/4).

The independent schools

There are 166 independent schools in Greater London, according to ISIS (Independent Schools Information Service). They vary from the august halls of Harrow, which competes with Eton for the crown of most distinguished boys' public school, to the East London premises of the Italia Conti Stage School. As one might expect, independent schools cluster most thickly in the southwest postal districts, with Putney and Wimbledon having especially dense collections. Northwest, especially Hampstead and Highgate, is close behind, with a surprising concentration in the southeast segment around Dulwich.

ISIS (address above) will send you a copy of 'Choosing your independent school' if you prefer, and are able, to send your child to a fee-paying school. The many in London and its environs include single sex, mixed and some with provision for day, weekly or full-time boarders.

There are also a number of voluntary-aided schools. There are funded partly by ILEA or the local education authority and partly by an outside, often religious, body. Examples include the Cardinal Vaughan Memorial Roman Catholic school in Holland Park and the Jewish Free School in Camden. Although these schools do operate a catchment area system whereby they will take children from the surrounding area, they will also admit pupils from outside the area provided they are, for example, either Catholic or Jewish.

If you have come to London for a while from abroad, you may wish to send your child to one of the international schools here. LISA (London International Schools Association) publishes a directory giving details of some of these schools which is available from Lyle D Rigg, Tasis England American School, Coldharbour Lane, Thorpe, Surrey, TW20 8TE Tel: 09328 65252). Your embassy here will know of others. Some of the best known are listed below:

American School in London, NW8
Tel 722 0101
Japanese School in London, W3
Tel: 993 7145
Lycee Francais, SW7
Tel: 584 6322

German School, Richmond
Tel: 948 3410
Swedish School, SW13
Tel: 741 1751
Norwegian School in London, SW20
Tel: 946 2058

Decoding the post codes

London's postal districts are a matter first and foremost of Post Office convenience: they act as collection and delivery zones and are based around the location of sorting offices and the ease of routes. But those few letters and numbers also convey a powerful emotional and financial message. The difference between SW1 and SW2 is more than a digit: it is all of the gap betwen Belgravia and Brixton. Londoners absorb these subtleties with their mother's milk. But few natives appreciate quite how remote SE2 is, or that E4 is in Epping Forest while E14 is the upwardly-mobile Isle of Dogs. And the borders can be arbitrary: some of Brixton is SW2, agreed – but so are the solidly respectable mansion blocks of Streatham Hill. Some postal districts are more logical than others. The Post Office say the whole system is quite clear: it's alphabetical. It is not, and it is not. Use this list to check which areas a zone includes, and to spot anomalies. Estate agents quite frequently quote just postal districts in advertisements and by using this list you can get an idea if the area is one you want to look at. Follow the area names into the main A-Z in this book for a map, which shows post boundaries, and a profile of the area.

E1 The East End heartland, from the City E through Whitechapel and Stepney to Mile End. Also includes the smart warehouse conversions of riverside Wapping and City fringe areas like Spitalfields and Shoreditch.

E2 North from E1, Bethnal Green and council-flat-dominated Haggerston. Also a chunk of City fringe in Shoreditch.

E3 Bow, either side of the Mile End Road in the East End.

E4 The NE fringe of London on the edge of Essex beyond the North Circular, including the suburban streets of Chingford Green and Highams Hill.

E5 The N part of Hackney borough, with Lower and Upper Clapton and a good chunk of the Hackney Marshes. Also fringes of Stoke Newington.

E6 London's eastern edge, on the way to Southend: East Ham and the Docklands suburb of Beckton.

E7 Forest Gate, the S part of Wanstead. East of Stratford East.

E8 The W side of Hackney, on the border with Islington, including the area around London Fields and the SE corner of Stoke Newington.

E9 The E part of Hackney, across the the Lea Valley and the Hackney Marshes. Includes Victoria Park and Homerton.

E10 Most of Leyton, E of the Hackney Marshes from Hackney. Includes a corner of Walthamstow.

E11 Centres around Wanstead and Snaresbrook, residential suburbs where the M11 meets the North Circular.

E12 Manor Park and Little Ilford on the E fringe of the London postal district: E from here is Essex, Ilford in particular.

E13 West Ham and Plaistow on the Barking road E from the East End.

E14 Very diverse area including both the enterprise zone in the Isle of Dogs, centre of the Docklands regeneration and site of a hundred office and homes schemes, and big tracts of council housing in Limehouse and Poplar. Also the Limehouse riverside.

E15 Stratford, the metropolis of East London, and surrounding areas E of the Lea Valley.

E16 Contains the vast Royal Docks area, next on the hit-list for Docklands regeneration, as well as old-established industry and housing in riverside Silvertown and Canning Town.

E17 Walthamstow and Higham Hill in NE London.

E18 South Woodford on the suburban fringes of Epping Forest.

EC1 All four City postcodes are ECs. This is the biggest, covering the relatively less prosperous tract from St Paul's N to the City Road, and including large parts of Finsbury and all of Clerkenwell.

EC2 The money heart of the City, from the Bank of England N to Broad St. Includes the Barbican.

EC3 The E side of the City, including the Tower and the Lloyds building.

EC4 The riverside slice, including Fleet Street, the Temple, Cannon Street and Blackfriars.

N1 The classic Islington postcode, extending S from Highbury and Islington tube to the Angel. Includes Hoxton and De Beauvoir to the E, Barnsbury and Kings Cross to the W.

N2 By contrast, the leafy streets and semis of East Finchley and Fortis Green in London's Northwest. Also the 'Millionaire's Row', Bishops Avenue, and the 'new' part of Hampstead Garden Suburb.

N3 Further out still, the next suburb on, covering most of Finchley.

N4 Crouch End, Stroud Green, Finsbury Park and Harringay greyhound stadium, a widely contrasting chunk of North London.

N5 A small district covering Highbury, to the N of Islington.

N6 The centre of Highgate, Dartmouth Park to its S, some woods and a few streets of Fortis Green to the N.

N7 WHere the Seven Sisters Road crosses the Holloway Road is the centre, with parts of Tufnell Park and a corner of Highbury.

N8 Hornsey, most of the 'ladder' district of Harringay, plus the N side of Crouch End.

N9 The N slice of Edmonton, especially Lower Edmonton.

N10 Muswell Hill

N11 Friern Barnet, New Southgate and Bounds Green: residential districts straddling the North Circular.

N12 North Finchley and Woodside Park.

N13 Palmers Green, where the North Circular crosses Green Lanes due N of London.

N14 Southgate, on the northern edge of London on the Hertfordshire border.

N15 The southern part of Tottenham, at the NE end of the Seven Sisters Road.

N16 Stoke Newington and the S part of Stamford Hill.

N17 Most of Tottenham.

N18 A slice along the North Circular beyond Tottenham, including Edmonton and Upper Edmonton.

N19 Archway, from the fringes of Highgate and Crouch End in the N down to Tufnell Park.

N20 The semi-rural, prosperous and pony-infested Totteridge, Oakleigh Park and Whetstone, N of Finchley and S of Barnet.

N21 Winchmore Hill and Grange Park, suburbia plus a lot of golf courses on the fringe of North London.

N22 Wood Green, Alexandra Palace, the E side of Muswell Hill, Noel Park and the W edge of Tottenham.

NW1 One of London's most diverse districts, with the Nash villas of Regent's Park and the near-slums of Camden Town sharing the same post code. Starts in the S at the Marylebone Rd, takes in part of Lisson Grove in the W, the edge of Kentish Town in the NE, all of Camden Town and Primrose Hill.

NW2 One of the less helpful post codes. Covers Cricklewood, Childs Hill, Dollis Hill, an arbitrary slice of Willesden and a bit of Brondesbury.

NW3 The Hampstead postcode, and

one with hardly an undesirable corner. Includes Belsize Park, part of Primrose Hill, the Finchley Road – but not West Hampstead, which is NW6.

NW4 Hendon, from Brent Cross up along the M1 to the edge of Mill Hill.

NW5 Kentish Town, Gospel Oak and Tufnell Park, on the SE fringes of Hampstead and Highgate.

NW6 Once thought of as the Kilburn postcode – which it still is – but now associated more with West Hampstead. Also spreads W to include Queen's Park and Brondesbury Park.

NW7 Mill Hill and assorted golf courses, detached houses and green belt countryside out along the M1.

NW8 Clearly defined as St John's Wood, with only a few acres of council housing around Lisson Grove to lower the tone.

NW9 West Hendon, Colindale and Kingsbury, suburban areas NW of The Welsh Harp.

NW10 A large area extending W from Kensal Rise to the North Circular, taking in Neasden, Harlesden and parts of Willesden.

NW11 Golders Green and the older, smarter side of Hampstead Garden Suburb.

SE1 A big tract in the bend of the river opposite the City and Westminster. It extends from Vauxhall in the W to the Old Kent Rd in the E. Very varied: from the National Theatre to some dire council housing.

SE2 In Kent, really, E of Woolwich and even Plumstead, it comprises Abbey Wood and part of Thamesmead.

SE3 Blackheath, Blackheath Park, East Greenwich and Kidbrooke.

SE4 A small district S of New Cross and W of Lewisham, centred around Brockley.

SE5 Essentially Camberwell, though the SW end on Coldharbour Lane is better described as Brixton, the NW corner is in Kennington and the NE in Walworth.

SE6 Catford, and Bellingham to the S.

SE7 Charlton, on the river E of the Blackwall Tunnel and W of Woolwich.

SE8 Deptford, extending along the riverside opposite the Isle of Dogs and S of the Surrey Docks. Not part of the Docklands area, though similar to it. A corner of SE8 sticks down towards Lewisham, taking in St John's.

SE9 Far, suburban SE London, including Eltham and Mottingham.

SE10 Greenwich, except for East Greenwich which is SE3. SE10 also includes the industrial peninsula to the NE through which the Blackwall Tunnel motorway passes.

SE11 Most of Kennington, from the Oval N to the Elephant & Castle and W to the river at Vauxhall. More SW than SE.

SE12 Lee and Grove Park, SE of Catford.

SE13 Lewisham, plus Ladywell and Hither Green to the S.

SE14 New Cross and a slice of the inland side of Deptford.

SE15 Peckham, though part of Peckham Rye falls into SE22, and Nunhead.

SE16 Bermondsey and Rotherhithe, including the entire Surrey Docks district of Docklands. Away from the river SE16 includes streets on the edge of North Peckham. The NW corner, along the river, has some big new riverside developments.

SE17 Walworth, from the Elephant & Castle southwards. Includes part of Kennington in the W.

SE18 Woolwich, Plumstead and Plumstead Common.

SE19 Centres around the Crystal Palace hilltop, including Norwood New Town and the fringes of Penge.

SE20 Penge and Anerley, to the SE of Crystal Palace.

SE21 Dulwich, and the fringes of Tulse Hill. Most of East Dulwich is in SE22.

SE22 East Dulwich, part of Peckham

Rye and a bit of Honor Oak.

SE23 Forest Hill, to the E of Dulwich. Also Honor Oak.

SE24 Herne Hill, also extending N towards Brixton's Loughborough Junction and NW to Brockwell Park and the Poet's Estate. Some streets in the SE corner are really in Dulwich.

SE25 South Norwood.

SE26 Sydenham, from Crystal Palace E to Bell Green and S to the edge of Penge.

SE27 West Norwood and the S half of Tulse Hill.

SE28 Thamesmead, the new town on the Plumstead Marshes E down the Thames.

SW1 Perhaps the smartest code of all, the postal address of Buckingham Palace and 10 Downing Street, never mind the whole of Westminster, St James's, Belgravia, Victoria and part of Knightsbridge including Harrods, squeezed in by a dramatic jink in the frontier, forming an enclave in SW3. Pimlico is SW1 and now that has 'come up' there is hardly a scruffy corner left. Sloane Square is SW1 too.

SW2 Part of Brixton, the southern slice, and also Streatham Hill, the edge of Clapham Park and part of Tulse Hill.

SW3 Chelsea, though the HQ of Chelseadom, Peter Jones, is in SW1. Also a good part of Knightsbridge and some of South Ken – see the area map for the quirks of the boundaries here. SW3 stops in the W at Beaufort St and large tracts of Chelsea are in SW10.

SW4 Clapham, plus a portion of Stockwell W of Clapham Road and a corner of W Brixton.

SW5 A small zone, essentially Earls Court.

SW6 By contrast, the entire island cut off by the river and the railway which is Fulham. Only in the N, where the boundary runs along Lillie Rd, is there any doubt. Some streets N of here are really in Fulham though they have W6 and W14 codes.

SW7 South Kensington, Knightsbridge (though see also SW3) and the Museums.

SW8 A mixed area, much crossed by railways, between the river and Stockwell. Includes parts of Stockwell, the Oval, Vauxhall, the E part of Battersea's Queenstown neighbourhood, and the industrial zone of Nine Elms.

SW9 The northern half of Brixton, the E side of Stockwell and a corner in the N which is really the Oval.

SW10 The western end of Chelsea, plus a patch to the N which is really West Brompton and, by sheer good luck for the developers, the big new Chelsea Harbour development which physical, if not postal, geography places across the creek in Fulham.

SW11 A big slice of smart and not-so-smart South London, from Battersea Park, through Central Battersea to Wandsworth Common.

SW12 Balham, including the streets in the 'Nightingale Triangle' where people say they're in Clapham South, and the lower tier of the 'between the commons' neighbourhood of Battersea.

SW13 Barnes, well defined by common, river and White Hart Lane, which forms the boundary with SW14 and Mortlake.

SW14 Mortlake by the river and the suburban streets of East Sheen on the edge of Richmond Park.

SW15 Putney, plus Roehampton in the W and some streets which are virtually Wandsworth to the E.

SW16 Streatham, plus Streatham Vale and Norbury in the S.

SW17 Tooting.

SW18 Wandsworth, Southfields and Earlsfield.

SW19 A large area including Wimbledon, Wimbledon Park, Merton and Colliers Wood.

SW20 The further reaches of Wimbledon towards the Kingston

Bypass, including Raynes Park.

W1 Grandeur and commerce, including Mayfair, Oxford St, Regent St ... Essentially, the West End.

W2 Bayswater and Paddington, plus Little Venice S of the canal.

W3 Acton, though not Acton Green in the S or the industry of North Acton.

W4 Chiswick, including Bedford Park and Acton Green.

W5 The centre of Ealing, including South Ealing. Ealing has three postcodes: see area map.

W6 Hammersmith and the northern fringes of Fulham.

W7 The western slice of Ealing borough, including Hanwell and part of West Ealing.

W8 The heart of Kensington, around the High Street and Church Street.

W9 Maida Vale and Little Venice N of the canal, plus a sharply contrasting area to the W of Walterton Rd stretching up to Queens Park.

W10 North Kensington N of the flyover, plus Kensal as far N as Queens Park.

W11 Notting Hill S of the flyover and N of Notting Hill Gate. Includes the N part of Holland Park.

W12 Shepherds Bush, plus East Acton and White City.

W13 The middle slice of Ealing, W of Ealing centre and E of Hanwell.

W14 A slice squeezed between Kensington and Hammersmith, including some of the smartest parts of Holland Park, Olympia, West Kensington and the NE quadrant of Hammersmith.

WC1 Bloomsbury, St Pancras and the W part of Finsbury.

WC2 Covent Garden, the Strand, part of Holborn.

The Boroughs

The big change coming in 1990 is the takeover of education by the inner London boroughs, who inherit the task following the abolition of the ILEA (Inner London Education Authority). For details and comment see the 'Education' chapter. The profiles below give the facts known at the time of going to press about the boroughs' education plans.

The town halls already play a big part in Londoners' lives, especially since the Greater London Council was abolished. The boroughs control a range of services from housing through planning control to libraries. With the exception of the City of London, each one is controlled by one of the main political parties and London local politics is a microcosm of politics on a national scale. Indeed, in recent years the battles between the largely Labour inner London boroughs and the Tory central government have achieved a prominence out of proportion to the local issues involved.

So Londoners live in a political environment where the stance of the party controlling the Town Hall makes quite a difference to a household's bills and the quality of its day-to-day life. The profiles that follow have been compiled by local reporters who are in constant contact with the policies and foibles of their council. The aim is to give a picture of what each borough is like to live in, whether it will cost you more or less to live across a dividing line, and what the political prospects are.

The boroughs discussed are those in the zone covered by the detailed area profiles in this book. Information on London's schools system can be found in the 'Education' chapter, and an account of the planning and building regulations apparatus is in the Property Business section. Detail given on the composition of councils etc is current as we go to press, but by-elections and splits within parties can change things. The telephone number listed is the Town Hall enquiry number: many boroughs will on request send full details of their services and facilities.

Barnet

Controlling party: Conservative. Make-up: 39 Con, 18 Lab, 3 Alliance
Rates: 189.7 in £. Town Hall tel: 202 8282. Search: 4 weeks.
Director of Education: Neil Gill, previously the Deputy Director
of Education for Barnet. Education enquiries: 368 1255

As if to match the pace of life in this green and leafy borough, Barnet council could at first appear quiet and sleepy. It likes to think of itself as a bastion of Conservative ideals, and reckons that if anyone complains they shouldn't shout too loudly.

Until the 1986 local elections the political make-up of the council was dull with the shock results in May 1986, Finchley, the parliamentary seat of Prime Minister Margaret Thatcher, reeled back in horror as 18 Labour councillors filed back into the chamber – representing the whole of St Paul's, Woodhouse and East Finchley wards – plus three Alliance members. During the campaign the Tories had been accused of needing a shot of young blood. But after the dust had settled, the level-headed, middle-aged, middle-class majority was still in charge if somewhat chastened.

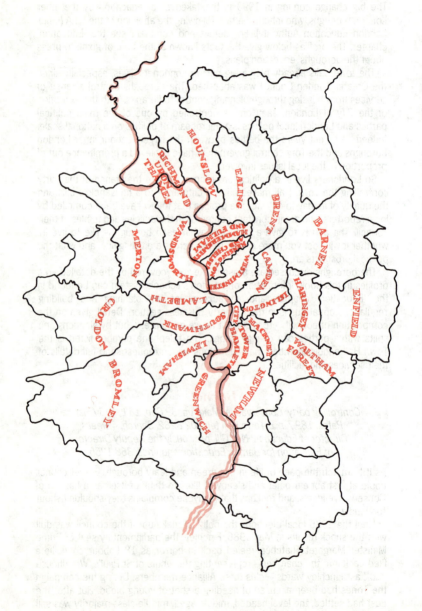

To give it its due, Barnet council is sensible and strong. It regularly languishes way down in the league of authorities assessed on their speed in dealing with planning applications. It is indeed slow – but it is thorough. The planning officers work hard liaising with applicants to make sure plans are fit for approval. That way time is not wasted as applications are referred back for amendments. Currently the schedule is being stepped up: with more frequent meetings the council should be able to escape the criticism of slow service.

The borough's biggest advantage for residents is the relatively low rates, which however rose in 1988 after years of stability. For that residents get a decent service. The refuse service is acceptable. People in communal flats who may have trouble with the large container bin collections need only phone to get it put right. And really that is the answer to any little niggles about borough services. If people just pick up the telephone and record their complaint, Barnet is quick to act. That's what Barnet would really like: putting things straight for individual enquiries. When people club together to demand action it acts like a wounded animal.

The schools are full to bursting, as anyone would expect for family suburbia, but Barnet prides itself on examination results – at the expense of reform, according to its critics. But it was one of a handful of authorities to take on the pilot project for the Certificate of Pre Vocational Education and in the '60s had primary schools involved in the Nuffield courses.

There is one major sports centre at Copthall, with an Olympic sized swimming pool, training pool. diving pool, gym and running track. It was tipped for a massive development as a national centre, but thrown out at a public enquiry last year.

In a word Barnet is conscientious, if pedantic.

Brent

Controlling party: Labour. Make-up: 42 Lab, 20 Con, 1 SLD. Rates 261.1 in £. Town Hall tel: 904 1244. Search: 5-6 weeks.

Brent is a borough for enterprising people. To live there, you have to be. So say many locals, at once exhilarated and exasperated by dealing with a council its (Labour) MP compared to Pol Pot's Cambodia, yet which at the same time shows every sign of being truly concerned to do the right (or left) thing.

The borough of Brent lies in the north-west corner of London, sandwiched between the edge of the West End and the 'Metroland' of John Betjeman's poems and writings. It was formed in 1965 by the amalgamation of the old Wembley and Willesden councils. The merger has never been a particularly harmonious one as the (generally Tory) north and the (generally Labour) south of the borough are very different in composition and character.

The borough is also effectively divided in two by the great swathe of the North Circular Road – a far greater barrier than the natural one of the River Brent, from which the council takes its name, which has now been reduced to the level of a stagnant trickle.

Brent has the highest ethnic population of any local authority in the country. About 60% of the borough's population are non-British. The largest single ethnic group are the Irish who make up some 20% of the population. In the last three or four years there has been a fresh exodus of Irish people to Brent rivalling anything that has happened in the past. Thirty fresh refugees from the economic problems of the Emerald Isle are thought to arrive in Brent each day of the year. Most end up living in the Kilburn/Cricklewood/Willesden areas in the south of the borough, drawn there because it has had an Irish population in residence since the original influxes at the time of the Great Famine.

The other main ethnic communities are black, mainly West Indian, but with a not insignificant African population, and Asian, mainly Indian. The Asians live mainly in the north of the borough around Wembley where many are owner-occupiers. The black population is scattered throughout the borough but is particularly concentrated in the Harlesden area and its attendant estate, Stonebridge. Stonebridge is one of several large council estates built in the 1960s in the borough. Along with Chalkhill in Wembley and the South Kilburn estate, they suffer some of the worst deprivation in what is officially the eighth poorest borough in Britain.

Apart from these large council estates there is a large proportion of other council-owned property, particularly in the south of the borough. There is also an increasing amount of property in the hands of housing associations such as Brent Peoples and the Paddington Churches.

Particularly in the north of the borough there are a lot of private owner-occupied houses. In the south there is more conversion going on of large old houses, although in some areas the council has not been keen on this because of the amount of extra parked cars multiple occupancy is thought to engender. It also means fewer homes for families.

Kenton and Kingsbury and other areas in the north of the borough have always been attractive to house buyers with their tree-lined avenues and their proximity to the green belt. In recent years areas in the south, such as Queen's Park and Brondesbury, have become progressively more gentrified as professional people, unable to squeeze into Hampstead and West Hampstead on the other side of the Kilburn High Road, are forced further west.

Brent's rates are high – for those of its 225,000 residents who pay rates – at 261p in the pound. Political control has changed hands in the past, but at the moment it is firmly in the hands of the Labour party who have a reputation in Fleet Street for being 'loony left'. For 1988/89 the council has escaped rate-capping for the first time in several years. This could, of course, mean large rate rises on the agenda. Rates rose from 242 to 261p in the £. At the start of 1989, rent arrears and budget over-runs totalled £25m.

Brent's radical leadership has taken a lot of criticism for some of its policies. Its libraries have been criticised as some of the worst in London and the education service has suffered a vote of no confidence with 25% of Brent children not educated within the borough, but sent by their parents to schools outside. Brent counter this by saying that the borough's education service has received an unfair press. The council claim the borough's 72 primary schools and 18 secondary schools have the lowest teacher-pupil ratio in the country.

1988 saw radical closures of amenities such as libraries as Brent tried to balance the books. Demonstrations against these cuts led to violence at Town Hall meetings. Other services are suffering, such as rubbish collections: local groups are banding together to collect their own rubbish. One group made their point by dumping their garbage on the Town Hall steps. As a resident observed "if you're enterprising, you can have quite good fun with Brent council."

Brent is a borough of contrast, with its fair share of greenery, but with some areas where insurance companies will refuse house insurance because of the high crime rate.

If some locals have their way, it would not exist at all. A petition signed by 10,000 residents of the northwest part – respectable suburbia, mostly – has been sent to the Boundary Commission which is looking at the London Boroughs. They want independence.

Camden

Controlling party: Labour. Make-up: 44 Lab, 13 Con, 2 Alliance.
Rates: 211.68p in £. Town Hall tel: 278 4444. Search: minimum 12 weeks.
Director of Education Designate (Director, 1990): Peter Mitchell, previously Chief Education Adviser to Leicestershire Council; Head Teacher of Quintin Kynaston School, NW8, 1972-83. Education enquiries: 860 5910.

Camden was created in 1965 by the amalgamation of the three old London Boroughs of Hampstead, St Pancras and Holborn, and thus stretches from the busy shopping and commercial areas around the famous Inns of Court and New Oxford Street, all the way to Highgate and the highest point in London at the top of Hampstead Heath. It's an enormously varied area which includes some of the most economically and socially deprived parts of London, such as Somers Town, Kings Cross and parts of Kentish Town and Camden Town, as well as some of the most affluent and attractive districts in the capital, like Hampstead and Highgate.

The northern part of the borough is particularly well supplied with public amenities, shopping areas, recreational facilities, entertainment centres, famous buildings, tourist attractions and many beautiful parks – as well as the famous 800 acres of Hampstead Heath. There are thriving areas further south, however, and parts of the borough are enjoying a resurgence of commercial and residential activity. Camden Town and Chalk Farm have experienced a particular rejuvenation, fueled by the thriving Camden Lock market area which has become an important centre for street markets, antiques and specialist shops, and because of the plans for major commercial and shopping developments in Camden Town itself, such as the new Sainsburys superstore which opened in December.

Politically, the council has been controlled by the Labour Party ever since its creation, with the exception of a brief period of Conservative rule between 1969 and 1971.

In its early years Camden Council gained an enviable reputation as a fiercely modern and progressive borough, building up social services and other council departments in a way that set the pace for other London boroughs and, indeed, boroughs all over the country. Its library services, for example, have been widely praised, and the annual Camden Festival has become an important event in the international music calendar.

But in the late 1970s the council began to run into financial problems and these are still the central issue in Camden politics today. Camden became one of the first boroughs in the country to have its Rate Support Grant withdrawn by the Conservative Government because of council 'over-spending', and also among the first to be 'rate-capped' under the legislation which allowed the Environment Secretary to place a limit on the amount councils could extract from their ratepayers. The result of rate-capping has been that although rates in the borough have risen only marginally in the last three or four years, the council has encountered major financial crises as councillors attempted to continue providing services at the same – and even higher – level, without sufficient income. Councillors resorted to heavy borrowing and 'creative accounting' schemes in an attempt to close the gap but, in 1987, it was finally forced to begin cutting its expenditure and reducing its town hall workforce. The main cuts have now been made, but there are still very rough financial waters ahead such as the estimated £23.4m deficit looming for 1989/90.

Ealing

Controlling party: Labour. Make-up: 47 Lab, 20 Con, 3 SLD. Rates: 197p in £. Town Hall tel: 579 2424. Search: 6 weeks.

Ratepayers in the London Borough of Ealing are still recovering from the shock of having elected a Labour council in 1987 after eight years of Tory rule. The Tories in Ealing were often accused of having just one policy – keeping the rates down. This meant that householders enjoyed one of the capital's lowest domestic rates, but other residents complained of poor housing, education cuts and general neglect.

In May 1987 Labour was elected with a huge majority – and immediately started work to meet election promises to increase spending on education, social work and housing. More controversially, councillors also created hundreds of new Town Hall jobs: they set up a race unit, a women's unit and a police unit, they discussed teaching schoolchildren that homosexual lifestyles were equally valid to heterosexuality, they invited Sinn Fein leaders to the Town Hall and generally became a target for Tory gibes of 'loony left'. The gibes were well-aired in the national press, where they were used to embarrass Ealing's most famous resident – Labour leader Neil Kinnock.

The ratepayers counted the cost of their new leaders in February 1987 when Ealing's rates rose by 65% – the highest rise in the country. Although neighbours were still paying less than they would have in long-established Labour boroughs like Camden and Brent, the outcry was furious – and the boroughs two Tory MPs, Harry Greenway and Sir George Young, made enormous political capital out of the row.

The 'London effect' backlash was felt keenly by Labour at the general election of June 1987, when Sir George Young and Harry Greenway both increased their majorities, and claimed that the rates were the main issue of concern to voters. In Ealing Southall, veteran Labour MP Syd Bidwell kept his seat, thanks mainly to the solid support of the large Asian community.

The inevitable result was that Ealing was 'rate-capped', and its rate was reduced by Whitehall decree from 234p to 197p in the £.

Greenwich

Controlling party: Labour. Make-up: 42 Lab, 12 Con, 6 SDP, 2 SLD. Rates: 230.68p in £. Town Hall tel: 854 8888. Search: 8 weeks.
Director of Education: appointment awaited. Education enquiries: 854 6003

Greenwich has given up its fight with Whitehall over rate-capping and applied, with success, for its rate to be 'redetermined', meaning that rates will be allowed to rise and spending to increase. The council was in the first batch of big spending local authorities to be rate-capped in 1985 following a decision by its Labour rulers to expand services to unheard of levels. But the joys of ratepayers at being spared massive annual rate rises – although rates are still very high – is now overshadowed by the impending arrival of the Government's

Poll Tax. For people in Greenwich will be some of the hardest hit in England when rates are replaced by the poll tax in the early 1990s. Under the new scheme the council are quoting £258 per person in 1990 rising to an estimated £587 by 1994, compared to an average household rates bill now of £464. That's very bad news for the small band of opposition Conservative councillors who have only once held control of the council, back in the 1960s. They know a second spell of Tory town hall rule is almost an impossibility as long as council tenants – who make up a majority of Greenwich's 200,000 or so inhabitants – continue to vote Labour in large numbers. Greenwich council threatened a 'won't pay' revolt against Poll Tax – but jaundiced locals recall they said the same about rate-capping. And indeed by December they had reached an accord with Environment Secretary Nicholas Ridley.

But while the Conservatives are hemmed into places like true blue Blackheath and suburban Eltham, Labour does face a growing challenge from the Alliance. The Alliance now boasts two out of three of the constituency's MPs (the other is a Tory) having snatched the Labour stronghold of Greenwich with Rosie Barnes in a famous by-election victory in 1987. The Alliance has made gains from Labour by pitching at working class voters worried by the council's 'loony left' image.

The council hits back by pointing to impressive records on improvements to social services, house building and leisure centres, but traditional Labour supporters seem unimpressed. Like many other inner London authorities Greenwich has refused to cut back spending in the face of the government rate-cap. Instead it preferred to carry on expanding services paid for with creative accounting techniques in the misplaced hope that Labour would triumph in the last General Election. Cuts in spending now look certain in 1989, following those of 1988, as councillors ponder a gap between income and expenditure of some £33m, with Greenwich's rents – among the lowest in London – a certain target.

Greenwich has tried in the past to shy away from the 'loony left' label, but has quietly followed the same policies of rapidly expanding its services and workforce. Now the council is having to get to grips with cutting services and raising rents (several childrens' homes have closed). That's hardly popular with Labour voters, and the Conservatives are saddled with being the party of the widely-feared Poll Tax.

No wonder the SLD is waiting in the wings with high hopes of making the kind of impact at council level which it has already made on Greenwich's parliamentary scene.

Hackney

Controlling party: Labour. Make-up: 50 Lab, 4 Con, 5 SLD, 1 vacant. Rates: 229.4p in £. Town Hall tel: 986 3123. Search: 16 weeks.
Director of Education: re-advertising as we went to press.

The current borough of Hackney was created in 1964 by the amalgamation of the three old London boroughs of Stoke Newington, Shoreditch and Hackney. In the past two years it has seen a massive increase in new residents, mostly owner-occupiers, and experienced spiralling property prices, which rose an average 38% during 1987 and 25% in 1988.

There is a population of 190,000, spread between prosperous areas such as De Beauvoir and Victoria Park, as well as the deprived dwellings found in

Haggerston and Hoxton. Hackney has a tradition of radical politics, and in 1987 Hackney North elected Britain's first black woman MP, Diane Abbott. In the GLC's heyday, Hackney was in the forefront of the Labour boroughs opposed to the Government's rate-capping laws which were used to restrict council spending, and the council was among those which used so-called creative accounting methods to circumvent the laws.

But in 1988 the council had to make £42 million of cuts, with library services among services curtailed. And in 1988/89 a further £17m must be cut. There are many good (ILEA-run) schools in the borough but high property prices have led to a chronic shortage of teachers, particularly in junior schools. Staff shortages have also had a bad effect on health services, which have trouble attracting clerical and nursing staff. A new district hospital was opened in Homerton in 1986, but health service cash cutbacks have already placed a question mark over its future.

Burglary rates in the borough are very high, and the police have set up special squads to tackle the problem. The huge increase in property buyers has led to lengthy delays in carrying out property searches. In 1987 these could take as long as 20 weeks, and resulted in many house purchases falling through. Hackney Council had to take on extra staff to tackle the problem, and managed to reduce the waiting time to four weeks by this January.

Sales of council homes started sluggishly in the borough, but have slowly picked up. In December 1987, the total sold stood at 800, a year later it was 1,226. A limited range of home improvement grants are available for tenants, but there is nothing available for owner-occupiers. The council is not keen on conversions of family-sized houses into small flats. It is hard to get planning permission unless one of the resulting flats is big enough for four.

Rates in Hackney are high, although rate-capping laws mean that the increase in rates has been more gradual for the past two years. The borough will be one of the hardest hit by the introduction of Poll Tax in 1990, when each resident will be asked to pay an estimated £347 charge, rising to £578 by 1994, though questions over rate support grant and education could change this.

The change in population is reflected in the up-market shops which have recently sprung up in the borough. This is exemplified by the rapid rise of Stoke Newington Church Street, which now boasts restaurants, antiques, designer clothes shops, art galleries and a clutch of smart estate agents. Nowhere is this affluence more apparent than on Stamford Hill, where shopping giants Safeway have decided to open two Superstores within a few hundred yards of each other. They are confident that both can attract enough custom to prosper. There is also an historic open air market in Ridley Road. In January Dalston acquired Hackney's first purpose-built shopping centre.

Although sometimes portrayed as an inner-city wasteland, Hackney has its fair share of green open spaces, ranging from Clissold Park with its engaging mini zoo in Stoke Newington to the sprawling Victoria Park, which borders on Tower Hamlets. And the River Lea, which boasts its own marina, runs through Springfield Park and the Hackney Marshes. There is even a prosperous city farm within its borders.

The diversity of the borough is reflected in the re-emergence of the Hackney Empire. Once, it was a prime date on the music-hall circuit and everyone of any note 'played The Empire'. It fell into decline, along with its neighbourhood, in the post-war years. Re-opened in 1986 after many years as a bingo hall, its highly popular mix of old style entertainment and alternative cabaret mirrors the shifting pattern of Hackney's population. And Hackney is now gaining a name as the jazz and cabaret capital of London.

Hammersmith and Fulham

Controlling party: Labour: Make-up: 40 Lab, 9 Con, 1 Lib
Rates: 228p in £. Town Hall tel: 748 3020. Search: 1-1½ weeks.
Director of Education: Christine Whatford, formerly
head of Abbey Wood School.

One of the smaller London boroughs, resulting from the fusion of Hammersmith (to the north of Hammersmith flyover) with Fulham. The marriage was an uneasy one, especially at first when the name Hammersmith was given to the whole area, leaving Fulhamites bereft of their identity. The twin name was brought in to mollify them.

The local council, whose slogan is 'serving the community', is currently Labour after a period of unstable coalitions and is suffering from infighting between various elements of the Labour Party. Their wings have been clipped for the last two financial years by a self-imposed rate-capping exercise and reduced capital spending following a 50% rise in rates in their first year in office. At present, services are generally good, but residents report a noticeable decline in services such as street cleaning and rubbish collection. Some estate agents, apprehensive about future rate increases, suggest the main disadvantage of living in Hammersmith and Fulham is the Labour council.

There is relatively little council housing in the borough, and this is located in pockets. The council's planning policies are quite stringent, with most applications needing to go before committees, which means considerable delays – up to six months for a simple extension.

Hammersmith returned a Labour MP in the 1987 election, and is regarded as a safe Labour seat. Fulham changed from Labour to Conservative, followed by a brief Labour by-election victory, but was Conservative again after the 1987 General Election. Cynics suggest Tories got back in to Fulham because of the 50% rise in rates. Realists suggest it reflects the changing population structure of the area.

Hammersmith still retains the more traditional types of shops. Hammersmith Centre has chain stores and a shopping precinct; to the north Shepherds Bush, with its market, Goldhawk Road, Uxbridge Road and Shepherds Bush Road have numerous small shops. Shepherds Bush and Brook Green are changing fast as residential areas since they are only 20 minutes from the City.

Fulham, apart from the North End Road market, has been taken over by 'unreal' shops. It is reputed to have the highest density of estate agents in London – over 70 around Parsons Green alone. Fulham Road and New Kings Road – and even parts of Dawes Road and Lillie Road – are full of specialist furnishing shops, picture galleries, antique shops, dress boutiques. In the evening the density of car parking along Fulham Road and New Kings Road indicate the bon viveur restaurant and wine bar set have truly arrived.

Major commercial developments planned in the area include Fulham Centre, where new developments are rising piecemeal out of long-blighted vacant sites, and Hammersmith Centre, which suffered for years from planning blight but where full-scale demolition now in progress precedes the big redevelopment planned. Chelsea Harbour, a luxury residential and leisure development, is nearing completion. Future redevelopments planned for the area include

Fulham and Chelsea football grounds, though it is too early to say what form these will take (except the council has pledged that football will remain).

The West London Relief Road is the major traffic improvement scheme affecting West London, a north/south motorway type road running beside the railway lines along the eastern borough boundary. The question everybody asks is where will all the traffic go when it gets to the river?

Haringey
Controlling party: Labour. Make-up: 39 Lab, 19 Con, 1 SLD.
Rates 226.83 in £. Town Hall tel: 975 9700. Search 3-4 weeks.

Haringey was created by the merging of the former boroughs of Wood Green, Tottenham and Hornsey. With Tottenham as its core, the borough extends north towards the North Circular Road, west to Muswell Hill, Harringay and Wood Green, south to Finsbury Park and South Tottenham, and east to Tottenham Hale and Tottenham marshes. The geography of the borough ranges from the heights of Muswell Hill and Alexandra Palace to the flat area of Tottenham marshes, and from the open spaces of Finsbury Park to the densely populated urban areas in central Tottenham.

Haringey is also marked by cultural and social diversity, ranging from the economically deprived parts of central and northern Tottenham to the generally more prosperous areas stretching towards the southern and western borders.

Some members of Haringey council have been portrayed by the media as the loopiest of loony lefties, squandering valuable money on obscure minority organizations. But word is that the council as a whole 'is getting saner all the time.' Given that the Tottenham area is a multi-ethnic community – and given all the problems that arise in such a community: language barriers, racism, high unemployment and crime rates – the council's task is by no means easy. In an attempt to solve these problems, the council has introduced a number of policies to revitalise the more deprived areas, including a wide variety of educational, employment and housing redevelopment schemes. The sports and cultural centre off the High Road should be finished by the end of this year, and efforts are being made to encourage small businesses.

Politically, Haringey has been Labour-controlled since its inception, apart from a brief Conservative spell between 1968 and 1971. The reputation of Haringey Council has not been helped by unfavourable media coverage – the Tottenham riots acted as the catalyst for public criticism, and the Council's often controversial educational and racial stances have not helped matters. The media, however, make little attempt to investigate the real situation in the area and the inflammatory nature of the news stories in the national papers has often misrepresented the Council – and increased its justifiable paranoia.

In addition, the constant battle between the government and the Council over rate-capping has prevented Haringey from drawing up firm plans for the future. When the Council was rate-capped for the first time in 1985, it immediately adopted, like other rate-capped authorities, 'creative accountancy' measures to provide £20 million for local services over and above the funds allowed by the government. The Council was rate-capped for a second time in 1986, again using creative accountancy to provide an extra £40 million, and was hit for a third time in 1987. The Council overspent its budget, rates became very high, a financial crisis resulted, and court procedures were threatened.

The situation came to a head in 1987 when the Council finally agreed to implement 'a balanced and lawful budget'. As a result, there has been a substantial cut in planned spending and an increase in charges of £15 million including an average £4 per week rent increase for Council tenants, a freeze on hiring and a selective increase in charges for Council services. But by late 1988 a new money crisis had blown up with the discovery of an overspend of £7.25m. Most of this was a loss sustained by the council's building organisation. There were fears that further spending cuts would be necessary.

Although Haringey is by some measures the seventh most deprived borough in the country, and despite the fact that the Council has lost over £100 million in government grants over the last eight years, Whitehall has still called for the Council to adopt much stricter administrative and spending policies. Council housing will be affected by these new developments – rents for garages will increase by £4 per week, refunds for properties undergoing repair will be withdrawn, and the work done on maintaining grounds surrounding council property will be halved. Last winter rubbish collection became the hot local issue, with residents complaining of an inadequate Council service.

Despite these drawbacks, Haringey's decision to adopt a spending policy in line with the government's guidelines may indicate that there will be less conflict between the two sides in the future, allowing the implementation of more long-term solutions to Haringey's problems.

Islington

Controlling party: Labour. Make-up: 37 Labour, 15 SLD/SDP.
Rates: 184.33p in £. Town Hall tel: 226 1234. Search: 2 weeks.
Chief Education Officer: Christopher Webb, 1974-1988,
Director of the Notting Dale Technology Centre, the ITEC
Consultancy Unit and the Notting Dale Urban Studies
Centre, and a former teacher in Kings Cross.

The modern borough of Islington, created out of the old metropolitan boroughs of Islington and Finsbury in 1965, faces most of the inner city problems experienced by many London councils – but without many of the resources of its richer neighbours like Camden and the City of London. It stretches from Clerkenwell and the Old Street area in the south all the way to the lower reaches of Highgate in the north. On the east is the equally deprived borough of Hackney, and on the west are Camden's bordering areas of Holborn, Bloomsbury and, further up, Kentish Town.

Despite its lack of resources, Islington has always been an extremely popular borough for its indefinable London 'character', and there are still large areas where traditionally working class families still form the majority of the population – even if it's in council estates nowadays instead of the old terraced houses. There are, too, some extremely smart and expensive areas in Canonbury and Barnsbury and surrounding areas where 'gentrification' on a large scale has dramatically altered the nature of the environment. And the spill-over effect from these parts is resulting in more and more of the borough becoming a prime target for young people looking for housing. Its close proximity to the City makes it a very attractive proposition.

The core shopping centre around Islington High Street, Upper Street and Essex Road contains everything from old-fashioned ironmongers' shops to the most up-market and trendy stores imaginable. Restaurants and good pubs abound, and the area is also famous for its markets – notably the Camden Passage antiques, and the fruit and vegetables in the colourful Chapel Market. There is also Steve Hatt, in Essex Road, claimed by many thousands to be London's finest fishmonger.

Politically the borough is totally dominated by the Labour Party. It is many years since Conservatives held any seats at all on the council, and today the only opposition on the 52-seat council are the 16 SDP and Liberal Alliance members. In the early '80s the council became known as The People's Republic of Islington because of its uncompromising left-wing policies. But often the council attracted most criticism purely for its enlightened approach to minority groups, ethnic minorities and gay organisations, even though the amount of ratepayers' money spent on these groups was negligible in terms of the overall spending budget.

However, like the other free-spending Labour councils, Islington's wings were severely clipped by the Government's rate-capping legislation. Expenditure was cut back dramatically, to the extent that the borough is no longer on the rate-capping blacklist.

Kensington and Chelsea
Controlling party: Conservative. Make-up: 39 Con, 14 Lab, 1 Independent Lab.
Rates: 98.9p in the £. Town Hall tel: 937 5464. Search: 7 days.
Director of Education: Michael Stoten, previously Director
of Education for Brent, 1987-88; Senior Assistant Director of Education
for Coventry, 1983-87

Kensington and Chelsea is a true-blue Tory stronghold with tinges of red around the edges. The Conservative rulers have more than twice as many councillors as their Labour rivals, confining them to the socially-deprived neighbourhoods in the north and south-west of the borough. Although the council's political complexion never alters, its image recently underwent a radical change. Out went the old guard of ageing and retired Tories and in came the young upwardly mobile professionals to give the party a youthful, go-ahead image. Mostly in their late '20s and early '30s, they brought down the average age of the council to 40. The architect of the image change, council leader Nicholas Freeman, said he wanted the borough to be run by councillors who worked for a living. Freeman, leader since 1977, is a barrister outside the council chamber.

Although the council is staunchly Tory, it does not always toe the Government line. Freeman is an outspoken critic of Government interference in the affairs of democratically-elected local councils. The Tories have also joined the Labour Opposition in condemning the proposed poll tax as unfair, admitting that the wealthy will benefit at the expense of the poor. Local amenity groups see the council as their ally in a battle with Whitehall to protect the borough's environment. The Town Hall is a staunch foe of over-development – but many planning applications it turns down go through on appeal to the Government.

The council's main aim to retain Kensington and Chelsea as an attractive residential area and to make it possible for middle-income groups to continue living in the borough. Such people have been squeezed out over recent years by high property prices, rents and rates. (The population dropped by 31% between 1971-84, to 136,000.) To help stem the inflationary flood, the council reduced rates by 30% in 1986/87 and froze them in 1987/88 and 1988/9.

Over the years the council has encouraged the growth of housing association developments and co-ownership schemes, both as an alternative to council housing and to help people on low incomes to get a foothold on the property ladder. As part of its drive to enhance the borough's appeal as a residential area, the council has designated 65% of Kensington and Chelsea as conservation areas. 'A place without old buildings is like a person without a memory', it argues. The council also runs a 24-hour noise complaint 'hotline' Fourteen gardens, parks, cemeteries and streets in the borough are included in the register of notable gardens and landscape compiled by the Historic Buildings and Monuments Commission.

The council's most controversial proposal at the time of writing is its decision to opt out of ILEA and run education itself. Labour opponents warn that the borough is too small to set up its own education service with the necessary back-up youth and careers services which that entails. Another fight the council has taken up is the battle against AIDS. It has led the way among local authorities in recognising the needs of sufferers of the disease. As well as giving planning consent for Britain's first AIDS care centre/hospice in Notting Hill, it gave a £100,000 grant towards building costs.

Lambeth

Controlling party: Labour. Make-up: 40 Lab, 21 Con, 3 SLD.
Rates: 187p in £. Town Hall tel: 274 7722. Search 10 weeks.
Chief Education Officer: Bebb Burchell, previously the Assistant
Education Officer (Equal Opportunities) for ILEA, 1987-88; Senior Officer
for Race Equality, 1983-87.

Government ministers often refer to Lambeth in the same breath as Liverpool when talk turns to the hotbeds of intransigent Labour council control. Council leader 'Red' Ted Knight and 30 Labour colleagues trod the same path as Derek Hatton on Merseyside when rate-capping hit the headlines in 1985. They were surcharged and banned from office for five years for refusing to set a rate – and their stance appeared to be vindicated when Labour's share of the vote in the ensuing council elections jumped from 34% to 44.5%. Since then resistance to Government spending restrictions has collapsed and the present Labour council made cuts of £60m.

Former council leader Linda Bellos reduced the council workforce from 10,400 to 9,400 in 1987 to comply with Government spending restrictions, but set spending at £152m. The council also cut social services, housing offices and library opening hours. Councillor Bellos and her closest colleagues resigned after the cuts went through.

Her more moderate successor, Cllr. Dick Sorabji, took over after a hastily scrambled compromise without a majority in his own Labour group. Despite this, he beat off a challenge from left-wingers who wanted to defy the Government over Poll Tax which might have led to Lambeth councillors being surcharged and banned from office yet again. Sorabjis' administration has started efforts to develop inner-cities areas like Brixton in conjunction with private developers and the Government. A Lambeth-commissioned report by independent property consultants Debenham, Tewson and Chinnock has suggested Brixton could be exploited as a tourist attraction and it recommends building a major shopping mall in the High Street.

Lambeth, however, will always be a borough of contrasts. The council boundaries cover 10 square miles and three Parliamentary constituencies. The southernmost, Streatham, has long been a Conservative seat and pockets of the two Labour-held constituencies, Norwood and Vauxhall, are decidedly gentrified. Nearly a third of housing is owner-occupied, with 44% council rented and 15% held by private landlords.

Preserving the present population balance in Lambeth is high on the council's list of planning priorities. Pressures for luxury flats and offices in the north of the borough and conversions of houses into flats in the south are disapproved of, although there is little the council can do to stop them. There is strong commitment to environmental and housing improvements, with more than 20 Conservation Areas and 14 General Improvement Areas. About £1 million a year is spent on upgrading housing in GIAs and roughly £300,000 a year is made available in grants for home restoration and other improvements in Conservation Areas.

With a housing waiting list of 20,000 and 600 homeless families in bed and breakfast accommodation or council hostels, Lambeth is in principle opposed to the Right-to-Buy for council tenants. But it cannot legally prevent sales and about 300 homes a year are sold, compared with 1,000 in neighbouring Wandsworth. It is also worthwhile to compare rates in the two boroughs. The rate in Lambeth is 187 pence in the pound as against 130.8 pence in Wandsworth.Town Hall predictions on Poll Tax put the likely charge per head in Lambeth at £490 in 1990, rising to over £1,000 in 1994.

Lambeth would say the higher charges reflect a political decision for more and better services for a low-income population, although an authoritative comparison of the quality of council facilities and services in the two boroughs has never been carried out.

At the moment, voters are backing Labour's approach in Lambeth. With Labour increasingly aware of the need to appear businesslike and efficient, control of the council is unlikely to change.

Lewisham
Make-up: 48 Lab, 17 Con, 1 SLD, 1 Independent Con.
Rates: 226.44p in £. Town Hall tel: 695 6000. Search: 6 weeks
Director of Education: to be appointed.

Ratepayers in Lewisham frequently complain that they have a lot to put up with. Their rates bills are among the highest in the capital and some will increase even further when the feared Poll Tax arrives. And on top of that they are saddled with a council seemingly intent on promoting London's image as being the home of the 'loony left'. Despite being rate-capped several years running, council officers came up with a series of creative accounting techniques to keep the ship afloat. That led to impressive records of new house building, extra home helps and other back-up services such as lunch clubs for the elderly and nurseries for the under fives. But at the same time Lewisham welcomed in more than its fair share of women's and race advisors and succeeded in diverting attention from its solid achievements.

But the council ran out of ways of dodging the government's spending curbs, and a large deficit had to be faced. The council estimates that Poll Tax will work out at £320 a head in 1990, rising to £603 in 1994. They further calculate that 74% of Lewisham's inhabitants will be worse off under Poll Tax.

Two out of three of the borough's MPs are now Conservatives with fairly comfortable majorities, although Labour's grip on the town hall remains as firm as ever. The unanswered question concerning local politics in Lewisham now is, can the council knuckle down and concentrate on the basics like rubbish collection and leaving the crusades to someone else?

Southwark

Controlling party: Labour. Make-up: 40 Lab, 15 SLD, 7 Con, 1 Ind,
1 councillor suspended
Rates: 195.68. Town Hall tel: 703 6311. Search: 8-12 weeks.
Director of Education: Gordon Mott, previously Assistant Education Officer
for ILEA Secondary Schools; Divisional Education Officer
for the Southwark area. Education enquiries: no special number;
ask for the Education Action Unit

Politically speaking, the London Borough of Southwark is a mess. Labour-controlled since it was formed in 1965, the borough takes in the Parliamentary constituencies of Bermondsey, Peckham and Dulwich. Back in 1965 all three had Labour MPs – but the picture is very different now. Leafy Dulwich in the south of the borough went Conservative in Mrs Thatcher's landslide year of 1979. The Prime Minister has now bought a £500,000 retirement home there. Next to go was Bermondsey in 1983, covering the decaying docklands on the Thames. Simon Hughes' victory for the Liberals is remembered as the 'Tatchell By-election' when Labour's choice of a gay Australian candidate lost the party thousands of votes in this no-nonsense, working-class area. Labour still hold Peckham, with well-known MP Harriet Harman, and have solid control of Southwark Council. Seats are split 40 Labour, 15 Alliance and seven Conservative.

But the Labour Party nationally recognises its problems in Southwark and temporarily closed down its Peckham branch last year while inquiries take place into violence at meetings and financial trouble. Bermondsey Labour Party has been closed by Labour HQ while an inquiry into Militant Tendency infiltration is under way.

Southwark is London's biggest landlord with 61,000 council flats and houses – 65% of all housing in the borough. Relatively few properties have been sold to tenants under Right to Buy – 1,700 by the end of 1987. The council admits it does not agree with Right to Buy, but rejects Conservative claims that sales have been purposely delayed. There is no hard policy line on housing conversions and run-of-the-mill planning applications for garages and loft extensions go through easily. There have been complaints about delays on applications – largely due to Southwark's consultation procedure with neighbours, which is more extensive than most councils'.

Planning policy in the borough was brought radically up-to-date with the arrival of the London Docklands Development Corporation in 1981. The corporation now controls planning over one-tenth of Southwark's 7,115 acres. Derelict warehouses preserved by Southwark for light industry have been demolished to make way for offices or converted into luxury flats, business centres and museums.

Rates have dropped somewhat since 1985, with reductions because of ratecapping and GLC abolition made up for by increases in the police and fire brigade charges. No sharp rate increases are likely, with the expectation that

Southwark will remain ratecapped at least until the introduction of Poll Tax. Financial restraint on the council is now causing serious concern as numbers of social workers are cut and facilities for the mentally handicapped and elderly are closed down. Cuts in council spending have to be seen against the background of severe poverty. A Department of the Environment report in 1982 ranked the borough the tenth most deprived area in the country. Average household incomes are half the national average, with 20% of families living on less than £50 a week. The council is owed £34 million in unpaid rent (a £10m increase in a year). The results are seen in the bleak complex of council estates north of Peckham High Street and around East Street market in Walworth. These are rough areas with high crime rates and rampant drug abuse amongst teenagers.

Southwark Council's Labour leadership is now admitting that their inability to get to grips with the worst problems must take some of the blame for the state of the borough. But Labour insists that its new-found commitment to good management and cost-efficient services will not succeed in tackling South-wark's problems unless it is coupled with a massive injection of Government cash. Southwark predicts massive cuts and closures unless they get £39m extra. One in five teachers are leaving in inner London schools.

Tower Hamlets

Controlling party: none (Mayor has casting vote). Make-up: 25 Lab, 25 SLD.
Rates: 217.89 in the £. Town Hall tel: 980 4831.
Search 3-4 weeks.
Chief Education Officer: Anne Sofer, ex-SDP education spokesman and
ex-special adviser on education to Paddy Ashdown.
Education enquiries: 790 1288

The borough of Tower Hamlets was created in 1965 by the amalgamation of the three old boroughs of Poplar, Stepney and Bethnal Green and covers the area traditionally known as the East End. It's a place of dramatic contrasts: Spitalfields, home of Britain's largest Bangladeshi community and the most overcrowded ward in the country, also contains spacious Georgian houses built by Huguenot silk-weavers, many of which have been lovingly restored by the 'New Georgians'. Run-down tower blocks stand next to multi-million pound developments in the Docklands Enterprise Zone.

Tower Hamlets has the second largest public housing stock in the UK: at present 71.5% is council-owned although home ownership is sharply on the increase. The gentrification process has taken longer here than in neighbouring boroughs like Islington, which has more Victorian terraced housing. But proximity to the City, tax incentives for investing in Docklands and the new Docklands Light Railway has recently made Tower Hamlets one of the most sought-after boroughs in the capital. House prices have risen fast, and new private housing developments proliferate.

Soaring land values have fuelled concern over the threat to green space, but the 280 acre Victoria Park, bordered in the south and west by the Regent's and Hertford Union Canals, remains the finest in east London. Other open spaces include Mile End Park, started in 1949 and not yet completed, the Mudchute, Europe's largest urban farm, and several smaller parks like Island Gardens at the bottom of the Isle of Dogs with its magnificent view of Greenwich. The many canals, basins and docks provide excellent facilities for watersports.

Street life is vibrant with the famous East End markets while the shopping and leisure complex at St Katharine's Dock gives a taste of major developments to come in Wapping, the Island and Spitalfields, where a Covent Garden style scheme is planned for the £200 million site now occupied by the fruit and vegetable market. Culturally, Tower Hamlets is an exciting place: it holds the largest community arts festival in the country and claims (how do they know?) it has more artists per square mile than anywhere else in Europe.

Traditionally, the East End has been a Labour stronghold, but in May 1986 the Liberals gained control of the council. There are now 25 Labour members, and 25 SLD, with the mayor holding the casting vote. However Labour easily held on to both parliamentary constituencies in the 1987 General Election with former Environment Secretary Peter Shore in Bethnal Green and Stepney and Mildred Gordon replacing veteran MP Ian Mikardo in Bow and Poplar. Once in power, the Liberal council embarked on London's most ambitious and innovative decentralisation programme, dividing the borough into seven 'neighbourhoods'. As part of the campaign to 'cut through the red tape' local advice centres, called First Stop Shops, are already running, there are plans for seven Mini Town Halls and even the refuse lorries are being repainted in seven distinct neighbourhood colours. The SLD rule in Bethnal Green, Bow, and Globe Town, while Wapping, Poplar, Stepney and the Isle of Dogs are Labour-controlled. However, the most important policies are still determined centrally and Labour's power in the south of the borough is seriously undermined by the London Docklands Development Corporation.

Rate-capped for the third successive year, the borough is in serious financial trouble, partly because it is forced to spend one-seventh of its total revenue budget on hotel accommodation for homeless families. Meanwhile, after much effort, fewer council flats stand empty because they need major repairs or are too small for the Asian families who represent 90% of homeless households. Tower Hamlets' acute housing crisis was recognised by the 1986/87 all-party Home Affairs Committee report, 'Bangladeshis in Britain', but as yet, pleas for more cash have been in vain and the council faces a big cash shortfall, in common with many Labour-run councils. Recently more controversial measures included heavy cuts in grants to voluntary sector groups and selling off estates and land to private developers. But Tower Hamlets is aiming to become 'a centre of excellence for multi-cultural education'. And they have the biggest school building programme in the country.

Tower Hamlets' radical breed of Liberals are not affiliated to the national SLD Party and remain unimpressed by advice from politicians outside the borough. At present, the average rates bill is between £500-£600. But under new Poll Tax system, it is estimated that every adult could be charged over £600, making Tower Hamlets the second hardest hit borough in London. A recent report by the Association of Metropolitan Authorities warns the figure could be as high as £800 if 20% of residents evade the poll tax register. But with discounts of up to 70% for council tenants, home-ownership has become increasingly popular.

Despite high crime levels and severe social and economic deprivation, the East End has a tradition of friendly, close-knit communities. The last year has seen wide-spread development; new homes, new roads, new public transport, all catalyzed by Docklands. Indeed, the area is referred to by some as 'The Docklands-City Triangle'. If long-term gain is not sacrificed to quick profit, Tower Hamlets could become an exciting and civilised area to live and work.

Wandsworth

Controlling party: Conservative. Make-up: 31 Con, 30 Lab.
Rates: 130.8 in £. Town Hall tel: 871 6000. Search 3-4 days.
Director of Education: Donald Naismith, previously Director for Croydon and
prior to that, Richmond.

Wandsworth, the largest of the Inner London boroughs after Greenwich, was created in 1965 through the amalgamation of the old London Boroughs of Battersea and Wandsworth. In common with any inner city area it is a place of contrasts taking in the industrial zones of Nine Elms and York Road and the leafy avenues of Putney, the high-rise council estates of north Battersea and the quietly affluent suburbia of Southfields.

Although Wandsworth has the highest population of any inner London borough – 252,000 at the last census – it also has more than 700 acres of park and common land. To the east the borough boundaries are marked by Clapham and Tooting Bec Commons, to the south by Wimbledon Park and Wimbledon Common and to the west by Richmond Park and Barnes Common while lying entirely within the borough are Battersea Park, King George's Park and Putney and Wandsworth Commons.

Until recently the borough was split both politically and socially between the middle-class areas of Southfields and Putney and the working-class strongholds of Battersea, Balham and Tooting. But the last ten years have seen an influx of newcomers, mainly young professionals, moving south of the river and the 1987 General Election saw Battersea return a Conservative MP, John Bowis, an event which surprised Conservative Central office almost as much as it shocked Labour who lost their long-serving front-bench MP Alf Dubs.

The process of gentrification looks set to continue and the Tooting seat of veteran Labour MP Tom Cox is now highly marginal. He survived the 1987 General Election with a sharply reduced majority of under 2,000, due in part to a strong personal following. Yet just ten years ago all three Parliamentary seats in Wandsworth were held by Labour.

In the years following the amalgamation of Wandsworth and Battersea, control of the council oscillated between Conservative and Labour. But in 1978, following a decision by the then hard left Labour Council to impose a 20% rate rise, the Conservatives won control of the Town Hall. They have held control ever since with a radical brand of politics that has won favour with the Government and seen a number of councillors move into Parliament.

Since the Conservatives took power rates in Wandsworth have moved from being among the highest in London to one of the lowest. The average householder now pays a rates bill of just over £300 a year – almost half that faced by residents in neighbouring Lambeth. Wandsworth residents are among the few in Inner London to be seen smiling in April when their rates are fixed. Rates have been held down by the sale of more than 12,000 council properties, by large-scale privatisation of council services and by the sale of land to private developers.

The council pioneered Right to Buy for council tenants in advance of government legislation and the scheme extends to first-time buyers living or working in the borough who can register for the Priority Group Sales Scheme which offers discounts on council houses and flats of more than 30 per cent. Today local people seeking a home are more likely to be able to buy a council property than to rent one.

There have however been complaints from leaseholders of high service and repair charges while modern council-built houses and flats generally tend to fetch around 20% less when resold than privately built properties. Would-be buyers of ex-council properties should note the council is currently selling off for development what it considers 'underused' open spaces. These have included play areas and parking and open spaces.

Wandsworth Council has also sold a number of its less popular council estates to private developers, most notably to Regalian, and this policy has further weakened Labour's grip on its traditional strongholds and contributed to the Conservative victory in Battersea.

Virtually all Wandsworth Council services are automatically tested against private sector competition and all major contracts, from refuse collection and street cleansing to catering in old people's homes, are now privately run.

As a result of capital receipts from property sales and careful use of government grants Wandsworth remains one of the few boroughs in Inner London to be able to offer home improvement grants in areas targeted for special attention. The council is spending huge sums on the council estates – notably where it is bidding to extend home ownership – while the Brighter Borough campaign has a True Blue council laying red paving stones.

But although the Conservatives succeeded in holding onto power at the 1986 borough elections their majority over Labour was reduced to just one. The Government's Poll Tax proposals could also damage Conservative prospects in the 1990 elections. The council's high profile in determining to opt out of ILEA has also lost the Conservative's some friends. But the Council may have scored in poaching radical-right educationalist Donald Naismith from the Borough of Croydon as Director of Education. Naismith is particularly well-known for his calls for children to be educated in their 'civic responsibilities'.

Although when Poll Tax is introduced Wandsworth is likely to have a low level of payment compared with neighbouring Labour-run boroughs, it is now becoming uncomfortably clear that local businesses will be among the worst hit by the government's new Unified Business Rate proposals.

But there are however more Labour-held marginal seats than Conservative and a by-election last autumn in Southfields saw the Conservatives increase their majority – at the expense of the then SDP/Liberal Alliance – and it seems likely the borough will remain Conservative.

City of Westminster

Controlling Party: Conservative. Make-up: 32 Con, 27 Lab, 1 Independent.
Rates: 136.4 in the £. Town Hall tel: 828 8070. Search 4-6 days.
Chief Education Officer: Gwyn Robins; 1981-88, ILEA Divisional Education Officer for Camden & Westminster; Area Education Officer for Oxfordshire.
Education enquiries: 798 3338

The present-day City of Westminster was born in 1965 when the former Metropolitan boroughs of Paddington and St Marylebone were merged with the 400-year-old Westminster City. In many ways it was an unlikely marriage, because it combined the staunchly socialist Paddington with the more conservative City. Westminster is traditionally a Conservative stronghold, but the Labour opposition has recently made inroads on the council's majority.

Westminster Council is caretaker to London's West End and home to many of the capital's most famous landmarks including Westminster Abbey, the

National Gallery and No 10 Downing Street. Its central location dictates much of its policy; it is responsible for such varied duties as policing Oxford Street's pavement traders, inspecting the health standards in the kitchens of the country's most famous establishments such as the Dorchester and the Ritz, and instituting planning controls on the capital's 'red light' districts.

Residents include many of the country's rich and famous with homes in fashionable Little Venice, Regents Park and Hyde Park. At the same time there are pockets of great poverty in Paddington and Pimlico. Housing has always been a political hot potato for the borough: in the early '60s the notorious slum landlord Peter Rachman's empire was based in Paddington in the area now occupied by the Wessex Gardens estate. Local campaigns led by the then Labour MP Ben Parking led not only to new rent control initiatives but to the development of low-rent council homes. The controversy around these continues. The '60s-built tower blocks of North Paddington's Mozart Estate and Marylebone's Lisson Green estate were hailed as architectural triumphs at the time of their construction; the Mozart Estate was given a design award. But both the structure and the design were discovered to be faulty. Extensive works have been carried out to remedy dampness and major efforts were required to remove walkways and increase safety on the estates. The creation of General Improvement and Housing Action Areas have assisted in the upgrading of many privately-owned and rented properties in the borough. One of the side-effects of these has been the 'gentrification' of some parts, most noticeably around Paddington Station.

Since Lady Porter became council leader, the keynote of council policy has been 'value for money' and the target to cut red tape and inefficiency. At the same time the council has adopted a high profile, public relations approach to local government. More services are now de-centralised and 'one stop' centres offering a range of public information have been instituted at two of the council's buildings. Hand in hand with this has gone increased privatisation. The renovation of some tower blocks is being funded by the sale of others. The management of leisure centres and of parks and gardens has already gone out to private tender; the cleansing service is about to follow suit. This approach backfired after the City was censured for the 'cemetery sale scandal', when three large council-owned cemeteries were sold off for virtually nothing in an attempt to save their running costs.

A welter of council campaigns has marked the last few years: the Cleaner City Campaign, Westminster City Watch and the latest, the Quality of Life campaign. All genuine residents are entitled to a 'Rescard' ticket, which offers them discounts at local venues. More emphasis is being placed on facilities for the disabled. Like all central London boroughs, Westminster's population is declining and growing older. Alarmed by the fall in a decade from 240,000 to 180,000 residents, Westminster launched its latest campaign designed to build a stable community via the use of planning restrictions, encouraging more low-cost homes in new commercial developments. It is now carrying out a review of parking restrictions in the borough to allow more parking spaces on main roads, and has introduced more stringent checks on those entitled to residents' parking permits.

Parliamentary Constituencies and MPs

London is represented in the House of Commons by MPs elected by 84 constituencies. These areas are parts of the local government boroughs. See the boroughs chapter for details of the party controlling the town halls.

Barking and Dagenham
Barking: Ms Jo Richardson (Lab)
Dagenham: Bryan Gould (Lab)

Barnet
Chipping Barnet: Sydney Chapman (Con)
Finchley: Mrs Margaret Thatcher (Con)
Hendon North: John Gorst (Con)
Hendon South: John Marshall (Con)

Bexley
Bexleyheath: Cyril Townsend (Con)
Erith and Crayford: David Evennett (Con)
Old Bexley and Sidcup: Edward Heath (Con)

Brent
East: Ken Livingstone (Lab)
North: Rhodes Boyson (Con)
South: Paul Boateng (Lab)

Bromley
Beckenham: Sir Phillip Goodhart (Con)
Chislehurst: Roger Sims (Con)
Orpington:Ivor Stanbrook (Con)
Ravensbourne: John Hunt (Con)

Camden
Hampstead and Highgate: Sir Geoffrey Finsberg (Con)
Holborn and St Pancras: Frank Dobson (Lab)

Croydon
Central: John Moore (Con)
North East: Bernard Weatherill (The Speaker)
North West: Humfrey Malins (Con)
South: Sir William Clark (Con)

Ealing
Acton: Sir George Young (Con)
North: Harry Greenway (Con)
Southall: Sydney Bidwell (Lab)

Enfield
Edmonton: Ian Twinn (Con)
North: Tim Eggar (Con)
Southgate: Michael Portillo (Con)

Greenwich
Eltham: Peter Bottomley (Con)
Greenwich: Mrs Rosie Barnes (SDP)
Woolwich: John Cartwright (SDP)

Hackney
North and Stoke Newington: Ms Diane Abbott (Lab)
South and Shoreditch: Brian Sedgemore (Lab)

Hammersmith and Fulham
Fulham: Matthew Carrington (Con)
Hammersmith: Clive Soley (Lab)

Haringey
Hornsey and Wood Green: Sir Hugh Rossi (Con)
Tottenham: Bernard Grant (Lab)

Harrow
East: Hugh Dykes (Con)
West: Robert Hughes (Con)

Havering
Hornchurch: Robin Squire (Con)
Romford: Michael Neubert (Con)
Upminster: Sir Nicholas Bonsor (Con)

Hillingdon
Hayes and Harlington: Terry Dicks (Con)
Ruislip-Northwood: John Wilkinson (Con)
Uxbridge: Julian Shersby (Con)

Hounslow

Brentford and Isleworth: Sir Barney Hayhoe (Con)
Feltham and Heston: Reginald Ground (Con)

Islington

North: Jeremy Corbyn (Lab)
South and Finsbury: Chris Smith (Lab)

Kensington and Chelsea

Chelsea: Nicholas Scott (Con)
Kensington: John Fishburn (Con)

Kingston upon Thames

Kingston upon Thames: Norman Lamont (Con)
Surbiton: Richard Tracey (Con)

Lambeth

Norwood: John Fraser (Lab)
Streatham: William Shelton (Con)
Vauxhall: Stuart Holland (Lab)

Lewisham

Deptford: Joan Ruddock (Lab)
East: Colin Moynihan (Con)
West: John Maples (Con)

Merton

Mitcham and Morden: Mrs Angela Rumbold (Con)
Wimbledon: Dr Charles Goodson Wickes (Con)

Newham

North East: Ron Leighton (Lab)
North West: Tony Banks (Lab)
South: Nigel Spearing (Lab)

Redbridge

Ilford North: Vivian Bendall (Con)
Ilford South: Neil Thorne (Con)
Wanstead and Woodford: James Arbuthnot (Con)

Richmond upon Thames

Richmond and Barnes: Jeremy Hanley (Con)
Twickenham: Toby Jessel (Con)

Southwark

Dulwich: Gerald Bowden (Con)
Peckham: Ms Harriet Harman (Lab)
Southwark and Bermondsey: Simon Hughes (Lib)

Sutton

Carlshalton and Wallington: Nigel Forman (Con)
Sutton and Cheam: Neil Macfarlane (Con)

Tower Hamlets

Bethnal Green and Stepney: Peter Shore (Lab)
Bow and Poplar: Ms Mildred Gordon (Lab)

Waltham Forest

Chingford: Norman Tebbit (Con)
Leyton: Harry Cohen (Lab)
Walthamstow: Hugo Summerson (Con)

Wandsworth

Battersea: John Bowis (Con)
Putney: David Mellor (Con)
Tooting: Tom Cox (Lab)

Westminster (& City of London)

City of London and Westminster South: Peter Brooke (Con)
Westminster North: John Wheeler (Con)

Architectural Styles

by Soo Ware

Foreigners coming to London have been known to express surprise that so many homes here are 'second-hand'. It is true that the majority of the city's houses are pre-1919. The only chance to buy a totally new house in Inner London comes with comparatively rare developments in odd corners.

The nearest most London buyers get to a 'new' home is a newly-converted flat or a heavily modernised house. Even then, the facade will usually be carefully restored 'old' and many of the original features inside retained.

New homes are being built on a large scale in only one area: Docklands. At the very top of the market, there are also modern houses around Hampstead and new blocks of flats there and near Regents Park. Pockets of 'mews' type developments are taking place on infill sites on other areas, and riverside sites are being developed with luxury flats upriver from Docklands, for example in Pimlico, Vauxhall and Fulham. Some new estates of conventional family homes are being squeezed into surplus land beside railways in parts of South London.

A glance at London's skyline, with its many tower blocks of flats, shows that homes have been built since the war and on a large scale. These have been built by London's local authorities, and until very recently were effectively outside the mainstream housing market as they were rented. Now, however, the Right to Buy laws are bringing these flats, and the many council houses down at ground level, onto the market. This adds a new dimension to the choice of homes: modern properties (some simply convenient, some in fact excellent in both style and soundness) in central locations.

Most buyers, now and in the future, will be buying 'period' homes. This is a phrase widely used by estate agents who have no idea how old a house really is. It is often useful to know the vintage of a property, not just for interest but because different kinds of homes were built at different periods. Some are spacious, some cramped. Some were usually well-built, others a hurried response to fashion. Some kinds of architecture throw up more maintenance problems than others.

It should be said that there is some cause for sympathy with the agents' 'period' tag. First, some styles – eg 'Georgian' – were built, with little discernable evolution, for decades. Some were derived from earlier periods than when they were built – take the turn-of-the-century 'Queen Anne'. And this is still going on, with new London 'mews' popping up where none were there before. So the illustrations here are a starting point, a framework for reference. It can literally be impossible even for experts to date a London house by appearance only.

Soo Ware is an architect with a special interest in London's homes.

18th Century Georgian

These very elegant and much sought-after houses are found in small pockets. There are some in Mayfair, but most are now used as offices. Islington, Hackney, Greenwich, Kennington, Clapham, Battersea, Kew, Richmond, Hampstead and Highgate have some still used as homes. Detached or, more often, in terraces, each house slightly different. Flat-fronted, of classical proportions, 2 or 3 storey with a slate mansard attic storey, usually 3 or 5 sash windows on each floor, often very simple in appearance, soft yellow or red bricks weathered with time. Often a fine front door with a carved wood door case with classical details – pediments, columns and fan lights. Principal rooms on the 1st floor reached by an elegant staircase. These buildings are invariably listed.

Georgian, late 18th and early 19th centuries

Built from the 1780s to the 1840s: often hard to date accurately without local knowledge. Found in Islington and Camden Town, Chelsea and Kensington, Kennington, Stockwell and parts of the West End. Usually in terraces, sometimes in squares and crescents. Three or 4 storeys; sometimes an attic behind a parapet and a basement behind railings. Ground floor often stucco in a rusticated design. Other features: fanlight above front doors and ironwork balcony. Two sash windows per floor, brickwork usually soft London stocks. Rooms are often modest-sized, main ones on 1st floor.

Regency villas and cottages

Built in the early 19th century, these pretty villas and terraces were intended to reflect a rural idyll in urban or suburban surroundings. Normally 2-storey, terraced or semi-detached, with ironwork canopies and wooden or cast iron conservatories, trellises, sash windows and decorative railings. The front doors and porches often have delicate canopies. Slate roof,shallow-pitched with wide eaves. Rooms pretty but small. Found in small pockets (for example, Richmond, Kew or Twickenham), though a few survive in Chelsea, Mayfair, Regents Park. A style much sought-after.

Regency terraces

In contrast to the picturesque Regency villas and cottages, there are also the more formal and magnificent terraces around Regents Park and elsewhere in London (Belgrave Square, the riverfront at Richmond). These are buildings of classical proportions, 3, 4 or 5 storeys in sweeping crescents, terraces or lodges and substantial villas. Terraces are formed by a number of identical houses joined together, with the end of the terraces being defined separately like full stops. They are generally part of large estates, and are stucco faced with identical decorations. Some are still single homes of truly magnificent proportions, others are converted into smart flats. Many are now used as offices or as company/diplomatic accommodation. Some have been rebuilt behind the original facade. Sometimes they are hard to distinguish from the early-Victorian equivalent (see right).

Early Victorian

Vast areas of London were built at this period, forming a ring stretching from Kensington and Chelsea through Camden and Islington, down through Hackney and to a lesser degree in South London: Blackheath, Camberwell, Kennington. They form part of the great estates of the time: Grosvenor, Gunter, Pimlico. Three-, 4- or 5-storey flat-fronted terraces or squares, usually with semi-basements, with classical leanings: porticoes, Doric or Ionic columns, pediments and brackets. Almost always with a stucco, symbolic rusticated ground floor storey, and sometimes painted above. Now mostly flats, but planned as family homes for the middle classes. Rooms often very large and well-proportioned, with fine plasterwork, fireplaces and staircases.

Mews

Surviving mews date mostly from the 1830s to the 1890s. They were built to provide stabling and servants' housing, behind the terraces and squares in Belgravia, Knightsbridge, Mayfair, Marylebone and other parts. Today, they are converted to cottages in a hotch potch of styles, with the coach house or stable used for garaging and the upper floor(s) forming 1 or 2 bedrooms. Some have been virtually rebuilt as larger houses. Usually brick, maybe painted or rendered or with a stucco finish. Conversion often adds features such as bay windows, shutters, ironwork, window boxes, hanging baskets. Some are still cobbled streets entered through an arch.

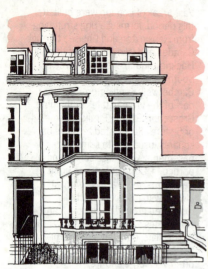

Mid-Victorian

These large villas were typically built in pairs with the front door to the side, usually approached up some steps. They have a pitched roof with elaborate overhang or eaves. Detailing is 'classical' stucco around windows and on the ground floor, with some being clad in stucco all over. Vestigal balconies, with ironwork, are found below sash windows. These are found in Chelsea, Kensington and other areas. Terraced houses in the same style, with similar classical details, are widely seen. They are the result of a building boom in the 1850s and '60s and are found all round inner London. Some, in less fashionable areas, fell into disrepair but many are now being restored. They are frequently turned into flats.

Late Victorian

Houses of this period fall into 3 kinds: small, medium and large. Together, they are by far the most common type of house found in Inner London and many outer suburbs. It is difficult to imagine what London must have been like towards the end of the 19th century, with thousands of these houses being built all within 20 years. While the middle of the 19th century saw the construction of houses decorated with classical 18th century architectural details, the houses of this later period follow the Gothic fashion, with columns decorated with foliage, stained glass windows, pointed arches and generally fussy detailing. They are usually built of yellow London stock brick or with stucco or red brick dressing, mostly with slate roofs. Their front doors are set back in decorated porches. However, despite the Gothic detailing, most have sash windows.

The smallest houses (pictured below left) were working-class terraces, 2 storeys high, usually with white stucco bay windows on the ground floor to the front parlour with columns carrying foliage capitals, a narrow frontage and with rooms usually arranged 2-up, 2-down.

The medium-sized house are the most commonly found (pictured right) Also usually 2 storeys, sometimes with an extra room in the roof with dormer windows. These houses are found either in terraces or semi-detached. They often have stucco bay windows on both ground and 1st floors, with a small pointed hip roof to the gable. These houses have wider frontages, often extend quite far back and usually have 3 or 4 bedrooms. The principal rooms have high, moulded ceilings and cast iron fireplaces with marble surrounds.

The large detached, semi-detached or terraced versions (pictured above) can be very grand, like the red brick 'lion' houses of Peterborough Estate, Fulham and the similar ones around Barnes Pond and Tooting Common. They have 5 or 6 bedrooms, are usually 2 storeys plus basement and/ or attic, with attractive decorative mouldings inside and out. They have square bay windows with big gables, large rooms with high ceilings and attractive proportions. About half of all these 3 sizes of house are still family homes, but many have now been converted into flats.

Late 19th century Dutch style

These tall, usually narrow-fronted soft terracotta-coloured brick houses, with elaborate moulded brick or faience decorations, are found in Knightsbridge and tucked away in Holland Park, South Kensington or Chelsea. Now softened with weathering, they were built at the end of the 19th century in a very free and eclectic style, usually in terraces (although sometimes semi-detached), but each house having varied features. Normally 4 or 5 storeys, with enormous chimneys and wiggly 2-storey gables (decorated with everything but the kitchen sink), and an elaborate porch up a few steps. The main rooms are on the 1st floor, very much following the plan of the mid-19th century stucco estates. The windows have a different design on each floor, often with fiddly glazing patterns. The 1st floor sometimes has decorative ironwork, and rather fine railings separate the semi-basement from the street.

Mansion flats

These very large blocks of flats, usually 4, 5 or 6 storeys high, were built from 1880-1910. Usually built of red bricks, with a horizontal stripey appearance formed by white stone banding and rows of windows. Facades are broken up with elaborate gable ends, bay windows, balconies and other features, giving an overall exuberant effect. They often have 'interesting' window designs, with glazing bars forming attractive patterns for both sash and casement windows. Arranged with 2 or 4 flats off a central staircase, often with well proportioned rooms on the street frontage and secondary rooms facing rather dreary light wells. Mansion blocks range from very scruffy and poorly maintained to the extremely luxurious. Found all over London, examples include Prince of Wales Drive facing Battersea Park, around Baker Street, in Mayfair and behind the Royal Albert Hall in Kensington.

Early 20th century

These large detached and semi-detached houses were built for the wealthy middle classes who commuted from the healthy suburbs by train or tube. Many are found in such areas as Wimbledon, Putney, Hampstead, Dulwich, Greenwich, Streatham. A wide range of features were often used in one house. Usually 2 or 3 storeys with 5 or 6 bedrooms, large reception rooms and entrance halls and generous staircases. Often double fronted, built of brick or brick with render, Features include bay windows, steep gabled pitched tiled roofs, a variety of different types of casement window. Fewer Gothic touches than the late Victorian buildings. More modest versions have a similar approach.

Nondescript 'Georgian'

Much loved by estate agents, who call them 'period', which means they are unable to date them accurately or to define precisely the architectural style. Built early this century, in the '20s and '30s, and still being built. Very large, 2-storey, double-fronted houses, detached, with attic rooms in the steep pitched roof. Set back from the road, with a sweeping drive, a full flight of steps, an imposing classical front door. Many 'Georgian' features are incorporated: pediments, the Palladian window. Several large reception rooms, bedrooms with en suite bathrooms as standard, staff quarters, large gardens. Found in Bishops Avenue in Hampstead, St John's Wood, Wimbledon Common, Bromley and Finchley.

Mock Tudor

Built in large quantities around the perimeter of London mainly during the 1930s. More interesting examples occur nearer the centre of London in and were built early in the century. And even now, still a popular style with the speculative developer. 1930s examples are found in ribbon development along arterial roads and on large estates. Detached, semi-detached or terraced, many with garages, and almost all family houses with 3 or 4 bedrooms and often substantial back gardens and smaller front gardens. Features: leaded lights in casement windows, steep pitched tiled gabled roofs, black and white timber decoration on white rendered walls, red brick on ground floor, often with brick decoration. Many now heavily altered with new plastic or aluminium windows.

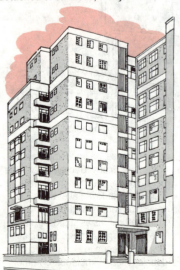

1930s blocks of flats

These very large and rather anonymous blocks of flats, 5 to 7 storeys high, were widely built during the 1930s. Some were private developments (for example, those around Baker Street, Maida Vale, Dolphin Square, Streatham). Others were built by the LCC or charitable trusts and are now coming on the market as individual flats. Built from yellow or red bricks with horizontal and vertical bands of render giving a stripey effect. Often they have balconies or bay windows. Windows sometimes are Georgian type sash, but steel casement windows with very thin glazing bars are also common. Flats vary from 1 to 4 bedrooms.

Glossary of architectural terms

Bricks: London Stock bricks are the most common, made from yellowish clay in Kent, they weather down to greyish black but are often cleaned up and have a soft appearance. Red bricks are also widely used, often with London stocks as a decorative feature.

Casement window: a window with the opening part hinged on one side. Traditionally wood, but in the 1930s they began to be made of steel and now also of aluminium or plastic.

Columns and capitals: vertical pillars with decorative tops. These can be either in Doric, a simple geometric style, or Ionic, a more elaborate style with curled motifs. Occasionally the third order, Corinthian, is seen, elaborate designs decorated with leaves.

Doorcase: a wooden surround to a door opening, often very elaborate with carving or mouldings and classical decorative features – for example, pediments or columns.

Dormer window: a vertical window (sash or casement) with upright sides coming thorough a sloping roof, having its own pitched or flat roof.

Faience: decorative moulded bricks, usually terracotta-coloured or yellowish, sometimes glazed; used in late Victorian times for picking out features.

Frieze: a band of mouldings around a building, usually at high level.

Gabled end or gable: a triangular end wall of a pitched roof, often becoming a decorative feature in their own right, for example, Dutch gables.

Glazing bars: the narrow strips of moulded timber or metal which hold the panes of glass together.

Leaded lights: small panes of diamond-shaped glass held together with narrow strips of lead.

Mansard roof: first rises steeply, almost vertically, with windows in it, and then has a flat top.

Moulding: continuous groove or ridge which forms a decorative feature with an original functional purpose, to throw water away from the face of a building. Can be in any material – brick, timber, stone, stucco. Internally, the term applies to decorative plasterwork or joinery, externally to many design features.

Palladian window: a composite window, designed to look like one big window, but made up of three of which the middle section has a semi-circular fanlight over.

Parapet: a small wall guarding the edge of a roof or, alternatively, the wall of the building extended above the roof line to conceal the gutters.

Pediment: triangular decorative motif usually found over doors and windows.

Render: a thick finish, usually sand and cement or pebble-dash, which covers all the brickwork and can be painted as well. Popular on Edwardian or mock-Tudor houses with areas of brickwork or tile hanging.

Sash window: a window in which the opening parts slide up and down. They are usually balanced with ropes and weights concealed inside the frame. Traditionally wood, but replacement windows are now aluminium or plastic.

Slates: thin sheets of grey rock, once used extensively for roofing in London.

Stucco: similar to render, but popular in the 18th and 19th centuries as a smooth finish covering large areas of a building (often the whole wall) sometimes with classical mouldings or details. Normally painted cream or white.

Tiles: made of clay, traditional plain tiles, small rectangular rusty red and flat in shape, have been used in some areas for hundreds of years, and are seen on all periods of houses. They are used on roofs or can be hung vertically on walls as a decorative feature. In modern times, a wide variety of much larger profiled clay tiles have been used for replacement of old slate or tile roofs.

Velux window: a manufacturer's name for a window inserted into the sloping part of a roof, frequently used in loft conversions.

The

Property

Business

Property is an industry. It has its producers: builders and developers; its marketing side: estate agents; a host of professionals: financiers, surveyors, lawyers. And its consumers – you and me. This section is an outline of how London's property market works, what is going on in it now and how buyers and sellers can get the best out of it.

First comes an explanation of the historical factors which govern the way we hold property. Americans, in particular, are puzzled by our leaseholds: they cannot understand a system in which a large proportion of Londoners do not, in fact, own their homes outright. Shirley Green looks at *Who Owns London*.

Next, buying and selling a London home in 1989, at a time when the whole industry is changing fast. The steep rise in property values in the past few years brought about a new breed of developers. A different order of skill is needed to sell homes both old and new, from estate agents whose own profession is in a state of flux with mergers, takeovers, expansion – and some contraction – the order of the day. The 'Buying and Selling' chapter explains and discusses the whole process. This includes advice on how to sell your home: particularly how to choose and instruct an estate agent. (There is limitless advice for the first-time buyer, but a lot less available for the first-time seller).

Also in this section is a look at the other processes involved: different ways of getting onto the housing ladder; how to look at a property with a critical eye. David Spittles unravels the mortgage market, Daniel Taub outlines the conveyancing process: the legal side of transferring ownership of a home. The sale achieved, an Englishman's home is his castle – until he wants to build an extra turret or demolish the keep. Then there are building regulations to consider, if not planning permission to be sought. Soo Ware explains.

Renting your home used to be an alternative to buying. Or rather, to be accurate, the other way around: renting was the norm. The last few years has seen a great resurgence in the rental market – but not for the average Londoner. It has become the province of high-flying foreigners, both jet-setters

94 *The Property Business*

passing through and top businessmen here for a month, a year, or ten. Now in 1989 there is new legislation aimed at encouraging the return of the private landlord, letting to 'real people'. Details of the new types of tenancy are in the 'Rental' chapter.

This section leads on to that other, complementary, side of London's recently-acquired crown of luxurious rented homes – the investment aspect. The 80's have seen the widespread practice of many more people investing in London's homes – not by capitalising on the one they live in but buying houses and flats in anticipation of a rise in value, and renting the property out to cover its outgoings and with luck make a modest profit. John Brennan of the *Financial Times* charts the course of the investors and the newer phenomenon of the speculators – and asks what their fate will be in 1989's uncertain market. This chapter also sets London's property market in its international context.

Who Owns London?

by Shirley Green

One of the nastier shocks of looking for a home in central London is discovering that most properties can only be bought leasehold. Strictly speaking, this means you don't own what you buy. You're just a tenant who pays the landlord a one-off premium to live in his property for as long as the lease lasts, plus an annual ground rent for the land it stands on.

How leasehold/freehold came about

To understand how this situation has arisen, you have to go back to when London was small, and much of the land around it owned by a mere handful of landlords who rented it out to farmers or market-gardeners. However, from the 17th century, as London's population grew, their land became ripe for development with housing.

Since the landlords tended to be too rich and noble to want to involve themselves directly in trade, they didn't develop the land themselves – but they weren't prepared to sell it either. So they retained the freehold of the land but granted building-leases to developers in return for receiving an annual ground rent. The developers laid out the streets and built the houses, and then sold slightly shorter leases on the houses to the public at slightly higher ground rents.

If a building lease was for 100 years, for instance, and the houses took a year to build, they'd be sold on 99-year leases. And if the ground rent the developer paid the landlord worked out at £5 a building plot, the developer would ask a ground rent of say £15 from the housebuyers to provide himself with an income as well as capital. Finally when the 99-year leases ran out, the houses reverted to the freehold landlord, who could sell a new lease to a developer or new leases to the public.

Basically, this freehold/leasehold pattern has remained unchanged – and so have the original landlords, whose vast estates have stayed largely intact. In fact if anything the pattern has become more extensive, because even in those parts of London where you used to be able to buy freehold houses, many properties have been converted into flats, and flats are almost always sold leasehold.

Why the length of leases varies

Leases can be for any length of time, and obviously the shorter they are, the lower the price. Most landlords sell new or newly-modernised properties on 99-year leases, but the purchasers can sell the leases whenever they want to move elsewhere. Furthermore, they can usually sell for a good profit, because although the lease will be several years shorter, property values will have risen during those years. This explains why a long leasehold can be nearly as expensive as an equivalent freehold property. In general, however, when a lease has less than 40 years left to run, it's a diminishing asset and is cheap to buy. But you need capital because building societies won't give mortgages on short leases. However, leaseholds in really prestigious areas are an exception. They keep their value right to the end – and even new leases can be as short as

60 years. Short leases on expensive homes are viewed by purchasers, which are often companies, as rent paid up-front rather than an outright purchase. See the Rentals chapter for the economics of this.

Head-leases, sub-leases and sub-sub-leases

As a leaseholder, your landlord will not necessarily be the freeholder. This was true in the past. For example, when a freeholder granted a lease to a developer, the lease the developer sold to the public was a sub-lease, making him the sub-leaseholders' landlord. But today the chain of leaseholds can be even longer, and rather confusing.

When the Church of England sold literally thousands of houses in Paddington in the 1950's, for instance, they tended to be sold in batches rather than to individual owner-occupiers because so many of them were full of sitting tenants. In some cases the new freeholders sold long head-leases to companies which specialised in getting vacant possession, and as houses fell empty, these companies sold sub-leases to development companies which converted them into flats. Once the flats were finished, they were sold to owner-occupiers on sub-sub-leases.... But although being a sub-sub-leaseholder sounds horrendously complicated, all it really means in practise is that the ground rent will have been bumped up a bit at every stage.

Service charges – a necessary evil

Building societies seldom, if ever, give mortgages on freehold flats, which is one reason why they're such a rarity. The thinking is that if flats were sold freehold, when the house needed painting or the roof repairing, some flat-owners would want the work done whilst others would refuse to spend the money, and the building would fall into a state of neglect.

To ensure a building is well-maintained, each leaseholder, as a condition of his lease, has to pay a bi-annual or annual service charge. This generally covers his share of any outgoings on the following: carrying out structural repairs; having the exterior painted; heating (if the central heating is communal); keeping common parts like the hall and stairways cleaned and lighted; and seeing that the building is fully insured. The service charge is usually made by a managing agent who arranges for work to be done when needed, and includes his fee – usually 10% to 15% of the money spent.

Query low service charges

Buying a flat over-stretches many people financially, so they're often tempted to choose one where the service charge is low; but unless the flat was recently converted, it's probably low because maintenance has been neglected. As a result, they get hit with an astronomical service charge once the neglect becomes too serious to ignore.

This problem can be even worse in big blocks of flats – the type that date from the late 19th and early 20th century, and were built for letting rather than selling. Such blocks remained let until the 1960s but since then, as flats have fallen vacant or sitting tenants have been bought out, they've been modernised and sold on long leases. Here, the trouble arises where only a minority of the flats have been sold – say 40 out of a block of 100. The landlord may be reluctant to have repairs done because he'll have to foot 60% of the costs, and will try to delay until more flats have been sold.

The 1987 Landlord and Tenant Act gives leaseholders the opportunity to get bad managing agents changed or, in extreme cases, to buy out the landlord altogether. (You can get the relevant DoE leaflet at your local town hall.) But as litigation is nerve-wracking and expensive, the best way to get an idea of future service charge commitments is to ask your surveyor, when he surveys the flat, to check the structure of the building as well. Or if this isn't possible, knock on a few doors and ask existing leaseholders about the standard of management.

Leases and the law

The new 1988 Housing Act aims to encourage the provision of rented housing. It does not however, affect the status of existing sitting tenants. Sitting tenants have the right, by law, to remain in their rented homes for life. They pay 'fair rents', which are artificially low, so the properties they live in tend to be neglected. The Leasehold Reform Act gave certain leaseholders of entire houses as opposed to flats (depending mainly on low rateable values and ground rents) the right to buy their freeholds at bargain prices. This right has been exercised at the expense of, among others, the Grosvenor Estate.

What to expect on the traditional estates

The oldest of the traditional landlords is the Queen, whose Crown Estate, over the past decade, has been carrying out massive improvement schemes. Her magnificent Nash terraces surrounding Regent's Park have virtually all been renovated now – some by the individual leaseholders who live in the houses. They were sold (relatively) cheap 62-year leases on condition that they renovated, and the Crown controlled how they set about it, from the obligatory use of Welsh slates on the roofs to the Crown Cream paint on the stuccoed exteriors. These often Grade 1 listed houses – among the most beautiful but most expensive in London – trickle onto the market as leaseholders sell. Very occasionally a flat is available, but few houses have been split in this way.

The Queen's properties at Millbank, between the Thames and Pimlico tube station, are a mixture of new apartment blocks (like Crown Reach overlooking the Thames), renovated 19th century terraces, and newly-built facsimile terraces. They have already been sold on 60-year and 99-year leases, but several come back on the market each year.

The flats recently built by Regalian on the Crown's Kensington Barracks site in Kensington Church Street were snapped up before they even reached the market.

The Crown's Victoria Park estate at Hackney in the East End is taking longer to improve. This is because most of the existing houses are 'fair-rented' and can only be renovated as money comes in from the sale of building leases to developers, who, where sites have become vacant, convert old houses or build new ones. Wates have already sold several new houses on long leaseholds, and Ideal Homes have sold new mews houses and new or newly-converted flats. Prices are cheap by Crown Estate standards, and the 280 acres of Victoria Park provides a considerable local amenity.

Prince Charles owns the Duchy of Cornwall estate, which includes 45 acres of South London at Kennington – 10 acres taken up by the Oval cricket ground.

It's a very mixed area architecturally and socially. Most houses are small, Edwardian artisan type, but a few, most notably along part of the noisy Kennington Road, are Georgian. Except for two small post-war developments, blocks of flats are Edwardian or 1930s. All properties were 'fair-rented' until recently, but current policy is to sell whenever the Duchy gets vacant possession: freehold in the case of houses; or 99 year leases in the case of individual flats. But entire blocks have been sold freehold to housing associations, and the ultimate aim in other blocks, once all the flats have been sold individually, is for leaseholders to take over the freehold themselves and own it on a management basis. In other words, the Estate will eventually be broken right up.

The Church as landlord

The Church of England is the next-oldest London landlord, but with the exception of its 90-acre Hyde Park Estate (see Bayswater), policy since the 1950s has been to sell freehold. What's left now, apart from a scattering of houses and flats in Kensington, is about 500 properties in Maida Vale – the Church Commissioners only started selling here in 1981. These range from 19th century houses, still full or part-full of sitting tenants, to Victorian or Edwardian blocks of mansion flats, which are partly tenanted.

The Hyde Park Estate is a very different proposition. It's an up-market mixture of Georgian terraces like those in Connaught Square, and 1960s-developed blocks of flats and town-houses. Although many of the properties are rented rather than sold leasehold, most are too luxurious to fall within 'fair rent' legislation, and high rents have meant a high standard of maintenance. Recent policy is to sell on 99-year or 125-year leases whenever rented flats or houses fall vacant; also to sell long leases to sitting tenants.

The land-owning schools

The next oldest landlords are the public schools. Tonbridge School, Bedford School and Rugby School all own small pockets of WC1, but Eton College works on a grander scale, owning 60 acres around Swiss Cottage. In the rectangle formed by King Henry Road, Fellows Road, Winchester Road and Primrose Hill Road, 20 of these acres were redeveloped with about 300 modern town houses in the 1960s. The leases still have 75 years left to run. They prove popular when they come on the market, but popularity can vary according to proximity to four 1960s tower-blocks, which Eton College leases to the local authority for letting to Council tenants. The estate is known as the Chalcot Estate, and its remaining 300 or so houses are 19th century. Although some of them are 'fair-rented', the vast majority were sold to head-leaseholders long ago. As many of them require major improvements, when leases revert, Eton College sells 85-year leases to developers, who usually convert them into flats.

The school with the biggest estate is Dulwich College in South London. Its land stretches from Denmark Hill in the north to Crystal Palace in the south, including Dulwich Village which is a conservation area, and Dulwich Park, Bel Air Park and Dulwich Common, which provide literally hundreds of acres of leafy green. Until the 1967 Leasehold Reform Act, Dulwich owned 3,100 Victorian or Edwardian houses and 1,400 post-war houses or flats.

Since then, it has been forced to sell the freehold of 2,800 houses, which leaves it with about 300 old houses which are 'fair-rented', and the 1,400 modern houses or flats, which were sold on 99-year leases between the 1950s and 1970s.

Nevertheless, Dulwich College still retains control over the estate as an entity. It operates a special Scheme of Management, whereby even freeholders are not free to change a window or cut down a tree without approval.

The aristocratic landlords

The best-known of the traditional freeholders are the aristocratic landlords. Their estates, which include some of London's loveliest garden squares, tend to fall within conservation areas and are liberally sprinkled with listed buildings. This not only makes the properties expensive to buy but means maintenance requirements – and therefore service charges – are high. As always though, good maintenance upholds the value of leaseholders' investments as much as the freeholder's.

Lord Portman's family owns the 110-acre Portman Family Settled Estate. This is bounded by Oxford Street to the south, Edgware Road to the west, Crawford Street to the north and Manchester Square to the east. About half its mainly 18th-century buildings are in residential use, but most of them were sold leasehold about 30 years ago to head-leaseholders who converted them into flats and then sold sub-leases. These, which sometimes come on the market, only have about 15 years left to run.

Current policy is to encourage sub-leaseholders to get together and buy out the head-leasehold of their house on a management company basis. Then the management company can surrender the balance of the existing head-lease and get an extension of 50 years, making a head-lease of about 65 years. Leases are so strict on this estate that as well as laying down the law about house exteriors, individual flats have to be decorated inside every seven years.

The biggest of the aristocratic landlords is the Duke of Westminster whose Grosvenor Estate owns 100 acres of Mayfair and the entire 200 acres of Belgravia. The Mayfair acres are bounded by Oxford Street to the north, Park Lane to the west, Mount Street and South Street to the south and South Molton Street to the east, and about a third of the mainly 18th century buildings are still in residential use. Belgravia is almost entirely residential, and its superb Regency terraces stretch virtually unbroken from Hyde Park Corner in the north to Chelsea Bridge Road in the south; from Buckingham Palace in the east to Sloane Square in the west.

Both areas are amongst the most sought-after in London, and although even new leases are only 60 years long, the sky's the limit when it comes to prices. The Grosvenor Estate occasionally sells an unmodernised house to the public, but usually it either modernises itself, or sells to a developer who modernises. New or existing leases of flats and houses often come onto the market and, much more rarely, a freehold property is available – one of the smaller houses the Estate had to sell under the provisions of the Leasehold Reform Act.

Like Dulwich College, the Grosvenor Estate operates a Scheme of Management which covers freehold and leasehold properties alike. Its results can be seen most spectacularly in Belgravia, where all stuccoed terraces gleam with the regulation magnolia paint, applied by rule every three years.

The 120-acre Howard de Walden estate lies just to the north of Oxford

Street, bounded by Marylebone High Road to the West, Marylebone Road to the north, Hallam Street to the east and Wigmore Street to the south. Although it's home to the many private doctors who practice from plush consulting suites (most notably in Harley Street and Wimpole Street), the medical profession is usually confined to ground-level. Upper floors of the mainly 18th century buildings are residential, and when they've been modernised by the Estate or other developers, flats become available on 75-year leases. Recent developments elsewhere have included remodelled mews houses and a new block of flats. Throughout the estate, parking is virtually impossible by day but evenings and weekends can be as calm as the country.

The Duke of Bedford's London estate is small – only 20 acres of Bloomsbury in London University-land. It's divided into two long strips: one extending widthways from Tottenham Court Road to Gower Street; the other from Montague Street to Southampton Row. Most of the buildings are 18th century, but only about a quarter are residential: most are offices or small hotels.

Viscount Chelsea's Cadogan Estate still comprises 90 acres. Some of them are in the big chunk of Chelsea bounded by Sloane Street to the east, the SW3-stretch of the Kings Road to the south, Draycott Avenue to the west and Walton Street to the north; others in streets to the south of the Kings Road; and they're about 80% residential. The estate has recently completed a policy review, and one of its main results is that it now carries out direct refurbishment and redevelopment projects. Work in progress involves six houses in First Street and five houses in Pavilion Road, all to be sold on a leasehold basis.

This more active approach could affect existing leaseholders whose leases have only a short time to run, because, whereas previously, the estate usually negotiated new longer leases, now it will only do so if it has no plans for the property itself. Where new longer leases are negotiated with existing leaseholders, they are normally for a period of 60 years.

The majority of properties are already on long leases, which are always coming on the market. The terms of the leases are strict with regard to maintenance and alterations.

In aid of charity

The only other traditional estate in central London to rival the riches of the aristocratic estates belongs to the low-profile Henry Smith's Charity, whose annual millions go mainly to medical research. It was founded in 1627 with £2,000, and the Kensington farmland where the money was invested was developed in the 19th century with some of London's most elegant housing.

Well-known charity-owned streets include Cranley Gardens, Onslow Square, Pelham Crescent, Egerton Gardens and Lennox Gardens, and management is possibly the strictest in London. In the case of the many stuccoed terraces, for instance, the Charity paints them all white itself and then puts the cost on the service charge. 'For Sale' boards are forbidden except for new conversions. The 18 acres of garden-squares and crescents are kept impeccably. And when conversions are carried out by developers instead of the Charity, if the developers can't be bothered with managing the houses once they've sold the flats, they can surrender their head-leases back to the Charity.

Existing leases often come on the market, and those on the western half of the estate have about 50 years left to run; about 28 years on the eastern half.

New leases are usually 65 years long, and should be available in Onslow Gardens, where several new conversions are nearing completion.

The inescapable fact about buying leasehold property is that when the lease does eventually run out, that's the end of it. It has no value whatsoever. As far as leasehold houses are concerned, it is always possible (but only remotely so) that the scope of the Leasehold Reform Act could be widened. Equally, it's just possible that the 1954 Landlord and Tenant Act (which already gives leaseholders of certain flats, where rateable values and ground rents are low, the right to become sitting tenants when their lease ends) could be widened in its scope.

Shirley Green is the author of 'Who Owns London?' (Weidenfeld & Nicholson, 1986) and an award-winning book on the slum landlord Peter Rachman.

Buying and selling in London

It is safe to assume that most people reading this will be in the position of not having enough money to buy exactly the home they want in their most preferred part of London: safe, since expectations escalate with income and everyone feels that way until they hit the multi-millionaire bracket.

So most people will undertake a fairly prolonged search, for one or more of several reasons. One, they are really pushed to afford the place they need. Two, their freedom of movement is restricted by the need to be near certain schools, fast routes into work, relations, etc. Three, they want to make the most advantageous move possible, and find a place that will maximise their investment, hoping perhaps to spot an area which is on the way up – which, if correct, can mean that it will move smartly ahead of the rest of the town until its prices catch up with other 'acceptable' areas.

Whether our theoretical searchers are first-time buyers or already own a home, unless they have moved within the last five or six years they will find London a different place. In those years, a quiet revolution has happened. The obvious symptoms have been the rocketing prices and the advent of homes of such marble-bedecked, gym-and-Jacuzzi-clad luxury that they seemed totally divorced from the lives of Real Londoners.

And so, to begin with, they very largely were. At one stage there were two distinct markets, top and everyday, with foreign buyers accounting for quite two-thirds of the top level. This prompted the outward wave of 'gentrification' as people were priced out of the centre of town. The high prices also made economically possible the restoration of great tracts of decaying housing. Now UK buyers are once more in the majority and things are less frenetic: but the town has been transformed. Today's buyers are faced, then, with a far wider choice of areas: once it was unfashionable to live north of the Park, unthinkable to move south of the River. Now both fashion and lines of communication (following necessity, as ever) have re-drawn the map of London. Are still, indeed, redrawing it – see, for a start, the 'Transport' chapter. And we have a far wider and better choice of properties. First, then, a look at two important aspects of this new situation, London's new developments and the people responsible for them, and the way that they are sold.

London's homes and their development

One intriguing point about buying a London home in 1989 is that all that interior-designed opulence at the millionaires' end has had a knock-on effect. Homes are not merely more expensive; they are different. Standards have risen and expectations demand not just modern kitchens but more than one bathroom per large family house. In new homes, design and layout have altered immeasurably – and across the board. It wasn't simply that we were backward in such respects compared to other countries (though we were). House prices didn't allow such fripperies.

But the enormous difference made by the advent of the new, moneyed buyers at the top of the market was that as prices rose ahead of inflation, it became economically viable both to build new homes and to convert older buildings, grown too large for modern families. To invest not only cash but increased amounts of time, imagination and care which at their best have produced results that range from the refreshingly inventive and ingenious through to the downright brilliant: cleverly-planned homes that will be tomorrow's classics.

This scope for good work has attracted some of the large builders back into London, and has also produced a crop of first-class indigenous developers, some small, some large. Their work is beginning to be referred to by name, as it were. 'Developer' in the Rachmanite '60s and '70s was virtually a dirty word; a low profile has until recently been maintained by even the best. But now it is worthwhile to know who is responsible for the conversion of a flat or the building of a house, and the developers are starting to come out of their shells.

It is hard, now, to remember that at the start of the '80s hardly any new homes were being built in London at all. Now the likes of Wimpey, Wates, Bovis and Barratt are seen around London – not just building at one price level, but right across the board, and converting as well. The ultimate irony is probably provided by the Wimpey homes built, at the behest of the Crown Estate, as so good a replica of the classic white-stucco Pimlico terraces that sales staff had some difficulty getting prospective buyers to believe that they are totally new and not a conversion. And others are coming onto the scene: Trafalgar House is no longer synonymous with just newspapers and civil engineering: they are now developing under their own name as well as that of Ideal Homes London. Kentish Homes are making a splash in Docklands and Bow as well as Kent. The shipping company P&O, with Globe Investment Trust, are responsible for Chelsea Harbour. Fairclough, McAlpine and Taylor Woodrow have moved into development from building.

Some of the names you will come across are Rosehaugh Copartnership, independently-minded offshoot of the large commercial developers; Merivale Moore, Broadwell, Jacob's Island Company, Roger Malcolm, Regalian, London & Edinburgh Trust, Town & City, Heron, Skillion, Conran Roche, Declon Kelly, Lovell, Fairview . . . you'll find their names and others cropping up in the A to Z section of this book, building, converting and generally renewing London.

Overall verdict: the large builders and developers are getting better by the minute; though too many still fall down on detail – a syndrome known as leaving the choice of finishes to the site manager. What is happily dying out is the tendency of some of the mass builders to use their standard house and flat layouts, fine for Essex, with a gloss of London style. The smaller specialist developers are expanding their scope, though not all have proved as adept at new-build as at the conversions they excelled in, or vice versa.

For all developments, a chat with existing dwellers as to the standards of after-care service can be informative. And ask the selling agents for names of schemes the developer has done before. Go and have a look to see how they are faring. Whoever you are buying from, check carefully the specifications in the brochure. Do not assume you will get the standard of fittings in a show flat unless they are specifically listed. Small print in specifications repays attention. 'You could shoot cannon-balls through some brochures' comments a leading agent. This means watching not just the obvious like kitchen appliances and colour of bath but the standard of joinery, the solidity of doors and cupboards, the depth of skirtings. In any newly-built home, there are certain simple checks: like, for example, jumping up and down in the centre of the floor. See if the pictures fall off the show-flat walls. Send your partner to the next room and upstairs and see if you can hear footsteps or conversation. Note that new homes should carry the 10-year National House Building Council guarantee.

Marketing and estate agency

Once, there was selling. Now there is marketing. London's estate agents have also had to come to terms with the enormous range of properties and the commensurate range of prices – and the sophistication of clients. This, too, has reverberated through the whole market; as glossy brochures began to be appropriate, the use of pictures for 'ordinary' details became more usual and then expected. (Though sadly, the day of the scruffy, badly typed and printed list, all too frequently inaccurate, illiterate or both, has not yet entirely passed.) New technology began to mean computer link-ups – which should soon make their presence even more felt – and also videos for top schemes, and the production of everything from in-house newspapers to glossy magazines. Now agents fly to Hong Kong and Taiwan to sell London property; professional services, advising developers, investors, etc, is an increasingly important part of their business. The bigger firms have marketing departments, carry out intensive research; they are involved, these days, from the early stages of a new development and advise on the probable buyers and their wants, the layouts, the finishes, the appropriate marketing.

Meanwhile the agencies themselves have been bought up by financial institutions, following deregulation and fierce competition between building societies, banks and the like. Enormous national chains have appeared – but note that these big players have more in mind than estate agency commissions: their main concern is to use these networks of High Street branches to sell you mortgages, insurance, even pensions. The remaining independents have gone 'public' to finance their own expansion. Smaller firms are merging or taking over each other; more offices means reduced overheads, more clout to negotiate reduced advertising terms, more safety, in short.

With estate agency changing so fast, customers may be under the occasional misapprehension. For instance, the big national name over the door may be a recent change: Amalgamated Insurance PLC may have bought Bloggs & Co of Station Parade only last month, changed the fascia, painted the office in house colours and left the former partners as managers. You walk in, confident in your faith in Amalgamated, but is it them you are really dealing with? For a year or so, until the corporate culture has time to seep down to Station Parade, you are still buying the strengths and weaknesses of Bloggs. There are two sides to this: some well-respected London firms have lost their identity in Amalgamated's anonymity. And Amalgamated's good name has been attached to some pretty second-rate concerns which were bought just because they had a couple of well-placed offices.

While all this expansion has been going on, there have been more and more small players appearing on the scene. These mushroomed in the wake of the rising prices and profits; some have aggressively modern methods far removed from the gentlemanly old school. Some are good. Some are not. Some have been sued. One or two have been convicted of criminal offences.

Happily, the (at best) confused and unsatisfactory state of both estate agency and of the buying and selling process, which came under the spotlight in this Guide and in the national press last year, is seriously under review.

In July, the government finally threatened legislation if the profession couldn't keep its own house in order. There is now an 'inter-professional working party on the transfer of residential property' at work, composed of agents, lawyers, conveyancers, building societies, local authorities and, to represent the rest of us, the Consumers' Association. Issues under discussion include estate agency, local searches, gazumping, house-buying 'chains', registration of title, financing and the Estate Agents' Act 1979. We await events. Meanwhile, the quieter market will in itself begin to sort out the genuine agents from the used-car salesman. Anyone can sell when there's a boom on; it takes skill, care and experience when the advantage swings back towards the buyers. (See Selling, below, for the choosing and instructing of an agent.)

As regards the selling process, it is clear that it must be simplified and speeded up, and soon.

The professional bodies to which most agents belong, the Incorporated Society of Valuers and Auctioneers (ISVA), the Royal Institution of Chartered Surveyors (RICS) – who are planning to amalgamate – and the National Association of Estate Agents (NAEA), are a useful source of information. Members will have undergone courses and passed professional exams (the NAEA's members are not necessarily qualified, with the other two it's a condition). The bodies also guarantee deposits held by their members and can be approached if you have a dispute with a member.

Buying

Buying your first home may seem an overwhelming step; in fact, once you have scraped up enough cash for a deposit and enough evidence of reliability to persuade a building society or equivalent to lend you three or three and a half times your salary, it will likely prove the most straightforward property deal you will ever make. You will find a wealth of advice, in print and in person, on this subject. Everyone smiles kindly on you and offers anything from free leaflets to better mortgage terms, special rates, money-off deals.

This is only partly tender solicitude on your behalf: you have, as a first-time buyer, one inestimable advantage: you are not encumbered with a home to sell before you can buy their client's. It is worth remembering this advantage that you have: it can clinch you a good deal if the seller is in a hurry to move. The other point to remember when looking for the first time is that an estate agent is just that – an agent. Not yours, but the seller's (or vendors, as they are known). It is the agent's job to present the goods in the best light. He is bound not to lie; he is *not* bound to point out that the tube line passes underneath, shakes the foundations and rattles the windows. Nevertheless a good agent with a reputation to maintain is concerned to have satisfied customers on both sides. His clients will then often come from people to whom he has sold. If, though, he treats his customers shabbily, then they will be living in his patch and talking about him. Loudly.

General pointers: London is luckily a very well-mapped city. Many people – and not just first-time buyers – will need to keep an open mind about their choice of areas. If you are free to live anywhere within reasonable lines of communication, it's worth bearing in mind that some areas have been changing well ahead of their reputation; the road you remember as the scruffy place where a friend had a bedsit may have changed out of all recognition. But journeying to far-flung corners can be frustrating if you find the place backs onto a mainline station. A good look at a good map alongside this book can fill in the gaps in the property details.

That being said, one man's drawback is another soul's way in to an area above his means. If you are hell-bent on a certain area, there are likely to be cheaper corners; the essential thing to remember, though, is that anything inexpensive for an unalterable reason – views over graveyards, for instance, seem to be a minus-point – will likely not just stay relatively cheaper but also take longer to sell. Always look at a home with a view to having, one day, to sell it to somebody else – fast.

The more estate agents' details (which are at least free) and newspaper ads you can wade through, the better idea you will get of what is going on in the market in a given area at a given time. The one golden rule when looking at a procession of properties is always to make brief notes at the time or immediately on leaving; three flats further on and you won't be able to recall which was the one that smelt damp, which overlooked a noisy playground. When you think you've found the one, visit the locality at different times of day. Many people who only have weekends for homehunting can find on moving in that the street is a solid traffic-jam on week-days.

Briefly, the anatomy of a purchase goes:

1. Talk to building society or other lender as soon as you start looking, if not before. They will advise on how much you are likely to be able to borrow. When looking, remember that you will be unlikely to be able to borrow the entire asking price and will therefore need money for a deposit. A mortgage of 80% over 25 years is the norm, though first-time buyers may get a better deal. Also remember that all the attendant fees – searches, stamp duty, valuation, survey, solicitor – and the cost of moving will absorb another £3,000 or more; that homes cost money to maintain: the Royal Institution of Chartered Surveyors have an invaluable booklet on the cost of improvements and alterations.

2. Make an offer through the agent, who will probably ask for a deposit (generally £100) to show good faith. If and when it's accepted, return to your lender with the details of the property. They will conduct (but you pay for) a valuation. You should commission a survey of your own – talk to estate agents and lenders about the several levels now available. Offers should be made 'subject to survey'.

3. Your solicitor starts the searches and conveyancing process (see Rudiments of Conveyancing). Alert him when you begin househunting.

4. Contracts are exchanged, and you pay 10% of the purchase price as a non-returnable deposit.

5. A month or so later (though it can be done in days) completion takes place and the deal is done. You are free to move in.

Selling

In recent years there has been limitless advice available for the guidance of first-time buyers, from free leaflets from the building society to whole books on the subject. Strangely, there is almost nothing to help the seller –first-time or otherwise. This is surprising: selling a home is an activity even more likely to be carried out in conditions of stress, since in most cases you will also be trying to buy the next, co-ordinate it with the sale, and arrange for the move. Yet there is much that can be done in order to get off to a good, fast start – and speed is generally all-important to one party or the other in a London property deal.

For example, a problem particularly peculiar to London is the length of time it takes to get the local authority searches carried out. Councils vary widely in the time they take to complete this bit of form-filling: the City of London, with hardly any private residents to speak of, have been known to reply in one day while last year one borough was taking some *23 weeks*. You will find average

search times at the bottom of each area's opening information page; check, though: particularly in the busy spring and autumn periods. This is a task generally undertaken by the prospective buyer, but there's no reason that the seller shouldn't get a search carried out: a small expense that can save weeks. The results are valid for three months.

Your solicitor can of course arrange this for you – which is a second point. Alert your solicitor to the fact that a move is impending: people often forget to do this, assuming that there will be time enough when a buyer is in view. That is a bad point at which to discover that your solicitor is on holiday or even – as has been known – has died since you needed him last. Once notified, he can also draw up a draft contract in readiness and retrieve the deeds to your property from bank, building society or other mortgagor. It all saves time.

A top London estate agent added the interesting rider that not only can such preparation hasten the conclusion of a sale, it helps the agent to test the true worth of the would-be buyer. If the seller's side isn't ready to proceed, it can be weeks before you discover that the apparently eager buyer's own home isn't, after all, quite sold, or that they haven't, after all, got quite enough money.

A good agent will point all this out to you, and in London there is no shortage of agents to choose from. Like the little girl in the old rhyme, when they are good they are very, very good, and when they are bad. . . .

A lot hinges on the seller's ability to pick the right one for him/her and then instruct them properly. You should see at least four. If you don't already have strong ideas on which are the most prominent locally, it can help to go window-shopping, checking for offices in a prominent position, with properties of the calibre of your own, well displayed, and run by welcoming staff. You can go in, describe your own place and ask for details of anything of that type on their books. This serves the dual purpose of finding what the competition is, and how much, and what their reception of your potential buyers is going to be.

Showing prospective agents is a good practice run for showing potential buyers. Remember that agents are human too: they, like buyers, are seeing many different properties; they, too, can be put off by an untidy, uncleaned shambles. Light, warmth, flowers and furniture polish (the old-fashioned smelly sort) can do wonders to underline a welcoming atmosphere.

Having thus set the scene and shown the agent over, what do you need from him? First, of course, you want to know what price he suggests. A house is worth what someone is willing to pay: there is no absolute. The agent needs to take into account not only what appears to be the going rate, but the state of the overall market and your personal circumstances, too. If you must sell by next week, both marketing and price will be different.

But how do you evaluate what he tells you? If four agents come up with different prices, which should you appoint? The answer is not necessarily the one who mentions the highest figure. Perhaps that agent does know something that the others don't – or perhaps he is tempted to promise you more in order to get your attractive home onto his books. Good properties attract more good properties – and bad luck the hapless owner, who has a long, slow wait and may in the end have to reduce the price on his by now 'stale' home. Buyers do notice, and wonder what is wrong with, homes that are inordinately slow to sell. Alan Collett, a director of the College of Estate Management's course for residential estate agents, summarized the sort of questions you should be asking the agents: 'the first thing you want to know is how they've arrived at that price. What evidence of sales at that sort of level is there to substantiate his view? He may be able to tell you straight away, he may need to go away and come back with some figures — that's fair enough. But if the attitude is "I've been in the market 20 years and I know everything", I'd want chapter and verse on how many houses he has personally sold in recent months which compare to mine. Then, you could ask what other properties there are on the market that will compete with yours. If he shows signs of not understanding the question, it'll tell you a lot!'

After that, ask what the agent proposes to do to sell your home — though, as Alan Collett points out, advertising is not necessarily the whole answer. If your home warrants it, you may find yourself asking about whether the agent has a regular contract with national magazines or newspapers. This can be a tangible benefit: regular contracts mean cheaper advertising rates and a saving to be passed on to you. It also indicates the level that the agency is working on, of course. Maybe expensive brochures will be appropriate (one, produced for the sale of St John's Lodge in Regent's Park, was a hardback book and cost £25 a copy). Some firms have press offices who will send out a release to the papers.

Fees come last. Some agents make a point of a lower percentage, but take this on the 'you get what you pay for' principle. A skilled agent's negotiating acumen can easily save you the half of a per cent extra he charges. What will vary the rate charged is whether you appoint one firm sole agent or, as you are perfectly entitled to do, instruct several at once. Agencies charge less if they get sole agency, and they work harder, because all the effort they put in will be rewarded if they get a sale. Appoint more than one, and only one will get a fee from the transaction; all of them will know this and it will be reflected in the intensity of their efforts.

You'll find that agents come in all shapes and sizes, from one-partner, one-office, old-established concerns, through brash, keen newcomers to big independent practices and the local offices of large chains. Each has its advantages. Weigh local knowledge against marketing skill, the personal touch against chain-breaking clout. With big firms, ensure that the people you deal with know your area and have not just been transferred from Sidcup. All this said, choosing an agent is a personal business. Whatever the firm, it is only as good as the staff in your local branch: choose the people who impress you.

However expert the agent, you know your home best. He should therefore look to you to check draft particulars. They should be set out clearly and logically, and remember that items mentioned in them are generally understood to be included in the price unless otherwise specified. If you are going to be showing people around, he should brief you, because he can provide an objective list of selling points to mention. If you are not showing buyers round, who is? Can you show them round first, and are they both personable and intelligent (an elusive combination in junior staff in estate agents)? Who should you contact for progress reports — you should expect regular news, but they have other places to sell too: don't ring every day.

Selling tends to be fraught with excitements, and it's wise to keep cool. But what if you have appointed an agent and nothing seems to result? Give the agent a set number of weeks of sole agency, and if there is no action call him in for a progress report. There may be good reasons for the dearth of buyers. At this point decide whether to give him a longer period of sole agency, appoint a second agent as well, or even drop the first entirely. Good agents are loud in their encouragement of clients who are forthright: if there is a problem, let them hear about it.

Mortgages

by David Spittles

There are more than 200 sources of mortgage finance available and a bewildering array of loans. Where do you start? How do you discriminate?

Building societies no longer rule the roost. The monopoly that enabled them to ration funds and dictate costs disappeared when the High Street banks took the market by the scruff of the neck and quickly grabbed a 20 per cent share. A pack of merchant banks, foreign banks, insurance companies and City conglomerates followed. The increased competition has brought refreshing innovation where loans are tailored to specific types and circumstances: pension mortgages for the self-employed, interest-only mortgages for the elderly, low-start mortgages for the first-time buyers, capped or fixed rate mortgages for those who prefer a set budget, unit-linked mortgages for borrowers prepared to speculate, foreign currency mortgages for the financially sophisticated.

Eight out of ten mortgages advanced are endowment-based. This means the amount you borrow is covered by life insurance. You make interest-only payments to the lender and pay a regular premium to an insurance company. The initial sum borrowed is eventually repaid from the proceeds of a maturing endowment policy. The size of this fund depends on how well the insurance company has invested your monthly premiums. If there is a surplus, you can take it as a tax-free lump sum. Hence the importance of choosing an insurance company with a track record for good investment. Among the top performers are Standard Life, Scottish Widows, Scottish Mutual and Norwich Union.

Insurance companies now have to provide two projections of maturity values – one showing a net growth of 10.5 per cent per year and another plotting an annual growth of seven per cent. But accurate forecasting is tricky as yields are influenced by stock market movements. The October 1987 Crash was disastrous for some borrowers because terminal bonuses on maturing policies were slashed.

The commission question

One reason for the popularity of endowment mortgages is the lucrative commission received by intermediaries and lenders (more than a quarter of the leading building societies' profits come from this source). Unfortunately, too many home-owners are talked into accepting inferior endowment contracts because of the juicier commission paid by some insurers. Mortgage brokers, which have been most closely identified with this unsavoury practice, still have a credibility problem, though it is evaporating as borrowers begin to recognise their worth in the home loan jungle. The belief that you visit a broker only if you have been unemployed for a decade and intend buying a disued lighthouse is misplaced. A reputable broker should be able to pinpoint the best deals in the marketplace. Indeed, some of the most competitive rates of interest, those offered by unfamiliar foreign banks and finance houses, are available only through brokers. Normally, brokers charge about one per cent of the mortgage advanced, though some reimburse any insurance commission they receive. The two biggest firms in London are John Charcol (01-589 2626) and Chase de Vere (01-930 7242).

Mortgages are not covered by the new Financial Services Act – an odd omission given the substantial asset property represents – so brokers are not bound by the "best advice" rules that govern other financial intermediaries. However, they must register with an authorised body if they sell insurance products. Avoid using a broker that isn't a member of FIMBRA.

Under the "polarisation" rules of the Financial Services Act, lenders have to decide whether to sell the products of one insurer exclusively or remain an "independent" intermediary dealing with various companies. Of the major building societies, only the Abbey National has become a "tied" agent, having joined forces with Friends Provident. This means that the Abbey National will give only that company's endowment quotations, though it cannot make a Friends Provident policy a condition of the mortgage. Most of the clearing banks are tied agents as well (NatWest and the Royal Bank of Scotland are not), and they tend to be pushy about borrowers accepting the endowment contracts they offer. Sometimes they are insistent that you transfer your personal bank account too. Some home-owners have no objection; others prefer not to put all their eggs in one basket. It depends on how you organise your finances.

Endowment or Repayment?

Research shows that borrowers are less bothered about the method of repaying a mortgage than they are about finding a lender quickly and conveniently, which means there is enormous scope for promoting endowments. Yet the difference in cost between an endowment mortgage and a conventional repayment mortgage (where you pay a combination of interest and capital each month) isn't usually significant – unless you suffer chronic illness or are elderly, which boosts the insurance premiums. One advantage of a repayment mortage is that it is more flexible should you fall into arrears: unlike an endowment loan, the mortgage term can be extended and the monthly outlay reduced. If you move house, it is possible to transfer an endowment to the new property. Surrendering (cashing in) the policy during the first ten years is unwise – the pay-out value will be poor.

Tax relief on endowment premiums was abolished in 1984 (the change didn't affect policies already in force), but relief on pension premiums is still claimable. A pension mortgage, which works in an identical way to an endowment loan, is the most tax-efficient method of buying a house, and should be considered by those in non-pensionable employment. Pension contributions need to be high enough to repay the capital sum borrowed *and* provide a decent retirement income.

Check the rate

Widening mortgage choice has made borrowers more interest rate conscious. Though the big lenders tend to shadow each other when pegging rates, the margin across the range can be hefty. With the typical London mortgage in excess of £60,000, even one percentage point difference amounts to a meaningful saving. Opting for a lender with the keenest rate is tempting, but always check the company's pedigree and credentials. Does the lender have a reputation for remaining competitive? Or is it just exploiting a marketing opportunity? Some of the new lenders, anxious to gain a foothold in the market, offer attractive deals that are unlikely to be sustainable. Also consider if you are comfortable doing business with an organisation without a branch network, or whose headquarters are based in Japan or Canada, for example. Are you content with the sales "culture"? You may like the reassurance of a High Street presence and a personalised service.

Building societies are inclined to believe that borrowers are not especially "price sensitive", and that they base decisions on the strength of the complete service – the availability of deposit and current accounts, credit cards, travel insurance and so on. Of course, building societies have a more cuddly image, which stems from their "mutual" status. In theory, they are owned by their borrowers and investors whose needs they serve. Other lenders are answerable to shareholders, and are therefore more likely to be guided by commercial considerations (if you cannot meet mortgage repayments, they may well be quicker to threaten repossession). Recent legislation does allow building societies to convert into public limited companies, though to date only the Abbey National has grasped the nettle.

If you do make a judgment solely on interest rates, always compare the annual percentage rate (APR) value of the loan. Sometimes the actual cost of a loan at a seemingly better rate is more. This is because lenders calculate interest in different ways. Building societies normally compound the interest on an annual basis, while banks do it monthly, making their APRs lower.

Savings are also possible if you pick a lender that discounts higher mortgages (usually deemed to be over £60,000 plus). The Abbey National, Halifax, Nationwide Anglia, Woolwich and the Girobank are among those that shave 0.5 per cent off the standard rate. Building societies introduced such sweeteners to entice those borrowers targeted by the specialist lenders (Household Mortgage Corporation, for instance) – unglamorous but highly computerised institutions that have gained a reputation for speed and efficiency, and have thus captured the yuppie market. "Vanilla" mortgages (as the trade calls modest loans) are not as profitable.

Brand loyalty is a disappearing virtue now that borrowers are more prepared to dump one lender and switch to another in order to gain an interest rate advantage. But be wary of ostensibly amenable new players. Most charge an initial arrangement fee, and having locked you into a scheme, will clobber you with redemption penalties if you choose to exit. Often the penalty is three months' interest, which on a £100,000 loan works out to more than £3,000.

First-time deals

First-time buyers underpin the mortgage market and there are always incentives on offer for them. These include interest rate discounts for a limited period (rarely beyond a year) and subsidised household insurance. Try to quantify the savings before being seduced. Selective payment mortgages are appetising if you are operating on a shoestring. These reduce the cost by as much as 30 per cent in the first few years, but the saving is really only deferred, ultimately the loan is recalculated so you have to be more confident that your earnings will rise enough to cover the increased mortgage debt.

Income multiples (the amount the lender will advance according to what you earn) vary. It shouldn't be difficult getting three times your salary. Some smaller lenders offer four times income, but then charge a higher interest rate or will limit the loan to, say, 80 per cent of the valuation. Building societies are still the best source of 100 per cent finance, though the maximum advance seldom exceeds £50,000. Remember too that the loan is based on the lender's valuation of the property. If this is lower than the agreed purchase price, you will still have to find the difference.

The abolition of multiple mortgage tax-relief has not bucked the trend of first-time buyers pooling resources and buying together. By law, only four people can be named as owners on the title deed – in any case, lenders are unenthusiastic about situations involving more than two buyers. Each person is jointly and separately responsible for the entire mortgage, so if one party defaults the other(s) have to pay up. Hence the importance of choosing a reliable co-habitant. It is also advisable to formalise the agreement by asking a solicitor to draft a trust deed specifying a buy-out provision. Without this, one person can at any time force a sale of the property, and there is no legal obligation to sell to the other(s).

If you are borrowing the entire purchase price, finding the customary ten per cent deposit on exchange of contracts is a predicament. Equally, if you are an existing home-owner whose cash is tied up in the property you have yet to sell. One solution is the Deposit Guarantee Scheme, now operated by thousands of solicitors in London and the South East.

Under the scheme, instead of the traditional cash deposit being handed over, a buyer pays a nominal sum to an insurance company. A £10,000 deposit requires a premium of £60, and a £30,000 means you have to pay £150. The buyer then signs a certificate, provided by the solicitor, which is the vendor's guarantee that the appropriate sum will be paid on completion. If the buyer withdraws from the transaction, the insurance company pays the vendor and then recovers the money from the defaulting buyer. The scheme is administered by Legal & Professional Indemnity (0892 862345), which will provide details of participating solicitors.

In a sluggish market, exchange of contracts is often delayed by owners trapped in property chains. Various organisations (including Prudential Property Services, Hampton's, Black Horse Agencies, Legal & General) now operate chain-breaking schemes, but emancipation means accepting between eight and twelve per cent less than the market value (though normal estate agency commission is included). Moreover, these organisations will only step in if they have a sole agency arrangement, and sometimes flats are excluded. A better facility is that offered by Norwich-based Home Exchange. It runs an independent service whereby it takes the average of two valuations and offers the seller 90 per cent.

David Spittles is a freelance writer on property and finance. He contributes a weekly column to the Evening Standard.

Rudiments of Conveyancing

Writing cheerfully, in order to stave off depression, solicitor Daniel Taub outlines both the process and the jargon of conveyancing.

You're moving house. This time the home improvement urge won't be satisfied with simply extending the extension or triple-glazing the double-glazed windows. So you've ignored the advice of your friends, listened to the pleas of your neighbours, and entered the deep and murky waters of the conveyancing transaction, the legal transfer of the ownership of a property.

Conveyancing is largely a matter of using the right words. For 'buyer' say 'purchaser', for 'seller' say 'vendor', and for 'I'd forgotten all about it' mumble: 'We're still waiting for the searches to come back'. With this vital information in mind, you're ready to begin.

In the outline of a conveyancing transaction which follows I've assumed that you're buying a house. Similar procedures apply if you're buying a flat, except that if the flat's above the tenth floor subsidence doesn't generally present an immediate worry. I've also assumed, for simplicity's sake, that the purchaser and vendor are handling the conveyancing themselves. Most people, lacking a spirit of reckless adventure, get a solicitor to act for them, or one of the new breed of 'licensed conveyancers'. Doing-it-yourself, though, is becoming more popular and not only saves you money, but also provides an endless source of fascinating dinner-party conversation, especially when you have to sue yourself for negligence. However you decide to go about it, though, the basic structure of the transaction is as follows.

In buying a house there are two stages. The first, up to signing the deal, and the second up to paying the money. In the legal profession these two stages are usually termed 'before and after exchange of contracts'; to the housebuyer they're generally known as 'before and after we discovered the dry rot'. The exchange of contracts by the purchaser and vendor seems hardly worth the effort since both contracts are exactly the same. What the purchaer and vendor are exchanging of course is their signatures. The contract itself is originally prepared by the vendor, or by a solicitor on their behalf. Solicitors have a hard time preparing documents since they never learn to read and write. Instead they're taught to 'peruse' and 'draft', which is very similar but rather more expensive. In order to draft the contract the vendor, or their solicitor, needs to see the documents showing the vendor actually owns the house. The type of document depends on whether or not the property is registered. All houses in England and Wales are either registered or unregistered. The unregistered system is the traditional one in which the vendor proves title by flourishing a pile of dusty deeds that trace the line of ownership back into the mists of antiquity (well, 15 years under the current regulations).

Not quite so much fun, but a whole lot simpler, is the system of registered conveyancing which has taken over from the unregistered system in most areas. Nearly all London homes are registered. Where this system applies, the Land Registry, a central government department, issues a single document for each property, bearing the name of the owner and listing any mortgages or restrictive covenants affecting the property. This document, called a land certificate (or charge certificate if the property is mortgaged), means the title to the property is guaranteed by the state, so the vendor can go ahead and frame his old title deeds to sell them to foreign tourists, or use them to paper over the cracks before showing the prospective purchaser round.

Having extracted the necessary information from the deeds or land certificate, the vendor drafts the contract and sends it to the purchaser. The purchaser must, of course, peruse the contract, and then respond by making preliminary enquiries. These take the form of an extensive list of questions about such things as rights of way, boundary fences and disputes with neighbours, to which the sly vendor gives such pertinent answers as 'Inspection will reveal', 'Please search' and, an old favourite, 'The purchaser must rely on his own enquiries'. The diligent purchaser will of course ask for more particulars – and get them: 'Look, we told you, the purchaser must rely on his own enquiries' . . . and so on.

At the same time as this vital information is passing back and forth, the purchaser will also have made a local authority search. This should reveal any new road developments in the area, any breeches of planning permission and other matters affecting the property. The questions are generally set out in a standard printed form. So, in the main, are the answers – but you may be lucky enough to get the personal touch when you find there's a compulsory purchase order to turn your dream home into a municipal car park.

At this point in the proceedings, the wise purchaser will arrange for a qualified surveyor to produce a full report on the structure and condition of the property. The even wiser purchaser will think twice before actually reading this report. For the surveyor fault-finding is a challenge, an instinct, an art. The verdict of a sound and stable structure that you were hoping for would be an insult to your surveyor's professional pride, and you would do well to be grateful if you're told the walls give negligible support, the roof's an acceptable risk and in place of a floor the house has 'a faulty loadbearing structure which necessitates extensive underpinning'.

Once contracts have been exchanged, and a deposit, usually 10% of the purchase price, has been paid over by the purchaser, a marked change is discernible in the sleeping habits of the vendor and purchaser. The vendor sleeps blissfully beneath his faulty loadbearing structure, while the purchaser tosses fitfully amid foreboding dreams of a life spent in the shadow of an acceptable risk.

The purchaser's solicitor, meanwhile, has no time for sleep of any sort now that the time has come to investigate the vendor's title. Not, that is, his social status (which should all be clear from the exchange of signatures) but whether the vendor actually owns the property. So, as the vendor did earlier, the purchaser now peruses the land certificate if the house is registered, or the deeds if it isn't. Either way the purchaser sends off 'requisitions on title', a list of requests for clarification or further information, to which the vendor responds with his usual helpfulness.

Title having been investigated, the purchaser can now prepare the document which will legally transfer ownership of the house – a 'transfer' if the property is registered, a 'conveyance' if it isn't – in readiness for completion. Completion, at which the actual sale itself takes place, usually occurs about one month after exchange of contracts. However this is subject to complex legal variables such as when the vendor's solicitor has booked his holiday or when the purchaser's new three piece suite is being delivered. For some reason quite beyond law or logic, Friday has become a popular day for completions. If you are tempted by the thought of moving in on the following Saturday, think again: should there be an unforseen hold-up it may mean a loss of three days' interest on your money, and it will definitely spoil your weekend.

With the date for completion fixed, the invitations sent out, and the drinks and savouries ready, the purchaser sends off a quick pre-completion search to check that nothing untoward, like a subsequent mortgage, has happened to the property while everyone's attention was diverted with all the perusing and drafting. If something should turn up, then completion may have to be postponed, and the drinks and savouries go down as 'general expenses'.

All the way along, the vendor and the purchaser have been pretending that they are selling and buying the property respectively. This may of course be true, but in most cases they come clean and let on that most of the money involved isn't theirs, but instead it comes from a building society or bank. Where mortgages are involved the procedure is still the same as outlined above, except that the title deeds will have been kept by the vendor's building society rather than the vendor, and that the purchaser's building society will also want to be in on the perusing of the various searches and documents relating to the property.

The completion part usually takes place at the office of the vendor's building society solicitor, and no-one's allowed in without a present. The purchaser's building society solicitor brings a bank draft for the mortgage advance, the purchaser brings another to make up the balance of the purchase price, the vendor brings the conveyance or transfer, and the host has the deeds or land certificate. When all present emerge from the scrum the mortgage on the property has been repayed, the vendor is left holding the balance of the sale price, the purchaser's building society is left with the deeds or land certificate, and the purchaser is left wondering where on earth the doorkeys are.

It's not, in fact, necessary for everyone to get together in the same room to complete the transaction. With the aid of telegraphic transfers beaming money from bank to bank, most solicitors or licensed conveyancers are now able to complete over the telephone, and some can even do it without moving their lips. The mechanics of the operation can become confusing, however, when the transaction is part of a chain – i.e. where either or both sides is using the proceeds of the sale of one house to buy another. A hitch in one distant transaction can cause a pile-up all the way along the line, and, in the unlikely event that a chain should be circular, then nothing would ever happen while everyone waited for someone else to make the first move. Many people are calling for a change in this aspect of the system.

Completion is not, of course, the end of the business. The purchaser has to arrange for stamp duty to be paid on the transaction, the vendor's building society has to produce a form certifying that its mortgage has been discharged and the vendor has to invite all their friends round to tell them about the dupe who bought the house no-one wanted. And you, the purchaser, have to sit down with a stiff drink in the middle of your acceptable risk, with its title deed wallpaper and faulty loadbearing structure, recovering from the news that the person who was foolish enough to buy your old place has just struck oil in the back garden. Welcome home.

YOUR NEXT MOVE

Well, it was a "terribly good buy", if you're partial to waking at the crack of dawn to the strains of cement trucks thundering out of the half built depot, jackhammers pounding incessantly and the neighbour's crazed alsatian. The local school is an hour's forced march, with buses as frequent as unicorn sightings, the handy local corner shop is only handy if you've broken the four minute mile of late, the nearest bottle of Mouton Cadet is a mere 20 minute jog down mugger's alley and the library is still operating a 4 day week. It's a cultural wasteland (unless you count the graffiti on our road sign) and the last rubbish collection must have been in Jubilee year, though how they found the place at all is a mystery, with the feeble street lighting—although the neon burger bar next door *is* a new local landmark.

Well......frankly, we're putting our "terribly good buy" on the market and moving. But this time we are going to start by talking to people with an established reputation for the quality of their service backed by years of experience, more than modicum of local knowledge and a very real understanding of just how traumatic selling and buying property can be.

RESIDENT EXPERTS

FARRAR STEAD & GLYN

 Residential • Furnished Lettings • Commercial • Management • Professional

Chelsea
152 Fulham Road, SW10 9PR.
Sales: 01-373 8425
Lettings: 01-370 4329
Management: 01-373 0066
Developments: 01-373 5075
Fax: 01-244 8914
Telex: 295845 FSAND G (all offices).

Commercial
22-25 Sackville Street, W1X 1DE.
All Enquiries: 01-434 9272
Fax: 01-434 9271

Kensington
281 Kensington High Street, W8 6NA.
Sales: 01-603 1221
Lettings: 01-603 9291
Fax: 01-602 3850

Fulham
656 Fulham Road, SW6 5RX
Sales: 01-731 4391
Lettings: 01-736 4851
Fax: 01-736 9816

Clapham
99 Northcote Road, SW11 6PL
Sales: 01-223 8111
Lettings: 01-223 8111

Hong Kong
1431 Central Building,
Pedder Street, Hong Kong.
All Enquiries: 5-252136
Fax: 5-8106815

Looking at a Property

It looks good, it seems cheap: is there anything wrong? A professional survey is essential if you are serious about buying a home, but a careful layman can take an organised look at a property and cut out the no-hopers. Here is a checklist prepared by an expert. The only equipment required is a cool nerve (to disarm outraged vendors) and a stout screwdriver.

Outside: take a good look at the next-door properties to see if there is any common fault. Check walls for any bellying in the brickwork or subsidence. Subsidence generally looks as if part of the building is out of plumb, or tilting. Cracks in walls can show subsidence; but not always: in some post-war concrete and brick buildings cracks in the brickwork occur because of the varying movement of the two materials. In buildings over 60 years old, lime mortar, which is flexible, was usually used, and this has allowed many to remain standing despite subsidence.

Check nearby trees; their size, type and age. Big trees near foundations could cause problems like subsidence, especially in long hot spells when the London Clay sub-soil dries and cracks.

Check for new extensions and alterations. This will show the possible further permissible development (see Planning).

Roof: if there is distortion in its shape or slumping, distrust the roof structure. Check the condition of the roof covering. Don't be afraid of asking for access to take a closer look as the view from street level is not always clear.

Gutters also need a close-up check: from the ground they may look fine, but they may be rusting away or badly fixed, causing unseen water penetration.

Get into the roof space or loft if possible; take a torch and check the soundness of the roof rafters and ceiling joists, eaves and ridges and the underside of the roof covering. Do they all look in good condition and sound? Likewise check the gable walls and chimney stacks. On your way down, turn off your torch and see if any daylight is coming through – a sign of slipping tiles. Check loft insulation and ventilation.

While in the roof space check the plaster under the ceiling joists – in older buildings lath and plaster was used and with age the plaster loses its grip on the laths, and the ceiling will eventually need to be replaced or covered with plasterboard fixed to the joists. Disturbing ceilings is a very dirty business.

Examine wires in the roof space: if they are untidy and not properly fixed, it is likely that the whole electrical system is the same.

Check that water tanks are insulated and pipes lagged – it gets cold in the roof in the winter. See that the tank is supported properly, preferably over an internal structural wall and not just the joists. Check that the size of the tank is adequate: an average (50 gal) tank is 3ft x 2ft x 2ft wide.

Outside walls: check pointing of brick walls to see if it is crumbly. With rendered walls, tap the wall with a screwdriver. If unsound, it will sound hollow and will probably crack and fall off. Close one eye and look up from one corner and down the length and height of the wall to see if it is bellying or out of plumb. Are the chimney pots leaning precariously to one side?

Foundations are hard to check, and most older buildings in London probably don't have them as such, but rather three or four courses of splayed brickwork two or three feet under ground level. Ask if any underpinning work has been done. If in doubt about newer buildings, ask the District Surveyor or Building Control Officer: if anyone is likely to know then he is. Give timber window sills a tap with the screwdriver to see that they are not rotting away under twenty coats of paint. South- and west-facing windows get most exposure so check them carefully.

Balconies: mostly these need a specialist inspection because there can be hidden problems. Does it look safe, or do the materials it's made of look decayed and badly maintained?

Floors: with timber-floored buildings, jump up and down in the centre of a room. If the floor feels springy or uneven, suspect inadequate joists, woodworm or other infestation or rot. To find out more take up two or three floorboards close to a wall.

NB. Just because a house is new don't assume it's well built.

With floorboards up, check wiring and pipework: does it look securely fixed? Does the ceiling plaster beneath look sound or is it falling away from the laths?

Do the stairs feel safe? Look out for unevenness and cracks opening up between the staircase and the wall, which may mean the wall is moving or the staircase has been poorly fixed. Look under the stairs for signs of woodworm.

Inside walls: tap plaster walls with your knuckles: if it sounds hollow then the plaster has blown, or lost its adhesion to the wall surface behind. If it sounds dense and is a little damp to the touch then it could mean water penetration or rising damp, when further specialised investigation will be required. Take another look outside in case gutters or downpipes are leaking.

Woodwork: do doors look straight and do they close properly? Have they been cut askew to fit the door opening, if so it is likely that there has been some movement in the building or it may be a sign of settlement after it was built. Tap the skirting boards to see if they are sound and look for signs of woodworm. Tap around window frames and sub-frames for soundness. Open sash windows to see if they work. Are they very draughty?

Drains: try to find the main inspection chamber (manhole) and lift the cover with the help of your screwdriver. Check which way the flow is going (by running taps) and the general condition of drains.

Check all external gulleys and downpipes: are they blocked or overloaded with pipes coming from all directions?

Onto the housing ladder

The removal of multiple mortgage relief for joint buyers who are not married was a blow to the home-purchase aspirations of many young Londoners. Rising mortgage rates, and yet higher house prices, added to the misery. While getting a foot on the first rung has always been hard, it is harder in London than it has been since owner-occupation became the goal of the majority. The typical London first-time buyer is on his or her own, with no discounts or special aid except personal savings and parental loans or gifts. There are, however, several ways to make that vital first step up easier. The first is to watch for low-cost schemes from builders and developers. The quieter market last winter prompted a revival of these. First-time buyers (ie, people unencumbered with a home to sell) are a useful part of the market so developers are keen to ease the pain of purchase. Look out for low-start mortgage offers, packages to cut legal costs, discounts for quick completions, even offers whereby you can do without the fitted kitchen and carpets and get a reduction on the house price.

Joint mortgage

Shared purchase is now widely practiced. Today's sharers are not necessarily couples but two or more friends who buy a property jointly and split the costs. This needs careful drafting of a legal agreement setting out terms of ownership and making clear what happens if one participant wants to sell up. Building societies and other lenders are increasingly flexible about such shared loans and will give advice. Men seeking to buy together may face the need for an AIDS test. Note that Poll Tax will mean higher bills because each occupant will have to pay rather than splitting the rates on the property.

The 1988 Budget made sharing more expensive by removing the right to mortgage tax relief for each joint-owner. Tax relief is now applied to the property not the person, and the £30,000 ceiling is a smaller and smaller fraction of the price of even a studio flat in London.

Sheller Publication's book *Buying your home with other people* by Dave Treanor (£5.95) investigates all aspects of joint purchase, including housing cooperatives, trusts and co-ownership.

Shared ownership

A more formal scheme whereby you can buy a share in a home, with the other share held by a housing association, council or other body. You pay this shareholder rent on the portion of the home it owns. You can buy extra shares when you can afford it at the price set on the home by the District Valuer. When you come to sell, the profit on the share you own is yours. It is best to go into shared purchase with at least a 50% stake, otherwise the rent payable, and the small proportion of the profit gained on resale, make it uneconomic. Shared purchase is available in London, as is the related scheme allowing tenants of charitable housing associations to buy private homes at a discount. The Housing Corporation (see below) and your borough council (see The Boroughs) are the people to consult.

Building societies are developing new variants on shared ownership. The

Woolwich, for instance, has Equity Mortgages. As a buyer, you get full title to the home but pay normal interest on 60-80% of the mortgage. On the rest, the rate is very low and can be zero. In return, the Woolwich are entitled to get a proportion of the rise in value of the home. The Woolwich aim this scheme at young buyers who will probably earn good salaries in the future, but at present can't take on the full commitment of a mortgage in the area they live in. Councils are working with the building society on finding housing list applicants who could benefit from the scheme. Loans are tied to special new-build or council refurbishment schemes. Eight schemes are under way, including two at Chelmsford and Harrow.

National Provincial have another scheme, whereby it lends to a housing association which builds low-cost homes. Buyers pay 5.5% deposit, which goes towards their rent for the first three years. After two years, the occupier has the right to buy the house at the price it was built for, regardless of any rise in value. This allows people who are unable to save for a deposit to get a toe-hold.

Nationwide Anglia have a Partnership Mortgage scheme designed to give NHS staff in London cheap home loans of up to 4.5 times their normal income in return for a share in the profits when the property is eventually sold. Urgent talks are going on in Government circles about the plight of similarly low-paid people like teachers and other essential workers.

Tower Hamlets council is active in the shared-ownership field, with 69 homes completed in 1988 and more on the way. The council will retain ownership of the land until the buyers complete payment for the homes, which they will do on the joint-mortgage-rent system.

Since deregulation in 1987, building societies can be housing developers in their own right. The Abbey National is building 1,000 homes a year, Nationwide Anglia aims for 2,000. A good proportion of these homes are built in partnership with councils, and sold at discount prices to people nominated by the council from their waiting lists. Docklands is a prime place for such developments, as it is for the rehabilitation of existing council housing by private firms like Barratt and Ideal Homes, again, often for sale at discount to housing list nominees – see below.

Councils

Tenants of councils have a statutory right to buy their home. For many in London, this has bought unforeseen windfall profits: tenants of 15 years' standing (less for flats) get a discount of 70% on the valuation price. This has led to Wandsworth tenants paying £10,000 for a 1-bed flat. Buyers can sell without penalty after having owned their home for three years. This, of course, is no good if you are not a tenant. But council resales are often cheaper than 'private' homes and can be a very good buy. In Roehampton, modern ex-council 3-bed maisonettes were selling last winter for around £88,000, a price that would seem cheap for a 2-bed flat in nearby Putney. Note, though, that unless exceptionally good, ex-council housing will, until most of the estate is privately owned, take longer to sell again. Beware too of certain 'non-traditional' homes built post-war by industrial techniques. Building societies can be reluctant to lend on them.

Councils vary in their enthusiasm for Right to Buy. Wandsworth, which pioneered the scheme before it became national policy, is very keen. They offer sons and daughters of council tenants the chance to buy vacant 1-bed flats. But a scheme whereby people who worked but did not live in the borough could buy has been abandoned: there were too many other applicants with higher priority.

It is no loss however to apply to be put on your council waiting list for both renting and buying a home. Occasional schemes come up whereby hard-to-let blocks of flats are sold or passed on to housing associations or cooperatives. Councils such as Westminster and Kensington & Chelsea have a declared policy to keep a 'social mix' in their area – which means they will help the hard-up young resident if they can. Council tenants in some boroughs can apply for House Purchase Grants of up to £15,000 to enable them to buy privately, thus freeing their home for another tenant.

More radical moves include the complete sell-off of Thamesmead, a GLC-built town of 22,000 people, to a non-profit-making board. The sale, at about one-tenth of what the place would be worth on the open market, was made by the government, which is eager than tenants should run their own affairs. Now nine of the 12-strong board will be elected residents, and right to buy is encouraged.

Docklands

As the place where most new London homes are being built, Docklands should feature on the list of anyone after an affordable first home. Not the smart warehouse flats of Wapping, but the Surrey Docks and Beckton. Housing associations are active here, often renovating run-down pre-war council flats. And all schemes for new homes on Docklands Development Corporation land must include some low-cost housing. This is usually allocated on a first-come, first-served basis to people on council lists in the Docklands area. This leads to people queuing for days to buy homes. Contact the LDDC and the local councils. To date, 1,600 housing association homes have been built in Docklands. Plans for the Royal Docks include 2,000 'social housing units' – the new euphemism for council and housing association homes. Some of these will be for shared ownership.

Renting

Private rented housing has sunk to a low ebb in London, but there are signs it will revive. More homes to rent would ease the plight of those who need a roof, but do nothing for those who see a home as an investment as well as a shelter. So renting means making a psychological adjustment: rent money is money spent, whereas we have got used to mortgage money being money invested. Nevertheless, there are times at which renting is much more appropriate than buying: when, for example, a move away from the area is likely in the near future; when your immediate prospects are hard to predict. And a good supply of rental accommodation would certainly help the sales market, too: being able to rent between selling one home and buying the next would help break many a chain in which no-one dare complete until they have somewhere to go.

The new Housing Bill, and the 1988 Budget's scheme to allow tax-breaks on investment in rented homes, should increase the stock available. Under the new law, rents can be set at a market rate by agreement between landlord and tenant – which inevitably means they will often be higher than current rents.

Planning

by Soo Ware

When buying a home, it often becomes necessary to know something of the law which affects development of residential property. There are, broadly, two sets of rules: planning permissions and building regulations. It may be that you are doing your own conveyancing, in which case your searches should reveal whether or not applications for planning permission and building regulation approval have been made. You may also be buying a property which has been modernised or converted – possibly over a number of years – and you may wish to reassure yourself or your building society that the conversion has been done with the full approval of the planning authorities and to the standards required by the Building Regulations.

And no matter how ideal the estate agents' particulars are, frequently some alteration or extension to new property is necessary to adapt someone else's lifestyle to your own. This brings you into contact with the planners and Building Control Officers.

There are two kinds of legislation which affect changes to buildings: first, the Planning Acts; secondly, the Building Regulations. Here we are only dealing with homes; rules for industrial and commercial property are different.

The last year has seen a change to the Planning Acts which could affect residential areas: This is an amendment to the "Use Classes Order" whereby land or property is defined as being suitable under the Borough Plan for a particular use – offices, homes etc. One of the classes, B1 light industrial/ studio use, can occur in or adjacent to residential areas and there are different interpretations of this in different London boroughs. This class does sometimes include residential workshops – places where people live and work in the same building. In some cases there are conditions attached to the use of these kinds of developments which restrict their use quite tightly. Check carefully if you are considering buying/leasing or renting something like this.

Planning Permission

The Town and Country Planning Acts are quite complex and often it may be necessary to obtain expert advice early on from architects, planning consultants or chartered surveyors (see below). This chapter deals only with controls on dwelling houses in terraces, semi-detached or detached houses. Blocks of flats are more complex and, more than ever, demand expert advice. The Acts are there to regulate development and protect the public interest in the development of land. Each application is looked at in context against the background of the general development plan prepared by each London borough. Copies of the development plan can be obtained for a very modest sum from Town Halls. Some areas within boroughs are designated conservation areas and usually the borough produces a separate policy document for such areas. Not all borough plans are totally up-to-date and in the LDDC area of Docklands different rules apply.

What might seem to the owner a very minor extension or alteration to a house can nevertheless have far-reaching effects on the amenities and appearance of the whole locality. Many boroughs provide design guides showing what is or is not acceptable in their area.

A planning application may be necessary for any of the following:

1 Building work, extensions, alterations, garages, conservatories, roof gardens, balconies, loft conversions.

2 Garden fences and the removal of trees (which are either the subject of preservation orders or in conservation areas). However garden sheds, greenhouses, swimming pools, sauna baths and summer houses generally do not require planning permission provided certain conditions are met.

3 Alterations to road access, drives and off-street parking. Consent from the highway authority (in London, Department of Transport) may also be required.

4 Alterations to a previous planning consent or a change of use – for example, dividing a house into flats.

5 If the building is in a conservation area or covered by an Article 4 direction (an order often placed on a whole street to maintain its appearance). This can include changing doors, windows and roofs, painting brickwork, pebble-dashing, sandblasting brickwork etc.

6 If the building is listed (as of historical or architectural interest), a separate listed building consent will also be required. Initial enquiries should be made to the planning department of the appropriate borough council, some of which have specialist historic buildings offices who will deal with your application and advise you as to whether or not you need to contact English Heritage at the Department of the Environment who may be interested in your proposals.

Early in 1989 amendments to the Planning Acts come into force under the General Development Order. There will be changes to what is considered "permitted development": work which does not require planning permission. An example which will affect many loft conversions which at present fall into the "PD" catagories is that windows will not be permitted in roof planes overlooking the highway – that is the front of the house to you and me. It is well worth checking at an early stage if the changes proposed affect the property you are interested in.

However, not all building work requires planning permission, and some quite modest extensions and alterations fall into the category of permitted development. Planning permission may not be required if you wish to extend your home by less than a certain volume, providing you can comply with certain conditions to do with height and location and (usually) make no changes to the front elevation.

The way in which the volume of a house is assessed is quite simple and relates to the 'original' house, that is as it was when first built or as it was on July 1, 1948 (if any extensions have taken place since then, the allowance may have been exceeded). The volume is based on the external dimensions of the house including the roof. At present, the allowance for extensions to a terraced house is 50 cubic metres or 10 per cent of the original volume of the house up to 115 cubic metres; for a semi-detached or detached house, it is 70 cubic metres, or 15 per cent of the original volume of the house up to 115 cubic metres. However there are no permitted development rights for flats. Planning permission for extensions or alterations will be necessary.

Even if the proposals fall within the volume for permitted development, it is advisable to make an appointment to see the council officer who deals with your area in the planning department to confirm that no permission is necessary. Increasingly, boroughs are insisting on applications being made for permitted development as a result of local borough policy, particularly for such things as loft conversions.

How to apply

All boroughs have a planning enquiry office and most produce leaflets explaining their requirements for different types of development. Whenever possible, it is a good idea to have preliminary talks with the borough before making an application. It is in theory possible to telephone the planning office and make an appointment to discuss your proposals in broad terms with the planning officer who deals with your areas before lodging a planning application. In some cases you may be able to arrange to meet the officer on site. However, the greatly increased volume of planning applications and appeals made in London means that many boroughs are no longer able to offer these services until a formal application has been lodged.

Four sets of forms should be obtained from the planning office, and it will also be necessary to provide four sets of drawings. These drawings are quite important and must be well done, and should include a location plan showing the street and surrounding area on the Ordnance Survey map at a scale of 1:1250, and clear plans, elevations and sections which are coloured to show the proposals and existing buildings. It is very useful to include photographs of both the property concerned and the surrounding buildings as well as a description of the proposed work.

There is also a statutory fee payable which varies according to the type of alterations. The planning officer will be able to advise you on the amount and your cheque should accompany the application.

How long should it take?

In theory, planning applications should be processed within eight weeks; this is a statutory requirement. However, many London boroughs are taking considerably longer than this – in some cases up to six months – before permission is granted or refused. The first hint of a possible delay over the eight weeks may come in the form of a letter from the council requesting an extension of time, although not all boroughs formally inform you in writing – you just don't get a reply. To further compound the problem, the eight weeks is counted from the time the authority acknowledges receipt of your application and again many boroughs are taking a considerable number of weeks just to send out the letter acknowledging receipt of the application.

On receipt of the letter asking for an extension of time, there is a choice: to accept the delay and hope it won't be too long before there is a result; or to consider appealing to the Secretary of State at the Department of the Environment on the basis that the authority has effectively refused the application because it has not issued a decision in time. If you are thinking of an appeal, it is certainly advisable to seek the assistance of a chartered town planner or architect or surveyor with special planning expertise. There are two types of appeal: a written representation, which is called a written appeal; and an inquiry which is like a court case and involves the appointment of a planning QC to act on your behalf.

Planning appeals are a very lengthy business and can be expensive. It is usually quicker to let the borough determine your application rather than appeal to the Secretary of State in an attempt to speed things up. However if you are reasonably certain the borough is going to refuse your application it is often quicker to appeal after the statutory eight weeks period even if you have had no reply. Once you have appealed to the Secretary of State because of 'non-determination', the borough cannot determine the application during the period in which the appeal is being considered.

It is possible to check up on the progress of your application over the telephone after about four weeks from receipt of acknowledgement and find out at which planning meeting of the council the application will be considered, although relatively minor issues can be determined by the planning department without the application going to the planning committee. Sometimes it may be necessary to post notice on the boundary of the property (a Town Hall euphemism for the front gate post or fence) so that local people are informed and can comment if they want to. Usually councils put notices in local newspapers about planning applications received. The procedures for public consultation vary from council to council.

Where to get help and advice

Councils produce free leaflets available from their enquiry offices which explain the borough's own planning policies in the form of the Borough Plan, Conservation Area Policy documents, Borough Design Guides, and often a handbook explaining the procedures.

There are two useful Department of the Environment booklets: *Planning Permission – a Guide to the Householder*; and *Planning Appeals – a Guide to Procedure*. These are often available from council offices or, if not, from the DoE, Tolgate House, Houlturn Street, Bristol BS2 9DJ.

The Royal Institute of British Architects provides leaflets describing services which architects offer in respect of planning applications. These are available from the Clients Advisory Service, Royal Institute of British Architects, 66 Portland Place, London W1N 4AD. Tel 01-580 5533.

The Royal Town Planning Institute has a number of leaflets about planning application procedure and appeals, lists of sources of planning advice in Greater London, and can put people in touch with 'Planning Aid for Londoners' which is a free advice service manned by Chartered Town Planners. Address: 26 Portland Place, London W1N 4BE. Tel: 01-636 9107.

Lists of architects, town planners and chartered surveyors can be obtained from: Architects: Clients Advisory Service of the Royal Institute of British Architects (address above) which can give lists of local architects with special planning expertise. Town planners: The Royal Town Planning Institute (address above) can give lists of Planning Consultants who will help with applications.
Chartered surveyors: The Royal Institution of Chartered Surveyors (12 Great George Street, London SW1, tel: 01-222 7000) also produce lists of Chartered Surveyors and Estate Agents with expertise in planning matters.

Building Regulations

To some extent, making an application for Building Regulation approval is more straightforward than making a planning application. There are two clearly-defined approaches which are detailed below. It is also worth knowing a little about the background to the legislation and the kinds of work which need building regulations approval.

The 1985 Building Regulations Acts introduced new building regulations which now apply to both inner and outer London boroughs and are run by each borough council's building control department. The new rules have reorganised and superseded all previous legislation relating to those building works that were covered by the old Building Regulations and separate local bylaws. New regulations have been introduced for Inner London covering matters such as sound and thermal insulation, control of condensation and energy, heat-producing appliances and provisions for the disabled.

What do you need building regulation approval for?

Generally the procedures for obtaining Building Regulation approval are now the same whether you are building in an Inner London borough or elsewhere in the country. Leaving aside for a moment the special additional Inner London requirements, the kind of work for which approval is necessary includes:

1 The erection of a building.

2 The extension of a building (conversion into flats, loft conversions, some forms of conservatory).

3 The 'material' alterations to a building – alterations to structural walls (for example, knocking two rooms together, taking down a chimney breast), means of escape and fire resistance, particularly in relation to conversions into flats and loft extensions for individual houses.

4 Provision, extension or 'material' alteration to sanitary equipment (putting in a new bathroom or shower or extra WC), drainage, unvented water systems and putting in a stove, boiler or fire which runs on solid fuel, oil or gas.

5 Provision, extension or 'material' alteration of energy conservation, insulation (including cavity wall insulation systems) and ventilation in dwellings (particularly when installing an internal bathroom or WC or internal kitchen).

Additional rules for Inner London

Since the Great Fire of 1666, there has always been special legislation in Inner London relating particularly to the rights of adjoining owners and covering joint concerns such as party walls, means of escape and special, temporary and dangerous structures. The new legislation introduced in July 1987 rationalised all the various London Building Acts formerly administered by the GLC through the District Surveyor's Office. With the demise of the GLC, the responsibility for administering the Inner London Regulations was vested in the boroughs.

These new regulations have now been in force long enough for test cases to be brought where differences of opinion arise. One example is the interpretation of Appendix B relating to means of escape in case of fire in residential buildings over 3 stories, which will affect you if you are proposing converting a property into flats or putting in a loft conversion. The interpretation of Appendix B can make the difference between a straightforward job and something rather more complex. Check first with the Building Control Officer before you get too involved in your new plans.

These additional new Inner London Regulations apply only to the Inner London boroughs of Camden, Islington, Hackney, Tower Hamlets, City of London, City of Westminster, Kensington and Chelsea, Hammersmith and Fulham, Wandsworth, Lambeth, Southwark, Lewisham and Greenwich.

In Inner London, there remains, in a modified form, legislation relating to:

1 Any works to adjoining owners' party structures – walls, fences, foundations shared or close to neighbouring property (for example, dividing walls between terraced houses). A party wall award would be necessary for this.

2 Means of escape and fire regulations, compartmentation to prevent spread of fire, etc (particularly for conversions into flats, loft extensions and rear extensions or for very large buildings which need special access for firemen).
3 Dangerous structures, relating to buildings likely to collapse.
4 Special and temporary structures, such as boundary walls over 8 metres, steel fire escapes or balconies, or other structures that are likely to deteriorate and which are not covered by building regulations. It may be necessary also to apply for a licence for these at the same time so that they can be checked up on from time to time to ensure safety.

In Inner London, if the proposals include any work that affects the adjoining owner (for example party walls) it is at this point that the procedures associated with what is known as a Party Wall Award commence. This involves serving notices on the adjoining owner and agreeing the appointment of architects or surveyors to act on behalf of both building owner and adjoining owner to ensure that the adjoining owner's property does not suffer as a result of the proposed work. This is a straightforward procedure, but professional help is required.

An architect or surveyor will be familiar with the regulations. Note that building control offices will pay particular attention to party wall matters when inspecting work in progress. Indeed, with so many London houses in terraces, all building work must consider the effect on adjoining buildings. As simple a step as knocking a wall down can have repercussions next-door.

How to set about it

In order to obtain Building Regulation approval, or where appropriate Inner London Building Regulation approval, apply to the Borough Council. Unless you intend to do very simple work, the services of an architect or chartered surveyor will be essential since detailed drawings are often required giving technical information on materials, drainage, fire protection and, in the case of any structural work, calculations are usually necessary.

It is possible to make an appointment with the building control officer before putting in an application to discuss the proposals and to find out if any particular information should be included (for example, specific calculations). Sometimes the officer (still called district surveyors in some boroughs) will be happy to meet the applicant on site if this is easier. There are two approaches: the Building Notice route or the Full Plan route.

Building Notice Route

Eighty per cent of building control applications involve a Building Notice. For buildings where it is not necessary to obtain a fire certificate before occupation – that is most homes – it is possible to serve a Building Notice. This is done by obtaining a standard form from the building control department, which should be completed and deposited with two sets of drawings and calculations, plus a fee, giving notice of the intention to start work 48 hours later without waiting for approval. It is usual to arrange a meeting immediately after submitting the Building Notice in order to establish whether or not there are any difficulties. As work progresses, the building control officer will pay regular visits to the site to ensure everything is done to his satisfaction.

A certain amount of confidence is needed to take this course, for if the regulations are not complied with, the local authority can enforce them up to a year after the work is completed, and this can prove to be extremely expensive for the owner. Less information needs to be shown on the drawings than on the Full Plan route, but the building control officer, during his inspections, can (and does) insist on additional works being incorporated to ensure that the regulations are complied with as the work goes along. These people have very wide powers, and they use them.

There are other types of building work which may require additional applications. For example, some structures require a licence (a boundary wall more than six feet high or a steel balcony or external fire escape). These are regarded as temporary and special buildings. In the case of flats or maisonettes over shops, separate applications have also to be made to the fire brigade, but your building control officer will give you details of these.

Full Plan Route

This is best used if you wish to have very tight control over the cost of the job and wish to have all details sewn up before the work starts to minimise the possibility of extra expenses. It's also necessary to have a reasonably long lead-in – at least five to eight weeks for the application to be processed.

Building regulation approval for the Full Plan route is in two stages:

1 The approval of the drawings (for which a fee is payable) and which should take from five to eight weeks. However, for complex submissions where a relaxation fo the regulations is required, or where inadequate information is provided, building regulation approval can take considerably longer.

2 On commencement of the work, a Notice of Commencement should be submitted to the building control officer together with a further fee to cover the building control officer's inspection of the works. It may be that the officer requires that he is informed when certain work is taking place (for example, building foundations, damp proof courses, laying new drains or covering up structural work), in which case further notices (but no fee) need to be served with one full working day's notice.

For the first stage, two sets of drawings and information should be submitted together with a letter or in some boroughs a form requesting that the proposals are considered for Building Regulation approval together with the appropriate fee. Details of the fees can be obtained from the building control department. During the five to eight week period before the full plan approval is given, a building control officer may ask for additional information or explanations and it is possible to have discussions with the officer about the best way of meeting requirements.

Whichever route is selected, when the works are completed, the owners or sometimes solicitors doing searches often write to the building control department requesting confirmation that the work was constructed in accordance with the regulations and a confirmatory letter is usually sent.

What happens if you decide to do without Building Control approval? You could find it difficult to sell your property when you come to move again, as solicitors' searches may reveal that the work was done without the proper approval, licences, or party wall awards. Or, you may be caught red-handed doing work for which approval has not been obtained, as building control officers take an eagle-eyed interest in the contents of skips. You may find the borough taking legal action.

The rental scene

This year sees the biggest change in the rented housing market since the First World War. From January, new tenancies can be at a market rent – the amount a willing tenant will pay and a willing landlord will accept. This seemingly basic economic law has to be spelled out, because for generations London homes have been set about with controls and legal restrictions. The idea of a free market, so readily accepted when it comes to buying, is totally unfamiliar when applied to renting. The new Housing Act changes the rules: in 1989 we will begin to see how the property world, and individual landlords, react to the new regime.

For the last decade in central London the only active market in rented property has been at the top end, the corporate sector, where the legal tenants are companies and the actual inhabitants their executives, usually foreign. This avoided the provisions of the old rent act, which gave individuals security of tenure. Tenancies by bona fide companies were not subject to rent act controls, and thus were the only tenants that prudent landlords would consider. Savills, who are active players in the top rental market, reported in 1988 that 93% of their tenants were companies, another 4% embassies, and only three in a hundred individuals. And 88% were foreign, with Americans alone making up more than half.

This company rent world has co-existed with the investment property business. It will not go away now the law has changed, indeed it is the hope of the more bullish of rentals agents that a new breed of tenant, the British one, will emerge to join the foreigners now that the new law makes renting more sensible a proposition.

The new Housing Act

The concept of the market rent, agreed between tenant and landlord and with provision for regular reviews, is central to the new law. Tenancies will be of two kinds: assured tenancies and assured shorthold tenancies. With the former, tenants have security, but there is more scope than before for the landlord to regain possession. Redevelopment of the building, or its sale, are now valid grounds for repossession. Rents of assured tenancies will be subject to review at regular intervals. If landlord and tenant cannot agree, the local rent assessment officer can be called in. These people now have the job of establishing what the market rate is in a given area. Thus a landlord can rest assured that his property will always command a market rent. BES schemes will use these new assured tenancies – see below.

There is a second kind of new tenancy, the assured shorthold. These are for a minimum of six months, and at the end of the tenancy the landlord has a right to possession. Shortholds too may be at market rents and the rent assessment officers can arbitrate.

It should be stressed that existing 'fair rent' tenancies, established under the old law, continue without change. When a property falls vacant and is re-let it will, however, be subject to the new rules. There is some doubt however about what will happen when 'fair rent' tenancies come up for review, as they have to every couple of years. Rent officers will have the double duty of setting 'fair' rents for these and 'market' rents for other tenancies. And the security of tenure can pass from husband to wife, or vice versa, but can no longer be 'inherited' by their children.

The purpose of the new law is, according to the Government, to liberate more homes for renting. It will certainly make it easier for landlords to let property without fear of never getting it back again. It will also increase their rent returns, until now artificially depressed by the law. And it will make it possible for owner-occupiers to let unused portions of their homes – think of the number of semi-self-contained basement flats about. What it will not do, at least straight away, is unleash a flood of rented homes. As is noted below, the company let sector is somewhat copiously supplied with homes at the moment. Landlords will be cautious about investing in a hypothetical market until they see real British tenants appearing to swell the demand.

The BES schemes

One of the surprises of the 1988 Budget was a concession allowing valuable tax breaks to companies renting out homes. The companies can buy homes worth (in London) up to £125,000 each and let them under the new assured tenancies. Investors in the Business Expansion Scheme companies get an effective 40 per cent discount on their investment as they can set the money against their tax bill. After five years the company can be wound up and the homes sold. Several millions have been raised under the BES rules. The London property world is waiting for this money to come into the market where, it is anticipated, it will make more buoyant the market for cheaper flats. Then we will see what effect the increase in the number of rented homes has on the rental market. Christine Davis of Radius predicts that the new tenancies will 'revolutionize the letting of property to individuals and should give landlords more confidence to let homes in this sector. It will be particularly significant in the areas where it is currently more difficult to get company lets, ie Hammersmith, Battersea and Ealing.'

Naturally, the tax breaks make it more attractive for individuals to invest in a BES scheme rather than buying property themselves – another dampening effect on the hoped-for rebirth of the small landlord.

The international market

The boom seen in company rentals over the last half-decade was sparked off by the economic upswing in the country's fortunes and grew to a flood of international executives arriving as a result of Big Bang. Since then the stock market has crashed and City redundancies have been seen, and in London at least the sales of residential property has also quietened. But though rents did not rise last year as they have in previous ones – indeed, tenants were able to haggle for reductions in the asking price – neither did this lucrative market go into decline.

By November Farley & Co were reporting their best-ever quarter. Winkworth had 'one of the busiest Decembers our office can recall, defying all the normal rules'. Initially the reason seemed to be that the cooling off in the sales sector had boosted the rentals side: 'It is becoming apparent that where some companies were encouraging their employees to buy property, they are now suggesting that they should rent', said Savills' Philippa Ramsay, whose firm had doubled the number of homes let as compared with the same time the previous year.

Conversely, Hamptons noted that there was some fall-off of central London lettings towards the end of 1988, 'probably', they thought, 'due to City redundancies'. The prime central areas may also have been noticing a slight draught from the east, as the smart new Docklands developments established a good lettings market. The area is less of a building-site now, and prices, points out Stuart Lawson of Keith Cardale Groves, are realistic compared with the West End. 'Tenants here are impressed by swimming pools – an integral feature of many developments – off-street parking and maintenance standards.' Christine Davis of Radius observes that 'there is also a growing demand for property in the Rotherhithe, Greenwich and Blackheath areas as prices here are still much lower than in Wapping and the Isle of Dogs.'

And there are other customers appearing in the rentals market: Savills note a marked increase in lettings to international corporations, not merely financial institutions. And Hamptons believe that the impact of 1992 on the residential lettings market will offer a greater mobility of senior executives and stimulate demand. In the shorter term, they can see a relative shortage of the types of homes most in demand: the houses and flats for senior personnel who often bring their families with them. They do not see BES assured tenancies affecting this end of the market at all. They predict that gross yields are likely to remain at or around 7 to 8 per cent of capital value.

This peculiar niche market is served by a band of property investors whose activities, and future, are profiled by John Brennan in the 'Investment' chapter. They work according to the motto concisely spelt out by agent Harold Phillips of Phillips, Kay & Lewis: 'remember to buy what the Americans will rent and the British will buy'. This has led to a concentration of rental activity in the most traditional and 'safe' of areas: Mayfair, Belgravia, Knightsbridge and Kensington.

The executives who make up the tenants come with fixed ideas, very often, about where they want to be. Areas like Battersea and Clapham have now joined this group, although foreign renters prefer to stay more central. Starting from the cheaper end, Docklands, Battersea, Clapham and Streatham come in a group. The next layer up has areas like Pimlico, Notting Hill, and Highgate; followed by Little Venice, Hyde Park and Wimbledon. Then come Hampstead, Kensington and part of Chelsea, with the top layer comprising Mayfair, Knightsbridge, Belgravia, Kensington, St John's Wood and the best bits of Chelsea. Docklands has become more popular but will only rise up the ranking with family tenants when the infrastructure of schools, shops and transport catches up with the quality of the property.

Rentals in late 1988 were running at £90-150 a week for a studio in Blackheath or Battersea, £250 for a 1-bed in Docklands, up to £100 a week more for the same size in Knightsbridge or Belgravia – more still if serviced. Two bedrooms would cost you £150-300 in Docklands or Battersea, up to something like £600 in Mayfair or Belgravia. For three bedrooms the comparison is £300-375 (the higher price brings a river view) in Docklands and up to £800 in Mayfair. A 4-bed Docklands town house would be around £400 a week, while in top West End areas this can rise to £1,500-2,000 a week for an exceptional property. For comparison, a double room at The Hilton currently costs £181 plus VAT. Per night.

The Investment Market
by John Brennan

Few would seriously argue with the American financier Bernard Baruch's warning that it's unrealistic to try to apply the investment adage to 'buy at the bottom and sell at the top.' "This can't be done...", said Baruch, "...except by liars." Since there are no obvious markers to the top and bottom of any investment market – until long after the event – 1989 looks set to be an intriguing, sometimes nail-biting year for the London property market.

There are now so many conflicting pressures on property values, and so many distinctive sub-markets within London, that there's plenty of scope for subjective judgement of what constitutes the 'top' and 'bottom' of the price charts. There is also an unparalleled interest in the investment value of London property, since the entire adult population of the capital, and a substantial number of people who have never set foot in the country, have a material interest in the way London property prices move this year.

After five years of often spectacular percentage increases, everyone with a London home has acquired the price sensitivity of an investor. There is an even keener interest in prices amongst the 80 to 90 per cent of adults under retirement age who are currently renting in the capital and who, according to the Building Societies Association's housing preference research, would like to own their own property if they could afford to.

Investment value has come to be ranked just below the traditional, basic criteria of location and size in every recent survey of property buying decisions. And that's hardly surprising after a decade in which the average London home has more than doubled in price, and when the nerve to borrow up to the hilt has enabled a significant number of people to trade their way up the market to a house or flat that they couldn't possibly afford on any straightforward calculation of their income and the money they'd need to borrow if they were to try to buy it today.

Homeowners and 'real' investors

This kind of conscious equity leap-frogging has turned quite a few homeowners into quasi-investors. But there are a number of profound differences between homeowners – even if they do have a keen, occasionally obsessional, personal interest in their property's value – and the pure investment buyer.

It's the differences in approach of these two distinct groups which help to determine the way different sections of the housing market react to changes in interest rates and to the ebb and flow of confidence in the economy as a whole, and property prices in particular.

Perhaps the single most important difference is that there is no safety net in the pure residential investment market. Unlike houses and flats that are bought by owner-occupiers, properties acquired primarily as investment counters have non of the live-in stability of a home. If there's a fair chance that prices are going to fall, investors rush to sell, and homeowners do the exact reverse.

Even if the consensus view is that prices are likely to remain comparatively stable, investors are still likely to want to sell, to re-invest in a better performing medium. In that situation homeowners who don't need to sell simply stay put and switch back to the weather as prime conversational topic after a few years in which it has been hard to string together a dozen sentences without some reference to house prices.

The other key difference is that successful investors have learnt the art of selling.

Equity-building owner-occupiers may become adept at buying by following their judgement of what constitutes an 'up-and-coming' area and by seeing the potential for improvement in a poorly-maintained property. But few of these own-home investors can resist the temptation to hold out for the last few pence of their asking price, however ambitious that might be. In contrast, a professional investor has to be a trader by nature since it is the uplift in the capital value of a property, rather than any rental income it might generate while it is being held for resale, that makes commercial sense of the deal.

The three-tier investment market

All of which suggests that, in an ideal world, we should be able to see a clear distinction between the way prices move on properties owned by the – in theory – coolly objective investment community, and those properties that are investments only in the eyes of their owner-occupiers.

That's true, but only up to a point.

As far as cool objectivity goes, for the companies and individuals who make, or at least substantially supplement, their livings by trading residential properties, the summer of 1988 was widely recognised as a good time to cash in earlier gains.

By that time every economic signal was flashing amber or red, yet prices were continuing to rise, disregarding the likely impact of what every city commentator agreed had to be a progressive and probably protracted period of high interest rates. Evidence that prices had overtaken, and were beginning to streak ahead of, their historic relationship with average earnings gave an additional spur to investors to sell while they were ahead.

By no means every professional managed to get their timing right in 1988. But those who listened to their advisers were either insulated from higher financing costs, having scooped up the fixed interest loans that became available for a period earlier in the year, or, if they failed to sell ahead of the autumn slump in buying activity, they've recognised the need to take the long view on the London market and settled down to wait and see how prices react over a number of years.

Unfortunately for this vision of an orderly market (and fortunately for those who did take the decision to sell into a still rising market) while there are plenty of people who have been keen to put money into London property, only a minority of these could be described as either true professionals, or as adequately advised investors.

In the 1980s, London flats and houses for rent have become a populist investment option. That is partially because so many people feel more comfortable putting surplus money and credit into bricks and mortar than into equities or fixed interest stock, and in no small measure because of the success of the sales agencies in presenting a picture of assured capital growth and guaranteed high rental income to a receptive audience.

As a result, what has for long been a two-tier investment market has acquired a third, much larger, and much more unstable layer of 'amateur' investors. The first two tiers consist of the internationally wealthy London home

TO GIVE ACCURATE, FAIR AND PERCEPTIVE ADVICE IT IS NECESSARY TO HAVE A THOROUGH AND COMPLETE KNOWLEDGE.

THIS SHOULD EXTEND NOT ONLY TO PROPERTY BUT ALSO TO PEOPLE AND THEIR REQUIREMENTS.

CHESTERFIELD & CO AIM TO ENSURE THAT EVERY CLIENT RECEIVES A PERSONAL AND INFORMED SERVICE BASED ON THIS KNOWLEDGE.

FURTHERMORE, WE CURRENTLY HAVE AVAILABLE ONE OF THE BEST PORTFOLIOS OF PROPERTIES AVAILABLE FOR SALE IN CENTRAL LONDON. CONTACT EITHER OFFICE FOR DETAILS OF THESE PROPERTIES OR THE SERVICES THAT WE OFFER.

CHELSEA OFFICE: 166 WALTON STREET, LONDON SW3 2JL
TELEPHONE: 01 581 5234

BELGRAVIA OFFICE: 28 CADOGAN PLACE, LONDON SW1X 9RY
TELEPHONE: 01 235 8008

Chesterfield & Co

buyers, and the serious, specialist property professionals.

For the transient population of seriously rich individuals, a London home has long been a necessary business and social base. Over a century ago there were complaints by the locals that Park Lane and much of the rest of Mayfair was becoming an international ghetto with every second house occupied by an American millionaire, Indian Rajah, or a South African diamond mine owner. Now, some of London's most expensive homes provide seasonal bases for Middle Eastern oil sheiks and the wealthier Iranian exiles, for South American landowners and Australian, Indian, and Hong Kong Chinese traders.

This top tier of the investment market is made up of people who are effectively collecting properties worldwide. They will often trade around from one home to another if a particular property that appeals to them becomes available. Otherwise, their decisions about a London home are influenced less by any year-to-year changes in the health of Britain's domestic economy than by their judgement of the country's political stability, by the dominant position of London's airports as a hub of the international air routes, and by London's status as one of the more civilised centres of world trade.

There is a considerable overlap between these internationally wealthy collectors of homes and the owners of long established central London estates. Neither are investors in the sense of being as active in selling as they are in acquiring or managing existing numbers of London homes. Both are relatively insensitive to short or medium term fluctuations in property prices.

The second tier of activity in the investment market involves the few remaining publicly-quoted residential property management companies, and the larger number of private, mainly family-owned estate companies, which are run by and which operate alongside a close community of residential property specialists.

Those specialists who are not managing the estate companies are often agents without particular interest in the prosaic business of handling people's home moves. Instead, they trade in and out of residential properties on their own account, sometimes holding them for rent, but more often buying in the hopes of being able to improve values by renegotiating leases or winning a planning permission so that the property can be sold to a developer.

Few ever get involved directly in the costly and uncertain business of residential development or refurbishment. They recognise that the bulk of any capital gain comes from rising site values, or when a planning consent for improvement is granted. Their skill is that of any trader, to buy wholesale, to add value – even if that merely involves timing a purchase and resale to take advantage of a general rise in values – and to sell retail.

These specialists haunt the auction rooms in search of the occasional bargain. They also frequently act as personal buying agents and advisers to a number of individuals who want a proportion of their money in London property, but who recognise that they haven't the time, the expertise, or the market contacts to manage that part of their investment portfolio themselves.

Crisis for the amateurs

That leaves the third, and what is now the largest tier of investors, made up of the tens of thousands of individuals who have been attracted to London property by the price increases of the 1980s, but who are not close enough to the market to join the ranks of the professional traders.

These are investors who have no option but to buy their properties retail, making them heavily dependent upon the quality of advice they receive. These are investors who, if they wanted to put money into the stock market would normally be directed into a unit trust, or into some other form of managed fund – yet the overwhelming majority of them have staked all in a single property.

Many are UK expatriates, with the income to support a substantial UK mortgage and the wish to retain a foothold in the British property market. Expatriate communities across the world have been heavily and successfully wooed by British agents selling London flat developments.

Few hotel conference rooms in Hong Kong and Singapore have not been drafted into use at one time or another in recent years to display travelling exhibitions of London property. And the arguments used to persuade high-earning exiles to borrow their way into new-built, or soon to be built, apartment blocks have worked just as well on Hong Kong Chinese families remitting money from the Colony ahead of the hand-over to mainland China, on the new generation of young City dealers racing after their first million, and on a mixed bag of business and professional people who have seen the value of their own home soar, and who have wanted their share of the seemingly certain profits in owning someone else's home as well.

There is a real crisis of confidence amongst these part-time investors right now, and for good reason. A few real-life examples help to illustrate the extent to which the past few months' change of pace in the London housing market has proved to be a financial minefield for ill-advised investors.

One investor who totally ignored all the advice he didn't want to hear recently ended his property career in the bankruptcy courts. Half a dozen private auctions in Mayfair acted as ill-attended wakes for this German buyer's mistimed confidence in the upward-only nature of London property values. Backed by a number of different, mainly US and Scandinavian banks, he had outbid his way through the agents' stock of Mayfair properties in 1987 and well into 1988, gathering as he went an impressive portfolio of refurbished town houses. Long-term, few would argue with him that the end of post-war temporary office consent on nearly a million square feet of Mayfair property in 1990, and the return of that space to residential use, will help to revive the area as one of, if not the, best addresses in London.

However, he proved to have committed to much, too quickly, too late in the market cycle. The banks ceased to share his enthusiasm for Mayfair houses when interest rates began to rise faster than property values. When efforts to resell a few of the houses to pay off the most pressing of his loans failed to attract offers within sight of his forward-looking asking prices, the banks lost their patience, and he was forced to go bankrupt.

Another equally expensive mistake, albeit on a smaller scale, was made by a Nigerian-based expatriate who contracted to buy a two-bedroom flat off-plan in a development near Regent's Park just over two years ago. He paid a 10 per cent, £46,000 deposit, and settled back to enjoy re-reading the sale agent's calculation showing that, assuming a reasonable rate of price inflation, he could expect to sell for £520,000 when the block was completed. That resale price would ensure a £60,000 – 130 per cent – clear profit in 18 months.

As the construction work neared completion, and apartments proved to have been fitted out to the impressively high specification shown in the initial sales material, all the flats on the Regent's Park side of the building were resold quickly, and at prices well in line with the agent's best forecasts. Unfortunately, the expatriate's flat was at the back of the block. It overlooked busy roads and an unappetising-looking tube station. He had bought sight unseen, and was to pay dearly for that mistake.

His flat just could not be sold before the completion date arrived, even at a deep discount to the hoped-for value. The expatriate then faced having to remit an extra £414,000 to complete the purchase or forfeit his deposit. The money couldn't be raised, and while the developers accepted that it would have been futile to try to enforce their completion rights on the contract, the investor lost his money.

Given the successful sale of so many of the flats in the block, any aggregate analysis of its value to those who put down deposits before the foundations were laid would probably show that it had been a good investment option. But aggregates and averages are of no comfort to the speculators who lost out on the deal.

The several thousand people who have bought similar 'futures' contracts on development properties have been biting their nails as their respective completion dates approach, and as the continuing price rises that so many of them based their buying decisions on begin to look impossible to achieve.

The major residential developments due to reach the market in 1989 were initiated at a time when there was an acute shortage of modern, high-specification flats for rent in Central London. Allowing a couple of years from first foundations to completion, most of the 1989 schemes were coming off the drawing board and being offered for forward-sale in 1987, at a time when central area property prices were racing up by between 20 and 30 per cent a year. Buyers who accepted completion prices anticipating a continuation of that rate of price growth through to 1989 could find themselves with contracts on unsaleable, or at least slow to sell units.

Unlike the expatriate whose UK assets couldn't match his completion costs, many of the people who have paid their deposit and contracted to buy a flat months ahead will find that it is not easy to walk away from the deal even if it no longer makes financial sense.

Developers who can see no obvious signs of an alternative buyer in what has become a highly competitive and increasingly price-sensitive market, are much more likely to want to enforce completion contracts than they were a year ago. Unlike an equity market option, which simply lapses if it isn't exercised in time, an agreement to purchase is as binding a contract if it is taken out 18 months or two years before the completion date as it would be if it related to an immediate sale.

A bargain hunters' year

High loan rates and general nervousness about the state of the world financial markets are expected to force the rate of house price inflation in London into line with, or even a point or two below, the general rate of inflation in 1989. Because of owner-occupiers reluctance to sell into a weak market, sales volumes are unlikely to pick up after an already unnaturally quiet late autumn and winter. And if any area of the London housing market is to record a serious drop in value, it has to be amongst the investment trading stock bought at prices discounting future rises that are not likely to occur for some years.

This creates a classical market for the bargain hunters. And many of the professional investors who were able to sell early in 1988 are hovering around the market ready to swoop on any distressed sale properties as cash buyers at the heaviest discounts they can get.

Which does, of course, beg the question – at a discount to what? If much of the London residential investment market really is facing a crisis year, why would anyone with ready cash be willing to commit their money at all?

The answer has to refer back to the basics of supply and demand. The bargain hunters are looking for discounts to prices that are quite firmly underpinned, albeit in the long run, by simple rarity value.

Only around 15,000 additional homes are expected to be built in the central London area in the next decade. Even allowing for the greater effect of a continuing transfer of housing from the rented to the owner-occupied side of the balance sheet, that's nowhere near enough to match the forecast increase in the number of households in London. It is certainly not enough to make even a marginal dent in the underlying demand for housing from 'concealed households' made up of people still living with their parents, otherwise sharing accommodation, or currently living beyond a reasonable travel-to-work distance.

This strong, unsatisfied domestic demand for London housing does feed through to the more rarified price levels of central area properties held for investment, and rented to company tenants.

Although the housing requirements of a couple reluctantly living with their parents in Acton or Wandsworth might seem to make no difference at all to the value of a prime central property in Kensington, that pent-up local demand for additional homes keeps up the pressure on building land prices throughout the London area.

That pressure on land prices underpins the long term value of existing properties of all types throughout the capital, raising the cost threshold for first time properties, increasing, in turn, the value of second and third resale homes up the price scale. Rising land costs feed through right to the top of the house price pyramid, and that helps to ensure that there is no impossible gradient in values between the prices of properties sold to home-grown buyers and to international buyers.

Without strong local demand right up through the price ranges, investment-standard flats and houses rented to international corporate tenants would represent a price-isolated ghetto of property within the London market. That is exactly what happens with international standard homes which stand apart from the rest of a city's housing in many less developed countries. In those third world situations high government officials are often the only local buyers who can afford to take on such properties, and any downturn in the investment markets there feeds directly and immediately through to property values.

There is a far greater texture to the London property market where a house in Belgravia may be rented at several thousand pounds a week to an American banker one year, and bought back into the local market by some successful British businessman the next.

Every element in the equation that leads to generally high property values in the centre of the capital – right back down the line to that home-hunting couple in Acton and their like whose needs inspire housebuilders to bid up the value of scarce development sites – helps to counter short term reactions to high interest rates and increased resistance to ambitious asking prices.

Since there are no signs of any early relaxation in development restrictions on greenbelt land around London, there is nothing to relieve the pressure cooker effect of such a marked imbalance of supply and demand on property prices can only continue.

Or at least it will as long as that demand is effective: that is to say, as long as people who want to buy can afford to do so. Which might appear to bring the case back full circle to those historically high levels of average house prices to average earnings.

On the basis of those figures, showing prices running at between 4.5 and 4.8 times average earnings, property valuations are way out of line with a thirty-year rolling average that shows properties selling for nearer 3 to 3.5 times average earnings.

That's the central plank of the argument suggesting that there has to be a major reaction in the property market and a sharp fall in sale prices before the averages get back into line again. But those historic figures take no account of changes in home-buying practice, particularly in London.

A closer look at the mortgage statistics show that first-time home buyers in London have been borrowing at much the same level as they always have, at levels equivalent to three times earnings. They've been doing that by raising larger deposit payments – with a significant amount of money being passed down the generations by home-owning parents – and by clubbing together to buy a property, despite the ending of tax relief on more than one mortgage.

It is probable that property values will tend to mark time until earnings do start to move back into line with prices, but at the same time, it would be overstating the case to suggest that the entire London housing market is about to grind to a halt in 1989. As the first-time buyers' evident willingness to adapt to changed market conditions shows, while the housing market may be log-jammed in theory, in practice, people do tend to find a way to beat the averages.

There's a similar resilience in the London rental market where rents in 1988 were offering investors around 8 to 8.5 per cent return on their money, net of financing costs. Nevertheless, tenants – even major international corporate tenants – have been increasingly selective and far more willing to bargain down asking rents, in a year when trading volumes in the world financial markets haven't recovered from the crash in October 1987. And when the upward spiral of interest rates worldwide has been pulling the reins on international trade. Higher mortgage costs now put even greater demands on capital appreciation to make a rental investment stack up in financial terms. Bargains apart, the yield gap between realistically achievable returns (allowing for greater risk of running into void periods as so much new rental accommodation competes with the existing stock) and financing costs in matching sterling loans, calls for a level of capital uplift that looks improbable in 1989. So there will be few investment takers for new rental space, unless its price reflects the changed rates.

That's another reason for concern for already over-stretched investment property owners, another reason why 1989 will be the year of the bargain hunters, and the most solid reason to treat all forms of property – even the super-hyped residential investment stock of the capital – as a long term proposition.

John Brennan is the residential property correspondent of the Financial Times.

London's
Areas
A to Z

This central section of the book is an alphabetically organised guide to London's areas. The system is a two-tier one: each section covers an area or areas, and in its turn is divided into the various neighbourhoods within them – Parson's Green can thus be found under 'F' for Fulham, of which it is a part. Below is an index which lists the areas for quick reference. Area and neighbourhood names are also found in the main index at the end of the book. If you know only the **postal district** of the place you're looking for, check the listing which starts on p 54 in the 'London in 1989' chapter for the areas it covers. This division, although less clear-cut than using the hard-and-fast boundaries of postal districts or boroughs, make for more logic since areas refuse to stop at bureaucratic boundaries.

● **Maps:** an outline map of London on the pages following the area index shows the areas covered. The first page of each area section has a map and a table of information. The map is specifically designed to be a guide to the *shape* of the place, its main roads, railways and stations, the neighbourhoods it divides into, what areas lie next door. Borough and postal district boundaries are shown (difficult things to chase over several pages of a street atlas – if they are shown at all).

There is a key to these maps on the next page. The maps are not designed to be street maps: to locate a particular street we refer you to the relevant page of the standard-sized edition of the *A-Z London Street Atlas* published by Geographers' A-Z Map Company. The first line of information beside each map in this book is a reference to the page and grid square of the *A-Z London Street Atlas* which covers a central point of the area concerned. Thus the first page of the Acton section has 'Map ref: p73 (1J)' indicating the page and grid square of Acton High Street.

● **Information:** the information at the top of the map pages can be used on its own and as a cross-reference to other sections of the book. The postal district is given, as is the borough and its controlling party. Further details on both postcode and borough can be found in the 'London in 1989' chapter which begins the book.

Household contents insurance rates vary from area to area according to scales decided by the insurance companies based on their assessment of the risk level. Here we have taken a consensus of large companies' scales and given each area a rating from 1 (high) to 4 (low).

Conservation areas are indicated where feasible. These are zones subject to special planning protection and where new building is generally not allowed unless in harmony with the existing architecture: this can restrict your freedom to alter your home, or add to the expense of so doing. Many inner London boroughs now have 20 or more conservation areas: check with the Town Hall (see Boroughs section for phone numbers) for exact extents.

Car parking restrictions are listed where information is available. Some places, such as Kensington & Chelsea, are almost wholly metered and residents' permits are needed. The note on parking refers to residential, not commercial, streets. In most areas, there are restrictions on parking in shopping districts and main through-routes.

● **Transport:** transport details give the tube stations and local British Rail stations, and the fare zone the tube stations are in. The London Transport network is split into Zones 1, 2 and 3a, 3b and 3c, with 1 at the centre. Times are given from a central station in the area to three key points: the City (Bank station), Oxford Circus and Heathrow Airport. Where local British Rail lines are available, their main destinations are given. Note that official journey times assume no hold-ups! Bear this in mind if you are planning a vital journey, rather than using these times as a point of comparison with other areas. See the 'Transport' chapter for news of 1989's transport developments.

The 'miles from centre' note under *Convenient For* is the distance to the centre of the area measured from Charing Cross (as in UK road signs). The purpose is to give an immediate picture of an area's relationship to the centre, and a quick point of comparison between areas. It does not indicate journey times.

● **Schools:** this gives the local education authority or division of the Inner London Education Authority (ILEA), the main secondary schools and local private secondary schools. Refer to adjacent areas for further schools. See also the 'Education' chapter.

● **Prices:** average price ranges are given for flats and houses of all sizes in the area. These prices give a 'freeze-frame' picture of where prices stood at the start of the 1989 season. They indicate the price range into which each size of home mainly falls – not the price of the meanest slum or the grandest palace. Thus a narrow or a wide price range for, say, a 2-bed flat is in itself an indication of the range of homes in the area. See also 'How to use this book' on p 14.

Below the price bands is a note on the kinds of homes found in the area and on the state of the property market there, and how long the local council is taking over searches. This varies widely across London.

● **Area Profiles:** The text on each area divides into an Area Profile and sub-sections on neighbourhoods. At the end of each area there is a list of some of the main estate agents active there. This is neither an endorsement of the agents mentioned nor does it (or could it) mention all of the ones you might encounter.

To find a particular street, refer to the main index, which lists streets, areas and neighbourhoods mentioned in the book.

Acton *148*
Archway *408*
Balham *152*
Barnes *161*
Baron's Court *534*
Battersea *166*
Bayswater *174*
Bedford Park *182*
Belgravia *186*
Bermondsey *587, 274*
Bethnal Green *190*
Blackheath *338*
Bloomsbury *193*
Borough *587*
Bow *199*
Brentford *300*
Brixton *203*
Brockley *418*
Camberwell *212*
Camden Town *216*
Catford *428*
Chelsea *223*
Chiswick *233*
City *240*
Clapham *245*
Clerkenwell *251*
Colliers Wood *453*
Covent Garden *526*
Cricklewood *259*
Crouch End *265*
Crystal Palace *269*
Dartmouth Park *408*
Deptford *461*
Docklands *274*
Dollis Hill *293*
Dulwich *296*
Ealing *300*
Earls Court *534*
Earsfield *307*
Finchley *315*
Finsbury *251*
Finsbury Park *571*
Fitzrovia *442*
Forest Gate *465*
Forest Hill *322*
Friern Barnet *578*

Fulham *326*
Gipsy Hill *596*
Golders Green *334*
Greenwich *338*
Hackney *343*
Hammersmith *348*
Hampstead *355*
Hampstead Garden Suburb *361*
Hendon *366*
Herne Hill *203*
Highbury *382*
Highgate *371*
Holland Park *376*
Isle of Dogs *274*
Islington *382*
Kennington *390*
Kensington *396*
Kensal Rise *417*
Kentish Town *408*
Kew *413*
Kilburn *417*
King's Cross *193*
Knightsbridge *421*
Lewisham *428*
Leyton *432*
Leytonstone *432*
Lisson Grove *442*
Limehouse *274, 493*
Maida Vale *436*
Marylebone *442*
Mayfair *448*
Mill Hill *366*
Mitcham *453*
Morden *453*
Mortlake *161*
Muswell Hill *457*
Neasden *293*
New Cross *461*
Newham *465*
Norbury *596*
North Kensington *471*
Notting Hill *471*
Palmer's Green *544*
Parsons Green *326*
Peckham *482*
Penge *269*

Pimlico *487*
Poplar *493*
Primrose Hill *548*
Putney *497*
Regent's Park *510*
Richmond *514*
Roehampton *497*
Rotherhite *274, 587*
Sheen *413*
Shepherd's Bush *520*
Shoreditch *190*
Soho *526*
Southfields *307*
South Kensington *534*
Southgate *544*
Stratford *465*
St James's *448*
St John's Wood *548*
Stepney *554*
Stockwell *390*
Stoke Newington *559*
Streatham *566*
Stroud Green *265*
Swiss Cottage *355*
Sydenham *269*
Thornton Heath *596*
Tooting *152*
Tottenham *571*
Totteridge *578*
Tufnell Park *408*
Tulse Hill *203*
Twickenham *514*
Vauxhall *390*
Walthamstow *452*
Walworth *587*
Wandsworth *581*
Wanstead *432*
Wapping *274*
Waterloo *587*
Westminster *487*
West Hampstead *592*
West Norwood *596*
Whetstone *578*
Whitechapel *554*
Willesden *601*
Wimbldeon *605*

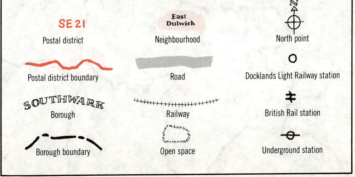

Key to area maps

Maps are not to scale and are intended for orientation and general guidance rather than detailed reference. Check north point for orientation. Only main roads are shown. The neighbourhoods are those discussed in the accompanying text.

To locate a map, see arrows for surrounding areas and see the key map at the start of the A-Z section. For full details refer to the A-Z London Street Atlas. Each map has a cross-reference to the A-Z page and map square covering the centre of the mapped neighbourhood.

SE 21
Postal district

East Dulwich
Neighbourhood

N
North point

Postal district boundary

Road

Docklands Light Railway station

SOUTHWARK
Borough

Railway

British Rail station

Borough boundary

Open space

Underground station

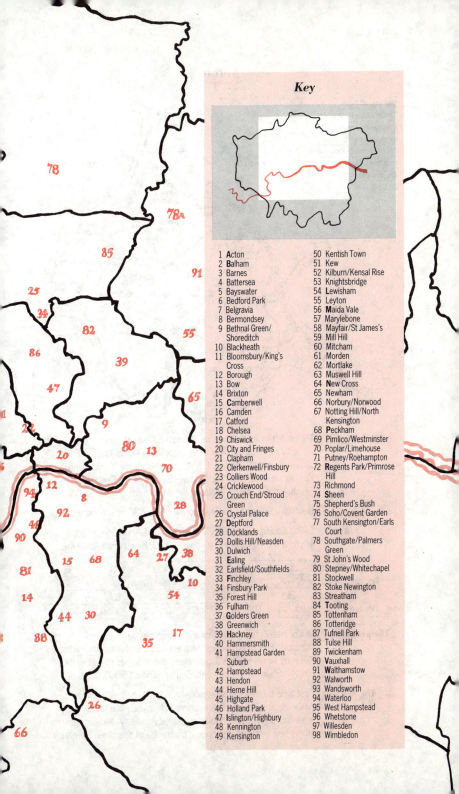

Key

1	**A**cton	50	Kentish Town
2	**B**alham	51	Kew
3	Barnes	52	Kilburn/Kensal Rise
4	Battersea	53	Knightsbridge
5	Bayswater	54	**L**ewisham
6	Bedford Park	55	Leyton
7	Belgravia	56	**M**aida Vale
8	Bermondsey	57	Marylebone
9	Bethnal Green/	58	Mayfair/St James's
	Shoreditch	59	Mill Hill
10	Blackheath	60	Mitcham
11	Bloomsbury/King's	61	Morden
	Cross	62	Mortlake
12	Borough	63	Muswell Hill
13	Bow	64	**N**ew Cross
14	Brixton	65	Newham
15	**C**amberwell	66	Norbury/Norwood
16	Camden	67	Notting Hill/North
17	Catford		Kensington
18	Chelsea	68	**P**eckham
19	Chiswick	69	Pimlico/Westminster
20	City and Fringes	70	Poplar/Limehouse
21	Clapham	71	Putney/Roehampton
22	Clerkenwell/Finsbury	72	**R**egents Park/Primrose
23	Colliers Wood		Hill
24	Cricklewood	73	Richmond
25	Crouch End/Stroud	74	**S**heen
	Green	75	Shepherd's Bush
26	Crystal Palace	76	Soho/Covent Garden
27	**D**eptford	77	South Kensington/Earls
28	Docklands		Court
29	Dollis Hill/Neasden	78	Southgate/Palmers
30	Dulwich		Green
31	**E**aling	79	St John's Wood
32	Earlsfield/Southfields	80	Stepney/Whitechapel
33	**F**inchley	81	Stockwell
34	Finsbury Park	82	Stoke Newington
35	Forest Hill	83	Streatham
36	Fulham	84	**T**ooting
37	**G**olders Green	85	Tottenham
38	Greenwich	86	Totteridge
39	**H**ackney	87	Tufnell Park
40	Hammersmith	88	Tulse Hill
41	Hampstead Garden	89	Twickenham
	Suburb	90	**V**auxhall
42	Hampstead	91	**W**althamstow
43	Hendon	92	Walworth
44	Herne Hill	93	Wandsworth
45	Highgate	94	Waterloo
46	Holland Park	95	West Hampstead
47	**I**slington/Highbury	96	Whetstone
48	**K**ennington	97	Willesden
49	Kensington	98	Wimbledon

Acton

Map ref:	p73 (1J)
Postal districts:	W3
Boroughs:	Ealing (Lab)
Rates:	197p in £
Constituencies:	Ealing Acton (Con)
Insurance:	Scale 2
Conservation areas:	–
Parking:	Free

| | | Transport | Tubes: Acton Town (zone 3a, Piccadilly, District); North Acton, (zone 2/3a, Central), others see map. From Acton Town: Oxford Circus 30 min (1 change); City 45 min; Heathrow 20 min. British Rail: Acton Main Line (Paddington 15 min), Acton Central and South Acton on North London Line. Miles from centre: 6.5. |

Convenient for Heathrow, routes to Oxford and the West, BBC in Shepherd's Bush.

Schools Ealing Education Authority: Acton School, Ellen Wilkinson (g), Twyford C of E. Private: Japanese School, King Fahad Academy.

Flats	S	1b	2b	3b	4b	5b
Average prices	52–60	65–72	77–100	90–120	–	–
Houses	2b	3b	4b	5b	6/7b	8b
Average prices	90–125	110–170	145–225	190–250	→350	300+

The properties Mix of late-Victorian and Edwardian terraces and inter-war suburbia. Few large houses. Ample 1 and 2-bed flat conversions. Recently some new-build and several big schemes to come. Best streets include those of 'Poets Corner' (add c £5,000 to prices).

The market First-time buyers' stepping-stone, and family homes. Best parts of Acton have caught up Ealing prices in last year, due largely to advent of Japanese School, King Fahad Academy, and proposal for smart new high street shopping centre. Local searches: 2 weeks.

Area Profile

Acton, for most, is a stepping-stone. Road- and rail-bisected, it is further out than Shepherd's Bush but not as comfortable as Ealing. The young people who find their first homes in Acton's many newly converted flats harbour hopes of cashing in on their property before too long and moving on to leafier Ealing or livelier Hammersmith, Fulham or even Shepherd's Bush. The only breed to get a buzz of excitement from Acton's drabber corners are the builders and developers. They have spent the last couple of years buying old houses and carving them up into flats as quickly as possible, in readiness for BBC TV's mass exodus from central London to their new HQ in Shepherd's Bush.

It's not only Acton's homes that are receiving attention. This year's talk is all of the transformation of the High Street, where a major redevelopment is planned which will supplement the less than remarkable local shops with a bright new shopping centre. Sheraton Securities' scheme should be started this year, and will add four national stores and 37 others, plus parking for 299 cars, between the *High St* and *Churchfield Rd*. The centre, plus other arrivals such as a new Habitat for North Acton on *Western Avenue*, will be welcome in an area so far devoid of major stores: Woolworths and a 7-11 are the Acton shopper's idea of big names.

For the present, the young people buying homes in Acton aren't the high fliers of Islington and Battersea. They are the not-so-well-off, those who lie awake at night fretting about their mortgages. Perhaps that explains Acton's lack of nightlife; there is little beyond pubs and good ethnic restaurants. Two further groups have their eye on Acton. Japanese families are following in the wake of the Japanese School, while BBC stage-staff and secretaries, now traipsing in to White City insted of Langham Place, are also out hunting.

Acton Central

Acton Central, between *Horn Lane*, *Hanger Lane*, *Uxbridge Rd* and the railway line, contains some large family houses, although many are falling to the Acton speciality – flat conversions. The people buying the family homes in central Acton – particularly *Rosemont Rd*, which is leafy and pleasant – are often Japanese. Attracted by the school that has recently moved here from Camden Town, Japanese families are gradually moving to West London, served by their own estate agency on the *Uxbridge Rd*. The area is also popular with families who want their daughters to go to Ealing Borough's only girls' comprehensive.

The general rule in central Acton, that prices rise the nearer you get to Ealing, means that flats in *Creffield Rd* and *Inglis Rd* are sought-after. Those in *Inglis* and some in *Creffield Rd* come with that dream of an Acton home-buyer ... a W5 postcode. Further E *Horn Lane* is a dirty, noisy main road. But *Pierrepoint Rd* and *Rosemont Rd* could be in another world – secluded, leafy and quiet. *Lynton Rd* is a mixture – some 1930s and '40s houses, some Edwardian property converted into flats. Parking is slightly easier in this long, wide road than in most of Acton's jam-packed streets. Central Acton does suffer from being a long way from tube stations.

Acton Town/South Acton

The neighbourhood S of *Acton High St*, E of *Gunnersbury Lane* and W of the railway line is dominated both physically and in reputation by the South Acton estate. The council estate's ugly concrete towers loom above the pleasant Edwardian terraces around Acton Town tube station; but now the first upmarket mews of Georgian-style new homes has appeared, and more sites have been pinpointed by developers.

The main attraction for buyers of the terraced Edwardian houses and flat conversions in roads like *Bollo Bridge Rd*, *Avenue Rd* and *Mill Hill Rd* is the nearby tube station. The terraced houses are in good condition, the roads are tree-lined, and *Mill Hill Rd* is particularly pretty in the summer, with flowery front gardens.

Poet's Corner

Estate agents wax lyrical about Acton's 'Poets Corner' – it is central, pleasant, full of converted flats and intensely gentrified. The area stretches N of the *High St*, between *Horn Lane* and *East Acton Lane*, S of the railway line and Acton BR station. Living in the streets named after the great, centred around *Shakespeare Rd*, can cost you an extra £5,000 above normal Acton prices. Home buyers are mostly looking at terraces in treelined streets. The houses in streets like *Cumberland Rd* and *Maldon Rd* were once grand family homes – but are now almost all 2- or 3-bedroom flats. Best roads in Poet's Corner are the Goldsmith estate around *Goldsmith Avenue* which has Edwardian houses, like most of Acton. Some of the houses in surrounding streets are later, built about 1950. *Shaa Rd* and around, N from Acton Park, are popular with Arab families, because of the road's exclusive school for Arab children and there's the Barbara Speake Stage School nearby in *East Acton Lane*. Around *Beech Avenue*, across *East Acton Lane*, there are some modern developments, including one very popular estate by Barrett which includes a stylish block of retirement flats.

To the S, *Cowper Rd* and *Milton Rd* have small terraced houses that were once the homes of Victorian workers. They are too small to be turned into flats, and have tiny gardens, but have a delightfully cottage feel. *Shakespeare Rd* is a better bet for conversions, and some have big rooms and elegant fronts. Be cautious in *Alfred Rd* and *Burlington Gardens*. The huge 3-storey Victorian terraces look imposing, but many are very run down – although there is a lot of building work going on. Some of the huge houses have been bought up and turned into hostels.

West Acton

West Acton was the scene of a property buyer's dream in the early '80s – 3-bedroomed semis were sold off for a fraction of the market prices, fetching just a few thousand pounds. The homes were the 'railway cottages', homes in and around *Saxon Drive*, built in the 1930s for rail employees to rent, and sold to the tenants years later. These homes are now coming onto the open market, obviously far more realistically priced but still cheap by London standards.

West Acton is dominated by the railway, being bordered by the Piccadilly tube and BR lines, and *Horn Lane* and the *Western Avenue*, and crossed diagonally by the Central line. To the W of West Acton station is the Tudor estate – different from anything else in either Ealing or Acton, with black and white mock-Tudor homes built between the wars. West Acton is popular, partly because it is greener than the rest of Acton, partly because it is close to Ealing. It is also well-served by public transport.

North Acton

North Acton might be called Leamington Park by some estate agents, but don't let the up-market name blind you to the area's drawbacks. Most of the property in the triangle between *Old Oak Lane*, *Victoria Rd* and the *Western Avenue* is run down, with a few unappealing purpose-built blocks of flats. But between Acton Main Line BR station and the North Acton tube, an area which straddles the A40 *Western Avenue* is seeing several developments. Laing are marketing 1- and 2-bed flats this spring in *Cotton Avenue*; in *Friary Rd* there is approval for over 40 flats, and in *Horn Lane* Mobil Oil have applied for planning permission for their site. In *Wales Farm Rd* Ealing Housing Association are building some 140 homes, and the big news is Laing's proposal to build 400-plus houses and flats on the National Freight Corporation's depot site in *Western Avenue*. But there are plans to widen the A40: check how this might affect you before buying in this corner.

East Acton

East Acton is a small area situated in the midst of railway lines and bordered to the S by the busy *A40 Western Avenue*. The neighbourhood lies on the Hammersmith borough boundary close to Wormwood Scrubs prison and the Common to the E. East Acton, a collection of two dozen or so roads, has a pleasant village feel – a mixture of council and private accommodation. Running N from the *Western Avenue*, *St Andrews Rd* offers 1930s red-brick terraces with square bays extending from the ground to first floor.

A

Council properties dominate *The Fairway* running W-E between the main line and *Old Oak Common Lane*. The majority are stone clad semis and terraces – but some are of a warmer brown brick. Nearby on the pleasant green the homes – 1930s once again – are privately owned and arranged in both terraces and semis. Moving N through *The Bye* to *Long Drive*, clusters of 12 semis are grouped around small greens in closes – creating a friendly atmosphere. Further down *Long Drive* towards the *Western Avenue* are one or two larger detached houses, some with gables, some with bays. However, these types are rare in East Acton. Turning left into the heart of the neighbourhood once more, *Brassie Avenue* offers a mixture of council and private semis. The main shopping area is situated in nearby *Old Oak Common Lane* to the E near the A40 intersection. All the essentials are there including a big Texas Homecare, snooker hall and Mecca bingo.

Borders: Gunnersbury

A no-mans-land between Ealing and Acton, trapped in the triangle of *Gunnersbury Lane*, *Uxbridge Rd* and *Gunnersbury Avenue*, Gunnersbury is a pleasant area, with some roads of detached family homes that fetch high prices. *Lillian Avenue*, *Gunnersbury Gardens* and *Gunnersbury Crescent* are good for family homes, with large gardens. And the area is very convenient for the huge Gunnersbury Park, with its stately home turned museum.

Among those estate agents active in this area are:
- Duncan Gray & Co
- Pocock
- Raymond Bushell

Balham and Tooting

Map ref: p108 (2E)	
Postal districts: SW12, SW17	
Boroughs: Wandsworth (Con), Lambeth (Lab)	
Rates: W: 130.8p in £. L: 197p in £	
Constituencies: Tooting (Lab), Streatham (Con)	
Insurance: Scale 1	
Conservation areas: include Heaver, Totterdown Fields, Trinity Rd	
Parking: free, if congested	

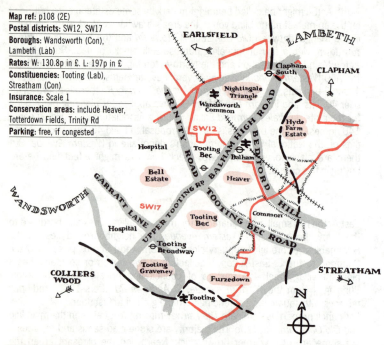

Transport	Tubes: Balham, Tooting Bec, Tooting Broadway (zone 3a, Northern) direct to City, Charing Cross, Waterloo. From Tooting Bec: Oxford Circus 30 min (1 change); City 30 min; Heathrow 90 min (1 change). BR: Balham: (Victoria 15 min). Tooting: London Bridge, Blackfriars.
Convenient for	South Coast routes and transport into town . Miles from centre: 5.
Schools	ILEA Division 10: Graveney, Ernest Bevin (b), Burntwood (g). Private: Upper Tooting High.

Flats	S	1b	2b	3b	4b	5b
Average prices	50–60	65–80	75–100+	88–120	–	–
Houses	2b	3b	4b	5b	6/7b	8b
Average prices	90–120	110–160	130–190	150–220	240–300+	275–350

The properties	Balham is Victorian, Tooting Edwardian/'30s, with a (very) few older homes in both. Terraced houses of all sizes (including very large), plus conversions and some p/b flats. Inter-war suburban homes, too, plus conversions and some p/b flats.
The market	Overspill from Clapham and Battersea drove prices up in early 1988 as sharers scrambled to buy before multiple mortgage relief ended. Buyers are first-timers plus families seeking big, affordable homes. Tooting is cheaper, more cosmopolitan: a much more local market. Local searches: Wandsworth 1 week, Lambeth 10 weeks.

B

Area Profile

In the late 19th century Balham and Tooting were merely small hamlets on the main road into London. Their popularity grew with the advent of the railway, and the extension of the Northern Line underground in 1926 was the final stage of metamorphosis from genteel settlement to inner-city. Late-'80s developments include a rash of new homes as well as widespread conversion.

Balham – Gateway to the South, as it was immortalized by the late Peter Sellers – was especially favoured as the ideal area for a country residence by the professional classes of the early 19th century, and this accounts for the impressive houses near to the commons still standing today. Now the lawyers and bankers are once more flocking to these suburbs, attracted by Wandsworth Borough's low rates, easy transport by tube and train into and out of town and the good supply of relatively cheap period properties. Prices have been rising, but there are still good buys around – particularly in Tooting Broadway and areas further from tubes. Other attractions are the sports complexes in *Elmbourne Rd*, SW12 and *Greaves Place*, SW17, and the commons (Tooting Bec and Wandsworth).

Insurance rates are high, however, and Wandsworth's current planning policies are strict; property conversions into flats *must* now (since 1988) include two family units comprising four bed spaces (was three). Anything less than 120 sq metres is deemed too small to convert – this excludes many 2-storey terraced houses. Beware though. Check whether your prospective property is in Wandsworth or Lambeth as the boundary runs through Balham.

Traffic-flow is frequently congested along the A24, and the many railway lines (with few road bridges) make car journeys tortuous and frustrating. A Savacentre hypermarket on the A24 at Colliers Wood, opening this Spring, will add to motorists' headaches. But traffic studies now on their way to the Department of Transport may help congestion in the future. Parking is the usual problem, as in any other part of inner London. One deficiency which developers could tackle is, with the exception of the sports centres, the surprising lack of leisure facilities.

There are no theatres or cinemas and very few decent pubs and restaurants apart from those in *Bellevue Rd*, E of *Nightingale Lane* and a recent rash of winebars scattered along the A24. Nearby suburbs are better served – theatre in Wimbledon and cinema, skating and bowling in Streatham.

Most homes in Balham are Victorian, whereas Tooting ranges from the 1800s to present day – mainly Victorian, Edwardian and '30s with some modern developments. Prices are generally higher near tube and train stations and opposite commons, and lower on main roads and (say local agents) near graveyards! The further S you go, the less you pay – Balham is slightly more respectable than Tooting Broadway.

Balham

Some time around 1985 a local estate agent confided 'it's all right to talk about Balham now'. The combined efforts of Peter Sellers and Nikolaus Pevsner ('nothing of interest on *Balham Hill* except the Odeon') had damned the place into a sort of property limbo. Half-hearted attempts were made to shift it into 'south South Wandsworth'. Clapham South tube station gave its name to a swathe of what is really Balham. The quiet and pleasant streets between *Nightingale Lane* and *Balham High Rd* migrated upwards to become the Nightingale Triangle and honorary Clapham, but are covered here.

Balham has all the attributes of a real place: a *High Rd*, a station (BR and Northern Line), a parish church (St Mary, 1805), a library. The BR line to Croydon, running W to E on its embankment, divides Balham in half and contributes largely to traffic congestion: there are only three bridges beneath it.

Nightingale Triangle

The most exclusive area in Balham; quiet, attractive and convenient for transport. Roughly bounded by *Nightingale Lane*, *Balham High Rd* and the railway. Roads running between *Ravenslea Rd* and *Chestnut Grove* contain neat Victorian terraced 3/4-bed houses, popular but smaller than some properties in the triangle. Larger gardens in *Calbourne* and *Mayford Rds*. *Nightingale Lane* starts on the brow of the Wandsworth Common railway bridge and contains very large and distinctive semi-detached 5/6/7-bed houses including some by T E Collcutt (1879) opposite *Endlesham Rd*. Flat conversions explain impromptu parking spaces in front gardens. Then come '30s 4-bed houses leading to mansion flats near Clapham South tube including Clapham Mansions (2/3/4-bed flats, mix of owner-occupied and tenants) and Hightrees House (art deco overlooking cricket-ground. Service charges are between £1,200-1,500 – but this includes insurance, porterage and use of gym and pool). *Western Lane*, leading S from the popular Nightingale pub, is a leafy alley with mid-19th century cottages, newly and attractively paved, with Victorian-style lamp-posts. Through to *Linnet Mews* – built '83 – smart 1/2-bed red brick houses and flats. South is the picturesque *Nightingale Square* – coveted large Victorian houses surrounding a garden for residents. Despite the bustle of two schools and a church at the far end, the square remains a popular corner.

Chestnut Grove, running on to the S, has pleasant cottagey terraces. Large school (Hydeburn Comprehensive) on W side. The *Grove* gets less popular as it nears busy *Balham High Rd* and the tube. *Ramsden Rd*, cutting through the middle of the Triangle, has a variety of Victorian houses and terraces, some flat-fronted, some red brick, large and small. The houses are generally larger at the two ends of the road, but the *High Rd* end does get congested with Safeway's car park entrance on E side. Heavy street parking adds to the confusion. Two-bed cottages (once workmen's quarters) feature in *Bellamy St, Pickets St, Balham Grove* and *Temperley Rd*. *Bracken Avenue* is leafy and pleasant. *Badminton Rd* has period red brick on E side, early 20th century unusual double-fronted maisonettes on W. Front gardens on E side smaller (Nos 1-54). *Balham Grove* has Safeway's supermarket's goods entrance at S end but then a couple of lovely Georgian houses – one recently converted into flats. Large Victorian houses follow with a small recent estate in *Ainslie Walk*. The Lochinvar Estate ('60s, concrete, low rise) is an affordable, if uninspiring, first-time buy. A mews development off *Malwood St*, at the apex of the triangle and just around the corner from the tube, is indicative of the popularity of this Clapham-borders corner. *Liberty Mews*, built three years ago, was marketed as a good investment opportunity as well as for straightforward owner-occupation, and a number of the units are rented out.

Hyde Farm Estate

A rectangle bounded by *Hydethorpe, Emmanuel* and *Radbourne Rds* in the eastern part of Balham and in Lambeth, not Wandsworth. This network of streets consists of red-brick Victorian 3/4-bed terraces and maisonettes, with only slight variations in style from road to road (eg, more 'bell-fronted' in *Haverhill Rd* than in *Scholars Rd*). *Emmanuel Rd* is popular – it overlooks Tooting Bec Common, the nearby railway line being screened by trees. Two schools – Henry Cavendish and Telferscot (both Junior Mixed and Infants). Building of the estate began in 1901 by speculative developers on land leased from Emmanuel College, Cambridge. Main developer was Ernest Hayes-Dashwood. Now parts of *Radbourne* and *Telferscot Rds* are set aside as rent-free accommodation for retired servicemen and war veterans.

The area N of Hyde Farm is more mixed with an industrial estate in *Zennor Rd*. *Weir Rd* is industrial on the W side but soon calms down to Victorian terraces on right and *Molly Huggins Close* on left – new development of 40 flats and houses for rent on an old hospital site. *Belthorn Crescent* has the smart Weir Estate. *Atkins Rd* has pleasant 20th century semi-detached and terraced houses on right – mainly in good repair, some mock Tudor. School on left – St Bernadette Catholic Primary School (girls).

The roads to the E of the *High Rd*, between *Englewood Rd* to the N (really in Clapham) and *Rossiter Rd* (S) are almost entirely quaint period terraces of 3/4/5-bed houses. Recent flats in *Hanson Close*; back to period in *Ravenswood Rd*. *Old Devonshire Rd* has a mosque and some industrial buildings giving way to a mix of period and recent properties. *Laitwood Rd, Ormeley Rd* and *Ranmere St* form a quiet, pretty enclave. On either side of the railway line, *Fernlea Rd* and *Byrne Rd* have attractive flat-fronted upper facades, early Victorian in style, leading to Victorian terraces.

Byrne Rd, to the S of the railway, and E of *Bedford Hill*, curves into the leafy *Culverden Rd* with its impressive 6/7-bed period semi-detached houses – some converted, some needing repair. Those on E side overlook Tooting Bec Common. Neat terraces in *Dornton Rd* (some purpose-built flats with balconies) and *Fontenoy Rd*. Smart new maisonettes on E of *Brierley Rd* opposite period terraces. The Ryde Vale Estate (entrance *Ryde Vale Rd*) has a mix of styles – small blocks of terraced flats, low-rise concrete blocks and bungalows.

Bedford Hill's notorious 'red-light' reputation is now largely unmerited, kerbcrawlers having been discouraged by blocking off E end of *Elmfield Rd* and making *Carminia Rd* one-way. The hill has large period properties – some very grand with ornamental brickwork. Recent developments include 14 new 1- and 2-bed flats on corner of *Culverden Rd* and 12 flats in the shadow of the railway bridge for the Wandle Housing Association. The Priory, on the edge of the common, dates from 1822 and is now flats.

Marius Rd, W of the *High Rd*, has attractive period houses and Marius Mansions – impressive Victorian flats, recently renovated – at far end. More mansion flats at S ends of *Nevis Rd* (Cecil Mansions) and *Wontner Rd* (Stanley Mansions). Many period terraces and some new developments – notably the pleasant brick houses in *Ashdown Way* and the not so pretty yellow Flowersmead council estate ('40s) opposite (now one-third private ownership).

Even the most ordinary corners provide quirky details for those who look. This unusual window, above the front door of a Balham home, shows its late-Victorian date with gothic-style carving and decoration and the pattern of the glazing bars in the sash windows. Attractive as they may be, such bays need careful maintenace if damp is not to be a problem.

The N end of *St James's Drive* boasts large covetable homes overlooking Wandsworth Common – popular as near BR and the amenities of *Bellevue Rd*, but pricey. *St James's Close* is an attractive new development of houses and flats round a central garden. *Balham Park Rd*, leading E from the *Drive* back to the *High Rd*, has a mixture of Victorian terraces, and towards the E end more modern flats and houses. Ducane Court on the main road is a '30s block of 650 one-bed and studio flats – once the largest block in Europe.

Balham Borders

The roads directly N of the Heaver Estate in Tooting, from *Ritherdon Rd* up to *Elmfield Rd*, are all neat period terraces apart from '60s flats at N ends of *Carminia* and *Childebert Rds*. At W end of *Elmfield Rd* there are mansion flats of impressive red brick, some needing repair. Ravenstone School opposite (primary) and Balham Leisure Centre (pool, gym, solarium, etc) are the other features of the road. *Cheriton Square* is opposite the leisure complex: its curving terraces always enjoy top billing in estate agents' ads, but look in need of some care and attention externally.

The area E of Hyde Farm, and S of the *South Circular Rd* with the wide *Kings Avenue* running N-S, has generally large, pleasant inter-wars and post-war housing with some flats scattered around. *Thornton Rd* – semi-detached mock-Tudor; *Thornton Gardens* – a small estate. The flats at the S of *Kings Avenue* give way to large attractive modern houses with garages and a one-acre site earmarked for homes. More 20th century houses in *Copthorne Avenue* and *Parkthorne Rd*. This area has aspirations to be Clapham Park, or perhaps Streatham Hill.

West of *St James's Rd*, in the triangle between *Bellevue Rd* and *Trinity Rd*, are neat, prosperous, grey-brick cottage terraces. In SW17 rather than SW12, and emotionally Wandsworth Common (which see) rather than Balham.

The roads N of *Nightingale Lane* and S of *Thurleigh Rd*, while still in SW12, have been annexed into the new 'area' of Between the Commons ('Betwixt' to the jollier estate agents). See Battersea – though whether it is in Clapham, Wandsworth, Battersea or Balham is to a large extent a matter of taste.

Tooting

The name Tooting excites a certain amusement, but the place has more history than nearby Balham and can boast a village history back to Domesday. Little remains of the villages of upper Tooting (Tooting Bec) and lower Tooting (Tooting Graveney). The place stayed small and rural well into the last century, and the big development of houses happened relatively late. The result is a district of orderly grids of late 19th-century homes, some spacious, some small, all well served by the Northern Line tube.

The two commons, Bec and Graveney, are sadly cut up by railways and roads. They do however give Tooting a clear boundary to the E. To the N is Balham and W, beyond the sprawl of Springfield Hospital and the oddly-placed Streatham cemetery, is Earlsfield. To the S, the railway line between Wimbledon and Streatham forms the boundary. Beyond is Colliers Wood. Tooting BR station is right on the (SE) edge of the district it is named after.

Heaver

By far the grandest and priciest neighbourhood in Tooting and Balham. Bordered by *Balham High Rd*, *Tooting Bec Rd*, *Ritherdon Rd* and *Hillbury Rd*, this turn-of-the-century estate was built by the Heaver brothers and consists of distinguished double and single-fronted 3-storey houses and some maisonettes, all in red brick with white detail. Approximately half have been converted, but the houses are enormous – typical interior for an intact property would be 6-8 bedrooms, 2 bathrooms, kitchen plus three other rooms and huge garden. Many original features remain inside and out – note the ornate front doors with stained glass insets. Largely untouched by modern developments, the main exceptions being infill maisonettes in *Manville Gardens* and *Carnie Hall*, smart flats at N end of *Hillbury Rd*, which also boasts some modern 3-bed town houses. The area is much in demand from families wishing to escape cramped modern housing. *Elmbourne Rd* overlooking Tooting Bec Common is popular, as is the wide, tree-lined *Streathbourne Rd*. Average prices for intact houses are high (c £235-320,000), with one going last year for £450,000, but prices settled back in the Autumn as mortgage increases began to bite.

Tooting Bec

Between *Tooting Bec Rd* and *Mitcham Rd* lies Totterdown Fields (roads between *Derinton and Cowick Rds*) which has the distinction of being the first cottage council estate in the world – started 1903. A pity, some say, councils didn't stick to this mood: now a conservation area, the houses are an 'olde-worlde' mixture of red brick and grey stucco. Above this, close to Tooting Bec tube, the roads N of *Foulser Rd* are lined with charming Victorian terraces in red brick. Edwardian and '30s in *Lynwood Rd*; more cottage-council in *Topsham Rd*. South of the Totterdown Fields comes more Victoriana. *Vant Rd* has modern maisonettes at S end. *Franciscan Rd* running S through the entire neighbourhood from *Tooting Bec Rd* to *Mitcham Rd* is mainly period with a few modern 'pockets' – eg, *Barringer Square* (yellow 7-storey flats surrounded by smaller, pleasant, brown-brick blocks. Communal garden for residents), *Bruce Hall Mews* (small, smart development of 20 houses and flats) and *Groomfield Close* (recent maisonettes opposite church).

The Rectory Triangle, between *Mitcham Rd* and *Rectory* and *Church Lanes*, is a pleasant estate mainly built by Laing in '84 on the site of the old St Benedicts Hospital. 1/2/3-bed houses and flats.

Furzedown

Running between *Links Rd* to the S, *Rectory Lane*, *Thrale Rd* and *Mitcham Lane*, Furzedown is filled with Edwardian/Victorian properties popular with families. No tube line nearby, so prices tend to be lower than elsewhere in Tooting. Approximately half is counted as Tooting – the area S of *Southcroft Rd* plus *Crowborough*, *Idlecombe*, *Salterford* and *Freshwater Rds*. The remainder is thought of as Streatham. The borough boundary runs E-W between *Southcroft Rd* and *Seely Rd*. *Seely Rd* and *Links Rd* running parallel have identical terraces of solid, deep-porched turn-of-the-century houses. East of the junction with *Eastbourne Rd* however, *Seely Rd* changes to less appealing, and often badly modernised, 20th-century terraces and then to bay-windowed, gabled homes. Crossing between *Seely* and *Links Rds* are orderly rows of uniform terraces. The only breaks in the regularity are the striking Links Primary School and the modern orange brick flats of St Andrews Hall at S end of *Hailsham Rd* – horribly inappropriate amongst such general order. *Vectis Gardens* surrounds a small rectangle of fenced-off grass. The whole section has an air of well-cared-for, quiet suburbia. The S side of *Links Rd* backs onto the railway. It is not, however, a very busy line.

Southcroft Rd has at its E end older terraces, giving way as you go W to post-war rows on right and a series of pleasant 2-storey ex-council red-brick flats on left. On the corner of *Nimrod Rd* is a low-rise block of modern flats. Both sides of *Southcroft* are now brick flats. Ditto *Freshwater Rd* and roads off; these are similar buildings, but in less attractive orange brick with stucco top halves. We regain Victorian terraces at the W end of *Southcroft Rd* and adjoining roads running to the N, parallel with *Mitcham Rd*.

Tooting Graveney

West of Furzedown is Tooting Graveney, named after the Gravenel family which owned the manor in the 12th and 13th centuries. The area, which is bounded by the Wimbledon-Streatham railway line to the S, *Tooting High St* to the W and *Mitcham Rd* to the N, is still comparatively cheap but prices are starting to rise. Good first-time buys in this area. At E end of *Longley Rd* there is a small block of red-brick flats/houses on the right – Kilmarnock Court – with a play-area for the kids. Opposite is Tooting Baptist Church and the intriguingly ugly Jubilee Villa (1887) – a pale green house with white trim and mosaic work insets. Handsome Victorian terraces continue left and right. Some later houses on the right. The railway runs behind S side of *Longley Rd*. Area to N of *Longley Rd* is a maze of period terraces and maisonettes with modern infills. *Bickersteth Rd*, leading N from *Longley*, contains a veritable cocktail of architecture in places, and thus looks a little ragged. *Otterburn St* (off *Byton Rd*) has well-cared-for large mock-Tudor houses opposite Edwardian maisonettes. School in *Sellincourt Rd* (Junior and Infants), while *Gravenel Gardens* in *Nutwell St* is a recent 6-storey block of council flats – pleasant but currently spoilt by intermittent graffiti.

Across the A24, (here *Tooting High St*) *Garratt Lane* leading W from Tooting Broadway tube is lined with large, flat-fronted period semi-detached houses (first few with front gardens) and smaller terraces. Parking is a problem on this main road and larger properties have the usual uneasy mixture of garden and parking space. Smaller terraces without gardens on the left side have garages behind in *Garratt Terrace*. Opposite these garages is a long row of Victorian 2-storey houses, curving round to *Tooting High St* (resembling a pale imitation of the Royal Crescent, Bath). A few smart modern houses stand at the top on the left. Roads S of *Garratt Terrace* have similar rows of period housing, but modern maisonettes appear in *Recovery St* and smart-looking '30s flats in *Tooting Grove*. Quaint cottagey terraces line *Aldis* and *Carlwell Sts*. Recent development in *Aldis Mews*.

Blackshaw Rd, S-W of St George's Hospital, has smart Edwardian terraces – these are cheap as they're next to Lambeth Cemetery (around £89,000 in 1988). Anderson House (1931) on the corner of *Fountain Rd* is a handsome-looking 3-storey block of red and cream brick flats (1931) with, as they say, scope for improvement inside. An archway in the block leads through to a public recreation ground. More Victorian terraces left and right in *Fountain Rd*, un-done-up as yet – which also goes for some earlier flat-fronted 2-storey stucco houses. *Cranmer Terrace*, off *Fountain Rd*, leads down to *Tooting Gardens* – a small park with swings, etc – not quite Regents Park, but quite a surprise among such intensive housing. Period terraces lie W of *Fountain Rd*, some quite quaint: for instance the cottage rows of *Bertal Rd*. *Alston Rd*'s Edwardian terraces seem in better repair on left. Occasional modern infills, including OAP hangout to right. At junction with *Hazlehurst Rd* on opposite corner is a school (Smallwood Junior and Infants) and on the left is the imposing grey concrete of the Hazlehurst council estate. *Greaves Place*, E of *Fountain Rd*, holds the striking 'geometrics' of Tooting Leisure Centre (swimming, gym, etc).

The Bell Estate

The Bell Estate, W of *Upper Tooting Rd*, belonged to an old family trust which was developed in the '30s and '40s by the Bell in question. Comprising *Fishponds*, *Ansell*, *Hebdon* and *Lingwell Rds*, its neat purpose-built 3/4-bed terraced houses are popular with families and convenient for Tooting Bec tube. Houses in *Ansell Rd* have small roof extensions. *Lingwell* and *Hebdon Rds* tend to be slightly cheaper as they back onto Springfield Hospital (built as Surrey County Lunatic Asylum, 1840s) and Streatham Cemetery respectively. Off *Hebdon Rd* at the E end is *Herlwyn Gardens* – a few pleasant brick bungalows

B

and maisonettes. Parking is a mystery as the road stops short of the buildings! *Holmbury Court*, at the N end of *Fishponds Rd*, has uninspiring maisonettes. *Fishponds* itself has the occasional Edwardian property alongside.

The roads between *Broadwater Rd* and *Garratt Lane* have Victorian terraces, most of which have been painted over giving a multi-coloured effect to the streets. Endearing cottage terraces at E end of *Graveney Rd* and modern maisonettes opposite the junctions with *Selkirk Rd* (Nos 26-32). Ungainly semi-detached maisonettes in *Rogers Rd* and at top of *Broadwater Rd* as it turns E to A24. On the corner of *Rogers Rd* and *Garratt Lane* stands Bellamy House – council flats, stylish in red brick and white detail.

Glenburnie Rd on the other (N) side of the Bell Estate has mainly smart Edwardian properties, but on S side of *Beechcroft Rd* there are some attractive large mock-Tudor detached houses. *Beeches Rd* has pleasant red-brick terraces (Victorian) both sides giving way to less attractive small beige brick maisonettes on the right (c '83). To the left is Parkhill Court – an impressive '30s block of large 2/3-bed flats, although not much to look at from behind.

The roads between *Trinity Rd* and *Beechcroft Rd*, to the N of the Bell Estate, are part of a conservation area filled with large, appealing Victorian properties lining leafy streets. Red brick dominates, although *Brodrick Rd* has some lovely Georgian-style 3-storey stucco houses. *Crockerton Rd* and *Dalebury Rd* have stately red brick courtesy of the Heaver brothers. Modern flats at S end of *Crockerton Rd*. Ernest Bevan School is opposite in *Beechcroft Rd*. To the N of the school is the College Gardens Estate, built '83, an attractive development of 1/2-bed houses and flats similar to Balham's *Ashdown Way* but slightly cheaper as further from the Northern Line tube.

At the N end of *Trinity Rd*, where it crosses into Wandsworth, are shops and restaurants facing a playing-field. Then, going S, come impressive mid-19th century flat-fronted stucco terraces and houses. Note No 172 – once home of Thomas Hardy. Victorian red brick continues. Tooting Bec fire station and police station are close to junction with *Trinity Crescent*, one of the most expensive roads in the area with magnificent mid-19th century stucco houses of 7/8-bedrooms and large gardens. Impressive mansion flats on right side (St Nicholas). *Holderness Rd* has mock-Tudor houses – terraced and semi-detached, and the faithful Victorian terrace reappears in *Chetwode Rd*.

Among those estate agents active in this area are:
- Barnard Marcus
- Bell Son & Co
- John G Dean & Co
- Richard Barclay
- Winkworths
- Jackson Property Services

Barnes and Mortlake

Map ref: p90 (2B)
Postal districts: SW13, SW14
Boroughs: Richmond upon Thames (Alliance)
Rates: 192.13p in £
Constituencies: Richmond & Barnes (Con)
Insurance: Scale 3
Conservation areas: include Barnes Pond, Green and Common; Mortlake Green.
Parking: Free

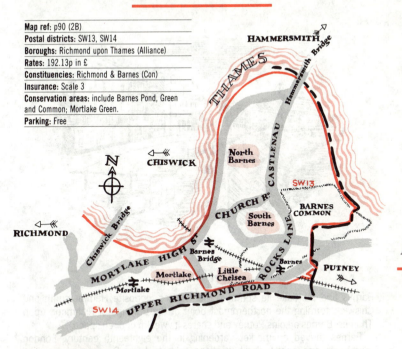

Transport	British Rail: From Barnes, Barnes Bridge, Mortlake to Waterloo 16–20 min.				

Convenient for	Richmond Park, River Thames, Kew Gardens. Richmond shopping. Heathrow via M4. M25. Miles from centre: 6.				

Schools	Richmond Education Authority: Shene School, Christ's School. Private: Swedish School, St Pauls School (b). See also Hammersmith.				

Flats	S	1b	2b	3b	4b	5b
Average prices	58–70	70–85	80–120	110–170	200+	–
Houses	2b	3b	4b	5b	6/7b	8b
Average prices	125–155	150–220	190–280+	280–350+	350–550+	750–900

The properties   Charming cottages and 3/4-bed terraces; some large early Victoriana in Barnes, also splendid 18th century riverside homes. Mortlake is more Victorian; some flat conversions under way here.

The market   Barnes is the more expensive area, but neither is cheap. Ex-council property can offer bargains. The actors and BBC-people living here are diluted by European (especially Scandinavians) and US businessmen/diplomats, who find the area conforms to their idea of Englishness. Local searches: 3 weeks.

Area Profile

Barnes and Mortlake lie south of the Thames, opposite Hammersmith and Chiswick, forming the northernmost point of the Borough of Richmond upon Thames. Barnes adjoins Putney and shares its wealth of open space.

Barnes thrived on market gardening in the eighteenth century. London merchants and nobility built weekend retreats here. Some survive – The Terrace – others are remembered in local street names; St Anne's, Elm Grove and Ranelagh.

Only five and a half miles from Hyde Park Corner, Barnes has a rural atmosphere: locals say this is because it has no tube station (Barnes and Barnes Bridge BR make up for it). Once south of Hammersmith Bridge urban grime gives way to Surrey village charm, with a village green, natural duck pond and the Sun Inn (crux of *Church Rd* and *Station Rd*).

Leafy riverside walks, more than 100 acres of pretty common, Lonsdale Reservoir (NW) where swans breed, Barn Elms Reservoir (NE) for fishing, make Barnes a family favourite. Good local schools include St Paul's public school (boys) in *Lonsdale Rd*; Godolphin and Latymer (girls) and St Pauls (girls) in nearby Hammersmith. The Swedish School (also in *Lonsdale Rd*) draws in expatriate and diplomatic families. Locals say the area lacks prep schools, forcing car journeys to Putney or Richmond. Some local comprehensives suffer the lack of bright pupils due to the large proportion of parents who send their children to fee-paying schools.

Large well maintained houses, many of architectural merit, mean it is not an area for buyers on a tight budget. There are a few black spots. One penalty of living 30 minutes' drive from Heathrow is some aircraft noise. An effective pressure group, supported by a local MP, monitors problems. Alternate use of the north and south runways at Heathrow ensures occasional noise relief, but inhabitants pray for an east wind which removes the planes entirely.

There is a sprinkling of council property throughout Barnes; all spruce and no grafitti and many now in private hands. A 2-bed ex-council flat can fetch between £75,000 and £80,000; more once the block becomes entirely owner-occupied. This is a sector of the market to watch as relative bargains can be had.

Prices rose in 1988 between 15 and 20% but levelled off in the autumn. Barnes has a good range of 5-8 bed houses but coveted locations near the river or common mean prices can start at half a million. Smaller family houses form the bulk of the market – expect to pay between £200-300,000 – and there is a limited supply of 2-bed converted flats. Larger flats will be found in purpose-built blocks and those with prime locations like Riverview Gardens and Elm Bank Mansions have prices in excess of £200,000.

The predominant home in Barnes is a Victorian or Edwardian terraced house. Houses greatly outnumber flats or maisonettes. Great difficulty is experienced in finding flats and detached 3- or 4-bedroomed houses. Conversion into flats is rare as most houses have been well-maintained and are in demand as family homes.

The most sought-after streets are *Castelnau, Lonsdale Rd, Woodlands, The Crescent, Vine Rd* and *Station Rd*. Values fall where properties are near the railway line. The most expensive homes in Barnes are in the £800,000 bracket with an odd one being offered at £2.1 million recently.

One of the few new developments consists of 40 flats of varying sizes near Barnes Bridge, due for completion early in 1989.

There is talk of a development near the Harrods Depository at Barn Elms, perhaps involving the filter beds site next to the reservoir, but there are no firm plans as yet. The Harrods building itself arouses continued speculation about its conversion potential.

B

North Barnes

Castelnau – a busy boulevard named after the French lands of the Boilieu family – forms the spine of Barnes leading busy traffic S from Hammersmith Bridge, via *Rocks Lane* down to the *Upper Richmond Rd*. This is a prime location with large houses set well back; driveways and trees mask them from the road. Early Victorian styles near the bridge lead to later double fronted towards the Red Lion pub (junction of *Rocks Lane /Church Rd*). Prices for the best approach the million mark.

Lonsdale Rd peels off W from *Castelnau* at the Old Rangoon (colonial style restaurant with garden). Another area for Victorian villas, some with stunning white exteriors and Italianate towers (next to St Pauls playing fields). As the road follows the river, property moves to the left (some flats, '30s and Edwardian houses) down to the Bull (jazz pub) and the Terrace.

Lonsdale Rd and *Castelnau* are linked by a lattice of roads – *Suffolk, Nassau, Lowther, Westmoreland* and *Baronsmead* – with a range of 3-5 bed family houses; a mix of Edwardian/Thirties/Victorian. Around *Verdun Rd/Barnes Avenue/Stillingfleet* there is a council estate. Some houses have come onto the market and can fetch £120,000.

South Barnes

South of Church Rd (with shops, art galleries and restaurants) are more 3-5 bed houses. Roads off *Glebe Rd* are gaining in popularity; their solid red brick Lion houses are at a premium (also found in Fulham). *Ranelagh Avenue* (some doubled-fronted Victorian property) faces the common. *Bellevue*, *Rectory* and *Elm Grove Rds* spill onto the common and have a touch of Little Venice as Beverley Brook passes beneath them. To the west *Laurel Rd* and *The Crescent* branch onto the green, bringing prices up to £300-500,000.

Opposite Barnes Green is *Station Rd*, S of *Barnes High St* leading to Barnes BR station; houses include 17th century Milbourne House where Henry Fielding lived, a mix of small bow windowed Victorian terraced houses; workers' flat fronted cottages; pretty 18th century cottages leading to the inevitable large Victorian houses close to the common.

Behind Station Rd and Barnes Bridge railway line is an area worth exploring. It was traditionally the 'wrong' side of the village but is rising in local esteem. Architecturally it is confused – small 2-bed cottages give way to flat fronted 3-storey houses in *Cleveland Rd* with an outcrop of eight Lion houses marooned at the corner of *Cleveland Gardens* – this is where 3/4 bed houses cost £250,000: a year ago they could be snapped up at under £200,000.

North of *Station Rd* is *Barnes High St* (with a good range of family-run shops and restaurants) which runs down to the river. Turn left into the riverside *Terrace* and a sweep of pastel coloured 18th century houses – wisteria wrapped around wrought iron balconies – gives a whiff of Brighton. These fetch around £750,000, but rarely change hands. Those closer to the bridge go for less. Past Barnes Bridge (said by the unkind to be the ugliest to span the Thames) are Elm Bank Gardens (large 5 bed houses), Elm Bank Mansions (red brick blocks of flats), and more ivy-clad Georgian houses. *The Terrace* ends at the White Hart pub, *White Hart Lane* cuts S; marking the boundary between Mortlake and Barnes. Barnes continues beyond the railway crossing down to the *Upper Richmond Rd*.

Barnes Bridge is included in one of the more ambitious SW London road proposals: the scheme would involve closing the railway and building a new road across the river along its route. It is far too early to know if this, or the other, schemes will come off: see also 'Transport' chapter.

Little Chelsea

East of *White Hart Lane* lie *Charles St*, *Thorne St*, *Archway St* and *Westfields Avenue*. The vogue for renovating these 2-bed cottages (some have three) was apparently started by a Polish builder in the '60s. His wife saw the potential of the area, comparing the brewery workers' homes with their mews counterparts in Chelsea. An irregular style – they were added to as the Victorian workforce grew – makes them less stately than their namesakes but prettier. Extensive renovation means some have an extra bedroom or conservatory and can fetch £170,000. Typical prices are around £150,000. Skirting the area are *Thorne Passage*, *Beverley Path* (reached by foot); cottages here are smaller or have the Hounslow loop BR line running behind their garden; factors which may give a discount. There are three pretty pubs within staggering distance.

Mortlake

Best known as the end of the Oxford and Cambridge Boat Race (rowed from Putney), Mortlake is historically more important than Barnes. In Medieval times the Archbishop of Canterbury built his palace here (long gone); brewing has been a local industry since the 15th century.

The most popular type of home in Mortlake is the 2-bed flat or maisonette. Large detached houses are scarce. The more expensive streets are considered to be *Avondale, Cowley* and *Ashleigh Rds*, with riverside houses when available rating highest. Prices generally fall away with proximity to the railway line and the brewery.

There are some developments taking place. The conversion of old property to flats at the bottom of White Hart Lane will be completed early in 1989, ten new flats in *Rosemary Lane* are now complete and the development of the old bus station in *Avondale Rd* into town houses and maisonettes is under way.

A victim of economic success, Mortlake lacks space and prettiness and is overshadowed by the Watney Combe Reid Brewery. It is troubled by busy roads during the rush hours and exposure to the busy Southern Region railway line. Bordered by *White Hart Lane* to the E, *Mortlake High St/Lower Richmond Rd* (N); W by *Clifford Avenue* (the South Circular) and S by *North Worple Way*, it comprises a grid of roads which vary in character.

Property is cheaper than in Barnes: a 3/4 bed family house costs between £135-210,000. There are some gems for those who care to look; *Victoria Rd* and *Wrights Walk* have large cottages with unusually large gardens. *Rosemary Cottages* (a row of pretty almshouses) is sandwiched between two grim blocks of flats and overlooks Mortlake Station. They sell for around £125,000 leasehold. *Cowley, Ashleigh* and *Avondale Rds* are mostly Edwardian terraces with 2-bed flats (about £100,000). Property along the *North Worple Way* overlooks the railway.

Current refurbishment along *Mortlake High St* and around The Green will bring up property prices. In 1988 the Green and the area to the E and W surrounding it were declared a conservation area. *Tideway Yard*, near the White Hart (The Times/RIBA award winner 1986) is a refurbished refuse depot. There is a busy wine bar (with fittings from Aintree race course) which has stunning riverside views. The site has been extended to include 18 flats, built in Victorian warehouse style to blend in with existing buildings.

Cowley Mansions, once a rambling eyesore, is being transformed to provide around 40 flats. Last winter a studio flat was listed at £69,500. Overlooking Mortlake Green, some Victorian shops have been refurbished into a small development of flats (£110,000 for 2 beds) and on the west side of the Green are some 2, 3 and 4 bedroom flats in a Victorian building overlooking the Green. The old bus garage at the bottom of *Avondale Rd* has been demolished and flats are being built.

B

Among those estate agents active in this area are:

- Barnard Marcus
- George Stead
- Hamptons Dixon Porter
- Kitson & King
- Black Horse Gascoigne Pees
- Knight Frank & Rutley
- Prudential
- Winkworths
- Allen Briegel
- Stephens

Battersea

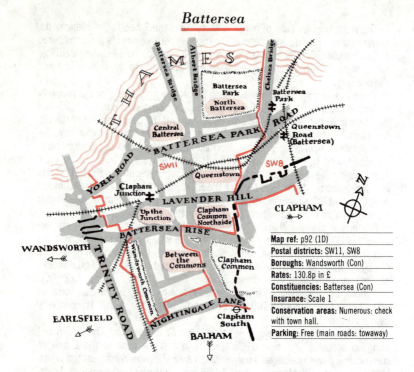

Map ref: p92 (1D)	
Postal districts: SW11, SW8	
Boroughs: Wandsworth (Con)	
Rates: 130.8p in £	
Constituencies: Battersea (Con)	
Insurance: Scale 1	
Conservation areas: Numerous: check with town hall.	
Parking: Free (main roads: towaway)	

Transport No tubes; nearest are Clapham Common, Clapham South. British Rail: Clapham Junction to Victoria 9 min, Waterloo 7 min; Queenstown Rd to Waterloo 7 min; Battersea Park to Victoria 5 min.

Convenient for Victoria and Waterloo; Gatwick Airport (28 min), South Coast. Thames, Clapham Common, Battersea Park. Miles from centre: 3.

Schools ILEA Division 10: Battersea County, Salesian College RC (b), Walsingham (g). Private: Emanuel School (b).

Flats	S	1b	2b	3b	4b	5b
Average prices	55–65	70–90	85–110+	95–130	150–200	–
Houses	2b	3b	4b	5b	6/7b	8b
Average prices	120–140	135–175	175–200	190–300	250+	–

The properties An area of terraced late Victorian houses, flat conversions and smart new townhouse/flat developments. Five-bed plus houses and larger flats are scarce (try round the Park for bigger, mansion flats). Riverside is this year's news, influenced by Chelsea Harbour.

The market Eager Wandsworth council is both selling its homes to tenants and doing deals with developers to transform scruffy blocks. Clapham Junction (despite the name) is in Battersea: this draws younger City types who compete with Fulham's children for the smarter homes. Good, cheap ex-council to be had. Local searches: 1 week.

Area Profile

Up the revitalized Junction, down by the penthouse-strewn riverside, Battersea is joining fashionable London with a vengeance. Even the sad council estates in the middle are changing as blocks get sold off wholesale by Wandsworth Council. In return, grateful developers are doing up the remaining homes for them. To add to the new shops and homes, Battersea has a rash of new commercial, often aimed at the new-style 'work where you live' buyers who don't see the point of the drive to West End or City.

From the roads surrounding Battersea Park it is only a five minute drive to Sloane Square – spiritual home of the new inhabitants of Battersea. And from Clapham Junction it is some 7 minutes to Waterloo and the City 'Drain'.

Battersea, especially the area between Clapham Junction and Battersea Park, suffered badly at the hands of German bombers aiming for Clapham Junction. Town planners during the late '50s and '60s, however, did more damage with their 'slum clearance' projects, replacing small terraces with worst-period high-rise blocks.

Historically, the northern part of Battersea was a mixture of working-class terraced housing and industry. The industry has relocated to industrial zones in *Nine Elms* (by Battersea Power Station) and to the west between *York Rd* and the Thames. The descendants of the old inhabitants are still there – but up on the 15th floor of a tower block, sometimes coming down to examine the residences of their new neighbours.

Until recently much of the housing in Battersea was rented, both from Wandsworth Council and from private landlords. The pool of rented property is however shrinking rapidly as landlords sell rather than re-let. Meanwhile Wandsworth Council's property sales policy is turning tenants into 'residents'.

Property in the area, with a handful of exceptions, is Victorian and Edwardian, with mansion blocks centred around *Albert Bridge Rd* and *Prince of Wales Drive* overlooking the Park; elsewhere are Victorian and Edwardian terraces. The major problem facing the area is that of an overloaded road system which sees main access roads to London such as *Queenstown Rd*, *Battersea Park Rd*, *York Rd* and roads leading to the Thames bridges suffering from considerable congestion, especially in the morning.

B

North Battersea

The favoured *Prince of Wales Drive* mansion flats run the entire length of Battersea Park. Service charges can be high, and there have been problems with maintenance charges, though leaseholders are increasingly getting together and buying up their freeholds. Behind are more such blocks in *Lurline Gardens* and *Warriner Gardens*. Roads leading off, like *Sudan* and *Kassala*, feature 3-storey 4- and 5-bedroom red-brick houses.

The *Prince of Wales Drive* area is not just popular for being close to the 200 acres of Battersea Park, complete with children's zoo, lake, running track, tennis courts and the splendid Peace Pagoda, gift of Japanese Buddhists. Even given Battersea's notorious traffic problems, Sloane Square and Knightsbridge are seldom more than a 10-minute drive. The mansion flats often have balconies from which to enjoy the leafy park views; best of all are those flats with sweeping windows in the corner turrets.

The mansion blocks are close to the high-rise Doddington and Rollo council estates on the other side of traffic-plagued *Battersea Park Rd*. A proximity made the more bizarre by the presence of Park South (formerly Jay Court), another tower block sold to developers by Wandsworth Council. Crime on the Doddington and around *Francis Chichester Way* has been cut – but it is still not an area in which to walk late at night with expensive jewellery. Here, too, Wandsworth Council has agreed to sell a 110 flat tower block (Park Court) to Laing Homes in return for a major estate improvement programme. Work starts this spring. A supermarket is also planned.

The mansion flats which run most of the length of *Albert Bridge Rd* face E and thus benefit from more light than *Prince of Wales Drive* and also overlook Battersea Park. Best blocks are probably Albert and Albany. The mansion blocks are interspersed with some fine, large, mid-Victorian semi- and detached houses. Council blocks lie just to the rear. *Parkgate Rd* runs between *Albert* and *Battersea Bridge Rds*. Large plain 3-storey houses, mainly converted to flats, some still awaiting modernisation. It suffers road noise.

The major question-mark facing the area is the ongoing conversion by Alton Towers of Battersea Power Station to a fantastic leisure centre expected to receive more than two million visitors a year. Near the power-station at the Chelsea Bridge end of *Queenstown Rd* now stands the mammoth, smoked-glass and shiny-white HQ of *The Observer* newspaper. Between it and the river, Parc Securities plan more than 300 flats and little houses on its £275 million Battersea Wharf project, which includes more than 400,000 sq ft of offices and a 3- or 4-star hotel, shops and restaurants.

Queenstown

Queenstown Rd leads from Chelsea Bridge past Battersea Park and Queenstown BR stations to *Lavender Hill*. The mainly flat-fronted Victorian houses and flats on either side are now being renovated and improved for sale. Between busy *Silverthorne Rd* and *Queenstown Rd* is the Park Town Estate, now a conservation area, much of which is still owned by the Peabody Trust. At the *Silverthorne Rd* end of *Tennyson St* the houses are 3-storey flat-fronted. Most of the estate, however, features Victorian cottage-style houses; some are purpose-built flats with roof terraces for the first-floor flat.

The larger houses with ornate carved balconies overlooking *St Philip's Square* and the church have been modernised and converted. The flat-fronted cottages with their distinctive high chimneys in *St Philip's St* remain very rarely available. Prices in this corner are still slightly lower than W Battersea – despite better transport.

On the other side of *Queenstown Rd* lie the perfect Gothic cottages of the Shaftesbury Estate (built in the 1870s by the Artisans, Labourers and General Dwellings Co), which runs across to the traffic-snarled *Latchmere Rd*. The Peabody Trust are also the main landlords in the area but an increasing number of the 2- and 3-bedroom terraced cottages are coming on the market. Popular with buyers seeking small, manageable houses – so small as to be better described as vertical flats – they have recently been fetching between £130-140,000. Rat-running in *Eversleigh Rd* soon to be eased with barriers at the *Stanley Grove* junction. *Eversleigh Rd* has the railway line on its northern side. *Eland Rd*, leading down into the Shaftesbury Estate from *Lavender Hill*, has some of the larger houses in the area.

Separated from the Shaftesbury Estate by the railway line behind *Eversleigh Rd* lies a triangle made up of *Poynz Rd*, *Knowsley Rd*, and *Shellwood Rd*.

Approached from *Latchmere Rd* and cut off by railway sidings on three sides are small 2- and occasionally 3-bedroom mainly flat-fronted cottages. The area is useful for access to the excellent (council-owned) Latchmere Leisure Centre off *Sheepcote Lane*. Prices are lower than in the Shaftesbury Estate – the noise from trains could well increase with Channel Tunnel traffic.

Busy *Latchmere Rd* features flats (3-storey blocks) at the upper (*Lavender Hill*) end, Victorian one side, newly built on the W. At the *Amies St* junction is large former Latchmere School, now adult education centre, overshadowing small Victorian cottages in *Amies St* (some railway noise). After come flat-fronted cottages, reasonably priced because of traffic noise.

Clapham Common Northside

South of *Lavender Hill* and bordered by *Cedars Rd*, *Lavender Sweep* and *Clapham Common North Side* is the grid of late Victorian terraced houses known by local estate agents as the *North Side Square*.

Lavender Hill offers adequate shopping with a good small parade close to the junction with *Cedars Rd/Queenstown Rd*. Increasingly shops being taken over by estate agents and restaurants. Easier to buy a house than a loaf of bread. The road is busy at all times – in non-rush hours some speeding.

Virtually the entire area consists of terraced 2- and 3-storey houses – although a growing number are being converted into flats. The exception is *Wix's Lane* (where both the SW4 and the borough boundaries run: check whether you're in Wandsworth or Lambeth) which offers spacious purpose-built Victorian flats (backing onto a school playground). *Nansen*

Battersea price trends 1984-88

60%				
55%				
50%				
45%				
40%				
35%				
30%				
25%			£59,926	
20%		£110,000	£132,000	£92,240
15%	£89,000		£73,295	
10%	£41,475 £47,698		£155,000	£185,000
5%				
0%				
-5%				
	1984	1985	1986	1987	1988

London average home: percentage rise on previous year, adjusted for inflation.

Typical home in this area, percentage rise on previous year, adjusted for inflation.

Four-bed, 2-bath terraced house in the Taybridge Road area, price change compared to London-wide average home. The price of this home fell behind the London average rise in 1986 and 1987, but has made up some ground this year. Battersea became 'established' quite early on – but it still offers more house per £ than across the river.

Rd and *Gowrie Rd*, running parallel to the Common, offer 3-storey 4-bedroom houses, as does *Garfield Rd*, where there is a thriving community centre. The area is within reach of Clapham Common tube.

Roads running between Clapham Common and Lavender Hill such as *Stormont*, *Sugden* and *Taybridge Rds* suffer slightly from rat-running, but *Elspeth Rd* is a through-route for traffic from the South Circular heading for *Latchmere Rd* and Battersea Bridge. *Parma Crescent* and *Eccles Rd* – more early Edwardian terraces – are also popular for their easy access to Clapham Junction station.

Larger houses, now mainly converted into flats, are found in *Sisters Avenue*, *Mysore Rd*, *Lavender Gardens* (once home to the Duchess of York) and *Altenburg Gardens*. This area has parking problems due to the proximity to Clapham Junction. Properties in *Lavender Gardens* near the junction with

Lavender Hill could experience late-night excitement from Jongleurs, a fringe cabaret venue above the Cornet public house. On *Lavender Hill*, the old Battersea Town Hall is now the home of the Battersea Arts Centre.

The flats in Avenue Mansions, *Sisters Avenue* (recently modernised) are unusually spacious, and the top flats offer good (N-facing) views across London. At the top of *Lavender Gardens* is The Shrubbery, a stunning late Georgian mansion, complete with ballroom, now converted to 16 flats, priced £95-300,000, under the watchful eye of conservationists.

Up the Junction

From *Lavender Sweep* down into Clapham Junction parking becomes increasingly awkward, with the situation likely to worsen with the opening of a major new shop-and-office development. But this is the price paid for being just five minutes from Clapham Junction (Gateway Superstore, Marks & Spencer etc). Wandsworth Council are considering a residents' parking scheme for the area.

Leading off *Lavender Sweep*, roads like *Barnard* and *Eckstein* offer spacious purpose-built early Edwardian 2- and 3-storey red-brick flats and maisonettes, the upper-floor flats with large roof terraces. *Ilminster Gardens* and *Beauchamp Rd* feature plain 3-storey Victorian houses, virtually all converted to flats, some still privately tenanted. Both suffer somewhat from their proximity to Arding & Hobbs, the area's very own department store, where a £50 million rebuilding programme launches this spring to bring the store in line with its new clientele. The scheme affects the entire block along *St John's Rd*.

In this area especially there are still some good buys possible, with the triangle between *Boutflower Rd*, *St John's Hill* and *St John's Rd* particularly still to improve.

Crime, particularly street robberies, remains a problem at night, notably in the area immediately surrounding Clapham Junction station and *Plough Rd*.

Off *St John's Hill*, past *Plough Rd*, are *Louvaine*, *Cologne* and *Oberstein Rds*, which feature some spectacular early Edwardian and late Victorian terraced houses – some, notably in *Louvaine*, ornate 3-storey-plus-basement with porticoes. Virtually all are flat conversions – only two houses are left intact in one road. The area is attracting interest and is a fertile hunting ground. Houses in the northern leg of *Harbut Rd* (smaller 3- and 4-bedroom Edwardian) will hear the passing trains from the Clapham Junction to Richmond & West London line.

Prettiest – and most popular – road in the area is *St John's Hill Grove* with a number of charming Regency and early Victorian cottages, some semi-detached. The road is a Conservation Area and the older houses command substantial prices for the area (a 3-bedroom cottage recently sold at £186,000).

Strathblaine, *Vardens* and *Sangora Rds*, running between *St John's Hill* and the railway line, are now fast improving. More large 3-storey Victorian houses here. Some, notably in *Vardens Rd*, exceptionally large semi-detached 3-storey semi-basement houses, some of which have converted into very pleasant flats. This road gains from having been cut off from the traffic at the S end. Houses to the S side of *Strathblaine Rd* back onto the railway.

At the top of *St John's Hill* and running down alongside *Trinity Rd* is the East Hill Estate. The low-rise flats and houses were built by Wandsworth Council in the late 1970s. When the Conservatives took power in 1978, the estate was designated for a low-cost home ownership initiative, and it is entirely owner-occupied.

Between the Commons

Northcote Rd is the centre of the residential area now known as 'Between the Commons' which runs from *Battersea Rise* to *Thurleigh Rd* and is bordered to E and W by Clapham and Wandsworth Commons. These protect the neighbourhood from through-traffic, and the leafy, peaceful streets are great favourites with families. No-one is ever quite sure if this tract is in Battersea, Clapham or Wandsworth. Most is in SW11, though the southernmost roads tip into SW12.

The mainly late Victorian/early Edwardian terraced houses sweep down from the Commons to *Northcote Rd* which, from *Battersea Rise* to *Salcott Rd*, features a daily fruit and vegetable street market: its popularity means congestion on Fridays and Saturdays.

B

The majority of houses are 2-storey, 3-bedroom Edwardian homes, some of considerable charm inside, and remain in single-family occupation. There are pockets of larger, 3-storey mainly flat-fronted houses (some with semi-basement) notably in *Mallinson*, *Bennerly* and *Salcott Rds*. A number of the houses in these three roads have been converted to flats. *Broomwood Rd* is the one through-road between Clapham and Wandsworth Commons, and *Webbs Rd* has traffic running N-S between *Battersea Rise* and *Broomwood Rd*.

This handsome gothic tower stands somewhat incongruously above a shop on the Shaftesbury Estate. One of a pair, it marks the entrance to the estate of little cottages built a century ago as low-rent housing for the working classes. Today, the neat little homes are fashionable with young buyers. Pointed gables and other cottage details set these terraces apart from the norm.

Chatham Rd boasts a row of attractive early Victorian cottages (facing a small, low-rise council estate) and one of the oldest pubs in the area, The Eagle. The private *Stonell's Rd*, (cul de sac off *Chatham Rd*) offers tiny flat-fronted early Victorian cottages. *Hillier*, *Devereux* and *Montholme Sts* are growing in popularity because of easy access to Clapham South Tube (with its direct if not always speedy Northern Line), as are *Kyrle*, *Broxash* and *Manchuria Rds*.

There are virtually no private purpose-built flats in the area with the exception of Broomwood Chambers off *Broomwood Rd*, but former council flats are increasingly coming available. Council property in the area tends to be flats and small houses. Most have been bought under Right to Buy.

Largest houses in the area are found on and just off *Bolingbroke Grove* which runs along the length of Wandsworth Common. Most are late Victorian semi-detached and terraced. Those on *Bolingbroke Grove* itself balance road noise with open views over the Common. The large 3-storey red-brick terraced or semi-detached Victorian houses of *Gorst Rd* and *Dents Rd* are quieter – and more expensive. Smaller mid-Victorian houses on *Bolingbroke Grove* are close to the junction with *Battersea Rise*. Separated from the road by a stretch of grassland, the mid-Victorian cottages overlook a cemetery.

Off *Chivalry Rd*, which forms an L-shape between *Battersea Rise* and *Bolingbroke Grove*, is Commonside, a small private estate (little red boxes) of houses and flats built by Fairview. A number of the houses and flats back directly onto the mainline railway to Waterloo/Victoria; those fronting the Common face a little children's playground. A council traffic scheme looks set to ease rat-running problems in *Chivalry Rd*. 3-bed 'Commonside' houses were fetching c£120,000 in the autumn. *Chivalry Rd* has attractive late Victorian houses (some semi-basement) and two large mid-Victorian houses (now converted to flats) overlooking Wandsworth Common. Rat-running by motorists trying to avoid the *Battersea Rise/Bolingbroke Grove* traffic lights.

South of *Thurleigh Rd* is SW12, but the streets between *Thurleigh* and *Nightingale Lane* belong to 'between the Commons'. These have the shops and services of Balham to call on, and the advantage of nearby Clapham South tube – which is probably where most newcomers think of themselves as living.

Central Battersea

From Clapham Junction shopping centre *Falcon Rd* leads N into the heartland of Battersea. To the right is the enclave of 'Little India', so called after its road names – *Cabul, Afghan, Khyber* and *Candahar*. Houses on the N side of *Rowena Crescent* are nearest the tracks.

Off *Falcon Rd*, with a fine view of Clapham Junction railway station, is Regalian's *The Falcons*, a '60s council estate bought from Wandsworth Council four years ago. The flats are reasonably spacious and facilities include a swimming pool, saunas and gym (included in the service charge). Although the awnings and ornate boundary railings do not disguise the estate's municipal origins, the place makes a great transitory roost for young City workers and the like, for whom the adjacent trains-to-everywhere Junction is a draw, not a drawback. Eminently unsuitable for families, which is why the council sold it. 2-bed flats were on the market last winter priced £90-120,000.

Frere St, off *Battersea Park Rd*, has some pleasant 2-bedroom 3-storey semi-basement houses and a small terrace of town houses (with garages). *Abercrombie St* – small late Victorian terraces – is another Battersea road embraced by a railway.

To the N of traffic-plagued, restaurant-ridden *Battersea Park Rd* lies the oldest part of Battersea, a sometimes uneasy mixture of high-rise council estates and conservation areas. At the heart is 'Battersea Square' – the junction of *Battersea High St* (almost entirely residential at this point), *Vicarage Crescent* and *Westbridge Rd*. The yellow brick flat-fronted 3- and 4-bedroom houses may look early Victorian but looks are misleading. Virtually all have been reconstructed by a sympathetic developer.

Valiant House on *Vicarage Crescent* is a popular development of early '70s brick-built flats overlooking the Thames and the new Chelsea Harbour development. On the other side of *Vicarage Crescent*, still overlooking the river, are some of the oldest buildings in the area, including the early 18th century Devonshire House and Old Battersea House.

'Battersea Village', at the junction of *Vicarage Crescent* and *Lombard Rd* (heavy traffic at rush hours), is a pre-war estate of brick-built flats, built around courtyards, sold by Wandsworth Council to Regalian. Across the road, Groveside Homes have built Albion Wharf, a block of 1-, 2- and 3-bed flats and maisonettes (£160-550,000). Nice spacious flats – but open access walkways (to tie in with the 'Village's' ex-council style?). Buy on end furthest from railway bridge: see 'Transport' chapter. Inland, Windsor Court is a charming conversion of an old school, gated parking behind, small park next door. Ten new houses, 4 flats to be built in *Orville Rd* alongside.

From *Lombard Rd* westwards past the Heliport, old industrial sites are being replaced by riverside homes and offices. Chief among these is the vast Plantation Wharf, Broadwell's mixed business/residential scheme in effect creating an entire new village. Architects Moxley & Frankl seem to be displaying their usual sure touch. River-view flats and 4-bed 'atelier' work-homes are exciting interest – but are not cheap. Next door, Price's candle works, long a landmark, has been bought by the same developers. Note that at the Wandsworth end of the site, the glucose works still scents the air. Chalmers House, another former Wandsworth Council block now privately owned, is directly on *York Rd*.

Off *Shuttleworth Rd* is a grid of five streets running from *Orbel* to *Octavia*, among the most popular locations in Battersea but hidden in an impenetrable road system. The roads offer 3- and 4-bedroom late Victorian semi-detached houses with creamy gold brickwork.

Battersea Church Rd has an attractive 18th-century church and small cottage-style, flat-fronted houses near the junction with Battersea Square. New homes are planned for the site of the burned-out Swan public house on the riverside. The *Morgans Walk* development by Wates features houses and flats, some, but not all, overlooking the Thames and the adjacent Battersea Bridge. Between *Battersea Church* and *Westbridge Rds* lies a recent (1986) development, Battersea Triangle, whose brick-built houses and flats are reached via electronically-controlled wrought-iron gates.

Westbridge Rd, another conservation area, has some attractive early Victorian villas and the late 18th-century Battersea Laundry (close to the junction with *Battersea High St*) now flats with a (small) outdoor swimming pool. It fronts the high-rise Surrey Lane Estate.

Across *Battersea Bridge Rd* to the E, Thames Walk is a plate glass office block with flats alongside the river. The future of Battersea Bus Garage next door is still under discussion, and developers have eyes on Majestic Wine's riverside site. A hideous block has appeared beside it at the head of *Ransome's Dock*; this already boasts a pleasant commercial warehouse conversion at the *Parkgate Rd* end. Rosehaugh, Merivale, Moore and Bovis are all at work on sites on the other side of the dock. On the riverfront, Waterside Point has £160-525,000 flats; the vast penthouses (own pools) have gone already. A block better to look out of than at.

Among those estate agents active in this area are:

- Barnard Marcus
- Bell Son & Co
- Courtenay
- John D Wood
- Farrar Stead & Glyn
- William Gyoury
- Winkworths
- Andrew Kent & Ptnrs
- Hamptons
- Bishop Beamish
- Raymond Bushell
- Edwin Evans
- John Hollingsworth
- Roy Brooks
- Prudential Property

B

Bayswater

Map ref: p59 (7K)
Postal districts: W2
Boroughs: Westminster (con)
Rates: 136.4p in £
Constituencies: Westminster North (Con)
Insurance: Scale 1
Conservation areas: Cover two-thirds of area
– check with City Hall.
Parking: Residents/meters. Clamps.

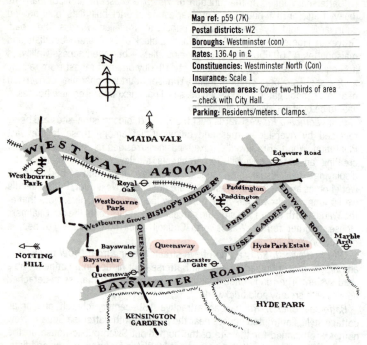

| | **Transport** | Tubes, zone 1: Bayswater (District, Circle); Lancaster Gate, Queensway (Central); Paddington (District, Circle, Bakerloo, Metropolitan). From Lancaster Gate: Oxford Circus 6 min, Bank 20 min, Heathrow 55 min (2 changes). British Rail: Paddington. |

Convenient for   Hyde Park, West End, City. M40 to West. Miles from centre: 2.5.

Schools   ILEA Division 2: Westminster North Secondary. Private: Pembridge Hall School (g).

Flats	S	1b	2b	3b	4b	5b
Average prices	65-85	80-140	115-285	145-400	300-600	400-1m
Houses	2b	3b	4b	5b	6/7b	8b
Average prices	180-340	240-450	330-500	400-600+	500-1.2m	→

The properties   Bayswater's image of seediness (fast altering) means its prettier corners and occasional quiet mews come as a shock to many. White terraces were once grand; currently a total mix: everything from pristine millionaires' squares (Hyde Park Estate) to hostels. Ramparts of flats along Edgware Rd. Freeholds scarce; flats most common.

The market   Move in now: the cannier developers have started Bayswater's restoration – while homebuyers haven't realised that it will shortly be a 17-min train ride from Heathrow. Local searches: 1 week.

B

Area Profile

There is probably no other area in London which has such a wide social mix as Bayswater. Some of the West End's most luxurious homes, bordering Hyde Park and Kensington Gardens, are matched elsewhere in the area by huge decaying houses still split up into scores of seedy bedsits.

Bayswater's southern boundary is the broad sweep of Hyde Park and Kensington Gardens. To the E the *Edgware Rd* is the frontier with the West One area. To the north, beyond the elevated M40 motorway, the railway and the canal, is Maida Vale. To the W Bayswater blends into Notting Hill. The entire area is within Westminster City Council's jurisdiction, and the W2 postcode also neatly surrounds Bayswater.

The area, being close to the Paddington railway station and to the West End, has always catered for a large section of London's transient population and for low-income workers and students. At the same time it is the established home for many long-term residents in council-owned homes, as well as those who can afford the Monopoly-money prices commanded by the better properties.

Bayswater is used to constant movement, and there is now a big change going on in the property market and in the area's planning future. Many of the older, run-down 5-storey houses are being converted into flats and sold on leaseholds – but estate agents warn to check the quality of developments. Most new developments are 2-bedroom or studio apartments. Because there is such a huge variety of properties and such a variation in the quality of the conversions, prices, taken in isolation, can often be misleading.

Values promise to rise in the Queensway district when the new Whiteley's store complex opens this spring. This is already reflected in the developments in *Kensington Gardens Square*. Several other major developments are due to affect the area. The plan to make Paddington Station the terminus of a high-speed rail link to Heathrow airport will certainly increase the area's residential attraction.

Major schemes are pending for the Paddington Goods Yards site, N of mixed commercial and residential development. London Transport has now dropped plans to include in the development a central coach terminal for the whole of London, following fierce local opposition. On the other side of the road to the station a £200 million-plus mixed residential, commercial and leisure scheme is planned for the Paddington Canal Basin site. Building is expected to start within the next year and take 4-5 years to complete. And N of the Westway the former St Mary's hospital in *Harrow Rd* is due for demolition and replacement by a large homes development.

Two-thirds of the Bayswater area is a conservation area, which means new developments must win special approval first. And four general improvement areas, where the council promotes housing improvements through grants, affect large tracts of the N-W end of the area.

An attempt to restrict residential roads being used as traffic thoroughfares is now being made by a pressure group called BATS – the Bayswater Area Traffic Study. Their plan aims to divide the area up into no-traffic 'cells' and will affect the whole of Bayswater.

As mentioned above, Bayswater is very varied. Neighbourhoods range from the highly salubrious SE corner, the Church Commissioners' Hyde Park Estate, to the council flats to the N.

Bayswater

Bounded by *Westbourne Grove* in the N, *Queensway* (E), the borough boundary (W) and *Bayswater Rd*, this is the heart of Bayswater's traditional bedsit land. Its many 5-storey stucco houses have long been split into rooms for letting to students, visitors and service workers in the hotel industry and the health service. The S part of the neighbourhood, close to Hyde Park and convenient for the West End, now shows signs of change. 'For Sale' signs proliferate in many streets as the larger houses are split up and sold off as flats.

Three large squares dominate the N part of the neighbourhood – *Leinster*, *Princes* and *Kensington Gardens*. Peeling stucco walls reflect the deterioration of many of these old houses; one large block of three has been taken over by the council, others are empty pending development. *Kensington Gardens Square* contains a number of busy hotels. Each square has a large communal garden to which neighbouring residents have access. Nearby in *Moscow Rd*, Alexandra Court is the latest Rosehaugh Copartnership flats development.

In contrast to the run-down houses around the squares, *St Petersburg Place* further S contains an attractive brick terrace of period maisonettes. A 2-bed flat here fetches around £190,000 and with it comes the use of another communal garden. Further W is *Hereford Rd*, which contains a mixture of properties. They are smaller, less ornate, brick houses with wrought-iron balconies; the road is serviced by a few small local shops. A development of 28 new flats, with car park, was under way last winter. *Hereford Mews* also has new homes.

Westbourne Grove itself is a cosmopolitan centre: here you can eat Chinese, Malaysian, Indian, Greek or Lebanese food – or buy the ingredients from a late-night grocer. Dotted among this gastronomic mecca are a few specialist shops for cooks or collectors of Oriental furnishings, an Arabic bookshop and several clothes shops catering for the cheaper end of the market (*Westbourne Grove* was known in the 1860s as 'Bankruptcy Avenue'). Nearby *Queensway* – see below – has a similar character. This is an ideal part of town for the nocturnal, rivalling Earls Court in its ability to stay up late.

Queensway

The neighbourhood bounded by *Queensway* in the W, *Bayswater Rd* to the S, *Gloucester Terrace* (E) and *Bishops Bridge Rd* (N) reflects the tremendous social mix that is characteristic of this part of town. In the N of this area is the council-owned Hallfield Estate with its strong community feeling, its own health centre and school. The estate is bordered by *Inverness Terrace* and *Gloucester Terrace*. In the S, *Lancaster Gate* sports some of the neighbourhood's most luxurious developments, facing Kensington Gardens.

Gloucester Terrace is a wide, sweeping road which brings much traffic off the A40 motorway and into Central London. S from the Hallfield Estate the road features large, well-kept stucco houses, most already divided up into luxury flats. These are broken by terraced brick houses. Where the road meets *Craven Rd*, another small 'village' begins. Going W along *Craven Rd*, a cluster of small shops provide local services as well as fresh fruit and flowers. And on either side are two sets of mews with steeply sloping entrances (*Gloucester*, *Smallbrook*, *Upbrook* and *Craven Hill Mews*). In *Westbourne Terrace* a derelict former hotel on a corner has become 12 flats priced from £115-350,000.

Around the corner off *Leinster Gardens*, *Craven Hill Gardens* and *Queens Gardens* contain more large, 5-storey multi-occupied houses in varied states of repair. *Cleveland Square* and *Devonshire Terrace* have smaller 3-storey houses. Bed and breakfast and holiday lets are still widely advertised in the area.

The most desirable homes in Bayswater, beside those on the Hyde Park Estate, are to be found in the *Lancaster Gate* and *Porchester Terrace* areas. *Porchester*, which runs N from the Park, contains an intriguing mixture of period town houses with well-maintained gardens. Many of the cars along this road bear diplomatic plates, and anti-burglar bars are evident on many of the ground floor windows. Dotted among the detached houses are some flat-fronted brick apartment blocks. The modern Hyde Park Towers apartment block affords wide views across Kensington Gardens. In *Inverness Terrace* is Park Gate, a major new development of 37 flats by Broadwell, priced from £165,000 up to £340,000. 1 Porchester Gate is a new block of 27 flats completed last year, with park view penthouses priced at £1.6m.

Lancaster Gate is a street of surprises. Here the large hotels have solid, respectable frontages; among them are two owned by the Transport and General Workers Union and the Merchant Navy. The square itself, surrounding an eye-catching development of luxury flats, created from a former church, contains the College of Law and the headquarters of the Unification Church. On the corner, another luxury-level development has been completed: 24 flats have been carved out of several 5-storey colonnaded terraced houses. More properties are up for sale in the square as lettings give way to sales.

In contrast to the atmosphere and scale of *Lancaster Gate*, neighbouring *Lancaster Mews* is reminiscent of a small country village. Its sloping entrance is topped by the Mitre pub. The cottages here are beautifully maintained and colour-washed in attractive pastels. Mediterranean blue paintwork and abundant window boxes complete the picture of the busy light industrial/residential 'village'. The twin mews on the opposite side of *Craven Terrace* is smaller but equally well maintained. There are few signs of sales down here.

Back on *Queensway* itself, at the W end of the neighbourhood, the traditional

B

night life continues with restaurants pulling in tourists and visitors, and small shops catering for local residents. Thirties brick apartments, served by walkways, top the shopping arcades at the lower end of *Queensway*. Here a major reconstruction is now taking place. The famous Whiteley's department store – London's first, opened in 1863 – is, after several years of uncertainty, due to reopen this spring. The developers promise to 'recreate the legend' of the store as a heart to the area's shopping centre.

Paddington

Paddington station is the hub of the neighbourhood bounded by *Eastbourne Terrace*, *Harrow Rd*, *Edgware Rd* and *Sussex Gardens*. Like those surrounding most major main-line stations, the area contains a mixture of expensive homes and more run-down properties catering to the transient population.

Most of the Victorian brick cottages S of *Praed St* in *Sale Place*, *St Michael St* and *Star St* were once owned by St Mary's Hospital, *Praed St*, or by the railway companies to house their workers. Over time they fell into disrepair. Some were acquired by housing associations but many benefited from the declaration of a Housing Action Area to encourage private owners to improve their properties. Now they are coming up for sale and with their period charm and central location command high prices. Five new houses in *Praed Mews* will this year add to the air of revival.

But *Praed St*, next to the station, reflects the dominant trend of the area; exchange bureaux, instant photos, heel bars and dealers in gold, silver and second-hand goods abound. *Norfolk Square* lies S of *Praed St* and contains mostly small hotels surrounding a communal garden. Westminster Council has taken over the square gardens, which it claims were neglected and is doing them up. South again, *Sussex Gardens* is a major road connecting *Lancaster Gate* and the *Edgware Rd*. Its 4-storey terraces are now mostly given over to bed and breakfast hotels, many used as temporary homes for homeless families. Adjoining *Sussex Place* contains a private apartment block, Sussex Lodge. N of Paddington station, a new luxury block has been completed in Holy Trinity Court, on the site of Holy Trinity church in *Bishop's Bridge Rd*.

Westbourne Park

Porchester Rd takes you N from the *Queensway* neighbourhood and up towards the motorway and *Harrow Rd*. Leaving *Bishop's Bridge Rd*, go N into *Porchester* and you are heading towards Royal Oak tube station. Pass by the local landmark of Porchester Hall, council owned and always busy. Behind the hall is the Porchester Baths, a well-known steam and sauna spot with swimming pool, newly modernised after a £1 million facelift.

To the E *Gloucester Terrace* is the motorway access route: large 4-storey houses form what was once an elegant terrace; now their facades are crumbling. The buildings have attractive wrought-iron balconies. *Porchester Square* to the S has another busy communal gardens with playground for local residents. In *Orsett Terrace* 90 new flats range from studios at £77,500 to 3-beds at £185,000.

To the W of *Porchester Rd*, *Westbourne Park Rd* discloses a curious mixture of properties ranging from the flat-fronted brick apartment blocks to detached villa-style houses with ornate, oriental-inspired decorations and colonnaded entrances. Heron Homes have built 8 new houses and some offices in *Celbridge Mews* off *Porchester Rd*. Prices from £150-310,000.

West of the triangle bounding the church, *St Stephens Crescent* contains an attractive terrace of stucco 5-storey properties with steps up to front entrances guarded by columns. St Stephens Gardens have recently been improved by the council. Around the corner, just off *Talbot Rd*, and E of *Chepstow Rd*, lies *Bridstow Place*, a tiny roadway of colour-washed Victorian cottages. Climbing roses and trailing plants splash colour over the pastel brickwork of the cottages with their small gardens. But turn the corner, and you're back with the peeling stucco and scaffolding of *Chepstow Rd's* 5-storey houses. Even these are being converted: a recent scheme, 'West Park', carved 25 flats from 3 houses.

To the S of *Talbot Rd*, *Artesian Rd* is a hotbed of activity: skips are in abundance as the homes in this tree-lined street are undergoing extensive work. Nearby *Courtnell St* contains more attractive colour-washed, brick-fronted properties overlooked by copper beeches. W of here is the boundary of the W2 district and of Westminster borough.

North of the motorway in *Harrow Rd* a major development is planned on the site of the old St Mary's Hospital. The development, to be called 'Carlton Gate', will include about 580 flats, houses, a nurses' home and old people's home. The first 80 flats are due for completion by late summer. Prices will range from £100,000 to £600,000 (1-3 bedrooms). Just opposite is the Paddington Basin project, a 13-acre site being developed by Trafalgar House and the British Waterways Board. There will be offices, shops, industry, a cinema and boating facilities, plus homes. Completion date is 1995.

Hyde Park Estate

Should you find yourself at Marble Arch – the famous landmark originally built as an entrance to Buckingham Palace, but which today stands at the western end of *Oxford St* as an entrance to nowhere – you might feel like taking a short walk. Go up busy *Edgware Rd*, turn left into hotel-lined *Sussex Gardens*, left again at the towering Royal Lancaster Hotel onto *Bayswater Rd*, and back along the Park to Marble Arch. You have thus circumnavigated the Hyde Park Estate. It is like an island adjacent to Paddington Station on one side and the West End on the other. Inside its boundaries you feel a million miles from the hustle and bustle of central London. Leaving *Edgware Rd* is almost like travelling in time – going from a weekday to a Sunday.

The Estate owes its character to its landlords, the Church Commissioners. Once, the Bishop of London owned nearly all of Paddington. At the start of the 19th century the Bishop's architect built an elegant estate of squares and crescents, called Tyburnia. The Church Commissioners, heirs of the bishops, sold off all their Paddington land except the Hyde Park triangle in the 1950s. Much of ecclesiastical Paddington had sunk into a slum, populated largely by prostitutes: one corner, W of the station, was known as 'Sin Triangle'. Concentrating on the Hyde Park Estate, the Commissioners started widespread rebuilding. The result is a neighbourhood mixing early 19th century stucco terraces, handsome (some, anyway) modern houses and – forming a protective rampart along *Edgware Rd* – tower-block apartments. The Regency street-plan has remained despite redevelopment. The Estate's lack of through-routes and clearly defined borders keeps it quiet and pleasant. It is a tribute to the

B

Commissioners, or more especially to their agents and architects, that the Estate is still a desirable place to live.

As is common in residential Central London, garden squares are a feature of the Estate, each with a character and atmosphere of its own. *Oxford* and *Cambridge Squares* for example, are bordered by modern town houses and tall blocks of flats with underground garages. *Hyde Park Square* on the other hand is larger and has a range of styles surrounding it, from grandiose 5-storey stucco houses to spacious modern family homes to blocks of flats. *Sussex Square* has an even more spacious feel about it, with a circular green at the centre. One of the handsomest is *Connaught Square*, enclosed by Regency town houses. While being just a stone's throw from the Marble Arch madness, it manages to retain its dignity and leafy peacefulness. But the jewel in the crown is probably *Gloucester Square*. One can walk around the perimeter and not always be aware that it is a square: some of the (highly priced) houses have the luxury of backing directly onto the central green, concealing the garden square to the untutored eye. A recently completed block of de-luxe flats added onto the end of a cream stucco terrace were all eagerly snapped up.

Many of the Estate's large town houses, once occupied by the wealthy families from the pages of history books and by the merchant classes and empire builders, have now been converted into ultra-luxurious flats. Some of the most exclusive are the stucco-fronted Regency buildings in *Hyde Park Gardens*, having their own huge communal garden opposite Hyde Park. In contrast to this quiet elegance and opulence, there are a variety of purpose-built modern blocks on the estate, ranging from the workaday Park West in *Kendal St* on the E fringe, to the fountain-laden Water Gardens and the Quadrant, both bordering on Sussex Gardens. The *Water Gardens* estate is a complex of towers and smaller blocks, with a '60s split-level feel and a profusion of pools and fountains.

Sussex Gardens forms the northern border of the Hyde Park Estate. It is lined on either side by cheap hotels and bed and breakfast houses filled with homeless families and young travellers – but if you're looking for somewhere cheap and central to stay, you can't beat it. *Sussex Gardens'* other claim to fame was that of being a red light district – obviously encouraged by its proximity to both Paddington and Marylebone stations. The Hyde Park Estate is genteel and reasonably safe, with *Sussex Gardens* acting like a divide. On the other side of the road, you're no longer on the Estate – there is a different atmosphere, the pace is faster and more commercial and the streets dirtier as you near Paddington Station and *Praed St*.

Mews houses are becoming increasingly popular, here as elsewhere in London. They were originally built behind the big houses of the gentry as accommodation for horses, coaches and coachmen. It is only since the last war that they have been converted into homes, providing compact, easily manageable houses in village-like cobbled streets, retaining their period frontage and last-century atmosphere. Some of the most charming and coveted mews on the Estate are *Hyde Park Gardens Mews*, off *Hyde Park Square*, and the two smaller mews off *Albion St*. The Hyde Park Estate is lucky to have a mews that is still used for its original purpose; *Bathurst Mews* houses a riding school, where you can hire horses and go riding in Hyde Park. Smart conversions in Hyde Park Square have recently added 20 flats to the local stock. Sample prices: 1-bed flat £200,000, 4-bed flats £650,000-1m.

One of the gems on the Hyde Park Estate is *Hyde Park Crescent*, and the lovely old church of St John's, which can be seen as a long-distance vista from as far as *Sussex Square*. The Crescent adds space and dignity to the church.

Complementing *Hyde Park Crescent* is *Norfolk Crescent* to the E. The two form part of a circle embracing the church, the two squares (*Oxford* and *Cambridge*) and two high-rise blocks. *Norfolk Crescent*, a post-war development of tall thin family houses, in contrast to *Hyde Park Crescent* feels slightly crammed and congested, due to the parking meters opposite, which narrow the road and create permanent traffic problems.

One of the disadvantages of living so centrally is the problem of parking. Some mews houses have their own garages and nearly all the post-war flats and houses have underground garages. But parking meters and parking permits put considerable pressure on movement, on space and on life in general. Then again, living in such an attractive and convenient location must have drawbacks somewhere.

Most of the land on the estate is owned by the Church Commissioners who historically have been reluctant to part with their freeholds, so that all the flats and most of the houses are leasehold properties. But since the advent of the Leasehold Reform Acts (1965-1974) many small leaseholders have managed to purchase their freeholds. But in order to enjoy some benefit from the Acts tenants must apply very soon, as the number of remaining properties qualifying is diminishing day by day. (Only homes with a rateable value of less than £1,500 qualify.)

B

The centre of life in the Estate is the Connaught 'village', with its mix of small shops, offices and homes. It's a varied corner: *Connaught Place*, a mixture of new hi-tech offices and homes reconstructed behind their original stucco facade overlooking Marble Arch and Hyde Park, for example, houses the headquarters of a large multinational. And quietly camouflaged into the white stucco front of *Hyde Park Gardens* is the Sri Lankan embassy.

The corner of *Sussex Place* and *Hyde Park Gardens Mews* is another picturesque hive of activity for eating, meeting and drinking, where on warm summer evenings people sit out at tables on the pavement – in (almost) Parisian style. And if you're in dreaming or decadent mood, there's a chandelier shop on the same corner where you could fritter away more than just a few odd pounds.

The atmosphere on the Estate, once genteel, slow moving and village-like, has become more cosmopolitan and anonymous. The variety of languages that you can hear within a few paces ranges from Filipino to Swahili: many diplomats live here. The latest and largest influx has been that of Arabs, many of whom only come for the summer months, but keep their flats and houses throughout the year. This has led to changes – the top end of *Edgware Rd* now has estate agents, banks, clothes shops, cinemas and restaurants, all catering for Middle Easterners.

Prices on the Estate are much influenced by the length of the remaining lease. And, with much modern property among the stucco, check that the homes on offer are from a period you favour. The modern houses often have a key advantage in this crowded corner: a garage.

Among those estate agents active in this area are:

- Browne Beck & Flindall
- Druce
- Foxtons
- Lurot Brand
- Marsh & Parsons
- Plaza Estates
- Prudential Property
- West One Property
- Winkworths

Bedford Park

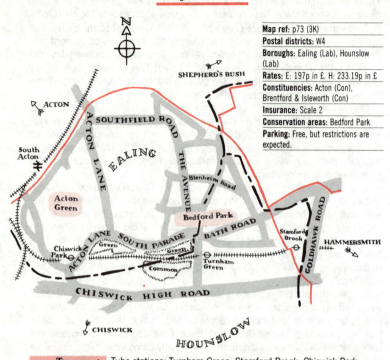

Map ref: p73 (3K)
Postal districts: W4
Boroughs: Ealing (Lab), Hounslow (Lab)
Rates: E: 197p in £. H: 233.19p in £
Constituencies: Acton (Con), Brentford & Isleworth (Con)
Insurance: Scale 2
Conservation areas: Bedford Park
Parking: Free, but restrictions are expected.

Transport — Tube stations: Turnham Green, Stamford Brook, Chiswick Park (zone 2, District). From Turnham Green: Oxford Circus 25 min (1 change); City 40 min; Heathrow 25 min (1 change). British Rail: South Acton on North London line.

Convenient for — Heathrow and M4. Miles from centre: 4.

Schools — Ealing and Hounslow Education Authorities: Chiswick School, Acton School. Private: Latymer (b), Godolphin & Latymer (g), St Paul's (g).

Flats	S	1b	2b	3b	4b	5b
Average prices	65–75	70–120	85–150	85–190	→	→
Houses	2b	3b	4b	5b	6/7b	8b
Average prices	130–200	160–250	190–375	250–500+	300–800	→

The properties — Distinctive enclave of late 19th century Queen Anne-style houses, from 3-bed cottages up to large houses. Bordering streets are more usual Victorian/Edwardian.

The market — Always fierce competition for the small number of genuine, conservation-area homes. Surrounding streets are also popular family homes. Local searches: Ealing 6 weeks, Hounslow 1-2 weeks.

Area Profile

It is, of course, quite possible to live in Bedford Park without being keen on architecture, but it would be rather a waste. For this was London's first purpose-built aesthetic suburb, laid out, and the houses designed, in the 1870s to high artistic standards. It has survived virtually intact, an island in the less creative sprawl of West London. And a good number of the inhabitants spend a good part of their time protecting their neighbourhood against philistine encroachment.

Convenient position (it lies just N of Chiswick, and the M4 is close at hand), pleasant character and family-sized houses are other attractions of this green corner. Corner it is: Bedford Park is not very big, and its cachet leads to a stealthy extension of the name into Acton. 'Bedford Park Borders' is a term to beware of. Some roads outside the original estate belong in spirit, but to the true Park residents, the world outside their carefully conserved corner is, and will remain, forever Acton. True Bedford Park consists of a mere dozen streets. The L-shaped area to the N and W is the 'borders' and is considered below.

Founded in 1875 by Jonathan Carr, a cloth merchant with a taste for speculation and art, Bedford Park was the prototype garden suburb. Carr employed such well-known architects as R Norman Shaw, E J May, E W Godwin and Maurice B Adams to design houses in the Queen Anne Revival style – all red brick, dormer windows, Dutch gables, hanging tiles, balconies and pretty porches. Some 400 buildings, mostly Grade II listed, now make up the conservation area. Despite the odd bit of war damage and modern in-filling, the estate remains remarkably homogenous; the most obtrusive new building is St Catherines' Court, a 1930s block built on the site of Carr's own magnificent house. There is great variety in homes, from little 2-storey 3-bedroom cottages to 6/7-bedroom detached houses, semis and terraces of up to 4 storeys. There are a couple of large mansion blocks, and some of the larger houses have been converted into owner-occupier flats – only a few remain as rented accommodation. Despite its sobriquet of garden suburb many of the gardens are disappointingly small ('though not for central London, which for practical purposes we are!' objected one resident), and prices reflect garden as much as house size and position. Garden flats also fetch proportionately more. Because there is such a good size mix, residents often move within the area and many properties are sold through the grapevine – which is why some people move to Bedford Park borders before working their way in. Larger houses may come onto the market via major London estate agents.

The whole estate with its irregular layout (to preserve existing trees) was modelled on the idea of a village complete with shops, pub, church of St Michaels and All Angels, church hall and club. The village atmosphere remains, which means plenty of social and cultural activities plus a friendly atmosphere where everyone seems to know everyone else's business. The community spirit is further fostered by the Bedford Park Society which fiercely protects the area's architectural heritage. Originally built as homes at modest rents for the aesthetic middle classes, Bedford Park first attracted many artists and personalities. Nowadays it is more likely to house media folk, professionals such as architects, and others who can afford the considerably less than modest buying prices.

Just about every house in Bedford Park is listed, and the whole place is a conservation area. So splended details like this assemblage of gable, balcony and bay will survive. The wooden railings, close-set glazing bars in the square bay, heavy gable and tiled roof are typical. The houses are late Victorian, but they hark back to Queen Anne.

Carr chose the spot because of its proximity to the newly-opened Turnham Green station; these excellent links to the West End and City remain, with the added advantage of being 20 minutes' drive from Heathrow down the M4. The area is within walking distance of the shops and restaurants on *Chiswick High Rd*, as well as other W4 facilities. Acton Green, adjacent to the tube line, is the nearest open space, but the river, Kew Gardens and Richmond Park are only a few minutes' drive away. *Bath Rd*, *The Avenue* and *South Parade* are main roads with bus routes, while the latter, along with *Flanders Rd*, runs adjacent to the tube line. Streets round the station suffer commuter day time parking but there are plans for a parking scheme to favour residents. *Abinger Rd*, *Blenheim Rd*, *Bedford Rd* and streets leading off *South Parade* become rat-runs during the rush hour, though there are tentative proposals for a traffic scheme. It follows that roads in the heart of the conservation area, such as *Queen Anne's Gardens*, are the quietest, but all the roads have desirable houses.

Bedford Park Borders

Non-listed houses, such as those in streets leading off *Flanders Rd*, along with mansion blocks and houses just outside the conservation area *Vanbrugh Rd*,

Esmond Rd, *Fielding Rd*, *Blandford Rd*, *Rusthall Avenue*, *Ramilles Rd* and *St Albans Avenue* were built a little later than Bedford Park proper, with some inter-war additions. They are cheaper in both design and price, forming the lower price brackets of our price chart. *Esmond Rd*, however, has some substantial houses – in both size and price – at its S end. Beyond these streets, all in the Ealing borough part, are more conventional red-brick Victorian terraces and inter-war semis. By a quirk of post office geography they are all in W4 and thus dubbed Chiswick by estate agents, although strictly speaking they are in Acton. Really unscrupulous agents, aided by upwardly mobile clients, call everything up to *Greenend Rd*, *Hatfield Rd* and the railway line Bedford Park. That said, this is the only section where there are still (comparative) bargains. Similar properties and prices pertain W of *St Albans Avenue*, an area known as Acton Green but still considered Chiswick for estate agents' purposes.

These streets run off *Acton Lane*, but are indeed kept distinct from Acton proper by a railway line to the N-W. The streets of variously-styled, neat suburban villas have Chiswick Park tube to hand, but beware mini-traffic jams caused by school runs, confirming this leafy corner's popularity as a family area. Indeed, the schools are mentioned again and again as plus-points for the whole area, with private prep schools like Chiswick & Bedford Park on *Priory Avenue* putting up impressive numbers of candidates for the academic groves of Westminster, Latymer, St Paul's and Godolphin & Latymer. Close to South Acton station, off *Church Path*, there are plans for nearly 50 homes on a 1½ acre site.

A final point: unlike neighbouring Chiswick, Bedford Park is far enough from the flight paths to escape aircraft noise being a nuisance.

Among those estate agents active in this area are:

- Barnard Marcus
- John Granville
- Knight Frank & Rutley
- Raymond Bushell
- Prudential Property Services
- Tyser Greenwood
- Winkworths

B

Belgravia

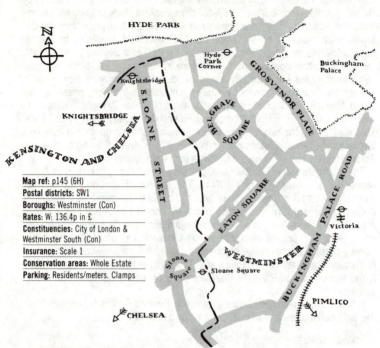

Map ref: p145 (6H)
Postal districts: SW1
Boroughs: Westminster (Con)
Rates: W: 136.4p in £
Constituencies: City of London &
Westminster South (Con)
Insurance: Scale 1
Conservation areas: Whole Estate
Parking: Residents/meters. Clamps

Transport   Tubes: All zone 1, Knightsbridge (Piccadilly), Sloane Sq (District, Circle) Victoria (District, Circle, Victoria). From Sloane Sq to Oxford Circus 15 min (1 change), City 20 min, Heathrow 55 min (1 change).

Convenient for   West End, Hyde Park, Gatwick Airport. Miles from centre:1.5.

Schools   ILEA zones 1/2: Pimlico School, Grey Coat C of E (g). Private: Francis Holland (g), Southbank – The American International School, Westminster School (b), More House School (g).

Flats	S	1b	2b	3b	4b	5b
Average prices	–	150–300+	250–550+	450–900+	500–1m+	→2m+
Houses	2b	3b	4b	5b	6/7b	8b
Average prices	360+	425+	500+	550–2.5m+	→	→7m

The properties   Owned by the Grosvenor Estate: almost all leasehold. Grand Regency homes provide equally grand converted apartments. Also houses of all sizes from mews cottage to Embassy.

The market   'Average' prices here are a very general guide: all depends on length of lease and location. Discounting embassy-sized houses, Eaton Square commands highest prices. Short leases, c 8–15 years, equate to rental, rather than sale prices: those above are for reasonable leases. Rare freeholds of (relatively) smaller houses. Local searches: 1 week.

Area Profile

This pristine, gleaming part of London must rank among the best property investments of all time. The sole proprietor of this patch of enviable real estate, the enjoyer of its rents and revenues, is the Grosvenor Estate, personified by a youngish man called Gerald Grosvenor, the Duke of Westminster. His family has owned the land for generations and in Regency times developed it with the help of builder and architect Thomas Cubitt. Much of London was built up at this time or a little later, but no other district has kept its character in quite the same way. The credit goes partly to Cubitt, whose building standards were, if not exactly high, then better than those of Nash. But the main upholder of the Belgravian character has been the Grosvenor Estate, and the snowy sweep of stuccoed terraces and squares stands seemingly unchanged. The estate office is still very much in charge, controlling tenancies, developing its own properties through its own restoration company and stipulating just how the inhabitants behave. The control of the estate office may be discreet but it is firm. Whatever their personal tastes, householders must paint their facades cream, and not just any old cream but British Standard 3033 Magnolia, the official estate paint.

The Duke's inheritance has been nibbled at of late by tenants exercising their rights under the Leasehold Reform Acts (see Who Owns London). The estate contested the buy-outs and took the case to the European Court of Human Rights under the complaint that the Acts infringed the duke's right to freely enjoy his property. But the estate lost and for the first time in two centuries the word 'freehold' appears occasionally in Belgravia.

B

Belgravia is almost wholly residential. The estate's policy is to use the fringes for offices and shops and hotels, but to keep the heartland free of commerce. Shops are to be found in a few streets: *Elizabeth* and *Motcomb Sts* have the majority. There are a few discreetly hidden pubs in mews. But the rest is houses and flats – or, as Belgravia calls them, apartments. The properties within this enclave vary considerably in size. The grandest homes, those in *Belgrave Square*, have nearly all become embassies or institutes. Most of the only slightly smaller *Eaton Square* mansions are now flats. Smaller-scale houses often survive as single homes, as do many of the mews cottages built to serve the grand streets and squares.

The standard commodity on sale here is the lease, either direct from the estate or a sub-lease. Some leases can be very short, but those expecting a 15-year lease to be one-fifth the cost of a 75-year one are doomed to disappointment: buyers of short leases, usually companies, view the sums demanded for these enviable London bases as rent paid upfront, rather than a purchase. The area is very popular with foreign diplomats and business people. Due to the positive ghetto of embassies in and around *Belgrave Square* there is a plethora of police, including the always-armed Diplomatic Protection Group. This presence reassures foreigners, say estate agents. There was a time, not more than a couple of decades ago, when Belgravia's grand houses were considered too big to inhabit. And by modern standards so they are: they were designed with the assumption of dozens of servants. What has happened is the great improvement in the art of conversion. The grand old buildings are often just facades, concealing flats which are in some cases very big and equally grand. Sometimes the conversions are lateral, running behind two or even three house facades. Belgravia buyers, and renters, put stress it seems on cleanliness and entertaining space: agents always make a point of the number of bathrooms and the size and grandeur of the reception rooms.

To live in Belgravia is to be seriously rich – or at least to have someone else (like your company or embassy) paying the rent. For your money you get unrivalled ambience, discreetly excellent estate management, and a position mid-way between Harrods and Buckingham Palace and a short taxi ride from everywhere you would ever want to be. The key to Belgravia's charm is its changes of scale, from minute mews homes through low-storeyed rows to the grandeur of the set-pieces of *Eaton* and *Belgrave Squares*.

Southern Belgravia

Once, the dukes owned the whole tract S from Victoria Station down to the Thames. The Pimlico area was developed at the same time and was once considered more or less part of Belgravia. The railway cut Pimlico off, and it never achieved the same exalted status as its senior neighbour. The Grosvenor Estate sold Pimlico about 30 years ago. Belgravia thus starts at busy, slightly seedy *Buckingham Palace Rd*, which runs alongside the station. The strip between this road and *Ebury St*, another busy through-route, contains little of the Belgravia character. The occasional mews, and some flats in *Ebury Square*, compete for space with the Victoria Coach Station.

Ebury St has small (for Belgravia) early terraced houses, many of which are hotels. Until recently it was quite run-down, but now it is improving though still mixed – and paradoxically has the area's largest gardens. The houses are mostly brick, not stucco. To the W *Bunhouse St*, tucked behind *Bourne St*, has a row of '70s neo-Georgian townhouses: quiet and popular. Between *Ebury St* and *Eaton Square* is the first slice of Belgravia proper. And how proper it is, with quiet, pretty *Chester Square* as its showpiece. These houses were built as 'second rank' homes but are today thought to be some of the best in the area. Quite a few are still single houses. *Chester Row* is similar. Typical houses hereabouts have 4/5 beds and ample reception rooms. Last year, though, an eight-bedroom house in the square, unusually still having its own cottage in the mews behind, came up for sale: the price was £900,000 for the 22-year lease. The differing lease-lengths make price comparisons a tricky sport in Belgravia: last year £250,000 could have bought you a family-sized *Ebury St* maisonette – but only for 27 years; £345,000 spent in *Chesham St* would have netted a 2-bedroom flat (albeit a luxurious one) for 1,000 years.

Eccleston St, which bisects *Chester Square*, is a busy one-way road taking traffic up to *Hyde Park Corner*. This is where the mews begin, the Belgravia mews where the little cottages, built as stables, can cost half a million pounds and more. *Ebury Mews* is typical, running through from *Eccleston* to *Elizabeth Sts*. It has a mix of converted mews cottages of greater and lesser degree of opulence, plus some new-build homes in mews style. Quite a few of these homes have kept their garages. *Elizabeth St* has a selection of very up-market shops, including some serving quite everyday needs. It is also the site of one of the Grosvenor Estate's restoration projects: it produced 4 luxurious apartments, priced at £475,000 to £1.5m. *Gerald Rd* has a small police station.

To the W, *Eaton Terrace* and splendidly-appropriate *Caroline Terrace* have more handsome houses, many made into apartments. *South Eaton Place* has one or two freehold houses. It also boasts pretty Chantry House, a low-built corner house lovingly restored from its wine cellar to its roof garden and for sale last winter for £2.5 million (52 years). The far SW corner of the area has some smaller homes. *Bourne St's* 2-storey and semi-basement houses have 2 or 3 beds. *Graham St* too has more modest sizes. *Eaton Square* is the centrepiece on which the area turns. It has, to say the least, considerable presence. The buildings are enormous, and are virtually all apartments. Penthouses top most of them, and prices are in the 'if you have to ask…' bracket. it could more properly be called 'Eaton Squares': it is on so large a scale that inhabitants hardly seem to notice the slight disadvantage of the main *King's Rd* running through towards Chelsea. And two smaller roads cross at right angles, dividing the central garden into six – all of good size. 1988 saw one of the six remaining entire houses come on the market: its silk-lined, seven-bedroomed (not counting staff quarters) splendour called for 'offers over £7 million' – for a 57-year lease.

Central Belgravia

Belgrave Square was planned as homes but is now mostly embassies. The four enormous corner mansions, as big as any in London, are occupied by the likes of the Portuguese Ambassador. One unconverted house came on the market a year ago, giving a chance to see just what these enormous places used to be like. The 6-storey house has 21 rooms including a ballroom and the attached mews cottage half a dozen more, plus garage. A price of £3.5m was mentioned – and the place was not even restored. So *Belgrave Square* is unlikely to figure on your shortlist unless you are the envoy of a new and very rich country. It is such embassies which saved the square from decline: since the last war, several dozen 'new' countries have set up shop in London, and all, to the relief of the Grosvenor Estate, needed imposing buildings.

B

North of *Eaton Square* are more mews, on a grander scale this time, with the stucco continuing behind the scenes. The arched entrances cut the mews off from the busy main streets. *Wilton Crescent* is the queen of this corner, its Regency sweep re-faced with stone at the turn of the century. The N end of *Wilton Place* has some rare early, pre-Cubitt brick houses. *Kinnerton St*, leading off, has concealed surprises: it is the entrance to an unusual warren of old and new cottages in mews and courtyards. To the S are some big blocks of purpose-built flats with car parking, then *Motcomb St* with more shops. The succession of mews and terraces continues on past *West Halkin St* back to *Eaton Square*, passing gems like *Grosvenor Cottages*.

The E corner of Belgravia has a cut-off collection of mews and little streets with a village feel, a couple of good pubs and even a general store. Streets like *Groom Place* and *Wilton Mews* have all the Belgravia assets plus a little more atmosphere. The NE corner is dominated by the old St George's Hospital, now at last being redeveloped. A nest of little mews cottages behind it offers more charming, cramped and very desirable homes. To the W, the borough boundary running down *Lowndes* and *Chesham Sts* marks, more or less, the end of the Duke's remit: often referred to as Belgravia, *Lowndes Square* is more properly Knightsbridge. The end of the estate's control is marked.

Among those estate agents active in this area are:

- Best Gapp
- Chesterfields
- Friend & Falcke
- George Trollope & Sons
- Hamptons
- Debenham Tewson
- Knight Frank & Rutley
- Savills
- Aylesfords
- Cluttons
- De Groot Collis
- Harrods Estate Offices
- W A Ellis
- Plaza
- Strutt & Parker

Bethnal Green

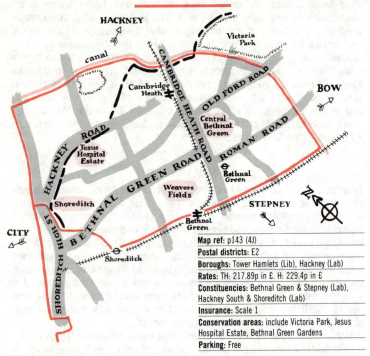

Map ref: p143 (4J)
Postal districts: E2
Boroughs: Tower Hamlets (Lib), Hackney (Lab)
Rates: TH: 217.89p in £. H: 229.4p in £
Constituencies: Bethnal Green & Stepney (Lab), Hackney South & Shoreditch (Lab)
Insurance: Scale 1
Conservation areas: include Victoria Park, Jesus Hospital Estate, Bethnal Green Gardens
Parking: Free

Transport	Tube: Bethnal Green (zone 2, Central); Shoreditch (zone 2, East London Line). From Bethnal Green: Oxford Circus 15 min, City 5 min, Heathrow 1 hr 20 min (1 change). British Rail: Cambridge Heath, Bethnal Green: trains to Liverpool St, Essex and Herts.
Convenient for	The City, Docklands. Miles from centre: 3.
Schools	ILEA Divisions 4 & 5. Daneford School C of E, Morpeth Secondary School C of E, St Bernards Secondary School RC.

Flats	S	1b	2b	3b	4b	5b
Average prices	55–65	55–78	60–110	65–110	–	–
Houses	2b	3b	4b	5b	6/7b	8b
Average prices	90–135	→	100–150	–	–	–

The properties	Two-and 3-bed terraced houses increasingly available, plus new and ex-council flats. Large houses rare. Increasing smaller flats, including the new 'work/homes'. Also now smart, Docklands-style warehouse conversions. Owner occupation rate: low but rising.
The market	Caught in the middle of City's expansion and Docklands regeneration. Bargains to be had so close to both areas – but buy the best as you'll have plenty of competition when selling from all the new developments. Local searches: Tower Hamlets: 4 weeks, Hackney: 16 weeks.

Area Profile

Bethnal Green in London's East End is one of the most cosmopolitan areas of town with almost every race, colour and creed among its inhabitants. A century ago it was the poorest quarter of London. Today it retains a strongly inner-city air, though the population has fallen by two-thirds since the turn of the century.

Docklands, with its booming developments, is a mere mile or so to the S but Bethnal Green's rows of 2-storeyed 1840-60s terraces, interspersed with the Model Dwellings of the Victorian philanthropists and later council-build, remain reasonably priced. Now new flats and dual-purpose work/homes are appearing: watch for names like *City View*, *London Terrace*, *Lion Mills*, *Bowbrook*, *The Minstrels*. The City is just one stop away; City souls even cycle to work. Now locals are getting involved in self-build, with the aid of developers Rosehaugh, and nearby Spitalfields Housing Co-operative is at work on handsome houses.

Bethnal Green lies alongside the City: Hackney lies to the N, Bow to the E, and Stepney to the S. *Cambridge Heath Rd*, *Hackney Rd* and *Bethnal Green Rd* are the three main thoroughfares. Busy *Cambridge Heath Rd* runs from Stepney through to Hackney and includes pretty Bethnal Green Gardens, one of Bethnal Green's four conservation areas, and the Bethnal Green Museum. The Green is the centre of the old village.

Shoreditch, to the W of Bethnal Green, forms the boundary with the city. This area is mainly commercial but there are flats in the Boundary Estate conservation area off *Shoreditch High St*, which includes *Arnold Circus* with its bandstand. The imposing landmark of Shoreditch Church, which houses the impressive St Leonard's Gardens in its grounds, stands on the corner of *Shoreditch High St* which runs S to *Bishopsgate* and Liverpool St Station. *Sclater St*, at the W end of *Bethnal Green Rd*, includes several pet shops and has an animal market every Sunday morning. Shoreditch has long been famous for furniture makers, and their workshops are still much in evidence dotted round the area. A new amenity for the area is a big leisure pool planned as part of the new Whitechapel Rd Shopping Centre. Completion: 1990.

B

Bethnal Green

The Victoria Park conservation area forms part of Bethnal Green's NE boundary; it is edged, on the Bethnal Green side, by the Grand Union Canal: homes in the conservation area with views over canal and park command a premium. *Sewardstone Rd* and *Approach Rd*, where 3- and 4-storey Victorian houses have been converted into flats, are popular but *Cyprus St* is more sought-after. Some of these neat terraced houses, built before the First World War, are grade II listed, with original shuttered windows adding to their tidy appearance. The well-kept Victorian terraced houses have immense character and a plaque, dedicated to the memory of the men of *Cyprus St* who died in two world wars, hangs between Nos 76 and 78. The terrace is continued by the Duke of Wellington pub and further S is the Cranbrook Estate of council homes.

Roman Rd, a busy thoroughfare which runs E into Bow, has more council homes to the S and Meath Gardens, a welcome relief from the blocks of flats. It runs W to *Cambridge Heath Rd*, where Bethnal Green tube station is situated in the splendour of Bethnal Green Gardens, another conservation area. *Victoria Park Square*, behind Bethnal Green Museum, leads to *Sugar Loaf Walk* and then a cluster of close-knit red-brick terrace houses in *Moravian St*, *Gawber St*, *Welwyn St* and *Globe Rd*. Opposite York Hall Baths in *Old Ford Rd* is an imposing Georgian house, part of which has been converted into two flats. Terraced houses, many refurbished, are on either side. Further E down *Old Ford Rd* is *Bonner St* with a row of impressive new council houses.

North along *Cambridge Heath Rd* are more council homes in *Patriot Square*, opposite the town hall, and then Bethnal Green Hospital for Geriatrics. At the junction with *Hackney Rd* is Cambridge Heath BR station and to the NW are some of Bethnal Green's most run-down council flats in *Pritchard's Rd, Coate St, Teale St* and *Emma St*. However, Wharf Place has a canalside warehouse conversion: London Wharf's 2-bed flats are around £90,000.

In complete contrast, the coveted Jesus Hospital Estate is on the S side of *Hackney Rd* and includes *Columbia Rd, Baxendale St, Quilter St, Elwin St, Durant St, Ezra St, Wimbolt St* and *Wellington Row*. These two-up, two-down Victorian terraced houses have trebled in price in recent years. Many have hanging baskets of flowers outside in summer, in keeping with the area which has a flower market in *Columbia Rd* on Sunday mornings.

Bustling *Bethnal Green Rd* has a famous street market but a short stroll to the S is another contrast in *Derbyshire St* where delightful 2- and 3-storey Victorian terraced houses fringe the green space of Weavers Fields. In *Wilmot St*, opposite Hague Primary School, is The Waterlow, a development of a large Victorian terrace converted to studio, 1- and 2-bedroom flats. The project will eventually provide nearly 400 homes including some sheltered homes for the elderly. At the bottom of *Wilmot St*, in *Three Colts Lane*, is Bethnal Green BR.

E along *Bethnal Green Rd*, at the junction with *Punderson's Gardens* and almost opposite Bethnal Green police station, is the City View development. This recently-converted bakery now holds 110 flats and 25 of the new, dual work/home units. *Paradise Row*, where *Bethnal Green Rd* meets *Cambridge Heath Rd*, lives up to its name, with 3- and 4-storey Georgian terraced houses.

Shoreditch

Shoreditch, a stone's throw from the City, is a busy commercial area W of Bethnal Green. Much of the residential property is council-owned and situated around the Boundary Estate conservation area which includes *Palissy St, Rochelle St, Navarre St, Calvert Avenue* and *Montclare St*. These streets contain mostly flats ranged around *Arnold Circus* with its bandstand. *Calvert Avenue* leads W to *Shoreditch High St* and Shoreditch Church, surrounded by the picturesque St Leonard's Gardens. North is the Mildmay Mission Hospital while *Sclater St*, which has an animal market every Sunday morning, is to the S. Shoreditch is bordered to the E by the Bethnal Green part of *Brick Lane* which is densely populated by Asian immigrants in run-down tenement flats. This area is the heart of the Asian garment industry. *Brick Lane* has been home to successive waves of immigrants: a chapel built for protestant Huguenots in the 1740s has been used in succession by Methodists, Jews and now Muslims. Some houses in the street date back to the first decade of the 18th century. It is also just about the only place in London where you can buy bagels all night. Connoisseurs say *Brick Lane's* bagels are London's best.

Among those estate agents active in this area are:
- Alan Selby & Ptnrs
- Cornillie & Co
- John Barber & Mrs Jones
- John Neville & Co
- Land & Co

Bloomsbury and King's Cross

Map ref: p140 (3C)	
Postal districts: WC1, N1	
Boroughs: Camden (Lab), Islington (Lab)	
Rates: C: 211.68p in £. I: 184.33p in £	
Constituencies: Islington South & Finsbury (Lab), Holborn & St Pancras (Lab)	
Insurance: Scale 1	
Conservation areas: Several, check town hall.	
Parking: Residents/meters. Clamps	

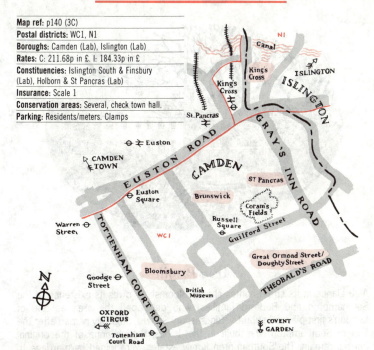

B

Transport   Tubes, all zone 1: Kings Cross (Victoria, Piccadilly, Northern, Metropolitan, Circle); Russell Square (Piccadilly); others see map. From King's Cross: Oxford Circus 8 min, City 15 min, Heathrow 1 hr 10 min. British Rail: King's Cross, St Pancras, Euston.

Convenient for   British Museum, West End. Miles from centre: 1.5.

Schools   ILEA Division 2/3: Sir William Collins, Samuel Dowrey School, Starcross School, Maria Fidelis Convent RC (g).

Flats	S	1b	2b	3b	4b	5b
Average prices	55–80	77–140	95–175	125–230	–	–
Houses	2b	3b	4b	5b	6/7b	8b
Average prices	125–250	150–260+	→	→450	–	–

The properties   Many of Bloomsbury's Georgian and early Victorian houses are now offices. Flats, however, abound in mansion, '30s or more recent blocks. King's Cross has some surprising corners of handsome Victoriana. King's Cross redevelopment will boost area, but is blighting nearest streets.

The market   Young, single people and businessmen find homes here to buy or rent, from student-poor to quiet luxury. King's Cross is the cheaper end of the scale, and scene of much development. Local searches: Islington 2 weeks, Camden 12 weeks.

Area Profile

As a glance at its street-names shows, Bloomsbury owes its existence to the Southampton and Bedford families, who developed the area as one of London's first planned suburbs. Bloomsbury Square, originally named after the Earl of Southampton, was built in the 1660s, though none of the original houses remain. The Southampton family estates were joined by marriage to those of the Russells, the Dukes of Bedford. Add in the Gower who married the 4th Duke and you have a complete gazeteer of Bloomsbury names.

Bloomsbury's early start as a residential area gave it gracious architecture, but fashion left it behind at the end of the last century. Commerce and culture moved in – though the British Museum has been there since 1755. The University of London now takes up large tracts, and there are several hospitals. Many of the surviving Georgian buildings are used as offices. Despite the incursions, much of Bloomsbury retains a pre-19th century air of seedy graciousness. It remains a popular place to live, especially among academics, writers and professional people.

King's Cross, Bloomsbury's neighbour, is the site of London's biggest redevelopment scheme: see below.

But one of Bloomsbury's most striking features – *Bedford Square*, built in the late 18th century and combining creamy stucco facades, Coade stone keystones and other delightful Georgian detailing – is now solely used for commercial purposes. If, that is, 'commercial' is the correct term for the gentlemanly publishing houses gathered here, hoping no doubt to attract a little Bloomsbury Group brilliance.

The most common dwelling in Bloomsbury is the flat, with houses an almost impossible luxury. Studios, 1- and 2-beds are easily obtainable either in purpose-built blocks (mostly from the 1930s) or as new conversions.

The area, for our purposes, is bounded by *Tottenham Court Rd* in the W, the *Farringdon Rd* in the E, *Theobalds Rd* and *New Oxford St* in the S and the *Euston Rd* to the N. This is a larger area than 'traditional' Bloomsbury, taking in streets which are allied to, but not quite part of, the old estate. King's Cross to the NE is also considered here.

Bloomsbury can be divided into four distinct neighbourhoods; St Pancras in the NE, Great Ormond St/Doughty St to the SE, and Brunswick and Bloomsbury to the W. It is almost impossible to find a private house in the area, but those that do exist are mainly in the E, with council and private flats being the norm.

Great Ormond St/Doughty St

Sheltering between the busy main routes of *Southampton Row*, *Guildford St*, *Theobalds Rd* and the *Gray's Inn Rd* is a lovely quiet part of London with wide pedestrian-only streets and an abundance of patisseries, cafés and small boutiques. *Doughty St*, which runs S from *Guildford St*, is most famous for once housing Dickens at No 48. But now the street has few private residents – although the lucky ones have 3- and 4-storey Georgian buildings with attics, mosaic steps and large portals for porches. *John St* is a continuation of *Doughty St* to the S.

Also running S, to the W of *Doughty St*, is *Doughty Mews*, which has a number of small houses with roof gardens above garages and a cobbled road. There is also a '30s block of flats at the junction with *Roger St* called Mytre Court, which is in very good condition and overlooking a primary school. There are a number of other mews in the neighbourhood, but they are used solely for commercial purposes.

Millman St runs S from *Guildford St*, and has a row of modern maisonettes opposite some converted flats in Victorian 3-storey houses. This runs into *Rugby St* which combines shops and offices with very ornate, terraced 4-storey Victorian houses converted into flats. *Lambs Conduit St*, which is partly pedestrianized, is the centrepiece of the area with a new block of flats above the shops at the N end. This links with a conversion of several houses on the corner into flats. The remaining property is shops with flats above. *Dombey St* leads W off *Lambs Conduit St* with houses built in 1884 and quiet courtyards at the back.

Orde Hall St, running north from *Dombey St*, again has 19th century 3/4-storey sand coloured houses decorated with red brick. These have now been converted into flats. *Orde Hall* runs into *Great Ormond St*, which splits the area roughly in half. The W part of this has the hospital, but there are still some 18th century houses scattered either side, with flats at the E end.

St Pancras

Judd St forms the border in the W, and *Guildford St* in the S. A lot of the N part, around *Cromer St* and *Argyle Walk*, has old council buildings from the turn of the century, but with wide open courtyards often decorated with small trees, plants and bright wall paintings.

Judd St runs S from *Euston Rd*, and has some flats above shops and three large blocks of private flats (studios, 1-bed and 2-bed). Continuing S into *Hunter St* there is another large block of 63 apartments (1930). The best homes in this corner are in the S and W: there are some lovely 3-storey houses on *Mecklenburgh Square* (1880). However a few have been converted into flats and there is a purpose-built block, also on the square, facing the open space of

B

Corams Fields. (Coram was a philanthropist who left the land to charity.)

Guildford St has the familiar office and flat developments side by side. But crossing the *Gray's Inn Rd* E into *Calthorpe St* are flats in large 4-storey houses (late 19th century). There is some development work here too and a number of derelict and poorly kept properties. The adjacent *Wren St* has a number of smaller 2-storey houses with white facades and basements. Also in this area on the mostly commercial *Gray's Inn Rd* is an 8-storey purpose-built Mediterranean-looking block of flats, which lies incongruously in its surroundings.

Brunswick

The Brunswick neighbourhood, to the W of St Pancras, is arranged around the busy crossroads at *Tavistock St* and *Marchmont St*, which run W to E and N to S respectively. There are a number of small bookshops, an art gallery, grocers, barbers and fishmongers at this junction, with flats above the shops.

Leigh St runs W to E out of *Marchmont St* and again has a number of converted flats in 3-storey buildings above antique shops and restaurants, with a new development of flats and shops on the corner. *Thanet St* and *Sandwich St* which run N from *Leigh St*, have some small 2-bed houses, and there is a large block of flats on the corner of *Hastings St* and *Thanet St. Leigh St* leads into the elegant crescent of *Cartwright Gardens* which features tennis courts surrounded by hotels. In the S the Brunswick Centre dominates; built around 1970 in a striking stepped pattern, this enterprise encompasses flats, shops and pubs. The hotel district starts here around *Bernard St* and Russell Square tube station. There is very little private housing from here S, except occasional flats above shops. However, *Russell Square* itself has seen a series of recent developments along the southern side. The latest is a £3 million refurbisment of Nos 54-56 as a mix of offices and flats.

Bloomsbury

Bloomsbury covers the rest of the area, W to *Tottenham Court Rd.* Many of the streets in Bloomsbury have purpose-built blocks consisting of studios, 1-, 2- and 3-bed flats. Typical of these blocks, which normally charge service fees ranging from £300-£600 per annum, are Endsleigh Court on *Woburn Place* (60% studios, 30% 1-bed and 10% 2-bed flats) and Russell Court (95% studios, 5% 1-bed).

But there are a number of flats in converted houses in many of the area's quiet backstreets. Running N, off *Store St* is *Ridgmount St*, which has a number of new flats above garages. These are a development of the Bedford Estate, which is still the ground landlord in this area. Further N, the entire block between *Ridgmount* and *Huntley St* is a vast mansion block. N again, several of the mansion blocks are council-owned: Gordon Mansions E and W of *Huntley St* for example. *Chenies St* also has Camden Council-owned mansion flats. *Store St* has flats over shops. *Chenies Mews* is part residential with a mansion block and the back gardens of *Gower St*. The N end of the mews is light industrial, with hospital and college premises. Three of the mews buildings are being redeveloped. At the N end of *Huntley St* a row of flat-fronted 3-storey houses are converted into flats.

Chenies St runs E into *Gower St*. The buildings in this busy road are mostly early 19th century and are now used as hotels or for commercial or university purposes, with a few rather run-down flats. The hotels have a period air: notices proudly announce their possession of central heating, which must puzzle foreigners. One of the quieter streets in the neighbourhood is *Gower Mews*, with Gower Mews Mansions, small '30s flats above garages. And S of here is *Bedford Square*, which is nearly all commercial – though 19 new flats were created behind an original facade in 1987. But *Adeline Place* and *Bedford Avenue*, which run directly off it, have Bedford Court: blocks of well-appointed 1900-vintage flats. Penthouses have been added to these in recent years.

King's Cross

The massive scheme to develop the land N of King's Cross and St Pancras Stations has become clear. The 200 acres will become a major new London neighbourhood, with everything from a deep-level British Rail station serving the Channel Tunnel to a new park. Around 1,400 homes feature in the plans alongside shops and offices. Work is scheduled to start in the summer of 1990. The area extends N over the canal as far as the E-W railway at Camden Town.

King's Cross is already a surprise: the area around one of the larger rail termini is a blend of commercial and small business premises, with a scattering of residential property. Last year a tidying-up was evident: now the spotlight is firmly on the area and worries about the side-effects of the development conflict with anticipation of its benefits.

B

There are some delightful roads in the neighbourhood, including *Swinton St* in the S and quiet backwaters like *Keystone Crescent* and *Balfe St* off the *Caledonian Rd*. Both streets will be affected by the proposed cut-and-cover rail tunnel which forms part of the giant King's Cross scheme. One draft plan involved demolition of houses, but the alignment has been changed in the latest plan and the houses should survive.

Their greatest advantage is of course their extraordinary convenience. Apart from King's Cross BR, St Pancras is next door, Euston station down the road. You can stroll to the City. King's Cross also runs Oxford Circus a close second as the single most useful tube station on the entire network: the Northern, the splendid Victoria, the Circle, the Piccadilly (direct to Heathrow) and even the Metropolitan lines pass through here. By the late 1990s, trains will take you straight to Paris.

Across the Grand Union Canal which acts as the northern boundary lie the select realms of Barnsbury and Islington. The other boundaries are formed by *St Pancras Rd* to the W and *Calshot St* to the E. The southernmost part infringes the Borough of Camden ending at *Argyle St* and *Swinton St*.

Because the council is reluctant (unlike Hackney) to stop developers from splitting up houses into 2-bedroom units, anything like a 3-bedroomed flat or 4-bedroomed house is now extremely rare. But 2-bedroomed houses and small flats predominate with new conversions constantly under way.

To spot them in time, though, requires a careful watching brief. Not many estate agents at any given time have properties on their books in King's Cross because of the shortage of private houses and flats.

The best houses tend to be in small, secluded groups and can surprise with the quality of their architecture. *Northdown St* has little flat-fronted Victorian houses and modern replicas. *Balfe St's* 3-storey houses have been well converted into 1-bed flats behind the early Victorian facade. This street also has some modern homes. *Keystone Crescent*'s curve is echoed in the rounded windows of its pretty 2-storey houses. These streets apart, most of the King's Cross station hinterland combines flats above shops, commercial property and council flats like the Derby Lodge estate on *Britannia St*.

The *Caledonian Rd* runs S-W to King's Cross and splits the area into two, with most of the residential property on the S-E side. The road has a number of converted flats and flats above shops – almost exclusively studios and 1-bedroomed – with many in a poor state of repair.

The southern part of *Northdown Rd* runs S from the *Caledonian Rd* and features a major development of mostly 1-bed flats with original facade intact. And the northern part over the *Caledonian Rd* has 2-bed houses dating from 1845. This is probably one of the nicest streets in the area. *Balfe St* runs south from *Wharfdale Rd* and is similar to *Northdown Rd* with recently modernised flats and some small houses.

Other areas of small 2-bed houses include those of *Southern St*. There is a new 14-flat conversion on the *Kings Cross Rd* by Tilbury and a number of 3-storey Victorian houses clustered at the bottom end of *Wicklow St*, which look to be in good condition.

There is also a new development across the canal at *Thornhill Bridge Wharf* (see also Islington) which epitomises the new breed moving into the area – young couples without children. The northern part of the *Gray's Inn Rd* is mostly commercial with a few flats above offices. But the area bounded by *Argyle St*, *Gray's Inn Rd* and *Euston Rd* is dominated by the Birkenhead Estate which is a complex of seven 1960s blocks. The remaining property is a mixture of private 3-storey Victorian houses (some split into flats), bed-and-breakfast establishments and private hotels.

The railway lands redevelopment has already pushed up prices – but anyone living here has got to be ready for several years of disruption.

Among those estate agents active in this area are:

- Aspen
- Batty Stevens Good
- Copping Joyce
- Debenham Tewson & Chinnocks
- McHugh & Co
- Salter Rex
- Bairstow Eves
- Browett Taylor
- Cornillie & Co
- Ideal Homes
- Prudential Property Services

Bow

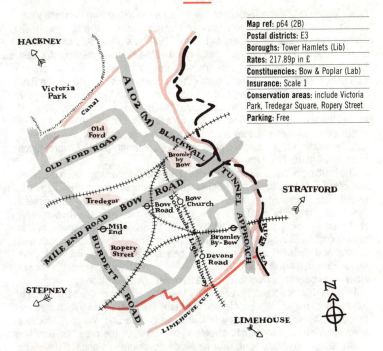

Map ref: p64 (2B)	
Postal districts: E3	
Boroughs: Tower Hamlets (Lib)	
Rates: 217.89p in £	
Constituencies: Bow & Poplar (Lab)	
Insurance: Scale 1	
Conservation areas: include Victoria Park, Tredegar Square, Ropery Street	
Parking: Free	

B

Transport Tubes: Mile End (zone 2, Central, Metropolitan, District), Bow Rd, Bromley-by-Bow (zone 3a, Metropolitan, District). From Mile End: Oxford Circus 20 min, City 10 min, Heathrow 75 min (1 change). Docklands Light Railway: links to Stratford, Tower, Isle of Dogs.

Convenient for City and Docklands, East Cross Motorway route and Blackwall Tunnel. Miles from centre: 4.5.

Schools ILEA Division 5: Central Foundation Girls, St Paul's Way, Bow boys.

Flats	S	1b	2b	3b	4b	5b
Average prices	48–65	55–75	60–105	70–100	–	–
Houses	2b	3b	4b	5b	6/7b	8b
Average prices	90–140	100–180	110–200+	150–250	→	–

The properties Bow's Georgian glories, among the many 2-/3-bed terraced houses, have long since been rediscovered. Tredegar, CVOBORN, Rhondda, Chisenhale, Campbell are names to watch for. Away from quarter-million Georgian, there are still no-bath houses for the DIY man. Many new developments; but the most important is Kentish's conversion of the Bryant & May factory: 700 homes at good prices.

The market Owner-occupation is higher than other parts of Tower Hamlets, and rising in this increasingly popular East End heartland. High demand for the best properties, mainly N of Bow Rd. Local searches: 4 wks.

Area Profile

Bow's Victoria Park and *Tredegar Square* have been well known for some years as places where fine houses can be bought for a lot less than their counterparts in smarter corners of London. 1988 saw a veritable boom in the provision of new homes at the cheaper end of the scale, cementing this East End heartland's status as a residential area attracting locals to owner-occupation as well as 'refugees' from other, pricier, areas of London. The Bow Quarter, the grand re-naming and re-building of a giant Victorian factory, will add 700 homes to the local stock. Other major schemes, now at hole-in-the-ground stage, will bring close on a thousand more, and hundreds of existing council-owned homes are set for rehabilitation. The new developments include homes with work-space attached, an increasingly popular hybrid much in evidence in the East End.

The building boom is taking place in an area which has always been the tidier end of the East End, but is still a widely varying mixture of gaunt council towers, ostentatious Victorian terraces, industry, railway tracks and street markets. Residential property in Bow is not grouped in tidy neighbourhoods, it is scattered in pockets between all the other things jostling for space in this crowded corner. Typical Inner London, in fact. Transport is fairly good, with Central and District Line tubes and the new Docklands Light Railway for the rapidly-growing north-south traffic: Bow, like much of the rest of Tower Hamlets, is benefiting from its new role as hinterland to Docklands.

Bow, as described here, is essentially the E3 postal district, but the name is used rather sporadically. People who live in the Tredegar conservation area are proud to say so, others nearby talk of living in Mile End. Victoria Park is a prestigious name attached to streets in the north of the area, while in the south, along Limehouse Cut, new canalside developments annexe the name Limehouse, made smart by Docklands. Of the old village of Bow, a crossing place over the River Lea, virtually nothing survives except the name.

The Lea Valley, to the E of Bow, is earmarked for major housing development in a Government study which sets out to spot the places where London's new homes can be built. This sprawling floodplain at present holds industry, gasworks, railways and sundry waterways. The name of Rosehaugh, ubiquitous developer of wide inner London spaces, has been mentioned, in conjunction with Tower Hamlets council, to handle the regeneration of all of 650 acres.

Tredegar Square

Tredegar Square, N of the busy *Bow Rd* and within a stone's throw of the busy Mile End tube station, is the pride of the East London property market. This delightful Georgian garden square is another conservation area and boasts the area's most impressive – and expensive – houses, some of which have 5 or 6 bedrooms. It also boasts seven new ones, just built, with basement flats. But these, tucked on the corner, don't disrupt the unbroken Georgiana overlooking the central gardens. For one of the smaller, 3-bed originals you might have to pay a quarter-million.

The *Square* is the centrepiece of a conservation area which includes *Lichfield Rd*, *Alloway Rd*, *Aberavon Rd*, *Rhondda Grove*, *Tredegar Terrace*, *College Terrace* and *Coborn Rd*. Sometimes referred to by estate agents as Mile End village, the area is made even more distinctive by its blue lamp posts in keeping with the period. In *Coborn St*, Tredegar Villas, a recent development of 2-bedroom terraced houses, and flats built around a central courtyard, were carefully built in a similar style to neighbouring houses, with capped iron railings, brick arches over front doors, etc. Morgan St, too, has new houses appearing.

At the S end of *Aberavon Rd*, almost opposite Mile End tube station and on the site of the old cinema, is *Eaton Terrace*, a row of new luxury 4-storey houses with ornamental pillars at each entrance.

South of Victoria Park

Over the railway line, N of the *Tredegar Square* conservation area, are the popular 2-storey bay-fronted Victorian houses of *Antill Rd*, *Strahan Rd*, *Lyal Rd* and *Medway Rd*. In nearby *Arbery Rd* is the award-winning development of *School Bell Mews*, a converted school that provides a perfect setting for new flats and houses. Three-storey Victorian properties, some of which have been converted into flats, in *Old Ford Rd* and *Chisenhale Rd* are made more appealing by backing onto the canal. Victoria Park, which divides Bow and Hackney, is one of the largest parks in London. It was laid out in the 1840s and has several lakes as well as the canal. This at present has rather a sad aspect, being short of water. But this is due to work on a 4-acre site to the S which is being redeveloped in a big way. It runs from *Parnell Rd* in the E to *Gunmakers Lane* in the W. Assured Developments have an ambitious plan to refurbish close on 400 existing council tower-block and low-build homes and build nearly 500 new homes. Victoria Park is just across the canal to the N.

B

The canal runs along Victoria Park's S border to *Cadogan Terrace*, near Bow's E boundary. Three-storey Victorian properties in *Cadogan Terrace*, overlooking the park, command a premium although parking in this road can be a problem. The East Cross route is just behind. The Hermitage, a new development of flats and houses in *Wrexham Rd*, behind Bow bus garage, is appealing despite being so close to the East Cross Route motorway which leads to Blackwall Tunnel to the S and Hackney and Leyton to the N. *Brymay Close*, one of The Hermitage streets, is named after the old Bryant and May match factory nearby. The factory is itself being developed by Kentish Homes into nearly 700 new flats around landscaped, fountain-filled squares. It will boast two swimming pools and a sports complex. This extraordinary old factory is vast, stretching back over 6 acres from *Fairfield Rd*. It will create its own environment, and give a considerable boost to the area. There is a lot of local excitement for Keith Preston's scheme – not least for his pricing policy: from £60-105,000. No yuppie ghetto, this. Also in *Fairfield Rd* is a Tillbury Homes development of 12 2/4-bedroom houses.

In *Tredegar Rd* is Yallops Yard, the site Prince Charles was seen knocking down on television last year. An archaeological dig held up progress last autumn, but 180-odd houses and flats are forecast, some for sale, some for shared ownership, some to let. Along *Bow Rd*, which is part of the main route E to Stratford, there are some handsome early Victorian and Georgian houses. One site on the N side has planning permission for 40 flats behind a reproduction facade. A conversion of an existing building will produce 200 flats close to the Town Hall – and opposite the Bow Bells pub.

Red brick bay-fronted houses in *Baldock St*, *Ridgdale St* and *Jebb St* lead to Grove Hall Park with its children's playground and football pitch.

Bow Church

Bow Police station, which has stables for horses, is on the opposite side of *Bow Rd* to the *Tomlin's Grove* conservation area where steps lead up to the 2-storey Victorian houses, some with attic rooms. The new Docklands Light Railway station of Bow Church stands on the corner of *Campbell Rd*, part of which falls within the conservation area. *Ropery St*, another conservation area, lies S of *Bow Rd* and E of *Burdett Rd*, has Victorian terraced houses as do *Mossford*, *Maritime* and *Lockhart Sts*.

Cantrell Rd, lined with scrap merchants' yards, leads E under the railway to the Lincoln Estate which includes council flats and houses in *Rounton Rd*, part of *Campbell Rd*, *Devons Rd*, *Blackthorne* and *Whitethorn Sts*, *Tidey St*, *Bow Common Lane*, *Fern St* and *Swaton*, *Spanby*, *Fairfoot* and *Knapp Rds*. These are some of Bow's less desirable properties and, similarly, the Coventry Cross council estate, on either side of the East Cross Route motorway, is far from appealing. The Coventry Cross estate includes *Devas St*, *Brickfield Rd*, *Empson St* and *St Leonard's St*. A large tract of land beside the DLR between the Limehouse Cut and *Devons Rd* has been recently designated residential. No news yet, but an area to watch. The canal is the focus for several work/home schemes, including Enterprise Works, in *Hawgood St*, a scheme where houses and flats include their own workspaces. This is an increasingly popular idea across town, but particularly this end of it. See also the Poplar and Limehouse chapter. Off *St Paul's Way*, 27 3-storey houses are planned, while flats are proposed for the Way itself.

Between the Blackwall Tunnel approach road and River Lea is Bow's fifth conservation area, situated in *Three Mills Lane* behind the giant Tesco's supermarket. Here there are facilities for weight training, floodlight football and fishing along the River Lea towpaths.

Among those estate agents active in this area are:
- Alan Selby & Ptnrs
- Anthony Gover
- Cornillie & Co
- John Barber & Mrs Jones
- John Neville & Co

Brixton

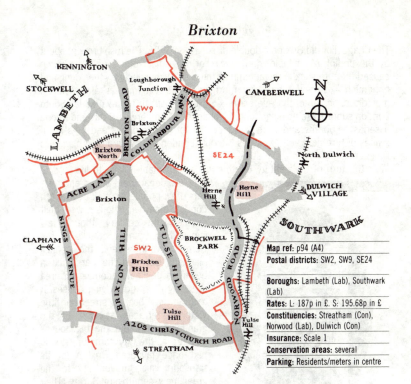

Map ref: p94 (A4)
Postal districts: SW2, SW9, SE24
Boroughs: Lambeth (Lab), Southwark (Lab)
Rates: L: 187p in £. S: 195.68p in £
Constituencies: Streatham (Con), Norwood (Lab), Dulwich (Con)
Insurance: Scale 1
Conservation areas: several
Parking: Residents/meters in centre

B

Transport Tubes: Brixton (zone 2, Victoria), to Oxford Circus 15 min, City 20 min (1 change), Heathrow 1 hr 10 min (1 change). British Rail: Brixton to Victoria 10 min; Herne Hill to Victoria, Holborn Viaduct, Tulse Hill to London Bridge, Holborn Viaduct. Both on Thameslink.

Convenient for Victoria BR, South Circular Rd, A23/M23 for Gatwick Airport and Brighton. Miles from centre: 3.5.

Schools ILEA zones 8/9: Dick Sheppard; Tulse Hill (b). Private: Streatham Hill & Clapham High School (g).

Flats	S	1b	2b	3b	4b	5b
Average prices	46–59	55–72	68–85	75–95	90–125	–
Houses	2b	3b	4b	5b	6/7b	8b
Average prices	85–120	95–135	105–160+	115–180+	130+	→

The properties Wide range in Brixton: rows of Victorian houses – some of real quality. Also lots of council-build – ditto. Flats are conversions; some '30s blocks. Tulse and Herne Hills have Victorian-'30s family homes, often in quiet streets. 3-bed flats converted from roomy Edwardian houses can have larger rooms than p/b 3-bed houses.

The market Young people move here to swap flats in pricier areas for roomy houses. Brixton prices are slightly cheaper; gap widens as size increases: Herne/Tulse houses range higher, esp. near stations. Local searches: Lambeth 10 weeks, Southwark 8-12 weeks.

Area Profile

The Chancellor did Brixton a double disservice in 1988. The rush brought about by the ending of multiple mortgage relief drove flats prices up – and then caused them to stick in the autumn as the area's likely buyers – the young and bohemian – were hit by rising mortgage rates. Brixton has always led a melodramatic, larger-than-life existence. Not content to be a workaday South London suburb, like its neighbours Clapham and Camberwell, it has undergone a series of booms and busts, a succession of rags-to-riches and rags again swings of fortune. Even today, it's the only London area with a blue plaque to Dan Leno.

At the turn of the century Brixton was a fashionable place to live and to shop. Its department stores and markets drew people from all over South London. Many large houses were built in the 19th century, though few survived the pincer attacks of the German bombers and the council planners. Between the wars Brixton began to decline, becoming an area of seedy flats and lodging houses. It had, and still has, its streets of little Victorian terraces as well as the grander homes. But the big houses suffered as the City commuters, who had once favoured Brixton for its transport links, moved out to the green new suburbs of Surrey. Their place was taken by a transient population; the latest and most permanent (and noticeable) wave being the West Indian immigrants of the '50s and '60s. Melodrama reasserted itself in Brixton once more as street life, local politics and rhetoric took on a distinctly Jamaican tone. Many of the West Indian families settled down in Brixton, and the third generation of black Londoners is now in its teens.

Brixton's most prosperous period was the mid-Victorian, when houses of all sizes were built, many with interesting detailing such as this elaborate porch and balcony. The carved leaves are typical. Stone or brick in contrasting colours was used for details, with stock brick and/or stucco for the walls themselves, the whole under a slate roof behind, in this street, a large gable.

Brixton today is cautiously enjoying one of its upswings. Things got pretty low in the early '80s, with well-publicised riots, a theatrically entertaining, well-meaning but inept council and heated words (and deeds) between locals and the police. But sense reasserts itself quickly in Brixton. Violence seems less likely and cooperation, even between police and council, more evident. The council is in constructive rather than confrontational mode.

But a crucial component in the Brixton revival is its discovery by would-be home-buyers. It forms one of the last areas of cheap, unconverted housing in Inner London. The seductive charms of a proper house, with room to move, are not lost on cramped flat-dwellers in more fashionable areas. The incomers are viewed with some alarm by the council, who say with reason that as house prices go up, key workers such as teachers and nurses are priced out.

Whatever the fears of its elected leaders, Brixton is responding to the market-place. The homes market got very brisk in 1987 and roared on through the first half of '88, till the curtailing of mortgage relief and rising interest rates dampened the market. Initially some sellers found it hard to entice prospective buyers into the area. It is the sort of place you have to visit, to spend time in, to get to know – before you buy. There are many minus points: the uneasy history of racial tension, the high crime rate, the very many ugly modern estates, some seedy and depressing streets. The plus points include a really friendly atmosphere: racial tension in the abstract never seems to affect day-to-day street life. The Victoria Line tube is a major plus, as is the bustling, cheerful atmosphere of the town centre.

And it is a proper centre – not, as with so much of South London, a shapeless grey sprawl. The imposing Town Hall looks out from the corner of *Coldharbour Lane* and *Brixton Hill* over a wide green triangle, with St Matthews (church turned community centre) as its focal point. The triangle's apex points N, to the high street shops of *Brixton Rd* and the famous market. By the station is the new leisure centre; there are lots of good sports facilities in the area (not to mention the popular ice rink in neighbouring Streatham). Nightlife includes independent cinemas, clubs like the renowned Fridge, even a Brasserie, and an up-market restaurant in *Trinity Gardens*. And there's the pleasant expanse of Brockwell Park with its swimming pool and running track, scene of such community festivals as the annual Lambeth Show.

Plenty of people live in Brixton by choice, plenty more by necessity. It is a lively (only occasionally too lively) and entertaining place. Some say hopefully that it could become the Left Bank of London. Others fear it is doomed to be forever peripheral, a place for people who can't afford to be elsewhere.

The image of Brixton as the centre of London's Afro-Caribbean life is true enough, but that is only one side of Brixton's personality. Black people make up less than a third of the residents. Whites are the biggest single group, but these broad figures conceal a place where everyone is a minority, where there are communities of Chileans and Chinese, City workers and anarchist squatters. In Brixton you will never be bored.

The Post Office confuses the geography of Brixton considerably. It is often thought that Brixton equals SW2, but a glance at the map shows that Brixton station, and most of the town centre, lies in SW9, while SW2 takes in the positively suburban swathes of Streatham Hill as well as Acre Lane. Much of *Railton Road*, the melodramatically-named 'Front Line' street where police/black tension is highest, is in SE24 – a district known more for the solid respectability of Herne Hill. And chunks of West Brixton stray into SW4.

House prices in Brixton have been rapidly catching up with those in the more desirable districts south of the river. Prices rose by 25 per cent in 1986, compared to the London average of 21 per cent, and kept pace last year. There are now few 'cheap' areas in Brixton, although properties east of the town centre near the notorious *Railton Rd* can sell at a marginally lower price than the average.

There are several conservation areas in Brixton protecting districts of outstanding architectural quality. Properties in these streets command a premium. Examples are Angell Town, Loughborough Park and Trinity Gardens.

Studio and 4- or 5-bed flats are rare, there are few 2-bed or 8-bed-plus houses in Brixton. Lambeth Council has tight controls on house conversions to maintain as much accommodation suitable for families as possible. Developers

B

are under pressure to provide at least one three-bedroom flat in each converted property. In some neighbourhoods such flats can offer better proportions than either purpose-built 3-bed flats or some 3-bed houses in this area – they sell at a premium, especially when they also include a garden.

This area has become increasingly popular with young people, who are mainly first-time buyers with parental backing, or buying together with one or two friends. Two-bed flats and 2-, 3- and 4-bed houses, preferably with period features, are most popular. The most desirable homes lie just off either side of *Brixton Hill*, handy for the frequent bus services to the town centre, the tube and central London. There are however pockets of interesting houses all over Brixton, though their surroundings can sometimes be on the grim side.

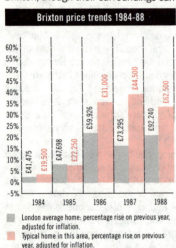

Brixton price trends 1984-88

£41,475 £19,500 £47,698 £22,250 £59,926 £31,000 £73,295 £44,500 £92,240 £62,500

- London average home: percentage rise on previous year, adjusted for inflation.
- Typical home in this area, percentage rise on previous year, adjusted for inflation.

One-bed purpose built flat close to the centre, price change compared to London-wide average home. This flat shows one of the biggest price leaps this year, reflecting the buoyant market for flats in spring and summer of '88 caused by the Budget mortgage tax changes. And, of course, by the steady rehabilitation of Brixton.

Acre Lane is a broad, busy street linking the centre of Brixton with Clapham. The neighbourhood to the N, bounded by *Bedford Rd* to the W, *Ferndale Rd* to the N and *Brixton Rd* to the E consists of small 3- and 4-bed houses and larger 3- and 4-storey Victorian ones, many converted into flats. The W side of the neighbourhood, including the W half of *Ferndale Rd*, is in SW4 and has aspirations to be Clapham. Indeed, many of these streets are closer to Clapham North tube than they are to Brixton. *Ferndale Rd* is wide and busy and backs onto a railway line. Good-sized 3-storey Victorian terraces predominate, getting bigger still at the W end, as they do on the parallel - *Sandmere Rd*. The railway N of *Ferndale* is a busy one, taking the Dover trains into Victoria and carrying a lot of goods traffic. When the Channel Tunnel opens this will be part of the route from it to the new terminal at Waterloo. *Tintern St* is mainly small 3-bed flat-fronted Victorian terraces as are *Ducie St*, *Medwin St* and *Allardyce St*. *Ducie St* has unusual gothic-style houses with pointed arched doorways and windows and decorative brickwork. *Plato* and *Solon Rds* are similarly terraced, though less interesting architecturally. Many of these houses have been split into two or more flats. The quality of the conversions varies considerably.

The showpiece of the neighbourhood is *Trinity Gardens*, a Regency square of cottages tucked away behind *Acre Lane* and close to Brixton centre.

Southwest Brixton

South of *Acre Lane*, across to *Lyham Rd* in the W, *Brixton Hill* in the E and Windmill Gardens to the S lies a mixture of large Victorian houses, Edwardian maisonettes and inter-war semis. The land rises gently towards the S, where a carefully-preserved windmill stands in a small park. Beyond again is Brixton Prison. All this is SW2. It is one of the quietest, least remarkable parts of Brixton. To its W is Clapham Park, and some estate agents have taken to using this name for the *Lyham Rd* corner. *Lyham Rd* branches off *Kings Avenue*. Streets of small Victorian terraces – *Kildoran, Margate, Mauleverer Rds* – run off to the E. Going S, *Lyham* has council homes on both sides, with the spreading low-rise *Ramilles Close* estate running up to the windmill. *Lyham* then has some pretty flat-fronted brick cottages, followed by the back wall of Brixton Prison, which is less overwhelming than some prisons one could mention.

South of the prison, *Dumbarton Rd* has 1914-ish purpose-built flats, 2-storey terraces with gables and fancy porches. Some of those on the N side of the road back onto the prison. *Doverfield Rd* has similar flats, while *Felsberg Rd* has more – this time with an arts-and-crafts air. Dumbarton Court, a big block of inter-war flats, runs round onto *Brixton Hill*. *New Park Road* has a neat parade of shops. This district is quite high up, and some homes in these peaceful, hilly streets have good views to the N and W. It is convenient for the buses that run down *Brixton Hill* to the tube station, and for Streatham's shops.

East of *Kings Avenue* in the furthest S-W corner of the neighbourhood lie more streets of small 3-bed Victorian terraced houses. *Rosebery Rd, Thornbury Rd, Wingford Rd* and *Kingswood Rd* are typical of this area of clean, narrow streets full of family housing. There are relatively few conversions here. Nearby Windmill Gardens and the sports ground provide a welcome bit of greenery.

Back down the hill to the N, in the angle between *Brixton Hill* and *Acre Lane*, another grid of streets is almost cut off from those off *Lyham Rd* described above. *Hayter Rd* is typical, with large 3-storey double-fronted Victorian houses, many converted to flats, and eight very large 6-bed-plus 4-storey detached Victorian houses have recently been converted. *Bonham Rd, Lambert Rd* and the tree-lined *Haycroft Rd* follow a similar pattern. *Baytree Rd* in the N is a good example of suburban-type inter-war semi-detached housing, a quiet leafy street yet close to Brixton centre.

B

Brixton Hill

The biggest concentration of desirable properties in Brixton lies to the E of *Brixton Hill* around the *Brixton Water Lane* conservation area. In *Josephine Avenue* and *Helix Gardens*, a fully modernised large, 3-storey Victorian terraced house with 75 ft of garden frontage reaches the market at about £220,000. These grandly curving, leafy streets were spaciously planned by their Victorian builders, and they have been the subject of a highly successful community architecture scheme. The long front gardens have been reclaimed from the dumped-car-dotted wastelands they had become. New reproduction railings, improved street lighting, car parking spaces – it's all been done and has made a dramatic difference. The houses are 3-storey and quite wide. They make spacious family homes but many are flats.

The nearby loop of *Appach Rd* is made up of small 3-bed Victorian terraces, with some charming two-storey double-fronted houses on one side. Many houses in this area have retained their original period features such as marble fireplaces and ornate ceilings and picture rails.

Brixton Water Lane itself is busy, but has some of the area's most charming homes. A Georgian farmhouse, a few similar-period cottages – and all with Brockwell Park close by. The enclave of *Brailsford* and *Arlingford Rds* has big Victorian houses, some converted to flats. A quiet corner, and the homes on the E side of *Brailsford* back onto the Park.

The area further S, between *Brixton Hill* to the W and *Tulse Hill* to the E, is disputed between the neighbourhoods named for both those roads. One patch that does belong to Brixton Hill is *Holmewood Gardens*.

Holmewood Rd, which runs E from *Brixton Hill*, is a wide road of rather ordinary Victorian terraced brick and stucco houses. But it leads into surprising *Holmewood Gardens*, where the same terraces suddenly open out to surround an irregular green. The road is wide, the general effect spacious and cut-off. *Maplestead Rd*, running off to the E, has similar houses. E of here is covered under Tulse Hill below.

Upper Tulse Hill winds across these slopes, with its E end in Tulse Hill, while to the W are a mixture of big mid-Victorian detached houses (now flats), 1920s terraced homes, and council blocks. Tree-lined *Athlone Rd*, which runs off to the E, has '20s terraced homes, square-bayed. The neat, cared-for atmosphere is maintained in *Elm Park* where topiary features in one front garden. *Claverdale Rd* is more Edwardian. Further down *Elm Park* is a mix of Victorian homes of varying sizes, some flat-fronted ones being quite attractive. *Elm Park* meets *Brixton Hill* opposite the prison entrance. On the *Hill* here is Tudor Close, a large block of '30s flats.

Somers Rd leads, somewhat unpromisingly, into the unexpected, hidden corner of *Archbishop's Place* with its pretty little early-Victorian semi-detached 2-bed cottages. The Place is a cul-de-sac, with a few of the cottages tucked down paths at the end. *Brading Rd* has more ordinary Victorian houses. *Upper Tulse Hill* nearby, at the junction with *Ostade Rd*, has pairs of pretty early-Victorian villas facing mock-Tudor inter-wars terraced homes.

Central Brixton

Central Brixton is mostly shops, offices, railways and council flats. There are pockets of private housing, though. South of *Coldharbour Lane* to *Morval Rd* and between *Effra Rd* W and *Railton Rd* E are streets of 2- and 3-storey Victorian housing. North of *Coldharbour Lane*, a new development of studio, 1- and 2-bedroom flats is expected in spring '89.

North of the railway that divides Brixton in two are some streets of 3- to 4-storey Victorian housing between *Dalyell Rd* and busy *Stockwell Rd*. Between *Stockwell* and *Brixton Rds* is a triangle of council homes, with Stockwell to the N. *Brixton Rd* was once lined with solid early-Victorian houses, and some still survive, though many are in commercial use.

East Brixton

East of the centre are neighbourhoods that have been changed most by Brixton's unruly past. Railways, abortive motorway schemes, the Blitz and the council between them have virtually destroyed what were once two smart Victorian suburbs, Loughborough Park and Angell Town. *Loughborough Park*, the road, survives in part, wide and leafy, with pairs of Victorian villas of varying sizes. There is a small park, then a modern low-rise council estate off *Moorland Rd*. Here too there are some cream stucco Victorian villas that would be worth a million each in St John's Wood. The giant reversed ziggurat council slab of Clarewood Walk, S of *Coldharbour Lane*, makes more sense when you realise it was designed to turn its back on an eight-lane highway, planned but never built.

North of the railway, the street pattern is that of the mid-19th century Angell Town estate, but most of the buildings are '60s council flats. A few Victorian homes survive in *Villa Rd*: a tall, rather run-down terrace. Lambeth Council is restoring some more original Angell Town detached double-fronted houses in *St John's Crescent*. *Vassall Rd* in the extreme N of the area has some handsome early-Victorian terraced homes.

Many houses in this part of Brixton are owned by, even if not built by, the council. Lambeth is a reluctant seller, even under the Right to Buy laws, but some of these surviving period homes will probably find their way onto the market eventually.

Brixton/Herne Hill Borders

Railton Rd has one of the worst reputations in Brixton. At the N end, where it runs into *Atlantic Rd*, it to a large extent deserves it. But further S there is a grid of pleasant streets between *Railton* and *Dulwich Rds*. With the inevitability of estate agents, these roads, each named after a literary giant, have been dubbed the Poets estate (London has several other such).

B

Despite its position, Poet's Corner, as the area between *Dulwich Rd* S and *Railton Rd* N is alternatively known, is highly desirable, residents seemingly ignoring its proximity to the riot 'front-line' of *Railton Rd*. Indeed one could be miles away from trouble of any sort in these tree-lined, well-cared-for streets. It is a short walk from the town centre and borders on to Brockwell Park in the S. The Victorian houses here were built on spec for letting. They are much sought-after for each one is largely unique – they were purpose built and architect designed – most are detached 3, 4- and 5-bed houses.

Most of the streets are short and homogenous, but *Shakespeare* runs on E beyond *Railton Rd* and the railway. This eastern section is decidedly scruffier than the 'poets' bit, with a single row of houses facing wasteland, depots and a railway.

Herne Hill and Tulse Hill

South of Brixton are two more areas with subtly different personalities. Their boundaries with Brixton are hard to define, but once in the centres of either Herne Hill or Tulse Hill you will know you are in another place. The bustle of Brixton is lacking, and some streets, especially in Herne Hill, have a solidly suburban feel. Another difference is the lack of a tube – though if London Transport get their way there will be one – one day. Both places have British Rail stations on the new Thameslink line, with trains to Blackfriars and Kings Cross.

House prices are similar to those in Brixton, though Tulse Hill is slightly less desirable than Herne Hill because of the latter's border with expensive and fashionable Dulwich. Both districts are convenient for Brockwell Park. Large 3-storey Victorian houses are very common, though most are being converted into flats. They are popular because they are spacious and full of character. One- and 2-bed flats find ready first-time buyers, while the young couples who inhabit the smaller 2-and 3-bed houses move on to the roomy 4- and 5-bed houses when the children come along.

The smaller 2- and 3-bed Victorian houses and Edwardian maisonettes are largely concentrated in Tulse Hill, while the larger family housing of 4- and 5-beds plus is more characteristic of Herne Hill – particularly along *Norwood Rd* facing Brockwell Park and in the streets running directly off *Herne Hill* and *Half Moon Lane*.

Tulse Hill

Along *Tulse Hill* S from *Brixton Water Lane* council housing gives way to private properties on the E side at *Craignair Rd* and the W side at *Trinity Rise*. Properties are a mixture of inter-war semis, some with mock Tudor fronts and smaller 3-bed Victorian houses.

Inter-war semis line *Craignair Rd* and *Claverdale Rd*, giving way to small 3-bed Victorian houses at the W end. *Trinity Rise* comprises 4-bed Edwardian houses and inter-war semis, leading to the very desirable *Brockwell Park Gardens*, 3-bed Victorian terraces overlooking the park. *Deronda Rd*, *Deerbrook Rd* and *Romola Rd* contain semi-detached and detached Victorian houses with 4-, 5- and 6-beds. Going W, *Upper Tulse Hill* is mostly council housing, some of the more attractive in this part of London. Some of these homes, and some on nearby *Tulse Hill*, are starting to come onto the open markets as former tenants sell. *Tulse Hill* is a good place to look for the now-fashionable 'Art Deco' 30s houses with flat roofs and steel windows.

Herne Hill

Brockwell Park, a wide sweep of grassy hill surrounding a Victorian mansion, edges Herne Hill to the W. To the N-W is the 'poets' district on the borders with Brixton (which see). A railway line from Herne Hill station N to Loughborough Junction forms a barrier against Brixton. The ground rises to the E of this line, forming a pleasant quarter of solid red-brick houses between *Herne Hill* and *Milkwood Rd* and the railway. The area consists of predominantly Victorian and Edwardian 3- and 4-bed houses as in *Kestrel Avenue*, *Gubyon Avenue*, *Shardcroft Avenue* and *Woodquest Avenue* and larger double-fronted Victorian and Edwardian houses as in *Rollscourt Avenue* and *Fawnbrake Avenue*. Some are handsome examples of their period, some have good views, and all are well-placed for the station and shops.

There is a mixture of housing types strung along *Herne Hill*, from very large Victorian and Edwardian detached and semi-detached houses and inter-war detached and semi-detached housing to mansion blocks. To the N, the area between *Herne Hill Rd* and *Milkwood Rd* has smaller Victorian houses, the area merging into Brixton around the multiple railway bridges of Loughborough Junction.

To the E of Herne Hill's central parades of shops around the station, the atmosphere becomes strongly suburban. *Stradella Rd*, *Winterbrook Rd* and *Burbage Rd* off *Half Moon Lane* are on the Dulwich border and much sought after. They are wide tree-lined and quiet predominantly late Victorian/ Edwardian terraced and semi-detached houses with small front gardens and 60 ft back gardens. *Burbage Rd* holds many surprises, with several large period-style detached houses with large gardens and driveways.

The area bounded by *Half Moon Lane* to the S, *Herne Hill* to the N and *Red*

Post Hill to the E contains many delightful streets of family housing, a mixture of Victorian, Edwardian and more modern terraced, detached and semi-detached homes. *Holmdene* is a good example with its wide roadway, trees and hedges and 3-storey Victorian houses with some modern semi-detacheds at the *Herne Hill* end. 'Dulwich Mead', off *Half Moon Lane*, is a new development of smart 1-, 2- and 3-bed retirement homes.

Beckwith Rd, *Ardbeg Rd* and *Elmwood Rd* are more exclusive and expensive. These streets are even quieter, and stand on the Dulwich border. They have very popular 3-bed Edwardian terraced houses with small garden frontage. They are close to a charming, well-kept public park, Sunray Gardens, with its duck pond, tennis courts and children's play area.

Back N of *Herne Hill*, on the slopes which lead along to the Ruskin Park neighbourhood of Dulwich, *Brantwood Rd* and *Dorchester Drive* are very quiet and could be anywhere in suburban London with their '30s built semi-detached housing and rose gardens. Becoming increasingly popular are the '20s purpose-built architect-designed blocks in Dorchester Court. *Milkwood Rd's* S end is very convenient for the station and contains small 3-bed Victorian terraced housing.

To the S of the station, *Norwood Rd* runs down towards Tulse Hill, with Brockwell Park on the W side. Just off *Norwood Rd*, but still well placed for Herne Hill station, lie *Guernsey Grove* and *Harwarden Grove*, next to a small estate of Peabody Trust housing. Mainly small houses and flats on *Guernsey*, 4- to 5-bed houses on *Harwarden*. Both back onto the railway which can be noisy. Facing Brockwell Park along *Norwood Rd* lie large 3-storey double-fronted Victorian houses, some detached, some semi-detached, turning into smaller 3-storey and 2-storey houses nearer to Herne Hill.

B

Tulse Hill Borders

The area bounded by *Christchurch Rd* – the busy South Circular – on the N, *Palace Rd* and its side-streets to the S is very pleasant. The roads stand on the Streatham/Norwood borders and are spacious, tidy and tree-lined. *Palace Rd* is by far the most expensive, with conversions becoming more widely available in these huge Victorian and Edwardian properties. *Christchurch Rd* is mainly lined with large 3-storey and 5-storey Victorian houses of 5-beds plus, though there are some double-fronted 2-storey 5-bed houses available, and a large council estate in *Coburg Crescent*. The shorter roads between, like *Probyn Rd* and *Perran Rd*, are predominantly small 3-bed Victorian terraces. *Lanercost Rd* is the exception with larger 5-bed Victorian houses, many retaining their original internal features.

Among those estate agents active in this area are:

- ABC Estate Agents
- Bryce Curtis
- Burnet Ware & Graves
- Galloways
- Houldings
- Priors
- Property and Finance Centre
- Prudential Property Services
- Shannons
- Walter Elms
- Winkworths
- Ramsey Robertson

Camberwell

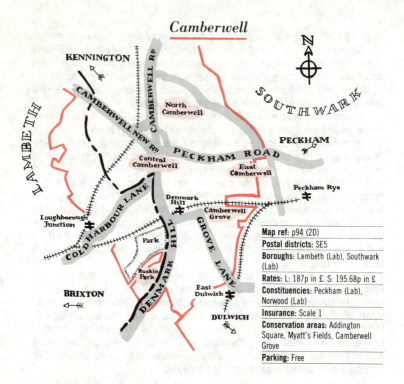

Map ref: p94 (2D)
Postal districts: SE5
Boroughs: Lambeth (Lab), Southwark (Lab)
Rates: L: 187p in £. S: 195.68p in £
Constituencies: Peckham (Lab), Norwood (Lab)
Insurance: Scale 1
Conservation areas: Addington Square, Myatt's Fields, Camberwell Grove
Parking: Free

Transport	British Rail: Loughborough Junction to Holborn Viaduct 10 min, East Dulwich, Denmark Hill to Holborn Viaduct, London Bridge, Victoria. Nearest tube Oval
Convenient for	City, Westminster, Dulwich. Miles from centre: 3.
Schools	ILEA Divisions 8/9: Archbishop Michael Ramsey C of E, Sacred Heart RC. Close Dulwich (which see).

Flats	S	1b	2b	3b	4b	5b
Average prices	45–50	55–80	70–85	75–120	–	–
Houses	2b	3b	4b	5b	6/7b	8b
Average prices	80–100	90–150	100–200+	120–200+	110–300+	250+

The properties	Scruffy main roads conceal pockets of fine Georgiana. Also ordinary terraces and converted flats. New developments appearing, adding town houses and flats to an area which mixes some of the best and some of the worst of London homes.
The market	Large new developments show level of interest in this convenient spot. Buyers hoping that long-awaited tube will make it even more so – one day. Unconverted Georgian coveted. Price range dependent on location and architecture as much as size. Local searches: Lambeth: 10 weeks, Southwark: 8 weeks.

Area Profile

In a rather crowded corner of southeast London you suddenly come across Camberwell Green, clearly a former village centre but now rather more of a traffic island, surrounded by shops. It takes time to get one's bearings around here as every street seems to be called 'Camberwell Somethingorother', but persistence is rewarded with the discovery of some fine and interesting residential corners tucked away amongst the drab streets and dire council buildings. Camberwell is very much a place of enclaves.

Camberwell is where the ground starts to slope up from the flat ground of Walworth and Bermondsey towards the southern heights of Dulwich. This means streets with unexpected views of London. What Camberwell still lacks is a tube – although this is now a 'when' rather than an 'if'. For now locals make do with traffic jams, the copious buses and Denmark Hill BR station, where the old ticket office, lovingly restored after fire, now houses the Phoenix & Firkin pub to tempt weary travellers.

The main shopping street is *Denmark Hill* (with *Walworth Rd.* not far away). There is a very large new Safeways supermarket with car park. Wine bars are non-existent, restaurants are mainly Indian, with a Chinese and a Caribbean in *Camberwell Church St.*

Parking in Camberwell is restricted to side streets off the main roads and is especially difficult around *Denmark Hill*: a lot of the spaces are taken up by people visiting the local hospitals, King's College and the Maudsley. Because of King's College Hospital, Maudsley Hospital, Camberwell art school and Dulwich college the area is rich in student rented property.

The contrast between *Camberwell Grove* and *Champions Hill* half a mile to the S of the Green, and the streets to the N, is marked. That's to ignore the disaster zones of E Brixton on one side and N Peckham on the other. *Camberwell Grove* has some of the handsomest Georgian houses S of the Thames. There are leafy, quiet streets of villas of every period from Regency to '30s. And there are some of the nastiest of ex-GLC flats interspersed with very ordinary late-Victorian terraces of the ubiquitous South London sort.

Camberwell Green, the centre of the area, sits at the junction of *Camberwell Church St*, *Camberwell Rd*, *Denmark Hill* and *Camberwell New Rd*. These busy roads define the various neighbourhoods of Camberwell, which is further divided by two railway lines. The boundary with Brixton to the W is ill-defined, and Camberwell fades into Walworth to the N.

Camberwell Grove

The area S and E of the Green, on the gentle slopes up towards Herne Hill and Dulwich, was the first to be developed as Camberwell began its expansion from village to suburb. *Camberwell Grove* survives virtually intact as a street of late Georgian houses. Some, at the N end, date from the 1770s; others further up the street, such as *Grove Crescent*, are early 19th century. Used by rush-hour motorists as a means to avoid Camberwell Green, it is subject to various "traffic experiments" which tend to clog it up further or concentrate even more traffic around the Green. The Georgian atmosphere continues on into *Grove Park* (largely lined with particularly peaceful Edwardian houses) and *Grove Lane*. Some new red brick homes have been built E of *Camberwell Grove* alongside the railway, and Rialto have built 137 more in 'Springfield Grove' E of *Grove Park* and N of *Chadwick Rd.*, again on land between two railway lines. These run from studios to 2-bed maisonettes. The last few maisonettes were priced last winter at around £98,000.

West of *Grove Lane*, *Champion Hill* and surrounding streets were developed in the 1840s. Some of these elegant villas still survive. The Longford Green estate of 1968 is built in a Regency style, and has large town houses in pleasant stock brick: highly desirable. Off *Champion Hill* itself is Ruskin Park House, a pair of large blocks of '20s mansion flats.

Ruskin Park

The bulk of King's College Hospital and the E-W railway line form a frontier cutting off the Ruskin Park corner in S Camberwell. The park is the centre of an enclave of 20th-century streets with a strongly – but pleasingly – suburban feel. *Denmark Hill* itself is a busy but pleasant road. To the E are large brick council blocks and further on the *Sunray Avenue* estate of 1920s homes on the borders of Herne Hill, built by the government as part of the post-First World War 'homes fit for heroes' campaign. West of *Denmark Hill*, roads like *Deepdene* and *Sunset*, with their '30s semis – not to mention a green-roofed, Spanish-style bungalow – slope peacefully down to Ruskin Park. *Ferndene Rd* lines the E side of the park, its 1920s gabled and bay-windowed villas having fine views across it and the rooftops towards central London.

West of the park, *Finsen Rd* has handsome (c 1914) terraces looking out over the green park from particularly pretty square-bayed windows. To the N, *Kemerton Rd* and surrounding streets have neat little Victorian cottages.

East Camberwell

Between *Peckham Rd* and the railway line to the S, there are several streets of late-19th century terraces, such as *Bushy Hill Rd*, *Vestry Rd*, *Crofton Rd* and *Shenley Rd* – a corner to watch when Camberwell's communications improve.

North Camberwell

Most of the area E of *Camberwell Rd* is taken up by large council developments. A few older streets survive, notably around *Addington Square*. The square itself is early 19th century, its irregular houses of the classic, tall, late-Georgian style – plus a pair of low, Regency villas. It is, of course, a conservation area. Nearby is *Rust Square*, a pleasant Victorian corner. Other streets where private housing remains include *Havil St* and *Ada Rd* with its little flat-fronted cottages. A former hospital site off *St. Giles Rd* has been largely cleared for the building of new town houses, while one imposing section of the Victorian institution has been retained for conversion into luxury flats.

Georgian houses line long stretches of both *Camberwell Rd* and *Camberwell New Rd*. The latter leads directly to Vauxhall Bridge, passing the Oval tube: Camberwell is very close to central London. Both roads are busy, however: *Camberwell New Rd* leads E to the Old Kent Rd and the Dover Rd. South of *Camberwell New Rd*, Camberwell merges with Brixton. There are big council estates but also the conservation area around Myatt's Fields. The 1890s Minet Estate houses here, in roads such as *Knatchbull Rd*, are attracting interest.

Central Camberwell

You could drive through the area's traffic-filled heart every day without discovering Camberwell's most surprising corner. Off *Denmark Hill*, a tiny turning called *Love Walk* is, indeed, a no-through-road for cars. At this end traffic can only penetrate, alongside a short terrace, as far as the entrance to a tucked-away group of 3- and 4-storey brick blocks of flats, owned by the Orbit Housing Association. Walk on, and the *Walk* reveals its surprise. On the left is Selbourne village, a 1982 Wates estate of small cottage houses built with great attention to materials and detailing in the highest flight of village vernacular. It is undoubtedly pleasant, peaceful and a highly successful human-scale, well-hidden corner, but an extraordinary stylistic jolt in so urban an environment. Cars can enter from the E end: garages are hidden in groups between the houses.

On the other side of the walk are older, but equally unlikely homes. First comes a little row of earlier versions of the country cottage, tile-hung, gabled – and hidden behind an older wall, reached only through two arched gateways. And further on are splendid, double-fronted small Regency detached houses with garages, which lead out onto *Grove Lane* where some dignified larger Georgian terraces still stand.

C

Among those estate agents active in this area are:
- Andrews & Robertson
- Jacksons
- Whitehall Estates
- Roy Brooks
- Burnet Ware & Graves
- Shannons
- Winkworths

Camden Town

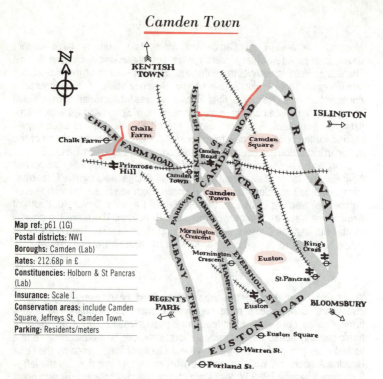

Map ref: p61 (1G)
Postal districts: NW1
Boroughs: Camden (Lab)
Rates: 212.68p in £
Constituencies: Holborn & St Pancras (Lab)
Insurance: Scale 1
Conservation areas: include Camden Square, Jeffreys St, Camden Town.
Parking: Residents/meters

Transport	Tubes: Camden Town, Chalk Farm, Mornington Crescent, Euston (zone 1/2, Northern). From Camden Town: Oxford Circus 15 min (1 change), City 15min, Heathrow 1 hour (1 change). British Rail: Camden Rd to Liverpool St 20 mins.					
Convenient for	City & West End, Euston & Kings Cross BR, Euston Rd to M40, M11, Cambridge, Chelmsford. Regents Park. Miles from centre: 2.5.					
Schools	ILEA zone 2: William Ellis (b), Camden School for Girls, Private: London International School					

Flats	S	1b	2b	3b	4b	5b
Average prices	60–75	65–95	85–150	100–170	–	–
Houses	2b	3b	4b	5b	6/7b	8b
Average prices	120–180	140–200	190–400+	200–450+	→	→

The properties	Victorian housing of all shapes and sizes, with wide variations in status and condition. Lots of converted flats. Quite a few modern homes and more on the way: flats and mews–style houses. Lots of council homes, some (rehab period) very desirable.
The market	General flat market centres on conversions. Best family homes change hands quickly. Population shift as middle classes replace Irish, Greek and Italian families. Local searches: 12 weeks.

Area Profile

Camden: convenient, central, still cheap in parts – and in the news. Historically a poor, seedy part of the inner city, it is slowly undergoing a modest transformation. Its best homes look hopefully at the status of neighbouring Islington; much renovation is in hand but unmodernised flats and houses, now rare in most 'up-and-come' areas, can still be found here.

It is bracketed by railway lines – but this means that it will eventually border not a desolate hinterland of derelict goods yards but the brave new world of the King's Cross (which see) development, set to create a virtual new town. And Paris, via the Channel Tunnel, may well be on the doorstep.

As yet, however, Camden is a highly mixed area. There is a high proportion of council housing (particularly in the southern part); many light industrial factories, workshops and commercial buildings; modern purpose-built blocks of flats and town houses; conversions in Victorian terraces and substantial Victorian family houses now selling at around the half-million mark. For playground, however, it has Regent's Park; and there's also the canal.

Camden Town is flanked by its satellite areas of Chalk Farm, Mornington Crescent and, to the S, what little housing there is in Euston. Camden residents often have to put up with noisy main roads or the sound of tube or BR trains; as a result, each road commands a different price. What attracts them to the area, apart from the central location, is the high availability of popular Victorian properties and conversions – new purpose-built flats and maisonettes sell less well here. The narrow-fronted Victorian houses give no more than 1-, possibly 2-bedroomed flats; larger flats tend, therefore, to be maisonettes.

One of the main advantages of the area is that it is so central. Young professionals are moving in, and the traditional inhabitants – Greek and Irish families mainly, and some Italians – are moving out. Nevertheless, Camden retains its cosmopolitan atmosphere, with lots of excellent restaurants and specialist food shops. The weekend markets at Camden Lock draw the crowds, and venues like the Camden Palace and Dingwalls Club ensure a consistently high proportion of young people. An ambitious new development opposite the tube station of excellent up-market food and book shops points to the direction in which Camden is heading.

Camden Town

Camden High St, running N from *Mornington Crescent*, is Camden's main shopping street, lively and always busy, with Camden Palace – venue for discos and concerts – at S end. There are flats and maisonettes above the shops in flat-fronted Victorian terraced buildings at the S end, and red-brick mansion blocks near Camden Town tube station. Plans for the *High St* include 35 flats with parking and a new library. *Delancey St*, also busy and wide, is one way going W and has shops at *High St* end, with flats above; thereafter terraces on either side, the narrow, flat-fronted Victorian buildings providing flats, maisonettes and houses, some with gardens. The W end overlooks the main railway line into Euston. A new office development in *Carlow St* has been crowned with 14 penthouse flats: 'The Carlows', ultra-smart, ultra-modern, have roof terraces and prices up to £295,000. 12 new houses, in excess of £300,000, will be for sale in *Beatty St* from mid-1989.

Parkway is a colourful, crowded three-lane street going W towards Regents Park: a good range of shops and restaurants on either side and some terrific bookshops; 1- and 2-bed flats and studios above. *Jamestown Rd*, used as cut-through by traffic, has a recent development of period-style properties and older terraces opposite commercial buildings, providing flats and maisonettes.

Albert St, Camden's most attractive and expensive road, is wide and has elegant and beautifully maintained terraces on both sides, providing large 4-, 5- and 6-bed family houses. In some, basements have been sold off separately. *Arlington Rd*, parallel, has similar middle section with large terraced houses along either side, though prices are lower in this less attractive street. The N end has a hostel for the homeless on the corner with *Jamestown Rd*, a large bingo hall next door and some terraced housing opposite. At the S end, after *Delancey St* junction, is a large NCP car park and council housing on E side, more large terraced Victorian homes opposite. Large 4-bed family houses on 4 storeys can be picked up in this street for around £250,000.

Mornington Terrace is council in S part; the N part has housing in Victorian terraces on E side only; the W side overlooks main railway line into Euston. Terraces are pleasantly situated behind main streets; most are still single houses, both modernised and unmodernised. *Mornington Place* ditto. In the triangle formed by *Camden High St*, *Hawley Crescent* and *Kentish Town Rd*, small new developments of town houses and purpose-built flats rub shoulders with the vast TV AM complex and large, ugly commercial and office buildings. In the triangle on the other side of *Kentish Town Rd*, bounded by *Camden St*, a huge new Sainsburys opened in December, served by a Dial-a-Ride bus and with parking for 300 cars. 10 mews houses on the site are due mid-1989, backing onto the canal. *Camden St*, the main southbound highway into the West End, has period terracing at N end providing converted flats and maisonettes; plus mix of old and new council housing. Greek Orthodox church on E side, and London International School at the end of the W side. *Bayham St* is similar, with heavy traffic southbound, and has small light industrial factories and council housing on E side; shops with flats above in period terracing opposite, and Victorian terraces backing onto Camden Palace.

Greenland Rd is a quiet tree-lined street with yellowish-grey brick flat-fronted Victorian terraced houses; these are 3-storied, with gardens both front and back, providing 3-bed houses. Some are privately owned, some housing association and some council-assisted, resulting in varying conditions of housing and a good mix of residents. *Carol St*, *St Martin's Close*, and *Georgiana St* ditto. *Lyme St* has a pleasant row of early Victorian terraces on E side overlooking canal. Both *Lyme* and *Georgiana Sts* are blocked off to traffic which pushes prices up slightly. *Pratt St* only has private housing between *Bayham St* and the *High St*, in flats and maisonettes over shops, and some individual houses. *Plender St*, with a small fruit-and-veg market at its W end is similar, though it also has housing in some purpose-built blocks of flats. The roads S of *Pratt St* to *Crowndale Rd* are mainly council with the exception of *College Place*, which has large Victorian terraced houses in the northern section only – a mix of modernised and unmodernised family houses, interspersed with council-assisted properties. *Royal College St* (main through-road, northbound only) has council housing at its S end; then terraces on both sides, some still single properties, most converted into flats and rooms.

On *Baynes St* a new development of mews houses and flats, Reachview, occupies the S side overlooking the canal. Built in 1985, it attracted a lot of interest when new. *Rossendale Way* has conversions in period terrace to right, new mews houses beyond; it overlooks the canal at the rear. At the bottom of *Rossendale Way* is Elm Village, a development of town houses, flats and maisonettes built three or four years ago, where some of the cheaper homes in Camden are to be found (2-bedroom flats around £85,000; 2-bed houses from £110,000). *Rousden St*, a narrow street running up to Camden Rd BR station (the tracks run on the S side), has run-down aspect but also some terraces of new town houses, purpose-built flats and maisonettes and conversions in period houses. *St Pancras Way*, which runs S from *Camden Rd*, is a through-road with industrial and commercial buildings only on both sides.

C

Tall Victorian terraced houses reappear on the northern part of *St Pancras Way* and *Royal College St*. *Jeffreys St*, through road to *St Pancras Way*, has 3- and 4-storey Victorian terraces on either side with basements, black railings in front and small balconies on first floor. *Prowse Place*, closer to the railway line, has four brick-fronted cottages to the right, and is cobbled. *Ivor St* is a quiet, tree-lined street with brightly painted 2- and 3-storey houses, most still single occupancy, and many recently done up or being renovated. *Bonny St* is very mixed; some period houses offer conversions. A development of town houses has recently been built, and there is British Rail housing next to the bridge. In *Jeffreys Place* there are a dozen substantial new town houses with garages.

To the N of St Pancras Way lie 'the Rochesters', a group of streets tucked in beneath the borders of NW5 and Kentish Town, which rank next in desirability and price to *Albert St* and *Camden Square*. *Rochester Rd* is part of an Environmental Area and a no through road. It overlooks a small playground area, which lies between *Rochester Rd* and *Rochester Terrace*. Here prices are slightly higher, thanks to S-facing gardens and larger, grander houses. *Rochester Place*: very narrow street in which are council blocks, small workshops and a school. To the W, *Reed's Place* is a tiny, hidden-away street, blocked off to traffic at both ends. Square, stucco-fronted Victorian houses, most still in single occupation, set the tone; most have pretty front gardens. *Wilmot Place* has substantial pairs of brick and stucco-fronted houses and terraces – developers are moving in. *Rochester Mews* has several little, white-painted mews houses in its E section. *Whitcher Place* is low brick-built halls of residence for London University. The remaining 'Rochester' – the *Square* – lies across the *Camden Rd*: see below.

Camden Square area

The area on the Kentish Town borders, bounded by *York Way* to the E, *Camden Rd* to the W and *Agar Grove* to the S, is fast becoming a very popular corner, and prices have been rising accordingly. *Camden Square*, where substantial houses, good-sized flats and maisonettes are to be had in a quiet attractive setting, sets the tone. *Camden Rd* is a huge main road, but Victorian properties

Camden Town has many houses of mid-Victorian date, which feature sash windows such as this, often with vestigial 'balconies' in wrought iron. The window surrounds, of classically-detailed stucco, form a pleasing contrast with the London stock brick of the walls. The sash windows have large panes, in contrast to the earlier Georgian small ones, which staged a reappearance late in the century.

on E side, almost all conversions, are well shaded by trees and set well back. Some garden flats available. *Camden Park Rd*, *Cliff Rd* and *Cliff Villas* are a mix of council blocks, Victorian terraces currently being converted into flats, and mid-Victorian semi-detached cottages, sold as single houses.

North and *South Villas* run N from *Camden Square* and have huge grey brick villas on both sides. Garden flats available in deep basements. All these villas are now conversions, providing 1-, 2- and 3-bedroom flats and maisonettes, *Camden Terrace* likewise. *St Augustines Rd* – pleasant, wide tree-lined and quiet – has large pairs of villas to either side in varying conditions of repair. Unmodernised examples still available; conversions yield garden flats, flats and maisonettes. *Marquis Rd*, *Cantelowes Rd* and *St Pauls Crescent* ditto.

Camden Square itself – an elegant, leafy, subdued square – provides large family houses, especially on the S side, and flats and maisonettes in conversions. *Murray St* has a period terrace at its N end, modern parade of shops on W side with flats above. The narrow 6 ft wide entrance to *Agar Grove* restricts heavy traffic. Stratford Villas, council at S end, thereafter has tall grey brick and stucco-fronted terraces, up to 5 storeys high on both sides. Many are undergoing conversion.

Rochester Square has private homes on two sides; some in pairs of Edwardian-style villas, 2-storied with raised ground floors plus semi-basements below, some in Victorian terraces, many also in the process of renovation. In *Camden Mews*, a pricy backwater, is a handful of brick-fronted mews houses. *Agar Grove* is a busy thoroughfare and prices here are £10,000-£15,000 cheaper than in Camden Square: noise from the road is augmented by noise from the railway lines. Mix of old and new council blocks on S side particularly, interspersed with modern town houses and tall Victorian terraces which yield lots of converted flats and maisonettes. *St Paul's Crescent*, a crescent no longer, leads to a low-level white painted council estate. On either side are terraces of grey brick houses, 2 storeys with basements. St Paul's Mews, 25 town houses, is currently being built here. Council housing S of *Agar Grove*.

Chalk Farm area

Going N, *Camden High St* becomes *Chalk Farm Rd* as it reaches the canal and Camden Lock. This one-way street holds a cinema (the Camden Plaza) and a lively fruit-and-veg market to left, and Saturday market to right. *Hartland Rd's* 2-storey brick- and stucco-fronted brightly painted late Georgian terraces provide 3-bedroom houses on 3 floors, with small gardens. First section on S side, new buildings will provide council housing in low-rise blocks. The railway line runs overhead at the end of the street; much of the area is being rebuilt, which gives it a slightly derelict air. No private housing beyond the junction with *Clarence Way*. Similar terraces are found in the N part of *Clarence Way*.

Hadley Street, to the E of the railway line, runs up to the borders of NW5 and Kentish Town. The street is divided in two by road block; the S end is a peaceful cul-de-sac of narrow-fronted terraced houses, some Victorian, some built six years ago in original style. The railway line passes overhead on N side; council housing surrounds. The N section of street is pretty, tree-lined and not used by traffic; rows of brick- and stucco-fronted 2-storey houses on both sides. Trains using Kentish Town West station pass behind; the street has an up-and-coming air. *Healey St* likewise, though houses here are slightly grander and taller.

Grafton Crescent, tucked in behind the main road, has large grey brick and stucco-fronted terraced houses on both sides; many are recently modernised, though original ones can still be found. Homes here are mostly 3-bedroomed, some with gardens. The E end of *Prince of Wales Rd* is a busy, noisy road, but grey brick and stucco houses, mostly conversions, are well set back. Homes in flats over the shops on *Kentish Town Rd* going N. *Hawley Rd* is a mix of old properties restored into spacious houses and new purpose-built flats, with more being built. Prices are lower here because of extremely heavy traffic.

Chalk Farm 'proper' lies W of *Harmood St* taking in the area around the tube station. It is a small and highly convenient corner with a good deal of council housing intermingled with homes which borrow some of the aura of Belsize Park and some of the trendiness of Kentish Town.

Most of the homes here are in the huge blocks of mansion flats in *Eton College Rd*, or in small Edwardian villa-type houses in roads off the *Chalk Farm Rd*. The area is currently being developed: new blocks are planned for the *Chalk Farm Rd*, and one appeared last year on the corner of *Adelaide Rd*.

Prince of Wales Rd: the N side has large blocks of red brick council flats; on the S side are three terraces of period houses, some in good condition, others run down. Best terrace of the three is Nos 131-151. *Crogsland Rd*, likewise, is council on one side; on the W side, a short terrace of 4-storey houses have been laterally converted into flats. Further along the *Prince of Wales Rd* going E there are terraces of period properties on both sides of the street; some single houses, some maisonettes, some flats. *Harmood St*: rows of low 2-storey Edwardian terraced houses here, very mixed: some done up, some run down. Average prices for 3-bedroom houses are upwards of £160,000 in good condition. Chalk Farm bus garage and more council housing towards S part of street. *Clarence Way*, a pretty street, has rows of brick terraced houses similar to *Harmood St*, railway bridge for the North London line passes over the middle of the street. *Chalk Farm Rd*, the busy main road, has new developments of purpose-built flats and offices; flats over shops on E side.

Just to the W of the Chalk Farm tube station is *Eton College Rd*, a very pleasant, quiet road which has three huge mansion blocks known as The Etons. Flats in these blocks change hands regularly. A major 5-year refurbishment programme is still under way, so service charges are exceptionally high – but prices, correspondingly, lower than normal. Two-bedroom flats were around £80-85,000, 1-bedroom around £70-75,000, in December.

This end of *Adelaide Rd* is also regarded as part of Chalk Farm. The houses here are large, stucco-fronted terraces, converted into flats, usually geared for first-time buyers. *Adelaide Rd* is busy, and these houses overlook the railway.

Mornington Crescent and Euston

To the S, on the other side of Camden Town, lies another area centred on a convenient tube station. Mornington Crescent (the tube stop) is actually on the junction of busy *Hampstead Rd* and *Eversholt St*. *Mornington Crescent* (the street), once a grand, semi-circular terrace of tall stucco-fronted Victorian houses, has fallen into disrepair. Now, however, it's gradually being renovated and converted into flats. Prices here are lower than in central Camden.

Crowndale Rd, E of *Eversholt St*, has tall brick and cream stucco terraces on either side, mostly conversions: thereafter there is council housing and a small parade of shops. The N end of *Eversholt St* also has 4-storey high terraces.

Oakley Square's S side is council; the N side is a pleasant terrace of Victorian houses, brick and stucco-fronted with elaborate detail on doors and window-frames, black railings in front, and deep basements. In keeping with the rest of area, this is gradually being restored and renovated. At the N end a purpose-built block of luxury flats, St Matthews Lodge, has apartments of all sizes including studios. Both flats and houses face onto the leafy, green, small public garden. *Harrington Square* has a terrace of Victorian houses, most new conversions, on section running N-S only; in front runs a busy one-way street carrying traffic into the West End. Hurdwick Place, off *Hampstead Rd*, provides new conversions in period terraces, and garden flats in some basements.

The Euston area, bounded by *Euston Rd* to the S, *St Pancras Way* to the E, *Hampstead Rd* to the W, and *Oakley Square* to the N is virtually all council-owned, except for some privately-owned flats and maisonettes over shops on *Churchway* and *Chalton St*, which have the benefit of this very central location. Many of the council homes are handsomely-restored period houses. Similar housing, too, on the S part of *Eversholt St*, in *Starcross St*, *North Gower St*, and *Drummond St* to the W, where there is privately owned housing in Victorian terraces, well-sheltered from the main road and centrally located.

This southern part of Camden will eventually benefit from all the amenities of the vast King's Cross (which see) development.

Among those estate agents active in this area are:

- Bairstow Eves
- Druce
- Ellis & Co
- Elliot Ross
- Hotblack Desiato
- Beauchamp Estates
- Stickley & Kent
- Sturt & Tivendale
- Hirschfields

Chelsea

Map ref: p76 (4D)
Postal districts: SW3, SW10, SW1
Boroughs: Kensington & Chelsea (con)
Rates: 98.9p in £
Constituencies: Chelsea (Con)
Insurance: Scale 1 (SW1), Scale 3 (SW3,SW10)
Conservation areas: most parts – check.
Parking: Residents/meters. Clamping.

C

Transport   Tube stations: Sloane Sq (zone 1, District, Circle). South Kensington (zone 1, District, Circle, Piccadilly). From Sloane Sq: Oxford Circus: 15 min (1 change), City 20 min, Heathrow 55 min (1 change).

Convenient for   West End, Victoria BR, Thames, M4 to West. Miles from centre: 2.

Schools   ILEA zone 1: St Thomas More. Private: More House School. Many good prep schools. See also neighbouring areas.

Flats	S	1b	2b	3b	4b	5b
Average prices	80–100	110–140+	140–200+	160–300+	200–500	–
Houses	2b	3b	4b	5b	6/7b	8b
Average prices	220–360	225–450	350–700	500–1.8m+	→	→

The properties   Lovely Georgian/early Victorian homes in garden squares, small streets and mews are the archetypal Chelsea properties. Also, N of Kings Rd/Sloane Sq, red-brick, Dutch-gabled mansion flats.

The market   Five years ago there were still scruffy streets in Chelsea. Now prices reflect the depth of the facelift, the length of the lease. Exceptional properties go well over the mainstream averages above. Local searches: 7 days.

Area Profile

Chelsea is more than a place, it is a byword, a symbol for a rather special kind of urban living: smart yet artistic, prosperous yet individual, expensive yet free-wheeling. The image of bohemian Chelsea, home of artists and their models, site of studio parties, has not survived the rise in property prices. The painters and sculptors have moved out, and their studios are owned by the usual mix of international residents found in any rich London area. But that special Chelsea flavour lives on in the little pastel-painted streets, the elaborate mansion blocks, the occasional superb Georgian house.

It is also easy to forget that until a decade ago quite a few of Chelsea's people were very ordinary, even poor, living in tenanted homes. Gentrification has done its work here too, with West Chelsea, spurred on by Chelsea Harbour and adjacent developments, the last enclave to be 'improved'.

Chelsea, strung along the *King's Rd* and the river, has a self-contained air. It has its own department store, a shop which is a way of life as much as a source of supply. You need not leave the area to be fed or entertained: restaurants abound, it has its own theatre. Shops sell most things, especially if it is ephemeral or expensive. The *King's Rd's* fortunes wax and wane with fashion: a recent trend is the arrival of big-name food and fashion stores (several branches of Next, and Gateway food store) which displace small boutiques.

The *King's Rd* may be busy, even tawdry at times, but a street away all is quiet: you are in a Georgian village, or a Victorian square. Chelsea keeps the villagy air which Fulham and such places somehow never quite attained.

The area was first made popular by Sir Thomas More, who went to live there in the 16th century. The aristocracy followed, building large country houses. They stayed and, over the years, their rural retreats have been replaced by their townhouses. To reach his country estate, Sir Thomas travelled by boat: the all-important Road, genuinely as royal as its name implies, came later when King Charles II had a farm track cleared so he could journey to Putney to catch a boat to Hampton Court and, presumably, visit Nell Gwynn in Fulham en route.

The track became, literally, the *King's Rd*, later famous throughout the world as a symbol of the swinging sixties.

King's Rd remains the main thoroughfare. It runs the entire length of Chelsea, W to E, 'playing every note in the social scale', as one of the area's most famous former inhabitants, writer/wit Quentin Crisp, observed.

As it wends its way from fashionable *Sloane Square* in the E to World's End in the W, the restaurants, pubs, bars, boutiques, galleries and smart shops make way for handsome squares of traditional terraced houses.

As Chelsea is one of the most desirable and sought-after addresses in London, properties are among the most expensive in the capital. Even in W Chelsea, until recently the area's poor relation, prices have soared.

Chelsea's added bonus is the River Thames, which flows along its southern border. Once an inspiration for the likes of Turner, Whistler and the Greaves brothers, it now excites estate agents, who are well aware that anything with a view of the river commands a premium. The river is back in business as a highway, with Thamesline boats calling at Cadogan Pier and Chelsea Harbour.

Sloane Square, Cadogans, Pont Street

C

This is the neighbourhood bounded by *Pont St* and *Walton St* in the N, *King's Rd* and *Sloane Square* to the S, *Sloane Avenue* to the W, and the borough border in the E.

Unlike the rest of Chelsea's squares, *Sloane Square* is a busy shopping area/traffic junction with roads converging from Knightsbridge, the *King's Rd* and Pimlico. The paved square has plane trees and a fountain.

Lining the square are hotels, pubs, Peter Jones department store, the Royal Court Theatre and Sloane Square tube station. Many of the commercial uses occupy lower floors of the 19th century residential blocks overlooking the square. These flats are convenient, if noisy. *Lower Sloane St* and *Sloane Gardens* to the S are dominated by the tall red-brick and stone-gabled mansion blocks found in most of the E chunk of the neighbourhood.

Heading north, *Sloane St* is the main thoroughfare to Knightsbridge. It is lined by a jumble of modern and period buildings, mainly flats, with concentrations of shops and some embassies. The private square gardens of *Cadogan Place* (car parking beneath), spread along most of the E side of the street, overlooked by terraces of mixed-style period houses. An exclusive flats development, Royal Court House, is being built on the S side of *Cadogan Place* (24 2/5-bed flat/maisonettes, starting at nearly £600,000 and rising to £1.85 million for a 5-bed penthouse). These are due for completion Spring '89.

Tucked away behind *Cadogan Place* on the borders with Belgravia is quiet *Cadogan Lane* with its appealing mix of mews-type cottages and small houses.

West of *Sloane St*, in *Pont St*, are classic examples of the late 19th century red-brick style which Osbert Lancaster dubbed 'Pont St Dutch'. These tall houses with stone detailing and splendid gables were derived from 17th century Flemish and Dutch architecture. They form the predominant style in most of the area from *Cadogan Square*, a select address overlooking leafy gardens, W to *Lennox Gardens*, which curves round central gardens. Most of the houses have been converted into flats but leases can be short. Some new leases can be had. The Cadogan Estate, for instance, has just marketed 75-year leases on a high-standard conversion in Margaretha House, *Draycott Place*. Hidden behind these tall buildings are occasional quiet mews (*Shafto, Clabon*).

West of *Lennox Gardens* between *Walton* and *Cadogan Sts* lies an enclave of much sought-after smaller freehold houses. *Ovington*, *Hasker* and *First Sts* – the most popular group – and *Moore*, *Halsey* and *Rawlings Sts* all have similar terraces of attractive 2/3-storey plus basement period brick and stucco houses. Running between the two groups is *Milner St* with its ornate 5-storey stucco terraced homes.

Walton St, a twisty, busy little thoroughfare between South Kensington and Knightsbridge, is a mix of up-market shops/restaurants and stretches of pretty terraced houses. West of the freehold houses enclave are the private Marlborough Buildings, the tall backs of which create a cul-de-sac in *Donne Place*, with its charming little mews-type houses. To the S, *Cadogan St* is a mix of late Georgian terraced properties on the N side, with St Mary's Church, St Thomas More secondary school, St Joseph's Catholic primary school and the Guinness Trust Estate to the S.

More red bricks and a pocket of 2/3-storey terraced Victorian houses (*Coulson*, *Lincoln* and *Anderson Sts*) lie between *Cadogan St*, *King's Rd* and *Sloane Avenue*.

Royal Hospital

Between the *King's Rd* and the river, W of *Lower Sloane St/Chelsea Bridge Rd* and E of *Smith St/Tedworth Square/Tite St*.

The most sought after address in this neighbourhood is *St Leonard's Terrace*, which boasts some of the oldest houses in Chelsea (18th and early 19th century). Most are listed, with leafy front gardens. But their main attraction, along with the grand mansions in *Durham Place*, is their view over *Burton's Court* (sports ground) and Wren's famous Royal Hospital. This imposing home for old soldiers forms the centrepiece of the area, with its extensive grounds (public tennis courts, handicapped children's adventure playground) and the neighbouring *Ranelagh Gardens*, stretching towards the river. Residents of *Embankment Gardens* have the best of both worlds with views of both the Royal Hospital and the Thames – the latter over the embankment traffic. A housing association is active here.

Dividing the neighbourhood in two is *Royal Hospital Rd*, lined by a mix of period and modern houses, flats and shops. At its W end stands the National Army Museum and the drab modern concrete St Wilfrid's Convent. *Tite St*, running down to the river, boasts studio houses (ie homes with artists' studios, not today's one-room flats) which betray Chelsea's Bohemian past. Now their 2-storey glass windows stare glumly at the side of the Convent. Across *Royal Hospital Rd*, the 1930s mock Tudor houses in *Ormonde Gate* give way to tall red mansion blocks. The redevelopment of the river end of Royal Hospital Rd will provide smart flats with splendid views along the river.

In *Tedworth Square* the new, ungainly brick development (1981) on the N side contrasts sharply with the traditional 4/5-storey terraces of brick and stucco/red-brick houses on the other three sides of the central gardens.

Head back along *St Leonard's Terrace* to reach *Royal Avenue*. This tree-lined, gravelled parade is flanked on both sides by gracious terraces of 19th century houses, except for a post-war development at the *King's Rd* end. Its peace is guarded by the sensible barring of this end to traffic.

Just a few steps from the hustle and bustle of *King's Rd* stands *Wellington Square*, a fine group of 4-storey ornamental stucco Victorian houses. Despite its position, the terraces are set back from the road and the tall trees in the central garden give an air of seclusion and privacy.

Beyond the brick and stucco terraces in *Walpole St* is the huge Whitelands House flats complex in *Cheltenham Terrace*, which dominates the terraces further along the W side of the street. Facing *Cheltenham Terrace* is the Duke of York's Headquarters, S of which lie blocks of flats and modern townhouses. The mansion flats in Sloane Court E and W share expanses of communal gardens: ground-floor flats have direct access from graceful living-rooms.

Old Chelsea

As its name suggests, this area takes in the oldest parts of Chelsea and contains the most expensive properties. It is bounded on the N by *King's Rd*, by *Cheyne Walk/Chelsea Embankment* in the S, *Beaufort St* to the W, and *Smith St/Terrace/Tedworth Square/Tite St* E.

Beaufort St is a main road N-S leading to Battersea Bridge. Most of the W side is lined by the red-brick and stone-gabled blocks of Beaufort Mansions with the council's Thomas More Estate opposite. More mansion blocks with shops beneath front the *King's Rd*.

Neighbouring *Paultons Square* is one of the best-preserved examples of its type in the borough. Here handsome terraces of 1840s with decorative black iron balconies and railings are arranged on three sides of an elongated central garden square. Terraces of a later date continue down *Danvers St*.

Turn E along *Cheyne Walk* with its fine 18th century townhouses past Chelsea Old Church into *Old Church St*, the oldest in Chelsea. It now contains a hotch-potch of residential/commercial/light industrial uses in period and modern styles. Cut through the alleyway into *Justice Walk*, a delightful lane leading to the traditional heart and most exclusive part of Old Chelsea, *Lawrence St* and the *Cheynes*: quiet little streets with picturesque groups of houses and cottages, and fine brick and stucco terraces. Many of the houses are dotted with blue plaques commemorating famous residents ranging from Rossetti and Isambard Kingdom Brunel to Thomas Carlyle.

The crossroads of *Cheyne Row/Upper Cheyne Row* and *Glebe Place* form one of the prettiest spots in the area. From here, *Glebe Place* follows a dog-leg course through to *King's Rd*. On the W side of the first leg, the high-walled Libyan School borders West House, a Queen Anne-revival studio house and one of the landmarks in the history of 19th century British architecture.

The W-E leg of the street has a mix of highly individual studio houses and the main N-S leg has purpose-built artists' studios (late 19th and early 20th century) facing a long terrace of 3-storey plus basement 19th century terraced houses to the W (large rear gardens). Between *Lawrence St* and *Oakley St* lie more red-brick mansion blocks.

Oakley St is another major through-route N-S, leading to elegant *Albert Bridge*, *Cadogan Pier* and *Battersea Park*, Chelsea's adopted open space. On the W corner of the bridge stands Pier House, a vast modern red brick development stretching well up *Oakley St* to merge with older red brick blocks. The E side of the street is lined with tall formal terraces of stucco, or stucco and brick houses. Behind *Oakley St* lie smaller terraces in *Margaretta Terrace* (more than £20,000 has been asked for private parking spaces), *Phene St* and horseshoe-shaped *Oakley Gardens*. Here 3-storey brick and stucco terraces in leafy streets with pretty gardens convey a village character.

C

At the top of *Chelsea Manor St* stands the Old Chelsea Town Hall, housing the library and the sports centre (swimming baths, sports, sauna-solarium, multi-gym). Behind the town hall is the prestigious Swan Court apartment block, stretching through to *Flood St:* nine storeys built around a central courtyard. In *Flood St*, 3-storey brick houses with tall hedges and established front gardens lead to more brick and stone mansion blocks near the river and an attractive new top-of-the-market townhouse development in similar traditional style on the corner of *Alpha Place* (1986), which won a borough environmental award.

The scene changes again E of *Flood St* with a network of neat roads of smaller houses and cottages. Prettiest is *Christchurch St* with its 1830-50s artisan cottages, some with front gardens. Christ Church stands at the W end of the street near the infants' school. Between the gaily-painted cottages in *Smith Terrace* and the *King's Road*, 52 3/4-bed freehold houses set around a cobbled court-yard are due for completion at the end of 1989 (marketing from March). Developers Harry Neal.

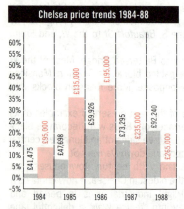

Chelsea price trends 1984-88

[bar chart showing values:
1984: £41,475 / £95,000
1985: £47,698 / £135,000
1986: £59,926 / £195,000
1987: £73,295 / £235,000
1988: £92,240 / £265,000]

■ London average home: percentage rise on previous year, adjusted for inflation.

■ Typical home in this area, percentage rise on previous year, adjusted for inflation.

Two-bed flat in a purpose built block in SW3, price change compared to London-wide average home. A modest increase in 1988 in an area which showed very steep rises in '85 and '86. In the five years to 1987 this flat was the best buy of those charted, but this flat, like other middle-rank properties and areas, seems to have run out of steam.

The S-E corner of the neighbourhood is covered largely by the famous Chelsea Physic Garden, founded 1673. *Swan Walk* with its glorious, and rare, detached Georgian houses, and *Dilke St* with its rows of mews and studio houses, lead to *Paradise Walk*. The W side is lined by a long terrace of new brick 2-storey townhouses (Wates 1986). Price of a 4-bed house rose £100,000 in a year. Phase 2 of the development is Physic Place, a newly-created mews behind the completed houses, through an arch off *Royal Hospital Rd*, next to the noted La Tante Claire restaurant.

West Chelsea

West Chelsea, until recently the area's poor relation, is coming up in the world fast and prices rocketed during 1986 and 1987. It is bounded by *Fulham Rd/King's Rd* to the N, the Thames (S), West London railway line (W), *Edith Grove/Beaufort St* (E).

The reason? The ultra-exclusive Chelsea Harbour development taking shape immediately across the borough border in Fulham (which see). As soon as the development was announced, prices in the *Lots Rd* area (between *Lots Rd* and *Edith Grove/King's Rd* and the river) began climbing. Houses with a garden in *Uverdale Rd* and *Burnaby Sts* now sell for as much as houses without a garden in posh neighbourhoods to the E.

The area faces further major change when the *Lots Rd* power station closes in 1990. The seven-acre site will be sold for development and the signs are that Chelsea Harbour will expand over Chelsea Creek into *Lots Rd*. London Underground, who own the land, have held talks with the developers over three acres of the site lying idle. More action is forecast for the old gas-works site to the west, across the railway and the borough border in Fulham (which see). Although the *Lots Rd* area is poorly served by public transport because of the distance from a tube, Chelsea Harbour is also bringing services to the neighbourhood, benefiting existing residents. A mini-bus now runs to Earls Court and Kensington High Street and a riverbus to Westminster, the City and the South Bank.

One major development which has so far failed to influence prices here is the Government's proposed Westen Environmental Improvement Route (WEIR). It will run alongside the West London railway line on the borough's western boundary, slicing through part of Chelsea College and branching in two at Chelsea Harbour. The development will be sandwiched between the W fork passing through Fulham and the E fork through Chelsea. Most of the W side of the *Lots Rd* area would probably be shielded from the road by the light industrial/commercial buildings. But the extreme E leg of *Lots Rd* looks like bearing the brunt of the traffic, together with *Cheyne Walk*. See also Transport elsewhere in this Guide.

C

Channel Tunnel trains will also run along the West London railway line. Trains carrying nuclear waste already use it.

L-shaped *Lots Rd* comprises mainly light industrial/commercial uses ranging from Bonhams auction rooms to a scrap metal yard in the W leg. The exception is a modern townhouse development, *Poole's Lane*, walled off from the street on the E side. Where *Lots Rd* meets *King's Rd* a new commercial development for owner-occupiers has been built.

Turning the corner past the Ferret and Firkin pub (real ale), the S leg is dominated by the *Lots Rd* power station, S side, with its tall chimneys and vast wall of arched glass windows. Next to it stands a refuse transfer station, water pumping station and Chelsea Wharf – a complex of small businesses and light industrial studios. The residential part lies along the extreme E end of the leg. Most of the brick and painted houses overlook the public Cremorne Gardens fronting the Thames (fishing off the jetty, kayak pool and training).

Lying inside the L-shape is a network of small streets lined with terraces of predominantly brick and stucco houses in varying styles and conditions. Many converted into flats/maisonettes. Much accommodation owned by council and Notting Hill Housing Trust. A new park, West Field, cuts across the northern corner of the neighbourhood behind the World's End Health Centre in *King's Rd*. South of the park in *Uverdale Rd* is the Ashburnham Community Centre, which also houses the Heatherley School of Fine Art. A handful of red-brick/stone mansion blocks are found in *Ashburnham Rd*. The N end of the street merges with *Cremorne Rd* to form the S end of the one-way traffic system, known locally as Juggernaut Alley. It runs N up *Gunter Grove*, S down *Edith Grove*. New homes are planned for part of the Chelsea College site between *Gunter Grove* and *Hortensia Rd*. London & Edinburgh Trust, which redeveloped Billingsgate Fish Market, was seeking planning consent at the time of writing to build 12 houses and 10 flats. First show houses should be ready summer 1989.

The one-way system creates a dividing line between the *Lots Rd* area and World's End, dominated by the World's End council estate with its unusual angular red-brick tower blocks. World's End Place, a landscaped piazza facing *King's Rd*, leads into the estate. Standing within the piazza are the Chelsea Centre, a purpose-built community centre for the area (adult education classes), and Ashburnham Primary School. St John's Church is incorporated into the flats complex. East of the estate, behind the 1950s Cremorne parade of shops, lie modern low-rise council flats, some now coming up for sale by former tenants who bought their homes.

Across *Milman's St* on the S-bend in *King's Rd* stands 355 King's Rd, an ex-council block which has been rehabilitated and converted into 50 luxury apartments (Ideal Homes). In a Cinderella-like transformation, the 13-storey tower was given a new, aluminium outer skin, and indoor gardens were planted on every third floor behind a glazed atrium. The final release was last summer, the prices £210-395,000.

Down *Milman's St* on the former St George's hostel site, Oxford-based Guardian Housing Association is building a sheltered housing development for sale to the elderly (49 units). Prices start at £155,000 for 1-bed, £230,000 for 2-bed. Completion March '89.

At the S end of the street, the houseboat colony moored on the river at *Cheyne Walk* comes into view. Houseboats offer a cheaper way of securing a smart Chelsea address. Prices range from £25,000 for a small one up to £300,000 for a luxury boat with all mod cons. You can buy a cheap boat to obtain mooring and bring in a better one. Advantages: price and no stamp duty (houseboats are considered chattels). Disadvantages: no mortgages; mooring and service charges; road proposals could displace the colony, though there is a strong local lobby in their favour.

Elm Park/North Stanley

This prime residential neighbourhood between the *Fulham* and *King's Rds* to the W of *Sydney St* includes some of the choicest streets and best squares in Chelsea. It also boasts some of the world's top specialist hospitals, as well as Chelsea's only general hospital, St Stephen's, which is to be replaced with a new 665-bed hospital.

Sydney St, the broad N-S link between South Kensington and *King's Rd*, has dignified terraces, some listed, at its N end. Opposite St Luke's Church, the new National Heart and Chest Hospital is being built. South of *Britten St* sits the Chelsea Gardener gardening centre and Chelsea Farmers' Market – an off-street colony of smart food, arts and crafts shops and outdoor cafés.

Through the back of the market, fronting *King's Rd*, is *Dovehouse Green*. It backs on to the council's Thamesbrook home for the elderly, adjoining the Heart and Chest Hospital development. The Brompton Hospital and Royal Marsden cancer hospital stand each side of *Dovehouse St*, stretching through to *Fulham Rd* (main entrances).

Tucked in behind the Marsden is *Chelsea Square*, one of the area's most prestigious addresses, with 3-storey 1930s brick houses overlooking a tree-lined garden square. The E leg of the square becomes *Manresa Rd*, home of the Chelsea School of Art. The S-W leg leads into *Carlyle Square*, the jewel in the neighbourhood's crown. The beautiful mid-19th century brick and creamy stucco houses overlooking the square gardens change hands for between £800,000 and £1 million-plus. The square is unique in that it is blocked off from the traffic in the *King's Rd* by a barrier of iron railings, trees and shrubs. A site for two large new houses, one in *Chelsea Square*, one in *Carlyle Square*, has been sold by the electricity board. Building should start this summer.

Turn W into *Old Church St*, a main through-route between *Fulham Rd* and the *King's Rd*, and head N to *Queen's Elm Square*, where a group of mock-Tudor houses sit in a semi-circle off the street. They back on to the Queen's Elm pub on the corner with *Fulham Rd*, haunt of writers and artists. Another of their haunts, the Chelsea Arts Club, is a short walk W along *Old Church St*.

Between here and *Beaufort St* many of the big houses have been converted into flats. *Beaufort St* and *Elm Park Rd* are the main areas of multi-occupation. In *Elm Park Gardens*, the borough is planning to turn basement storage roms in 24 council-owned properties into luxury flats. Private developers wil be invited to do the conversion work and in exchange wil be allowed to sell the flats on long leases. The council will retain the freehold.

The more desirable *Vale*, *Mulberry Walk* and *Mallord St* form a uniform colony of houses and purpose-built flats blocks, developed in the early part of the century for artists, architects, musicians and writers of modest means.

At the S end of *Beaufort St* are the two parts of *Chelsea Park Gardens*, a development of 1920/30s 3-storey brick suburban villas. These much sought-after houses stand well back from the road on the E side behind a screen of trees and gardens. West side ones have leafy front gardens and the central section backs on to a communal garden. One 6-bed house was bought by a German baron last summer for over £2 million.

C

Park Walk is dominated by the huge Elm Park Mansions, unique in the area in that the freehold is owned by the residents. The mansions are undergoing major repairs and renovation. Revamped flats have almost doubled in price. More expected to come on market as existing leaseholders realise profits. Leases 100 years. Good investment for first-time buyers or for letting out. (Managing agents: Keith Cardale Groves.) A car park site in the *Walk* is earmarked for 15 new flats and houses.

At the bottom of *Park Walk* is Park Walk primary school, opposite the Man in the Moon pub on the *King's Rd* S-bend (pub theatre).

Between *Park Walk* and *Edith Grove* can be found an increasingly popular residential area of big mid-Victorian family houses with gardens (*Limerston*, *Gertrude*, *Hobury*, *Shalcomb* and *Langton Sts*). Surprisingly uniform terraces of mostly 4-storey brick and stucco houses. The big disadvantage is distance from the underground.

Backing on to *Gertrude St* is St Stephen's Hospital, which takes up the N half of the block. It is to make way for a new £80 million-plus 665-bed hospital with a 300-space car park in the basement. A new exit is to be created in *Netherton Grove* to allow one-way traffic through the site. Ambulances will have their own entrance in *Fulham Rd*. Building is scheduled to finish by April 1992. Beside the site is the new Kobler Centre, Britain's first day care/out-patients' AIDS clinic.

Chelsea Green/St Luke's

From *Sydney St* eastwards to *Sloane Avenue*, this largely residential neighbourhood N of *King's Rd* is characterised by big 1900s flats blocks to the N and a mix of bijou 'dolls house' cottages and '30s brick houses S of *Cale St/Elystan Place*.

Sloane Avenue, a main N-S through-route between Chelsea and South Kensington, is lined by sprawling flats blocks like Nell Gwynn House (E),

Cranmer Court and Chelsea Cloisters (W). The latter has been refurbished and converted into luxury pied-à-terre apartments with back-up business services. *Draycott Avenue,* which runs parallel to *Sloane Avenue,* is similar. The buildings are smaller and the street somewhat quieter. Many conversions are under way.

Around the corner in *Lucan Place* (across the road from Chelsea police station) stands a new Regalian development, Crown Lodge, set in an acre of landscaped gardens with fountains, waterfalls and pergolas. The building was once housing for policemen: now flats range from £185 to £540,000. Covering the whole block, bounded on the other three sides by *Petyward, Elystan St* and *Ixworth Place,* it contains 130 1/3-bed flats with a Romanesque-style swimming pool and gymnasium in the basement. Permission is sought for 24 flats in another development in *Petyward.*

Across *Elystan St,* the NW corner of the neighbourhood is dominated by Sutton Dwellings and Samuel Lewis Trust Buildings, with the exception of narrow lanes of houses in *Pond Place* and *Bury Walk.*

At the S end of *Elystan St* at its junction with *Elystan Place* and *Cale St* lies *Chelsea Green,* heart of the area with its pleasant village green atmosphere. The tiny green is encircled by up-market food shops, restaurants, art galleries and a general store, among others. On the edge of the green between *Whiteheads Grove* and *Sprimont Place* is a surprise: the ivy-clad Gateways – a development of '30s brick houses, formally laid out cloister-style around fountain courtyards.

South of the green lies a series of much-favoured small-scale streets – *Bywater, Markham* and *Godfrey Sts,* with their colourfully-painted 19th century 3-storey houses, and around the corner *Burnsall St* with its painted, gabled houses.

Caught up between them is *Markham Square,* one of the six formal squares facing the *King's Rd,* laid out in terraces of 3-storey plus basement brick and stucco houses with black iron railings.

In contrast are the 1930s brick houses in *Astell St* and *Jubilee Place* with their leafy front gardens. Different again is *St Luke's Street,* lined with tidy terraces of 2-storey plus basement brick and stucco houses. The terraces on the W side back on to the public *St Luke's Gardens,* the leafy 'lungs' of the area. They were once a graveyard for St Luke's Church, a 19th-century Grade One listed building fronting *Sydney St.* North of the church lies St Luke's public playground.

Among those estate agents active in this area are:

- Allsops
- Aylesfords
- Beauchamp Estates
- Druce
- W A Ellis
- Farleys
- Farrar Stead & Glyn
- Friend & Falcke
- Gascoigne Pees
- Hamptons
- Jackson-Stops & Staff
- John D Wood
- Knight Frank & Rutley
- Marsh & Parsons
- Prudential Property Services
- Roy Brooks
- Savills
- Winkworths
- Jacksons
- Cluttons

Chiswick

Map ref:	p73 (5K)
Postal districts:	W4
Boroughs:	Hounslow (Lab)
Rates:	233.19p in £
Constituencies:	Brentford & Isleworth (Con)
Insurance:	Scale 2
Conservation areas:	include Grove Park, Chiswick Mall, SHRAND%ON%THE% Green.
Parking:	Free – but restrictions expected this summer

C

Transport	Turnham Green (zone 2, District, Piccadilly – restricted service); Stamford Brook (zone 2, District); Chiswick Park, Gunnersbury (zone 3a, District). From Turnham Green: Oxford Circus, 30 min (1 change); City 30 min; Heathrow, 25 min (1 change). British Rail: Chiswick to Waterloo 20 min, Gunnersbury (North London Line).
Convenient for	Heathrow, M4 and routes to the West. Kew Gardens. Miles from centre: 6.
Schools	Hounslow Education Authority: Chiswick School. Private: St Paul's (g), Godolphin & Latymer (g), Latymer (b)

Flats	S	1b	2b	3b	4b	5b
Average prices	60–70	70–100	85–150	100–160	→	–

Houses	2b	3b	4b	5b	6/7b	8b
Average prices	120–180	135–300	160–400+	200–650+	350+	–

The properties	Solid family homes, some smaller terraces; riverside has superb Georgian, plus cottages and new developments.
The market	Grove Park and riverside are smart, with high prices for family homes; the best riverside ones rarely change hands (and prices reach the £850,000 to £1 million-plus bracket). The peaceful streets inland popular with young families. Local searches: 1-2 weeks.

Area Profile

Chiswick is a community divided by the A4 *Great West Rd*. Although the twain meet frequently there is a slight difference of orientation between those who live between the A4 and the river and those who reside on the other side. The riverside community uses Southern Region railway and looks as much towards Richmond and Sheen as *Chiswick High Rd*, while the other half has easier access to District Line tubes and the *High Rd* shops.

The A4 is, however, boon as much as bane. Lying on the most direct route out of London saves Chiswick from being a mere suburban backwater: dwellers here can live in its leafy, sleepy streets and yet get to Heathrow Airport in as little as 15 minutes.

Old Chiswick began as a riverside village whose traces can still be seen in *Church St*, where St Nicholas parish church has parts dating back to the 15th century. A few earlier houses survive, but Chiswick really began growing in the mid-19th century, the bulk of development happening between then and the Second World War. The result is a variety of choice from tiny early Victorian cottages to large turn-of-the-century properties, from inter-war semis and mansion blocks to the odd in-fill of modern town houses. The more recent the property the tinier it is likely to be – even 1960s town houses are positively roomy compared with the toy boxes of the '80s. Some of the larger houses, especially in the western half and N of the *High Rd*, have been converted to flats. Established locals prefer the spaciousness of older houses and mansion flats, for which they are prepared to put up with lack of garage and consequent parking problems. Hounslow has plans for controlled parking in residential streets, to deter commuters, plus meters and a pay and display scheme.

Prices, high even by London standards, reflect the wide range as well as location. The biggest and most expensive houses are on *Chiswick Mall* (see below), but Grove Park conservation area, streets surrounding the Chiswick House conservation area, and roads between the *High Rd* and A4, all contain good-sized houses with generous gardens.

In the heart of Chiswick, just south of the *High Rd*, is the Glebe Estate (between *Duke* and *Devonshire Rds*), tiny 2- and 3-bedroom workmen's cottages now trendified into fashionable residences which sell for anything between £120,000 and £200,000. There are other pockets of bijou homes, such as Chiswick Common, N of the *High Rd*, plus plenty of solid houses built just before and after the First World War in neighbourhoods such as Stamford Brook on the Hammersmith borders. One of the top purpose-built flat blocks is Watchfield Court, often used as a pied-à-terre by television stars. Outline planning consent has been given for a mix of 21 houses and flats on part of the former Queen Charlotte's Hospital stores site in *Stamford Brook Avenue*, which is expected to be sold off by Riverside Health Authority. A nursing home is planned for the rest of the site.

South of Stamford Brook, on the other side of the *High Rd*, *Netheravon*, *Airedale* and *Homefield Rds* are desirable streets with larger houses, close to transport and Hammersmith. Westwards, down towards the Gunnersbury station end of the area, mansion blocks and houses of varying sizes, styles and periods are to be found.

Bovis Homes have fashioned 'Devonhurst Place' from a splendid Victorian warehouse: now 51 flats surround a central atrium in what was the Army and Navy depot in *Heathfield Terrace*, south of Turnham Green. Another six penthouses perch above offices on the site. Prices for the 1, 2 and 3-bedroom flats range from around £130,000 to £300,000.

C

Chiswick has attracted artists of all types ever since Hogarth bought a house (still standing, and open to the public) in 1749, along with leading businessmen. The current mixture remains much the same; it is popular with media people, City types, well-heeled executives, actors and professionals, especially architects. Young couples move into a flat or small house then progress to a larger house with a garden. They contribute to various cultural and social activities and patronise the Riverside Studios and Lyric Theatre in Hammersmith, as well as Richmond Theatre, the Watermans Arts Centre, Brentford, local pub theatres or the almost professional Questors Theatre in Ealing. They play hard at the Hogarth Health Club or Riverside Club – both private – or Fountains Leisure Centre, Brentford, and still yearn for the re-opening of Chiswick's open air swimming pool. It is a predominantly middle-class family district, where it still feels safe on the streets at night.

An immediate attraction is the greenery; apart from the river and open spaces of Dukes Meadows, many parts of Chiswick have their own little green, while the deer-filled acres of Richmond Park and Kew's famous botanical gardens are an easy drive away. Note, too, Ravenscourt Park on the Hammersmith borders: prized by mothers (1 o'clock club, adventure playground, etc) who probably discover it on visits to the adjacent Queen Charlotte's maternity hospital. The resultant atmosphere is a combination of busy city and green suburb – even the *High Rd* is tree-lined and runs by Turnham Green. This is the main shopping street – although there are many little local parades of shops scattered all round the area – with a large Sainsburys (enormous car park, open late daily) and token-size multiples including a mainly food-purveying Marks & Spencers. *Turnham Green Terrace* and, increasingly, *Devonshire Rd*, have a range of up-market specialist shops, with many late hours to suit working customers. There are a number of wine bars and restaurants, from takeaway to moderately expensive. Good transport to the City or West End with Heathrow only 15 minutes' drive away complete the list of pluses; the east side uses Stamford Brook and Turnham Green tube stations while the west has Chiswick Park and Gunnersbury, the latter being both tube and rail station. Those south of the A4 use BR's Chiswick station.

No part of Chiswick could be described as unpleasant, but higher density housing with more conversions and rentals are clustered round Turnham Green and Gunnersbury stations, along with the area by the Hogarth roundabout and flyover. Council estates are small, scattered and low-rise, with an increasing number of owner-occupiers. The main industrial area is a small estate by Gunnersbury, but this is separated from the bulk of the residential sector by the railway and *High Rd*. Office developments is confined to the *High Rd* environs. In general terms, any home too close to the railway, A4 or *Great Chertsey Rd*

loses a little value because of noise and dirt from traffic. This is a growing problem as these roads suck more and more drivers from the West into London, increasing pressure on surrounding roads. Certain parts of Chiswick are also prone to aircraft noise (the local paper even lists flight-path schedules).

Grove Park

Grove Park takes its name from Grove House, in whose grounds the Duke of Devonshire built Chiswick's first large housing estate as a high-class area for wealthy merchants. Some of these earliest houses are in *Grove Park Rd*. Over the years further tracts were developed, and in some cases redeveloped, following war damage and demolition of bigger houses and gardens. It is quintessentially Chiswick, with its wide, tree-lined roads (some specimens dating back to the original Grove House gardens) and range of properties. It is

Grove Park has long been popular for its solid, gothic-looking late Victorian villas. As this detail shows, they were designed as a piece, with even the front gate in style with the rest of the house. Note too the stone window surrounds, the stone detailing on the corners and the ecclesiastical note conveyed by the perforation in the balcony over the bay window.

particularly rich in Victorian architecture, from mid-19th century terraces to Gothic, and from red-brick timber frames with hanging tiles to later brick and creamy stucco terraces. The last big chunk of the estate was developed between the wars with roomy semis, detached houses and the odd bungalow, while since the war there have been various small estates of town houses and even the occasional striking example of modern brick and glass architecture. Flat-hunters can choose between the prestigious 1930s Hartington Court right on the river or modern small-scale blocks. There are virtually no conversions of bigger houses into smaller units. Some of the best houses are in *Hartington Rd*, despite its busy rush hour traffic, with a few having huge gardens which sweep down to the river.

Grove Park commuters use Chiswick Station to reach Waterloo and the City; they may drive to Chiswick Park or Turnham Green District Line tube stations;

some even commute outwards to satellite towns in the Thames Valley. Whatever their choice their wives need a car to cross the A4 divide for school runs and shopping.

The original estate was roughly bounded by the *Great Chertsey Rd*, on the other side of which is Dukes Meadows, the river, the North London Line railway, which effectively marks the start of *Strand on the Green*, and the Southern Region Waterloo line. Estate agents today, however, are insistent that Grove Park extends north of this railway and up to the A4. In terms of house style and price this is not totally unreasonable. Streets around Chiswick House, once the home of the Dukes of Devonshire, are spacious turn-of-the-century dwellings, often with gardens to match. *Park Rd* is generally considered one of the best addresses in Chiswick, while *Staveley Rd* is famous for its avenue of flowering cherries. Barratts is building 74 houses and 42 flats on the former Chiswick Lower School site in the street. The first of the 1-4 bedroom units should be ready this spring.

The Duke began selling off this part of his estate in 1884, but the charming little neo-Palladian Chiswick House remains in its 66-acre garden, open to the public now and a haven for urban wildlife such as foxes, squirrels and 20 different types of bird. Extra green space in the form of school grounds, allotments and playing fields makes it a particularly low-density neighbourhood. Much to the satisfaction of its predominantly owner-occupier residents the whole district north of the BR Waterloo line between *Sutton Court Rd*, the A4 and the *Great Chertsey Rd/Burlington Lane*, was declared a conservation area in 1977. This includes a little corner – *Paxton Rd*, *Sutherland Rd* and *Short Rd* – of early Victorian terraces once inhabited by Chiswick House gardeners and Reckitt & Coleman employees. Further west, new houses and flats are proposed for land off *Fauconberg* and *Hazeldene Rds*.

Grove Park also includes some modern riverside developments:

Chiswick Quay, a 1970s development of 4- to 6-bedroom town houses round a marina, was designed to appeal to boat owners, although tidal variations do not allow for spur-of-the-moment sailings. The long (c 999 years) leaseholds may fetch anything between £140,000 and £350,000, depending on size and whether it includes a river view. Despite their size these homes are unsuitable for younger children since there is no garden and the sheer sides of the marina make playing near the water highly dangerous.

Chiswick Staithe: the word 'staithe' meant embankment, an appropriate name for these 69 3- to 4-bedroom houses, built in 1964 around a landscaped, traffic-free centre facing the Thames. The very long leases cost around £200,000 to £300,000, and come with stringent regulations concerning activities and development. The estate attracts couples (often both working), with older children, or retired couples.

Thames Village: the peace of this low-density estate is much appreciated by its mainly retired residents. Built in 1955, the 2-bed maisonettes are set amidst immaculate lawns and flower beds. Prices are in the region of £95,000 to £170,000; the residents' association holds the freehold, and strict covenants apply.

Chiswick Mall/Old Chiswick

This riverside corner, where Chiswick began, is a paradox: it has remained a hidden time capsule, cut off and somehow protected by the *Great West Rd*.

Winding *Church St*, with its pretty houses and parish church, spans the centuries: the Hogarth Roundabout is at one end, the glorious *Chiswick Mall* looks tranquilly out over the Thames at the other.

There is still very much a village feel to this tiny strip. Houses range from little add-on cottages to magnificent brick or stuccoed residences in a charming jumble of periods and styles facing on to the river. The facades indicate every century from the 17th to the 20th: some, however, are even older than they look, having been modernized 200 years or so ago.

There have been three smallish modern developments where houses with up to four bedrooms go for between £230,000 and £450,000: *Eyot Green*, built in 1960 round a green just off the Mall; *Millers Court*, a 1970s square leading directly to the Mall; and *Church Wharf*, 1980s brick town houses facing the river on the west side of *Church St*. At the west end of the area, a 3½ acre site in *Pumping Station Rd* is earmarked for 105 new homes, mostly large houses. Just across the cemetery is a former nurses' home in *Dartmouth Place* which, it's proposed, will become flats. Despite the apparent dangers of water – not to mention the greedy eyes of developers – this remains a predominantly family area where neighbours know each other and children play together. Several houses have vast gardens behind, while others have a garden patch across the road bordering the river. Virtually none of the houses has been converted into flats. They are usually owned by big families who sometimes even pass a house down to the next generation; these are plum properties and if they ever come onto the market they go through West End agents at prices up to £1.5 million. For this you would get a 4-storey house with library and music room. The list of residents, past and present, is a roll call of aristocratic, artistic and industrial names. Their community spirit is fostered by the shared fear of flooding; the river comes right over the road and there is a neighbourhood warning system so cars are not marooned. Despite invasions from visitors strolling down the historic Mall residents still love their pretty riverside pubs, not to mention the birds and other river life which pass their windows.

Strand-on-the-Green

At the other, Kew, end of Chiswick is *Strand-on-the-Green*, another ancient riverside village mirroring Chiswick Mall in the E. Where fishermen once caught eels and boatyards and breweries plied their trade, now tourists throng the popular towpath pubs. Strand-on-the-Green was a working riverside village up to 15 years ago, and there is still a bit of light industry to make this a deliberately unpretentious community. Here too many houses are older than they look; the village dates back to the 15th century. The medley of styles ranges from quite grand to a row of Arts and Crafts cottages, while little passages between the houses down to the towpath add to the informality. Artists (the most famous was Zoffany) were often attracted to the area and some houses have studios at the back. Many desirable residences have humble origins, having once been shops, pubs, a post office or tea house. Gardens tend to be small. It is now a conservation area, with many listed buildings along the river frontage. Flats are rare; the main inhabitants are families who stay for years, watching their children grow up messing around with boats on the river, which is the area's main hobby and focus. Anyone with less than 10 years' residence is considered a newcomer. This, however, is changing, as the odd well-off young couple discovers the cachet of a riverside address without quite the prices of Chiswick Mall – a 4-bedroom house would cost from £300,000. There is the occasional modern development, including *Magnolia Wharf*, which offers 4-bedroom houses for around £300,000 to £350,000. The roads behind were developed in late Victorian red brick; once occupied by the working classes, they have been taken over by young middle-class families who find around £160,000 good value for a 3-bedroom home. *Oliver Close* is a 1980s estate of tiny houses and flats. North of the railway, the McAlpine development in *Wellesley Rd* has 61 studio, 1 and 2-bed flats. Last autumn's prices were £63,500 for a studio, £96,000 for a 2-bed flat.

Residents use Kew Bridge BR Waterloo line or take a 10 minute walk under the *Great West Rd* for *Chiswick High Rd* buses, or Gunnersbury on the District Line tube and BR's North London Line. Like other inhabitants on this side of Chiswick they find a car invaluable; most houses have garaging at the back since unlike the Mall, which has a proper road running alongside the river, they only have a towpath. Flooding is not a problem here since the advent of the Thames barrage. Parking is only difficult at the beginning and end of the school day as mothers sweep up in the car to collect their off-spring from school (Strand-on-the-Green Primary has a reputation which extends beyond the immediate district), while *Thames Rd* is a dangerously busy rat-run. Unlike most of Chiswick they are free of aircraft noise, although Kew Bridge produces a background drone. The only other drawbacks seem to be bums and beermugs on their window sills during the summer tourist season.

C

Among those estate agents active in this area are:
- Barnard Marcus
- John Granville
- Raymond Bushell
- Prudential
- Tyser Greenwood
- Winkworths

City and fringes

Map ref: p142 (6D)
Postal districts: EC1, EC2, EC3, EC4, E1
Boroughs: City of London, Tower Hamlets (Lib)
Rates: C: 124.9p in £. TH: 217.89p in £
Constituencies: City of London and Westminster South (Con)
Insurance: Scale 1
Conservation areas: Several - check with Corporation/Council
Parking: Residents/meters

Transport	Tubes, all zone 1: Liverpool Street (Central, Circle, Metropolitan); Holborn (Central, Piccadilly); Bank (Central, Northern); Blackfriars, Cannon Street, Monument (District, Circle); Moorgate, (Metropolitan, Circle, Northern). Others see map. From Bank to: Oxford Circus 10 min, Heathrow 1 hr 15 min (1 change).

Convenient for   West End, Docklands & City Airport. Miles from centre: 1.5.

Schools   ILEA zone 5: no secondary schools in City, see neighbouring areas. Private: City of London School (b)(g)

Flats	S	1b	2b	3b	4b	5b
Average prices	75–95	85–170	110–260	160–300	280–600+	–
Houses	2b	3b	4b	5b	6/7b	8b
Average prices	180–260	200–470	→	–	–	–

The properties   Hardly any homes in jam-packed office-land. Barbican has modern flats and houses. A very few period homes in fringe areas like Spitalfields and Smithfield, plus company flats.

The market   Barbican homes, originally rented, are now bought and sold. Prices can be good value compared with West End. Rare period homes and a very few (and pricy) new developments likely in fringe areas. See also Docklands for plentiful homes to E and S; Islington for family ones to N. Local searches: City 1-2 weeks, TH 3-4 weeks.

Area Profile

When considering a place to live in London, the City does not readily spring to mind. It is a place to work, not sleep, one feels. Yet for centuries its densely-packed acres held homes as well as work-places, and it is still possible to live there today. Indeed, the City's fringe areas, Spitalfields and Smithfield, will gain new homes as redevelopment takes place.

The true City, enclosed by *Commercial St* in the E, *Old St* in the N, *Chancery Lane* in the W and the River Thames, has few places to live. The sprawling Barbican complex N of *London Wall* represents the largest residential area in the City – and that thanks only to war damage.

A quick walk through the City soon determines just how great is the pressure on available land. Developments are sprouting up at an alarming rate but only the world of finance can afford the ever-increasing land prices. Virtually every major street in the Square Mile can boast a new office complex – but finding somewhere to live is often a thankless task. For those house hunting in the City it is often a case of take what you can get. This makes the property market in the City definitely one for the sellers and a bad one for discerning buyers. People are prepared to sacrifice their ideals of space and amenity to live in the City, however. Often it is a necessity because many major financial firms are now insisting that their top dealers live as near to the City as possible.

But life in the City definitely has its advantages. Transport is excellent during the week and all other parts of London are within easy reach. Close by is the world-renowned Barbican Arts Centre, and the 'village' atmosphere of the City is prized by all its residents. The City is unique in that its local council is entirely independent and non-political. The Corporation governs the Square Mile and its members are voted in by a mediaeval system. This entirely independent body is in charge of the City's day to day business, and the Corporation contributes greatly to the area's feeling of independence from the rest of London. While the City is certainly an exciting place during the day, it is definitely a 'Jekyll and Hyde' neighbourhood. After eight at night the Square Mile resembles a ghost town as all the office workers retreat to the suburbs. Night life is almost non-existent in the City and the few shops are very expensive. Even the pubs close. Weekends are also a problem, when local transport services are severely reduced from the levels of the weekday rush. But for all the drawbacks people are still prepared to pay a lot of money for that exclusive EC address. One luxury block, Norfolk House, has appeared on the riverside in *Trig Lane*, near the steps to St Pauls, with prices from £285,000 to £1,550,000.

Finding somewhere to live in the City is difficult but actually finding an estate agent to help you if often harder. In most areas a quick look through the phone book is enough, but in the City 99% of estate agents deal with purely commercial property. Only in the fringe areas of the City is there any sort of residential market. The sprawling Barbican complex accounts for the vast majority of homes. Just to the N is the council-owned Golden Lane Estate. There homes may sometimes appear on the market: since the Government reforms on council house ownership, allowing purchase by tenants, those who bought their properties on the Estate have shown a very handsome profit if they care to sell. Small residential markets also exist in the Smithfield and Spitalfields areas where an increasing number of properties are coming onto the market.

Barbican

The Barbican complex is bordered by *London Wall, Aldersgate St, Moorgate* and *Chiswell St.* Described by the developers as a 'city within a city', the three main towers of the Barbican – just some of the 21 residential blocks – dominate much of the Square Mile's skyline. To those expecting a world of penthouse flats and luxurious living, first impressions of the Barbican can often prove disappointing. The promotional literature promises so much but the exterior reality is often a let-down. The complex presents a picture of rather drab, grey, concreted uniformity in its outward appearance. Between the dull-looking buildings are token open spaces that seem to have been put there as an afterthought.

But the inside of many Barbican flats tells a completely different story – they belie their outward appearance and provide some of the most luxurious living in central London. Biggest prices are paid for the luxury penthouses of *Lauderdale, Cromwell,* and *Shakespeare Towers.* The *Shakespeare Tower* is listed in the Guinness Book of Records as the tallest residential building in Britain. The view from the top reaches clear to the hills surrounding London.

The Barbican contains over 2,000 homes with a roughly 50/50 split between leasehold and rental. Leasehold is definitely the growing trend and the estate's managers are keen to sell as many homes as possible. The turnover of properties is very slow for prospective buyers, and unless prepared to wait it is very much a case of having to settle for what is currently on the market. Types of home range from bed-sitters right through to a small number of town houses. The majority of properties available are 1- and 2-bedroomed flats. As would be expected, services such as estate cleaning and security are given a high priority and are of an excellent standard. The Barbican also has a very strong and active residents' association which presents a powerful voice at local council meetings.

The centrepiece of the whole complex is the magnificent Barbican Arts Centre. It is the home of the London Symphony Orchestra and the Royal

Shakespeare Company and is the largest development of its kind in western Europe. Theatres, concert halls, cinemas, an art gallery, library, bars, restaurants, exhibition and conference facilities are all here.

The Barbican provides a home for over 6,000 people and is a much coveted place to live. Although it look rather dull and lifeless, the complex is ideally located for those who want to be near the artistic and financial centres. Business is however flexing its muscles in the residential market, buying up Barbican flats for important members of staff. The outlook therefore is one of increasing scarcity for housing in the Barbican.

Spitalfields

Spitalfields is where the City merges with East End. *Commercial St, Middlesex St* and *Bishopsgate* form the boundaries of this unique part of London. A big wholesale fruit and vegetable market has dominated the area for years, but after much wrangling the market will be moving some time in 1989 to Temple Mills in East London. A vast commercial complex will be built on the 11-acre site. The plans include over 500 homes. There are existing homes in Spitalfields, some beautiful early Georgian ones with interiors to make a classicist swoon. Some have been lovingly restored, and will be retained in the area's redevelopment.

C

Just to the W, the multi-million pound *Broadgate* development is being completed. Both these developments illustrate the desire of firms to locate in this area just on the eastern fringes of the City. Commerce can therefore be seen to be pushing domestic usage out and, apart from the homes in Spitalfields, there are no purely residential developments being built. Just off *Bishopsgate*, the area around the market site seems a million miles away from the City. The atmosphere is purely East End, enhanced by the street market.

Spitalfields is beginning to attract attention as a place to live. The few Georgian houses go for £250,000 and a brisk market in pieds-à-terre is developing. Prices for small flats equate with those with no river view in Wapping. Conversions of old buildings provide nearly all the available homes. An example is Pennybank Chambers, *Great Eastern St*, which has 65 small flats priced last winter at around £75,000. The Cloisters, *Commercial St*, a purpose-built portered block, commands a few thousand more for its 1-bed flats. Further south, the *Leman St* area has a few homes. Leybourne House is a modern block with swimming pool and that ever more vital City amenity, an underground car park.

Smithfield

Smithfield, at the NW edge of the City, is a neighbourhood dominated by the world-famous meat market. Contained within *Charterhouse St, Aldersgate St* and *Newgate St*, it has a few homes amid the commercial buildings. Smithfield is definitely one of the City's up-and-coming areas following the Corporation's recent publication of several reports aimed at regenerating the neighbourhood. The meat market's future was in doubt, but it is now confirmed that it will remain. The Corporation is committed to an £18 million refurbishment programme that will also include small office units. The Corporation's latest amendments to the Smithfield plan include the policy "to encourage an increase of residential accommodation in suitable locations within Smithfield." The largest recent development is "Florin Court" in *Charterhouse Square*.

Regalian refurbished the 9-storey 1936 building to provide over 100 luxury flats. Prices started at £92,500 for a studio up to £255,000 for a 2-bed flat. The volume of property on the market at any one time is very small, but several new residential complexes have sprouted up recently. Typical of these is the small development in the little side street of *Cloth Fairs*. A parade of 10 mews-style homes has been built and they represent one of the largest residential developments in the area. A further 10 flats were built last year in *Charterhouse St* and these modern homes were snapped up very quickly.

Of all the areas in the City, Smithfield offers the greatest potential for developers to create a significant domestic property market. The neighbourhood consists of many small streets and side roads which lend themselves to domestic use. Also significant for potential buyers is the fact that local estate agents have set up residential departments. Another growth area here is businesses buying, rather than leasing, their office buildings. This trend was fuelled by recent dramatic City rent increases, and by the prospect of capital growth in the property investment: prices around Smithfields rose 30% in 1987 and again in 1988.

While the majority of presently available flats are represented by rather run-down Victorian homes above shops and offices, the future definitely lies in new developments. The majority of Smithfield's current residents are located in the halls of St Bartholomew's Hospital but the population seems set to grow as more people are attracted to this picturesque and colourful part of London.

Fleet Street

In a whirlwind of redundancies, riots and lucrative property deals, the newspapers have left the Street of Shame for the dank open spaces of the Isle of Dogs and Battersea. What's left is an area exciting flurries of interest from property developers. There are few homes there now, barring the odd penthouse built by yesterday's press barons. But this could change in the future as the street and its picturesque hinterland is re-vamped. An area to watch: most of the buildings are listed, so conversions to flats may occur. A block in Cliffords Inn, *Fetter Lane*, has purpose-built flats in a modern block: a studio was £85,000 in December. The 'Ludgate corridor' along the N-S railway is to be redeveloped, though no homes are envisaged.

Hoxton

An area which should not go un-mentioned is Hoxton, lying due N of the City. Blighted by well-intentioned post-war council monstrosities, it yet manages to cling to the remnants of its vigorous past: the music hall in the high street still stands as a thriving theatre/community centre. There are signs of a renaissance and even a few homes for sale. North of here are Islington and Hackney, W is Finsbury. The canal which bounds the area has spurred some residential/commercial developments W towards Islington and more could follow. Long-term, this corner's position must make for inner-city revival.

Among those estate agents active in this area are:
- Alan Selby
- Barbican Estates Office
- Ian Lerner
- Jarvis Keller
- Tarn & Tarn
- Halls Property Centre

Clapham

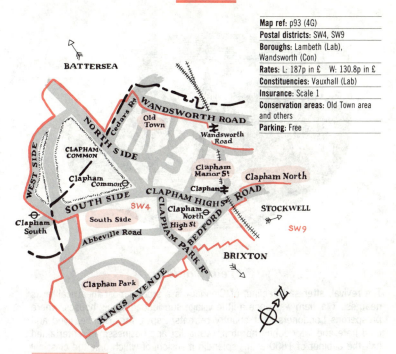

Map ref:	p93 (4G)
Postal districts:	SW4, SW9
Boroughs:	Lambeth (Lab), Wandsworth (Con)
Rates:	L: 187p in £ W: 130.8p in £
Constituencies:	Vauxhall (Lab)
Insurance:	Scale 1
Conservation areas:	Old Town area and others
Parking:	Free

B

Transport Tubes: Clapham South, Clapham Common, Clapham North (zones 2/3a, Northern); Oxford circus 20 min (1 change),City 25 min, Heathrow 1 hr 10 min (2 changes). BR: Wandsworth Road, Clapham

Convenient for City, West End, Sloane Square. Miles from centre: 3

Schools ILEA zones 9/10. Henry Thornton School, St Francis Xavier RC 6th form college, Chestnut Grove School

Flats	S	1b	2b	3b	4b	5b
Average prices	50–60	65–85	75–110	90–130	130+	–
Houses	2b	3b	4b	5b	6/7b	8b
Average prices	95–140	120–170+	140–220	155–300+	→	–

The properties Many Victorian terraces, some splendid Queen Anne, Georgian and Recency around the Common, Old Town and Crescent Grove, lots of converted flats (incl good large ones) and some 20th century flats blocks. Large houses in The Chase, Macaulay Rd, Rodenhurst Ave; typical house is 3/4 beds terraced, 4/5 beds around Abbeville.

The market South Side and Old Town are well 'discovered', former attracts families wanting space, latter has older, more character properties For lower prices try to N and E, though some SW4 streets are really Brixton. Local searches: Lambeth 10 weeks, Wandsworth 1.

Area profile

The revival, after sad decline, of Clapham is a story almost theatrical in its neatness. Clapham was once a little village surrounded by big houses, where prosperous Londoners kept country retreats. Pepys, for instance, lived and died here and later John Thornton, evangelist and businessman, entertained half the cabinet of 1800 at his splendid mansion, of which only the classical orangery survives amid a grim council estate. In early Victorian times more grand houses appeared as the ubiquitous Thomas Cubitt built a whole suburb of them and called it Clapham Park. But as the century went on, and trams and later tubes made Clapham cheap and easy to get to, the houses got smaller and smaller. By the turn of the century, Clapham was a byword for ordinariness. 'The man on the Clapham omnibus' became a judicial simile for all that was everyday and reasonable.

The tube, the arrival of which abetted the demolition (begun with the railways) of so many grand houses and their replacement with modest terraces, has more recently been Clapham's salvation. For thanks to the Northern Line, Clapham, unlike most parts of South London, has a direct link to the West End and particularly the City. A decade ago, housebuyers began to discover that Clapham is as close to Sloane Square as Fulham is, and that the journey to the City is a lot quicker. Clapham was re-established, after spending most of the 20th century in steady decline into seediness. In recent years Battersea has perhaps pulled ahead in the respectability stakes, helped primarily by its Tory council which charges lower rates than Labour Lambeth.

Clapham began as a village at the north end of the wide Common. The old village is still there, with a pleasant mix of buildings that includes a row of fine Queen Anne houses. From here the fine houses spread out S and W, beginning with a handsome 1820s row and going on to Cubitt's 250 acres of 'capacious detached villas' in Clapham Park. Later Victorian times saw the growth of *Clapham High St* and a shift in Clapham's commercial centre of gravity from the *Old Town* eastwards. This has reversed itself in recent years as Clapham

Junction to the W has boomed as a shopping centre. The Junction, by the way, is in Battersea not Clapham, a source of confusion for a century.

Today, Clapham divides into several distinct neighbourhoods radiating out from the Old Town, which is both a street-name and the name for the old village and nearby streets. The area W of the Common is Battersea (which see), or more normally now 'between the Commons'. The flat, low-lying streets N of *Wandsworth Rd* are thought of as Battersea too: Clapham is proud of being on a low but distinct hill. To the S the roads around Clapham South tube are now called 'Clapham South' but were Balham (which see): it would have been less confusing if the tube people had stuck to their original name for the station, Nightingale Lane. East, beyond Clapham Park, is a zone debated with Brixton.

Old Town

Strictly speaking, *Old Town* is a street, but the core of old Clapham has annexed the name. As with all such desirable tags, estate agents try to stretch it as far as possible. *Old Town* proper has Clapham's oldest and handsomest houses, a row of three dating from 1705. A new mews development has been promised off *Old Town* for over a year: no action yet. To the E is *Grafton Square*, a pleasant, rather untidy garden square surrounded on three sides by tall white stucco houses, which often have attractive semi-basement flats. There are three pretty 2-storey stucco houses, plus some new-build in the road off the Square: three new houses by Berkeley Homes. Broadwell are building 29 flats, with offices behind, in a smart development on the site of a garage at the W end of the Square. On the NW corner four new flats have just been finished. North of the Square are several streets of solid, 3/4-storey Victorian houses: *Offerton*, *Liston* and *Fitzwilliam Rds*. *Rectory Grove* runs N from the Old Town to pass the old parish church and link with *Larkhall Rise*. This is a busy traffic route, but has some attractive houses of varying periods. *Rectory Gardens* belies its name: a virtual slum of tiny mews cottages, it is about to be modernised by a housing association. *Turret Grove*, named after a prominent feature of the Elizabethan manor which once stood here, has some pretty cottages as well as the Victorian terraces it shares with *Rozel* and *Ively Rds*.

West of *Old Town* and its continuation *North St* is a quiet network of streets. *Macaulay Rd* was built in late Victorian times with very large gabled detached and semi-detached houses, many of which survive. Most are flats but some are still vast single hopmes. A 2-bed, 2-bath garden flat was on sale last winter for £135,000. Macaulay Court is a block of '30s flats, nicely positioned, always with some for sale. *Macaulay Square* is a small council estate. *The Chase* has similarly vast Victorian houses. *Lillieshall Rd* has some substantial Victorian terraces and some pretty, very small cottages (and the area's nicest pub) at the E end. Parallel *Broadhinton Rd* has some attractive early Victorian cottages. *Orlando Rd* has 3-storey Victorian houses, many flats. One 5-bed house was on the market for £235,000.

The *North Side* of Clapham Common has a succession of terraces of various periods, from early Georgian through mid-Victorian to 1930s flats. The two commanding blocks on either side of *Cedars Rd* are remarkable examples of 1860s grandiose. Several of the enormous houses are now flats which have fine views across London to the N and the Common to the S. *Cedars Rd*, once lined with villas, is now mostly council housing. A new development of mews houses is planned in *Victoria Rise*. *Wix's Lane* to the W marks the border both

C

of Lambeth borough and the SW4 postcode.

The continuation of *Old Town* to the S is *The Pavement*, a curve of increasingly smart shops facing Holy Trinity church on the Common. There are some flats above shops, and a couple of popular interwars blocks of flats. The Common is the area's outdoor sitting room, used by small and not-so-small boys to fly kites and model aircraft, to fish and to sail boats on the ponds. Across the Common, *West Side* scrapes into the SW4 postcode though its hinterland is SW11. The tall, popular houses stand in their quiet road facing the Common: traffic is deflected down *The Avenue*, which is part of the South Circular.

Clapham Manor Street

The Old Town area is bounded to the E by a tract of council housing around *Cubitt Terrace*. These are nicely-designed, brick-built, mainly 2-storey, and arranged in pleasant closes and green squares. A few are appearing on the resale market, though Right to Buy has not caught on in Lambeth as it has in neighbouring Wandsworth. To the N of *Larkhall Lane* are some sloping streets of terraced houses: *Brayburne Avenue*, with 4-bed houses, *Netherfold Rd* and, E of the railway, *Killyon Rd*. The little Wandsworth Road BR station has a restricted service to Victoria and London Bridge. The railway line will be used by Channel Tunnel trains.

Clapham Manor St, especially at its N end, is handsome with 2-storey Cubitt terraces, much in demand as family homes. The S end, towards the *High St*, is more mixed. The little roads off to the E have later Victorian terraces, and *Edgeley Rd* has rather looming 3-storey Victorian ones, most flats. The E side backs onto the railway. The corner between *Old Town* and *Clapham Manor St* has some 3-storey purpose-built Victorian flats in *Bromells Rd* and some flats in smaller terraces in *Venn St*, two minutes from Clapham Common tube.

High Street

Clapham's *High St* is hanging on, just, as an all-purpose shopping centre. To the annoyance of locals its Woolworths was closed in 1987, but a large Superdrug replaced it. The street is a busy but convenient collection of banks, building societies, restaurants, small supermarkets and a post office. A question mark hangs over the 5-acre site occupied by the disused bus garage S of the *High St*. Lambeth council has earmarked the site for a large supermarket, but a long delay by LRT led to tenders coming in only late last year and no sale decision at the time of writing. There is local speculation that a supermarket is unviable there and homes may be built. S of the *High St* is a mixed area of Victorian terraces and council housing. It is very close to tube and common, and offers better value than the more 'tidy' areas of Clapham. *Nelson's Row* with its dozen flat-fronted Victorian cottages leads on down to a '30s redbrick council estate, then to the attractive modern council houses of *Haselrigge Rd*. *St Luke's Avenue* and the roads to the E are mostly 3-storey Victorian, many now flats, which are cheaper here than in other Clapham neighbourhoods. New business units have been built in mews style in *Tremadoc Rd*. The NE end of this corner is close to Clapham North tube.

The streets S of *Clapham Park Rd*, down as far as the corner with *Abbeville Rd*, are council homes. A new mews of 'business units' has just been completed in *Clapham Park Rd*. *Northbourne Rd* has some well-preserved detached and semi-detached mid-Victorian houses on a handsome scale. These are some of the nicest houses in Clapham, but are tucked away in rather drab surroundings. A smart 4-bed one was on the market for £575,000 in December. *Park Hill* has some '20s gabled terraces, some modern flats and a few large 19th century houses. It runs up to Clapham Park.

Clapham North

East of the tube station and N of the railway, and in the SW9 postcode, is a rather cut-off corner of Victorian terraces and council housing. The Southwestern Hospital, which may be redeveloped, forms the border with Brixton. Housing in this district is cheaper than in other parts of Clapham, but it is further from the Common and some streets are distinctly down-at-heel. However, roads in the little network N of *Landor Rd – Atherfold, Hamberton* and *Prideaux* – are worth investigating. Along *Clapham Rd* towards Stockwell are some fine but neglected Georgian houses, most used as offices.

West of *Clapham Rd, Gauden, Bromfelde, Sibella* and *Chelsham Rds* have some big Victorian houses. Some good flat conversions can be found, including one in *Gauden Rd* where several houses have been split into flats which share the large communal garden and a swimming pool. Some houses, however, are still single homes: they are large and can be spectacular – and £300,000.

C

Clapham Park

Cubitt's elegant suburb of detached mansions has vanished, leaving as its legacy large trees and the occasional surviving square early 19th century house, now flats. *Kings Avenue* has several blocks of flats – Queenswood Court includes one of the Victorian houses – Robins, Oakfield and Thorncliffe Courts are '30s blocks, Peters Court is '60s. A 3-bed flat in one of the '30s block was on the market for £95,000 last winter. Interwars detached houses punctuate the flats. *Kings Mews* is a modern group of houses tucked behind an old house. East of the Avenue is in SW2 and is a border zone between Brixton and Clapham Park. There are several quiet streets of Victorian terraces. Brixton Prison dominates the E end of *Thornbury Rd*. *Kingswood Rd* has some larger, 3-storey houses. These streets are fairly evenly split between single houses and flat conversions. A typical price in January was £85,000 for a 2-bed garden flat in *Thornbury Rd*. The S end of *Kings Avenue* and W to *Clarence Avenue* is all council housing, houses and low blocks set in a pleasant green space. The N end of *Clarence Avenue* has some 1930s semi-detached houses.

South Side

This is the largest residential neighbourhood in Clapham and the most uniform, consisting almost entirely of Victorian terraced housing. The grid of streets runs down a gentle slope from *Clapham Common South Side* to *Abbeville Rd* then on up again towards Clapham Park. The parade of shops at the junction of *Abbeville Rd* and *Narbonne Avenue* has recently been dignified with the name 'Abbeville Village', but though the road makes a pleasant neighbourhood shopping centre the name is an estate agents' conceit and has no local roots.

There is no way through from *Clarence Avenue* in Clapham Park to the next road W, *Rodenhurst Rd*, which belongs to South Side. This divide is architectural as well as physical: much of *Rodenhurst* (except the S end) is large, popular Edwardian semi-detached double-fronted houses set well back from the wide road. *Poynders Rd* forms the S boundary of Clapham – and is also the South Circular Road. It has some rather depressed-looking interwars flats, some modern town houses and some Edwardian ones. Its equally busy continuation, *Cavendish Rd*, has big turn-of-the-century houses.

West from *Rodenhurst Rd* is *Elms Crescent* which is lined with late 19th century bay-windowed terraced houses. It and the roads off it to the W are very uniform: exceptions to the 2-storey terraced rule include *Elms Rd*, which has some handsome tall-gabled, wider than average houses on the N side. A 6-bed semi was on the market for £395,000 in January. *Leppoc Rd* has 4-bed houses, typical for the area, which were selling in the winter for around £150,000. A 4-room flat in *Elms Crescent* was £90,000. The number of trees, width of the road (and thus ease of parking) and distance from the tube are the variables around here. *Abbeville Rd*, which carries a fair amount of traffic, has some bigger than usual houses, many divided into flats. There are also flats above the shops in the parade and a few nice big purpose-built flats in Edwardian blocks. The W end of *Elms Rd* runs up towards the Common and has some large 1880s houses, some detached and double-fronted. Five large square Victorian houses at the W end are flats. Opposite is the new Berkeley Homes mews development, to which 2- and 3-bed houses will be added this spring.

The Common at the junction with *Elms Rd* is lined with big Victorian terraces set back behind a strip of grass. These are South Kensington-like houses with pillared porches, all flats. A surviving detached villa is about to be developed, having been sold by London Transport. *St Gerards Close* is a little estate of 4-storey flats built within the last 10 years. Opposite, on the Common, is the popular Windmill pub with a few tall houses behind it. Some are splendid flats, their roofs partially glazed to form big rooms with wide views.

Narbonne Avenue runs back down towards Abbeville. Its 4-bed houses were changing hands around the £175,000 mark last winter. Very smart ones with 2 baths were £220,000. *Eagle House Mews* off the Avenue is a neat group of mews cottages tucked behind a gate. *Hambalt* and *Mandalay Rds* are mostly terraced housing with quite a few purpose-built flats, which can be spotted by their pairs of front doors under a single arch. The streets S of *Narbonne* are mostly Victorian terraces, but with some post-war 3-storey flats.

Crescent Grove is a splendid Regency crescent facing a row of grand semi-detached villas of the same period, the whole forming a private road entered through a gateway. These splendid homes used to be cheap but are now well 'discovered' and command prices of £½m. The coachhouses which link the big villas have themselves become sought-after small homes. The neighbour of this enclave is the hideous Notre Dame Estate: gaunt brick blocks at odd angles, looming over the Common. *Crescent Lane* has a few council homes, some in pleasant cottage style are appearing for sale. Once it crosses *Abbeville Rd*, *Crescent Lane* becomes Victorian, with 3-4 bed terraces.

Among those estate agents active in this area are:

- Andrews & Robertson
- Barnard Marcus
- Folkard & Hayward
- Hugh Henry
- Morgan Gillie
- Bell Son & Co
- Callows
- Friend & Falcke
- Jacksons
- Price & Co
- Cornerstone
- Roy Brooks

Clerkenwell

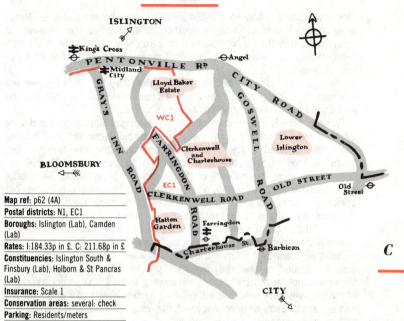

Map ref: p62 (4A)
Postal districts: N1, EC1
Boroughs: Islington (Lab), Camden (Lab)
Rates: I:184.33p in £. C: 211.68p in £
Constituencies: Islington South & Finsbury (Lab), Holborn & St Pancras (Lab)
Insurance: Scale 1
Conservation areas: several: check
Parking: Residents/meters

C

Transport	Tubes: Angel (zone 1, Northern); Farringdon (zone 1, Circle, Metropolitan). From Angel to: Oxford Circus 10 min (1 change), City 6 min, Heathrow 1 hr 10 min (1 change). British Rail: Farringdon (Moorgate 10 min and Thameslink).	
Convenient for	The City, King's Cross, St Pancras and Euston stations. Miles from centre: 1.5.	
Schools	ILEA zones 2/3: Central Foundation (b).	

Flats	S	1b	2b	3b	4b	5b
Average prices	55–75	65–100+	90–130+	135+	–	–
Houses	2b	3b	4b	5b	6/7b	8b
Average prices	150–200+	210–350+	→	→	–	–

The properties	Handsome Regency and Victorian houses, conversions of commercial/warehouses, council flats. Homes scattered amid offices and industry and very varied in quality. Some gems.
The market	Dearth of homes makes market patchy. The real gems command a premium, but otherwise prices marked time last year. Period-home lovers and City people have discovered the area, which has a charm all its own. Some of the best houses have long been council-owned: watch for un-refurbed resales. Local searches: Islington 3 weeks, Camden minimum 12 weeks.

Area Profile

Clerkenwell and Finsbury have at first sight enormous potential as a residential area, ideally situated with a high proportion of Georgian buildings. However, in recent years demand for homes has always exceeded supply, due to the high percentage of commercial property. What homes there are tend to be let to council tenants.

The area is N of the City and *Fleet St*, E of the *Grays Inn Rd*, St Pancras and Bloomsbury, S of *City Rd* and the Angel. It's convenient for the City, West and East Ends and Docklands and the mainline railway stations.

Property here is a curious mixture, mainly Georgian and modern, and fairly evenly divided between commercial and residential. Much Victorian housing was either bombed or has been demolished since the war. Streets often contain a mixture of architectural styles and periods, and residential and commercial uses. The majority of the homes are 1- and 2-bed flats; large houses and studios are rare. Two-, 3- and 4-bed houses are available, but scarce — most agents seem to sell only between four and five houses a year. However, it is difficult to be precise about the exact nature of housing stock since so little property comes on to the market. For the moment, all property is scarce and the percentage of owner occupation is low.

Being adjacent to the City but outside the walls, the area developed as a pleasure ground, a favourite execution site for political prisoners and a favoured haunt for archery practice and bowling. In the 18th century, a number of the old wells were rediscovered, including Sadlers Wells and Bagnigge Wells, and the area rapidly developed a reputation as a fashionable watering place, with an array of theatres and tea gardens.

This part of London divides roughly into four neighbourhoods: Clerkenwell and Charterhouse, Lower Islington, Hatton Garden and the Lloyd Baker estate. These are all approximations, areas are difficult to define since there are no clear boundaries and no consensus among either inhabitants or estate agents as to what to call them. No agent uses the term Finsbury, once the accepted local name, since it is too easily confused with Finsbury Park, a couple of miles to the N. Finsbury was a separate borough from 1900 to 1965, when Islington took over. No estate agent deals with the whole area, most deal with a portion adjacent to a surrounding area, thus Islington agents will deal with the Lloyd Baker estate but not Clerkenwell.

Lower Islington, between *Old St* and *City Rd*, is almost exclusively council housing with a large number of very high '60s-style tower blocks with 20-plus floors. Some lower-rise housing occurs towards the Clerkenwell border, and there is a lot of commercial property. Good, quiet estates, private ownership, it seems, unheard of.

Lloyd Baker estate, on the W edge of the area, and North Clerkenwell include the Georgian Lloyd Baker estate proper, and the area to the E of *Goswell Rd* and W of Lower Islington which has no official designation but is sometimes referred to as North Clerkenwell. The architecture is mainly Georgian, some modern high-rises, a little commercial, a high proportion of council housing. The Lloyd Baker estate was originally built by the Lloyd Baker family in 1819, and was partly sold to the Islington council on the death of Miss Lloyd Baker in 1975. It consists mainly of Georgian flat-fronted brick terrace houses, retaining an old charm with its fine squares with central gardens. Streets are wider here and houses larger, generally 3/4-bed houses and 2-bed flats. This neighbourhood has a higher percentage of home ownership than most of the area, but still not a majority. Still not as select as parts of Islington, but getting there. This area has enormous potential. The cultured find it to be conveniently close to Sadler's Wells.

Clerkenwell and Charterhouse, much of it inhabited from the Middle Ages, has roads which retain their medieval flavour, twisting and turning like snakes and ladders upon a board. They are districts of narrow, dense streets, with concealed alleys and arches and mixtures of architectural styles and residential and commercial uses. There is a high percentage of Georgian; many other buildings have been given Post-Modern spruce-ups. The area is increasingly popular for office space, since it is close to the City but rents are not as high. Lots of small shops and businesses, generally 1- and 2-bed flats; although there are some houses here, finding them is like pulling plums out of the pudding.

Hatton Garden is traditionally London's centre of the jewellery trade, especially diamonds. It's next door to Holborn, and so has a distinctly upmarket, big-business feel; streets are wider and less medieval in appearance. There may be flats concealed above shops, but property here is mainly commercial with enclaves of council housing and some new developments dotted about. Nevertheless, there's still a high proportion of Georgiana.

The most expensive areas tend to be on the Smithfield and Barbican borders, and Clerkenwell Green and Lloyd Baker estate. In the last category prices are still below those in Islington. If you want to buy more cheaply try the Kings Cross (which see) borders – especially in the streets with dense traffic such as *Kings Cross Rd* or those near railway lines – for example *Britannia St*. Or near densely populated housing estates such as Wynatt St or Exmouth Market. It's a good place to buy now; property is increasingly in demand because of proximity to the City, and prices can only go up. But until local authority houses are sold on a large scale there'll be no great increase in supply, and it is unlikely that the two local boroughs Camden and Islington will overcome their reluctance to sell in the near future. Even if they did begin to change their attitude it would still require a 50-60% owner-occupation level before the resale market for council properties would be viable.

The large amount of council homes contributes a continuity in the population now missing from other corners of town – most tenants have lived there all their lives, often working in the printing trade. But there are also a lot of academics from the University, City types since Big Bang, plus publishers because of Bloomsbury and designers and typesetters.

The area's advantages are its location, close to the West and East Ends, 5-10 minutes from the City, and close to major stations which makes it ideal for dormitory living. Its disadvantages are obtaining property in the first place, obtaining planning permission, and the housing stock itself which is very mixed, and uneven even within streets. In addition, despite a large number of squares and parks, it remains essentially urban, and the area is dead at weekends; there is little in the way of shops, restaurants or nightlife. And parking, especially around Clerkenwell, can be a nightmare.

C

Lower Islington

The *Old St* roundabout is the most easterly point of the area; from it *City Rd* runs NW and *Old St* SW. The area between the fork is Lower Islington, almost exclusively modern council housing mixed with some commercial property.

Bath St runs N-S between the two. Entering at the *Old St* end, property is modern low-rise maisonettes which extends W towards *Lizard St*. Continuing N, you enter the high-rise estates, tower blocks of between 16 and 20 storeys, including roads to the E and W: *Peerless*, *Galway*, *Radnor*, *Mora* and the lower portion of *Lever St*. Turning W along *Lever St*, roads to the N are mainly commercial – with a large derelict area to the E of *Macclesfield Rd*, and a car park to W. The new Barbican Hotel is off *Dingley Rd*. Further W, *King Square* has 4- and 6-storey tower blocks, with shopping precinct and a large rose garden.

To the S of *Lever St* is commercial property in *Ironmonger Row*, followed by the Turkish baths and more offices in *Europa Place*, at the back of which is a 5-storey tenement building. Further S past *Norman St* is a park and rose garden, and the Finsbury Leisure Centre, which borders on *Mitchell St*, which together with *Bartholomew Square* runs W to E. Both have commercial buildings although the streets at right angles to them off to *Old St* are residential, including the refurbished tenement block in *Anchor Yard* and the 3-storey Georgian terraces in *Helmet Row* (partly offices).

Goswell Rd, to the W, is one of the main thoroughfares (marked by the Triangle development, 5 storeys on the corner of *Percival St*). The rest of the housing is mainly scruffy Victorian and Georgian terraces with a multitude of small shops beneath.

To the E of *Goswell Rd*, running like the rungs of a ladder, are *Seward St*, *Pear Tree Court*, *Bastwick St*, *Ludlow St* and *Gee St*, all of which have commercial developments of between 3 and 5 storeys. *Gee St* also has a 12-floor tower block, Parmoor Court, to the S, and a large City University hall of residence off *Bastwicke St*.

To the W of *Goswell Rd*, street patterns are a little more diverse. *Compton St* has a row of low Georgian terraces to the S, and an 8-storey tower block to the N. Running at a diagonal to *Compton St* is *Cyrus St*, which has low '30s-style tenement blocks at the *Compton St* end and the Triangle development at the junction with *Goswell Rd*. Percival estate continues on the other side of *Percival St* with Harold Laski House, and tower blocks continue on both sides ending at College Heights on the corner of *St John St*.

The end of *Goswell Rd* forms an acute angle with *City Rd*. In the angle to the E, *Moreland St* is dwarfed by the enormous London Gin Distillers building and other commercial premises, including Finsbury Brewery. *Gard St* and *Masons Place* to the S, and *Pickard St* to the N, have large '60s tower blocks to flamboyant heights.

St Marks Hospital is opposite Kestrel House tower block in *Pickard St*. Continuing N, *Hall St* has the 25-storey Peregrine House. The area to the W up to the Angel is commercial. *City Rd* is mainly 3- and 4-storey Georgian terraces, set back from the road on both sides with shops and offices down to *Nelsons Terrace*; from here the height drops dramatically and standard becomes more uneven, and begins to include modern developments. Some of the *City Rd* terraces are being redeveloped as homes.

The Lloyd Baker estate and North Clerkenwell

The neighbourhood is bounded by *St John St* and *Rosebery Avenue* in the S and E, and Kings Cross and *Penton St* in the W. It includes two distinct estates of early 19th century houses, the Lloyd Baker and New River Estates. From the

Angel tube, *St John St* runs N-S along the E edge of the neighbourhood. At the top on the W side is the large smoked glass British Telecom building, on the E are a scruffy array of Late Victorian commercial properties with ornate gables. After this the road has flat-fronted Georgian terraces on both sides. Past the *Chadwell St* junction is a row of gentrified little shops, and on the corner of *Rosebery Avenue*, an exclusive Thai restaurant. *Rosebery Avenue* has the Sadler's Wells theatre on the N side and some fine Georgian terraces on the S, which command good prices when they come up for sale. Further down, past the theatre, is the imposing Thames Water Authority HQ. The site is that of the New River Company's former building. *Rosebery Avenue* continues in a mixture of predominantly industrial Victorian buildings and Victorian workmen's flats; at the intersection with *Rosoman St* is the old Finsbury Town Hall with its distinctive stained glass and wrought iron porch.

Chadwell St runs from *St John St* into the centre of the New River estate, built in the 1820s. The street has modern Georgian-style mews development through an arch on the right, the rest is tall Georgian terraces which open out into the vast *Myddleton Square* with its central garden and church, surrounded on all sides by tall Georgian terraces – one of the finest squares in the area. The roads running off to the W – *River St*, *Inglebert* and *Mylne Sts* – have fine wide streets and terraces of large houses. *Claremont Square*, which completes a right-angle with *Amwell St*, is particularly fine and imposing. It runs NS to join *St John St*, and has Georgian terraces of varying sizes and states of repair, and a number of small shops.

Amwell St marks the boundary between the New River and Lloyd Baker estates. Three roads run parallel to each other W from *Amwell St*. First is *Great Percy St*: tall Georgian terraces, 4 storeys with first-floor balconies. The road is steep and drops sharply just before *Percy Circus*, giving a superb view over the W of London. *Percy Circus* is a fine square with a park in the centre, two-thirds encircled by a long crescent of terraces. But it is sadly marred by the last third, which is a low-level tower block and car park. Parallel to *Great Percy St* and *Wharton St* and *Lloyd Baker St* which converge at *Lloyd Square*. This is the heart of the estate, with a railed garden in the centre: a fine view across to the Post Office Tower, and spacious double-fronted Georgian houses. The style continues down *Wharton St* (both sides) and *Lloyd Baker St* and NW of *Rosebery Avenue* is composed of large Victorian and Edwardian tenements and modern commercial and residential blocks, until *Wilmington Square* and *Tysoe St* which border on *Rosebery Avenue* and mark the limit of the area. *Wilmington* is the last fine period square with tall Georgian terraces and a large central garden. *Tysoe St* has smaller and slightly scruffier terraces.

The area E of *Rosebery Avenue* up to *Goswell Rd* and N of *Skinner St* and *Percival St* is not part of the Lloyd Baker Estate but has some similar features. It is composed of two approximate triangles, the first formed by *St John St* and *Rosebery Avenue* as they diverge S from the Angel, and completed by *Skinner St* which runs W-E along the bottom. The area enclosed is predominantly council tower blocks: *Gloucester Way* has the 23-storey Michael Cliffe House on stilts. *Myddelton St* which forms a cross with *Gloucester Way* is the only period street with neat Georgian houses and a handful of tidy shops at the bottom. *Lloyd's Row* has another large tower block. The point where it joins *St John St* also marks the end of the Georgian terraces there, which are replaced to the S by more modern commercial and academic buildings.

The last part of North Clerkenwell is closed by *St John St* and *Goswell Rd* as

C

they diverge away from the Angel, forming another triangle which is bounded by *Percival St* in the S, which is a continuation of *Skinner St* to the E. The whole of this area is very mixed. In the S, on the corner of *St John St* and *Percival St*, is the 4-storey College Heights development. Originally an old warehouse, now stylishly refurbished with royal blue awnings into a 24 flat complex with gym and car park. One-bed flats were selling in late '88 for around £95,000 and 2-bed flats for £130-£165,000.

To the N, forming a circle with roads radiating off it, is *Northampton Square* and the central core of the University. The quiet square, with a garden and folly in the centre, is bounded on the N by the 7-storey University complex and on the other side by a crescent of 4-storey Georgian terraces with first floor balconies. The streets leading off to the E, *Ashby* and *Sebastian*, are also mainly Georgian terraces. *Spencer St* to the N has anonymous University buildings on one side and *Earlstoke St* council estate on the other. Among the best ways of buying into the area cheaply are either to pick up ex-council property or to find property which overlooks modern council estates. This is possible in North Clerkenwell since there are many small clusters of Georgian houses dotted about. *Rawstorne St* up to *Friend St* is a mixture of low modern mews developments and small period terraces. The last remaining streets up to the Angel are commercial.

Clerkenwell and Charterhouse

Clerkenwell is centred around the *Green* and the surrounding small streets. The very overcrowded *Clerkenwell Rd* cuts through the neighbourhood from W-E, and *Farringdon Rd* runs N-S. To begin from the N, from the crossroads of *Rosebery Avenue* and *Farringdon Rd*, the area to the NW up to *Calthorpe St* is on the NW boundary of Clerkenwell and houses a variety of commercial buildings, including the old Times newspaper building in *Coley St* and *Gough St*, and the vast Mount Pleasant Post Office which dominates *Farringdon Rd* and the top of *Mount Pleasant*. A large part of the Post Office site is being redeveloped. Continuing S down *Rosebery Avenue* there are a number of Victorian commercial buildings with shops beneath, followed by Rosebery Square Buildings, a large Victorian workmen's flats development which dominates both sides of the *Avenue* as it goes to join the *Clerkenwell Rd*. It is currently being refurbished by the St Pancras Housing Association to provide 100 flats.

Clerkenwell Rd runs W to E, with *Rosebery Avenue* forking off to form a triangle. The area between the two is typical Clerkenwell. A warren of narrow, densely packed streets running higgledy piggledy, their names betraying their mediaeval origins: *Herbal Hill*, *Vine Hill*, *Baker's Row*. The architecture is mainly Georgian or early Victorian and uses mainly commercial – though now four new blocks in *Topham* and *Warner Sts* will provide some rare flats as well as shops and offices. There is a car park in the centre off *Warner St*. This part of Clerkenwell terminates with *Farringdon Rd*, which completes the triangle in the E. Just E of the *Farringdon Rd* and the railway in its deep cutting is *Clerkenwell Green*. This is the centre of old Clerkenwell, gathering place for the Peasant's Revolt and now home to the Karl Marx Library. This is the very heart of Clerkenwell, a jumble of Victorian, Georgian and modern architecture, with a smattering of upmarket restaurants, pubs and posh design studios, and a quietly prosperous atmosphere.

The two main streets of central Clerkenwell are *Clerkenwell Close* running NW from the *Green* and *Sekforde St* running NE. *Clerkenwell Close* retains a number of small Georgian terraced homes, but there is much building work in progress. To the left is a new commercial and residential development by Islington Council with shops below and 28 new flats above. To the right is the imposing St James's Church with its clock tower spire and surrounding small garden. Building work goes on both sides on commercial projects. At the end of the *Close* are the distinctive yellow and white brick Peabody flats which go on round into *Pear Tree Court*. To the E *Clerkenwell Close* twists round to meet *Bowling Green Lane* and *Corporation Row*, with their mainly commercial buildings of mixed periods, after this *Clerkenwell Close* becomes *Rosoman St*. On the left hand side past *Northampton Row* is the Red Lion pub and on the right an adventure playground, followed by the gardens of *Rosoman Place* on the left, opposite is a high tower block. Continuing along *Rosoman St* the turning to the left is *Exmouth Market*, while straight on is the junction with *Rosebery Avenue*, marked by Finsbury Town Hall.

Returning to the *Green*, *Sekforde St*, one of Clerkenwell's finest streets, runs NE. It is made up of 2- and 3-storey Regency terraces, the middle portion of which have balconies. Residential and commercial uses mingle. Towards *St John St*, *Woodbridge St* to the N has 3-storey Georgian terraces overlooking a school. Forking to the N from *Sekforde St* is *St James's Walk*, on one side a mixture of Georgian homes and Victorian commercial buildings and on the other a children's playground and the garden surrounding St James's Church. The originally fine network of mediaeval streets which made up the middle of this area has now been obliterated, and the area is bordered by *Sans Walk* in the N and *Clerkenwell Close* in the W.

The area S of *Clerkenwell Rd* down to *Charterhouse St* and W to *Farringdon St* is also Clerkenwell, although the streets to the E of *St John St* up to *Aldersgate* are more commonly termed Charterhouse. Anything in this area or along Smithfield border is at a premium because of its proximity to the City. There are virtually no houses, what homes there are being predominantly flats used as pieds-à-terre. Charterhouse proper centres on the Charterhouse, originally a mediaeval Carthusian Monastery and now home to the medical students of St Bartholomews. The site is located on the corner of *St John St* and *Charterhouse St*, and stretches back to the *Clerkenwell Rd*. It has a central park with plane trees and the students' residences on two sides, with tall commercial property in the W and down *Charterhouse Mews*. In *Charterhouse Square* – one of London's last private, gated squares – Regalian has been busy refurbishing a '30s Art Deco block to provide nine floors of pieds-à-terre for City folk, complete with its own pool, gym, etc, and roof garden. There were a few remaining units and re-sales in Florin Court at the end of 1988; prices started at £97,500 for a studio, £165,000 for a 1-bed flat and £255,000 for a 2-bed flat. To the E *Charterhouse Square* becomes *Carthusian St*, site of a modern commercial and residential development which should be ready in the spring of '89, comprising 3 shops and 10 flats (two 1-bed and eight 2-bed). Roads to the N off *Aldersgate* are solidly commercial.

To the W off *St John St* roads continue in a familiar Clerkenwell pattern, though a little more orderly. The lower end of *St John St* is largely commercial with many tall Victorian and Georgian buildings, some adapted in a post-modern style to provide posh office space close to the City, some concealing flats. Parallel to *St John St* is *St John's Lane*, which terminates in the

C

N at *St John's Gate*, a stone arch dating from 1504 and the original entrance to the Grand Priory of St John of Jerusalem. Most property in this area is commercial, varying in date and size. What residential property there is is either one-off rarities or refurbished office space which has had some residential included into it.

Britton St to the W runs parallel to *St John's Lane*, with mainly 4-storey Georgian and Victorian commercial. In the middle is Mountford House, a 4-storey office block which has some flats at the top. At the end of 1988 a penthouse was sold for £190,000 while a 2-bed flat was available for £155,000 and a 1-bed for £109,000. Continuing down *Britton St* to the junction with *Brisset St*, there is a modern 5-storey office/residential building in progress with intriguing post-modern exterior, being built for a well-known showbiz client. Further down at the corner of *Benjamin St* is tiny St John's Garden, to the S is Eagle Court which joins *Britton St* to *St John's Lane*. It is mainly modern commercial, but has one 3-storey Georgian mews house which was recently sold. Continuing down *Benjamin St* and left into *Turnmill St* brings you to Farringdon Station, the tube and BR link for the area. It is in the process of expansion, being on the BR north-south link which was recently re-opened. *Charterhouse St* runs W to E, forming the southernmost boundary of the area, beside Smithfield Market and on down to *Holborn Circus*.

Hatton Garden

The area to the north of Holborn and *Charterhouse St* is *Hatton Garden*, traditionally the home of the diamond business. It is defined by the *Grays Inn Rd* in the W, *Farringdon Rd* in the E, and *Clerkenwell Rd* in the N. Its streets are wider, less densely packed and more logical in layout than Clerkenwell's. *Hatton Garden* leads N from *Holborn Circus*, and is a mixture of imposing modern office blocks, including the sumptuous New Garden House, and smaller Georgian and Victorian terraces. It houses the best and most expensive jewellers of the area. The district to the E is exclusively commercial, save for *Viaduct Buildings*, a cul-de-sac (entrance at the corner of *Charterhouse St* and *Saffron Hill*). Here a 4-storey flats block has been refurbished in a smart post-modern style with planted walkways and wrought iron entrance gates.

To the N are *Dorrington* and *Beauchamp St*, which form a quiet square with plane trees, mainly commercial with a row of modern maisonettes at the end. At right angles to *Greville St* is *Leather Lane*, site of the famous market, which runs down the length of the street. There are Georgian terraces with shops at the bottom. To the W of *Leather Lane* is *Baldwin Gardens*, mostly commercial, but St Alban's Church Hall has been recently purchased for conversion into 20-25 homes. Further W, running off the *Grays Inn Rd*, is Brookes Court, a new 3-storey maisonette development by Ideal Homes in dark brown brick with facing gardens.

Continuing N along *Leather Lane*, the streets to the W between *Verulam St* and *Clerkenwell Rd* surround the Bourne Estate — '30s-style 5-storey flats entered by arches from the surrounding roads. Quiet, exclusively council.

Among those estate agents active in this area are:
- Frank Harris
- Holden Mathews
- Hotblack & Co
- Roy Brooks
- Stickley & Kent

Cricklewood

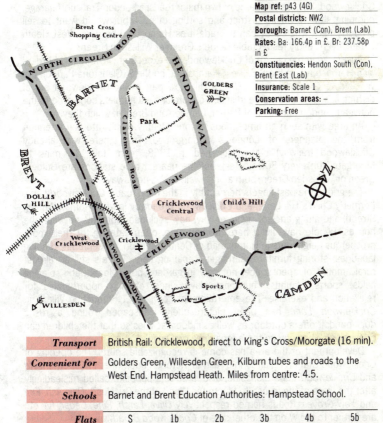

Map ref:	p43 (4G)
Postal districts:	NW2
Boroughs:	Barnet (Con), Brent (Lab)
Rates:	Ba: 166.4p in £. Br: 237.58p in £
Constituencies:	Hendon South (Con), Brent East (Lab)
Insurance:	Scale 1
Conservation areas:	–
Parking:	Free

Transport	British Rail: Cricklewood, direct to King's Cross/Moorgate (16 min).
Convenient for	Golders Green, Willesden Green, Kilburn tubes and roads to the West End. Hampstead Heath. Miles from centre: 4.5.
Schools	Barnet and Brent Education Authorities: Hampstead School.

Flats	S	1b	2b	3b	4b	5b
Average prices	45–65	58–75	70–95	80–100+	–	–
Houses	2b	3b	4b	5b	6/7b	8b
Average prices	80–95	90–125	130–250	185–250+	→	→

The properties	Wide range, from prestige Hampstead-fringe detacheds and mansion flats via '30s semis to Victorian and Edwardian terraces and conversions.
The market	Steady business in good-value converted flats and terraced houses as buyers discover that this area is only three miles from Marble Arch. Smarter corners gain from Hampstead spillover as prices there have risen. 70% owner-occupied. Local searches: Barnet: 4 weeks, Brent, 5-6 weeks.

Area Profile

'Rather a no-man's land', says the estate agent dismissively when asked about Cricklewood. Yes, it's the name of two major roads, a London Transport garage, pumping station, postal district and sorting office – but who'd want to sell property here when they can upgrade it as Hampstead borders, West Heath Estate, even solidly respectable Golders Green or Willesden Green?

Prices sag in the centre of Cricklewood, rise expectantly towards its borders with Hampstead on the S-E, West Hampstead on the S, Gladstone Park on the W, Golders Green to the N. Child's Hill, now part of the Cricklewood postal district, lies on the Hampstead side. Both are ancient hamlets compared to the nouveau London boroughs of Barnet, Camden and Brent in which they lie.

An area with such an amorphous historic identity didn't rate any attention from the planners of London's Underground. True, there was already Cricklewood (railway) station (opened in 1868, trains take 16 mins to Moorgate, run every 30 minutes), but the nearest tube stations are Golders Green or Willesden Green, both a brisk walk or bus-ride away.

The grid of the past lingers perceptibly in the main roads: *Cricklewood Lane*, (formerly Child's Hill Lane) and *Cricklewood Broadway* (part of Roman Watling Street), and along ancient rights of way, now secluded footpaths between the houses. People have lived here, worked here, often catering for their more prosperous neighbours in Hampstead or Central London, for centuries: running laundries, storing furniture, carriages, repairing cars. There's still an almost rural amount of open space, not only in gardens but in local parks, playing fields, sports grounds, municipal playgrounds, offering opportunities for relaxation and exercise. The entertainment complex at Production Village in *Cricklewood Lane* has been picturesquely landscaped round a rustic duck-pond; it offers outdoor as well as indoor facilities so that the children can come along when you go there for a drink or a snack.

Development of the area has come in recognizable spurts. The opening of Cricklewood Station resulted in a rash of Victorian brick villas in *Claremont Rd* and *Cricklewood Lane* alongside, also in streets opposite called misleadingly after the trees of the forest (to fit into the Wood of the Crickles?): *Oak*, *Ash*, *Elm* and *Yew Groves*. Roads named respectively *Olive*, *Larch*, *Pine*, *Cedar*, *Ivy* etc are further to the W on the other side of *Cricklewood Broadway*.

Hendon Way to the E followed in the years between the wars, a bypass, precursor to the roads leading northwards, now the M1. Ribbon development spread alongside: semi-detached houses with garages for the new mobile motor age. Council housing from those years, and post-1945, is now slowly trickling onto the market as tenants cash in on their right to buy.

In-filling in such a long-established area has produced some apparently unselfconscious mixes of residential property cheek-by-jowl with industrial development. There is a great deal of shopping available, but local shops along the main road arteries are mostly specialist and mini-market: Brent Cross, one mile or so up the road, throws a large shadow. But a number of classy restaurants, antique shops, mail order company, and surely London's only pine furniture shop to sell rocking sheep, seem to indicate that people from outside the area come here for at least some of their services.

An area within three and a half miles of Marble Arch where properties are available at so many levels must be worth looking at, especially if access to the City is important.

Child's Hill and more particularly Cricklewood are mixed areas, predominantly-though not exclusively residential. Shops and local industry may detract from the value of houses nearby, even when they provide services and employment for locals within (often) walking distance of their homes.

This residue of neighbourhood facilities also enables elderly and relatively immobile residents to find many of their requirements locally: an open-air market outside the Crown pub in *Cricklewood Broadway*, shops, historic pubs. Churches of various denominations include St Agnes' Catholic Church and primary school in *Cricklewood Lane*, a Mosque and Islamic Centre stretching from *Chichele Rd* to *Howard Rd*. There are two local libraries, half a dozen primary schools, and Hampstead (comprehensive) School in *Westbere Rd*.

The disadvantages include lack of access to London's tube network, to local hospitals and fee-paying schools, all outside the area.

Child's Hill

On the electoral map, Child's Hill is a Barnet Ward extending well into NW11. Not so in estate agents' descriptions, where it's usually defined as the NW2 area of Hampstead.

Semantics apart, the select Hocroft estate certainly includes some very prestigious and expensive houses, one-off brick built neo-Georgian, detached in *Ranulf Rd*, semi-detached and detached in *Hocroft Rd*, *Hocroft Avenue*, *Farm Avenue*, *Harman Drive*. Even the semis here have 5 beds, usually 2 bath and car ports for the second car. *Harman Close* is a surprise: it has some half dozen architect designed 1970s houses, all individual, young, smart.

Most of the area's blocks of purpose-built flats are in Child's Hill; Vernon Court at the corner of *Finchley Rd* and *Hendon Way*, Wendover and Moreland Courts about 30 yards further on at the top of *Lyndale Avenue*. All three were built in the 1930s: mock Tudor red brick with 1/2/3-bed flats. Ground floor flats have access to the garden. Some of the original protected tenants still live here, slowly giving up the ghost and their tenancy . . . but other flats have been modernised, and come on the market with regularity every few years. They're popular with the newly retired, some of whom may always have lived nearby, or have children living there. *Finchley Rd* dwellers also have the option of a longer bus-ride down to Finchley Rd tube. It's further away than Golders Green, but reckoned worth it for the Jubilee Line (half the stops to Charing Cross) – and the large Waitrose for shopping on the way home.

Further along the *Finchley Rd*, Orchard Mead has been spruced up by Regalian: now has all the '80s mod cons including porters, gymnasium, sauna, small garden to sit out in – and commensurate prices; it is at least partly let for investment. Heathway, at the corner with *West Heath Rd* has 54 flats, about a quarter of them protected tenants, but these too come on the market, sometimes already modernised. Opposite, Portman Heights is a new development by St George PLC; its 20 flats will be ready this spring. 1-, 2- and 3-beds, with balcony and parking space, but maybe not for the average first-time buyer at £200-340,000 for a 125-year lease. Note that the outgoings in purpose-built blocks include service charges which also cover elements of maintenance and can run well into four figures.

The former Child's Hill House, near the junction of *Hermitage Lane* and *Pattison Rd* is still in single occupation, but most of the Victorian 3-floor houses in the latter street have been converted into flats and/or maisonettes. There's an intermingling of older houses with others built pre-1914, between the wars,

C

and in the last twenty years or so in these sought-after roads which lead up to Hampstead Heath. Often, as in *Hermitage Lane*, there has been a deliberate attempt to adapt to existing spacious pre-war houses with latticed windows and mock antique touches, but there are also two terraces of newer, more frankly functional, houses for people who prefer equipping their homes to looking after them full-time. More enthusiastic gardeners live in the bungalows of Hermitage Terrace, a secluded place where children and/or grandchildren can play in safety.

Back across the *Finchley Rd*, there's concrete jungle Sunnyside House above shops and motor car showrooms. Opposite, *Crewys Rd*, sometimes known as Little Sicily, has little turn of the century houses, mostly terraced with gardens and lovingly spruced up by owners, apparently oblivious of industrial premises nearby. More light industry, and less space for housing, in *Granville Rd* though this includes Granville Nurseries at its junction with *The Vale*. Nurseries are useful in areas with so many individual gardens, and locals with space and taste for keeping their gardens looking better than the Jones' next door.

This is also the place to find council properties coming onto the market. Barnet has encouraged tenants to exercise their enterprise this way, and has already sold off close to 29% of its housing stock. Look for 2-3 bed houses, terraced, in *Garth* and *Cloister Rds* off *Hendon Way*, 2-3 bedroom flats in *Longberrys*, *Cricklewood Lane*; 2-bed flats in Hermitage Court. Some agents say these sell at up to 20% discount, especially in larger configurations of council housing, but it's sometimes difficult to tell at today's prices.

An oddity in Cricklewood is the 'Village' complex given over to entertainment of various kinds, including a little theatre. The complex is in part a conversion of some old industrial buildings. The rest of Cricklewood's architecture is straightforward inner London, with some interesting small railway cottages, and plenty of solid commercial Victoriana.

Cricklewood Central

This area covers a broad band each side of *Cricklewood Lane*, starting from *Hendon Way* to the N-E, the *Farm Avenue* sports ground on its N side, and with its other two sides bordered by *Cricklewood Broadway* and the *North Circular Rd*. The railway runs right through the middle.

It includes vast areas of council housing in the *Claremont Rd* area, also the Westcroft Estate in *Lichfield Rd* which is Camden Council housing on land leased from Barnet. Main kinds of property to look for: pre-1914 housing near the railway station (as already mentioned) and the semis built between the wars at the time the *Hendon Way* was being developed.

Often the two mix and mingle, 1930s 3-bedroom semis alongside and opposite Victorian villas in *Cricklewood Lane*, solid residential semis with gabled entrance lobbies and steep-sided roofs, sometimes joined up in terraces of four and six as in *Somerton* and *Gillingham Rds*. Then there are stretches of widely-spaced semis in *Greenfield Gardens, Purley* and *Sanderstead Avenues*, roads which are incongruously wider than the main thoroughfares. Most of the semis are owner-occupied, although there's also a certain amount of letting. Some former bungalows in *The Vale* and nearby have had their roofs opened up and extended, and indeed, much individual attention, money and ingenuity has gone into changing and adapting these houses and gardens.

But building land is scarce here now. Two 3-floor blocks of flats have been built (Avenue Court and Manor Court), and planning permission has now been given for 32 new flats to be built between *Pennine Drive* and *Brent Terrace*. Forty new terraced houses between *Somerton Rd* and *The Vale* form a rather inward-looking private estate – *Elsinore Gardens* – clustered round a landscaped parking area. There are more homes to come here: this large development by Dancon will, when complete, have 170 flats and houses. Prices from around £90,000 for a studio flat. The final phase will include 5-bed houses. Quite a lot of industry remains in these residential streets, but rubs shoulders fairly unobtrusively with placid suburban semis in *Somerton Rd* and *The Vale*, less so in *Dersingham Rd*.

C

Most of the houses in these streets are well maintained, often on a do-it-yourself basis. Indeed the stadium-shaped roads round *Pennine Drive* could well feature in the colour magazine ads for double glazing or spray-painting the pebble dash. Not so the older houses in the *Cricklewood Lane* end of *Claremont Rd*. Many are subdivided for letting.

It's a different, more crowded world on the other side of the railway bridge, already partaking of some of the characteristics of Cricklewood-in-Brent (see below). More cosmopolitan, too: shops near and in *Cricklewood Broadway* include Halal butchers, sari shops, jewellery and Oriental greengrocers, grocers and bakers.

The 'Groves' (already mentioned as the 'tree' names in Cricklewood) are all turn-of-the-century 2-storey houses which seem to have been rebuilt, converted, improved and adapted as if to show just how many variations on the original could be achieved: dormer windows, balconies, teak and glass doors, cladding. They must be among the most economically priced 2-bed conversions within three miles of Marble Arch.

But there's simply not enough pavement and kerbside space for residents, shoppers and railway users to park their cars. They try, which helps to explain why the council sweepers don't seem to be able to keep these streets litter-free. There's not much they can do to sweep behind and under parked cars.

So far, so predictable. But the former Railway Cottages some 300 yards up *Cricklewood Broadway* on the Barnet side are a surprise. Sold off to the then residents some 15-20 years ago, these five parallel terraces of 2- and 3-bedroom houses have pretty gardens, sometimes one large communal lawn on one side, individual private patches on the other. Access by car is limited, but it's a cosy spot where residents have shrugged off the original railway grime and coal dust, and a good place to get your feet on the property ladder. That's the rationalisation, but many get to love it and stick, and even start families in accommodation where it might not be easy to swing a cat or a baby. Still, Victoriana is in, and these houses are collectors' pieces.

West Cricklewood

Streets named after trees to the E of *Cricklewood Broadway* were the Groves; here, on the W (Brent) side, are the Roads. Most of them contain 2-storey houses built at the turn of the century, so there has been plenty of time for *Pine*, *Larch*, *Cedar*, *Olive*, *Ivy*, *Oaklands* etc, *Rds* to have developed leafy mature trees (not of appropriate species) and for conversions into flats, maisonettes, garden flats. More conversions still being carried out, often by landlords who continue to live on the premises.

Multi-occupation usually means parking problems, especially in streets built before cars – or indeed bathrooms – were considered necessary, so it's worth considering the width of any road before deciding to live in it. Ashford Court is the only really large blocks of flats, with 180 1/2/3-bedroom flats at quite moderate prices. Negotiations are under way for members of the Lessees' Association to participate in the Management Company's decision-making – useful when servicing, maintenance and repair bills will involve them all.

Purpose-built flats, two to each house, were built pre-1914 in *Wotton*, *Temple* and *Langton Rds*. Note the double front doors: one leads to the staircase for upstairs. There's also a two-year-old Laing development of houses and flats in and off *Langton Rd*, tribute to the growing attraction of shopping in and around Brent Cross.

More conventionally up-market are the wide leafy roads near *Gladstone Park* with comfortable 4/5-bed houses, some of them detached in *Anson Rd*, *Oman Avenue* and many of the roads running into the former. Some, ie *Oman Avenue*, also have blocks of flats where elderly parents of local residents can live near, but not with, their children.

These are sights for the eyes for anyone who thinks that civilization stops at the boundary of Brent (which includes at least one Child's Hill estate agent). It's true that this area contains a larger percentage of industrial buildings, also garages, workshops and even itinerant sellers of produce and textiles. *Hassop Rd* is totally industrial. But what seems to be happening to the better roads is that they're renamed Willesden Green. No wonder Cricklewood is said to be shrinking. Note, though, that aspiring yuppies Chas and Beatie (in the Independent's Saturday magazine strip) have now sold their residence in 'Cricklebois'. Even they were astonished at the price it fetched.

Among those estate agents active in this area are:
- Anscombe & Ringland
- Bairstow Eves
- Gladstones
- Ellis & Co
- Gordon Matthews
- William Nelhams
- Winkworths

Crouch End and Stroud Green

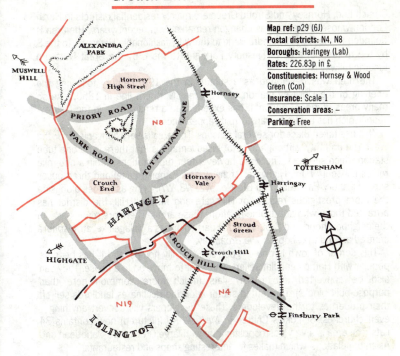

Map ref: p29 (6J)
Postal districts: N4, N8
Boroughs: Haringey (Lab)
Rates: 226.83p in £
Constituencies: Hornsey & Wood Green (Con)
Insurance: Scale 1
Conservation areas: –
Parking: Free

C

Transport	Tubes: Finsbury Park (zone 2, Victoria, Piccadilly). Oxford Circus 11 min; City, 30 min (1 change); Heathrow 1 hr. British Rail: Finsbury Park (Moorgate 13 min), Hornsey, Haringay, Crouch Hill.
Convenient for	Wood Green Shopping City, Alexandra Park. Miles from centre: 5.
Schools	Haringey Education Authority: Hornsey School, St David & St Katherine. Private: Highgate Boys School.

Flats	S	1b	2b	3b	4b	5b
Average prices	60	63–77	70–130	90+	–	–
Houses	2b	3b	4b	5b	6/7b	8b
Average prices	90–110	120–165	140–250	180+	→	–

The properties	19th century suburban houses, many now converted to flats. Largest and smartest close to Highgate, smaller ones elsewhere. Some p/b flats. Also ex-council bargains.
The market	Fast being discovered by those priced out of areas like Islington and Highgate. Crouch End in particular is popular with Hampstead flat-dwellers in search of whole houses. Hornsey is still the cheapest corner, and parts of Stroud Green: smaller houses, narrower roads – though some, eg Nightingale, have good views. Local searches: 4 weeks.

Area Profile

Crouch End, Hornsey and Stroud Green are mainly residential districts in North London whose character has changed remarkably in recent years. The area is bounded to the N by Alexandra Park, to the W by fashionable Highgate, to the S by the residential area of Finsbury Park and to the E by the Great Northern Electric railway line.

The area was developed as a suburb in the 19th century following the opening of the Hornsey station on the Great Northern line in 1850. Like so many areas of inner London, it has experienced a renaissance in the last few years which has begun to transform its appearance.

This has taken place for several reasons. The area is very convenient for the West End and City, although a major disadvantage is that there is no one tube station which serves it. There are however four tube stations within a one-mile radius (Finsbury Park, Highgate, Archway and Turnpike Lane) and three buses serve Finsbury Park tube and BR (Nos W2, W3, W7). Lying as it does alongside the more prestigious regions of Highgate and Muswell Hill, the district has attracted those who are unable to afford these areas. There are many parks in the neighbourhood and Crouch End in particular has a 'village-like' atmosphere centred around the shops in *The Broadway*.

This corner of town is one of good-sized family homes, and it has become popular with Hampstead flat sellers who want to move on to a house. They can also be converted into roomy flats (much more common here than purpose-built blocks). The rented sector is on the decline as landlords sell off their properties to the developers. These developers will convert anything — even churches: St Luke's Church in *Mayfield Rd* (pictured) now contains 34 flats. The area is a very cosmopolitan one with large Greek, Afro-Caribbean and Asian populations, which makes for interesting shops and restaurants.

Crouch End

This area (the name means 'cross end': it referred to the crossroads at the boundary of the Bishop of London's Manor of Hornsey with Brownswood Manor in modern Stroud Green) is officially part of Hornsey, but forms its own distinct neighbourhood. The many tree-lined streets lend Crouch End a rural appearance, but it also offers a good shopping centre along *The Broadway* and round *Tottenham Lane* and *Park Rd*. (Wine bars et al appearing fast.)

Highgate Borders

The most expensive homes in Crouch End are found to the W of *Park Rd*, *The Broadway* and *Crouch End Hill* because of their proximity to Highgate. Roads such as *Glasslyn Rd*, *Coolhurst Rd* (where a new development of flats and maisonettes rates prices up to £187,000) and *Clifton Rd* going down to *Coleridge* and *Crescent Rds* are tree-lined and mainly contain large Victorian Gothic and Edwardian 3-storey semi-detached or terraced houses. Most of these have been converted into flats, although a few houses do remain. Similar houses, too, are to be found in the streets between *Crouch End Hill* and *Crouch Hill*, in for example *Christchurch Rd* and *Haslemere Rd*. A development of 16 flats is under way in *Crescent Rd*. This area is particularly well off for open spaces, which include Crouch End playing fields off *Park Rd* and the Parkland Walk along a former railway line. An entrance to the walk is at *Crouch End Hill*.

Further S, in the N19 postal district, roads between *Crouch Hill* and *Hornsey Rise* such as *Warltersville Rd*, *Heathville Rd* and *Shaftesbury Rd* have some purpose-built council blocks and large 3-storey Victorian houses, also mostly reborn as flats.

There are a few roads W of *Hornsey Rise* and S of *Hornsey Lane*, such as *Sunnyside Rd* and *Beaumont Rise*, which are on the borders of Crouch End and Archway. See also the Highgate chapter.

Middle Lane

The triangle of roads N of *Tottenham Lane* and *Park Rd*, which is dissected down the middle by *Middle Lane*, is a hotch-potch of different types of houses, reflecting the different stages of growth and function of Crouch End. There are the large Victorian and Edwardian houses which are quickly being converted into flats such as in *Hillfield Avenue*, *Harold Rd* and some in *Middle Lane*, and the more modern ones like those found in *Rokesly Avenue* and *Elmfield Avenue* – which are more likely to remain intact. There are also some original cottage houses to be found in *New Rd*. The bus route to Finsbury Park tube goes up *Middle Lane* from *Priory Rd* and then turns up *Rokesly Avenue*. In *Priory Rd* 11 new houses around a courtyard back onto parkland.

C

Hornsey

The Hornsey High Street neighbourhood lies N of *Priory Rd* and *High St Hornsey*, and S of Alexandra Park. *Nightingale Lane* divides the district in two: to the E are mainly council properties and to the W mainly private. Streets such as *Linzee Rd*, *Redston Rd*, *Clovelly Rd* and *North View Rd* contain 2-storey terraced houses, many of which have been converted into flats. Some have beautiful views of Alexandra Park: a rarity in London.

Hornsey High St is hardly a great shopping centre – it has suffered from the growth of such centres as Crouch End, Muswell Hill and the famous Wood Green Shopping City, all of which are within easy reach.

Hornsey Vale

This neighbourhood lies S of *Tottenham Lane* and E of *The Broadway* and *Crouch Hill*. From *Weston Park* there is a steep incline up to *Mount View Rd*, which forms the border with Stroud Green. The roads either side of *Weston Park* contain mainly 2- (but some 3-) storey terraced houses which are being converted into flats, but efforts have been made to retain the external character of these well-detailed properties. *Ferme Park Rd* is on the bus route to Finsbury Park tube, so proximity to this road may be useful.

Stroud Green

This neighbourhood forms a triangle which lies to the S of *Mount View Rd* and is bordered by *Stroud Green Rd* to the W and the railway line to the E. It used to have large areas of sub-standard housing but this area is now definitely on the way up. People are starting to talk about Stroud Green Village, which is a sure sign of gentrification in progress. The houses on *Mount View Rd* overlook a large park and, as they are at the top of *Crouch Hill*, the rest of Stroud Green.

The roads coming down off *Mount View Rd* are wide and tree-lined: roads like *Mount Pleasant Villas*, *Granville Rd* and *Oakfield Rd* contain large 3-storey terraced houses which are almost all converted into flats. Crouch Hill BR station, with trains into St Pancras, serves this area.

The roads to the E of *Lancaster Rd*, like *Cornwall Rd* and *Connaught Rd*, contain 3-storey houses decorated with white stucco – again, good flat-hunting territory. Moving down towards Finsbury Park tube, the roads and the houses in them are not in such good order, with more crowded streets and more of an inner-city feel, but they are in the process of being done up and their proximity to the tube makes them increasingly attractive.

Inner London has an embarrasment of 19th century churches – but many, including this, have found other uses. This gothic edifice is now flats, popular because the conversion provides interesting room shapes and some dramatic windows. Architects have become adept at such conversions: buildings that have become homes also include a vinegar factory in Vauxhall.

Borders

The frontiers with Highgate and Muswell Hill are fairly well-defined; *Shepherds Hill* marks the border with Highgate, and *Muswell Hill* the road leads away from the southern tip of Alexandra Park to Muswell Hill the area, but elsewhere the borders are slightly more fuzzy.

'The Ladders' are a group of roads which have the N8 postcode but which geographically belong more with Harringay than Hornsey, being E of the railway. They are so-called because they run parallel to each other off *Wightman Rd*, and so give the appearance of a ladder on the map. The houses here are cheaper than those further W so might be a good way of getting into the area.

West of *Stroud Green Rd* Stroud Green merges with Finsbury Park. In roads such as *Evershot* and *Marriot* you'll find 2- and 3-storey terraced houses, many of which have been converted into flats. The N4 postal boundary runs along the *Hornsey Rd*. N and W of here is in the N19 zone.

Between *Hornsey Rd* and *Holloway Rd*, there is a tract which does not really belong to Crouch End but is not quite Tufnell Park either. Once it was Holloway, but this is a name that today seems less used. North of the railway there are flat-fronted Victorian houses in *Fairbridge Rd*. The rather mixed area around about is said to be coming up. South of the railway the houses are smaller. Housing associations are active here. The streets with Tollington in their names form a fairly distinct district: wide roads with big churches and solid houses.

Among those estate agents active in this area are:
- Dennells
- Ham Estates
- Hornsey Agencies
- Martin Gerrard
- Nicholas Shepherd
- Warmans

Crystal Palace

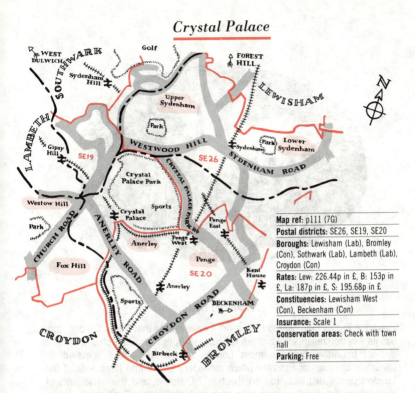

Map ref: p111 (7G)

Postal districts: SE26, SE19, SE20

Boroughs: Lewisham (Lab), Bromley (Con), Sothwark (Lab), Lambeth (Lab), Croydon (Con)

Rates: Lew: 226.44p in £, B: 153p in £, La: 187p in £, S: 195.68p in £

Constituencies: Lewisham West (Con), Beckenham (Con)

Insurance: Scale 1

Conservation areas: Check with town hall

Parking: Free

Transport	British Rail: Crystal Palace to Victoria; Penge West, Sydenham to London Bridge and Charing Cross; Sydenham Hill, fast line to Victoria.
Convenient for	Crystal Palace Park. Miles from centre: 7.
Schools	ILEA zone 7 & Bromley Education Authority: Kentwood (b), Rock Hills (g)

Flats	S	1b	2b	3b	4b	5b
Average prices	45–55	49–65	65–85	70+	–	–
Houses	2b	3b	4b	5b	6/7b	8b
Average prices	76–90	79–135	110–200	150–200+	→300	–

The properties	Grand Victorian villas, many now flats; smaller terraced Victorian, flats blocks and inter-war homes. Quite a few modern houses and flats. Gardens and long, long views.
The market	First-time buyers find value here in flats and smaller houses. Larger houses popular with families. Few very large houses left: most now flats. 1- and 2-bed flats are plentiful, both p/b and conversions. Local searches: Lewisham 6 weeks, Bromley 4-5 weeks, Lambeth 10 weeks, Southwark 8 weeks.

C

Area Profile

Everyone knows Hampstead is on a hill. Fewer realise that South London, too, has its wooded heights. Sydenham Hill rises abruptly from Dulwich and forms a distinct boundary between inner London to the NW and the essentially suburban borough of Bromley which meanders off SE into Kent. Indeed the London postal districts stop on the hills' SE slopes, and the inhabitants of Beckenham put 'Kent' on their notepaper, as if they were in Canterbury.

Crystal Palace, which took its name from Paxton's great glass-house which stood on the hill-top until 1936, is the name of a park and a landmark (the soaring TV masts) rather than a place. Anerley and Penge slope away to the SE, Sydenham is to the E, Upper Sydenham to the N, Gipsy Hill to the W and Upper Norwood along the ridge to the SW.

Five boroughs meet at the summit of the hill, making it more than usually necessary to enquire about who gets – and spends – a given property's rates.

The hills and valley of this interesting landscape give character to the area, define the neighbourhoods and influence the type of property. Large houses occupy lofty vantage points with compelling views; modest terraces cluster the lower reaches. Property is predominantly owner-occupied.

The Crystal Palace, saved from the Great Exhibition of 1851 and re-erected (much enlarged) in the park in 1854, burnt down spectacularly in 1936. Its popularity persuaded wealthy Victorians to build large mansions in the locality. The 1960s construction of the National Sports Centre and Bromley council's recent ambitious plans to upgrade the park have contributed to an upturn in fortunes. And now, indeed, the Palace looks set to rise again, phoenix-like, from the long-cold ashes. But the 22 metre-high hotel/1,000-seat multiscreen cinema/health club is rousing fiery responses from conservationists who condemn this 'meagre, impoverished pale imitation'.

At the summit of the Crystal Palace Hill is the area known locally as the 'Triangle', bordered by *Westow Hill* to the N, *Westow St* to the W and *Church Rd* to the E. It's part of Croydon but abutted by Lambeth, Southwark and

Bromley boroughs. *Fox Hill* and *Belvedere Rd* make an elegant descent from *Church Rd* parallel to the busy *Anerley Hill*. N of Anerley Hill, beyond Crystal Palace BR station, Crystal Palace Park acts as a barrier with Penge.

The King William Naval Asylum (1847) and Tudor almshouses raise *Penge High St* above the suburban commonplace.

Sydenham, to the N of Penge, is an elegant suburb which enjoys a good community spirit – the Sydenham Society is very active. Upper Sydenham historically had more lavish properties – surviving examples on *Westwood Hill* and *Sydenham Hill*. Other hill-climbers here are *Wells Park Rd* and *Longton Avenue*. Historic *Jews Walk* enjoys repute.

Sydenham today still has the atmosphere, which it shares with the other slopes of the hill, of having strayed from an Edwardian novel. A character from H G Wells, perhaps, or even Sherlock Holmes himself, seems likely to emerge from the pillared drives lined with laurels. Houses of that period were lavishly spacious, and even flats made from them are as big as any in London.

Lower Sydenham has the sought after turn-of-century *Thorpe Estate* but ends modestly round *Bell Green*. To the S of *Westwood Hill*, the roads starting with the name *Lawrie Park* are popular. Some parts are Bromley: low rates.

The even spread of BR stations across the area makes for convenient commuting – there is also good provision of bus routes, many terminating on Crystal Palace Parade. Escaping to the country is quick (the M25 is a mere 10 miles away) although the vast Crystal Palace Park offers respite from city hassles. The proximity of the National Sports Centre for spectator events and use of facilities is an added bonus.

C

Westow Hill

Westow Hill, Victorian and villagy in character, has a good selection of shops and better than average restaurants – some quite chic. The buildings bristle with aerials – rumour says pirate radio stations operate from here. To the N, the bay-fronted Victorian semis of *Farquhar Rd* are bedsit and flatland. Further down, large detached Tudor-timber-style houses in *Dulwich Wood Avenue*. *Jasper Rd* has large Victorian terraces. *Westow St* to the S has small shops and new supermarket and community centre complex. There are luxury 1- and 2-bed retirement apartments here. Upcoming *Church Rd* (which runs S towards Croydon) has Nesbitt Square, a small, new development of 5-bed homes. Also Nightingale Court, luxury sheltered retirement apartments. In the 'Triangle' between *Westow Hill* and *Church Rd*, *St Aubyn's Rd* has recent bay-window-style houses. Modern terraced houses in *Brunel Close*.

Fox Hill

This leafy district slopes down from the hilltop between *Church Rd* and *Anerley Hill*. *Fox Hill Rd* starts with small cottages and a modern development. It's steep (20% gradient) and offers a truly panoramic view. Large Victorian houses, semis and detached, as well as '60s town houses, complete the road. A low terrace of stuccoed almshouses with unusual iron canopy starts *Belvedere Rd*. Composition of the road is similar to *Fox Hill* – No 73, Tower House, is a striking property. 'For sale' boards are common in *Hamlet Rd* – Victorian detached and semis, many converted into flats. This tree-lined neighbourhood is further enhanced by small greens. Trees shield the large houses in *Auckland Rd* – also private flats, Victorian detached and semis. *Auckland Rd* travels down past playing fields and South Norwood Lake. *Sylvan Rd* has modern terraces as well as Victorian – also Sylvan High School and sports centre.

Anerley

A busy thoroughfare, *Anerley Hill* starts loftily at the roundabout with *Westow Hill* – commanding views of South London and beyond. Victorian detached and terraced properties – many converted into flats – and '60s town houses make the descent. Midway, there are a number of council estates. Shops near Anerley BR provide for basic needs. *Thicket Rd* (Victorian detached houses – mainly multiple occupancy) follows the S edge of Crystal Palace Park. Here, Rialto Homes have just built 176 homes in 'village-style' on a 5-acre former goods yard. The 'Orchard Park' homes (studios-3 bed houses) were selling fast last year for between £50-90,000. Second phase has studios, 1- and 2-bed flats from £58-78,000. *Anerley Park* has large Victorian semis – multiple tenancies. Terraced cottage-style properties are found in *Trenholme Rd*.

Penge

Modern shopping facilities in *Penge High St* contrast with the quiet dignity of the King William IV Naval Asylum and the almshouses of *Watermens' Square*. More almshouses are found in *King William IV Gardens* – sadly fronted by a council block. *Wordsworth Rd* has bay-fronted Victorian terraces. Parallel is *Parish Lane* – cottage-style terraced dwellings. Swallows' Court (Blenbury) is a new 2-bed town apartment development in *Morland Rd*. Larger properties are found in *Lennard Rd* (Victorian; Tudor-timber-style semis), *Cator Rd* (Victorian detached) and *Woodbastwick Rd* ('30s semis).

Roads parallel to A213 *Croydon Rd* provide opportunities. *Maple Rd* suffers from use as a street market at the *High St* end. To the E, *Kenilworth Rd* has bay-fronted 1930s terraced houses with wooden porches. *Clevedon Rd* is similar. Quiet and popular roads are *Chesham Crescent* and *Chesham Rd* – '30s semis. *Ravenscroft Rd* and *Birkbeck Rd* have more Victorian terraces.

Sydenham

The N-S railway line divides Sydenham Park from Lower Sydenham to the E. Quiet and leafy *Sydenham Park* starts with Victorian but also has some council blocks. *Sydenham Park* crosses with '30s bay-fronted and large Victorian terraces. Also some cottage-style dwellings and large semis. Renovation work has restored Farnborough House, an early 19th century villa on the corner of *Kirkdale* and *Jews Walk*.

Wells Park Rd runs W from *Kirkdale*, starting modestly with Victorian terraced housing – most with small ground-floor shops. Off on the right, narrow *Halifax St* comes as a surprise – variously bright-painted Victorian terraced cottages with white wooden fences. Council house building and estates occupy the lower part of the hill. Further up on the left is the hilly *Sydenham Wells Park* (Sydenham was a minor 19th century spa). Halfway up the hill, modern private flats start to appear – they have balconies, and raised gardens protected by fences and hedges. *Canonbury Mews* is a modern estate with neatly tended lawns. Right at the top is the large, modern St Clement's Heights estate.

Sydenham Hill skirts the N-W edge of the neighbourhood. *Kirkdale*, the wide, busy, road continues S-W with a private modern block on the left and detached houses on the right. Castlebar is a French-looking mansion. To the right is woodland. On the left is a walled off, modern Corporation of the City of London estate. Lammas Green council estate has some stuccoed terraces. No 34a, Sydenham Hill House, has an entrance tower and Jacobean roofline. The 'Cedars' is another very imposing building – bay-fronted, with balustrades and stained glass. Council estates make an appearance – including high rise blocks. Other properties found along here are Victorian and '30s detached, modern terraces and town houses. Also the occasional, almost enchanted, wooded cul-de-sac. Impressive, sweeping views of London are another plus. Near the roundabout with *Westwood Hill*, back on the hilltop by the Park, there's the recent *Wavel Place* development. The television mast soars into view.

Westwood Hill descends to the E towards central Sydenham with modern town houses on the left and mansions on the right. Torrington Court is a '30s mansion block. Also Sydenham High School here. Off *Westwood Hill* to the left is popular *Jews Walk*. On the right are large Victorian villas; on the left are modern town houses then retirement apartments on the corner with *Kirkdale*.

Sheltered from main traffic is *Beaulieu Avenue* – '60s town houses with neat handkerchief-size front lawns. Also small fenced off green in the middle.

Wide *Longton Avenue*, beside the Wells Park, has large Victorian bay-fronted semis and modern terrace house infills. Further up on the left are '30s semis with sloping front gardens, on the right park railings. Higher still come larger 1930s semis and the occasional detached house. Delightful views of the park.

South of *Westwood Hill*, *Lawrie Park Rd*, wide, tree-lined and gently undulating, offers a variety of Victorian properties – mansions, detached, semis, bay-fronted terraces with upper balconies and some balustrades. Many flat conversions. Also modern terraces and flats. Work is under way on Wicklow Court (Addley Homes) – luxury 1/2-bed apartments – diametrically opposite *Lawrie Park Crescent* (large Victorian semis, Tudor timber-style '30s detached, modern semis). Behind hedges on the corner of *Lawrie Park Crescent* and *Lawrie Park Rd* is Sydenham Lawn Tennis & Croquet club. Facing is St Christopher's Hospice. *Lawrie Park Rd* ends by *Crystal Palace Park Rd* with mansion blocks – '30s Park Court and the more modern Ashley Court.

On *Crystal Palace Park Rd* large Victorian redbrick mansions were built overlooking the park – many now converted into flats. Also large detached '30s infills. *Sydenham Avenue* (mock Georgian and big Victorian semis) has a bucolic air – there's a bench beneath the protective branches of a tree on the green and it looks towards St Bartholomew Church in *Westwood Hill*. It continues as *Lawrie Park Avenue* – Victorian mansions and 1930s detached. *Lawrie Park Gardens* has Victorian mansions, modern flats and Tudor-style detached.

Sydenham Rd, Victorian red-brick, has a useful range of shops in the upper part. Behind lies the popular *Thorpe Estate* of turn-of-century terraces.

In lower Sydenham, *Sunnydene St* climbs a gentle hill – Victorian/turn-of-century terraced cottages – also an unappealing council block. *Highclere St* is similarly terraced. By no means down at heel.

C

Among those estate agents active in this area are:
- Assheton & Co
- Childs & Co
- Cooper Giles
- David Baxter
- Jacksons
- Hampton Levens
- Winkworths

Docklands

Area profile

The most striking view in London this last winter was on the Isle of Dogs, where a thicket of Thames barge masts acted as foreground to a veritable forest of giant cranes on the site of Canary Wharf. Canary Wharf, the biggest office development in Europe, is actually happening. Lighters are processing up-river loaded with bricks and cement, piles are being driven, foundations laid. Soon the towers will be rising at the rate of two floors a week. By late 1990 the first phase will be occupied.

Canary Wharf sets the seal on Docklands. It is the biggest thing happening by a factor of ten. And, after all the talk and the politicking, it is actually getting built. The sheer scale of the scheme injects a new note into Docklands. It is a note of confidence, of long-term, serious, enormous, investment. The Reichmann brothers, the reclusive trio who are the owners of property firm Olympia & York, are renowned for taking the long view and for getting it right. They bought large chunks of Manhattan when everyone else had written off the Big Apple as a bankrupt mess. They virtually created the commercial heart of their home city, Toronto. And here they are in London, building an alternative City within view of the first. And they intend to keep it, to let the space. They are not traders but investors.

There are many predictions that 1989 will see a glut of new office space in London. It's the nature of property to suffer dearth and glut. If it happens, it will last a year or two or three. But the Reichmann brothers are thinking of the next century. And pundits agree that Canary Wharf's sheer scale will set it apart and go a long way to ensuring its success, despite events elsewhere in town.

Canary Wharf is an offices and shops scheme. 50,000 people will work there when it is complete. They will have to live somewhere, they will want amenities ranging from transport to dentists to pubs. Amenities are what the Isle of Dogs is still very short of. The presence of this workforce will have unpredictable but obviously major effects on the homes market in the whole of Docklands. What looks now like a positive oversupply of new homes may swing round radically when even a tenth of those thousands decide to live close to the office.

Meanwhile, people are at last moving into the myriad new homes developments to live. This is distinct from the speculators who bought in droves before Black Monday with no intention of ever occupying their investment. Thanks first to Black Monday and then to the general slow-down in the London house market, Docklands is no longer a place for get-rich-quick speculation. While things are quiet, though, it may well be a historically good time for a medium to long-term punt, if this is where you want to live or work. Docklands is too big to be dismissed as a yuppie-palace ghetto, and in 5-7 years people may well look with envy at those who bought into a good, well-placed development in the quiet months of 1988/89.

The reality of Docklands

Despite Canary Wharf, despite all the publicity and the rows, most Londoners have little or no idea what is happening east of the Tower. This is the biggest urban development project in Europe and the biggest supply of new homes in Southeast England. It is a giant shopping centre within sight of Tower Bridge: new homes for sale ranging from skyline penthouses to family houses with gardens. It is property prices that, when compared to the western side of town, can often look surprisingly reasonable. And the most important thing, both good news and bad, about Docklands is that it is still being built.

D

The good news is that this is an exciting, fast-changing place to live, where every week brings something new to applaud or abhor and where liveliness is becoming a way of life. After the tedium of some of London's smarter suburbs (one thinks of those interminable streets of overpriced, swagged-curtained Victorian terraces in west and south-west London) Docklands is a literal breath of fresh air. The views are wider, the river air keener, the skyline more exciting.

The bad news is that 1989 is going to be the year of the Docklands traffic jams. Things are bad enough now. They will get worse. New roads are coming, but they are only on paper. Already the Isle of Dogs can get literally cut off from the 'mainland' because there are only two ways in and out. The prices of some otherwise desirable homes on the east side of the Isle have been held back by the awful access road. Olympia & York, who are not fools, have a Thamesline riverbus on exclusive charter, and are bringing in building materials by barge.

It will be some years before the transport systems – roads, rail and river – catch up with the demand. (The plans for doing so are described in the 'Transport' chapter at the front of this book.) And the other elements of an infrastructure, such as entertainment and shopping, are equally far behind. Surrey Quays, a big shopping centre developed around a Tesco hypermarket, opened in the autumn of '88 and is already a major success. Tobacco Dock, Wapping, which is aimed more at the leisure shop-and-stroll market, was due at the same time but was held up. Fears that the place will be more a theme park than a shopping centre were heightened when the developers announced plans for 'special themed events' and 'full-sized replica sailing ships'. On a smaller scale, useful shops appeared among the Isle of Dogs offices.

The new inhabitants

Legend – and the newspapers – have it that Docklands is a community of confrontation, with hard-edged Yuppies glaring at cloth-capped unemployed ex-dockers. Savills, never content to take other peoples' word for things, did some research to find out who is really moving in. They surveyed the people enquiring about buying in Docklands and listed them by their current home address. And they came up with the intriguing fact that east London is the biggest single category (17.2%), with Essex next (9.6%). More than half currently lived in London, only 3.6% were from overseas, with Europeans, not Americans or Japanese, coming top. Another stereotype was exploded when Savills asked people how much they wanted to spend on a Docklands home. Sixty per cent said less than £225,000, 20% less than £125,000. Only 8% were able to spend more than £400,000. So much for the free-spending, jet-setting new Docklanders. The reality is someone from an East London or Essex suburb and someone rather careful with his or her money.

It is widely recognized that 1988 saw people buying homes in Docklands to live in, rather than to invest in. October '87 – Black Monday – put paid to the out-and-out speculators, and a new mood of caution scared off many of the investors who buy and then rent homes out. So those left were the people who actually plan to live in their homes. And who complain, loudly, if the developers' promises are not kept, if the trains and buses do not run and the traffic gets too bad. In other words, they form a community.

The neighbourhoods emerge

One key achievement by the LDDC has been to get the rest of London to think of 'Docklands' as an entity. This is valid: it is a new place overlaying a clutch of

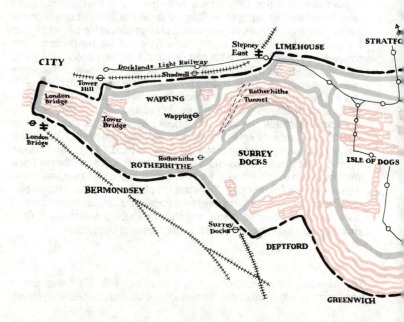

old ones, and newness and the attitudes it engenders are common to places well apart, in geography as well as character. But from the Docklands collective the local neighbourhoods are happily starting to re-emerge.

By the 1970s, the docks, from the City to Woolwich, had one thing in common: decline. So after much talking and several abortive attempts at cooperation, the government imposed a new kind of body, a development corporation, on a great swathe of riverside London. The London Docklands Development Corporation (LDDC) wields wide powers. It took over planning powers from the boroughs, acquired vast amounts of redundant land and began to install the infrastructure necessary – roads, water mains, sewers, electricity – if it was to be developed. Fierce rows arose with the established communities, and more especially their politicians, opposing the centralised, undemocratic LDDC.

The LDDC's achievements are many. It has acted as a pump-primer, getting things started and producing the initial momentum which has allowed private money to come in and invest. This was greatly helped by the Enterprise Zone status of much of the Isle of Dogs: businesses pay no rates here until 1992, and planning laws do not apply. Londoners used to decades of paper-shuffling before action were surprised to find that the Docklands Light Railway, an LDDC initiative, was up and running within a couple of years of the idea being mooted. 'Six years old and we've got a train set' said the LDDC ads with justifiable pride. And it was hardly their fault if the whole thing is having to be virtually rebuilt to allow more and longer trains to use it. No-one predicted success in Docklands. The area had a strong tradition of decline, it was almost

D

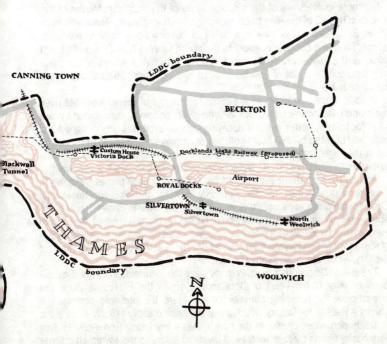

General map

built in. So many well-meaning attempts to revitalize first the docks, then their empty shells, had failed. There are those in Docklands who find the LDDC's dynamism misplaced. Criticisms are that the Corporation ignores the needs and aspirations of locals, and that its failure to plan has led to a jumbled mess of mediocre developments. There is force in both complaints, though the LDDC's record on housing is defensible.

For a fuller account of the recent history of Docklands, see the 1988 Guide.

The seven areas of 'Docklands' are lumped together for convenience under that one, all-embracing title. But like Shakespeare's Seven Ages they may be adjacent but they are not the same.

Start from Tower Bridge and work eastwards – the neo-colonists did the same. This takes you first to *St Katherine's Dock* – the area's first and most pleasant leisure spot. New flats, both local authority and private, were built as part of this marina scheme, on its eastward, Wapping, side. *Wapping* and beyond it *Limehouse* are where to look for the enormous flats created out of the lovely old riverside brick warehouses. The nearest London gets to the New York loft apartment, these are big, often galleried flats whose dimensions can be vast enough to merit a (literal) change in pace: an early resident swears she developed a loping stride to get from end to end of her living space. ('When visiting friends in town, I had to consciously change gear – otherwise I arrived at their back walls in two and a half strides, very likely knocking ornaments over as I went.') Here, too are the handful of old Georgian houses remaining, at *Wapping Pierhead* and in Limehouse's *Narrow St*, plus lots of new homes, both riverside flats and, on the old London Docks inland, houses.

For more conversions of the old, and some of the most spectacular of the new, next head S of the river to *Bermondsey*. Stretching, again, eastwards from Tower Bridge along the river is a range of buildings only now receiving its rebirth. From the *Courage Brewery* to the award-winning *New Concordia*, this, I think, is the place which will most quickly establish itself as a complete neighbourhood – a part of London, not just of 'Docklands'. Strategically, this is the place to be.

Beyond it, the *Surrey Docks* is a complete change of scene. Along the river, the hidden, Georgian-centred *Rotherhithe* is fast becoming surrounded by new sites for homes; better yet, the decaying council estates, badly designed and built, and blighted by the recent collapse of employment, are also being caught up in the regenerative urge: local authorities, with building societies, housing associations and large private builders are undertaking the work of renewal.

Around the waterfront everything from restored council homes for locals to very serious schemes for the seriously rich by the likes of Rosehaugh Copartnership are appearing this year; inland, the filled-in *Surrey Docks* gives open, greenfields sites for newly-built homes – many schemes here, from inexpensive family units to top luxury, are creating almost a new town: in places more Milton Keynes than Marylebone, it is yet within spitting distance of the City. A comprehensive range of homes.

The *Isle of Dogs* comes next. In many ways this peninsula in its great oxbow bend of river is the heart of Docklands. Here is the Enterprise Zone, the powerhouse for returning commercial life. Here the business centres, the offices – the site for Canary Wharf, a gigantic business city in itself. Around the riverside perimeter, chiefly, lie the new homes – from early (some now looking very basic) efforts through increasing layers of luxury to the asymmetric tower of *Cascades* and the conversion/new-build *Burrell's Wharf*, on its historic shipbuilding site. Conversions are rare here: most Isle homes are new.

Last comes the *Royals* and the future. Several schemes are under consideration: at least 6,000 homes should result. For now, housing here is the greenfields estates of *Beckton* where major builders are turning out relatively inexpensive family homes by the hundred. The planned Docklands Light Railway extension, the East London River Crossing and the proposed shopping centre will complete the transformation.

Prices in Docklands are impossible to generalize about, but there are a few basic principles. The older the conversion the bigger the flat: land and warehouses were cheap, once. But newer schemes have secure parking, a feature much in demand. The newer homes may be smaller but there is more luxury and more communal features such as swimming pools. Resales in the larger, older conversions can be better value in terms of £ per sq ft than new releases (perhaps because you are not paying for the marketing?). Water views command a premium. Prices in winter 88/89 seemed to have stablized as follows: benchmark prices for an 80 sq ft Wapping flat were £250,000 for a riverside position. £210,000 for an oblique river view and £160,000 with no river view at all. And as more and more homes get built, a smaller and smaller proportion will have that magic glimpse of Thames or (less valuable) a dock. Over in the Surrey Docks, a 4-bed family house on an inland site might cost around £160,000, while in Beckton such a home would be £80-120,000. But individual developments break the rules if and when they capture the public's imagination. And, say agents, prices in Wapping and Bermondsey have made their big leaps and now equate with similar properties in established parts of West London. The rental market is becoming well established in Docklands, with a wide choice of modern or period conversion homes. It will grow along with shops and services, though foreign executives' families, the staple of the renting market in other areas, have been slow to move in.

D

Wapping

Wapping starts, in the shadow of the Tower, with *St Katharine's Dock*. The *North* and *East Quays*, at present a car park for St Katharine's are to be developed with a mixed commercial/homes scheme, giving 220 flats, for completion around 1990. Housing already built includes 351 new homes, and there are 300 local authority homes – 80 already bought by tenants. *Mews St* has 10 small cottages; *Marble Quay* has 4 flats in an office development. At the entrance to the dock *Harrison's Wharf* will have a crescent of 6-bed, 5-bath 'Nash' style stucco houses amid a large commercial scheme, due this year.

President's Quay is a particularly stylish development by Bovis; the twin glass-roofed pyramids of its penthouses a new riverside landmark. Last autumn's opening prices were from £117,000 (studios) to £750,000 for those penthouses. As is now common, the launch was delayed until the scheme was totally finished: buyers who plan to live in, not speculate on, a Docklands home want to see what they're buying. Next door, *Miller's Wharf* has 22 homes in a warehouse conversion due in the spring. Selling started off-plan: £275-480,000 for 1-, 2- and 3-bed flats; penthouses at £1.5 million, and launch prices are forecast at much the same level. *Tower Bridge Wharf* is a new-built complex: 64 homes by Trafalgar House. One end is semi-circular, with a central courtyard, which gives the opportunity for some unusual shapes and two differing but equally enviable penthouses at either end of the crescent. It was

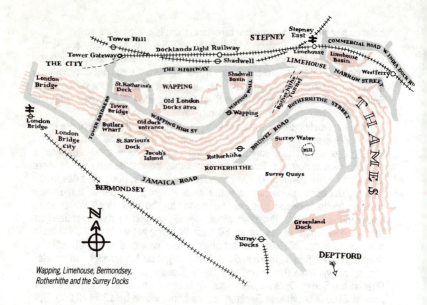

Wapping, Limehouse, Bermondsey, Rotherhithe and the Surrey Docks

completed and largely sold last year, though some of the non-riverside flats hung fire until pre-Black Monday prices were re-thought.

Inland, *Thomas More St* will have 150 homes in a big, high-rise scheme that will be mostly offices. Ready 1990/91. *Hermitage Basin* has 81 homes around one of the surviving London Docks basins: water, if not river, side. Developers Regalian are also building 90 sheltered council flats for the elderly in the scheme. The riverside end of the *Hermitage* scheme is the last big waterfront development in Wapping. It will have a riverside garden and shops for its 216 homes, ready 1990/91 with prices up to £1.75 million, heights up to 14 storeys. The scheme includes *Orange Court*: 17 houses on *Wapping High St* due in '91; from around £250,000.

Next door, and on the inland side of *Wapping High St*, is *Hermitage Court*: 97 homes over shops and offices, by Bovis/Berkley House; ready early this year. On the river front, *Black Eagle Wharf* is becoming 96 new homes, all with river view, in a development by Fairclough. *The Sanctuary* is inland, but with some good river views and modest prices: £112,000 for 1-beds, £142,500 for 2-bed, 2-bath. It boasts rooftop pool & gym, parking and was selling last winter with typical Docklands deals of 95% mortgages and money off for quick completion. Next comes the glorious *Wapping Pierhead*: the area's one remaining enclave of Georgian houses. (One sold last year for £425,000.) Extending inland, new local authority houses match the Pierhead style exactly.

Inland are new council homes. Back on the river side, *Oliver's Wharf* has some of the most coveted flats in Docklands: it was converted in 1973 by a group of architects and artists. This is the one that started the whole warehouse conversion fever off. The group each paid some £14,000 for their industrial space. Today they remain some of the largest of Docklands (or, indeed, London) flats – a typical one has a 54 x 38ft galleried living room. Now they generally change hands for around £350-400,000. Last year a Swedish rock star bought a top-floor one for half a million.

Orient Wharf is new flats let by a housing association. On the inland side of the *High St, Dundee Wharf* is a Berkley House scheme of 48 flats; most were sold off-plan before the scheme even had planning permission. The next-door *Red Lion Court* is scheduled for 1989. *78 Wapping High St* was better known as Oddbins wine warehouse; now the riverside warehouse is transmogrifying into 16 homes. Declan Kelly are the developers and prices run from £124,000 for a studio to £385,000 for a penthouse. The '60s apparition nearby covered with abstract heiroglyphs and bound to be listed one day is the river police's boathouse.

St John's Wharf was turned into 22 large (some are nearly 3,000 sq ft) flats in 1984. Resales are sought-after. The same owners, Samuel Smiths, possess *King Henry's Wharves* next door, as yet unconverted. Barratt's *Gun Wharf* conversion provided 68 flats in '85. They are now regarded as the 'benchmark' for generalisations about Wapping prices. At the start of this year riverside flats were from around £210,000 for a 1-bed one, £280,000 for a 2-bed. The adjoining *Gun House*, by the same developer, 8 flats plus penthouse, is newbuild. *Gun Place* is on the inland side of the *High Street* and has 73 flats in a conversion. Alongside, *Bridewell Place* is also Barratt: this one is a mews-style scheme with 52 homes. Also on the inland side – and close to Wapping tube station – is *The Carronade*, 42 flats, some double-height and galleried, by Broadwell Land. *Moran House* has 8 more flats in Wapping Lane. Sample price: 2-bed duplex with covered parking, around £140,000. *Towerside*, by Wates, straddles the *High St*; the waterside part is new; the rest – *Prusom's Island* – refurbished warehouses. The total is 97 flats. Although not the most sophisticated of Wapping schemes, it does provide among the least expensive riverside flats here (1-beds c £130,000, 2-beds c £165,000). *St Hilda's Wharf* is a new riverside scheme of 39 large, especially for newbuild, flats.

New Crane Wharf is a warehouse conversion with a courtyard, around which are grouped 143 homes plus offices, shops, restaurants. The developers are Conran Roche/Capital & Counties/Heron Homes; completion 1988/9. There are high hopes for this one: as you might expect of Sir Terence, the site is excellent and will boost the area's facilities. Three adjoining wharves along *Wapping Wall*, named *Lower Oliver's*, *Jubilee & Lusks* (which sold last year for office development, despite its waterside position) and *Metropolitan*, are all scheduled for development after 1990.

Pelican Wharf, next door to the Prospect of Whitby, has 13 large 2,000 sq ft apartments – each bigger than a normal family house. Walkways round an atrium and a whole-floor penthouse with three roof gardens are among its attractions. The painstaking Roger Malcolm had problems with this tricky site (taking due care of the historic pub not least among them). Prices from £345,000.

On the other side of the pub *Prospect Wharf* is a new scheme in warehouse style, built by Trafalgar House in an enviable position between the river and Shadwell Basin. Great views, therefore, on both sides, though some eccentrically-shaped rooms. Another plus is the open courtyard between the river and the curve of the buildings: a rare commodity in crowded Wapping. The flats are 1- and 2-beds; from £135,000. *Prospect Place*, N of *Wapping Wall*, has 70 houses and flats next to a Regalian refurb of a block of council flats, *Riverside Mansions*, which were sold to waiting-list locals at a discount. These 750 sq ft 2-bed maisonettes (many with views over Shadwell Basin) still provide great value at around £90,000.

D

Shadwell Basin consists of 172 flats and houses, some with 6 bedrooms, grouped round the dock, home to a youth watersports club. The gabled brick buildings with their distinctive semi-circular windows and red detailing are virtually all sold: not surprising, given their attractive dockside position. Heading W, *Wapping Lane* has a 6-acre business park, *Sovereign Court*, due for 1990, and *Tobacco Dock*, opening (at last) this year, is a smart shopping centre around a listed warehouse. *East Quay* (the award-winning Laing scheme) and *Waterman Quay* (Ideal) have 170 homes grouped around a new canal. *Quayside* is multi-tenure. *Portland Square* is a 1986 Barratts development with some (rare) large houses grouped around a private square with fountain, and a range of other homes. Also on the old site of the London Docks are *South Quay* – 182 low-cost (originally) homes by Brosely (some houses are shared-ownership through a housing association); handsome *Sir Thomas More Court*, 196 flats and houses by Heron; and *Quay 430*, a 300-home Regalian scheme due for completion this year: this will include family homes and priority will go to local residents. It's worth noting that this inland corner is a very convenient one, and that in some of the earlier, less fancy developments you can pick up a 2/3 bed home from around £125,000.

On *The Highway*, Wapping's main road, *Telford's Yard* has 68 particularly spacious flats in a warehouse conversion. Next door *Breezers Court* was divided, in 1985, into 38 flats. Further along *The Highway*, Barratt's *Pennington Court* is a 1987 scheme. Resales last winter were around £80,000 (studio), £110,000 (1 bed), £140-150 (2-bed).

Limehouse

Regalian's orange ziggurat landmark *Free Trade Wharf* stands sentinel at the end of Wapping, the beginning of Limehouse. This is a big scheme of new, and a few luxurious converted-warehouse, apartments, of which Phase 1 is now complete. These will have their own gym, swimming pool and an infrastructure of offices, shops, restaurants ... and riverside inn. Part of the Wharf dates from 1795 – an old salt-petre store. *Keepier Wharf*, a re-clad warehouse with 24 spacious flats completed in 1987, stands at the beginning of Limehouse's best-known corner, *Narrow Street*, a warehouse-lined road running the length of the Limehouse waterfront. It is also famous for its short surviving run of Georgian houses: one, home to Dr David Owen, saw the birth of the SDP; another – even more notably – is the venerable Grapes public house. On the inland side, between *Narrow St* and *The Highway*, is *St George's Square*, a newly-built complex in a remarkable mixture of architectural styles from Docklands vernacular to Mock-Tudor, executed in red brick. 41 houses and flats surround a small courtyard. Along the riverside are several smaller new buildings and conversions: *Ratcliffe Wharf*, which is new, and *London* and *Commercial Wharves*, both conversions. Both *Ratcliffe* and *Commercial* are by the hand of the unquenchable Mrs Rae Hoffenburg, a Docklands pioneer who has been converting warehouses (and living in them) since the 1970s. *Sun Wharf* is new, but in repro style, and is one enormous home built by a film director. Across the road is a newbuild inland scheme with 16 flats, *Eagle Wharf* (marketing this spring; prices for the 1- and 2-bed flats c £140-260,000). *Narrow St* still has some commercial uses, including Tower Hamlets' cleansing depot, where a superb riverside site is currently enjoyed by dustcarts and rubbish skips – but not for much longer.

Limehouse Basin itself is a large area of water which has been patiently awaiting its renaissance. Huntingate and British Waterways are joint developers, and the first phase of the 430 homes, all with water views, is due in the autumn. But first there is the little matter of the *Limehouse Link*, the new highway onto the Isle of Dogs, which must pass beneath the Basin in a 'cut and cover' tunnel (see 'Transport' chapter). This is a big scheme with shops and offices as well as community facilities, social housing and leisure space – but the local convent is worried about the nightclub ...

On past the Basin are some semi-derelict industrial buildings where work has begun on a mixed scheme, including 279 homes and restoration of a small canal. Now known as *Victoria Wharf*, Danish developers Danbuild forecast first completions mid-1990. One small and charming Georgian house survives here, at right-angles to the river by an inlet.

Commercial & Residential, known for their smart South-West London conversions, are at work on a mostly new-build riverside scheme of 52 homes, due early '89. Nearby, *Blyth's Wharf* is an unfortunate-looking fake warehouse with 16 large houses – this was the scheme that ill-advisedly decided to give away the odd Porsche or two as sales inducements last year. On the river frontage it boasts an extensive pier, giving a promenade. Inland from this *Roy Square* has 73 1- and 2-bed flats in regrettable beige brick, around a courtyard.

Past these two are the real thing: the Georgian waterside homes and the Grapes pub. Opposite is another pub, once part of a Victorian terrace but now alone and called, with accuracy, 'The House They Left Behind'. *Duke Shore Wharf* comes next, a much more successful new-build riverside development in a horseshoe shape. *Dunbar Wharf* ends *Narrow St;* owned by a shipping company at present, it lines an inlet, Limekiln Dock. Work on the Limehouse Link road tunnel will affect this site and the large *Dundee Wharf* on the far side of the creek. Both sites have plans for homes – not to mention a marina, shops, restaurants, etc. The LDDC has approved the *Dundee* scheme, but it has gone to Environment Secretary Nicholas Ridley since it departs from the Tower Hamlets Borough Plan and there are strong criticisms from that council. The plans include 162 1- and 2-bed homes, 46 3- and 4-bed ones. *Limehouse Wharf* is a small 1840 warehouse, an early conversion into flats/working studios: large with unusually high ceilings. *Lime Kiln Wharf* at the head of the inlet has 6 flats in a renovated building, and 23 new ones being built in an L-shaped block.

London Bridge

The westernmost tongue of Docklands intrudes right into the heart of London, facing the City, between London and Tower Bridges. As you might expect, the new, emerging *London Bridge City* has a million square feet of offices, plus shops, restaurants and a private hospital. It is thus outside the remit of this book, except to note that 78 expensive rented flats are included and that the riverbus stops there.

Bermondsey

The Bermondsey riverside, the south-bank stretch downstream from Tower Bridge, starts with one of the river's most splendid buildings. Not another warehouse, but an old Courage Brewery. The Anchor Brewhouse is a 10-storey edifice rising sheer from the river right next to the bridge. The interior has been totally rebuilt: the shell of the old Boilerhouse, with its towering landmark chimney, has 35 flats including the spectacular treble-decker penthouse (yours for £2 million) ... The Malt Mill, nearest the bridge, has more large flats in process of construction, all with river views. Here too is an amazing penthouse: this time on 4 floors, and boasting the original cupola and belvedere gallery. Where the first was glass-walled modern, its main room like the deck of a '30s liner, this one will be more like owning a Georgian house – set high in the air.

Directly behind the brewery lies *Horsleydown Square*, where unlovely '50/60s buildings have been cleared and shops, offices, workshops et al are emerging, courtesy of Berkley House, around an open landscaped square. 178 homes, some conversion, some new-build, are involved. Names to look out for in this corner are: *Eagle Wharf, The Cooperage, Crown Court* and *Horsleydown Court. Tower Bridge Square*, on *Gainsford St*, was built for sale by the Nationwide Housing Trust: 1- and 2-bedroomed flats and townhouses.

Next along the river from the brewery is *Butler's Wharf West*, a warehouse already converted, already inhabited – and nothing to do with the main *Butler's Wharf* scheme which runs on from here all the way to *St Saviour's Dock*. This huge site, which encompasses several existing streets including the Dickensian *Shad Thames* (the street will be preserved – but will its singular atmosphere?), runs inland to *Gainsford St*. It is being developed by a consortium headed by Sir Terence Conran, Jacob Rothschild and Fred Roche, who have planned for everything from homes through a hotel, businesses, shops, etc, to a museum of modern design – a complete neighbourhood, in fact. Already completed are the 66 homes in *Cinammon Wharf* beside St Saviour's Dock. A quality conversion of a fairly modern building, it sold briskly. And last year saw the launch of the first vast sybaritic apartments in the 1880s riverside *Butler's Wharf Building* itself. With river or dual aspects, they were released at £275,000 (1-bed, 931 sq ft) up to £700-750,000 (3-beds/2-bath, 2,561 sq ft). A student residence for the LSE is also included in this 14-acre scheme. At the riverside corner of the site will be an hotel, which will have a riverbus pier.

Christian's Warehouse is a Bovis conversion and newbuild scheme, promising 87 flats overlooking *St Saviour's Dock*. Next door are *Java Wharf*, also Bovis, and the splendidly-named *Butlers, Grinders & Operators* building (bought by Butler's Wharf). Plans to partially dam the dock to ensure it has water at all state of the tide seem to have evaporated. Prospective buyers should pester their developers on this point.

Straddling *Queen Elizabeth St* a scheme has just been begun which will certainly be, and remain, distinct from the rest of the Docklands gamut. *The Circle's* fluid lines and blue brick fascias caught the imagination of off-plan buyers a year ago, and the almost-immediate stock market slide seemed to do nothing to halt it despite some of the highest prices seen for an off-river site. Its provenance is good: developers Jacob's Island Company of *New Concordia*.

On the E side of the creek Bovis are building a courtyard of shops, offices and 93 flats at *Scott's Sufferance Wharf. Lloyd's Wharf* has 24 flats sold as shells in 1985 for £30-60,000. *Unity Wharf* has four gloriously large work/flats. *Vogan's Mill* is Rosehaugh's conversion of an old flour mill; a complete community is planned with 65 homes and 5,000 sq ft of office space. Thanks to the existence of the mill's tall silo, Ian Rowberry gets the chance to replace the unlovely structure with a new 18-storey high-tech tower – a south bank Cascades? *St Saviour's Wharf*, a Berkley House scheme, is a refurbishment which provided 47 flats. Downstream, at the creek's mouth, is the award-winning *New Concordia Wharf*, discovered on the point of demolition by young developer Andrew Wadsworth; his 1985 conversion sparked the revival of the entire Bermondsey bank. The final phase, the newly-built *China Wharf*, lies alongside: smaller rooms, glorious views, architecture loved by some, not by others. *Reeds Wharf*, adjoining has flats and offices. Wadsworth's company is about to develop *Jacob's Island* itself, the rectangle of land E of *Mill St*. The mix of homes, commercial and retail units are planned on avenues angled to give as many water views as possible and should be spectacular. Back to *Bermondsey Wall* and the river, where inland, *Hobbs Court* in *Jacob St* will have 30 homes. *Springhalls Wharf* is yet another Bovis development: 24 flats, ready early 1990. The future of the large *Chambers Wharf* site downstream has yet to be decided. Next comes *Cherry Garden Pier*, with 64 riverside council houses and five new terraces of flats and town houses by Lovell Farrow. They sold well to occupiers rather than speculators: the Thamesline waterbus already stops here. Flats from £72,000. *Corbetts Wharf* was converted to flats back in 1984.

Rotherhithe

D

This surviving waterside hamlet boasts a glorious 1715 parish church, St Mary's, whose internal pillars are not stone but old ships' masts, plastered over. Surrounding the church, the old school, rectory and some of the warehouses – not to mention the Mayflower pub – also date at least from Georgian days. On the western edge of the village *Elephant Lane/Mayflower Court* has 76 houses and flats, plus offices, built in 1984 in an avenue running away from the river to the Rotherhithe Tunnel roundabout. Around the old village are several blocks of pre-war council flats. The historic, award-winning *Thames Tunnel Mills* is a riverside warehouse converted into fair-rent flats, while *Ronald Buckingham Court* is sheltered housing. *Isambard Place*, whose name recalls the tunnel's builder, is an Ideal Homes development with 94 homes for sale and 44 for a housing association successful in attracting both locals and City commuters. Across the road, the same firm's *Atlas Reach* scheme adds a further 100, all of which were quickly reserved. Inland a little, The Jacob's Island Co are building flats and houses at *The Pump House, Renforth St*.

Surrey Docks

From Rotherhithe on E, round the great bend of the river, is the frontage of the old Surrey Docks. Nearly all the docks were filled in, and now large areas of new housing have been built. These differ markedly in character, if not in style, from the river-front schemes: houses with gardens predominate, rather than warehouse flats. New flats are following, but families should look here. Good, hardworking schemes, some interesting architecture. Last year saw a landmark: the opening of the Surrey Quays shopping centre provided the first major retail centre for this corner of SE London.

The long river frontage here has plans afoot for nearly every inch. *Clarence Wharf* is at present a busy gravel depot with ships unloading still. An inlet leads through a disused lock to Surrey Water, an ornamental lake surrounded by homes (see below). *Island Yard* by the lock, will be mixed homes and commercial, including a youth hostel and a pub. Local firm C J Sims are developers. The next gravel depot along is *Bellamy's Wharf*. *King & Queen*

Wharf is nicely detailed newbuild by Fairclough: 131 flats with swimming pool/leisure complex. Completion in September; prices around £80,000 (studios), £100,000 (1-beds), £150,000 (2-beds), £170,000 (3-beds). Fairclough also own neighbouring *Globe Wharf*, which they plan to convert into 139 smart flats, a luxury shopping complex and a gym. Opposite these, on the inland side, the *Amos Estate* has 131 housing association flats.

The northern tip of the peninsula is the 5-acre *Burmah Castrol* site: Barratts and Rosehaugh working jointly on a 350-home scheme, *Lavender Wharf* – the first of several similarly named schemes. Next comes *Lavender Quay*, 1985 Wimpey houses, inland. At Lavender Dock East *Pageant Steps* (riverside) and *Lavender Place* (inland) are the complementary halves of an important scheme by Heron, centred on a new park they are creating from the river, across *Rotherhithe St* to *Salter Rd*. The first of the 228 homes sold last year. *Lavender Green* is 1981 low-cost housing by Lovell. Long-term plans for the river bus to call at Lavender Pier.

Acorn Walk has 44 fair-rent flats, again council re-hab, with some of the flats and maisonettes for sale. *Canada Wharf* awaits development by Rosehaugh Copartnership. *Columbia Wharf*, *Nelson Dock* and *Lawrence Wharf* are all part of a major scheme by Islef on either side of an old ship repair dock: in its midst Nelson House, the firm's HQ, is a rare and charming Georgian survival.

Inland, *Acorn Yard's* 56 homes were sold in 1985. More rehab of a council block forms the heart of Regalian's *Silver Walk*, which has rehabilitated and newly built flats for sale. A tiny, peaceful park gives access to the riverside plus views to the Isle of Dogs and the Cascades tower. *Barnard's Wharf* and *Commercial Pier Wharf*, next to the splendid Surrey Docks Farm, are sites for Southwark council housing and a business centre. Here is Downtown, for years a very depressed corner of council flats, at last feeling the wind of change. In contrast is the emergent Rosehaugh riverside scheme, *New Caledonian Wharf*, 104 luxurious new flats, with sports centre, extensively sold off-plan in 1987; ready in the autumn (2-beds: £220-275,000). Some offices too: part of the work where you live movement. Next door is *Custom House Reach*, a 1970s 9-storey block of undistinguished flats.

Greenland Dock in the SE corner of the Surrey Docks area is the only surviving, un-filled in dock. Several developers are at work. The Islef scheme at the dock's mouth, *Greenland Passage*, boasts 152 homes, many of family size, and more expensive than others in the area so far. This made for a slowish start to sales, but these picked up as soon as Phase 1 neared completion and the river bus service began to run from the nearby pier. Prices now start c £180,000. *Rainbow Quays* the last site left on the S side of *Greenland Dock*, will also be an Islef development.

Other schemes afoot are: *The Lakes* – a new name for the entertaining scheme originally *Norway Dock* (177 houses and flats grouped around a lake, with the largest villas actually on pontoons, Ideal Homes), *Finland Quay*: 1- 2- and 3-bed flats and duplexes, from £80,000 (Lovell). *Russia Court East* (Heron) juts into the dock, with a circular 7-storey tower of flats on the point. Now complete, the scheme also includes further homes, shops, offices – and a pub. *Greenland Quay* (Ideal) uses open courtyard layout to give everyone water views. *Swedish Quays* (Roger Malcolm) sits between *Greenland* and *South Docks*: 96 flats and houses *Brunswick Quay* and *Russia Court West* are both by Daniel Homes; the former in 1985, the latter (43 homes) last year. The *Surrey Quays Marina*, which will be London's biggest, opens this spring in *South Dock*.

The interior of the Surrey Docks has large areas of 'normal' housing: put up by large builders, the wide open expanse giving them more familiar greenfield sites, and the result has a strong flavour of Milton Keynes. No new town however, has the dramatic view of the City towers offered by the artificial hill at the centre of the area. A tree-lined walk, flanked by block after block of new houses, leads from the hill to Surrey Water, an artificial lake with a tall fountain. The walkway is cleverly aligned to point straight at the City skyscape across the river: a view which contains more of London's landmarks than almost any other. The *Surrey Quays* interior has several hundred homes, mostly houses with gardens. This is the affordable side of Docklands, with 4-bed houses still available at around £150,000 – which would barely buy you a studio in some of the top-flight Docklands developments. There's plenty afoot close to the new *Surrey Quays Shopping Centre*. Schemes include *Marlow's Landing* (Lovell): 4-bed houses from £145,000; *Hithe Point* (Barratt) has 1- 2- and 3-bed flats and houses in a nicely-detailed stock brick development. And *Wolfe Crescent* (Lovell again) is a striking red-brick semicircle curled around four pale-coloured octagonal blocks, designed by fashionable architects and said by its agents to be out-performing the competition in the area. It includes homes for sale to local tenants, too.

There is not space here to detail all the local authority, housing association and self-build work in progress in the area. Nor yet the commercial schemes and industrial developments; the careful retention of green space; the provision of car parking; the work of the likes of Regalian and Barratt who have been refurbishing sad council estates. Here are homes genuinely aimed at every level.

D

The Isle of Dogs

The Isle of Dogs is indeed an island, cut off by a great bend of the Thames and with its isthmus severed by the West India Docks. Unlike the Surrey Docks it has kept its water, providing vast lengths of quayside. The Isle is special in two other ways: it has the most cut-off indigenous community, hardly part of London at all and only tenuously involved in the rest of Docklands, and it will have Canary Wharf. This giant office complex is a product of the Enterprise Zone (EZ), a government tax-break concession which was the catalyst for the first phase of the Isle boom.

For by now, a short decade after the start, the Isle renaissance is old enough to have a history. The hesitant days of light industry and warehouses, timidly built on land almost given away by the LDDC and with no rates to pay thanks to the EZ, were succeeded by homes schemes and then by taller, smarter, more self-confident commercial. By the time the Docklands Light Railway arrived, buildings put up in the early '80s were being torn down: they no longer earned their keep on the rapidly-appreciating sites.

The Isle's riverside has a wide and varying range of homes developments, encompassing both homes less imaginative and well-built than much modern council housing and the state-of-the-art palaces which have been exhaustively chronicled in recent years. The first thing to watch for is the date of the development, since nobody could at first believe quite how smart the Isle was going to get. Things built as late as 1985 can fall into this group.

Most Isle housing, by the way, is newbuild: there were no old riverside warehouses to convert. The exception to this are the listed buildings of

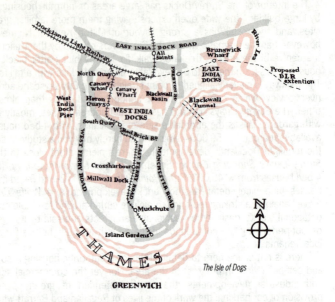

The Isle of Dogs

GREENWICH

Burrell's Wharf, the major new Kentish Homes development (see below). The second point is that housing is around the 'coast' of the Isle: the centre, much of which is in the EZ, is nearly all commercial – and is becoming more so as Canary Wharf begins.

Coming onto the Isle from the NW, Limehouse, direction, the *Canary Wharf* site dominates. This enormous 'city within a city' spreads from the river across the Isle between two of the West India Docks. It will be entirely commercial, but its enormous employment potential has guaranteed the health of the Isle's residential schemes. The developers, Olympia & York, are however joint developers with Regalian of the *Heron Quays* site next door as housing for some of the 50,000 who will eventually work at *Canary*. *Cascades*, already complete, is also close: a new landmark, a stepped, 21-storey riverside tower with 171 luxurious flats. Keith Preston of Kentish Homes travelled to America for inspiration for his dream; the off-plan selling in the spring of 1987 of this exciting new block sparked much of the investment fever and speculation in Docklands homes. Equally, when those buyers completed their deals last year amid talk of a Docklands collapse all the developers heaved sighs of relief.

Next door, beside the Thamesline River Bus pier on *Cuba St*, Rosehaugh have begun work on 129 homes at *Sufferance Wharf*, of which 30 were sold when it was a hole in the ground. Christened *The Anchorage*, the eight houses and the 1- to 3-bedroomed flats will be completed next year. The big Lenanton Timber Importer's site is earmarked for around 300 homes for 1990. Seacon seems likely to keep their riverside site industrial, but Merion are developing *Hutchings Wharf* with a wide-ranging mixed-use scheme to be called *The Point*. Its stylish design was 'tempered by a sense of dignity and restraint we felt was lacking in some of the more frenetic neighbouring schemes.' It includes 87 homes. A welcome open riverside space will remain a park. Opposite, *Glengall*

Place is an early inland estate by Barratts with 79 houses. The River Park Trading Estate goes back to the times when commercial use made sense on the waterfront. Unusually for a riverside site, it is in the EZ, as are *Arnhem* and *Kleins Wharves*.

South of the old Millwall Dock entrance, the Danish group Islef is planning to construct 250 homes on the *Winkleys Wharf* site. *Cyclops Wharf* is a popular newbuild Fairclough development with 176 waterfront flats and 24 houses, inland, grouped around a square: marketing now, completion September. The largest homes scheme on the Isle is under construction by Ideal Homes at *Timber Wharves*, which will boast 190 houses and 300 flats in total. First completions have taken place in this reasonably-priced scheme, aimed at providing 'real homes, not just pied-à-terres' around the central lagoons. Sizes range from 2-bed flats to 4-bed townhouses, prices from c £90-£165,000. A 3-bed terraced house (small rooms, but garage and garden) is around £158,000.

Other inland sites are *Island Square* next to the Daily Telegraph, with 31 homes by Laing last year, and a second phase under way will bring the total to 95. *Clipper's Quay* is a popular scheme by Roger Malcolm, where 256 homes around an old dock are now complete. *Quay West* comprises 127 homes by Wimpey in a surprisingly undistinguished style.

Back at the water's edge, Jacob's Island Company have paused while building *The Circle* and crossed the river to buy a site called *Ferguson's Wharf*, which they intend for homes. ('Knowing them, they'll come up with a very different and dramatic scheme indeed' commented a local agent.) Nearby once stood the tall outlines of an old mast house; its shape, though not its job of lowering masts into ships, may reappear in the form of a new tower of flats above a riverside pub. *Masthouse Terrace* should, if permission comes through, be the site of 350 homes for sale plus others for rent in a joint venture between Countryside Homes and the local council, Tower Hamlets.

One of the few remaining historic sites in the Isle is *Burrell's Wharf*. Here the Great Eastern, the largest ship of its time, was built in the 1850s. The piles of its launching slipway can still be seen, and will remain on public view. The range of buildings which saw the forging of its plates and its creation are being converted into apartments by Kentish Homes. Two new blocks will flank the river, each with 70 flats, while behind the listed buildings are grouped around a courtyard. This important scheme, among the most interesting on the Isle, came in for a re-think and a re-launch last year after the initial one which coincided with Black Monday. The original leisure complex has grown into an enormous health club (free membership for residents) with indoor running track and 20-metre pool. There will be shops, offices, and the river bus will stop at Masthouse Pier. *Burrells* has been selling well – not surprisingly: so bullish are Kentish that they've guaranteed buyers a 15% increase in value after nine months of completion, or they'll make good the difference.

Maconochie's Wharf next door is the site of a self-build project, where local people have created their own houses. *Clyde* and *Langbourne Wharves* belong to British Steel, but it's expected that around 175 homes will be built by 1990. The southernmost site on the Isle is the seven-acre *Lockes Wharf*, where outline consent exists for 107 houses and 225 flats. The inland partner to this is *Lockes Field*, where 90 homes (c £85-165,000) will be finished in spring. *Felstead Wharf*, a 1984 Wates scheme of 28 homes in an open square onto the river, has great views across to Greenwich: a handsome scheme, but used the

D

standard Wates flat layout with no concession to a rather different market. Next to it is the 14-house *De Bruin Court*. Wates' *Horseshoe Court* has 80 homes, mostly flats, on an inland site very close to the DLR station. Inland are terraces of pre-war cottage council houses, with large gardens. Some occasionally come up for sale. Back on the river, Barratt's *Luralda Gardens* scheme of 48 flats, their first Docklands venture, also shares the views of the Cutty Sark and Greenwich. Homes from here on E have less enticing views of the gasworks and industry of E Greenwich.

Cumberland Mills is architecturally one of the most pleasing new-build developments anywhere in Docklands. Its tiers of roof gardens step courteously down to the riverside from the high point of its four quarters without looming over its surroundings, which include a fine church. The level of specification and finish is reflected in the sale of the 1,150 sq ft show flat (not counting its two large terraces) for £350,000. Phase 1 of the 87 flats was launched last year. The award-winning *Caledonian Wharf* comes next; an earlier 104-home scheme by the same developer, Bates. *Cubitt Town Wharf* awaits development. Inland is the Tower Hamlets Cubitt Town Estate; on the riverside is *Plymouth Wharf*, 62 homes around a square.

Compass Point by Costain is now finished with 134 houses and some flats, stretching inland across the road. Unusually, the riverside has 5-bedroom townhouses rather than flats. Two rows of houses reminiscent of early Victorian brick villas face each other across a central garden; across the road the square is completed by a white-rendered crescent of flats. *Millwall Wharf* is an 8-acre site where 333 homes are planned by Roger Malcolm. *London Yard*, one of the earlier schemes on the eastern bank, consists of very large orangey brick buildings grouped around ornamental water. Neither design nor finish can compare with more recent development. Inland from this is *Friars Mead*, 72 houses built two years ago by Comben. The attractive 'pagoda' blocks of four houses are also unusual in having gardens: the developers, now part of Ideal homes, went to the trouble of treating the toxic, ex-industrial land.

At the entrance to and around Blackwall Basin is *Jamestown Harbour*, by Wates, with 73 homes finished and a third phase (£99-235,000) launching this spring. A picturesque site, making good use of the water – which offers private mooring as well as watersports. It should get a fine view of the towers of *Canary Wharf* which will soon rise to the W. At the moment traffic congestion on this side of the Island is affecting this corner. But road schemes now under way (see 'Transport'chapter) will help.

By now we are at the top NE corner of the Isle of Dogs. This corner is one to watch: Rosehaugh Copartnership have major plans afoot, including the demolition of an enormous power station. And the 8-acre Charrington site, on the riverside at *Blackwall Way*, will have homes and business space. And for those tired of tales of the riverside, it should not be forgotten that there are some homes between the dramatic commercial schemes in the Enterprise Zone in the centre such as *Glengall Bridge* and *Heron Quays*. *Heron Quays* gained new prominence in late 1988 when Canary Wharf developers Olympia & York joined with Regalian to buy the undeveloped part from Tarmac. Proposals include 1,000 homes and office space.

There have been many complaints about traffic on the Isle of Dogs, many stemming from the narrow (though very expensive) 'red brick roads' built by the LDDC. These will be widened this year in a £5m scheme. Work is also going on to upgrade the light railway.

The Royals and Beckton

To most Londoners the Thames Barrier, the strange structure designed to stop the sea flooding London, is a long way off. Well past Greenwich, east of Canning Town, it is virtually on the Thames Estuary, not the river. And the Royal Docks, touted as the next Docklands area for regeneration, are further east still.

The Royals were the last, largest and easternmost of the great docks complexes. They were still growing in the '50s, but closed for good in 1981. What was left was so enormous even the LDDC didn't quite know what to do with it. From end to end, the Royals cover as far as from Hyde Park to the Tower. They make the Isle of Dogs, with its wide spaces and long views, look as claustrophobic as Kensington.

But things did happen to the Royals, and will go on happening. The airport has happened and may this year get permission to handle small jets with longer range. The other big news was and is low-cost housing. Beckton, to the N of the docks and S of the A13, is a burgeoning district of neat little houses with gardens. It is just about the biggest area of owner-occupied new housing in London with 4,000 homes either built or on the drawing board. These are quite different to the warehouse conversions of Wapping: family houses in closes and winding streets on a greenfield site. Many were sold to local people and at prices which now seem astonishingly cheap. Everyone, including the LDDC, was surprised at the level of demand from East London people for new homes at affordable prices. Beckton is hardly Docklands in the sense that Limehouse, or even the Surrey Docks new-build is Docklands. But it is a vast increase in London's new homes stock and it's a short commute to the City: shorter still when the DLR extension is finished in three years' time. Future housing plans for the Royals, too, will include at least 1,500 'social units': homes for rent or shared ownership.

D

The Royals themselves are the focus of several giant schemes. One of these, at the eastern end, has been given the green light. Rosehaugh Stanhope's £500 million scheme covers 264 acres and centres around a vast shopping centre. There will be over 1,000 new homes, half for rent or shared ownership. The shopping centre will be right next to the ELRIC bridge, enlarging the catchment area well south of the Thames. Further west, another consortium led by Laing and Vom plan the Londondome Arena, an exhibition hall, two hotels, 1,750 homes and business use along the north and west sides of the Royal Victoria Dock. Negotiations with a third group fell through last August. They wanted to develop the south side of Royal Victoria Dock but could not agree a price with the LDDC. The proposals included 2,360 homes.

Much of the Royals' plans are on paper. For now, homes schemes exist as follows. The one riverside site with homes under construction is *Waldair Wharf*, E of the Woolwich Ferry. Here Hastingwood have built 29 flats and houses. Mowlem are about to start a 9-acre scheme on the S side of the King George V dock. Ideal for transport buffs: the homes will have fine views of the river lock (which will be modernised to allow ships into the dock once more) and of the airport.

All the other homes schemes under way at present are in Beckton, where a lively resale market also exists in modern homes. Jerram's *Robin Crescent* is in its final phase, with flats now around £85,000. Ideal Homes' *Tollgate Mews* has 55 pleasing 3-5 bed houses centred around a crescent. *Tollgate Green*, next door, is shared ownership. *London Green* is a large scheme by Daniel Homes with 237 homes, mostly houses, of varied styles: prices ranged in 1988 from

£53,000 for a 1-bed flat to £120,000 for a 4-bed house. Laing's *Tollgate Square* is also big, with 160 homes. Lovell have a nearby site, *Connaught Park*: 1- and 2-bed flats; houses including semis and detached. Prices of 3- to 4-bed houses: £125,000 and £150,000. Roger Malcolm's *Hogarth Mews* has 36 stylish semi-detached houses in *Nightingale Way*. These large schemes are all N of *Tollgate Rd* and thus a good half a mile from the actual docks.

A last thought about the Royals: Woolwich and Plumstead, S of the river, are on rising land and will have fine views of the developing 'water city' if and when it gets built. And with ELRIC these areas will get dramatically improved communications. As the Isle of Dogs has benefited Greenwich, so the Royals may boost Woolwich. But take care with your searches and keep well clear of ELRIC and its attendant highway.

Among those estate agents active in this area are:

- Carleton Smith & Co
- Knight Frank & Rutley
- Prudential
- Alex Neil
- Egertons
- Hamptons
- Keith Cardale Groves
- Cluttons
- Savills
- Collins Druce
- Barnard Marcus

Dollis Hill and Neasden

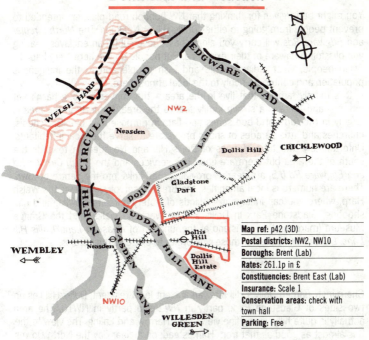

Map ref: p42 (3D)	
Postal districts: NW2, NW10	
Boroughs: Brent (Lab)	
Rates: 261.1p in £	
Constituencies: Brent East (Lab)	
Insurance: Scale 1	
Conservation areas: check with town hall	
Parking: Free	

D

Transport	Tubes: Dollis Hill, Neasden (Jubilee, 3a). From Dollis Hill: Oxford Circus 35 min, City 40 min, Heathrow 1 hr 15 min.
Convenient for	North Circular Rd, Brent Cross Shopping Centre, Edgware Rd. Miles from centre: 6.
Schools	Brent Education Authority: John Kelly (b)(g), William Gladstone High School, Neasden High School..

Flats	S	1b	2b	3b	4b	5b
Average prices	52–55	60–70	65–80	80–90+	–	–
Houses	2b	3b	4b	5b	6/7b	8b
Average prices	80–90	95–150	125–160+	–	–	–

The properties	Thirties semis dominate in Neasden, plus smaller blocks of flats, private and council. Dollis Hill is more spacious, similar to Neasden plus some older turn-of-century properties to the south: converters active here. Some early 20th century terraces.
The market	Families and DIY enthusiasts dominate this self-contained area. Flat-buyers moving in on conversions spilling over from Willesden Green. Families on restricted budgets buy here for schools, gardens and open space. Local searches: 2-3 weeks.

Area Profile

You might be forgiven for thinking that NW London road planners intended to prevent people from going to either Dollis Hill or Neasden. The *North Circular* and *Edgware Rds* will carry you along, past these suburban enclaves, leaving you blissfully unaware of their existence. But people do live here. Very happily. Asian people, West Indian people and Irish people add to the indigenous population and contribute richly to the local atmosphere.

It is mostly families that live in the area – the conversion bug hasn't yet bitten – and there is a strong family feel to the area. Property in the area is largely in the form of 3-bed semis and flats in purpose-built blocks. Schools, churches and little parades of shops proliferate to serve the local inhabitants. Unfortunately, the tube stations of Dollis Hill and Neasden lie towards the south of the area but there are good bus services and the *North Circular Rd* and *Edgware Rd* (A5) are nearby, providing road links into the centre of town. There are numerous local amenities; the Brent Reservoir, known as the Welsh Harp, where you can indulge in all kinds of watery pursuits, bowling and rifle shooting, Gladstone Park in Dollis Hill for weekend walks, and the Grange Museum (marooned on an island at the junction of *Neasden Lane/Dollis Hill Lane/Dudden Hill Lane*) for those who prefer to exercise their brains.

Dollis Hill

Charmingly named Dolly's Hill after an ancient local resident, Dollis Hill lies on two sides of Gladstone Park, partly in NW2 and partly in NW10. The area actually is quite hilly, giving fine views over Harrow and Ealing. The view to the S is almost as good as that from Hampstead; on a clear day the North Downs are visible. The NW10 neighbourhood – roads such as *Fleetwood*, *Ellesmere*, *Dewsbury* and *Burnley Rds* – has been named the 'Dollis Hill estate' by estate agents who have started to take an interest in the area. Neighbouring Willesden, particularly Willesden Green, is quite up-and-coming and those who can't afford property there are prepared to look N of the tube line in Dollis Hill. Increased demand leads to increased prices which means increased commission for agents on these older-style, Edwardian, 3-bed houses. Don't confuse the agents' estate with the Dollis Hill Estate on *Brook Rd* which is council-owned and on the other side of the park. *Dollis Hill Avenue* and *Gladstone Park Gardens*, with small neat semis at around £130,000, lead off the busy *Edgware Rd* towards the park where Prime Minister William Gladstone often stayed with Lord and Lady Aberdeen in the late 19th century. The Regency building here – known as Gladstone House – is now owned by the local authority and used for civic receptions. *Dollis Hill Lane* is the best road in the area, a busy thoroughfare linking Dollis Hill and Neasden. As well as houses and bungalows, this is the place to look for purpose-built blocks of flats. In particular, look at Dollis Heights and Neville's Court where some flats will have views overlooking the park.

Neasden

Neasden is not really a name to conjure with. In fact, as a local estate agent observed, 'Everyone makes fun of Neasden', which is rather unfair. Neasden boasts one of Tesco's largest superstores at Brent Park, the Ikea home furnishings warehouse opened in 1988 and a drive-in MacDonalds on *Blackbird*

Hill. What more could you possibly want?

The first homes in Neasden were built for workers on the Metropolitan Railway in 1876 and there was further development in the late 1920s and '30s when the *North Circular Rd*, which bisects the area, was built. A new EMI leisure development may be built along the *North Circular Rd*, on the old Neasden sidings, comprising cinemas, a theatre, restaurant and bars.

The majority of property in Neasden is 3-bed terraced and semi-detached houses in roads such as *Tanfield* and *Cairnfield Avenues*, though there are also some purpose-built blocks. Two built by Fairview are Hazelwood Court in *Neasden Lane* and Birse Crescent in the semi-pedestrian Neasden Shopping Centre: here a 2-bed flat will fetch around £73,000. The best block in the area is on the Neasden/Dollis Hill border, Hawarden Hill in *Brook Rd*. Built by Barratt, it is a modern red-brick block of 1- and 2-bed flats at prices around £72 and £82,000 respectively, very near to Gladstone Park. Costain have also built Shepherds Walk here, a development of 1- and 2-bed flats and 2- and 3-bed houses. Prices from £72,000. Agents also talk about the Brent Water estate to the north of Neasden which includes roads such as *Review*, *Dawpool* and *Warren Rds* but communications here are not as good as other parts of the area. For the top houses in the area, 4-bed Victorian homes, find *Prout Grove*, couched in between *Dudden Hill Lane* and *Neasden Lane*.

D

What Neasden lacks in charm it makes up for with shopping facilities. Not only is there the Tesco superstore (markers along the *Edgware Rd* tell motorists how far they are from the store) but also the huge stores at Staples Corner, the junction of the *North Circular* and the *Edgware Rd*. The Staples bed shop has long since gone and in its place are all manner of DIY furniture and home improvement stores.

Coles Green Rd runs all the way from the stores at Staples Corner to *Dollis Hill Lane*. Here there are purpose-built blocks such as Coles Green Court, the Ox and Gate pub by *Oxgate Lane*, and a delightful surprise, a little ivy-covered cottage called Oxgate Farm, last remnant of a more rural Neasden.

Among those estate agents active in this area are:
- Camerons Stiff
- Dennis
- Winkworth
- Gladstones
- Hoopers
- Dutch & Dutch
- Mendoza

Dulwich

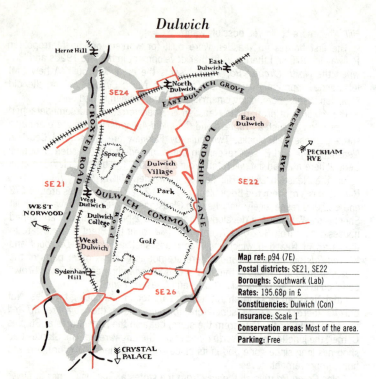

Map ref:	p94 (7E)
Postal districts:	SE21, SE22
Boroughs:	Southwark (Lab)
Rates:	195.68p in £
Constituencies:	Dulwich (Con)
Insurance:	Scale 1
Conservation areas:	Most of the area.
Parking:	Free

Transport British Rail: East Dulwich, North Dulwich (to London Bridge); West Dulwich, Sydenham Hill (to Holborn Viaduct, Victoria).

Convenient for Brockwell Park, South Circular Rd. Miles from centre: 5.

Schools ILEA zone 8: William Penn School (b), Kingsdale School, Waverley School (g). Private: Dulwich College (b), Alleyn's School, James Allen's Girls School.

Flats	S	1b	2b	3b	4b	5b
Average prices	48–60	55–75	70–100+	80–120+	–	–
Houses	2b	3b	4b	5b	6/7b	8b
Average prices	80–140	95–160+	120–200+	165–300+	190–400+	200–500+

The properties Centuries-old Dulwich Village has carefull-tended family homes from 18th to 20th centuries. Some 'country' cottages. Very few flats. Fringe areas were developed later, and have late-Victorian terraces, converted flats and some new property.

The market Family homes within Dulwich College Estate always popular: large gardens, lots of open space, close schools. E Dulwich attracts flat-dwellers and buyers of Victorian terraces. Lower prices above are E Dulwich – but also some very large, very expensive houses which range from modern £500,000 mansions to glorious Georgiana which can approach a million. Local searches: 8 weeks.

Area Profile

Dulwich is unique: a country village with its mill pond and cottages, finger-post road signs, its tollgate and its wide sweep of green space – an island in the South London sprawl.

The village gains its character, and its history, from the charitable foundation set up by Edward Alleyn, an actor-contemporary of Shakespeare's who prospered in the reign of James I. Alleyn was a successful businessman, and spent his money on the manor of Dulwich, leaving the 1,500-acre estate as an endowment for a school. Dulwich College still exists, and its playing fields are among several extensive green expanses which surround the village. The College (in the person of the Estate Governors) is a major landowner still: many Dulwich homes are on long Estate leases, and it owns all the freeholds to purpose-built flats.

There is more to Dulwich than the village. East Dulwich – really NE of the old centre – is straightforward 1880s suburbia. There are fringe areas to the W and S too. Everything within the Estate boundary has a certain leafy unity, though the ages of the houses vary. The Estate has sold off various of its acres for development over the last century, and in consequence Dulwich has houses from the Victorian, Edwardian, inter-wars and modern periods.

As with any reputable area, bits of surrounding neighbourhoods try to edge into Dulwich. The catchment areas of the (private) schools in Dulwich have been extended by the (private) school bus service which picks up pupils from as far away as Clapham. All of Dulwich proper is in SE21, with East Dulwich spreading into SE22. The whole area relies for commuting on BR, with stations all around – but not in – the area. The Estate Commissioners were reluctant to let the railways near the place at all. When forced to concede, they stipulated that all railway bridges should be to their own architect's design.

The Estate Governors maintain a strong interest in their 1,500 acres, be it built on or open space. Leaseholders have to adhere to strict conditions. About a third of the 6,000 houses on land owned by the Estate have been bought by leaseholders under the Leasehold Reform Act – but even then the Estate keeps control: it has retained powers over the appearance of houses and (a major concern of the Estate, this) the trees in their gardens. Touch a tree in Dulwich and the Estate Governors will have something to say about it.

So between *Croxted Rd* in the W and *Lordship Lane* in the E, the heights of Crystal Palace to the S and Denmark Hill to the N, you are in Dulwich Estate Country. Owning a home here means playing by their rules – but you get to live in one of the tidiest, and most charming, corners of London.

Dulwich Village

The denizens of Dulwich confuse outsiders by calling their village a hamlet, their main street *Dulwich Village* – and *Dulwich Common* is not an open space but a stretch of the *South Circular Rd*. The Village (the neighbourhood) starts abruptly. A busy W-E suburban road, starting from Herne Hill as *Half Moon Lane*, then *Village Way*, then *East Dulwich Grove*, skirts the village centre. Turn S into *Dulwich Village* and you are instantly in the old village. Houses are Georgian (or 20th-century Georgian pastiche) and highly desirable.

Noteworthy roads within Dulwich village are *College Rd* (possibly the most coveted street), *Pickwick Rd* and *Aysgarth Rd* (about the only smaller terraced houses in the area), and *Roseway*, picturesque 1920s semi-detached with private entrances to the sports ground. Try Homes are adding some new half-million pound mansions to *College Rd. Turney Rd* has open ground to the rear of the houses on both sides, a fairly common feature in Dulwich. Desirability continues S and W past Picture Gallery and College (Reynolds and Latin). *Alleyn Park* runs close to West Dulwich BR and the College and is very choice. *Alleyn Rd* ditto. *College Rd* runs S across the *South Circular* (a regrettable intrusion) with the modern 5/6-bedroom homes of *Frank Dixon Way* in the angle. On S, on the slopes of Sydenham Hill, you find a mixture of a few older properties and big inter-war and modern detached homes. Hereabouts, views across much of London are an extra bonus.

Despite the Village's ancient air, there are not many truly old houses. It was not a very big place, Dulwich, until the railways came. Even the College is 19th century, the foundation having fallen into positively Trollopian corruption and disrepute until it was reformed.

To the E of the village, roads of large, smart inter-war semis and detached houses run as far as *Lordship Lane*. On the W side of *Court Lane* they overlook Dulwich Park. There is so much green space in Dulwich that many houses back onto parks, sports grounds or golf courses. This includes Barratt's Dulwich Gate, which won prime ministerial approval but had some early teething troubles.

East Dulwich

To the E and NE of the old centre there is *Lordship Lane* and East Dulwich. *Lordship Lane* is the main shopping area; it has most shops necessary for everyday existence and a fantastic variety of restaurants. The Lane itself meets at the S with the A205, which is of course the South Circular.

East Dulwich really describes the area that flanks *Lordship Lane*. Properties are mainly early Victorian terraced or semi-detached houses. At the N end the properties are smaller 2- or 3-bedroom terraces. To the S, in for example *Friern*

Rd and *Upland Rd*, the houses are larger 4-bedroom family style. Many of these have been converted to flats, but this trend is now slowing up and large un-developed houses can still be found. All the above streets with the exception of *Lordship Lane* have unrestricted, on-street parking.

Goose Green, a little patch of grass with a parade of shops, forms a centre for East Dulwich. The neighbourhood stretches a good way E towards Peckham Rye Common. North of *Goose Green* and *East Dulwich Rd* are streets of turn-of-the-century terraces. These streets are considered to be Peckham Rye, not Dulwich, and are consequently cheaper.

West Dulwich

The final neighbourhood, West Dulwich, is the southern tip of the area meeting Sydenham. There are few properties here as it is mainly occupied by the golf course and the sports ground belonging to the College. As Dulwich meets Sydenham there are some blocks of purpose-built maisonettes and flats to be found on the borders: these can command superb views.

Dulwich borders

D

The allure of Dulwich leads to a slow spread of the name into neighbouring areas. One border district that has a good claim to the revered name is the neighbourhood W of *Croxted Rd* and centring around *Rosendale Rd*. This road runs down from Brockwell Park and Herne Hill, and the railway bridge which crosses it perhaps marks the true Dulwich frontier. There is a local shopping centre, a sports ground with tennis courts, and attractive streets of mixed terraced houses. The neighbourhood is equidistant from West Dulwich and Herne Hill stations. New developments here include a cobbled mews (just building, as yet un-named) of 12 traditional-styled houses with garages in the angle of *Croxted* and *Thurlow Park Rds*. Also in *Thurlow Park Rd* is Lincoln's Mews, again in period style, but with a mix of new flats, maisonettes and bungalows, plus a conversion of the original Victorian house. Prices from c £80,000 up to some £175,000 for a 3-bed bungalow.

In the N of the area, the two railway stations of North and East Dulwich confuse the geography by being a mere few hundred yards apart – and, if that were not enough, East Dulwich station is N of North Dulwich station. Some call the streets off *Half Moon Lane* North Dulwich. Those E of *Beckwith Rd* perhaps qualify, but the other pleasant streets further W, such as *Stradella, Winterbrook* and *Burbage Rds* with the spacious family homes, are really closer to Herne Hill and are dealt with under that area. *Burbage Rd* S of the railway is indeed Dulwich. The houses have green sports grounds behind them.

The tract bounded by *Half Moon Lane, Herne Hill* and *Red Post Hill* is the subject of a promotion campaign under the newly-minted name 'North Dulwich Triangle'. Like all such estate-agent-speak this should be treated lightly. Whether the people who live there speak of their homes as Dulwich or Herne Hill (which see) probably depends on which station they use: Herne Hill for Victoria and Holborn Viaduct, North Dulwich for London Bridge or Waterloo.

Among those estate agents active in this area are:
- Burnet Ware & Graves
- Harvey & Wheeler
- Morgan Gillie
- Winkworths
- Roy Brooks
- Spencer Kennedy

Ealing

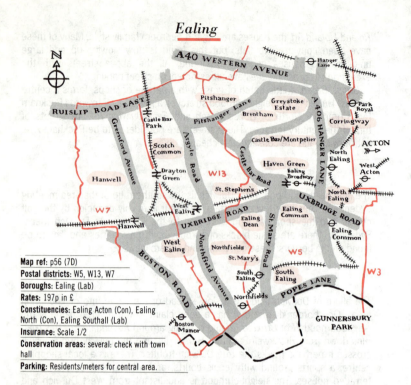

Map ref: p56 (7D)
Postal districts: W5, W13, W7
Boroughs: Ealing (Lab)
Rates: 197p in £
Constituencies: Ealing Acton (Con), Ealing North (Con), Ealing Southall (Lab)
Insurance: Scale 1/2
Conservation areas: several: check with town hall
Parking: Residents/meters for central area.

Transport	Tubes: Ealing Broadway (zone 3a, Central, District); Ealing Common (zone 3a, District, Piccadilly); From Ealing Common to: Oxford Circus 40 min (1 change), City 1 hr 10 min (1 change), Heathrow 15 min. British Rail: Ealing Broadway to Paddington 10 min.
Convenient for	A40 fast route to West End, Heathrow, M4/M40 and roads to the West, North Circular Rd. Miles from centre: 8.
Schools	Ealing Education Authority: Brentside School, Drayton Manor, Ealing Green (b) Ellen Wilkinson (g). Private: Ealing College Upper School (b), St Benedict's School (b), Notting & Ealing High School (g).

Flats	S	1b	2b	3b	4b	5b
Average prices	61–66	68–83	75–110	90–125	–	–
Houses	2b	3b	4b	5b	6/7b	8b
Average prices	95–130	110–165+	→325	185–375+	–	–

The properties	Late Victorian and turn of the century red-brick houses and terraces. Some '30s semis and modern blocks. Lots of conversions, a few mansion blocks. Hangar Hill (£1m mansions), Castlebar and Montpelier are the most favoured areas.
The market	Spacious houses and good schools attract families – including Japanese and Arabs, who both have schools in Acton. They are joined by those priced out of Chiswick. Agents tip Hanwell's canalside terraces for young couples. Local searches: 6 weeks.

Area Profile

'The Queen of Suburbs' is a title proudly claimed by Ealing and more or less deserved. The area famous for being Britain's film centre in the post-war years is now the 'BBC' borough, packed with BBC employees and often used as the backdrop for TV dramas and documentaries by the film unit based near Ealing Green.

Ealing's reputation for being pretty, leafy and genteel dates back to the 1880s, when a determined local authority only allowed solid, middle-class homes to be built. This aura remains – strongly in some areas. The borough has won the 'London in Bloom' competition two years running – and parks like Walpole Park, Lammas Park and Brent Lodge Park, as well as Hanwell's canalside walks, draw crowds from neighbouring boroughs. The 19th-century masters of Ealing would allow no workmen's dwellings to spoil the place, and today the council keeps up the tradition by severely restricting flat conversions.

Ealing's old guard of middle-class inhabitants are still holding strong, particularly in the Castlebar/Montpelier area, although quite a few old-timers are moving out, shocked at the high-profile left-wing policies of the Labour council, the badly-swept roads (which Labour have pledged to improve), the high rates of recent years and the large shifting population in the borough. Or simply taking advantage of the high price their homes will now fetch and moving to a smaller place.

In their place come young couples who cannot afford to be closer into town, or who like Ealing's pretty streets and good facilities – 'Polytechnic lecturers and advertising executives', according to one local estate agent, and workers from Heathrow airport who want a London base. The Japanese have been happily buying the family homes with gardens, following the Japanese School's move across town to Acton. There is also a large Irish community, and many Asian families are moving into Ealing and Hanwell, from the largely Asian area of neighbouring Southall. Ealing is also the centre of London's Polish community.

Ealing's main shopping area is near the Common, the new Ealing Broadway shopping centre and the up-market mall opposite, Waterglades. There are plans to demolish the shops in the *High St* opposite the Broadway Centre, and build yet another mall. The Broadway Centre has two department stores, and many main chains and smaller shops. It also houses a disco – Broadway Boulevard, which has drawn West London nightclubbers, and around central Ealing there are plenty of good restaurants, pleasant pubs and wine bars.

Ealing Common

A room with a view comes at a price on the Common. Ealing Common's outlook is so popular with housebuyers that they are prepared to pay through the nose for it – even though their land searches will find that a huge new road plan is afoot to widen the bottle-neck *Hanger Lane* (part of the North Circular). This has been mooted for the last 30 years or so, and has finally got the go-ahead. Work on Phase II, a dual 3-lane road from *Western Avenue* to Ealing Common via Hanger Hill, is unlikely to begin this year; the scheme for tunneling under their beloved common will never happen, vow residents.

The Common is convenient – for Ealing and Acton shopping centres, for the North Circular and the Hanger Lane junction with the A40 – not so much of a nightmare now it has traffic lights; and for Ealing Common tube station which is on the District and Piccadilly lines, and for the busy station at Ealing Broadway (District, Circle and BR).

There is a good mix of properties here, with plenty of conversions. To the NE of the Common there are large, expensive family houses. Slightly cheaper are the 4/5-bed semis to the E; while *Creffield Rd* and *Inglis Rd* are full of converted flats. *Tring Avenue* has some huge 1919 houses, with newer houses further down. South of the common there are mainly 1930s detached houses. *Elm Avenue* has some of the area's biggest and most impressive older properties, and to the S-W on the *Delamare Rd* estate '30s 3/4-bed houses sell for up to £200,000. Property overlooking the Common is sought-after – or rather fought-over: there is often fierce competition for homes, especially those near the up-market local pub, the Grange in *Warwick Rd.*

Greystoke/Brentham

Popular schools are a draw on this estate of semis in the N of the area, which is home for many young families. Homes on the Greystoke estate, S of the *Western Avenue* and just W of Hanger Lane junction, are being snapped up by parents who want their children to go to Montpelier First and Middle schools. The '30s 3/4-bed semis are not as imposing as the older homes further south. But they are spacious, with easy access for major roads, Ealing golf club, Helena Park and the pretty Hanger Hill park.

The Brentham estate around *Brentham Way* is for anyone who has the money to spend on a romantic rose-covered cottage. Prices are sky-high for these little houses, with young professional couples ready to spend £110,000-plus on a small cottage or £170,000 on a 3-bed house. They know they will have no problem reselling, as the estate is one of the most coveted in Ealing. The whole Brentham estate is a conservation area. The Brentham cottages are very popular and attractive, but certainly small.

Hanwell

Canalside walks and a popular animal park give a real village atmosphere to Hanwell, the district which borders the River Brent in the W of the borough. Prices and popularity are booming, and estate agents are mushrooming in the *Broadway* which splits the area. Hanwell prices moved up sharply in 1988. 'Sensible money will invest near the river, around St Marks and the Canal', agents say, pointing out that Hanwell will soon be wedged between two major shopping centres, Ealing and Southall.

Hanwell is bounded on the SW by the Grand Union canal. 'Old Hanwell' in the S (SW of *Boston Rd*) is a bit of estate agents' jargon, but the turn-of-the-century cottages around *St Marks Rd* and *St Margarets Rd* are charming and covetable. Old Hanwell has an excellent country-style pub, The Fox, and over towards Northfields is the popular Fielding First School. The St Marks canalside neighbourhood is a conservation area. Cottages sell for £109,000 down by the water.

Further S the area around Boston Manor tube station is popular with commuters. There are '30s semis in the roads off *Clitherow Avenue* – site of a disputed council development, proposed for housing. Older properties are in *Haslemere Avenue*. The area is convenient for two Piccadilly Line stations at Boston Manor and Northfields, and for shops in W Ealing and *Northfields Avenue.*

Close to *Hanwell Broadway* there is a mixture of properties around the tightly parked streets in the *Montague Rd* area, and neighbours report a friendly atmosphere. The *Broadway* itself has a mixture of basic shops, no big supermarkets or chains, a well-stocked delicatessen, a jewellery shop and a children's clothes store. The active Hanwell preservation society fears that it is being swamped by building societies and estate agents. Further W down the *Uxbridge Rd* towards Southall there are plenty of antique and house-clearance shops – a good hunting ground for bargains.

North of the *Broadway* are some streets with terraced turn-of-the-century homes – *Laurel Gardens*, *Myrtle Gardens* and *Conolly Rd*. These homes are close to one of Ealing's most popular beauty spots –the Brent Lodge Park bunny park, full of frolicking pets, adored by children and parents.

Backing onto the park, N of the railway, is the aptly-named Golden Manor estate – the jewel in Hanwell's crown, and the Park Lane of the village. The estate includes Hanwell BR station, with a direct line to Paddington. The park and gardens are beautiful and the houses large and well maintained. Flats in the purpose-built blocks on Golden Manor are priced in the £90,000s, and a 4-bedroomed house can cost up to £250,000.

To the N of Hanwell Station is a 'poets corner' – *Shakespeare*, *Milton*, *Cowper*, *Tennyson* and *Drayton Rds*, where 3- and 4-bedroom semis are sought after (not to be confused with the similarly-named enclave in Acton). Further N, around *Framfield Rd*, the prices sag thanks to the reputation of the large Cuckoo and Copley Close council estates. The High Lane estate to the W near the Brent Valley golf course has a similar reputation – but

Ealing is unashamedly surburban. Even the tennis club, hallmark of the thirties, has reappeard in a new development with an attractive clubhouse. This building has many of the features now fashionable on new housing: the deep eaves, round 'porthole' window. The overall result owes something to the mid-Victorian villa, something to the stable yard.

E

homes in *Studland Rd* backing onto the golf course were still selling last winter for around £130,000. Now, however, ex-council homes on these estates are starting to appear for sale: smaller houses can be had for under £90,000.

West Ealing

The run-down streets of the poor-relation neighbourhood of Ealing are hunting grounds for a bargain. North of the *Uxbridge Rd* the area is dominated by the troubled Green Man council estate, an area lacking in facilities. There are a few streets of owner-occupied homes backing onto *West Ealing Broadway* – *Ecclestone Rd*, *Endsleigh Rd* and *Felix Rd*. They have 2-bed terraced homes that sell for £100,000 – but prices are lower in *Felix Rd* where one side backs onto a main rail line.

South of the *Broadway*, West Ealing is more up and coming – particularly in the streets nearest *Northfields Avenue* in the E. The terraced houses that line the parallel streets E of *Grosvenor Rd* are showing the signs of huge improvements – although some are still rented. The craze for conversions has not yet hit West Ealing, though there is lots of potential for it.

Flats here go for upwards of £65,000 for a 1-bed conversion, £78,000 for 2-bedroomed ones. *West Ealing Broadway* is not too exciting as a shopping area, there are constant complaints about dirt and rubbish. Marks & Spencer, British Home Stores and Sainsburys are the main attractions; the rest is cheap and cheerful, although there is a health food store, a fishmonger and numerous pizza parlours.

An up-market Waitrose supermarket is being built on *Alexandria Rd*, near West Ealing BR station – despite controversy with neighbours about traffic problems. *Coldershaw Rd* has ceased to look like a bombsite now that the new service road (easy access to big Sainsburys) is complete. 2-bed terraces here range from around £110-145,000 – depending on degree of work needed.

Northfields

An old-style shopping *High St* is a major draw in the Northfields area. Young families (including Japanese ones, because of the Acton school) are buying up properties in the streets between Walpole Park and *Weymouth Avenue*, *Hessel Rd* and *Midhurst Rd*, the neighbourhood that centres on the main *Northfield Avenue*. They like the area's excellent transport facilities – a Piccadilly Line station, a bus depot and easy access by car to Brentford, the M4, the North Circular, West Ealing shops and Ealing Broadway. There are also two of the borough's nicest parks, a Cannon cinema in *Northfield Avenue*, an excellent Chinese restaurant and a pub, The Plough, which once won the Evening Standard's 'Pub of the Year' competition. A new night-club, however, was thought by residents to be going too far.

Home-buyers concentrate on houses – there are not many flat conversions because the houses are so small. The roads – *Altenburg Avenue* is typical – have rows of 2- and 3-bedroomed terraced houses, all very similar. Parking is a problem – and so is rat-running. But the shops are a definite plus – with a traditional butcher, fruiterers and fishmonger. *Churchfield Rd* and *Culmington Rd*, near Walpole Park, have large town houses, divided into flats: elegant, spacious and expensive.

Haven Green/Castlebar/Montpelier

Some would call this Ealing's best area – it is certainly the home of the 'old guard' of middle-class Ealing residents, who have often lived in the borough for generations. Haven Green is a pretty parkland patch just N of the *Broadway*, and the Castlebar/Montpelier area lies N of the Green, leading up the hill to Hanger Hill Park. Haven Green is the home of Ealing Broadway station (BR and tube), and Ealing's taxi rank. Homes on the green are mostly in luxury purpose-built blocks or, to the E along *Madeley Road*, in large red-brick detached houses – mostly converted into flats.

Haven Lane, leading N from the green, is a charming street of terraced cottage-style homes, each with a pretty flower garden. The lane is tight for parking, but also has two nice pubs: it is one of Ealing's most popular roads.

In *Eaton Rise*, *Montpelier Rd* and *Helena Rd* the houses are large, Edwardian and detached, with many conversions and a few purpose-built blocks. Prices are high, as befits the most popular area in Ealing. The homes of the new *Montpelier Mews*, with the benefit of Montpelier Park close by, are in the £300-£350,000 region. A 1-bed flat will cost at least £70-80,000 – a 4-bedroomed house a good £200-£250,000. In Minster Court, a luxury block of purpose-built flats on *Hillcrest Rd*, looking out over *Hanger Hill Gardens*, a 3-bedroomed flat can cost £200,000. Large houses such as those in *Corfton Rd* are over half a million. The status of Castlebar is confirmed by the recent Courtfield encampment of half-million pound houses on *Castlebar Hill*.

The area is particularly popular with the parents of young children, thanks to the excellent reputation of the state primary school, Montpelier, in *Helena Rd*. The Greystoke estate of '30s semis to the north of the Montpelier area, and the conservation area around the highly-priced cottage style Brentham estate area (for both see above) are also in the school catchment zone.

St Mary's

St Mary's is real village Ealing, the oldest part of the area. The roads around the parish church on *St Mary's Rd* are Victorian terraces and detached homes. The area is close to the *Broadway*, and to all the facilities of central Ealing. The Grange schools are popular, and Ealing College of Higher Education is in *Warwick Rd*. Most popular are the homes nearest Lammas Park, but all the streets are pretty, tree-lined and very expensive. A 3-bed house in St Mary's goes for £140,000 plus, a 4-bed can range between £165,000 (off *South Ealing Rd*) and £250,000 (off Lammas Park). *Clovelly Rd*, home of Neil Kinnock, is particularly popular with families anxious for the spacious detached homes. Further S, South Ealing around the tube station is less rarified, but still popular and expensive to buy.

Pitshanger

The northernmost area of Ealing, S of the A40, is a lively neighbourhood with a village atmosphere. Centred around bustling *Pitshanger Lane*, the streets are either '30s semis or Ealing's speciality – Edwardian detached homes, often split into flats. Pitshanger is good for access to the A40 and the Hanger Lane intersection, and backs onto Pitshanger Park and sports ground near the Ealing Golf Course.

Scotch Common/St Stephens/Drayton Green

The sprawling area between central Ealing and West Ealing, N of the *Uxbridge Rd*, is pleasant and popular. The main drawback is the lack of public transport, the nearest station is the BR one at Castle Bar Park.

St Stephens is named after the church that was at the centre of *St Stephens Avenue* and *St Stephens Rd*. The church has now been converted into plush and expensive flats that caused a stir when they appeared on the property market in 1987. The Draytons, also known as Drayton Green, is a group of roads with Drayton in their title – it is a good hunting ground for flats. West Ealing BR station is close by.

St Stephens and Scotch Common – the area to the N of *Drayton Green* around Scotch Common and *Kent Avenue* – are Ealing's best hunting ground for purpose-built flats. Some blocks are better built than others – check surveys.

Hanger Hill/Corringway

For those who live on Hanger Hill it is 'The Estate of Ealing' – large houses, with spacious gardens and garages. The estate is E of *Hanger Lane*, and its concentric rings of roads include *Corringway, Audley Rd, Beaufort Rd, Chatsworth Rd, The Ridings* and *Ashbourne Rd.* For those who do not live on the estate, Hanger Hill is sneered at slightly as 'nouveau-riche'. You certainly need plenty of money to buy one of the 1935-40 Haymills detached homes – over £800,000 has been paid for one sumptuous home on the estate. *Corringway* and *Ashbourne Rds* have the area's only drawback – they are a bit of a rat run.

Brentford

Brentford, to the S of Ealing, is divided in two by the M4 motorway. New Brentford, the part nearest Ealing and N of the motorway, has areas of suburban housing. The corner people get excited about is *The Butts*, a square in the old town, of which little else remains. *The Butts* has several late 17th and early 18th century houses: look here for genuine Queen Anne, with 4/5 bedrooms and huge garden. Posh central London agents solemnly make the journey to Brentford for these.

They may soon have another reason: nearby, in *Terry Lane*, an exciting new waterside development will bring smart homes to this riverside corner, and probably a footbridge across to Kew Gardens. Brentford, reckon the developers, is definitely a place to watch. This historic corner (Edmund Ironside fought Canute here in 1016, and the Royalists triumphed in 1642) certainly deserves resuscitation. It remains to be seen whether Broadwell can resist calling their new development Ironside Isle, or Canute Creek.

Among those estate agents active in this area are:

- Brendons
- Cole & Hicks
- Hetheringtons
- Raymond Bushell
- Prudential Property Services
- John Squire
- Jones & Co
- Barnard Marcus
- Black Horse/Acre Estates
- Grimshaws

Earlsfield and Southfields

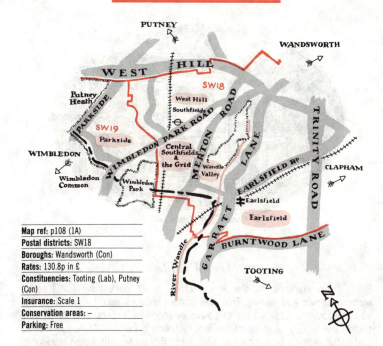

Map ref: p108 (1A)
Postal districts: SW18
Boroughs: Wandsworth (Con)
Rates: 130.8p in £
Constituencies: Tooting (Lab), Putney (Con)
Insurance: Scale 1
Conservation areas: –
Parking: Free

E

Transport Tubes: Southfields (zone 3a, District) to: Oxford Circus 30 min (1 change), City 30 min, Heathrow 55 min (1 change). British Rail: Earlsfield to Waterloo.

Convenient for Wimbledon Common and tennis. Tube to town via Fulham and Sloane Sq. Miles from centre: 5.

Schools ILEA zone 10: Southfields School, John Archer School (b), Burntwood School (g), John Paul II RC.

Flats	S	1b	2b	3b	4b	5b
Average prices	58–63	68–75	75–90	87–100	–	–
Houses	2b	3b	4b	5b	6/7b	8b
Average prices	90–125	115–160	165–210	225–350	–	–

The properties Edwardian terraced homes, including many p/b and converted flats, plus some larger houses towards Putney. Also (being in Wandsworth) ex-council from '20s cottages to '70s tower flats.

The market Southfields, with its tube, is more expensive, especially for flats: many young sharers seeking 2-bed flats pushed these up fast in '87 and '88. House prices in the two areas are more similar. Cheap buys in ex-council cottage estates and flat blocks: can be well below averages above. Local searches: 1 week.

Area Profile

South from Wandsworth, the River Wandle must once have run through watermeadows and woods. That was some centuries ago, for the river was soon discovered as a source of power by medieval millers, and the stream turned the wheels of some of the first factories in London. Now, the Wandle and its flat valley is best known as a barrier to E-W traffic rather than any kind of amenity. The valley has parks and playing fields, depots and factories – but only two bridges linking the Victorian suburb of Earlsfield, to the E, with its neighbour Southfields to the W. With the busy A3 and the notorious Wandsworth botttleneck to the N, the area is a traffic jam connoisseur's delight. Public transport is thus essential. Southfields is served by the Wimbledon branch of the District Line, while Earlsfield has a BR line to Clapham Junction and Waterloo/Victoria.

Overshadowed by the more obvious charms of neighbouring Putney, Wimbledon and Wandsworth Common, the area slumbered until recently. The quiet streets of sober, steady housing were neglected by buyers. This is changing as people find themselves forced to consider Earlsfield and Southfields by sheer lack of cash. And plenty like what they find.

Earlsfield

Earlsfield is bordered by *Allfarthing Lane*, *Garratt Lane* and *Burntwood Lane* and runs E up the hill from the Wandle Valley towards Wandsworth Common. Earlsfield, like Battersea, is trying to expand, as it becomes more fashionable, to take in areas that have been Tooting or Wandsworth since they were built.

Young professionals have been moving into the area for some years, notably around *Earlsfield Rd* which runs down from Wandsworth Common. Popularity shot up recently as an increasing number of buyers found themselves outpriced in Battersea and Wandsworth Common. Prices have risen but are still below Battersea and Putney levels, especially for houses.

The area between *Garratt Lane* and Wandsworth Common is essentially residential but note the land on either side of River Wandle, between *Garratt Lane* and *Merton Rd*, is mainly industrial. There are parks and playing fields, and a few streets of houses, but warehouses and light industry dominate.

Between *Magdalen Rd* and *Burntwood Lane* is a large 'cottage' estate running from *Tilehurst Rd* in the E to *Swaby Rd* in the W. The homes are a mixture of simple '20s and '30s style terraced and semi-detached houses, most with gardens much larger than average (50-80 feet is not unusual).

The council-built 'Estate' is, thanks to Right to Buy, now well over half owner-occupied, and resales are becoming frequent. The far-sighted have been buying 3-bed Estate houses (freehold) for the price of a 3-bed Victorian flat – and within easy reach of Earlsfield Station in *Magdalen Rd*. For example a 3-bed, unmodernised house with a 60 foot garden in *Dawnay Rd* went for £92,000 last winter. Get in now if you don't insist on Victoriana.

Open View and *Field View* overlook playing fields; *Tilehurst Rd*, marking the E end of the estate, suffers some rat-running. *Magdalen Rd* and *Burntwood Lane* suffer serious traffic at peak hours. Some buyers are prepared to put up with the traffic to live near the junction with *Garratt Lane* for closeness to the station. Majority of the mainly '30s semis in *Burntwood Lane* have open views over the school and the grounds of Springfield Hospital (mental).

E

Swaby Rd, running N towards the station, has generally late Victorian small terraced houses and some purpose-built Victorian maisonettes. Running between *Tranmere Rd* (late Victorian terraces, some maisonettes) and *Garratt Lane* are *Quinton*, *Isis* and *Littleton Sts*. There are spacious (for Earlsfield) 3-bed turn-of-century terraces increasing in popularity, especially *Littleton St* (Earlsfield third bedrooms tend to be very small). There is a large Victorian primary school at the junction of *Tranmere Rd* and *Waynflete St*. Some houses in *Quinton* and *Isis Sts* have been converted to 2/3-bed flats fetching £85-95,000.

Shopping facilities in *Garratt Lane*, between the junction with *Earlsfield Rd* and *Burntwood Lane*, are at last improving, with 'open late' supermarkets replacing grubby corner shops. Wine bars and deli's are appearing almost daily – and junk shops renamed 'antique'.

The railway from Earlsfield to Clapham Junction cuts Earlsfield in half diagonally. Properties between *Allfarthing Lane*, the N limit of the area, and *Earlsfield Rd* are generally small late Victorian and early Edwardian terraces with some small council infill blocks. *Earlsfield Rd*, running between *Garratt Lane* and *Trinity Rd*, suffers from heavy traffic during rush-hours and speeding traffic during off-peak. Like *Trinity Rd* this is not a road in which you would park your company's pride and joy without dreading dents on your return … It also figures in Transport Department road building papers (see 'Transport' chapter).

High numbers (*Garratt Lane* end) are small late Victorian houses set close to the road (no off-street parking and noise nuisance). Then modern council infill at the junction with *Inman St*. From the junction with *Dingwall St* houses are increasingly set back from the road (important given the volume of traffic) and grow from 2 to 3 storeys, many now converted to flats with off-street parking.

Odd numbers of *Earlsfield Rd* back onto the railway line but have large gardens and the fact that the railway line is set well below garden level means noise is reduced. Houses near *Heathfield Rd* junction enjoy a view across the railway line of Wandsworth Prison (which looks a bit like Windsor Castle). Here there are some larger, 5-bed semi-detached late Edwardian 3-storey houses to be found. *Bassingham, Bucharest* and *Brocklebank Rds*, leading off *Earlsfield Rd* to *Swaffield Rd*, are early Edwardian/late Victorian terraced houses, with ornate door surrounds and windows. They are mainly 3-bedroom houses, some converted into flats. At the junction of *St Ann's Hill* and *Garratt Lane* is a converted school house (early Victorian) now flats and renamed Earlsfield House. *Swaffield Rd* and *St Ann's Hill* suffer rat-running.

Aslett, Treport, Delia and *Daphne Sts* are all late Victorian terraces, some maisonettes, and popular with first-time buyers. Where conversions have taken place the second bedroom tends to be fairly small. A new development of 1-bed flats in *Aslett St* has prices which rise to £85,000. Some were being let, rather than sold, during the quiet months of last winter. There is a school on *St Ann's Hill* at the top of *Aslett St*. This part of Earlsfield is very convenient for the shopping facilities of Wandsworth (the Arndale Centre) and a new Sainsburys Homebase superstore on *Garratt Lane. Barmouth Rd, Swanage Rd* and *Cader Rd* E of *St Ann's Hill* are more Wandsworth Common than Earlsfield, 3- and 4-bed late Victorian/early Edwardian terraces with higher prices than the Earlsfield average. *Swanage Rd* has 4-bed houses around £175,000.

Southfields

Southfields proper is a wholly residential area which blends, with surprising success, classic 1930s suburbia with older Edwardian properties.

Between *Wimbledon Park Rd* and *Merton Rd* the houses are mainly Edwardian. From *Wimbledon Park Rd* W and N to *West Hill* (the A3) and Wimbledon Common come classic 1930s semi-detached and detached houses with some older Edwardian/Victorian ones. From *Beaumont Rd* W to *Wimbledon Parkside* are many large '60s/early '70s council estates. The smaller blocks and estates here are increasingly owner-occupied: Wandsworth Council was a pioneer of the Right to Buy principle.

The area has always been popular with families wanting good-sized houses in generally quiet roads. New arrivals to the area (notably to 'The Grid' – see below) are young couples, especially second-time buyers planning to start families.

Replingham Rd, near the tube station, offers the only shopping facilities of any note in Southfields, otherwise the nearest major shopping centres are in Wimbledon, Putney or Wandsworth. There are virtually no pubs in the area because of covenant restrictions when the land was sold for building. The area suffers some inconvenience from hordes of incoming tennis fans during Wimbledon Fortnight but enterprising locals can let their homes out for considerable sums!

Central Southfields and The Grid

The Southfields Grid, bordered by *Astonville St, Elsenham Rd, Revelstoke Rd* and *Replingham Rd*, is named for the grid layout of the streets (which run N-S) and roads (E-W). Properties are mainly spacious 3- and 4-bedroom Edwardian houses. A number of the houses in *Trentham St* and *Replingham* and *Revelstoke Rds* are actually purpose-built maisonettes. The supply of converted flats on the Grid drying up as Wandsworth Council has banned any more conversions. Houses closest to Southfields station suffer some daytime parking problems. There are some small council in-fill blocks in *Elsenham St* and even-numbered houses back onto the above-land tube line to Wimbledon – but have long gardens as compensation. Between *Merton Rd* and *Astonville St*, Courtfield plan 19 new houses designed by John Assael.

By Southfields station, *Crowthorne Close* is one of the few modern non-council developments in the area, with 2- and 3-storey blocks of flats, some backing onto the tube line. Almost opposite *Crowthorne Close*, and on the junction of *Pirbright Rd* and *Wimbledon Park Rd* is a snooker club. The roads between *Pirbright* and *Smeaton Rds* are mainly late Victorian/Edwardian terraces but *Longfield St* and *Smeaton* itself are smaller Victorian terraces (2-bedroom), recently priced at around £125,000. A small development of 2-bed bungalows is planned for *Longfield St*.

West of the tube line, *Gartmoor Gardens* has attractive large Edwardian houses with ornate metalwork balconies on the first floor, some now converted to flats. Proximity to Southfields station compensates for some noise from trains. Houses on the S side of *Southdean Gardens* back onto Wimbledon Park and are popular but rarely on the market. One recently (Oct '88) made £265,000.

The triangle bordered by *Granville*, *Pulborough* and *Merton Rds* features generally Edwardian houses in tree-lined roads slightly narrower than in the Grid. Odd-numbered houses in *Pulborough Rd* back onto the tube line but benefit from exceptionally long gardens and the large BR landholding as a buffer. From around (3-bed terrace) £130,000.

Sutherland Grove, running N from Southfields Station to *West Hill*, features 1930s semi-detached mainly 3-bed houses with off-street parking. Also a few large Edwardian houses (6-plus beds) not all of which have been converted into flats. These are extremely popular with prices ranging from £145,000 for good 3-bed semis.

The tube line (District) is above ground here and runs E of *Sutherland Grove*, crossing *Granville Rd* and going underground by the junction with *Melrose Rd* amd *Cromer Villas*. *Gressenhall Rd* has Edwardian-style houses and a Mosque. The roads leading off *Sutherland Grove*, notably *Skeena Hill*, *Cromer Villas* and *Girdwood Rd*, are larger '30s, the majority Tudor-style, with integral garages. Internally, the houses vary enormously.

Most, notably in *Coombemartin Rd*, are set well back from the road. From the junction of *Skeena Hill* and *Coombemartin Rd* there are small modern blocks of council flats, and the W side of *Coombemartin Rd* backs onto a (low-rise) estate. The triangle between *Coombemartin*, *Skeena Hill* and *Sutherland Grove* houses Wandsworth School (boys secondary), now being run down for closure.

Parkside

The area bordered by *Beaumont Rd* in the E, Wimbledon Common to the W, *Queensmere Rd* (the border with Wimbledon) to the S and *West Hill* is a complex mixture of council estates (high and low rise flats, some houses) and private detached and semi-detached houses, some very large which fetch very high prices.

The heaviest concentrations of council estates are between *Wimbledon Park Rd* and *Albert Drive*, *Augustus Rd* and *Whitlock Drive*. The area between *Beaumont Rd* and *Princes Way* from *Augustus Rd* to *West Hill* is almost exclusively council-owned. But all the estates are well-landscaped.

Wandsworth Council has sold two high rise blocks on the Edgecombe Hall Estate on *Whitlock Drive* to Ideal Homes for refurbishment. The 110 flats will be marketed this summer to first-time buyers registered on the Council's sales waiting list. The blocks feature stunning views out over Wimbledon Park across to Crystal Palace. Three more high-rise blocks, on the Argyll Estate off *Inner Park Rd* are being demolished and the site sold to a private developer for housing.

All the estates feature a rising rate of owner-occupation (many blocks now well over 50%) and an increasing number of ex-council properties are now coming on the market. Typically, 4-bedroom modern houses have been fetching up to £110,000, 3-bed flats around £80,000. Prices will rise, especially for flats, when the blocks are fully or mainly owner-occupied and common parts can be upgraded.

Beaumont Rd running between *West Hill* and *Wimbledon Park Rd*, has modern council properties on either side and a small parade of shops by *Keevil Drive*. *Albert Drive* runs between *Augustus Rd* and *Victoria Drive*. Again there is a mix of council and private blocks and good-size private houses (mainly detached). Between *Albert Drive* and *Wimbledon Park Rd* are mid and late '60s council blocks. On the other side of the road are some modern infill red brick detached houses, set well back from the road, then larger detached stockbroker Tudor red brick houses.

Midway down *Albert Drive* former police flats in 1950s block have been redeveloped as 'Southfields Village' with 2-bed flats on offer for up to £170,000 in 1988. The same developer also has a similar scheme: Augustus Court off *Augustus Rd*.

Augustus Rd runs W up the hill from Southfields station to *Inner Park Rd*, and has a mix of '30s houses and older, large detached houses. The occasional late Georgian house with 6 beds appears on the market. A number of private flat developments are grouped close to the junction with *Inner Park Rd*, including The Acorns (red-brick modern) and Dorada Court. There are also modern house and flat developments, brick-built, mainly '60s and early '70s in style. Increasingly, from junction with *Albert Drive*, large detached houses appear, mainly stockbroker Tudor but including older houses including the late Georgian-style 'White House'. Some '50s infill but all set well back from the road with large front gardens and off-street parking.

Princes Way runs roughly N-S between *West Hill* and *Wimbledon Park Rd*. From the junction with *Augustus Rd* towards *Wimbledon Park Rd* is Linden Lodge School for the Blind in large grounds, then private flats and an attractive town house development, *King Charles Walk*. *Weydown Close* is modern low-rise council properties.

Off *Augustus Rd* is John Paul II Catholic boys' secondary school, which has achieved reasonable exam results. The school buildings are followed by more mainly council property on either side of the road. A large pub and steakhouse (Burghley Hall) is in *Southmead Rd*. Off *Princes Way* at the N end is the private *Fleur Gate* development of attractive brick-built Victorian-style terraced town houses. Opposite the junction with *Castlecombe Drive* (council housing) is a small row of detached Tudor-style '30s houses.

Tree-lined *Victoria Drive* runs N to S parallel to *Princes Way* between *West Hill* and *Wimbledon Park Rd*. In character it is similar to *Princes Way* with a mix of (mainly) council and private property. Pines Court, a modern private block, has a selection of studio flats. *Oak Park Gardens* is a small attractive development of town houses followed by larger Tudor-style 1930s houses.

Inner Park Rd runs in a half-circle from *Wimbledon Parkside* to meet *Augustus Rd* and then back to Wimbledon Common, featuring a similar mix to the rest of *Parkside*. Close to the junction with *Parkside* stands a newly-built block of 16 red-brick 1- and 2-bed flats. Opposite are low-rise council flats (*Windlesham Grove*). Thereafter private blocks of flats in older style. 'Marlborough' has some studio flats. *Pilsdon Close*, with small town houses and flats, is set back, then comes *Holly Tree Close*, private flats currently suffering from high service charges. Some exceptionally large older Victorian detached houses have mainly now been converted into flats.

Opposite the junction with *Augustus Rd* is the Argyll Estate, a mix of high- and low-rise flats. *Limpsfield Avenue*, with 1930s-style houses, detached and semi-detached, some mock-Tudor, backs onto a council estate. *Kingsmere Rd* has detached mainly '30s houses. A spur of *Inner Park Rd* (easy to miss), close to *Parkside* marks the entrance to *Roundacres*, a small early '60s curved terraced house and flat development in communal gardens. Large, traditional style red-brick '50s-style houses stand at the entrance.

Queensmere Rd marks the border with Merton and is very much Wimbledon rather than Wandsworth. The fairly steep tree-lined road has mainly large modern detached houses set well back from the road. *Queensmere Close* is a bungalow development, Southlands College buildings are at bottom of the hill. Former police flats in *Queensmere Rd* sold off three years ago are now fetching £105-120,000.

Wimbledon Park Rd suffers heavy traffic at rush hour, some cars travelling exceptionally fast in off-peak hours. N from the junction of *Bathgate Rd* come blocks of flats, modern council and older-style private. Lakeview Court flats are very comfortable and well-run, looking over Wimbledon Park and its lake. Thereafter large detached '30s- and '50s-style houses are set well back off the road up towards Southfields station, where Edwardian semi-detached then terraced houses take over.

E

West Hill

The little triangle between the *West Hill* junction with *Sutherland Grove*, *West Hill Rd* and *Granville Rd* likes to considers itself West Hill (Putney) not West Hill (Southfields) and is fairly convenient for East Putney tube. It is a mix of large Edwardian semi-detached houses and 1930s semis with some modern infill and some early and mid-Victorian detached houses on *West Hill Rd*. Among most popular roads is the 1930s *Sispara Gardens* (large semi-detached houses with integral garages) while *Cromer Villas* has a mix of '30s and Edwardian semis (a 4-bed 1930s house was under offer in October at £230,000). *Coldstream Gardens* has '60s-style town houses and flats, *Valonia Gardens* is neat 1930s semis with some '50s infill built in '30s style. *Melrose Rd*, at the junction with *West Hill Rd*, has large terraced and semi-detached Edwardian homes.

Merton Rd to the E is a very busy through road carrying traffic between Wimbledon and Wandsworth and is also a commuter cut-through from the A24 to the Wandsworth one-way system. Large detached and semi-detached houses (some stuccoed) appear between *West Hill Road* and *Wimbledon Park Rd*. Thereafter going S the houses are semi-detached 3/4-bed late Victorian, set well back from the road. A primary school stands at the junction with

Standen Rd. Southfields Secondary School lies between *Burr Rd* and *Bodmin St*, with a modern townhouse development opposite. Then come old-style late Edwardian mansion flats, originally council, now owner-occupied. At the junction of *Burr Rd* and *Kimber Rd* is Coleman Mansions, an early '30s-style block of flats with views over King George's Park but industry and heavy traffic restricts prices. *Kimber Rd* is one of the few to cross the Wandle Valley and thus attracts considerable traffic. Improvements to the Wandsworth centre one-way system, planned for many years, may (or may not) help.

Wandle Valley

Between *Merton Rd* and *Garratt Lane* lie a handful of early Edwardian terraces bordered by King George's Park and *Ravensbury Rd*, which are the no-mans-land between Earlsfield and Southfields. Estate agents are unable to agree on where these roads are: Wimbledon Park, Southfields or Earlsfield.

Penwith Rd, being one of the few roads to cross the Wandle, suffers exceptionally heavy traffic which keeps prices for mainly purpose-built late Victorian 2-bed flats lower than the rest of area. *Acuba Rd* (Edwardian) and *Bodmin St* are quieter as is *Strathville Rd* despite a small industrial development. *Dounsforth Gardens*, a small modern townhouse development off *Strathville Rd*, backs onto the River Wandle. Acuba House, an Edwardian block of flats, was council, now mainly owner-occupied. It borders on King George's Park playing fields. Upper floors of *Bodmin St* have an open outlook over the park and playing fields. The nearby Kenco Coffee plant means a strong aroma of roasting coffee, notably in *Bodmin* and *Strathville Rds*. The playing fields N of *Bodmin Rd* may become homes if Wimpey, which has bought them, succeed with a planning application. However some open space seems likely to remain.

Among those estate agents active in this area are:

- Barnard Marcus
- Bragg & Co
- Hamptons
- Hooper & Jackson
- Richard Barclay
- Hitchcocks
- Kinleigh
- Sturgis
- Craigie & Co
- Bells
- John G Dean

Finchley

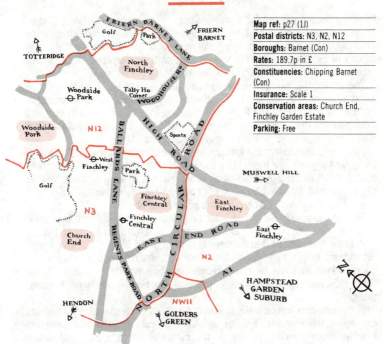

Map ref: p27 (1J)	
Postal districts: N3, N2, N12	
Boroughs: Barnet (Con)	
Rates: 189.7p in £	
Constituencies: Chipping Barnet (Con)	
Insurance: Scale 1	
Conservation areas: Church End, Finchley Garden Estate	
Parking: Free	

Transport — Tubes: East Finchley, Finchley Central, West Finchley, Woodside Park (zone 3a/b, Northern). From Finchley Central to: Oxford Circus 22 min (1 change), City 32 min, Heathrow 1 hr 20 min (1 change).

Convenient for — Brent Cross Shopping Centre, Wembley Stadium. M1 to the North, M25, North Circular Rd. Miles from centre: 7.

Schools — Barnet Education Authority: Finchley Manor Hill, Christchurch C of E, Woodhouse 6th Form College, Christ's College (b), Finchley Catholic High School.

Flats	S	1b	2b	3b	4b	5b
Average prices	58–65	65–80	75–160+	85–200+	125–300+	–
Houses	2b	3b	4b	5b	6/7b	8b
Average prices	90–120	110–200+	135–250+	150–400	225–400+	300+

The properties — Quintessential suburbia: typical home is the 3-bed inter-war semi. Also some terraced and larger older homes and modern flats in smart blocks, plus large houses in select streets. Higher flat prices in new luxury blocks: £400,000 penthouses appearing.

The market — A settled family community is changing as newcomers move in. Popular place to buy smart p/b flats: developers searching hungrily for land. Finchley's Japanese community could follow the school to Acton. Local searches: 4 weeks.

Area Profile

Londoners once headed for Finchley Common to escape the Great Plague. Three hundred years later the exodus starts at 5.30pm as commuters leave the City concrete and make their way north-westwards to the quiet, dignified, leafy suburb of Finchley, safe in the knowledge that their interests are being well represented by their local MP, Prime Minister Margaret Thatcher.

The woods that are echoed in names like Woodside Park and Finchley ('a wood frequented by finches') slowly disappeared when the Manor belonged to the Bishop of London, who found sheep-raising more profitable. The only elm trees now are those found in street names like *Elmhurst Avenue* and *Elm Park Rd.* Finchley is however one of the greener suburbs still.

Finchley Common was once a favourite haunt of highwaymen but these days vehicular travellers are more likely to be held up in streets lined with parked cars, a result of the age of flat conversions. Here is an area whose amenities run the gamut from a giant Tesco's ('every type of fruit *imaginable*') to a working farm, sandwiched between two polite suburban roads.

Finchley, originally defined as East End, Church End and North End, grew naturally as hamlets sprang up along the main *Great North Rd* from London.

With the train whistle that heralded the arrival of the Great Northern Railway, the suburb began to blossom and most of the large houses, estates and meadow land gave way to mainly middle-class housing. The first large villas of the 1860s are still in evidence to the E of the *High Rd* in North Finchley, though.

But developers were careful to retain the green open spaces and residents can enjoy the untethered Dollis Brook which cuts N to S and separates Finchley from Hendon, as well as the cultivated Victoria Park in Finchley Central, Friary Park in North Finchley and Cherry Tree Wood in East Finchley. The latter was once called Dirt House Woods but has sensitively been renamed.

Conservationists are hard at work improving a huge green sandwiched between *Summers Lane* and *North Circular Rd*, a nature reserve known as Coppetts Wood.

The manor house in *East End Rd* still exists, a fine listed building built in the early 18th century and now used as a private Jewish teaching centre and school. It was recently renamed the Sternberg Centre, but locals persist in referring to the manor house. Further along *East End Rd* stands Avenue House, once the home of 'Inky' Stephens, the philanthropist MP and pioneer ink manufacturer, and its public grounds almost opposite.

There is an abundance of 3-bedroomed semi-detached property throughout Finchley. Houses are larger and more spacious in Woodside Park; terraced and more picturesque in the 'county' roads of East Finchley.

Otherwise the area is bursting with flats. Many of the old suburban villas have been converted and more and more luxurious – and expensive – blocks are springing up, especially along *Hendon Lane* and *Regents Park Rd* in Church End. There are still many examples of 1930s blocks between Finchley Central and Tally Ho Corner shopping areas, and beyond North Finchley along the *High Rd* to Whetstone.

The area is very well served by the shops which you'll find along *East Finchley High Rd*, *Ballards Lane*, Finchley Central and at Tally Ho Corner in *North Finchley High Rd*. But local shopping has been affected by the huge Brent Cross shopping centre, just 10 minutes away by car or by the regular bus services. *Ballards Lane* and *North Finchley High Rd* have more than their fair share of building societies, estate agents and charity shops.

East Finchley

Row upon row of terraced houses within the triangle made by *East End Rd*, the *North Circular* and the *High Rd* give a distinct flavour to what was traditionally called East End; the name was changed by sensitive residents lest they be confused with the Cockneys of Bow Bells. Originally the centre for a weekly hog market, the area is probably the most quaint and affordable of all the Finchleys. It has a village-like atmosphere and residents are friendly and welcoming. In *East End Rd* itself, Wimpey and others are adding new flats and retirement homes to the area.

F

The terraces in the 'county' roads – *Hertford*, *Bedford*, *Huntingdon*, *Leicester*, *Lincoln*, *Durham Rds* – and in the roads S of *Church Lane* on the other side of *East Finchley High Rd* are popular with today's Dinkys (Dual Income, No Kids Yet). This younger crowd find it a convenient (good transport links) and attractive corner: Sunday mornings are busy with people painting and renovating the 2- and 3-bed Victorian/Edwardian cottages. The 'county' roads are fairly quiet although they are used as a shortcut around the traffic lights at the Bald Faced Stag junction. However, with no off-street parking at all or access to the back, the tarmac is littered with parked cars. prices on this (E) side of the *High Rd* tend to be higher too than those on the *Kitchener/Beresford Rd* side, where properties tend to be maisonettes rather than houses.

Finchley suburban makes constant reference to rural models in its streets and buildings, and due to generous gardens and plentiful trees goes a good way towards achieving the idyll. Mock-tudor touches such as half-timbering, leaded light windows and tile hanging add to the charm. Such houses are more appreciated today than they were, and purists deplore the excesses of DIY improvers.

Further away from the *High Rd* to the E in roads like *Creighton Avenue* you can find larger and detached houses with the luxury of their own drives and garages. And now there are plans to build 13 flats on the former Baptist Church Hall site in this road.

Fortis Green is particularly pretty with larger houses accompanied by their attached cottages, originally used as quarters for staff, along a tree-lined route to Muswell Hill (which also see). The larger houses are set back from what is a very busy thoroughfare. That central-London invention, the brand-new mews, has reached the area this year: Fortis Mews has 4-bedroomed townhouses, selling at around £220,000. Further new-build includes new flats behind the tube station.

South of *Fortis Green* roads like *Baronsmere* and *Ingram Rds* have the benefit of being very close to the tube and to Cherry Tree Wood. They are in the same league as the roads that run off *Fortis Green*, pretty, quaint cottages, some even with garages.

Back the W side of the *High Rd*, S of *East End Rd,* the houses are more expensive and the 3-bedroomed semis in the quiet cul-de-sacs like *Abbotts Gardens* have aspirations towards the Hampstead Garden Suburb and superb views of Hampstead and Highgate. Closer to *High Rd* and tube, Station House in *The Causeway* will be the site of six 3-storey houses.

East Finchley is also home to the area's currently most scruffy council estate, Grange Estate, set in small blocks surrounded by trees along the *High Rd*. Almost opposite, at the N end of the *High Rd*, is the Strawberry Vale Estate, a Camden council-controlled estate on Barnet land, sandwiched between the *North Circular Rd* and St Pancras and Islington cemetery. Outside, this estate looks like a prison, with its semi-circular wall shielding the noise of the *North Circular Rd* traffic. Inside, the estate – built in the late '70s -- is a haven: clean and pretty, with a mixture of houses and flats, many snapped up by tenants using the Right to Buy legislation.

East Finchley Village Society is very active, fighting long and hard against proposals to widen the *North Circular Rd* which, if successful, would divide the borough in half and kill off a beautiful avenue of golden poplar trees. So far the Department of Environment inspector's report from the most recent public inquiry has not been made public.

North Finchley

Beyond the *North Circular* and the famous Green Man pub on the *Great North Rd*, the site of two wells used for refreshment in the days of Finchley Common, the terraces begin to disappear and the suburban 3-bed semis spring up in roads like *Squires Lane* and *Queens Avenue*.

The division is more than clear. Here you see the family homes – two children and two cars. Until the Labour Party victories of 1986 in Woodhouse ward and St Paul's ward, the area was true blue. People here are conservative in nature, keeping themselves to themselves but working hard when called on for the PTA or the golf club.

The shopping area at Tally Ho Corner had taken on an air of resignation, having lived in the shadow of the crumbling and defunct Gaumont cinema for years while developers argued the future. But when the bulldozers finally moved in on the big screen and Sainsbury opened a new supermarket at the top end of the shopping centre (junction with *Ravensdale Avenue*) the smaller units started to perk up, new boutiques and record shops fitting in beside the established butchers, bakers and department store Owen Owen, and overlooked by the huge Tally Ho pub. New homes are following; for instance the neat 2-bed townhouses in *Castle Rd* (c £160,000).

To the E of the *High Rd* streets of terraces mix with avenues of late 19th-century suburban villas. Further E, in the tract bordered by *Woodhouse Rd* to the S and *Friern Barnet Lane* to the E the '30s suburbia is in full blossom, with many mock Tudor and modern town houses overlooking Friary Park.

To the W of the *High Rd* the picture is more of the large villas, converted into attractive and spacious mansion flats. *Lodge Lane* is particularly pretty (although busy and often impassable with lorries from the bakery and the Post Office sorting office), with rows of tiny cottages all beautifully modernised and spruced up.

Here and there on the sites of larger houses, knocked down before the present mood of conversion, are uninspiring but neat and tidy flats or town houses.

Woodside Park

On the W side of the tube track there is an air of affluence. Houses are larger, the cars are BMWs and Mercedes, the roads are wider. *Holden Rd* itself has changed its character in less than 20 years. What was once an avenue of enormous houses with gardens banking down to Dollis Brook, has been transformed. A section of the road is devoted to a mid-'70s development of square town houses facing luxury blocks of flats and the older, original houses.

Next door is another development of rows of early '70s houses – entirely council but nicely developed on the corner of *Holden Rd* and *Laurel View* – which was held up by an illustrious resident who refused to sell until almost the last bricks were laid all round his house and garden. There have been problems with a few of the units built too near the brook, but otherwise they are pleasant. Further substantial developments have been proposed for *Holden Rd*; Barratt want to build 100-plus flats with parking on a 2.5 acre site, Murphy Homes plan a further 32; Tudor Lodge is a Charles Church development: 16 flats with 2 beds/2 baths, around £150,000.

On the western side of the brook, *Southover* and *Northiam* are posh but characterless houses with pseudo column additions and plenty of roof extensions. The big advantage of Woodside Park is that it has a tube station, originally called Torrington Park. There is also a large synagogue next door.

To the W, the streets with South Downs names – *Lullington Garth*, *Walmington Fold*, *Chanctonbury Way*, *Cissbury Ring North* and *South*, etc, are ideal for families whose purse strings are a little more tied. Further away from the tube stations and the shops the prices can dip but they still command quite a price because of the open green aspect and the peace and quiet.

Back east across the tracks, those streets with 'Woodside' in their names – *Woodside Avenue*, *Woodside Grange Rd*, *Woodside Lane* etc – are all bringing gleams to developers' eyes: half a dozen schemes are planned, from studio flats to mew houses. Recent appearances include a development by St George of 14 2-bed flats, Woodside Park; Birch Court (*Woodside Grange Rd*): luxurious 2- and 3-bed apartments from £198,000; and Emerald Court (*Woodside Park Rd*) 2- and 3-bed flats from £155,000. Around the corner, *Gainsborough Rd* has a development with flats from studios up to 3-bed at prices from £63-225,000. This emphasis on flats reflects the popularity of Woodside Park as a place to settle into a comfortable flat after the children have left home.

F

Church End

The home of Finchley's most historic buildings: Avenue House, the manor house, Christ's College building, St Mary's school house; this is the area most often depicted in paintings and sketches representing old Finchley.

Church End itself surrounds St Mary's Church in *Hendon Lane*; this is the heart of the old village and the site of the turnpike on the old road from Marylebone. *College Terrace*, at the apex of *Hendon Lane* and *Regents Park Rd*, is still a picture of terraced cottages facing the playground of the school, which is currently being re-sited off the Manor Cottage roundabout in East

Finchley. Presently the Finchley Society is attempting to have the old building converted into an archives library.

Church End is Finchley's most visible conservation area, lying close to the centre and the tube. But to the W down *Hendon Avenue* is a more peaceful idyll, and another conservation area. *Village Rd* is the core of Finchley Garden Village, 54 semi-detached houses around a rectangular green in the early 1900s. It was the brainwave of architect Frank Stratton who lived there himself.

But the immediate triangle of Old England at Church End, around *College Terrace*, has become a virtual island, surrounded by the new, tasteful, luxury flat developments (Ibis Court, £300,000-plus, is one) down *Hendon Lane*, and an enormous development of top-priced red brick flats and office blocks in *Regents Park Rd*.

The luxury developments continue down this road, punctuated by the fields of the picturesque College Farm, once the Express Dairies showhouse farm, to the *North Circular Rd*, the famous Naked Lady statue, Henley's Corner – and the Kinloss Gardens synagogue. The Corner is the subject of controversy over Department of Transport plans to channel *North Circular* traffic through a tunnel which would also send pedestrians through a maze of subways.

Around the side streets like *Tillingbourne Gardens* the houses are impressive, detached and dear. Those in *Allandale Avenue* and *Fitzalan Rd* have the amazing bonus of overlooking what is still a working farm. Cars flock to the regular Sunday open days, but they are a small price to pay for this slice of the country.

Road experts at Barnet council have turned the streets to the east of *Regents Park Rd – Mountfield Rd*, *Stanhope Avenue*, *Cavendish Avenue*, *Holly Park* and *Holly Park Gardens* – into a maze of one-ways and no-through roads to stop rat-running, but there are those who feel that this has had the effect of making this corner faceless and less desirable, although quiet. The older houses here have gradually been converted into flats. A new development in *Mountfield Rd*, however, went for exclusivity in the form of a private court behind remote-control gates. St Luke's Court has as its star the refurbished 6-bed old vicarage (the developers built the vicar a new one), sold last summer for half a million. Two new houses, flats, and penthouses with 'cathedral-proportions living rooms' and £235,000 price tags, completed the scheme. New homes, too, for *Dollis Park*, near the tube: these are 5-bedroomed detached houses, from £320,000.

Finchley Central

Finchley Central is really just the name of the tube and belt of shops along *Ballards Lane*, but estate agents have seized on it to describe the area N of the railway line on either side of *Ballards Lane* before you come to the postal district of N12 and Woodside Park. Included in the area is the equally nebulous West Finchley which, again, covers the few streets around the tube station of the same name.

During the day side streets around here are packed with commuters' cars and those of workers in the offices above the giant Tesco development. The overwhelming appearance in the residential streets on either side of *Ballards Lane* is of being overcrowded. Again there are lots of flat conversions, although the further away from *Ballards Lane* you go, the more the 3-bedroomed semi dominates.

Victoria Park, N of *Long Lane*, is the outstanding feature of Finchley Central – a small but pretty man-made park rescued from the development of suburbia and surrounded by large houses and mushrooming luxury flats around *Etchingham Park Rd.* (For example Rosanne House: 2-bedroomed/2-bathroomed, from £175,000). Houses here have large gardens but no garages. Almost opposite the park is one of Finchley's most attractive developments of flats – Finchley Court. A spacious, well-maintained '30s development.

West of *Ballards Lane*, in *Moss Hall Grove* there are a few of the dull, everyday but sturdy '30s blocks of flats, plus a peacemeal row of '70s townhouses. At the bottom end of *Moss Hall Grove*, along *Ballards Lane*, is *Moss Hall Crescent* – a parade of mansions reclaimed from the ravages of the bedsit conversions of the last decade and now being restored.

Nether St joins Finchley Central to North Finchley and runs beside West Finchley tube station. In the past it has been used as a parallel short-cut to the high road and road planners have tried to stop this with a complicated junction at *Dollis Rd/Crescent Rd*. Traffic is a problem here, particularly on weekdays, by Moss Hall Junior and Infants Schools (junction with *Moss Hall Grove*) and by the West Finchley tube station which has no car park. From the N end, *Nether St* begins with terraces of neat houses which transform naturally to larger semis and, where these have been pulled down, blocks of flats. The latest example had 1- and 2-bed flats prices at £125-149,000 last winter, and more such are planned for this year. Some of the very large villas beyond the junction with *Argyle Rd* have been converted into old people's nursing homes or new blocks of luxury flats.

Among those estate agents active in this area are:
- Anscombe & Ringland
- Arthur Benabo
- Bairstow Eves
- Copping Joyce
- Winkworths
- Druce
- Ellis & Co
- Jeremy Leaf & Co
- Nicholas Shepherd

F

Forest Hill

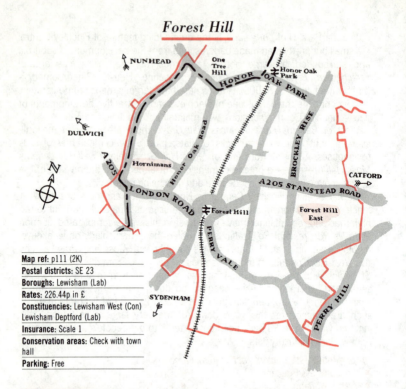

Map ref: p111 (2K)	
Postal districts: SE 23	
Boroughs: Lewisham (Lab)	
Rates: 226.44p in £	
Constituencies: Lewisham West (Con) Lewisham Deptford (Lab)	
Insurance: Scale 1	
Conservation areas: Check with town hall	
Parking: Free	

Transport	British Rail: Forest Hill to London Bridge 12 min.
Convenient for	Dulwich golf course, Crystal Palace Park and National Sports centre, Lewisham shops. South Circular Rd. Miles from centre: 6.
Schools	ILEA zone 7: Forest Hill School (b), Sydenham School (g).

Flats	S	1b	2b	3b	4b	5b
Average prices	46–53	55–66	65–80	75–85	–	–
Houses	2b	3b	4b	5b	6/7b	8b
Average prices	75–85	80–150	100–190	130–200+	150–250	–

The properties	Respectable Victoriana, larger homes in the W of the area, smaller terraces to the E. Three-bed houses most common, larger houses often converted into flats.
The market	Good supply of 3-bed houses and 1-2 bed flats. First-time buyers join families seeking space and greenery. Though market went quiet as mortgages rose, developers still had confidence to snap up big houses for conversion. They, and agents, reckon area is good value. Local searches: 6-7 weeks.

Area Profile

Forest Hill is E of Dulwich and Sydenham and S of Peckham and Brockley. Like Sydenham, it owes its development to the railway, which reached here in 1836. The 'forest on the hill' of ages past is long gone, but wooded areas and quiet, tree-lined roads continue to give the name meaning. Some impressive 19th-century villas have survived the depredations of developers. Late last century the tea merchant F J Horniman amassed an extensive anthropological and natural history collection from his world travels. His collection, a gift to the people, is in the museum he had built (1897-1901). Next to the Horniman Museum are delightful gardens with interesting views.

The area, which is essentially the SE23 postal district, divides roughly into two parts – the hilly ground in the W (between *Honor Oak Park* to N, the railway line to the E, *Thorpewood Avenue* to S, *Wood Vale/Sydenham Hill* to W), and the lower-lying ground to the E of the railway line. The centre and principal area for shops, pubs, restaurants etc, *London Rd/Dartmouth Rd*, meets basic needs but lacks the attractive character of, say, Blackheath Village. The centre has shown a modest upturn in the last year, though the advent of a McDonald's has brought mixed reactions. (The shopping centre at Lewisham is a direct bus ride or short car journey away.)

Most sought-after neighbourhood and most elevated – in price and geography – is Hornimans, the estate-agent shorthand for the roads N of the Horniman Museum and Gardens.

The south-eastern quarter between *Waldram Park Rd, Stanstead Rd* and *Perry Vale/Perry Rise* is generally flatter and has a mixture of property – detached and semis, terraced, Victorian/turn-of-century and '30s/modern as well as council blocks. Streets off *Honor Oak Park* near Honor Oak Park BR station have modest terraces.

The largest properties are usually found on the high ground but few roads are homogenous – you'll find Victorian houses next to bay-fronted '30s semis. Victorian properties predominate, though, and top the popularity list.

Mainly owner-occupied, Forest Hill is still an affordable area both for first-time buyers and those seeking a larger home. However, larger properties are declining in number as they are broken up into smaller, highly sellable units. The area still has a broad racial, age and social mix. Rising prices are tending to push out lower-earning, locally-born people to places like Belvedere. Professional families are moving in from more expensive areas like Battersea, Wandsworth and Clapham to acquire bigger homes. Young professional couples are also moving in (for example doctors working at King's in Denmark Hill) who now find Camberwell expensive. The area benefited from 1988's general rediscovery of SE London.

Forest Hill's leafiness and quiet tend to belie its inner-suburban location. It has a good share of gardens and parks, and Dulwich and Sydenham golf course is nearby. There are no real pockets of deprivation. London Bridge is 12 mins by train and connections to Gatwick are possible from East Croydon on the same line. The steepness of the hills demands fitness (some have 18% gradients) and in winter heavy snow leaves cars immobilised in the hilly parts.

G

Hornimans

One approach to Hornimans is up popular *Honor Oak Rd* at the *London Rd* entrance. *Honor Oak Rd* has surviving Italianate villas ('flats for sale' signs proliferate). The road is a mixture but not jarringly so – modern box developments, council, Victorian, and '30s semis. Dainty Ashberry Cottage was once home to William Duke of Clarence, later King William IV, and his actress-mistress Dorothea Jordan. The cottage dates from 1809.

Trailing hillward off *Honor Oak Rd* are *Westwood Park* and *Horniman Drive*. Desirable *Horniman Drive* has '30s detached homes with pretty front gardens and ends, by an entrance to Hornimans Gardens, with modern town house cul-de-sacs. It also has enviable views over London. *Westwood Park* starts with some large Victorian semis and later follows round the hillside with '30s bay-fronted detached and semis. Smaller '30s properties in *Tewkesbury Avenue*; larger, detached ones are in demand in *Ringmore Rise*. For spectacular views of the city and a mixture of Victorian, turn-of-the-century, '30s semis there's *Canonbie Rd*. Landmarks visible are the Houses of Parliament, St Paul's, Battersea power station, the Telecom Tower – even if the gradient is 18%, difficult for the elderly and impossible in snow. *Netherby Rd* (bay-fronted semis and occasional large Victorian ones) looks to the wooded One Tree Hill.

London Rd in the upper (W) stages near the museum has council blocks but also brightly painted classical terraces – now flats – lower down. On the N side is 'Horniman Grange', a 1988 redevelopment of some previously wrecked Victorian houses. Now there are studios, 1- and 2-bed flats. Off to the S is *Taymount Rise* (mansion flats, Victorian detached, '60s town houses), ending with dull '30s mansion blocks, Taymount Grange and Forestcroft. Parallel to *London Rd* is *Thorpewood Avenue* – here '30s semis outnumber the occasional Victorian houses.

Worth investigation is *Devonshire Rd*, running parallel to the railway line – Victorian semis, detached, turn-of-the-century, 1930s. Occasional property empty and boarded up, but plenty of renovation as evidenced by the number of skips. A small nature reserve comes as a pleasant surprise. Not the neatest road (though sprucing up) but very central and with BR stations at both ends. One new-built scheme, 'Forest Oak Lodge', offers 1- and 2-bed flats next to the nature reserve (from £70,000 to £82,500).

Forest Hill East

East of the BR station *Honor Oak Park* leaves behind the more illustrious properties. Shops line both sides – theatrical costume hire and a small gallery are curiosities here. Small roads such as *Ballina St* and *Gabriel St* have stolid, uniform turn-of-century terraces – also some '60s town houses in *Grierson Rd*. (The roads in the right-angle between *Honor Oak Park* and *Brockley Rise* are closed to traffic access from Honor Oak.)

Large Victorian houses on *Waldram Park Rd* have made for excellent flat conversions, close to Forest Hill BR and buses into town. *Stanstead Rd* is notoriously busy (it's part of the South Circular), but has large Victorian semis and cottage-style dwellings. The roads leading off both sides of *Vancouver Rd* are quieter and have terraced properties – Victorian and turn-of-century. Also some 1930s and modern infills.

Perry Vale, which runs S-E from Forest Hill BR, starts with Christchurch C of E primary school, and a concentration of unattractive council estates. Older type constructions with walkways, their impact is lessened by the surrounding trees. Large turn-of-century semis follow, with a parade of shops in the curve.

Sunderland Rd has large Victorian, turn-of-century detached, and '30s semis. *Woolstone Rd* starts with bay-fronted Victorian, turn-of-century terraces, and 1930s semis. Tree-lined: the leaves brush together in the middle of the road. Also some large Victorian detached houses down towards St George's church. *Allenby Rd* is quiet and leafy – large Victorian detached. Neighbouring *Garlies Rd* is less uniform – Victorian and 1930s semis. *Perry Rise* offers bay-fronted Victorian semis before giving way to small terraced houses near *Bell Green* with its gasworks. This area links up with Lower Sydenham, covered in the Crystal Palace chapter.

Queenswood Rd is terraced – Victorian, turn-of-century and '30s semis. Tucked away on old tennis courts, *Queenscourt (Rendon Estates)* – luxury 3-bed houses – appeared last year. A council estate, Forest Hill school and a town house development make up *Dacres Rd* until the right turn. Then come detached Victorian houses, leaf-obscured modern town houses and a modern mansion building.

The South Circular, which runs through Forest Hill in the guise of *London Rd, Waldram Park Rd* and *Stanstead Rd* is the subject of one of the Government's 'Assessment Studies'. A bypass for Forest Hill, which would certainly involve demolition of homes, is one of several proposals. A decision is unlikely before 1990. See the 'Transport' chapter.

F

Among those estate agents active in this area are:
- Woolwich Property Services
- Jacksons
- Hamptons Levens
- Mortimer & Hutchinson
- Robert Stanford
- Uniplan
- Wates

Fulham

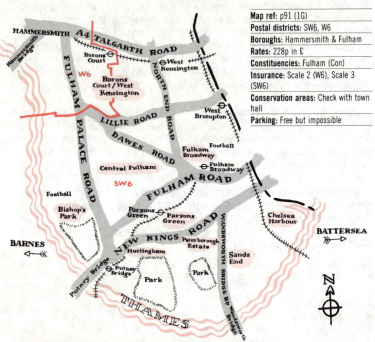

Map ref: p91 (1G)
Postal districts: SW6, W6
Boroughs: Hammersmith & Fulham
Rates: 228p in £
Constituencies: Fulham (Con)
Insurance: Scale 2 (W6), Scale 3 (SW6)
Conservation areas: Check with town hall
Parking: Free but impossible

Transport Tubes: Parsons Green, Fulham Broadway, Putney Bridge (zone 2, District). From Fulham Broadway: Oxford Circus 30 min (1 change), City 45 min (1 change), Heathrow 45 min (1 change).

Convenient for A4, M4, Sloane Square and Kings Road shops. Miles from centre: 4.

Schools ILEA zone 1: Fulham Cross (g), Hurlingham & Chelsea, London Oratory RC (b), St Edmunds RC, St Marks C of E, Lady Margaret C of E.

Flats	S	1b	2b	3b	4b	5b
Average prices	60–75	80–95	90–130	110–175	150–220+	–
Houses	2b	3b	4b	5b	6/7b	8b
Average prices	150–180	150–220	200–350+	260–400	400+	–

The properties Row after row of solid, late-19th century family houses of varying sizes. Also some Victorian/Edwardian/'30s p/b flats and many, many flat conversions. After a decade of energetic renovation, many houses boast top-flight interiors. Much newbuild on infill and river sites – including starry Chelsea Harbour and imminent neighbours.

The market More estate agents per sq ft than any other area mark the mass migration of families to Chelsea's neighbour. Prices rocketed and now equate with prime areas. Trend to re-convert flats back to houses as families displace first wave of singles. Few unmodernised houses left now: but council resales appearing. Searches: 2 weeks.

Area Profile

Fulham is the southern part of the Borough of Hammersmith and Fulham. Until 1880 almost all of Fulham was market gardens supplying London. With the completion of the District Line tube an enormous development took place – the bulk between 1880 and 1900, but extending up to the First World War in various small areas. These houses – almost entirely terraced with only a few detached and semi-detached in areas such as Hurlingham and Bishops Park – cover most of Fulham. There still exist a very few 18th-century buildings, mainly associated with the original villages of Walham Green (now *Fulham Broadway*) and Fulham (sited by what is now Putney Bridge) and extending along the *New Kings Road*.

After the pre-1914 building boom, Fulham relapsed into a condition of quiet respectability. A large proportion of the housing was let unfurnished: as late as 1971, more than 40% of the homes in most of Fulham were privately let. It was a stable community, with strong local loyalties and a tendency to stay put: three generations of the same family would live in the same group of streets. This pattern was shattered by the property boom of the early '70s. Demand by would-be owner-occupiers spilt over from Chelsea and Kensington, and the quiet streets of Fulham were 'discovered'. Landlords, beset by the Rent Acts, hastened to sell their tenanted homes as soon as the residents could be persuaded to leave. In came the young professionals (yuppies had not been invented then), out went the skilled workers and their families to new estates on the fringes of London.

The Sloaning of Fulham, as an unkind Labour councillor described it, has of course been repeated all over inner London. The process continues, as the builders work their way along scruffier and scruffier side-streets. A second wave is now coming through Fulham: the re-conversion of properties that were turned into flats in the early '70s and are now becoming smart 4-bedroom houses once again.

While Fulham historically had a large proportion of privately rented homes, it also had a fair sprinkling of council estates. These still exist and have, in the last year, begun to be affected by the 'right to buy' legislation. The biggest council estate is Clem Attlee Court in the north of the area, off *Lillie Rd.* These big blocks, named after Socialist luminaries of the 1940s, form a community of their own. In the S-E corner of Fulham, Sands End has more council blocks. Smaller clusters of council and housing association homes occur across the borough. Some, such as those by the river off *Stevenage Rd.* are very attractive.

The old Fulham turned its back on the river which curves around it on three sides. Or to be more precise it used the river rather than looked at it. The banks were lined with wharves and with industry. The Thames, two decades and more ago, was a working river, and barges delivered materials to many a riverside works. Few of these remain, and many of the industrial sites have been, or are being, replaced by housing. A by-product is the opening up of the riverside: public paths now follow much of the western bank.

The wide sweep of the Thames forms Fulham's southern and western boundaries. The river is crossed at two points to the S at Putney (the oldest and lowest fording point on the River Thames, and used by the Romans) and Wandsworth Bridges. The eastern boundary is defined by the main N-S railway line which runs from Kensington Olympia to cross the river to Chelsea Creek. The northern barrier which conclusively separates Fulham from Hammersmith is defined by the *A4 Hammersmith Flyover* and *Cromwell Rd Extension/ Talgarth Rd* which leads westwards to the M4 motorway. However, Fulham proper is SW6, which encompasses the whole bend of the river but stops just N of Lillie Rd. Above this divide lie West Kensington and Baron's Court.

Fulham is crossed by a number of E-W roads which have the effect of defining neighbourhoods. From S to N, they are: *New Kings Rd, Fulham Rd, Dawes Rd, Lillie Rd*. There are two main N-S routes: *Fulham Palace Rd*, leading to Putney Bridge; and *North End Rd/Wandsworth Bridge Rd*, leading to Wandsworth Bridge. Again these routes are neighbourhood demarcation lines.

New Kings Rd and *Fulham Rd* have developed in the last decade with fashionable shops selling antique

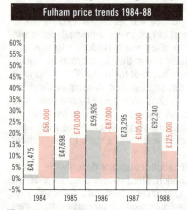

Fulham price trends 1984-88

London average home: percentage rise on previous year, adjusted for inflation.

Typical home in this area, percentage rise on previous year, adjusted for inflation.

Two-bed flat in the Radipole Road area of SW6, price change compared to London-wide average home. This flat did its briskest rising early in the period, then slowed as other areas caught up. The reasonably large increase in 1988 was in line with the year's trend for flats to move faster than houses.

furniture, clothing and specialist delicatessen, plus restaurants and wine bars. *Lillie Rd* and *Dawes Rd* still maintain many of the old-style small local shops, selling a wide range of goods, but they are changing fast. *Fulham Palace Rd*, especially S of *Lillie Rd*, is predominantly residential. *North End Rd* has a colourful street fruit-and-vegetable market, while *Wandsworth Bridge Rd* is a mix of residential and trendy shopping – it has been the stripped-pine capital of London for years.

Fulham has a number of open spaces and parks. In the S is Hurlingham Park with its sports ground. The Hurlingham Club, which adjoins it and has all the river frontage, is (very) private. It has a swimming pool and tennis courts and is centred around the 18th-century Hurlingham House. South Park, also in the S, has children's play areas, cricket pitch and tennis courts for public use. Parsons Green and Eel Brook Common are tree-lined open spaces overlooked by many attractive homes. To the W, Bishops Park borders the river above Putney Bridge: this was originally the gardens of the 16th-century Bishops Palace. In Bishops Park there are also a children's play area, paddling pool, tennis courts, a keep-fit trail and rose garden. To the N is the Queens Club private tennis club and Normand Park, which houses a modern swimming pool complex. Assiduous tree-planting along the streets has also helped to mitigate the main difference between Fulham and neighbouring Chelsea: the lack of the general leafy impression provided by Chelsea's square gardens. Fulham, built later, has rows of streets, not squares.

Fulham also boasts two football grounds. To the W is Fulham's riverside ground, while on the Kensington/Chelsea borders is Stamford Bridge, home of Chelsea. Both grounds are subject to a number of planning proposals for redevelopment, which may or may not continue to include football in part. They attract much traffic on match days and contribute to parking problems. At the time of writing, the council was being asked to ratify plans to compulsory purchase Fulham's Craven Cottage ground to safeguard its future. The council's policy is to retain all three football grounds in the borough.

There are three tube stations, with good connections into central London. Just outside the area, the two Piccadilly line stations at Baron's Court and West Kensington also have direct links to Heathrow. There are good E-W bus services into central London along the major routes. However, the borough is less well served with N-S bus routes. And large tracts are quite a distance from a tube station. A river bus runs between Chelsea Harbour and Charing Cross/the City/Isle of Dogs. The promoters say the service may extend further W to Putney Bridge this year if things go well.

There are good road connections out of London to the W along the M4 to Heathrow and the M25, to the S over Putney or Wandsworth Bridges to join the South Circular or A3, and to the N through Shepherd's Bush. However, the snag with the road system is that it is saturated with traffic, which affects the bus services and main routes out of London. Putney and Wandsworth in particular are choke-points on the routes S and W. The planned N-S road from Shepherds Bush to the river will run along the area's E edge (see Transport').

Although there are no meters or residents' parking systems operating in Fulham at present, parking in the residential streets is an increasing problem, as many owners of the narrow-fronted terraced houses now have two cars. Overnight double parking is a common feature of many streets. Council tow trucks are a recent innovation.

F

There was a time when Fulham was considered to be a poor man's Chelsea. People bought in Fulham because they couldn't afford the very high prices that Kensington and Chelsea addresses demanded. But now Fulham is seen as a highly desirable part of London in its own right; it has 'arrived', and this is reflected by the fact that Fulham has London's greatest density of estate agents – rumoured to be around 70 in the Parsons Green area.

In the days when Fulham was a Chelsea overspill, there was an enormous influx of 'Sloanes' and other prosperous young people, buying flats and houses and easing out the ageing indigenous Fulham population, who mainly rented their homes. These new arrivals have decided to stay rather than move on and have developed a new community. Evidence of this is the burgeoning of private nursery schools and playgroups.

As far as most estate agents are concerned, Fulham tends to end at *Lillie Rd*. The area to the N between *Lillie Rd* and *Talgarth Rd* has a very different character, centred around Barons Court and West Kensington tube stations. It is largely composed of big, late-Victorian houses and mansion blocks, and until recently rental property was dominant.

The neighbourhoods of Fulham can be divided into the expensive, the established and the up-and-coming, and they are dealt with here in that order.

Peterborough Estate

Perhaps the best-known neighbourhood in Fulham is the Peterborough Estate, an important conservation area between *New Kings Rd* and South Park bounded by *Peterborough Rd* to the W and *Bagleys Lane* to the E. The most sought-after roads are those to the W of *Wandsworth Bridge Rd*, with a series of N-S streets off the Parsons Green stretch of *New Kings Rd*: Perrymead, *Chipstead, Quarrendon, Chiddingstone, Bradbourne* and *Coniger*. There are matching rows of substantial terraced houses. Red brick, gable-ended, flat-fronted late Victoriana, of 3-, 4- or 5-bedrooms, many with additional space from sympathetic loft and cellar conversions, extensions and conservatories. They only have small back gardens. These are very distinctive houses, with attractive mullioned windows and terracotta lion statues decorating the party walls at roof level. The majority are still single-family houses. A variety of internal layouts can be found as many have been virtually rebuilt.

Hurlingham

Hurlingham, also S of *New Kings Rd*, is a much smaller conservation area,

consisting of *Napier Avenue, Ranelagh Avenue, Ranelagh Gardens, Edenhurst Avenue* and *Hurlingham Gardens*, bounded to the N by *Hurlingham Rd*. Predominantly, there are imposing late 19th century detached and semi-detached 5- or 6-bedroom houses, set back from the tree-lined streets, with drives and off-street parking, each with its own character and architectural style. In *Ranelagh Gardens*, there are two '60s apartment blocks – also much sought-after – and a new riverside development, Carrara Wharf, a private enclave of 20 houses and 69 flats. An unusual feature of this development is the number of 1-bed houses, which were snapped up by first-time buyers for £145,000-£170,000. Along the river on *Hurlingham Gardens* is a large inter-war luxury apartment block. The appeal of this corner is also enhanced by the nearby Putney Bridge tube and the proximity of Bishop's Park.

Fulham, at first sight a district of uniform terraces, has some unusual domestic buildings such as this splendidly ornate turret house near Hurlingham. The slate-capped turret, the romanesque detailing around its eaves, the handsome sash windows and the iron railings make up an attractive whole.

On the far side of Hurlingham Park with its exclusive club, Barratt have added a new square to the area. *Hurlingham Square*, in the angle of *Peterborough* and *Sullivan Rds* has fifty 4/5-bed homes in an enclave reached via electronic entry gates.

Bishops Park

Another small conservation area, bounded on the E by *Fulham Palace Rd* and on the W by *Stevenage Rd* facing Bishops Park, stretching from *Fulham Palace Gardens* and *Bishops Park Rd* to the S, into the pleasant tree-lined streets – *Cloncurry, Doneraile, Ellerby* and *Finlay*. Here you'll find terraced or semi-detached houses which were built at the end of the 19th century or later and have 4/5-bedrooms. Many have been extended upwards (not always sympathetically), with loft extensions, and to the rear with back extensions and conservatories. Most have substantial gardens. The later style of house found here reflects the stubborn hold-out of the last major market gardener.

Extending N of Fulham football ground (where there are various plans for homes on the riverside) along the river are a string of luxury apartment blocks built in the '70s, with fine views across the river to the Barnes water meadows, now used as reservoirs: River Gardens has 2/3-bedroom flats with spectacular terracing and balconies; Rosebank is a conventional high-rise block with 2/3-bed flats. Service charges must be considered in these blocks. There are more luxury blocks planned on this stretch of the river in the near future and it is likely the area will become even more up-market. (Indeed, a little further along the bank, on the Hammersmith borders, is the Richard Rogers-designed Thames Reach, whose living-rooms have floor-to-ceiling glass on the river side.)

Chelsea Harbour

Similar luxury apartments and houses are under construction at a development on the Fulham/Chelsea borders. Chelsea Harbour is a parable of the times. Only in very recent years could a developer take a triangular site cut off by a railway and a muddy creek and present these as advantages – even if the third side, as here, is river frontage. But this unpromising-sounding corner can thus, paradoxically, offer that goal of every really top-flight '80s development, complete security. Chelsea Harbour is the west side of town's answer to Docklands, a total of 400 homes in blocks, terraces, crescents and a landmark tower. Not to mention an apart-hotel, and commercial buildings on the railway side. The icing on the cake is to be a 3-floor penthouse perched on top of the Belvedere Tower, West London's newest riverside landmark. Valued at about £4 million at the time of writing, the exclusive eyrie with its 360 degree view of the capital will be sold on completion of the development in 1992. That is unless the developers are made an offer they cannot refuse in the meantime.

F

Chelsea Harbour is far from public transport – a minibus supplies the missing link to Earl's Court tube and High St. Kensington – and the proposed West London Relief Road scheme would sweep around it on two sides. But, the argument goes, it is alongside Chelsea, not the Isle of Dogs, and the waterbus makes commuting pleasurable; the advantages of a secure, self-contained and peaceful (largely pedestrian, no through traffic) community is reflected in luxurious homes at luxurious prices.

The centrepiece is the newly-reopened harbour surrounded by restaurants, shops, wine bars, etc. This provides the neighbourhood with a much-needed tranquil spot to relax by the river (a public walkway will run along the Thames) – not, of course, possible along the Chelsea embankment, nor yet the Sand's End stretch. Prices of normal homes in the area have already received a shot in the arm.

Moore Park Road

A pocket of large mid-Victorian stucco terraced houses and later Victorian detached and semi-detached houses on the Fulham/Chelsea borders, between *Fulham Rd* and *Kings Rd*. Some houses have been converted into flats. The proximity to busy Chelsea football ground is mitigated because the roads – *Moore Park Rd*, *Britannia Rd*, *Maxwell Rd* and *Rumbold Rd* – are barricaded off to through traffic.

Parsons Green

In estate agents' view, this covers a large area, bounded by streets either side of *Fulham Rd* to the N (up as far as *Bishops Rd*) and either side of *New Kings Rd* to the S, extending as far as Eel Brook Common to the E and *Munster Road* to the W.

This area is regarded as being that which is within easy walking distance of pretty, triangular Parsons Green and its tube station. It is made up of 1890s bay-windowed terraced houses, many of which have been extended upwards with loft conversions to provide a fourth bedroom. Popular streets include *Delvino Rd, Linver Rd, Guion Rd, Crondace Rd, Felden St.* There are more substantial houses of a different architectural style of 5/6-bedrooms in *Whittingstall Rd, St Maur Rd, Winchendon Rd, Lillyville Rd, Clonmel Rd.* In this latter area many of the houses have been converted into 1/2-bed flats or 2/3-bed maisonettes. *Mustow Place,* new homes in attractive mews style, have been squeezed in between the railway and *Munster Rd.*

On the fringes of Parsons Green are two neighbourhood pockets. To the E is Eel Brook Common with large late 19th-century terraced houses overlooking a pretty park with tennis courts: *Musgrave Crescent* and *Favart Rd* being particularly popular. To the W, *Fulham Park Gardens* is a small conservation area of very distinctive substantial red-brick houses of 5/6-bedrooms and considerable character.

Fulham Broadway

Known as Walham Green until London Transport renamed the station in 1948. Includes pockets of conservation areas – *Walham Grove* which is a street of 1840s semi-detached villas; and *Barclay Rd,* mid-Victorian terraced houses. The area is subject to a major redevelopment plan – the Fulham Centre Plan and part of the shopping area near the station has been pedestrianised to form 'Fulham Piazza,' intended to be a mini Covent Garden. An area full of character, which includes the *North End Rd* market as well as some of the oldest buildings in Fulham. The plan foresees a mix of preservation of the conversation areas and new developments of shops and offices. *Harwood Rd.,* just N of the *New King's Rd,* has an interesting development of offices and flats, the offices for owner-occupiers. Permission has been sought for 12 houses in *Epirus Mews* off *North End Rd.*

Central Fulham

Extending N from *Bishops Rd,* bounded by the river to the W (across *Fulham Palace Rd*), *North End Rd* to the E and up towards Charing Cross Hospital to the N are many streets of similar 3/4-bedroom terraced houses, all built between 1890 and 1910. Many of these have been converted into flats and there are several pockets of pretty streets (*Marville, Brookville, Rosaville, Parkville*) with occasional streets of unusual mansion blocks in yellow London bricks (*St Olafs Rd, Orbain Rd*). A number of interesting streets lead from *Fulham Palace Rd* down towards the river: *Inglethorpe, Kenyon, Lisia, Niton.* There are pockets of council development and the N part is overshadowed by the big Clem Attlee estate on *Lillie Rd.* A new mews has been built by Barratt off *Hartismere Rd.* In *Fulham High St,* Merivale Moore launched 'Parkview Court' in the spring: 51 flats backing onto the grounds of Fulham Palace.

Sands End

A most interesting up-and-coming area, much improved since it was declared a Housing Action Area 13 years ago. The E side around *Imperial Rd.,* formerly large-scale industrial and commercial, is being redeveloped with modern studio workshops, housing and flats. Along the S river frontage, on the site of the former Fulham power station, Bovis is building 250 flats due for completion this summer. they are expected to sell for roughly £250,000 for a 2-bed flat up to double that figure for a 4-bed penthouse. A leisure centre is also planned for part of the site. Barratts have built two developments off *Harwood Terrace* in the N corner of Sands End. *Chelsea Walk* and *Chelsea Lodge* – both named to stress proximity to the borough border – have a total of 20 4-bed houses. *Townmead Rd* may become part of the WEIR road scheme: see 'Transport' chapter.

There are small pockets of council housing and a large area of typical Fulham-type late Victorian terraced housing in somewhat dilapidated condition, still occupied by old Fulhamites, but clearly become sought-after: *Stephendale Rd*, *Broughton Rd*, *Lindrop St*, *Glenrosa St*, *Byam St*. The exception is a small area of *Wandsworth Bridge Rd*, where *Rosebury*, *Oakbury*, *Cranbury*, *Haslebury Rds* are smaller Peterborough Estate-type houses, many of which have been converted to flats and maisonettes and have in recent years 'come up' and are a very attractive corner. *Carnwath Rd* is rapidly switching from industry to homes: plans were announced late last year for homes on the Petrofina and Whiffen wharves. The gasworks in *Imperial Rd.* boasts a listed gasometer – though presumably it was not this public monument but the site's proximity to Chelsea that prompted the building of a smart modern development nearby. Tucked away behind the gasometer is delightful, restored *Imperial Square*: Victorian workmens' cottages.

F

Barons Court/West Kensington Borders

On the N-E fringe of Fulham, these two areas are not normally regarded as part of Fulham – by estate agents and in fact anyone else except the Town Hall: they're in the Fulham and Hammersmith borough. Barons Court has a large number of 19th and early 20th century mansion blocks, for example *Queens Club Gardens*, which are now being refurbished and the modernised flats marketed. Further N, but S of *Talgarth Rd*, are substantial red-brick late Victorian houses, quite decoratively detailed and with attractively designed windows, often with separate-access basement flats, which had mainly been converted into tenanted flats: *Comeragh Rd*, *Charleville Rd* and *Fairholme Rd*. These are now becoming owner-occupied and in some cases are reverting to family houses. For more detail see the Hammersmith chapter.

On the extreme E edge of Fulham, off *Seagrave Rd*, the Brompton Park estate of flats and houses, complete with its own swimming pool and health club, occupies the walled grounds of a former hospital. The proposed WEIR road and the Channel Tunnel railway run along the E border.

Among those estate agents active in this area are:

- Farrar Stead & Glyn
- Folkard & Hayward
- Friend & Falcke
- George Stead
- Hamptons
- Jackson-Stops & Staff
- Jackson
- John D Wood
- Prudential Property
- Vanstons
- Winkworths
- Lawsons & Daughters

Golders Green

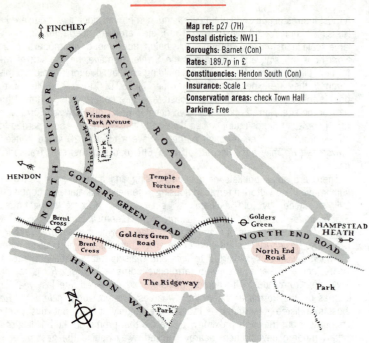

| Map ref: p27 (7H) |
| Postal districts: NW11 |
| Boroughs: Barnet (Con) |
| Rates: 189.7p in £ |
| Constituencies: Hendon South (Con) |
| Insurance: Scale 1 |
| Conservation areas: check Town Hall |
| Parking: Free |

Transport   Tubes: Golders Green, Brent Cross (zone 3a, Northern). From Golders Green to: Oxford Circus 20 min (1 change), City 30 min, Heathrow 1 hr 25 min (1 change).

Convenient for   Brent Cross Shopping Centre, Hampstead Heath, North Circular Rd. Miles from centre: 6.

Schools   Barnet Education Authority: Hendon School, Whitefield School.

Flats	S	1b	2b	3b	4b	5b
Average prices	60–70	75–100	80–125+	100–150+	–	–
Houses	2b	3b	4b	5b	6/7b	8b
Average prices	115+	140–170+	160–300	260–325+	375–500+	–

The properties   Mock Tudor suburban homes, large and comfortable, mix with prosperous blocks of flats and some conversions. Less pricy suburbia towards Hendon Way and Brent Cross.

The market   Primarily family; long-established community (largely Jewish; also Japanese). Good transport links and solid, peaceful family homes ensure its position. Market moves indicator: luxury flats appearing; prices well above average. Local searches: 4 weeks.

Area Profile

One of NW London's best-known suburbs, and a major rallying point for Northern Line commuters, Golders Green is home for many of London's Jews. The bustling *Golders Green Rd* which runs through the centre, from the tube up to the *North Circular Rd* and Hendon, is awash with delicatessens, kosher bakeries and take-aways – not to mention Blooms, an off-shoot of the famous East End restaurant. There are other benefits: most shops, and even a bank, are open on Sundays. At festival times, you'll see people in their holiday clothes strolling the streets and during Chanukah (December's festival of lights) the tube station houses a huge candelabra which is lit every evening. There are also sizeable Japanese, Malaysian, Asian and Nigerian communities, and these too are all reflected in the shops and restaurants in the area.

Unlike other areas which have merged with their neighbours into an amorphous suburban sprawl, Golders Green's boundaries are well defined. Its limits are the *Finchley Rd* to the E, the *North Circular Rd* to the N, the *Hendon Way* to the W as far as *The Vale*, and S to the NW11 border, which runs along *Dunstan Rd*, *Hodford Rd* and pleasant *Golders Hill Park*. Anonymous it is not: by and large people live here because they have chosen to live here. They are in Golders Green – not just some convenient corner of north London.

Property-wise, Golders Green is primarily an area of family houses, 3/4/5-bedroom properties which are large but not grand and speak of comfortable family life. These are Edwardian villas, not Victorian terraces: the area was mainly fields until the Northern Line bored its way through from beneath Hampstead Heath at the turn of the century. There are also many purpose-built blocks (along the *Golders Green* and *Finchley Rds* and in the area around *Woodlands*) and an increasing number of conversions around Temple Fortune. There's also a fair amount of rented accommodation, so there are lots of young single people in the area and also students – Golders Green is very convenient for several of the colleges of London University.

Golders Green is blessed with churches of every denomination, and synagogues, official and unofficial, of every shade of orthodoxy. Estate agents know the synagogues in detail since purchasers will often only consider properties in roads near to a particular one. There's plenty of park space too, if you'd rather commune with the Almighty in less formal surroundings, and the Hampstead Heath extension is nearby.

If godliness is its first name, convenience in the form of transport is its second. The Northern Line provides great links to West End and City; direct to Tottenham Court Road, Leicester Square and Bank. Buses are very good, too.

The Ridgeway

Some of the best houses in Golders Green are found in the area to the W of the *Golders Green Rd*, off *The Ridgeway*. In roads such as *Ridge Hill*, *Gresham Gardens*, *Armitage Rd*, *Basing Hill*, *Hodford Rd* and *Dunstan Rd* you'll find 4- and 5-bedroom houses, detached and semi-detatched, with large gardens. Basing Hill Park, the nearby tube station, cinema and shops are all attractions, though parking can be a problem in *Rodborough Rd* and *Helenslea Avenue*, where there are plans for a new block of 5 flats. Jewish residents have often chosen to live here because of the proximity to synagogues in *Dunstan Rd* and *The Riding*. The busy *Hendon Way* runs past the bottom of *Wessex Gardens* and *Ridge Hill*, so prices may be lower at that end.

Brent Cross

Brent Cross does not yet constitute an area by itself though it houses the famous shopping centre and has a tube station (the two aren't as near to each other as you might think). *Highfield Avenue*, with the tube station, is one of the nicest roads in Golders Green and *Highfield Gardens* is where you'll find one of Golders Green's most popular purpose-built blocks, Windsor Court.

In *Hamilton Rd* prices may be more modest since the street runs parallel to the *Hendon Way*; houses on the *Sandringham Rd* side won't suffer from noise as much as those right by the main road but will still be relatively inexpensive for the area. Also look out for 3-bed terraced houses and semis in *Woodville Rd* and *Elmcroft Crescent* for properties at the lower end of the price scale.

Golders Green Rd

This runs northwards like a main artery through the area from the station and the Hippodrome – first a music-hall, then a theatre, now a BBC studio. Very good shopping, much of it seven days a week, causes parking problems; triple-parking in Golders Green is legendary. Busy residents can buy a suit on Sunday and toiletries till midnight every day. Heading towards Hendon, the flats above the shops give way to large family houses around *Ravenscroft Avenue*; some of those towards the North Circular are rather run down. A housing association is planning to build on the former cinema site in *Golders Green Rd*. It is embroiled in a planning battle, but it plans a 32-unit home for the elderly, as well as nearly 40 sheltered flats. Building should start this year. Golders Green isn't usually noted for exceptionally pretty houses, but there are some surprises in *Brookside Rd*. You'll find conversions and family houses in streets off the *Golders Green Rd*, *Gainsborough* and *Powis Gardens* to the left and *Beechcroft* and *Elmcroft Avenues* to the right, where there are also a couple of blocks of flats and small hotels. A new development of 16 flats and 2 penthouses was completed last year in *Beechcroft Avenue*, when 2-bed flats were selling for £250,000. There are larger purpose-built blocks along the main road – Gloucester Court and Eagle Lodge, for example.

Princes Park Avenue

As with the streets around *The Ridgeway*, there are some very large houses to be found in the vicinity of Princes Park, to the N of *Brookside Rd* between the *Finchley* and *Golders Green Rds*. Look for them in the *Princes Park Avenue/Leeside Crescent/Bridge Lane* triangle. Princes Park in the centre makes houses here particularly desirable; on Saturday afternoons the little park is full of children. Again, agents mention the synagogue factor; Jewish people who live here have often chosen the neighbourhood specifically. Coveted bungalows, some with extra rooms in the roof, are to be found in *Decoy Avenue* across *Bridge Lane*. Popular purpose-built blocks in the neighbourhood include Dolphin Court in *Woodlands* and the luxurious Riverside Drive on the *Golders Green Rd*. Not as convenient as the Ridgeway area, though buses to Golders Green are numerous and frequent on the main road.

G

Temple Fortune

This area brackets the *Finchley Rd* northwards from *Hoop Lane/Wentworth Rd* up to Henley's Corner, the junction with the *North Circular*. Don't look for Henley's Corner on the map, though it's a name you'll hear in the area; the junction is named after a garage that used to be there. Confusing but true. The neighbourhood takes its name from the *Temple Fortune Parade* of shops (amongst them the police station) which is slightly less frantic than the chic *Golders Green Rd* – where you have a choice of places to buy a compact disc or a pair of designer jeans, but nowhere to get a hammer or a light bulb. There's also the Templars Tennis Club for sporty types. Roads between *Hoop Lane* and *Temple Fortune Lane* have small houses and some conversions, cheaper even though they are nearer the prestigious Hampstead Garden Suburb because they back onto a cemetery. Further up on that side of the *Finchley Road* you find purpose-built blocks like Belmont Court. Roads on the other (W) side of the *Finchley Rd* – *Templars Avenue*, *St Johns Rd*, *Portsdown Avenue*, *St George's Rd* and further up, also on the left *Hallswelle Rd* and *Monkville Avenue* – have smaller family houses and some conversions. Across the *Finchley Rd*, Golders Green becomes Hampstead Garden Suburb.

North End Road

The neighbourhood to the S of the tube station, nestling in the angle between *North End Rd* and the *Finchley Rd*, sports Golders Hill Park (look out for the flamingoes and wallabies in the zoo). Enviable roads like *West Heath Avenue* and *The Park* triangle have lovely views of the park, which merges into West Heath. Flat conversions and blocks are gathered along *North End Rd* itself.

Among those estate agents active in this area are:
- Winkworths
- Ellis & Co
- Hutton
- Culwick Lerner
- Druce
- Glentree

Greenwich and Blackheath

Map ref: p80 (7E)

Postal districts: SE10, SE3

Boroughs: Greenwich (Lab), Lewisham (Lab)

Rates: G: 230.68p in £, L: 226.44p in £

Constituencies: Greenwich (SDP), Lewisham East (Con)

Insurance: Scale 1

Conservation areas: Several, check town hall

Parking: Free off main roads

| *Transport* | British Rail: Greenwich to; London Bridge 10 min, Charing Cross 15 min. Blackheath to London Bridge 12 min. See also map. |

| *Convenient for* | Docklands; Docklands Light Railway through foot tunnel at Island Gardens; City Airport. National Maritime Museum, Royal Observatory, Cutty Sark. Miles from centre: 5.5. |

| *Schools* | ILEA zones 6/7: St Ursulas's Convent RC (g), John Roan School, Blackheath Bluecoat C of E, St Joseph's Academy RC (b), St Theresa's RC (g). Private: Blackheath High (g), Thomas Tallis. |

Flats	S	1b	2b	3b	4b	5b
Average prices	52–65	60–90	80–130	95–200	–	–
Houses	2b	3b	4b	5b	6/7b	8b
Average prices	95–150	130–200	190–400+	230–600+	300–1m+	–

| *The properties* | Superb Georgian in Greenwich and Blackheath, mid-Victorian in Blackheath Park (prices to £1m+ here), plus more ordinary period and modern homes im E Greenwich and other fringe areas. |

| *The market* | Prices vary dramatically from E Greenwich (still cheap) to Heath views and top roads eg Crooms Hill. These are the nearest established residential areas to Docklands and thus attract more traditional buyers. ELRIC bridge (1994) will be big boost. Local searches: 8 weeks. |

G

Area Profile

The nicest way to arrive in this area is by boat. But by far the more impressive is to drive (or try to) across South London, through the congested, most workaday tide of Victorian expansionism. Suddenly you reach the hills and high heathland where Greenwich and Blackheath speak of an earlier, more gracious time. One must dispose of the history quickly: the whole place reeks of it, and any local will fill you in at length, beginning with Romans, Saxons and marauding Danes, via half the Kings and Queens of England (all the best died/were born/rebuilt the country palace beside the Thames) to romantic 18th century highwaymen.

As far as the streetscape goes, however, the period that has stuck is the Georgian/Regency one: glorious examples encouraged some of the better exponents of Victorian building in their wake.

Greenwich, gathered around its royal park by the Thames, has the bustle and air of a seaside, more than riverside, town. Summer trippers flock to the Cutty Sark, the Maritime Museum, the observatory. The narrow streets are clogged with traffic. It is a happily mixed area: here the property market can, and does, embrace everything from tiny two-up two-down terraces to a wing of a red-brick, battlemented castle, built by Sir John Vanbrugh for himself in 1719.

On the high plateau at the top of Shooters Hill, Blackheath, at heart a country hamlet, considers itself a cut above. Those with money can choose Georgian restrained elegance or even, tucked away, Dallas-level opulence.

Until now the drawback (or blessing, according to some residents) of Greenwich and Blackheath life has been its lack of good transport links. There is no tube, and you can be a good way from a station. You can reach the Kent countryside via the A2 more easily than Central London.

But now, there is Docklands. The Light Railway is at the far end of the Greenwich Foot Tunnel under the Thames. Extending the railway across the river is as yet a fond glint in the eyes of local MPs, but watch out for developments. Going through the planner's hands now, however, is the proposed East London River Crossing, a new road bridge to the east past Woolwich which would link the whole area to the motorway network, relieve the notorious Dartford Tunnel and get you to that other Docklands amenity, the City airport. This is to look to the future, but as soon as definite dates are bandied about, look for price rises – except, of course, if the traffic will pass your door too closely for comfort. Plans for the DLR extension were still under discussion, as we went to press, but it is looking increasingly likely to go ahead. LRT backs the idea, but is waiting to see if private capital can be found. The airport is pressing for permission to use jets, which may mean more noise.

Greenwich divides neatly into two. East Greenwich still retains a working identity through its riverside industry. Its cottages are quickly being snapped up by young professional couples who discovered that civilisation does exist south of the river about two years ago. It is the site of a very large development on the former gas-works known as the Greenwich Peninsula, a tongue of land until now noted only for the Blackwall Tunnel approach road. A consortium of 11 top developers has plans for 6,000 homes. There is speculation about a new cross-river link here.

West Greenwich is steeped in history and boasts 17th century masterpieces such as the Royal Naval College, National Maritime Museum and Royal Observatory. Shopping will improve with the £12m complex planned for *Stockwell St*, and a cinema is under way in *Burney St*.

Blackheath, over the hill to the S, has long been regarded as a more sought-after area than Greenwich. Native S-E Londoners cruelly regard it as a home for snobs; but Blackheathens say it attracts those who love culture.

Westcombe Park

Bargain hunters should run their eye over the streets to the S of *Woolwich Rd* and to the E of *Maze Hill* as far as the motorway which leads into the Blackwall tunnel. Here are many small terraced family homes in tree-lined streets around Westcombe Park BR station. Virtually all are owner-occupied and are more reasonably priced than their near neighbours in East Greenwich.

Climbing up the slopes away from the river are the larger 3- and 4-bedroom properties of peaceful *Mycenae Rd* and *Beaconsfield Rd*, which crosses the delightful ornate 2-storey Victorian mansions of *Westcombe Park Rd*.

East Greenwich

Down *Vanbrugh Hill* and N of the railway is East Greenwich. Around Greenwich district hospital, typical Greenwich homes – terraced workman's cottages – quickly reassert themselves. Land to the N of the hospital is largely filled by well kept, low rise council homes. But to the S and W the Coronation Street style abounds. To the S and N of *Trafalgar Rd* lies the heart of East Greenwich with its many street-corner pubs and its narrow terraces, increasingly converted by newcomers to include inside toilets and bathrooms.

Heading E along *Trafalgar Rd* the picture is largely the same, although there is some low-rise council housing. Most cottages are 2-bedroom, with tiled roofs and, increasingly, they sport smart front doors.

Many were formerly occupied by tenants of the nearby Morden College alms houses estate. But young City types are increasingly common, as tenants who bought their homes at a discount sell up and make a killing by moving to Kent.

West Greenwich

Heading W, past Inigo Jones' Queen's House on the left, Wren's Royal Naval College and the now closed, soon to be developed, Dreadnought Seamans Hospital on the right, you are soon into the heart of West Greenwich with its generous mix of Georgian style.

Croom's Hill is known as the pride of Greenwich, with its huge high-ceilinged properties – some with chandeliers – overlooking the park. The road is plagued by heavy rush-hour traffic, but near the bottom of the hill lies one of the prettiest streets in South London – *Crooms Hill Grove*. Thousands pass by its tiny entrance, not realising that a beautiful row of 2- and 3-storey terraced homes lies yards from the park's entrance.

Also off *Croom's Hill* and near to Greenwich Theatre lies the late 18th-century crescent of *Gloucester Circus*, with its 2-storey houses and fenced garden to the front. The perfect proportion of the Circus is, however, spoiled by the block of brick-built council flats which stand opposite.

From the Circus you can cross over *Royal Hill* and *Circus St* and the *Brand St* area where the grander mansions give way to the 2-up, 2-down Victorian terraces so common in the E. The cobbled *Dutton St* is popular.

The Royal Hill council estate stands at the base of *Royal Hill*, but is medium-rise and not too intrusive. Travel up the hill and pass the marvellous *Hamilton Terrace*, 3-storey with garden flats. The sudden appearance of six 1930s semis near the top of the hill serves as a reminder of how quickly – and totally – Greenwich was developed in Victorian times.

G

Blackheath

The best way to approach Blackheath must be from the W up the steep *Blackheath Hill*. Taking a right turn into *Dartmouth Hill*, drivers are rewarded with a breathtaking view of the heath and the village. A former house of the Bishop of Southwark is being converted into 1 and 2-bedroom luxury flats from £115,000-350,000.

The area is defined neatly to the N by the heath; by *Lewisham Rd* in the W; by *Lee High Rd* to the S; and by an upwardly curving arc which excludes the Ferrier Council estate before joining with *Kidbrooke Park Rd* in the E.

Cross the heath into *Hare and Billet Rd*, you first pass a small '60s development of box-shaped houses with flat roofs, and then some typical terraced 2- and 3-storey houses in a dip in the ground which appear from a distance to stand just a few feet tall. The Hare and Billet pub has an expensive clientele – and prices to match – but marvellous views of the heath.

Travel next towards *Blackheath Village*, complete with all its fashionable shops and restaurants, and the mansions of the super-rich – mostly unconverted – which are strung along the heath's fringes. Turn down the misnamed *Tranquil Vale* (it suffers its share of commuter traffic) – and then left on *Montpelier Row* to come upon the Georgian splendour of *The Paragon*.

This sweeping crescent-shaped building is nowadays home to a strange mix of the young professional classes, eccentric ex-Army types and artists. The gardens are expertly kept but anyone stretching their budget should beware of high maintenance costs.

From homes for the rich pass through one of the poshest council estates in Britain, built in square 3-storey brick blocks in imitation of the 'dolls house' type mansions on the heath. Residents of the *Fulthorp Rd* area like to keep the estate looking clean, and flats come complete with Downing-Street type doors and imitation gas lamp-standards. Some former tenants are selling up and agents report 3-bed maisonettes at £95,000.

Some new town houses in *Blackheath Grove* came onto the market in 1988. Local agents promote the area as close to Docklands yet civilized.

Blackheath Park

Go down *Pond Rd* and into Blackheath's surprise package – the exclusive Blackheath Park estate. This incredible array of private housing was first built by a developer called John Cator at the start of the 19th century and now has every conceivable architectural style. It is sometimes still known as the Cator Estate. Lodges at the entrance to the estate were originally designed to keep out undesirables, and although the lodge keepers have since gone, notices warning of Private Property are enough to deter passers-by. There are still only five entrances, with speed bumps to slow traffic.

There are Victorian and Edwardian mansions; mock-Tudor 1930s detached properties and a sprinkling of 14 small Span estates, highly praised for the high standards to which they were built. There are no shops, one pub, but one church. Many homes have swimming pools. New homes are still being built: Wimpey offered 15 5-bed houses in 1988 for up to £350,000.

To the S-W are more pleasant streets S of *Lee Terrace*. Heron has built 140 flats and houses in *Belmont Glade*: the final phase of 1- + 2-bedroom Georgian-style flats will be on the market by spring this year. Prices £82,950-£98,500 plus garages at £10,000.

Borders

Leave the Cator estate by *Manor Way* and turn down *Lee Rd* and then right onto *Lee High Rd*. Properties here are a jumble of council-built and terraced homes with the quality generally declining as you leave the heath behind.

On the steep slopes of the heath just to the N there is a fair sprinkling of 1- and 2-bed conversion flats, where incomers are replacing fireplaces ripped out by over-zealous workmen in the '70s. Property here is cheaper than those with a heath view – but *Crossingham*, *Boyne* and *Caterham Rd* residents are troubled by drivers who park for free and then walk into Lewisham to shop.

For a cheaper alternative with Victorian charm, try Charlton Village, a mile to the E of Blackheath, or Brockley conservation area to the W (see Lewisham). Beware of estate agents selling Kidbrooke as Blackheath. The only thing they have in common is the SE3 postal address. The Ferrier estate in Kidbrooke is a rough concrete jungle. Woolwich is cheaper to the E, but too industrial for most people's liking. However, this corner, and Plumstead and the 'new town' of Thamesmead beyond, could find their relationship to other areas changed, when eventually the proposed East London River Crossing gives them access to N of the river, the Docklands City Airport and the motorway network. Hundreds of homes being built on banks of Thames at Thamesmead now under control of a private company, having been sold off after the demise of the GLC.

Among those estate agents active in this area are:

- Jackson
- Dyer Son & Creasey
- GA Property Services
- John Payne
- Humphreys Skitt & Co.
- Prudential Property
- Winkworths
- Wookey
- Ellis & Co

Hackney

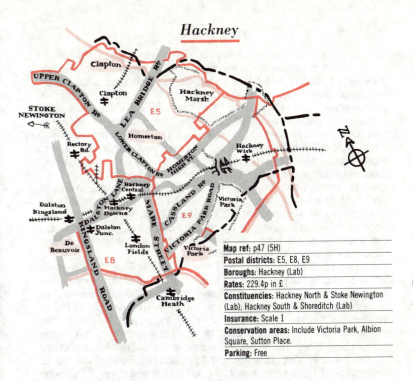

Map ref: p47 (5H)	
Postal districts: E5, E8, E9	
Boroughs: Hackney (Lab)	
Rates: 229.4p in £	
Constituencies: Hackney North & Stoke Newington (Lab), Hackney South & Shoreditch (Lab)	
Insurance: Scale 1	
Conservation areas: Include Victoria Park, Albion Square, Sutton Place.	
Parking: Free	

H

Transport   British Rail: Hackney Central, Hackney Wick, Homerton (North London Link); London Fields, Hackney Downs (Liverpool St). See also map.

Convenient for   Victoria Park, the City. Miles from centre: 4.

Schools   ILEA zone 4: Cardinal Pole School, Homerton House School, Hackney Free & Parochial School.

Flats	S	1b	2b	3b	4b	5b
Average prices	45–55	50–65	60–80	70–95+	–	–
Houses	2b	3b	4b	5b	6/7b	8b
Average prices	75–100	80–130	90–160	110–250	→	–

The properties   Many Victorian houses, some early and desirable, a few Georgian. De Beauvoir and Victoria Park now established residential zones, other parts more mixed with widespread council housing and 'gentrified' pockets.

The market   Owner-occupation low but growing: people who cannot afford Islington are taking advantage of Hackney's lower prices. There's lots going on here, including some smart new developments. Local searches: 16 weeks.

Area Profile

"Wiv a ladder and some glasses, You could see to 'Ackney Marshes, If it wasn't for the 'ouses in between", ran the old music-hall favourite. For a century, Hackney epitomised self-confident, working-class London: acres of tiny houses, corner pubs, music-halls and all. Then came the war and the slum clearances, and somehow Hackney lost its way. Now things are starting to change and change fast. It is not always to the taste of the locals, what's left of them after dispersal to new towns and far-flung council estates. But the change is coming in the shape of newcomers seeking out the remaining Georgian and Victorian housing, rediscovering Hackney's proximity to the City and its amenities of parks and open spaces. And discovering some of that community spirit in a new form. Hackney homebuyers seem fiercely loyal to their chosen home, far more than do the newly-arrived Fulhamites with their weekly exodus to 'the country'. They are adopting, and adapting, a place that has its faults, but also virtues in the shape of handsome houses, surprisingly usable communications (buses and trains, not tubes) and, of course, the amazing Hackney Empire music hall – still there and about to be reborn.

The borough of Hackney takes in Clapton, Homerton, Stoke Newington and half a dozen other former hamlets. Like most of north London, all was sylvan peace here once, interspersed with country seats and pleasure gardens. Then came the railways and the Victorian housing boom. The underground missed Hackney, but the many thousands of City clerks and respectable working men who rented the terraced homes found their way to work by horse-bus or train into Liverpool Street. The clerkly and respectably labouring classes were the heart of Hackney. Outright slums and filthy factories intruded into the SE corner, around Hackney Wick, but the bulk of the place was a commuter suburb for the great army of London's ordinary people.

Today Hackney council makes great and justified play of the area's poverty. But not all Hackney is poor. The 'gentrification' process has formed virtual islands of owner-occupation amid the council estates. A vociferous campaign against incoming 'yuppies' gave the area some notoriety in 1987, but the row seems, in retrospect, to have been more the creation of Fleet St than Hackney. Locals say there were only a dozen involved, and that tension has now eased. Most of the newcomers find the place a happy mixture of inner-city scruffiness and enlivening bustle. That is because, perhaps, the typical newcomer is a computer programmer, a social worker, a secretary or a teacher rather than a stockbroker (though 1988 saw more City people arriving). Hackney equals affordable homes for thousands of London's less well-paid young couples. It is noticeable, though, that local estate agents make much of secure car parking if such an amenity can be offered with a house or a new flats development.

Hackney, with its satellites such as Clapton and Dalston, is a large cosmopolitan area that offers most types of housing. Hackney may be poor and crowded, but it has a high percentage of parkland for inner London. Some areas stand out as attractive for home-buyers, usually because they are close to these parks but primarily because they have some surviving 19th-century homes. Properties around London Fields and Victoria Park are popular and, among the regulation 19th century terraces, some grander Victoriana and even some Georgian corners survive. The De Beauvoir area, W of the busy *Kingsland Rd*, carries a premium as it is near the border with fashionable Islington (which see) and has an N1 postal address.

Victoria Park, declared an outstanding conservation area by the Secretary of

State for the Environment, is divided between Hackney and the neighbouring borough of Tower Hamlets. The park forms part of Hackney's boundary while the River Lea provides the border with Waltham Forest to the E, with Islington to the W and Haringey to the N – and a site for smart new waterside developments (who needs Docklands?). Hackney Marshes is marshland no longer, but is another large area of welcoming greenery – its flat expanse makes for excellent football pitches. Properties around here can be much cheaper. The Marshes are in the SE part of Clapton; further N is Springfield Park, a much more attractive hilly area with Springfield Marina and City Orient Rowing Club on the Rive Lea. The *Ridley Rd* market area of Dalston, leading to busy *Kingsland High St*, is less enticing.

Hackney Central

The central spine of Hackney is the N-S road variously named *Mare St* and *Lower Clapton Rd*. Here are the Town Hall, one of the area's few wine bars, the famous Russian baths and Hackney Central station. Hackney Downs BR, with trains to Liverpool Street, is close by. Off *Lower Clapton Rd* is *Clapton Square*, a conservation area and one of several garden squares in Hackney. It is surrounded by various Georgian listed terraced houses, some of five storeys. The square leads on to *Clarence Place* and *Clapton Passage*, which both have a charming village feel and desirable period homes, large impressive 3-storied and ivy-clad terraced Georgian houses graced with entrance steps, railings and tiny wrought-iron balconies. This whole network of streets forms a green oasis in the midst of Hackney. The prices – a grade II listed Georgian house in *Clarence Place* can be had for £140,000-£150,000 – go a long way to explaining why Hackneyites are so possessive about their neighbourhood. West of the Duke of Clarence pub, at the junction with *Clarence Rd*, is the Pembury council estate which includes *Hindrey Rd*, *Shellness Rd*, *Bodney Rd*, *Pembury Rd*, *Dalston Lane* and *Downs Park Rd*.

From the southern edge of the estate *Amhurst Rd*, a busy bus route, leads back SE to the *Mare St* shopping centre. The Aspland council estate lies along part of *Amhurst Rd*. To the S of the railway serving Hackney Central, *Graham Rd*, another busy main road, provides good business for estate agents with numerous 3-storey terraced houses, some with basements, on both sides. A good number have been converted into flats. On the E side of *Lower Clapton Rd*, opposite *Clapton Passage*, more 2- and 3-storey Victoriana can be found in *Powerscroft Rd* and *Glenarm Rd*, near Hackney Police Station.

Another street worth a second glance in central Hackney is *Sutton Place*, backing onto the grounds of St John's Church, S of *Lower Clapton Rd*. This is another conservation area, with big Georgian listed terraced houses with steps, railings and basements. Several were bought about five years ago by intrepid DIY converters and turned into superb homes. The land behind these houses has been developed as *Sutton Square*. This is described by a local as 'an inward-looking social fortress'. It was conceived as an up-market development and is built around central gardens, with a courtyard and illuminated fountains. Recent resale prices have been: £65,000 for a 1-bed flat, £120,000 for a 3-bed, 2-bath house.

Other attractive streets in central Hackney include *Mehetabel Rd* and *Isabella Rd*. The former has well-preserved artisan cottages, while the houses in the latter are grander in scale. Both streets are S of *Sutton Place*.

H

Victoria Park

The park, laid out in 1845 conveniently in time for the Chartist rallies of 1848, is one of London's largest. It gives its name to a residential area containing some of the largest and most expensive houses in Hackney. Much of the housing is on land owned by the Crown Estate, so residents can claim to have Crown leases just like their grander counterparts in Regents Park. There are homes of all kinds, both Victorian and modern. Purpose-built flats in roads such as *Pennethorne Close*, near the Park, offer good value. Conversions of the big old houses provide flats with far more space than in higher-priced areas, and quite a number have lovely views of the Park and its several lakes. Another green space, Well Street Common, adjoins the park and provides open views for the Victorian and 1930s houses of *Meynell Rd* and *Meynell Crescent*. Homes here are priced up to £275,000 for 5 or 6 beds. In *Victoria Park Rd*, Ideal Homes refurbished six Victorian houses as 6-bed homes rather than flats, and tucked in the 'Sovereign Mews': 2- and 3-bed town houses and 1-bed flats. The disadvantage here is the lack of communications. Bethnal Green tube is a mile or so to the S and Cambridge Heath station gives access to *Liverpool St*.

Gore Rd, overlooking the N side of Victoria Park, has some of Hackney's most desirable properties. Imposing 3- and 4-storey terraced houses with steps to their front doors present a dignified front to the large and pleasant park. *Gore Rd* leads W into *Victoria Park Rd* and, at the junction with *Mare St*, a new development in *Earlston Grove* and *Northam St*. Flats and houses here are blessed with private garages – an important plus in such a busy area. A little to the N, the conservation area of *Fremont St* and *Warneford St* provides fine 2- and 3-storey mid-19th century terraced houses with basements, steps and railings. By contrast, nearby *Sharon Gardens* offers some of the few 1930s semis in the area. *Beck Rd* is also popular.

London Fields

The 26 acres of London Fields, successively sheep-pasture and cricket pitch, are the centre of a neighbourhood W of *Mare St* and N of the canal which is beginning to shadow De Beauvoir to the W in popularity. Here are streets of solid, readily-modernised houses which are popular with young couples. Impressive 4-storey Victorian terraced houses, some converted into flats, are found in *Lansdowne Drive*, W of London Fields. *Mapledene Rd* and *Lavender Grove* have smaller but attractive homes. To the N, *Navarino Grove* has neat flat-fronted terraced cottages. A development called The Old Vicarage, a conversion of a Victorian gothic parsonage beside the Fields, offers lavish flats with period features. The E side of London Fields is far less attractive with industrial units and London Fields BR station. *Middleton Rd*, *Albion Drive* and *Shrubland Rd* border the Fields council estate, but these roads too have pleasant 2/3-storey flat-fronted Victorian houses, some with 120 ft gardens. To the W, the conservation area of *Albion Square* is one of the finest garden squares in Hackney. Early 19th century semi-detached houses with pretty gardens lie away from the main traffic route.

Clapton

Clapton is an area to the N and E of Hackney on ground rising up from the Lea Valley. There are more streets of Victorian and Edwardian housing, modern council estates and an attractive park in the far N of the area, Springfield Park. Near the junction of *Lea Bridge Rd* and *Lower Clapton Rd*, two of the area's busiest thoroughfares, are *Thistlewaite Rd*, *Thornby Rd*, *Newick Rd*, and *Fletching Rd*: a cache of large 2- and 3-storey Victorian terraced houses in tree-lined streets. Among other corners worth noting is *Ashenden Rd*, W of Homerton Hospital in the SE of the district. This street includes Tower Mews, a warehouse converison of flats that have kept some of the original features. Parking space is provided in a tidy courtyard. Homes in the hilly Springfield Park area of Clapton, E of the Clapton Common conservation area, have the added attraction of the nearby River Lea. North of the park is *Watermint Quay*, on the river and reached via *Craven Walk*. This is a facing pair of terraces set end-on to the river towpath, with 77 houses and 18 flats at the river end. The houses have 33ft basements running the full length of the house, which can be used as play areas, storage or cellarage. 4-bed houses sell for around £150,000. Just to the S, rows of 2-storey Victorian terraced houses in *Spring Hill* lead down directly to the Lea with its Springfield Marina and City Orient Rowing Club. Similar homes are in *Lingwood Rd* and *Overlea Rd*.

Overlooking Clapton Common is *Clapton Terrace*, where large Georgian terraced houses with basements and big gardens give respite from the prevailing 19th century rows. By contrast, some of Clapton's cheaper properties are found to the S beside Hackney Marshes which also border the River Lea. Riverside Walk, a new development by Wimpey in *Mount Pleasant Hill*, has 1- and 2-bed flats. Close by, the massive Kingsmead council estate, encircled by *Kingsmead Way*, has just been renovated. The last year has seen renewed interest in the Lower Clapton/Homerton area. Homerton BR station (N. London Link line) is an asset. *Victoria Mews*, off *Swinnerton St*, is a new Fairview Homes scheme with flats and 3- and 4-bed houses (£68-125,000). In Hackney Wick, E of the A102(M), Kentish Homes has redeveloped a riverside factory site as 'Leabank Square': flats and houses from £61,000. The 3-acre site is off *Berkshire Rd*.

H

Dalston

Dalston is N of the London Fields neighbourhood, W of Hackney central and on the borders with Stoke Newington and Islington. *Ridley Rd* market, where anything and everything can be bought, is one of Dalston's best-known landmarks. The bustling market leads to more shops in busy *Kingsland High St* and the surrounding streets reflect the area's cosmopolitan image. Dalston Kingsland BR station is in *Kingsland High St*. *Downs Park Rd*, *Cecilia Rd*, *Ferncliff Rd* and *Sandringham Rd* are part of the Mountford council estate. Large 3- and 4-storey Victorian terraced houses with steps in *Sandringham Rd* and *Montague Rd*. *Colveston Crescent*, another of the streets around St Mark's Church, has more massive 4-storey Victorian houses. *Chester Gate*, a new development off *Ridley Rd*, provides some relief. Impressive 2-and 3-bed 3-storey houses are well sited away from through traffic. Dalston Cross shopping centre, off Dalston Lane, has just opened. Off *Wilton Way*, new homes have been built in *Walkers Court*. 'Independent Place' is a new work-homes development off *Shacklewell Lane*.

Among those estate agents active in this area are:
- Alan Selby & Ptnrs
- Strettons
- Winkworths
- Shaw & Co

Hammersmith

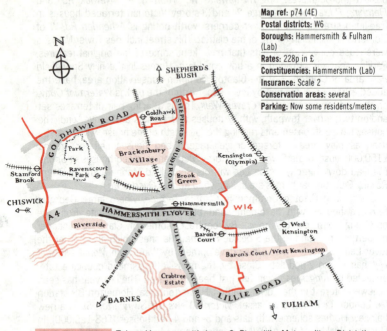

Map ref: p74 (4E)
Postal districts: W6
Boroughs: Hammersmith & Fulham (Lab)
Rates: 228p in £
Constituencies: Hammersmith (Lab)
Insurance: Scale 2
Conservation areas: several
Parking: Now some residents/meters

Transport	Tubes: Hammersmith (zone 2, Piccadilly, Metropolitan, District); West Kensington (zone 2, District); Barons Court (zone 2, Piccadilly, District). See also map. From Hammersmith to: Oxford Circus 25 min (1 change); City 35 min (1 change); Heathrow 40 min.	
Convenient for	Heathrow via M4, roads to the West. Miles from centre: 4.	
Schools	ILEA Division 1: Hammersmith School, St Edmund's, Sacred Heart (g). Private: St Paul's (g), Goldolphin & Latymer (g). Latymer (b).	

Flats	S	1b	2b	3b	4b	5b
Average prices	70–75	75–90	90–135	115–160+	150+	170+
Houses	2b	3b	4b	5b	6/7b	8b
Average prices	130	140–200	180–275+	230–350+	350+	–

The properties Very mixed but Victorian terraces predominate. Beautiful old riverside homes, modern flats, some new flats and houses. Many converted flats. Thames-side industrial giving way to luxury new developments towards Fulham border.

The market BBC work-force and City commuters keep the turnover brisk. Riverside homes scarce and expensive. Good location (tubes, M4 to airport) and BBC relocation to nearby Shepherd's Bush underpin house and flat markets. Local searches: 2 weeks.

Area Profile

The most outstanding thing about Hammersmith is how *everyday* it is. The whole area is average, apart from the presence of the prestigious Lyric Theatre on *King St* (and perhaps the Riverside Studios near *Queen Caroline St*, whose productions receive a lot of national media attention). In Hammersmith, the luxury properties (with a few well-known exceptions) are not that luxurious; and the down-market bits are not slums. It is a built-up borough, but, thanks partly to the river, not that claustrophobic. Its position in West London, on the way to Heathrow, means it suffers from heavy traffic, but public transport is good.

Hammersmith would be a large square on the map, if not for the curving Thames, which bites off the south-west corner. As it is, the boundaries are: *Goldhawk Rd* to the W and N, the river and *Lillie Rd* to the S, and to the E the borough boundary – reinforced by the much more physical barrier of the railway which runs N-S. Within this square lies Hammersmith proper (essentially the W6 postal district), Baron's Court and West Kensington. The latter, with Kensington's name but in Hammersmith's borough, is always good for confusing outsiders.

Hammersmith Broadway has been the focus of a classic local government conflict, which only goes to show how important the political complexion of your local council can be when it comes to property market developments in an area. Basically, the old Conservative council, convinced that Hammersmith Broadway needed a revamp at all costs (it does), gave planning permission for a £100 million town centre redevelopment on a site owned by LRT.

Shortly afterwards, however, Labour gained control of the council and slapped a conservation order on Hammersmith Broadway island, thus suspending plans to build a bus/tube interchange and high rise office complex on the site. This meant that developers Bredero, a Dutch construction company, had to apply for consent before any building within the area could be demolished. They appealed against the order and The Secretary of State for the Environment found in their favour, despite his own inspector's recommendation to the contrary. But following talks with the local MP, council and community groups, Bredero revised their plans. The amended scheme for offices, shops, restaurants, a bus terminal and a community centre has been welcomed by local people. Hammersmith Broadway will always be a very busy traffic interchange, but with luck the 20-year row about it will now end and the island site will acquire some more attractive buildings.

An upward swing in Hammersmith prices is now inevitable. And the BBC's plans to move Broadcasting House from the West End to White City have already led to increased interest in Hammersmith as a spillover residential area (neighbouring Shepherd's Bush is already full of BBC personnel because of the studios there).

A relief road, running from Shepherd's Bush along the Olympia line, past *Sinclair Rd*, past *Avonmore Rd*, to Fulham via West Brompton ... and eventually into Wandsworth, has been on the cards since 1914. An area of roughly 64 feet on either side of the planned road has been 'safeguarded' so that no development can take place there. With *North End Rd* and all main roads in the area getting busier and busier, a relief road will definitely improve the area (although it is affecting the prices of properties immediately on either side).

Yet again, this has led to a Tory (Kensington & Chelsea)/Labour (Hammersmith & Fulham) conflict. The Labour anti-relief road lobby sees itself

H

as a champion of the ordinary people whose lives will be disrupted by the building of a road. Searches are now being carried out, but some local estate agents say: 'Don't hold your breath … even if they could afford to buy all the houses in the way, even if the public enquiry was over and done with, even if the building started next month, the road will take another l0 years at least to materialise.' See, however, 'Transport' chapter. WEIR, as the road is acronymed, is a front-runner in the build new roads through London campaign. Perhaps because of the existing A4 and the planned WEIR, Hammersmith comes off lightly in the more long-term planning studies for new highways across south and west London.

Most common in the Hammersmith area are small 1- and 2-bedroomed flats; most in demand, overall, are flats with two large rooms. Unattractive, down-market modern office developments are dotted over the entire borough (it is estimated that these will attract an extra 3,000-5,000 people to Hammersmith over the next three years). Neighbourhoods with the fewest office blocks are the most in demand. But it is a general (very general) rule that those who want access to Central London will opt for the east side of Hammersmith, while those who are more interested in the airport opt for the area west of *Fulham Palace/Shepherd's Bush Rds*).

Hammersmith has a low-key cosmopolitan character and all social classes and most races are represented here; but there are no high concentrations of individual groups. Hammersmith divides fairly neatly into the following districts:

Barons Court/West Kensington (W14)

Fulham Palace Rd is the boundary to the W; *Hammersmith Rd* to the N; *Lillie Rd* to the S; the railway line to the E. The whole district is bisected by the A4 *Talgarth Rd*. The majority of buildings consist of 19th and early 20th-century houses converted into flats.

W14 is truly a hotch-potch, although most properties are Victorian. On almost every road there is a building that won't please the aesthetically-inclined, though council properties are not sprawling. The nearest park is Holland Park and foliage is in very short supply indeed. This is flatland. Those who can afford much larger properties might not want to live here: the least they will tend to aspire to is the more affluent Brook Green district (to the N). If they have the funds, they might well head for somewhere altogether less middle-market in tone than this neighbourhood. Although prices nudging half a million pounds have been fetched for properties in this area, this is far from typical.

So flats prevail. But floorspace is limited and little 2-bedroomed apartments are the norm: usually one large bedroom and a much smaller one. Three-bedroomed flats are rare, but occasionally they can be constructed out of the top two floors of a house, because, in this neighbourhood, one floor more often than not simply won't accomodate more than one or two rooms. North of *Talgarth Rd*, the 2-bedroomed flats are more spacious, but 3-bed places are still scarce.

A particularly popular segment of Barons Court/West Kensington is the grid bordered by *Gledstanes Rd*, *North End Rd*, *Barons Court Rd* and *Star Rd*. This district is popular because of its closeness to both Barons Court and West Kensington tube stations. People who don't even live in this neighbourhood flock to these stations and sometimes park nearby; so parking is a problem. It is worth noting that parking spaces are free to all: residents' permits are not issued in this area.

This *Gledstanes Rd* grid, thanks to the nearby A4, also offers relatively easy car access to Heathrow airport, the City and the West End. Local estate agents say that young, as yet childless, couples aged around 20 to 40 are moving in here in a big way – into flats bought by themselves or their doting parents. But so are investors, on the lookout for high rent yields. And so also are developers, on the lookout for yet more properties to convert ... they keep finding gems in places like *Gunterstone Rd*, lined with mid/late 19th century houses. Note, as you drive westwards along the *Talgarth Rd* highway past this corner, the splendid windows of a row of High Victorian artists' studios: it's a sad irony that such windows should have inherited such a view.

The most sought-after properties in Barons Court are the red-brick Victorian houses in *Queen's Club Gardens*, just south of the famous tennis club itself. *Queen's Club Gardens*, a conservation area, has a small central park; its aura of affluence and gentility makes it an oasis in an area not renowned for exclusive residences. *Fitzgeorge/Fitzjames Avenues* and *Queen's Club Gardens* contain rare examples of the few Victorian mansion blocks available in this district.

Purpose-built projects like St Paul's Court, which started off as a council brainchild but was turned over to private investors when funds ran low, are the sort of new development that is taking place here, side by side with the perennial conversions. Along *Hammersmith Rd*, a lot of modern buildings – both commercial and residential – are being erected from scratch.

The pastel-coloured 1930s villas on

H

Hammersmith price trends 1984-88

London average home: percentage rise on previous year, adjusted for inflation.
Typical home in this area, percentage rise on previous year, adjusted for inflation.

Three-bed terraced cottage in the Brackenbury Village area, price change compared to London-wide average home. Like its neighbour Fulham, price rises here were high in the early years charted. Last year saw only a modest rise: evidence perhaps that the house was a little above the price level of first-time and sharing buyers, 1988's dominant groups.

and around *Palliser Rd* are also in great demand. The triangle enclosed by *Palliser, Barons Court* and *Barton Rds* consists of about three-quarters of an acre of communal greenery. These villas, with garages, are rarely sold.

There are a lot of council properties – on *North End Rd* itself, as well as in the less popular part of this neighbourhood, the roads leading E off *Fulham Palace Rd* (W6) such as *Greyhound Rd*. There are modern/Victorian buildings which are rather grim-looking and patchy in quality, but relatively untouched by developers so far. *Greyhound Rd* is close to the big Charing Cross Hospital.

Riverside (W6)

The thin strip of river bank bounded by the roaring traffic of the A4 *Great West Rd* to the N, *Hammersmith Bridge Rd* to the E and the borough boundary to the W is an eastward continuation of Chiswick Mall. The river, here suddenly smaller-looking and more rural than in central London, runs to the S.

This slice of Hammersmith is the exception that proves the rule: as with neighbouring Chiswick Mall, some of London's rare surviving Georgian homes are here, strung along *Hammersmith Terrace* (which dates from the 1750s) and *Upper* and *Lower Malls*. The *Terrace's* homes have no road separating them from the river, but the two *Malls* are a little more public than the corresponding Chiswick stretch. Still, this most affluent and desirable corner of Hammersmith has estate agents reaching for words such as 'ambassadorial'. When the riverside houses do come onto the market (which is hardly ever), they can be snapped up for as much as £1.2 million. Two notable Georgian *Upper Mall* houses, Kelmscott House and Sussex House, were sold in 1988. Asking price for the first, once the home of William Morris, was £775,000; for the second £850,000. There is also one of the nicest, oldest riverside pubs, The Dove, originally a Georgian coffee-house. Because of a low tide, houseboats are not very much in evidence until you go further up the river towards Chiswick.

Just N of the riverside and just south of *King St* (Hammersmith's centre, complete with every type of high street retail outlet one could need, as well as a very useful shopping mall), is *St Peter's Square*, a conservation area that is full of unusually large (for Hammersmith), handsome stucco-fronted houses (5-6 bedrooms). These were built around 1825-30 in sub-Belgravia mode, and the surrounding streets of more modest houses are plainly of the same date.

Brackenbury Village

North of Hammersmith's shopping centre, this neighbourhood is bounded by *Paddenswick Rd*, *Hammersmith Grove*, *Glenthorne Rd* and *Goldhawk Rd*. It is a newly up-and-coming area with a delightful village atmosphere: little shops, pretty, unspoilt (and relatively undiscovered) Victorian street-corner pubs with hanging baskets, pavement seating or gardens. There is very little through traffic, but already a bit of a parking problem during the daytime with commuters and local people in these pretty streets – and at night with the residents' cars. Generally the homes are small 2- and 3-bedroom early Victorian terraced cottages and small villas on the western side of the area (for example *Carthew Rd, Cardross St* and *Dalling Rd*). A few larger houses are found towards the E on the streets leading to *Hammersmith Grove*. In the NW, *Greengate Rd*, *Wellesley Avenue* and *Dorville Crescent* are on the fringe of the Ravenscourt Park conservation area and are seen by their residents as being part of Ravenscourt Park. These very pretty streets contain early Victorian terraced houses or villas with many delightful features. And buyers, especially young couples, want them at their asking prices of about £165,000-£175,000 for 2-bedroom cottage type houses – and considerably more for the larger houses and those in the conservation area. The growing demand from the BBC in Shepherds Bush – more prosperous BBC persons are moving out from central London – seems certain to maintain the popularity of this area.

Ravenscourt Park

To the W of Brackenbury, on the Chiswick border, this neighbourhood is bounded by *Goldhawk Rd*, *King St* and *Paddenswick Rd*. Most of it falls within a conservation area centred around Ravenscourt Park itself, formerly the grounds of a fine 18th-century house bombed during the war. All that is left now are delightful gardens and formal lake, a pretty coach house (used as a tea house) and rather splendid gates. There are also a number of leisure facilities (including tennis courts) available for the locals to use.

Look for property backing onto the Park, for example along *Ravenscourt Rd* and *Goldhawk Rd*. There are pockets of pretty 18th- and 19th-century villas and terraces (*Ravenscourt Park, Ravenscourt Gardens, Hamlet Gardens*) and a rather pretty square (*Ravenscourt Park Square*) which has some lovely houses on three sides – the fourth side open to the park. There is not a great deal of residential accommodation in this area, since land is taken up either by the park or the Queen Charlotte's Hospital complex. The park is geared to children, which is not surprising: Queen Charlotte's is one of London's foremost maternity hospitals. On the fringes of Ravenscourt Park, it is worth looking at *Wingate Rd* (already mentioned under Brackenbury Village), *Dorvill Crescent* and *Wellesley Avenue*; and to the N on the other side of the *Goldhawk Rd*, (but still in the conservation area), *Ashchurch Park Villas, Rylett Rd* and *Ashchurch Grove, Minden Rd* and *Ashchurch Terrace*.

Ravenscourt Park has a very suburban feel to it and is more reminiscent of Chiswick's wide open spaces than of densely-packed Hammersmith. Though the two areas are neck and neck in the desirability stakes, because Brook Green (see below) is beside a commercialised thoroughfare, Ravenscourt Park has a definite edge. Besides, the houses tend to be more substantial in size and detached.

H

Brook Green

Strictly speaking 'Brook Green' consists only of *Brook Green* itself (a conservation area), plus a handful of immediately surrounding roads. But the term is often used to describe an entire area that stretches as far north as *Sinclair Gardens* and as far east as the Olympia railway complex.

Needless to say, properties on roads like *Sinclair*, which back onto the railway line, are not very popular with insomniac buyers. Prices have also suffered since the relief road plans were announced. (See 'Transport'.) But apart from properties which are bang next to the railway, the Olympia corner is not significantly less in demand than any other part of Hammersmith.

This area contains many larger terraced properties, frequently converted into 1- and 2-bedroomed flats. These houses often have semi-basement or garden-level flats which have the advantage of large back gardens, often with mature trees. In some cases, the semi-basement and ground floor are combined to form a more substantial maisonette. High-ceilinged rooms with ornate plasterwork on the ground floors are attractive features. Look out for property in *Addison Grove, Bolingbroke Rd, Milson Rd, Hofland Rd, Irving Rd* and *Lakeside Rd. Blythe Rd*, running E-W through the area, is up-and-coming. The final batch of flats at 8-storey Kensington West, a new luxury apartment block at the Hammersmith Rd end of *Blythe Rd*, are due to be released this spring. The 91 1-5-bedroom flats, including six penthouses, range in price from £160,000-£785,000. A sports complex is included in the development. The same firm, Brook Green Developments, was responsible for Windsor Way, 200 top-of-the-market houses and flats just round the corner.

Brook Green proper, despite its smaller houses and location just off the less than salubrious *Shepherd's Bush Rd*, is just as popular with house- and apartment-hunters as Ravenscourt Park. The scattered family houses overlooking the Green are splendid, and highly prized, but the neighbourhood on the whole is another outpost of flatland. And even good-sized mansion blocks are thin on the ground.

Detached houses are scarce. Developers are getting to them before eager private buyers can, and are chopping them up into smaller units (a good-sized Victorian terraced building with 5 storeys can be converted into five decent flats or 10 modest-sized studios).

At the southernmost end of the Brook Green area, near Olympia and fronting on to *Hammersmith Rd*, is the Collet Court site (formerly a private school). Notting Hill Housing Trust bought this with a view to a homes development, but have now sold it on: it is now likely to be primarily, if not entirely, commercial.

Crabtree Estate

This neighbourhood, built between 1910 and 1930, used to be predominantly industrial, but more and more homes – some luxurious by Hammersmith standards – are becoming available as Crabtree changes its image (signs of former industrial use are disappearing). The neighbourhood runs from *Hammersmith Bridge Rd* beside the river to *Crabtree Lane*, with *Fulham Palace Rd* as the E boundary. Leading the new developments is the Richard Rogers-designed Thames Reach complex, whose living roooms have floor-to-ceiling glass on the river side, giving them wide, uninterrupted views across to Barnes Reservoir and the picturesque Harrods Depository building. If, as has been rumoured, this too becomes flats – well, the river's wide enough for neither side to need net curtains.

Another riverside scheme is Chancellor's Wharf, a £10 million development of eight 5-storey town houses and 32 flats in *Crisp Rd*, just downstream from the bridge and the Riverside Studios. These, in the words of the developers, boast 'dramatic brick-clad elevations, slightly nautical in appearance, with large porthole windows....' Prices for the flats start at about £150,000 (2 bedroom) and the 4-bedroomed houses at £325,000.

Proposals for further riverside development are in the pipeline for the old Britvic Corona site in *Rannoch Rd.* Barclay's Bank and O & H Construction are planning a mixed residential/light industrial complex.

Among those estate agents active in this area are:
- Barnard Marcus
- Druce & Co
- James Anthony
- Marsh & Parsons
- Prudential Property Services
- Winkworths

Hampstead

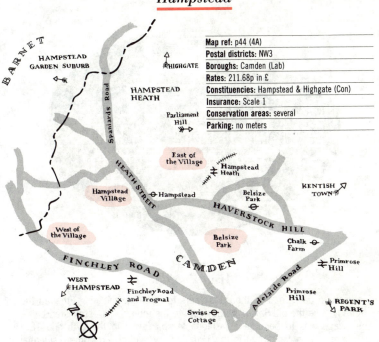

Map ref: p44 (4A)	
Postal districts: NW3	
Boroughs: Camden (Lab)	
Rates: 211.68p in £	
Constituencies: Hampstead & Highgate (Con)	
Insurance: Scale 1	
Conservation areas: several	
Parking: no meters	

H

Transport Tubes: Hampstead (zone 2/3), Belsize Park (zone 2), both Northern Line. From Hampstead to: Oxford Circus 20 min, (1 change), Bank 25 min, Heathrow: 1 hr 10 min (1 change). BR: Hampstead Heath, Primrose Hill, both North London Line. To Liverpool St: 20 min

Convenient for Hampstead Heath; M1, A1 to North. Miles from centre: 4

Schools ILEA Division 2. Hampstead School, Haverstock School. Private: University College School (b), South Hampstead High School (g)

Flats	S	1b	2b	3b	4b	5b
Average prices	70–80	90–140	125–250+	175–350	275–650	350+
Houses	2b	3b	4b	5b	6/7b	8b
Average prices	200–300	300–400	400–600+	500+	500–1.5m	500–2m+

The properties Georgian gems in heart of village and scattered among the surrounding gracious streets. New developments, generally towards Heath, are luxury-level: some innovative, some merely opulent. Victoriana reasserts itself down the hill towards Belsize Park.

The market Everyone wants to live here. Prices now stabilised having trebled in five years. Prices rise, with the hill, to ultra-luxury level: figures above reflect the wide spread of quality. Record in the Village: £3.5 million for Frognal house in early '88. Local searches: 12 weeks.

Area Profile

Hampstead dates back a thousand years to 986AD when King Ethelred the Unready gave the old Saxon 'homestead' to the monks of Westminster. Later, the village was to become a fashionable spa resort in the 17th and 18th centuries, a popular retreat in the 19th century, and now a prime residential area, its main attractions being its elevation above the smog of the city, and its proximity to the famous 800 acres of Hampstead Heath.

Hampstead deserves its reputation for prosperous intellectualism. Hardly a writer of note is published who does not live here, through the pressure on the intelligentsia's pockets has become intense as the merely wealthy have come after a share of the Hampstead charm. There is, nevertheless, still a strong community feeling about the way Hampstead looks. Residents resisted the advent of a MacDonalds some years ago by means of a heavily-supported campaign. Once roused, they are a force to be reckoned with.

Hampstead Village

One of London's most desirable residential areas, ranging from wide, leafy avenues with imposing detached Victorian mansions to classically picturesque, almost mediaeval lanes, squares and cul-de-sacs packed with a fascinating variety of architectural styles dating back 300 years and more – many with famous historical and literary connections.

Recent years have seen Hampstead very much a sellers' market, with demand far outstripping supply, and this resulted in property price rises probably not matched in any but the most exclusive areas of London. Values have nearly trebled in the last five years, but have now stabilised, say the agents. This has meant, inevitably, that the population has changed, as more traditional inhabitants are squeezed (or tempted) out by the high prices, and the proportion of high income professionals, businesspeople and foreign investors increases.

The population contains a remarkably high proportion of artists, writers, actors, musicians, diplomats and professionals, and the shopping centre reflects the cosmopolitan flavour of the area with many fashion boutiques, specialist food shops, bookshops, restaurants of all descriptions and some celebrated pubs, like the Flask and the Hollybush. Difficult to buy a needle and thread here, though.

From *Hampstead High St*, streets like *Gayton Rd* and *Flask Walk* (home of Hampstead's second-hand bookshops) lead to the old spa area where roads named *Well Rd* and *Well Walk* reflect the old attraction. Here, too, is Burgh House, the Grade I listed mansion built in 1702, now a community centre, art gallery and local history museum. The Everyman cinema is in *Holly Bush Vale*; with its daily changing programme it's a favourite of impoverished students and Hampstead's arty residents.

Houses in this area are mainly Georgian, Edwardian and Victorian terraces, the majority of which have been converted into flats. But there are still the occasional large and medium-sized detached and semi-detached houses in secluded streets like *New End*, *Cannon Place* and *Christchurch Hill*, where you'll find the New End Theatre. All the prices, however, reflect the area's close proximity (across *East Heath Rd*) to Hampstead Heath. Particularly attractive is the *Gainsborough Gardens* private estate, off *Well Walk*, a ring of houses on its own circular access road. Mansion block flats in The Pryors and Bell Moor, literally overlooking the Heath, are reckoned an excellent investment.

H

The other main road through the village is *Heath St* leading, on the N side, to the upper part of the old town, with beautiful houses in tightly packed squares such as *Golden Yard* and *The Mount Square*, and delightful secluded streets including *Windmill Hill*, *Hampstead Grove* and *Admiral's Walk*, with its unusually shaped houses with naval names. This area is a stone's throw from Whitestone Pond (next to the famous Jack Straw's Castle pub) which, at 440 feet, is the highest point in London. Generations of children have taken donkey rides here. Some of the houses have spectacular views over the city. Hawthorne House, a former nursing home in *Upper Terrace*, is now being replaced by a new block of 12 luxury flats, which are expected to be completed by February 1990.

The potential for other new developments of any size is limited by the extreme scarcity of available land, but there are currently two very large housing schemes on the cards – both involving former NHS hospitals. At the time of writing, developers Berkely House are embroiled in a planning row with Camden Council over its plans to build some 82 flats mainly in new blocks on the site of New End Hospital, off *Heath St*. Plans are being resisted by local residents and the council has turned down the first planning application. The company, however, is likely to succeed on appeal. A development of more than 50 homes is also envisaged on the site of The Elms (later a NHS hospice called St Columba's) almost in the heart of Hampstead Heath off *Spaniards Rd*. The bait for Camden is that the developers are offering to add two acres of land to the Heath if they get planning permission. They also intend to restore the badly run-down listed building. A third site, the old Mount Vernon Hospital in *Holly Hill*, is being vacated by its owners and will be redeveloped.

Heath St also leads, on the S side, to the splendid Queen Anne terraces in *Church Row*, past the ancient St John's parish church and *Frognal Gardens*, to *Frognal* – one of the oldest roads in Hampstead, and the site of University College School. There are some magnificent hidden 'pan handle' properties in this area. Further S are the very large houses in *Fitzjohns Avenue*, many of which have been converted into schools, B&B hotels and clinics. *Maresfield Gardens* also has large houses, the new Freud Museum in the house where Sigmund Freud died in 1941, and UCS's sister school South Hampsted High.

Look out, too, for terraced houses and flats in the *Vale of Health*, an exclusive enclave on the Heath itself. Once known as Hatche's Bottom, the land was drained in 1777 and a few of the houses, including an erstwhile hunting lodge on the market last year for £1.75 million, are Georgian. There are some new flats being built on one of the old fairground sites in the Vale.

West of the Village

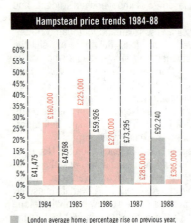

Hampstead price trends 1984-88

60%
55%
50%
45%
40%
35%
30%
25%
20%
15%
10%
5%
0%
-5%

£41,475 · £160,000 (1984) · £47,698 · £225,000 (1985) · £59,926 · £270,000 (1986) · £73,295 · £285,000 (1987) · £92,240 · £305,000 (1988)

London average home: percentage rise on previous year, adjusted for inflation.

Typical home in this area, percentage rise on previous year, adjusted for inflation.

Three-bed converted flat in the Hollycroft Road area, price change compared to London-wide average home. Prices in Hampstead have risen only moderately since 1985's big leap. In '87 and '88 this example only just beat inflation, another example of expensive homes doing less well last year.

These are the quiet, tree-lined avenues bounded by *West Heath Rd*, *Platts Lane*, *Finchley Rd* and *Arkwright Rd*, which have attracted so much attention from developers as it becomes more and more difficult for individual families to maintain large Victorian mansions. A steady stream of luxury flat conversions in this area will continue to be available for some years to come. There is some resistance, however, from existing residents against planning applications to demolish or convert the existing houses into flats.

A good example of the level of developments here is the 13 spectacular flats built on the corner of *West Heath Rd* and *Templewood Avenue*. Living rooms average 45 x 30ft, and the flats share a swimming pool – except for the 6,000 sq ft duplex, which has its own in a 50ft leisure complex. Similar schemes are destined to come onto the market in a steady stream. For instance, 20 flats with underground parking are being built in *West Heath Rd* in a development by St George called 'Portman Heights'. 1-bed flats from £199,000 2- and 3-bed up to £340,000. Ready this summer. Fairclough Homes have now built five opulent detached family homes in the *Westover Hill* enclave, with a swimming pool apiece, staff quarters, state-of-the-art appliances and air conditioning ... All sold for £1.3-1.7m.

The biggest houses – some positively ambassadorial – are in *West Heath Rd*, directly opposite the West Heath, all with price tags well in excess of £1 million. Most remarkable, near the junction with *Platts Lane*, is 'Sarum Chase', which Pevsner described as 'unashamed Hollywood Tudor'.

But there are also houses of all sizes and in all conditions in roads such as *Redington Gardens*, *Heath Drive*, *Hollycroft Avenue*, *Ferncroft Avenue*, *Templewood Avenue* and *Greenaway Gardens*, some with very large gardens. *Chesterford Gardens* has a particularly fine terrace of houses, as does

Redington Rd, an extremely graceful curving street which links *West Heath Rd* with *Frognal*. The Firecrest development, between *West Heath Rd* and *Templewood Avenue*, has exciting modern houses and flats on a beautiful, wooded site. The two largest houses have their own basement pools.

These roads also have easy access to *Finchley Rd* which runs N to connect with the M1 and A1, and S through St John's Wood and Regents Park to the West End. Bus services along the *Finchley Rd* are good and it's a short hop to Golders Green or Finchley Rd tubes.

East of the Village

Willow Rd and *Willoughby Rd* lead past pleasant Victorian terraced roads, now almost exclusively converted into flats and maisonettes, down the hill to what is sometimes known as the Downshire Hill triangle, comprising *Downshire Hill, Keats Grove* and *South End Rd*. One of the most elegant (and sought-after) areas in Hampstead. *Downshire Hill* has a pleasing number of stuccoed brick houses dating from the early 19th century, the majority of which have remained as single family houses. They are nearly all listed Grade III, and as a group they are listed Grade II as being of 'considerable merit'. *Keats Grove* contains lovely Keats House, now a public library and museum.

H

Further down the hill is *South End Green* shopping centre, Hampstead Heath BR Station (with North London Line trains eastwards to Liverpool Street and the City, and W to Richmond and Kew) and a three-screen Cannon cinema, giving access to *Pond St* and the giant, modern, Royal Free Hospital.

Also off *South End Green* is the attractive enclave of streets reached only via *South Hill Park* which contain a mixture of family houses and flat conversions, as well as a few post-war purpose-built blocks of flats in Parliament Hill. The chief attraction here is the lack of through-traffic and the instant access to the Heath and Parliament Hill itself. Most popular are the houses on the N side of *South Hill Park* which overlook the Hampstead Ponds on the Heath. Trying to find a parking place in this area can be a frustrating experience.

The streets around *Constantine Rd*, *Fleet Rd* and *Agincourt Rd* comprise the less expensive end of Hampstead, with a good mix of terraced houses and flat conversions, and many opportunities to acquire properties that have become run-down. Developers are active in this area too.

Also interesting, although not as reasonably priced, are *Parkhill Rd, Upper Park Rd* and *Lawn Rd*, which has a mixture of flat conversions, family houses and some modern council estates. The architecturally famous Isokon Flats block is in *Lawn Rd*, but is now owned by Camden Council.

Belsize Park

Originally from the French 'Bel Assis' ('beautifully situated'), Belsize Park was once regarded as the less desirable end of Hampstead, but now has a character and atmosphere all its own. It has two shopping centres, around the Belsize Park underground station in *Haverstock Hill*, and in what has become known as 'Belsize Village' in *Belsize Lane*, which also has some attractive mews developments and the arty Screen on the Hill cinema. The population density is high, and the streets can become very congested, but the architecture is charming and the typical Belsize Park flat will have generous-sized rooms and gloriously high ceilings. But like everywhere else in Hampstead, family-sized detached and semi-detached houses are becoming very scarce indeed.

The dominant road is *Belsize Avenue*, which runs from *Haverstock Hill* all the way to the Swiss Cottage end of the suburb. On the N side are the roads that lead up to the graceful, tree-lined *Lyndhurst Gardens* and *Wedderburn Rd*. On the S side, *Belsize Park*, *Belsize Park Gardens* and *Belsize Square*.

Also interesting are 'The Glens' – *Glenloch Rd*, *Glenilla Rd* and *Glenmore Rd*, only a minute or two's walk from the tube.

Englands Lane, with its own shopping centre, gives access to large houses in *Steeles Rd*, interesting terraces in secluded *Primrose Gardens*, and some new town houses in *Antrim Rd*. *Haverstock Hill* itself has a good selection of purpose-built blocks of flats, some quite modern. At its junction with *Belsize Grove*, Ideal Homes have built Egan Lodge on the site of – and in the style of – the old Elizabeth Garrett Anderson Hospital. Two-bedroom flats here are in the £164-200,000 range, 3-bed town houses c £275.

On *Belsize Lane*, Rosslyn Heights is an example of the imaginative conversion of a period house. Five out-of-the-ordinary apartments boast galleries, vaulted ceilings, conservatories and a terrace or a garden apiece.

Swiss Cottage

Long-standing Eastern European residents wistfully remember the days when Swiss Cottage was known as Schweizerhof, and they whiled away the hours drinking coffee and eating pastries in Viennese cafés like Louis. But the street market disappeared, they built a business complex, and the area lost most of its student party atmosphere and became a sharply-contrasting area between those who use the community centre and the City/estate agent types. In the last few months, Conservation Area status has enhanced the appeal.

The area took its name from the original Regency chalet-style tavern: this architectural oddity has been perpetuated by a more recent pub and restaurant complex opposite the tube station (Jubilee Line). It also has a large sports complex, one of the finest libraries in the country, a hotel, a three-screen cinema and close proximity to the thriving *Finchley Rd* shopping centre.

Much of the area – some 243 acres – was once owned by Eton College which was also responsible for a great deal of the housing development. The estate still owns a great deal of property in the area, particularly in roads like *Eton Avenue*, *Fellows Rd*, *Provost Rd* and *King Henry's Rd*. There are still large detached Victorian houses here, but most are subdivided into flats. The area gained over 100 flats and townhouses in the form of the Quadrangles development, between *Adelaide* and *Fellows Rds*.

The district is also characterised by a number of council estates and tower block developments, as well as a number of large privately-owned mansion blocks, including Regency Lodge in *Avenue Rd*, and Northways in *College Crescent*. There are some beautiful houses in the broad sweep of *Elsworthy Rd*, but the street does suffer a little from being an unofficial traffic through-route from Primrose Hill to St John's Wood. Some of the houses on the N side share a magnificent common garden with houses in *Wadham Gardens*.

Among those estate agents active in this area are:
- Anscombe & Ringland
- Benham & Reeves
- Druce
- Cluttons
- Goldschmidt and Howland
- Hamptons
- Knight Frank & Rutley
- Prudential Property
- Stickley & Kent

Hampstead Garden Suburb

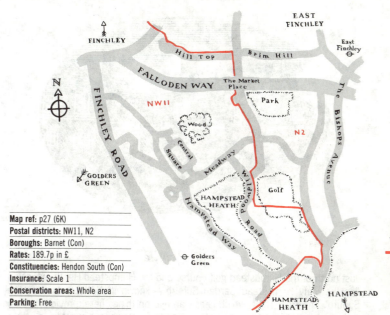

| Map ref: p27 (6K) |
| Postal districts: NW11, N2 |
| Boroughs: Barnet (Con) |
| Rates: 189.7p in £ |
| Constituencies: Hendon South (Con) |
| Insurance: Scale 1 |
| Conservation areas: Whole area |
| Parking: Free |

H

Transport No British Rail or tube, but Golders Green and East Finchley tubes are nearby. H2 bus does circular route via Golders Green.

Convenient for Brent Cross Shopping Centre, Hampstead Heath, North Circular Rd. Miles from centre: 7.

Schools Barnet Education Authority: Henrietta Barnett (g), Whitefield School.

Flats	S	1b	2b	3b	4b	5b
Average prices	–	70–90	80–130	100–200+	→	–
Houses	2b	3b	4b	5b	6/7b	8b
Average prices	120–180	180–350	200–450+	350–750+	→	900+

The properties Purpose-built turn-of-century suburb mixing picturesque cottages with houses of all sizes including mansion scale. A few flats. 'Old' suburb is smaller-scale, distinguished English-picturesque. 'New' (most in N2), has less distinguished, more ostentatious larger, later houses.

The market Inhabitants include international and Jewish families. Radical, doctrinaire past now a memory. Multi-million pound properties found on fringes of area – principally in the Bishop's Avenue. These attract princes, showbiz and tycoons. Local searches: 4 weeks.

Area Profile

Just north of the Hampstead golf course and the Hampstead Heath extension lies the leafy Hampstead Garden Suburb – known in N-W London as '*The Suburb*'. The HGS Trust, which keeps an eye on things here, provides a map with the boundaries of the area clearly marked, though less punctilious estate agents claim swathes of Golders Green and East Finchley as 'HGS borders'.

The Hampstead Garden Suburb came into existence at the beginning of the century; it was carefully designed by architects Parker, Unwin and Lutyens but the inspiration was Dame Henrietta Barnett who intended it to be an area where people of all walks of life and all ages would live together in beautiful tree-lined streets with woods and open spaces available to all.

Consequently you find a great variety of type and style of housing in the area from the terraced cottages around *Erskine Hill* and *Hampstead Way* (where 'artisans' were to live) to the double-fronted mansions of *Winnington Rd*, built later for those who didn't need to work quite so hard. Baillie Scott's purpose-built block, Waterlow Court in *Heath Close*, was originally intended for that strange phenomenon, the working woman.

The Suburb was once inhabited largely by eccentrics, 'crazy, freakish people', observed The Times, not mincing matters, but today its residents are much like those in the rest of N-W London – though probably rather richer. There are many Jewish inhabitants, and also Americans and South Africans who love the feeling of space here. Plot sizes are certainly larger than those in Hampstead, on the other side of the Heath.

Market Place, along the *Falloden Way*, provides some (expensive) shopping and a welter of estate agents, but you have to drive down to Golders Green/Temple Fortune or up to East Finchley for most things. There's a well-concealed post office along *Lyttelton Rd*, a library, schools, churches, a synagogue and – the Suburb's pride and joy – the Institute on *Central Square*, which is as old as the Suburb itself. Founded in the spirit of self-improvement, it's where you can take courses in everything from photography to pottery and where your au pair (this is very much au pair country) can learn English.

Suburb residents tend to stay once they've lived in the area for a while, and there are always people looking to move in. It's an estate agent's dream. The houses, particularly those in the Old Suburb or NW11 area, really are 'full of character' and there's no need for agents to take advantage of artistic licence when composing details. The major roads are wide and tree-lined, and hedges rather than fences divide the plots. Little secluded closes suit those who prefer more privacy. Living in the Suburb means you're close to Kenwood House and the Heath for summer walks and concerts, yet just seven miles from the centre of London, combining the advantages of both town and country.

When it comes to disadvantages the major one, apart from the price of property, is transport. Neither Golders Green nor East Finchley stations are close by and teenagers who don't drive or have access to a car are apt to feel stranded. There are certainly no amenities for them in the Suburb itself, though the area is great for small children. The Suburb mini-bus, the H2, does a circular tour from Golders Green station – prospective buyers might invest 50p on a round trip to see the area. Ask the driver to stop when you see a house you like the look of: he'll stop anywhere along his route.

Parking in the Old Suburb, which is full of closes and cul-de-sacs, can be problematic – particularly as few of the houses were built with garages. Residents in *Willifield Way* often have to resort to parking on the pavement, much to the fury of Barnet council officials. Residents were not intended to have carriages or cars – especially the 'contented artisans' the founders hoped would populate the suburb alongside the middle classes.

Depending on which way you look at it, another possible disadvantage of the area is that it is a conservation area and you have to apply to the Trust (862 Finchley Rd NW11 6AB) as well as to Barnet borough before making any alterations to your property – even if you own the freehold. Wily residents in need of extra living space have been known to develop very luxurious 'garages'. On the other hand, you can be sure that the character of the area and the price of property in it won't be massacred by unscrupulous types or those with a penchant for modern, incongruous architecture. Not that the Trust's is a lone voice: a proposed development near Hampstead Way which would be the first substantial addition to the Suburb has its would-be neighbours up in arms: see below.

H

NW11, Old Suburb

The area around Big and Little Woods and around *Central Square* and *Meadway* is known as the Old Suburb, although it is actually not that much older than the New. Generally, it covers the NW11 part of the Suburb, where the houses were built between 1907 and 1914, are full of character and are more expensive. Over 60 of them are listed.

Designed by Lutyens, *Central Square* is the heart of the suburb; a very green and peaceful centre, where you'll find neo-Georgian terraced houses and flats at prices guaranteed to give you sleepless nights. Here, too, you'll find the parish church of St Jude, the Free Church for Non-Conformist worshippers and the Institute which also accomodates the Henrietta Barnett School for Girls. In the corner of *North Square* is a Meeting House for the Society of Friends and in *South Square*, opposite St Jude's Church, is a purpose-built block where flats have only recently become available for sale. There's a memorial to Dame

Henrietta on the fourth side of the square, and one of the Suburb's many passageways (the aim was to keep pedestrian and motor traffic separate) leads down to *Willifield Way*. This is possibly the most charming road in the area, with a village green which is overlooked by Fellowship House where the over-60s meet. Many of the Suburb's younger residents attend the Garden Suburb School which is also in *Willifield Way*.

If your taste is for a cottage with roses round the door, then the roads around *Willifield Way* are where you should look. The first cottages to be built in the Suburb were at *Nos 140* and *142 Hampstead Way* in 1907. They were designed by Parker and Unwin who were strongly influenced by the Arts and Crafts Movement, hence the traditional East Anglian cottages with medieval German vernacular gable, dormers and wood window frames. Particularly charming are *Erskine* and *Asmuns Hills* where you'll find 2- and 3-bedroom cottages with pretty gardens. Some of the cottages in the Suburb are rented, a few have yet to be modernised and if you find one of these, get in quick. But you must ask both the Trust and Barnet borough for planning consents.

The cottages are favourites with first-time buyers and with older people. *The Orchard*, nearby, is still inhabited by elderly residents, just as Dame Henrietta intended, though the original buildings have been rebuilt. *Addison Way*, where the cottages and purpose-built maisonettes have slightly less character, leads into *Falloden Way*, the busy A1, where prices are lower because of the noise. Still, if you're immune to traffic or want to save money, the houses have lovely views over Northway Gardens where there are tennis courts. *Market Place* has flats above the shops and some purpose-built maisonettes tucked away on the *Ossulton Way* side but these can be noisy too.

Cross over the *Falloden Way* and you're on the 'wrong' side of the Suburb, although the roads are just as pretty and cottages in *Westholm*, *Midholm* and *Eastholm* (the names indicate how carefully planned the Suburb was) and in *Brookland Rise* are decidedly desirable. *Hill Top*, *Maurice Walk* and *Midholm Close* all have purpose-built maisonettes, usually with their own gardens.

Back in the main part of the Suburb, *Oakwood Rd* links *Addison Way* with *Northway* and the New Suburb. The road used to be something of a rat-run until speed bumps were built to dissuade motorists from using it as a short cut.

South of *Central Square* is *Meadway*, the Suburb's main thoroughfare which leads from *Hoop Lane* and Golders Green. Meadway Court, a Freshwater block around 60 years old, lies on the N side of the road and leading off on the S side are the prestigious Closes, some of them private roads, where the 6- and 7-bedroom houses are the largest in this part of the Suburb. Unless you knew they were there, you'd never come across *Linnell*, *Turner* or *Meadway Closes*. The same applies to *Linnell* and *Turner Drives* which have terrific views over the Hampstead Heath extension. For splendid views, and splendid 6-bed houses, look in *Wildwood Rd* where an outlook over the Heath and Hampstead Golf Course commands high prices. On the other side of the Heath Extension runs Hampstead Way where you'll find Heathcroft, a popular block not far from Golders Green station and *Wellgarth Rd*, where there's a youth hostel.

There are controversial proposals for a new development of as many as 20 to 30 homes on the site of a former garage in *Corringway*, near *Hampstead Way*, and behind Golders Green tube station. Controversial because it is being strongly resisted by neighbouring residents. Eventual development could be years away, but if it does go ahead it will be the first major influx of new homes since the Suburb was built.

N2, the New Suburb

Suburb snobs are rather patronising about the 'New Suburb' the N2 area, which lies E of *Ossulton* and *Kingsley Ways*, plus *Northway*, *Southway* and *Middleway* back in NW11. It's true that the architecture is less interesting and the area is more densely constructed, but the houses are large (and expensive) with grand gardens and plenty of space. Parking, which is difficult in the Old Suburb, is not a problem here. Cars were considered a normal adjunct to life when the New Suburb was laid out and were catered for (if not necessarily approved of) by the architects.

Holne Chase is the continuation of *Meadway* and off it run the elegant *Spencer Close* and *Neville Drive*. Houses on the 'right' side of *Neville Drive* have a splendid view of the golf course. *Linden Lea* and *Norrice Lea* (where you find the Suburb synagogue) both have large family houses, often detached, and are very popular.

North of the noisy *Lyttelton Rd* – where popular purpose-built blocks include Widecombe Court, set back from the road – are roads like *Gurney Drive*, *Widecombe Way* and *Edmund's Walk* which are quiet and pretty and have the advantage of being nearer East Finchley Station. Westwards, at the top of *Ossulton Way*, *Neale Close* is a favourite with first-time buyers and has purpose-built 2-bedroomed maisonettes kept private by hedges. Across the road, *Denison Close* has a popular block set around a pretty garden square.

Fanning out from *Central Square* and counted as the New Suburb despite their NW11 postcodes, are *Northway*, *Middleway* and *Southway* which are joined by *Thornton* and *Litchfield Ways*. Here you'll find large family houses with gardens to match in spacious hedge-lined roads. Harold Wilson once lived in Southway.

The most expensive roads in the Suburb are in *Ingram Avenue* and *Winnington Rd*, where prices resemble telephone numbers and the detached houses are huge and (particularly in *Winnington Rd*) rather ostentatious. Agents in the area also claim the famous *The Bishops Avenue*, known with reason as 'Millionaires' Row'. It is favoured by the ultra-rich international set as much for the privacy and security that the vast (for London) 2- and 3-acre plots afford as for the houses themselves, which are imposing but undistinguished 1950s mansions. There are more Middle Eastern royals here than in Marbella.

Among those estate agents active in this area are:
- Ellis & Co
- Gordon Hudson
- Prudential Property Services
- Selmans
- Winkworth
- Druce

H

Hendon and Mill Hill

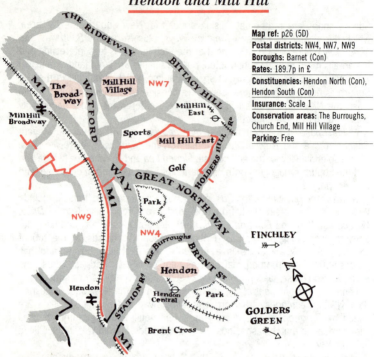

| Map ref: p26 (5D) |
| Postal districts: NW4, NW7, NW9 |
| Boroughs: Barnet (Con) |
| Rates: 189.7p in £ |
| Constituencies: Hendon North (Con), Hendon South (Con) |
| Insurance: Scale 1 |
| Conservation areas: The Burroughs, Church End, Mill Hill Village |
| Parking: Free |

Transport   Tubes: Mill Hill East, Hendon Central, (zones 3a/b, Northern). From Hendon Central to: Oxford Circus 30 min (1 change), City 30 min, Heathrow 1 hr 30 min (1 change). British Rail: Mill Hill Broadway (King's Cross 20 min, Moorgate 26 min).

Convenient for   Brent Cross Shopping Centre, Copthall Sports/Swimming Centre, Welsh Harp/Brent Reservoir. M1, North Circular Rd. Miles from centre: 7.

Schools   Barnet Education Authority: Copthall (g), Hasmonean (Jewish) Schools (b) & (g), Mill Hill County, St James' High RC, St Mary's C of E. Private: Mill Hill (b), The Mount (g).

Flats	S	1b	2b	3b	4b	5b
Average prices	55–65	65–85	75–150	80–200+	–	–
Houses	2b	3b	4b	5b	6/7b	8b
Average prices	100–140	115–250	150–360	200–450	500+	–

The properties   The 3-bed semi of inter-wars vintage is most common. Also flat conversions and smaller houses, including some ex-council. Some larger prestige homes and new flats.

The market   Popular for family homes: sizable Jewish and Indian communities. Also commuting flat-dwellers and first time buyers. Homes close to the many main routes are cheaper. Local searches: 4 weeks.

Area Profile

Somehow Hendon seems to be the crossroads for all roads that lead somewhere else. The area is dissected by the *Hendon/Watford Way*, the *Edgware Rd*, the *Great North Way* and the *MI* motorway, not to mention the *North Circular Rd* which forms an E boundary. Consequently, the N-W London suburb of Hendon divides into several old-style hamlets, each with their own identity. There is no real centre.

The area has a wide range of amenities to offer; the Brent Cross Shopping Centre, Copthall sports stadium, the RAF Museum and all the watersport activities associated with the Welsh Harp. Residents sleep safely in their beds since the Metropolitan Police training school is here, just off *Aerodrome Rd*.

Hendon has had its share of famous residents, among them Shakespearian actor David Garrick, who became Lord of the Manor in 1796 and rebuilt Hendon Hall in *Ashley Lane*, complete with the famous, but incongruous, brick columns which he reputedly won in a card game. Garrick Park is the only remnant of his estate. Hendon Hall is now a select hotel – the headquarters of the England football team during the 1966 World Cup.

Hendon also has a place in aviation history – the famous Hendon aerodrome was actually one of two in Hendon; the other was nearby in *Stag Lane*. Claude Grahame White established the aerodrome in 1910 and it was the site of the first British loop-the-loop, the first parachute descent and also the first British air mail delivery, a flight from Hendon to Windsor. The aerodrome now is the site of the council's Grahame Park Estate.

When Hendon Central tube station opened in 1923 it was surrounded by open fields – a scene hard to imagine in the bustling suburb today. One of the speculative builders who left their biggest mark on the suburban sprawl of the 1930s was locally-based John Laing, whose headquarters are in Mill Hill's *Pursley Rd*. One of Laing's regular homes was an award-winning design first used to build the *Sunnyfield* site, off *Lawrence St* in Mill Hill.

A focal point in the area is the Victorian town hall in *The Burroughs*. Hendon is the oldest part of the Borough of Barnet (where rates are among London's lowest) and it is fitting that it should be the political centre of the borough. Next door is Hendon's fine public library which also lends records and tapes, convenient for students at nearby Middlesex Polytechnic (Hendon campus of a very split site). Seventeenth-century Church Farm House is a museum.

Hendon has a strong community heart – residents were active in the campaign to stop the building of a national-size sports stadium on Copthall in 1986, and recently have been keeping an eye on the plans for a huge residential development behind the historic *Burroughs,* a space specially designated by the Department of the Environment. Outline planning permission has now been granted by the borough, so a sale of the site and building work is expected to start in 1989.

To the N lies Mill Hill – green and pleasant with plenty of wide open spaces. The original village stands on a hill and close by is Mill Hill School, built in 1807 with a splendid classical frontage. It was here that James Murray, a master at the school, edited much of the Oxford English Dictionary. The school was established for the sons of Protestant Dissenters and was known as 'an island of non-conformity in a sea of Roman Catholicism' because there are several Roman Catholic institutions in the area, most notably St Joseph's College in *Lawrence St.* Mill Hill is also home to the Medical Research Laboratory and to the Inglis Barracks.

H

Cut off from the rest of Mill Hill by the roaring *Watford Way* is *The Broadway*, a busy shopping parade with health food shops and a health and beauty centre. The BR station Mill Hill Broadway (26 minutes to Moorgate, 20 mins to King's Cross) is here too and there are buses to local and Central London destinations.

Hendon

If you take a detour from the speeding roads, Hendon has homes to suit everybody, from large detached houses in *Brampton Grove*, *The Downage* and *Cedars Close*, to luxury retirement flats in *Church Rd*, rows of suburban terraces round *Montague Rd*, West Hendon, and quaint cottages bordering picturesque *The Burroughs* in *Church End*.

Turning into *The Burroughs* from the *Watford Way* is a surprise. Immediately the grey commercial buildings which match the busy road make way for cottages and at least one of the larger, old houses converted into luxurious modern flats. Just along the road from the imposing Town Hall, flanked by a modern library and fire station, is the beautiful corner of Church End which has the Norman St Mary's Church in *Greyhound Hill* as a focal point. Next door, the old Church Farm House (dating back in parts to the 17th century) is home to the borough's museum, hosting displays all the year round. In fact, the house twice escaped the bulldozer, once to house council tenants after the Second World War and later in 1949 when they moved out and it became redundant. Between the museum and St Mary's stands the Greyhound Inn, originally the Church House and used for parish and vestry meetings. Further down *Greyhound Hill* the suburban semis are neat and tidy, just as the planners of the '30s imagined them, many with lovely green views; though the road is used as a cut-through from the *Watford Way* to *The Burroughs/Church Rd* and isn't as tranquil as it once was.

Heading down *Church Rd* towards *The Quadrant*, *Sunningfields Rd* and *Sunningfields Crescent* are to your left, both pretty, both with plenty of conversions. *Florence St* just off *The Quadrant* is a real find: not as cut off as the Sunningfields roads, it has charming little houses set along a narrow street. Probably the street in Hendon with the most character. The corner of The Quadrant, once the local cinema, is now sheltered housing. The area is well supplied with various types of homes and housing for the elderly.

Turning left down *Parson St* brings you to some of the premier streets in Hendon: *Downage*, *Ashley Lane* and *Cedars Close* with its mock-Tudor houses set in a circle around little private gardens. *Tenterden Grove*, *Close* and *Gardens* are also nice but homes at either end of *Tenterden Drive* may suffer a little from noise from the *Great North Way*. *Westchester Drive*, at the junction of *Parson St* and the *Great North Way*, is surprisingly unaffected by its proximity to the main roads, and has small houses and Westchester Court flats.

If Hendon could be said to have a high street then *Brent St* is probably it. Here you'll find the mini shopping centre at *Sentinel Square*, with plenty of parking. *Bell Lane* leads down towards the *North Circular Rd*, to the left roads like *Alexandra Rd* and *Albert Rd* have smaller semis and terraced houses. *Albert Rd* is the site of Jew's College with its fine library. To the right, *Green Lane* and the roads around have large family houses and a number of synagogues.

On the other side of *Brent St* lies the Shirehall Estate where many of the detached and semi-detached 4/5-bed houses have delightful views over Hendon Park. Unfortunately *Shirehall Lane* is used as a short cut by Hendon's shoppers on the Brent Cross trail.

Queen's Rd runs alongside the Park down to Hendon Central tube station. Home owners along here, of both houses and flats may be disturbed by commuters parking their cars here during the day: *Queen's Gardens* has the benefit of the park without the parking drawback.

To the N of *Queen's Rd* lie more of Hendon's best streets. *Brampton Grove*, *Wykeham Rd* and *Raleigh Close* have large family houses. They are particularly popular with Jewish residents due to the proximity of synagogues in *Egerton Gardens* (the YAKAR centre) and in *Raleigh Close* itself.

Station Rd, where you'll find the popular Highmount block, runs down from *The Burroughs* to Hendon BR station and provides a link between the *Watford Way* and the *Edgware Rd*. *Vivian Avenue* is home of the late-night bagel shop which is not terribly popular with local residents. Roads off *Vivian Avenue* have 4-bed semis which get less expensive as you near the *M1* motorway.

West Hendon, on the other side of the motorway, is the cheaper end of Hendon. Shopping facilities are not very good and the area, with its terraces and small semis, has a slightly run-down air. However, it is convenient for the *Edgware Rd* leading to Marble Arch, for the facilities of the Welsh Harp, and for Wembley Stadium. Welsh Harp Village, in Goldsmith Avenue at the northern tip of the Welsh Harp reservoir, is an award-winning modern development for first-time buyers where Hendon and Kingsbury meet. Brent Cross is the best local shopping for all West Hendon.

H

Mill Hill

A trip to Mill Hill is in order for London house hunters who would actually prefer to be in the country. There's plenty of space and open fields but not much in the way of leisure facilities. Mill Hill has a BR station, but the tube line ends in Mill Hill East (Northern Line) at the bottom of *Bittacy Hill*, definitely the cheaper end of Mill Hill. It doesn't venture up to the dizzy heights (in terms of altitude and price) of *Uphill Rd*.

To the N of Hendon, *Holders Hill Rd*, with its new blocks of flats, leads up towards Mill Hill East, the site of Mill Hill's only tube station. The original plan was to extend Mill Hill spur to Edgware, and then on to Bushey, but war intervened and the line stopped dead. Mill Hill East is an attractive belt of suburbia with a carefully planned grid of roads. Here the semis each have their own identity with a variety of modern windows and extensions. The main avenue, *Devonshire Rd*, radiates out from *Holders Hill Circus* and overlooks Hendon golf course and Copthall playing fields. One warning: the bottom end of *Devonshire Rd* is overshadowed by huge gasometers behind *Bittacy Hill*.

Moving W, you come to *Pursley Rd*, *Page St* and *Wyse Lane*. The houses here are fairly ordinary semis but, surrounded by green open spaces, they are very pleasant. From there, climb *Milespit Hill* to *The Ridgeway*. Here, Mill Hill Village stands quiet and glorious, still with its village pond, overlooking the green fields. Not all the houses are old: a handful are 'modern architect-designed', as the estate agents say, but all are very 'des res'. The *High St* belies its name: the nearest main shops are in *Mill Hill Broadway*. At *The Ridgeway* end, *Wills Grove*, which branches off to the left just before Mill Hill School, is charming, with larger houses and plenty of trees. Between *Daws Lane* and

Hammers Lane lies Mill Hill's 'poet's corner'. This one is a surprise, with pleasant 4- and 5-bedroom houses in roads named after literary greats such as *Tennyson*, *Milton* and *Shakespeare*. Further along *The Ridgeway*, at *Holcombe Hill* where the Old Forge stands, lies *Lawrence St* off which is Mill Hill's premier road, Uphill Rd. Home-owners in neighbouring *Sunnyfield*, *The Reddings*, *Uphill Grove* and the *Tretawn* roads have extended their houses in all directions. With spacious gardens and views over the grounds of St Joseph's College, they stand on gently undulating ground which enhances the feeling of space that they enjoy.

Highwood Hill has larger than average old cottages along just one side which therefore also have splendid views. It leads into picturesque *Marsh Lane* which takes motorists down to the busy *A1*. Roads to the N such as *Hankins Lane* and *Glenwood Rd* are equally pleasant up-market residential turnings.

On the other side of the *A1* lies *The Broadway*, a thriving, almost trendy, shopping centre which has come up considerably in the past year or so. *Flower Lane* has an estate of Georgian-style houses and *Russell Grove* and *Weymouth Avenue* are both good roads with detached houses. *Newcombe Park* is popular too.

Among those estate agents active in this area are:

- Alexander Jay
- Anscombe & Ringland
- Bairstow Eves
- Connell
- Ellis & Co.
- Cosway
- Gerald Linke & Co.
- Ian Hirschfield
- Martyn Gerrard
- Paul Press Assocs.
- Philip Phillips
- Russell Levine
- Seymours
- Spyer Johnston & Evans
- Talbots
- Winkworths

Highgate

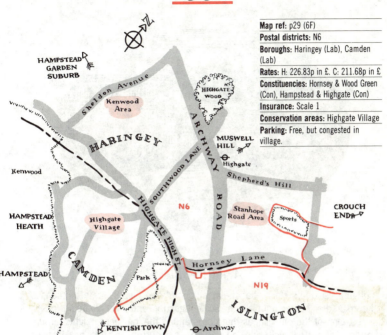

Map ref: p29 (6F)
Postal districts: N6
Boroughs: Haringey (Lab), Camden (Lab)
Rates: H: 226.83p in £. C: 211.68p in £
Constituencies: Hornsey & Wood Green (Con), Hampstead & Highgate (Con)
Insurance: Scale 1
Conservation areas: Highgate Village
Parking: Free, but congested in village.

H

Transport	Tubes: Highgate, Archway (zones 2/3a, Northern). From Highgate to: Oxford Circus 25 min (1 change), City 18 min, Heathrow 1 hr (1 ch).
Convenient for	Hampstead Heath, Kenwood. A1/M1 to North. Miles from centre: 5.
Schools	ILEA Division 2 and Haringey Education Authority: William Ellis (b), Acland Burghley, Parliament Hill (g), Highgate Wood. Private: Highgate (b), Highfield, Channing (g), St Aloysius (b).

Flats	S	1b	2b	3b	4b	5b
Average prices	60–65	70–90	90–150	100–200	145–300+	–
Houses	2b	3b	4b	5b	6/7b	8b
Average prices	125–175	155–260+	195–350+	250–400+	350–500+	450–1.2m

The properties	The roads around this ancient hill village hold not only 18th century houses but some 1680s ones. Victorian terraces and converted and p/b flats have been added, plus large mansions, town houses and coveted private estates, from '30s to present day.
The market	Musicians, media folk and the professions buy here, joined by exalted foreign potentates for the large sub-country mansions in vast grounds. Flat-buyers get glorious views. Prices vary widely as does the range of homes. Local searches: Haringey 4 weeks, Camden 12 weeks.

Area Profile

Highgate residents claim that their neighbourhood has all the attractions of Hampstead – but without the noise, congestion and over-inflated property prices. One of the old villages that commanded the 'northern heights' around London, Highgate is well sprinkled with places of current and historical interest, and with considerable charm. It was in Highgate Hill that the disillusioned young Dick Whittington heard the sound of Bow Bells and was persuaded to 'turn again'. The spot is marked with a stone and a statue of his famous cat, and the event gave its name to the adjacent Whittington Hospital and the Whittington and Cat pub.

But Highgate is certainly not cheap and there is little doubt that in recent years, as property prices in Hampstead went through the roof, values in Highgate began to rise more rapidly as a result of the 'overflow' effect of buyers looking slightly further afield.

Furthermore, the increasing buying pressure in Highgate created its own overflow areas in parts of the N6 postal area such as Muswell Hill and Crouch End (which see) which, until a few years ago, were fairly sleepy enclaves with relatively stable property prices – especially the section E of *Archway Rd.*

The population is well-heeled and traditional, with musicians and media folk among the area's most well-known residents. It is not quite as cosmopolitan as neighbouring Hampstead though there are, however, pockets of fabulously wealthy Middle Eastern residents – the vast Witanhurst mansion at the top of *Highgate West Hill* (the second largest house in London next to Buckingham Palace) is rumoured to be owned by King Hussein of Jordan, and the splendid Beechwood stately home in *Hampstead Lane* is owned by the Saudi Arabian royal family. The area also has more than its fair share of Russian diplomats and workers at the mysterious Soviet Trade Delegation building in *Highgate West Hill.*

Highgate shares with Hampstead the 800 acres of the Heath, plus the grounds of Kenwood where open-air concerts are held in summer. The Heath offers a semi-rural landscape of fields, woods and ponds plus sports pitches. Kenwood, a beautiful Adam mansion, houses the Iveagh Bequest, a notable collection of pictures including works by Van Dyck, Rembrandt and Gainsborough.

Highgate Village

Highgate proper is bisected by the *Highgate High St* shopping centre which is also the borough boundary between Camden in the W and Haringey in the E. The bulk of the residential section of the village is on the Camden side, including the marvelous *Pond Square* with its profusion of 18th century houses, late Victorian purpose-built flats, and the headquarters of the Highgate Society and the Highgate Literary and Scientific Institution, side by side in *South Grove* at one end of the square. South Grove House, opposite Witanhurst and the internationally famous Flask pub, is still one of the most desirable blocks in the village. Four new 5-bed houses are planned for the *High St*.

The premier address in the village is, however, *The Grove*; set back from the road behind an avenue of trees with a row of houses, a few of which date back to the 1680s. Distinguished residents have included William Blake and, more recently, violinist Sir Yehudi Menuhin. A house in *The Grove* last year sold for around £975,000.

H

Off *The Grove* is *Fitzroy Park*, an exclusive private road giving access to a number of sumptuous homes on the edge of Hampstead Heath, as well as to the dozen or so new luxury houses called *Highfields Grove* on the lower slopes of the grounds of Witanhurst, whose prices have recently been lowered by some 10-20% to range from about £650,000 to over £1m. There are still a few available.

More reasonable are the terraces in *Bisham Gardens*, almost all converted into flats which, on the S side, have stunning views towards the City over Waterlow Park (one of London's most delightful parks), Lauderdale House (one-time home of Nell Gwynn) and the extraordinary Highgate Cemetery which, apart from being the last resting place of Karl Marx, is a major tourist attraction – guided tours are given.

Swains Lane leads down from the village to the Holly Lodge Estate, an enormously popular residential area on the site of philanthropist Baroness Burdett-Coutts's estate, comprising a mixture of private houses and blocks of flats (now council owned) built between the wars in a mainly mock-Tudor style which is either smashing or vulgar, depending on your point of view. Also popular is *West Hill Park*, an award winning private estate of flats and houses built in the 1970s in *Merton Lane*, overlooking the Highgate Ponds.

The Haringey side of the village is slightly less dramatic, but attractive nevertheless, with some lovely leafy and secluded streets well supplied with a mixture of semi-detached houses and conversions, and even a few large post war purpose built blocks of flats such as Southwood Hall, Cholmeley Lodge and Northwood Hall. Particularly popular are *Southwood Lawn Rd*, *Cholmeley Park*, *Cholmeley Crescent* and *Cromwell Avenue*. The latter has a fascinating development of flats converted out of a disused church.

This area did suffer somewhat in recent years when it seemed inevitable that the government would insist on a dramatic widening of *Archway Rd* (which leads to the A1) as it went through Highgate, but extremely fierce opposition by a coalition of local groups at a series of public inquiries in the 1970s and '80s (together with the opening of the M25 orbital motorway, which has reduced the amount of heavy traffic using the road) managed to get the plan stopped. The scheme now appears to have been shelved indefinitely, but could conceivably be resurrected at some stage.

Kenwood

Hampstead Lane leads from the village around the N end of Hampstead Heath to the grounds of the Iveagh Bequest and Kenwood House, now owned and run by English Heritage. The house is an important art gallery, music and poetry venue, and the site of delightful open air concerts on summer evenings.

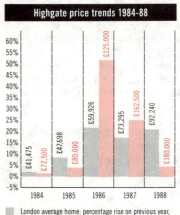

Highgate price trends 1984-88

London average home: percentage rise on previous year, adjusted for inflation.

Typical home in this area, percentage rise on previous year, adjusted for inflation.

Two-bed garden flat in a village centre location, price change compared to London-wide average home. The rise here has been very modest: prices performed well over the previous years (especially in '86) but in '88 it was already too expensive to benefit from the Chancellor's boom. Compare Pimlico.

Directly opposite are majestic roads like *Courtenay Avenue, Compton Avenue, Sheldon Avenue* and *Stormont Rd*, all a stone's throw from *The Bishops Avenue* (better known as Millionaires' Row) in the neighbouring borough of Barnet. These streets, almost exclusively with large detached houses, lead to Highgate Golf Club in *Denewood Rd.*

Other roads in the area encircle the large grounds of Highgate School (which also owns a lot of property in the vicinity), such as *Bishopswood Rd, Broadlands Rd* and *View Rd.* Mostly traditional large houses, but a sprinkling of new properties as well.

North Rd and *North Hill* have a number of large mansion blocks, including the architecturally renowned Highpoint block, which has the distinction of having the highest rooftop in London.

Also worth scrutiny are the well-mixed properties in *Talbot Rd, Bishops Rd, Bloomfield Rd* and *The Park* – although the *Archway Rd* ends of these streets suffer from the noise and vibration from the heavy traffic.

Stanhope

E of *Archway Rd* is a clearly defined area of Highgate bounded in the N by *Shepherds Hill* and *Priory Gardens* (a sought after cul-de-sac leading to Highgate tube station), in the E by *Coolhurst Rd*, and in the S by *Hornsey Lane.*

Shepherds Hill, with an increasing number of modern blocks of flats replacing the semis has unparalleled views to the N over Muswell Hill and Alexandra Palace and Park for those properties whose outlook is not obscured, and dramatic views to the S for others.

The area is bisected N-S by *Stanhope Rd* which carries most of the traffic, leaving other streets relatively free. Prime road is *Hurst Avenue* which has very large £1 million houses overlooking the playing fields of nearby St Aloysius Catholic boys' high school. It is now likely that all or some of the playing fields may be developed in the next year or two – which should bring *Hurst Avenue* prices down a little.

Avenue Rd, at the bottom of the dip, now has a row of fairly new blocks of flats on the south side – much to the disgust of the house- and flat-owners across the road.

The main drawback of this area is its distance from public transport – it's a stiff walk in either direction to Archway or Highgate tube stations, although there are buses along *Archway Rd*.

An important feature of this area is the Parkland Walk, formerly the path of the old railway which ran from Finsbury Park to Alexandra Palace, now turned by Haringey Council into a nature trail and wildlife reserve very popular with ramblers, walkers and joggers. Until recently houses adjacent to or with access to the Parkland Walk were much in demand (although some residents always saw it as a security hazard). But more recently blight has descended in the form of one of the more outlandish options put forward in the Government's East London Assessment Study – a major study of traffic problems and possible solutions in the area. The option envisages a six-lane motorway along the Parkland Walk, and the idea has not enhanced the value of nearby houses of late.

The smart money, however, may tend towards the viewpoint that the concept is so absurd and outrageous as to be unthinkable and politically impossible. So there could well be some bargains to be had during this period of uncertainty. Among the streets in this vicinity are *Avenue Rd*, *Hornsey Lane*, *Milton Park*, *Orchard Rd* and *Claremont Rd*.

'The Miltons': *Milton Park*, *Avenue* and *Rd* are popular with a good selection of smaller flats and houses which get less expensive the closer they are to *Archway Rd*. Lots of purpose built flats in *Avenue Rd* and *Hornsey Lane*, including the huge Northwood Hall block.

H

Borders

S of *Hornsey Lane* is an attractive group of streets called the Whitehall Park Conservation Area (in Islington) with beautifully preserved Victorian terraces in *Whitehall Park*, *Gladsmuir Rd* and *Harbeton Rd*. These have increased in value dramatically in recent years. The district is sometimes called 'Highgate borders' and even 'Highgate slopes', but is really Archway.

On the E side there are some pleasant streets more correctly called *Crouch End*, including *Crouch Hall Rd*, *Coleridge Rd* and *Birchington Rd*.

The boundary with Muswell Hill has some very interesting streets, including *Lanchester Rd* and *Woodside Avenue* behind Highgate Wood, and the group of street surrounding Haringey's Queen's Wood, including *Onslow Gardens*, *Connaught Gardens*, *Summersby Rd* and *Wood Lane*.

Among those estate agents active in this area are:
- Anscombe & Ringland
- Batty Stevens Good
- Lloyds
- Prickett & Ellis
- Prudential Property Services
- Hamptons
- Knight Frank & Rutley
- Sturt & Tivendale
- Winkworths

Holland Park

Map ref: p75 (1G)
Postal districts: W11, W14
Boroughs: Kensington & Chelsea (Con), Hammersmith & Fulham (Lab)
Rates: K: 98.9p in £. H: 228p in £
Constituencies: Kensington (Con), Hammersmith (Lab)
Insurance: Scale 1
Conservation areas: Holland Park
Parking: Residents/meters. Clamps.

Transport	Tubes: Holland Park, Shepherd's Bush (zone 2, Central); Kensington Olympia. To: Oxford Circus 12 min, City 22 min, Heathrow 50 min (2 changes). BR: Kensington Olympia, to Clapham Jct. and Intercity.
Convenient for	BBC TV Centre at Shepherd's Bush. M4/M40 to the West. Direct tube line to West End, City. Miles from centre: 3.5.
Schools	ILEA zone 1: Cardinal Vaughan School, Holland Park School. Private: Norland Place School, Notting Hill & Ealing High (g)

Flats	S	1b	2b	3b	4b	5b
Average prices	60–90	90–125	135–250	250+	350+	→
Houses	2b	3b	4b	5b	6/7b	8b
Average prices	200–275	250–350+	375–500+	600–850+	1–2m	→3m+

The properties	Vast, snowy-white villas and terraces, imposing Victorian red-brick, smaller-scale squares, modern townhouses, all gather round Park and Avenue. Rich source of family homes, flats converted and mansion, ambassador-level grandeur, in leafy streets.
The market	Recent years have seen rediscovery of the Park, and prices now reflect that it is N of Kensington rather than next door to Notting Hill. The embassy-size houses are reverting to multi-million pound single occupancy after years as tatty flats. Local searches: Kensington & Chelsea 7 days, Hammersmith & Fulham 2 weeks.

Area Profile

The desirable residential area known as Holland Park slopes gently away from Kensington, down the western flanks of Campden Hill. Leafy and spacious, it boasts the highest concentration of large houses in the Royal Borough.

'The area known as' is said with care, since there's Holland Park (the park) and also *Holland Park* (the road – which isn't: it's more a sort of square, in the middle of which is sandwiched *Holland Park Mews*). The grandest, largest, ambassadorial residences – some *are* embassies – are here. On one side is the park, on the other *Holland Park Avenue*, which runs westwards to busy Shepherd's Bush roundabout. 'The area known as' fans out on either side of the broad, tree-lined Avenue: southwards it runs between the park and *Holland Rd*, down towards the W end of *Kensington High St*; northwards it has, over the years, pushed upwards to take in the pleasant corners between *Portland Rd/St James's Gardens/Royal Crescent*.

Holland Park, wherever its frontiers, is one of the luckier parts of London. Lucky to have been in the right place at the wrong time.

Perhaps because Notting Hill, with its raffish connotations, was a little close, the area escaped the knock-down-and-build-flats boom of the '60s. Its early-Victorian elegance remained intact, if seedy. Now the grand old houses are once again fashionable, either as single homes or converted into unusually roomy flats.

Add to these a number of modern flats/townhouse developments, usually set in their own landscaped grounds, and the small mews cottages with their garages that are the legacy of the horse-drawn age in which the area grew up, and you have a neighbourhood with a good range of home sizes and styles.

This, over the last 10 years, has attracted families (schools, the park, communal square and crescent gardens), City people (the Central Line goes straight there) and Hampstead-style politicians, actors and media-persons (the BBC is down the road at Shepherd's Bush). And now ambassadorial-level personages have completed the circle and re-inhabited the ambassadorial-sized homes, reclaimed after years as rented flats.

Today, the pleasant, community feel is added to by small, villagy shops and good restaurants. Thanks to the neighbouring areas' amenities, there's been no incentive to clutter up the place with sprawling supermarkets and the like. Most streets are within easy walking distance of either of the two main shopping/entertainment centres of *Kensington High St* and *Notting Hill Gate*. Between them these boast three cinemas, clubs, pubs, restaurants and a wide range of shops. Several leading department stores line *Kensington High St*, which is currently undergoing a £400,000 facelift to improve its appearance and attract more shoppers. Another of the area's attractions is the vast amount of public open space in the shape of Holland Park itself and in nearby Kensington Gardens (riding and swimming). Holland Park covers 55 acres of woodlands and formal gardens, many sports, an adventure playpark and an open air theatre.

Holland Park South

Tree-lined *Holland Park Avenue* sets the tone for this choice neighbourhood of large houses and leafy gardens. Big stucco, or brick and stucco, mansions set back from the road behind sloping front gardens spread along the southern side of the busy avenue. Some have been converted into hotels. Pairs of large brick and stucco houses, split into flats, lie to the W, beyond the increasingly upmarket shops and restaurants clustered around Holland Park underground station.

The most coveted of imposing Victorian mansions are found in *Holland Park* (the road). Many of these double-fronted, detached, creamy stucco houses still have their decorative, highly ornate cast-iron and glass entrance canopies. (This delightfully idiosyncratic feature sits strangely, to be honest, on the dignified, pillared entrances: they look for all the world as if they were drawn in as an afterthought by Ronald Searle.) Many have been divided into flats, particularly popular with the diplomatic community. Some are indeed used as embassies. Whole houses, backing onto the park, fetch £3.5 million. Of those converted into large and luxurious flats, a current example newly completed has a 3-bed penthouse with a £625,000 forecasted price tag and other sizes ranging down to a 1-bed flat for around £220,000.

Lying between the N and S arms of the street through a stone arch is *Holland Park Mews*, lined by 2-storey cottages with ground floor garages.

Just S of here, *Holland Park* merges with *Abbotsbury Rd*, which runs southwards along the E side of the park itself. Most of the development on the W side of the street is post-war, from the 10-storey flats block, Abbotsbury House, at the NW end to the series of select private cul-de-sacs which make up *Abbotsbury Close*. Immaculate 2/3-storey terraced brick houses stand in neatly-landscaped enclaves set well back from *Abbotsbury Rd*. This is the deepest, most secluded part of Holland Park, select even for Kensington. Urban grime seems a world away.

The scene changes dramatically with the appearance of *Oakwood Court*, a development of 7-storey red-brick Victorian mansion blocks, which form the street of the same name. A strip of lawn, trees and shrubs divides the blocks on each side of the street. The mansions are being refurbished block by block. *Ilchester Place* opposite is leafy and salubrious. The big low-built houses, some with gardens backing on to Holland Park can fetch £2 million.

Melbury Rd to the S is particularly noted for its studio houses designed by the likes of Norman Shaw and Halsey Ricardo. An outstanding example is the eccentric red-brick Tower House, a copy of the Welsh Castell Coch. Built in the 1870s, it was renovated in the 1960s by actor Richard Harris. The houses are a legacy of the days when *Melbury Rd* and *Holland Park Rd* to the S formed a 19th century artists' quarter. Several more big red brick detached studio houses are found here, including Leighton House, once the home of painter Lord Leighton, now an art gallery and museum. The size of these Victorian mansions, built on the scale of country houses, makes for spectacular flats in those that are converted. These include the erstwhile home of pre-Raphaelite artist Holman ('Light of the World') Hunt, and most recently a pair designed by architect Halsey Ricardo for his father-in-law and his patron respectively. They are now six huge apartments of which the smallest, a mere 1,723 sq ft (3 beds, 3 baths, 3 receps) is £650,000. The vast 4-bed/4-bath/3-reception room one merits a £1,075,000 price tag for its 3,036 sq ft – excluding its two terraces, conservatory and 76ft private garden.

The S side of the street forms *St Mary Abbots Terrace*, a modern development of neo-Georgian townhouses. The 3-storey houses are set around a series of three cul-de-sacs. Some are turned sideways on to the street, their rear gardens adding to its leafy look.

Addison Rd S off *Addison Crescent* forms part of the S-bound one-way traffic system, which detracts from the character of this otherwise exclusive road. Detached and semi-detached stucco and brick/stucco villas, and a terrace of Gothic-style houses, sit on the W side. Opposite are two large modern flats blocks, 10-storey Monckton Court and 6-storey Farley Court. Both are set in landscaped grounds off the road.

The S curve of *Addison Crescent* forms the link in the one-way system between *Addison Rd* and *Holland Rd*. This short stretch of detached and paired villas consequently suffers from the heavy traffic and noise. By contrast, the N curve with its big 2/3-storey detached brick and stucco villas and walled front gardens is noticeably quieter and more desirable.

Grander white stucco-fronted detached villas line the W side of the N stretch of *Addison Rd*. They are set back behind walled gardens and small sweeping driveways. Security cameras are another feature of the street scene here. On the opposite side of the road is a group of detached and semi-detached houses, including the intriguing glazed brick and tile Richmond House, headquarters of the Richmond Fellowship. They lie between *Somerset Square*, a modern development of red brick townhouses and flats, and *Woodsford Square*, a 1970s development of large townhouses, considered particularly good value in local price terms. Both developments are set in landscaped grounds walled off from the road behind a shield of tall trees. Homes at the N end of *Woodsford Square* overlook the Holland Park tennis club, tucked in behind *Holland Park Gardens*. Holland Park Mansions, a 4-storey red and white block on the E side of *Holland Park Gardens*, also overlooks the courts.

At the N end of *Addison Rd* next to Cardinal Vaughan School stands Addisland Court, an 8-storey brick and stone block, which stretches around the corner into exclusive *Holland Villas Rd*. The choice 2/3-storey brick and stucco detached villas in this quiet, leafy street fetch up to £3 million plus. They have their own gates and driveways as well as large rear gardens. Off the N-W end of *Holland Villas Rd* are *Upper* and *Lower Addison Gardens*, both tree-lined streets of 3-storey terraced houses.

H

Holland Park North

Across *Holland Park Avenue* stands *Royal Crescent*. Two curving terraces of white-painted, 5-storey homes sweep around a tree-lined semicircular garden. Each of the end houses has graceful circular pavilions to finish the row, and the whole crescent appears to have been transported from Regency Brighton. Alas, it gazes out on the Kensington Hilton rather than the English Channel. Tucked in behind the W side is *Royal Crescent Mews*, a newly-built curved terrace of 2-storey brick and stucco cottages with their own garages.

St Ann's Villas, which leads off *Royal Crescent*, is a relatively busy local road with a mix of houses and flats – notably a group of Victorian Gothic detached brown-brick gabled houses. Cutting W-E through this street is *Queensdale Rd*, a pleasant and very popular street of Victorian terraced houses. The borough boundary runs across its W end, curving in from the line taken by the more physical barrier of the M41. *Queensdale Crescent*, *Swanscombe Rd*, *Norland Rd* and *Kingsdale Gardens* are thus under the jurisdiction of Hammersmith rather than the Royal Borough. The best stretch of *Queensdale Rd*, E of *St Ann's Villas*, has 3/4-storey and basement brick and pastel painted stucco houses. Off it, *Queensdale Place* is a pleasant little cul-de-sac of 2-storey plus basement stock brick and stucco terraces.

Addison Place, off the opposite side of *Queensdale Rd*, is a narrow cobbled crescent, lined by a variety of period and modern 2-storey mews-type cottages. It curves around into *Addison Avenue*, the showpiece of the area. The best stretch of this wide tree-lined street with its splendid vista of St James Norlands Church lies N of *Queensdale Rd*. Elegant paired stucco houses painted in pastel shades line both sides. The smaller paired stucco houses S of *Queensdale Rd* give way to an attractive parade of shops, offices and the Norland Arms pub. Green Victorian street lamps add to the avenue's period character.

St James Church sits in the central garden of *St James's Gardens*, another of the neighbourhood's choicest addresses. Pairs of attractive semi-detached houses linked by paired entrances are set around the gardens. The lower floors of these handsome 3-storey plus basement brick and stucco houses are painted in pastel shades, adding to the distinctive character of this Victorian square.

Return down *Addison Avenue* to *Queensdale Rd* and turn S into *Queensdale Walk*, a tranquil cul-de-sac of 2-storey painted cottages, E, facing a long garden wall with overhanging trees. One street away is *Norland Square* where three terraces of 4-storey with basement stucco-fronted houses stand around a large tree-filled private central garden (tennis court). Off the square runs *Norland Place*, a cobbled mews of 2-storey painted cottages which stretches through to *Princedale Rd*.

Princedale Rd has mainly Victorian terraces, a mix of houses and flats, interspersed with a sprinkling of speciality shops near the junction with *Penzance Place*. More brick and stucco terraces are found here, next to the new award-winning St Clements and St James primary school.

Penzance Place leads into *Portland Rd*, another popular street of Victorian terraced houses. Many of the 3-storey plus basement houses here have now been converted into flats. Properties on the E side are more expensive, being wider with larger gardens. The road is sealed off to traffic at *Clarendon Cross*, a delightful village enclave of smart shops, galleries, antique shops, restaurant/wine bar as well as old-fashioned newsagents and sub-post office.

Lying behind the N-W side of *Portland Rd*, across the road from Avondale Park, is award-winning *Hippodrome Mews*. Two terraces of 3-storey brown brick townhouses face each other across a narrow cobbled mews in this private cul-de-sac (1970s). The pleasingly bulbous shape of an old kiln, as high as the houses, is preserved among them, and no doubt accounts for the name of *Pottery Lane* which, running S from here, has an attractive group of 3-storey painted brick and stucco terraced houses at its junction with *Penzance Place*.

Clarendon Rd, which parallels *Portland Rd* to the E, marks the start of the climb up Notting Hill (which see), where graceful crescents still echo the shape of the race-course they replaced. Close to the tube station, between Holland Park Avenue and Lansdowne Mews, 12 new houses should be ready this spring. They each boast garages and 'high security', and prices, for 3 beds, start at £300,000.

Borders

Holland Rd (N/S), the area's western boundary, is a major traffic artery running down to *Kensington High St* from the M41, which ends at Shepherd's Bush roundabout. Its S end is one-way: the traffic flows northwards, while the south-bound stream dives down the bottom half of *Addison Crescent* into *Addison Rd*.

A series of small hotels cluster around the S end of *Holland Rd*. The rest is lined by mainly 4-storey and basement stucco, or brick and stucco, terraced houses of varying quality. In common with most properties in the neighbourhood, they are split into flats.

More bed and breakfast hotels are found in *Russell Rd* to the W. They are mixed in with further flats in the 3-storey and basement brick and stucco terraces overlooking the W London railway line and the glass facade of the Olympia Exhibition Centre. A high wall and trees hide the railway line at street level. A footbridge over the tracks links *Russell Rd* with the Kensington Olympia BR station, just across the borough boundary with Hammersmith.

Russell Gardens is a short parade of small local shops and restaurants, plus a pub. *Russell Gardens Mews* has several working garages at its entrance S, giving way to 2-storey brick/painted cottages towards the rear. The future of the mews is in doubt, however, because it lies in the path of the proposed West London relief road (see Prospects for London). The planned road would be built in the rail corridor, which is quite narrow in the N part of the neighbourhood.

Properties at the NW end of tree-lined *Elsham Rd* also back on to the railway.

Estate agents report difficulty selling homes in *Elsham* and *Russell Rds*. One resident in *Russell Gardens Mews* has succeeded in serving a 'blight' notice on the Department of Transport obliging it to buy his mews house. He had been unable to sell after six months on the market because of the road plans.

Among those estate agents active in this area are:

- John Wilcox
- Marsh & Parsons
- Prudential Property Services
- Alex Neil
- Callander Wright
- Cluttons
- Barnard Marcus
- John D Wood
- Savills
- Aylesfords
- Brian Lack

H

Islington and Highbury

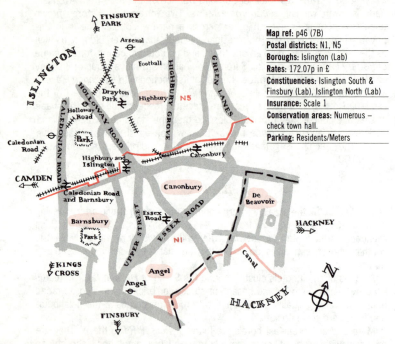

Map ref: p46 (7B)	
Postal districts: N1, N5	
Boroughs: Islington (Lab)	
Rates: 172.07p in £	
Constituencies: Islington South & Finsbury (Lab), Islington North (Lab)	
Insurance: Scale 1	
Conservation areas: Numerous – check town hall.	
Parking: Residents/Meters	

Transport Tubes: Highbury & Islington (zone 2, Victoria); Angel (zone 1, Northern). From Highbury & Islington to: Oxford Circus 8 min, City 18 min (1 change), Heathrow 1 hr 10 min (1 change). British Rail: Highbury & Islington (Liverpool St 10 min and North London Line); Drayton Park, Essex Road, Caledonian Road, Canonbury.

Convenient for Both City and West End, King's Cross, St Pancras and Euston BR. Miles from centre: 2.5.

Schools ILEA Division 3: Islington Green School, Highbury Fields (g), Highbury Grove (b), Elizabeth Garrett Anderson School (g), St Aloysius College.

Flats	S	1b	2b	3b	4b	5b
Average prices	55–75	66–95	90–160	100–160+	–	–
Houses	2b	3b	4b	5b	6/7b	8b
Average prices	130–220	160–300+	200–400+	220–450+	450+	–

The properties Good choice of early- and mid-Victorian houses in attractive areas such as Barnsbury and Canonbury. Highbury has more small houses. Two-bed converted flats in good supply.

The market Prices still reasonable compared to SW London. Character period homes in interesting area attract City workers and media types. Flats seem in shorter supply than houses. Highbury cheaper than Islington. New developments under way. Local searches: 2 weeks.

I

Area Profile

Islington, with Highbury to the N, is a most satisfactory place. It has a definite shape, which starts from the southern base-line of *Pentonville Rd/City Rd*, unfurls on either side of the central spine of *Upper St*, and is neatly capped by Highbury with its green, open Fields. Then, too, it is set on pleasantly hilly ground for variety; it boasts a village green to offset the commercialism of the S end, also theatres, pubs, restaurants, a canal – and real gems of residential corners which are made all the more pleasing by the fact that through-traffic can dash along the carefully unsmart main routes without suspecting their existence.

These are very British pleasures, and the inhabitants (wherever they may have hailed from originally) are somehow very British folk. The international jet-set do not appreciate, as do we, the inconvenience of the tucked-away, charming – but often narrow-gutted, many-staired – houses, however Georgian the terraces. Some arriviste City types were blown in by Big Bang, but by and large middle-class radicals (where else do you find an anarchist bookshop?) typify the house-buying classes.

Highbury and Islington, perched high above the City, are equally well located for the West and East Ends on either side of it. Their territory lies E of *Caledonian Rd* and Kings Cross, W of *Green Lanes* and thus Hackney and Stoke Newington, and S of Finsbury Park (*Gillespie Rd*). Notorious in recent years for the wilder excesses of its Labour council, this corner has been inhabited from Saxon times. What was 'Iseldone' developed rapidly in the 18th century as a spa resort, thanks to its mass of underground springs and rivers. It was also on the main route to Smithfield and developed a reputation as a market garden, providing cattle and produce for the whole of London.

The area divides into four neighbourhoods: Canonbury, Barnsbury and the Angel in Islington with, to the N, Highbury around the green, open spaces of its Fields – and prices tend to be in that order. Follow *Essex Rd* as it forks off to the E side of the Green to find Canonbury, Islington's heartland. A popular spot since Elizabethan times, it thrived in Georgian days and still has some fine terraces from this period set in its leafy roads. The cost of these can be as much as 10-15% higher than for a comparably-sized home in the other neighbourhoods. Mainly family houses here, but flats and some larger houses available.

Barnsbury is a little later: a stock-brick-and-stucco land laid out by Cubitt in the 1820s. This is almost exclusively family housing, quieter (thanks to a fiendishly maze-like traffic scheme) and more completely residential in character, arranged in pretty streets around half a dozen garden squares. The Angel corner, aside from the commercial area, is predominantly composed of small flat-fronted Georgian/early Victorian terraces. Front gardens are rare, but some streets have central greenery; roads tend to be narrower, broadening towards the N, and the area S of *Essex Rd* has larger property and more flats.

By contrast, Highbury is virtually completely Victorian, aside from the roads bordering on Highbury Fields. Generally you'll find ornate late-Victorian houses with broader avenues and gardens, evenly split between flats and family homes. Some very large properties in Highbury New Park and Highbury Hill – if you can get one before it is transformed into flats.

The majority of homes to be had are thus 3- and 4-bedroom houses and 2-bedroom flats. Larger houses (5/6/7-bedrooms) do exist, but are unusual – many, of course, have long since been converted into flats. Studio and 1-bedroom flats are rare and, if anything, decreasing. They tend to only be available on short-term leases; in part this is due to the nature of conversions in Highbury and Islington, many of which have tended to be unsophisticated. Lateral conversions are scarce, and the woodchip-and-avocado-suite variety still common. Now, though, the legacy of '70s conversions is giving way, particularly around Highbury, to newer, smarter, more professional developments. However, Hackney council recently decided against giving permission for conversion of recently acquired property into smaller than 4-person units in a bid to maintain family housing, and it's possible that Islington may follow.

It's a good area to buy into at the moment. You can walk to the City, and the Angel area is becoming a bustling commercial centre with new offices and the Business Design Centre having a smartening influence on the shopping street. Prices still tend to be slightly cheaper than comparably central areas. The disadvantages are the high rates, parking (which, especially around the centre, can be difficult due to narrow streets), and a busy, through-route main road, springing from the commercial *City Rd*. This main street at first glance seems to contain shops that are either somewhat tatty, are antique shops, or are wholemeal yoghurt purveyors. (In fact, appearances are, once more, deceptive: there's a good range of shops, and more to come.) Cheaper homes can still be found on the Highbury/Hackney/Stoke Newington borders, and Finsbury Park to the N.

The Angel

The Angel neighbourhood centres on the junction of *Upper St* and *City Rd*. *Islington High St, Upper St* and immediately adjacent streets are the main shopping areas in Islington. The area to the N of *Pentonville Rd*, from the *High St* W to *Penton Rd*, is mainly commercial property and offices. This is becoming an important office centre, with a giant hole in the ground in the process of becoming an office block next to the tube. Angel Square, as it will be known, will house a new ticket hall as part of a £20m improvement scheme for the station. At present, the tube is so crowded that getting to and from the platform is a major part of each journey. Running W-E is *Chapel St*, which has a large, well-known fruit-and-veg market – supplemented on the corner of *Mantell St* and *Liverpool Rd* by a large Sainsburys. Behind in *Tolpuddle St* (the re-named *Culpeper St*) is the only substantial car park in the vicinity. (Check with the council about a possible new one-way system for the Chapel St area, if looking at property near here.)

On the E side of *Upper St*, just before the Green, is the distinctive Mall antiques arcade; behind this, and running parallel, is *Islington High St* (a surprise: it is more of a charming lane) and *Camden Passage* (an equally confusing name), a great centre for antiques. Antiques and small, old-fashioned shops continue down *Essex Rd*. The area to the E of *Upper St* and *Essex Rd* is quiet and residential and almost exclusively glorious flat-fronted Georgian terraces. Streets are narrow and parking is restricted. *Colebrooke Row* has tall terraces set behind a strip of dignifying greenery, across which is *Duncan Terrace* and the imposing red-brick St John the Evangelist Church. Turning right into *Vincent Terrace*, fine Georgian houses give lovely views onto the Grand Union Canal; on the other side of it, *Noel Rd* houses turn their back on the water – and thus have raised gardens that stop at – or rather, above – the tow-path: the Hanging Gardens of Islington. S of *Vincent Terrace* and W of City Rd Basin, houses tend to be smaller, streets narrower. Some modern housing, particularly along the *City Rd* edge: *Elia St* has low Georgian terraces on right, low council blocks on left.

North of the canal, at the corner of *Packington St* and *Prebend St*, is the Packington Square Estate – modern '70s low-rise blocks (of currently unhappy repute). E from here, across to the *Southgate Rd* and the borough boundary, are some fine period terraces (mainly family houses). Streets are wider, squares and trees more common, parking easier and prices higher. *Arlington Avenue* and *Square*, with the tucked-away Clock Tower Mews development (among the first, and best, of the modern mews recreations), are typical. *Wilton Square* is also particularly quiet and fine. Eight new houses are planned in *St Paul's St*, though the scheme is at appeal after Islington vetoed it.

The streets between the *New North Rd*, *Essex Rd* and *Southgate Rd* are more mixed, with different periods appearing in the same road. Streets are wider and parking less of a problem, large houses and many conversions. *Queensbury St* and *Morton Rd*, adjacent to *New North Rd*, have stylish post-modern developments still in progress. *Elizabeth Avenue* has 8-storey tower block to the north of *Rotherfield St*. Roads are predominantly flat-fronted, substantial terraces, some double-fronted. Other streets are later in period, eg *Elmore* and *Northchurch*. Dover Court council estate is just beneath the *Essex* and *Balls Pond Rds* junction. In *Tilney Gardens*, four new houses were built in 1988.

I

Canonbury

Upper St is the main artery of Islington, running NE into its heart. At *Islington Green* (where 7 new houses are planned) the road forks: *Upper St* continues NW and *Essex Rd* NE. The sharp angle shelters little passageways and courtyards, up to the period terraces of *Florence* and *Cross Sts*. To the E of these are the red-brick mansion flats of *Halton Rd* and *Canonbury Villas*.

Running NW and intersecting with the *Essex Rd* is *Canonbury Rd*, forming a triangle with *Upper St* at the top. Georgian flat-fronted terraces on either side of *Canonbury Rd* give way to modern council blocks just before *Canonbury Square*. A superb Regency square with tall, thin terraced houses and a formal garden in its centre (and at the heart of Canonbury), this is one of its most prized corners – but not as peaceful a you'd expect thanks to *Canonbury Rd* which cuts straight across it. Round the corner we rejoin the main *Upper St* where *Compton Terrace*, a fine, lofty Regency terrace is sheltered from *Upper St* by a line of trees and a garden. New homes are appearing behind the S end of the Terrace. Just to the N, *Upper St* and *Canonbury Rd* meet at Highbury Corner, the vast roundabout beyond which Highbury begins. Eastwards from *Canonbury Square*, *Compton Rd* has tall Georgian terraces which give way to double-fronted period houses where it joins *Alwyne Villas'* broader-fronted rows. Here you'll find Canonbury Tower, romantic 16th century relic which now houses the famed Tower Theatre amateur company, which mounts ambitious rep seasons.

Continuing, *Canonbury Place* has the pleasant Canonbury Tavern and genteel little shops. To the N along *St Marys Grove* are a whole series of neo-Georgian developments, low flat-fronted terraces culminating in *John Spencer Square*. At the end of *Canonbury Place*, the road splits into *Grange Grove* and *Canonbury Park North* and *South*. The area is very mixed: modern semis nestle with mock-Georgian semis which rub shoulders with the real thing. At the corner of *Canonbury Park South* and *Willow Bridge Rd* is an imposing red-brick Victorian mansion which sets the tone for the rest of the street – spacious Victorian semis with quiet, unrestricted parking. This, along with *Alwyne Place*, form the two Victorian streets in Canonbury.

Running S, *Willow Bridge Rd* crosses *Alwyne Rd* and *Canonbury Grove*, which together enclose the New River walk and small, charming public gardens (quiet, covetable streets with superb period houses). To the NE, contained by *Essex Rd* and the *Balls Pond Rd*, is a quiet low-rise council estate with maisonettes and interconnected walkways. You'll have to cross the *St Pauls Rd* highway to find Canonbury's little BR station, which links with the North London line and has a handful of shops. *Wallace Rd*, which leads to it has fine, tall flat-fronted terraces on the right, and on the left later ones with good front gardens. To the E are the fine terraces of *St Pauls Place*, and the shabbier *Northampton Grove*. Much of the area to the W is unrenovated large period houses, especially along *St Pauls Rd* – not, however (despite proximity to the railway line), cheap.

Barnsbury

Liverpool Rd running N from the Angel is the main avenue, and is typically composed of flat-fronted brick terraces. To the east the junction with *Upper St* forms a thin strip of land up to Highbury. This is not strictly Barnsbury, but may well be referred to as such by estate agents. Predominantly Georgian, the lower section up to *Barford St* is semi-derelict. *Barford St* marks the site of the newly-restored Business Design Centre, with its glass arches. North is the fine *Gibson Square*, and above this *Milner Square*, an 1840s creation completely restored by the council in the 1970s. A recent private development around the corner mimics its rather eccentric, vertical style. East is *Almeida St*, home of the Almeida Theatre, and small period terraces continue up to Islington Park.

To the west of *Liverpool Rd* across to the *Caledonian Rd* is Barnsbury proper, whose homogeneous residential groves were laid out by Cubitt in the 1820s. In the best Islington traditions (see intro) it's a secretive corner. Its peace is unassailable, courtesy of an outsider-proof one-way system. Maps are issued to friends. To the south *Ritchie St* and *Bachelor St*, with their neat terraces and first-floor balconies, border on the Angel and end in Culpeper community garden. Continue west along *Tolpuddle* (*Culpeper St*), which intersects with *Barnsbury Rd* and *Penton St* running S to N. To the W *Copenhagen St* crosses *Barnsbury Rd* and curves round to meet the *Caledonian Rd*. S of here are Pentonville council estates. *Cloudesley Rd* runs N from Culpeper gardens, and to the W is Barnard Park – a rare open space for the Islington area, it boasts tennis courts. To the E is *Cloudesley St* with its wide avenues and dignified double fronted houses, leading into the superb *Cloudesley Square* (1820s Regency with the Celestial Church of Christ at the centre). *Richmond Avenue* runs W from *Liverpool Rd*, and connects with the *Caledonian Rd*. To the N is the secluded *Lonsdale Square*, substantial terraces of – a sudden shock – heavily Gothic styling: the only Victorian square in the area. N of this is the ivy-clad *Morland Mews*, one of the few modern developments. West is the delightful *Ripplevale Grove* – small, tidy terraces and gardens – and further W still *Thornhill Square*, a fine Regency square with substantial properties. Its curved end mirrors *Thornhill Crescent*. In *Barnsbury Square* 13 new houses are proposed.

I

Barnsbury ends with the *Caledonian Rd*, predominantly small, old shops, cheerfully and irredeemably scruffy, though conversions, such as the 24 flats proposed at No 465, are increasing. The junction with *Offord Rd* in the N which marks the top limit of the area. *Offord Rd* is full of large dishevelled Georgian houses, ripe for renovation; it travels E to join the *Liverpool Rd* at a junction marked by the Samuel Lewis red-brick flats.

Highbury

Highbury & Islington station (BR/Victoria Line tube) is at Highbury Corner, at the start of the *Holloway Rd*. *Highbury Grove/Park* runs north from *St Pauls Rd*, bisecting the area. To the W of the *Grove*, *Corsica Rd* and *Baalbec Rd* describes an area of late (1889) Victorian terraces with elaborate facades. Parallel with this is *Highbury Place* which marks the beginning of the green acres of Highbury Fields. Flat-fronted Georgian terraces overlooking the Fields are the poshest part of Highbury. The lovely open expanse of the Fields lives up to its name, a breath-of-fresh-air common with the civilised addition of a swimming pool at the S end, tennis courts in the N, and an award-winning adventure playground, staffed at certain times – but check. Bounded on the west side by *Highbury Crescent* and *Terrace* (respectively, vast detached mansions and tall period terraces), Highbury's only Georgian streets. Otherwise homes are exclusively Victorian terraces with bay windows, wide streets and few parking problems – though *Highbury Terrace Mews* is an exception. Tucked behind *Highbury Terrace*, this is a modern development with maisonettes, and 6 3-bed flats on the market last winter. The old Aberdeen Works in *Highbury Grove* is set to be redeveloped, the 1.5 acre site should yield new homes this year or next. To the N of the Fields is *Highbury Hill*, a pretty corner with St John's church to the E and a clock tower at the centre. Another coveted location, houses are large Victorian double-fronted, decreasing in size and becoming terraced towards Arsenal. A new mews, *De Barowe Mews*, has appeared in

Leigh Rd, with 2 of the 7 houses still for sale in December.

Roads to the N of *Highbury Hill* and W of *Highbury Park* are later Victorian terraces, again reducing in size and quality towards *Gillespie Rd* and Arsenal football ground. Many unrenovated properties towards the bottom, and prices around the football stadium are naturally cheaper (but not much). Victoriana continues NE of Highbury Park and *Riversdale Rd* to *Mountgrove Rd*. At the corner of *Highbury New Park* overlooking Clissold Park is the noted White Horse pub. The Highbury Quadrant estate covers the area from here down to *Green Lanes*; housing is low-level tower blocks. South from *Southeby Rd* to *Highbury New Park* in the south and east is late Victoriana: large terraces with ornate exteriors and quiet tree-lined streets. The exceptions are *Kerloss Rd*, off Highbury Park, which has modest 1930s semis, and *Fountain Mews* which opens onto *Highbury Grange*, an extensive new development of post-modernist and tower blocks. Acros the road are a series of large mansion flats, *Taverner Square* and *Peckett Square*, with interconnecting courtyards. *Aberdeen Rd* runs south to *Aberdeen Park*, the most secluded corner in the district: prices are high and styles range from 1930s semis to spacious Victorian mansions. *Highbury New Park* skirts the area to the E, broad and long, with newer property on right hand side, Quadrant estate in north to spring Gardens estate in south. On the left vast period mansions have mainly been converted into flats such as the sophisticated Belmont Court, on the corner of *Balfour Rd*. To the E, *Petherton Rd* runs north to *Green Lanes* with 4-storey Victorian terraces in a wide avenue with green shoulder down the middle. A grid of roads cross west to east to *Newington Green Rd*, made up of Victorian terraces decreasing in size from *Poets Rd* to *Green lanes*. This area, and nearby Stoke Newington, are catching up with Highbury in price and status.

Borders

Highbury and Islington have three main border areas. To the E of Islington lie 'the de Beauvoirs'. Still in the N1 postal district but just across the borough boundary (it runs along *Southgate St*), the pleasant corner around *de Beauvoir Square/Rd* has come up rapidly in the last few years, and its denizens look to Islington rather than Hackney. Its modern-sized semi-detached villas offer a rare chance to buy half a house rather than a slice of terrace. Even rarer is the size of garden these 2/3-bed homes enjoy: 75-100ft is not uncommon – some get 150ft. It lies to the N of *Downham Rd*, W of the *Kingsland Rd* and S of the *Balls Pond Rd*. Another sign of evolution is the way the place has changed its name: you'll find it labelled 'Kingsland' on maps, but that word seems to have dropped out of use. (The part to the S of *Downham Rd* labelled 'de Beauvoir Town' is now largely occupied by the high- and medium-rise tower blocks of the de Beauvoir council estate.) To the N of *Downham Rd*, the terraces resume. *De Beauvoir Square* is an 1840s Gothic square of smart pairs of 4-storey villas with bay windows and ornate gables, around a central garden. Is is the hub of a network of streets – similar homes can be found in streets like *Mortimer Rd*, *de Beauvoir Rd* (a busy thoroughfare), *Hertford Rd*, *Englefield Rd*. Those closest to *De Beauvoir Square* tend to be best; quality frays a little towards the edges, eg *Southgate Grove*. The old Gainsborough film studios, by the canal on *New North Rd*, were for sale last winter. There were hopes that the film industry might return, but homes are another possibility. Eagle Court, a Barratt development in *Culford Rd*, has 9 1-bed flats and 21 3-bed houses.

Lower Holloway, to the N of Barnsbury, lies N of the railway line and E of the *Holloway Rd*. Property is almost totally council-built (modern) radiating off *Paradise Passage*. The exceptions are *Arundel Place* and *Square* which are spacious flat-fronted terraces surrounding a central garden and playground; *Ellington St*, which has lower-level Georgian terraces, rising to the substantial. *Furlong Rd* runs E, with *Orleston Rd*, from *Liverpool Rd*: both have large semi-detached period houses. A development of 15 flats is mooted for the corner of *Orleston Rd* and *Orleston Mews*. N along *Liverpool Rd* are a few small Victorian terraces, *Morgan Rd*, *Ringcroft St* and *Sheringham Rd*, quality uneven.

The area to the W of Islington, between the *Caledonian Rd* and *York Way*, N of *Wharfdale Rd*, is also mainly low-level council homes, of various periods. The main interest here is Thornhill Bridge Wharf, a new development, post-modern in style, coral pink in colour, overlooking the canalside walk. Some 1-bed flats were on the market last winter. Phase 2, which will have larger flats, is due to be released soon.

Among those estate agents active in this area are:

- Bairstow Eves
- Baker Evans
- Bob Brooks & Co
- Folkard & Hayward
- Hamptons
- Copping Joyce
- Holden Matthews
- Hotblack & Co
- Prudential Property Services
- Stickley & Kent
- Winkworths

I

Kennington, Vauxhall and Stockwell

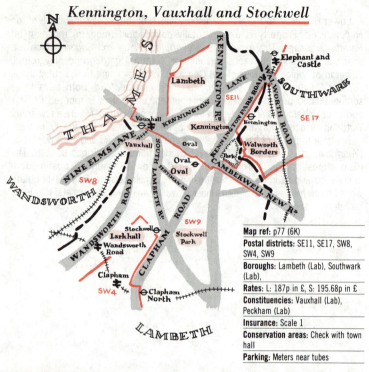

Map ref: p77 (6K)

Postal districts: SE11, SE17, SW8, SW4, SW9

Boroughs: Lambeth (Lab), Southwark (Lab),

Rates: L: 187p in £, S: 195.68p in £

Constituencies: Vauxhall (Lab), Peckham (Lab)

Insurance: Scale 1

Conservation areas: Check with town hall

Parking: Meters near tubes

Transport   Tubes: Kennington, Elephant & Castle, Oval, Clapham North (zones 1/2 Northern), Stockwell (zone 2 Victoria, Northern), Vauxhall (zones 1/2 Victoria). From Stockwell: Oxford Circus 10 min, City 20 min, Heathrow 1 hr 15 min (2 changes). British Rail: Elephant & Castle, Vauxhall, Clapham, Wandsworth Road.

Convenient for   City and Westminster. Miles from centre: 2.

Schools   ILEA zones 8/9/10: Lilian Baylis, Stockwell Park, Archbishop Tenison's C of E (b).

Flats	S	1b	2b	3b	4b	5b
Average prices	53–60	65–75	72–95+	80–115	110+	–
Houses	2b	3b	4b	5b	6/7b	8b
Average prices	89–130	125–195	150–235+	200–320+	→	–

The properties   Enclaves of handsome Georgian amid Victorian houses; some modern mews and flats, repro-Georgian of Duchy of Cornwall Estate. Widespread council housing.

The market   Good commmunications attract professionals, City people, MPs and doctors. Duchy is selling homes, some unmodernised. Location matters a lot here: select enclaves close to run-down inner city. Local searches: Lambeth 10 weeks, Southwark 8 weeks.

Area Profile

Homehunters have been slow to spot the advantages of this very central area, where a Georgian house in a handsome square can be had for half north-of-the-river prices. 1988 saw several new developments, however, and the area seems to be coming to the attention of the big developers.

This is the most urban part of South London and the only area with decent tube connections to the centre of town. It has quite large areas of surviving Georgian and early Victorian housing and its proximity to Westminster and the City attracts residents who put such assets above a fashionable postcode.

That said, these three areas are very mixed, with quiet squares only yards away from roaring, dusty through roads, with mews tucked into corners behind gasworks and with council tower blocks looming over the Georgian terraces. The heart of the area, Kennington, gains much of its character from the Duchy of Cornwall Estate. The Princes of Wales have owned land here since the Black Prince had his palace in Kennington. (Had he survived, would Kennington, rather than Kensington, have been the Royal Borough?) Today the estate is managed in the sensitive manner one would expect of the current landlord, and some of the houses and flats are being sold as they come vacant.

Vauxhall, once the site of a famous pleasure garden, has shrunk to be little more than a giant traffic intersection – and the Victoria Line tube. It does have a river frontage and homes are appearing here. Kennington is inland to the E, with the Oval district to the S. South again is Stockwell, an area which received a boost a decade ago when the Victoria Line brought it within minutes of the West End. Stockwell has some enclaves of fine houses, but does not seem to have kept up the momentum of improvement begun in the '70s. Over to the E, a few pockets of interesting housing are to be found on the borders with Walworth and Camberwell. There are no tubes in this direction, though, so distance from Kennington tube becomes a factor. This station has very good links with the West End and the City, being the junction for the E and W branches of the Northern Line. Much of Vauxhall and Kennington are in the Division Bell zone, and MPs favour the areas as being about the closest places to Westminster where one can find a family house. Partly because of the MPs, judges and other notables who live here, the area is considered part of inner London by cabbies, who don't mind making the trip across the bridges.

More than in most places this area demands careful use of the map when considering a purchase. There are two railway lines running through the area at high level. The W one, leading to Waterloo, will take Channel Tunnel traffic and will become even busier than at present. The main roads of the area are choked with traffic more often than not. The E-W route past the Oval to Vauxhall Bridge is signposted as an 'inner ring road' and therefore attracts much heavy through-traffic. There is also quite a bit of industry scattered around, though the premises of Sarson's Vinegar Works are now homes.

Transport is good, but other amenities are lacking. The only large shop is Sainsbury's flagship store at Vauxhall, although plans have been submitted for a major development to include a Safeway superstore on the Brixton Estates site at the corner of *Camberwell New Rd & Brixton Rd*. A decision on whether or not this will go ahead was due to be made at a meeting of Lambeth Council in January 89. A public meeting was held in November at which considerable opposition to the scheme was aired, particularly by local shopkeepers and residents. With Covent Garden and the West End minutes away not many wine bars or restaurants have been set up. And apart from one or two favoured

K

squares and quiet corners, the area lacks the community feel of other, more family-oriented parts of South London. It falls into no less than three boroughs – Wandsworth, illogically, sticks a finger into the W corner. Their rating and other policies differ, so look hard at the map.

Kennington

The road names around here are very confusing: it is hard to recall which is *Kennington Park Rd*, which *Kennington Rd* and which *Kennington Lane*. The first-named is the main road, following the line of the old Roman Stane Street and linking the Elephant and Castle in the N with the Oval and Stockwell, passing Kennington, Oval and Vauxhall tubes. To the W of *Kennington Rd* is the old heart of the neighbourhood, the 45-acre Duchy of Cornwall Estate. Ten acres is the revered Oval cricket ground, leased to Surrey Cricket Club and the scene of county and Test matches. The rest is mostly housing. A chunk stands NW of *Kennington Lane*, S of the site of the Black Prince's palace. This stood S of *Black Prince Rd* and N of *Sandcroft St. Courtney Square*, *Cardigan St* and *Courtney St* are Duchy homes in a neo-Georgian style. However authentic they look, they were built in 1913. *Woodstock Court* is an attractive enclosed square of homes which the Duchy rents to elderly tenants. The post-war flats in *Sandcroft St* and *Black Prince Rd* are also Duchy property.

Kennington Rd owes its existence to the building of Westminster Bridge (1750) and its regular rows of Georgian terraced houses are still largely in place. Many are flats, some offices, but some remain as large, potentially grand, houses. To the E of the road, in the angle formed by its intersection with *Kennington Lane*, is another part of the Duchy estate. Pretty *Denny Crescent*, *Denny St* and *Chester Way* are all 20th century Georgian. These, like other Duchy homes, come onto the open market and are considered a good buy although may well be in need of total modernisation. *Kennington Rd* has at its N end the park surrounding the Imperial War Museum. Just S of the museum, between it and the Lambeth Hospital, is *Walcot Square*, which dates from the 1830s. *West Square*, which is in truth to the E, has houses from three decades earlier, as does *St George's Rd* on the N edge of the area. This road carries heavy traffic from the Elephant. *West Square* and the surrounding streets are by contrast peaceful. Nearby *Oswin St* has solid 4-storey Victorian houses.

Much of the rest of the district E of *Kennington Rd* and W of *Kennington Park Rd* is council housing. One mid-'70s flats development is private, however: Vanbrugh Court on *Wincott St*. This popular complex has communal gardens and an underground garage. S of the hospital, a recent mews development by architects Moxley & Frankl has been slotted into the angle between *Gilbert* and *Renfrew Rds*. *Heralds Place* has underground parking for its compact 3-bed houses – and more than a hint of a mediaeval fortified town to match its name. To the E of the *Kennington Lane/Kennington Rd* junction is *Cleaver Square*, one of the best places to live in the area and the first to be 'discovered', allegedly by a '60s barrister trying to find his way back to civilization from a court hearing at Newington Causeway. The urban-feeling square has a mixture of houses, but all are extremely attractive. The square, like all the other worthwhile bits of the district, is a conservation area. South from here, in the angle of *Kennington* and *Kennington Park Rds*, is a neighbourhood of smaller terraced Victorian cottages. *Stannary St's* name makes clear the connection with Cornwall and thus the Duchy. *Ravensdon St* is popular, with many flat conversions. *Kennington Green*, a small widening of *Kennington Rd*, has a few pleasant old houses. *Montford Place* running off it is overshadowed by the gas works. The district to the W on either side of *Black Prince Rd* is nearly all council.

The Oval

Partly because of heavy traffic, and also due to the depressing influence of some pre-war council estates, the Oval neighbourhood has less charm than Kennington. Cricket fanatics might consider the period houses on the S side of the Oval itself, which have a view of the pitch but suffer from heavy traffic. The other sides of the Oval are lined with council blocks. S of the Oval, and sealed off from the traffic, *Ashmole St* and *Claylands Rd* have small terraced houses, rather overwhelmed by council developments. *Meadow Rd* has flat-fronted terraces. The prime street around here is *Fentiman Rd*, a long terrace of dignified mid-Victorian houses and a known address for MPs and the like. Most of the houses lack Kennington's Georgian charm, but are big and conveniently between Oval and Vauxhall tubes. Periods vary between Regency and mid-Victorian. Higher odd numbers overlook the park. Off neighbouring *Rita Rd*, where many down-at-heel terraces are now under conversion, is the contrasting *Regent's Bridge Gardens*, more popularly called the vinegar works. It is an expensive conversion of the early Victorian Sarsons works, the manager's house and his enormous ballroom. New homes have been built in a matching style. There is a wall round the whole place with security

Kennington is best known for its Georgian terraces, but the area also has some interesting survivals from other periods including these alms houses with their Gothic porches and windows. Other interesting architecture can be found on the Duchy of Cornwall estate, where small houses in Georgian style were built early this century.

K

gates. Since completion in 1986, a number of properties have been re-sold. Some are enormous, such as the conversion carved from the former ballroom and the loft apartments in the brewery itself. There are flats and town houses too; some are conversions, some are skillfully matched newbuild – it can be difficult to distinguish which is which. All have access to a large private swimming pool complex. Between *Fentiman Rd* and *Richbourne Terrace* is *Usborne Mews*, a recent development by Moxley & Frankl.

Close to the tube, *Hanover Gardens* is a pocket of Victorian 4-storey houses in a cul-de-sac. East of the Oval tube, a few streets such as *Handforth Rd* have 3-storey Victorian houses which convert into pleasant flats. The area is alive with skips and hammering as this goes on.

To the East again, in *Langton Rd* off the *Camberwell New Rd* is the new development of 'Salisbury Square'. This comprises 100 homes from studio flats to 4-bed houses, designed with a late-Georgian early-Victorian feel among cobbled courtyards and archways with variable roof-levels. (This is Moxley & Frankl again).

Vauxhall

Roads, railways and the New Covent Garden Market take up much of the floorspace in Vauxhall, and council homes dominate the rest. *Vauxhall Grove* looks promising on the map: a square tucked in off the Vauxhall Cross junction. The *Grove*, however, is rather scruffy, although developments are in the pipeline. Three-storey Victorian houses loom over the narrow streets, which are being improved with trees, new paving and bollards. Round in *Bonnington Square*, SELCHA – Southeast London Consortium Housing Association – is doing up some similar 3-storey flats buildings. Much of the square seems to be inhabited by young people in a sort of post-hippie timewarp. At the junction of *Langley Lane* and *South Lambeth Rd* is a turn-of-the-century mansion block, Park Mansions, which has a steady turnover of flats for sale. At the end of *Lawn Lane* is a council estate around *Ebbisham Drive*: 2-storey houses and two tower blocks. A new development of eighteen houses by Clements Property Developments is under way on the old Unigate Dairies site.

To the S, in what used to be called South Lambeth but is now a fringe area between Vauxhall and Lambeth, roads such as *Tradescant Rd* have a lot of flats carved out of 3-storey Victorian terraces. Some new mews houses in *Dorset Rd*. From here S is considered Stockwell.

A tract to the W of *Wandsworth Rd*, towards Battersea, is attached to Vauxhall – mostly because railway lines shut it off from anywhere else. Most is the Patmore Estate, council of varying sizes. Some are starting to sprout for sale boards: this is Wandsworth borough. N of the railway, 'The Stewartry' is a recent development of studio to 2-bed flats, built by Courtfield Properties on the Battersea borders. Back up *Wandsworth Rd*, a complex of streets entered from *Cowthorpe Rd* including *Crimsworth Rd* has rather scruffy late-Victorian cottages, some purpose-built flats. Round the corner in *Thornpatch Rd*, a development of town houses and flats was completed in October of '88. Along the river towards Battersea Power Station are some new blocks of flats with good views of Pimlico (better views, in fact, than the other way round). Phase 2 of the enormous Regalian development of "Elm Key" in *Nine Elms Lane* was launched in November '88. This large riverside block will include a sports and leisure complex complete with heated swimming pool, gymnasium, sauna and whirlpool spa for the health-conscious. It comprises 1, 2 and 3 bedroom flats and penthouses. Prices are from £180,000 to £½m.

The enormous twin sites on either side of Vauxhall Bridge are earmarked for development to include homes. Plans are not yet finalized.

Stockwell

Stockwell struck lucky in the early 19th century, with an expansive estate of Regency villas. Just enough survives to provide some gracious streets and architecturally interesting homes, but not enough to make Stockwell a fully-fledged gentrified suburb. The select streets have an air of being marooned in an ordinary patch of South London.

West of *Clapham Rd* is *Albert Square* and its associated streets. The giant mid-Victorian houses in the square loom over the central gardens, and are in turn dominated by nearby tower blocks. *Wilkinson St* and *Aldebert Terrace* have a more human scale. The former is the smarter. W of *South Lambeth Rd* is a mixed neighbourhood of pleasant new council houses and surviving Regency villas. Most of the period homes are clustered around *Lansdowne Gardens*, which opens up in the middle into a perfect circus. Sadly, it lost a large tree in the October hurricane of '87. The houses are double-fronted, detached, with big pillared porches. *Guildford Rd* and linking roads are similar. *Lansdowne Way* is a busy E-W road with a mix of properties.

East of *Clapham Rd* comes Stockwell Park, the surviving Regency suburb. *Stockwell Terrace* overlooks the roundabout and tube station: tall early 19th century houses. There are similar homes in adjoining *South Lambeth* and *Clapham Rds*. *Stockwell Park Rd* runs E with a mix of homes from small Regency to '20s gabled villas. At the junction with *Groveway* and *Stockwell Park Crescent*, the road opens out. All these streets have a mix of 1830s villas and terraces, with lots of trees and gardens. *Durand Gardens*, hidden away to the N, is a suprise: a pear-shaped square with big Victorian houses, mostly semi- and detached. A little gothic villa and an enormous detached house add variety. A few arts-and-craftsy 1898 gabled terraces stand on the way out to *Clapham Rd*. W of *Stockwell Park Crescent*, *St Michael's* and *St Martin's Rds* have 3-storey mid-Victorian brick terraces. South of Stockwell tube is a mixed district of council blocks and routine Victorian terraces. *Landor Rd* marks the border with Clapham North and Brixton.

K

Larkhall Lane runs through to Clapham, carrying a lot of morning and evening traffic. The housing off it is mostly council, though there are a few corners. The lane itself has some early Victorian houses, much interrupted by car sales yards and council blocks.

Priory Grove, overlooking the recently-created Larkhall Park, has some pretty small houses. To the S of the area, and virtually in Clapham (it's SW4) is a grid of streets such as *Chelsham* and *Bromfelde Rds* which have big houses, some with generous Victorian gothic gables, and mostly now flats. One or two are large family homes. *Gauden Rd* is similar, with some extensive flat conversions. Flats and two town houses have been built on *Larkhall Lane* by Higgs Development. From *Larkhall Lane* E to Stockwell is council.

Walworth borders

East from Kennington tube is mostly council housing. *Sutherland Square*, though, has some handsome early Victorian houses. These are popular despite the fact that the square is bisected by a railway line. Nearby streets such as *Berryfield Rd* to the N have Victorian terraced houses. *Lorrimore Square* has a mix of Victorian terraces and new houses. All the streets S of here are part of, or are dominated by, a vast council estate. The mostly post-war flats and houses are interspersed with restored Victorian terraces. A few handsome early Victorian houses survive – just – to the W in *St Agnes Place*, overlooking Kennington Park. This area also has several streets of rather run-down purpose-built Edwardian flats.

Among those estate agents active in this area are:
- Alan Fraser
- Barnard Marcus
- Daniel Smith
- Jacksons
- Winkworths
- Roy Brooks

Kensington

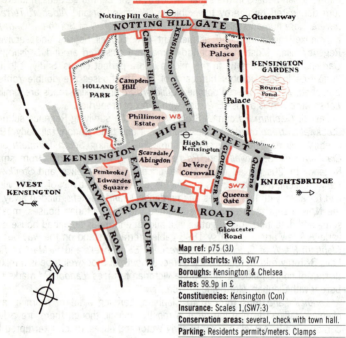

Map ref: p75 (3J)
Postal districts: W8, SW7
Boroughs: Kensington & Chelsea
Rates: 98.9p in £
Constituencies: Kensington (Con)
Insurance: Scales 1,(SW7:3)
Conservation areas: several, check with town hall.
Parking: Residents permits/meters. Clamps

Transport Tubes: Notting Hill Gate (zone 1/2, District, Circle, Central); Queensway (zone 1, Central); High St Kensington (zone 1, District, Circle); Gloucester Rd (zone 1, Piccadilly, District, Circle). From High St Kensington: Oxford Circus 15 min (1 change), City 25 min (1 change), Heathrow 40 min (1 change)

Convenient for Hyde Park, West End, Heathrow and West. Miles from centre: 3.

Schools ILEA zone 1. Holland Park, Cardinal Manning RC (b), Cardinal Vaughan RC (b), St Thomas More RC, Sion Manning RC (g) Private: St James' (b) (g), Falkner House (g), Queens's Gate School (g).

Flats	S	1b	2b	3b	4b	5b
Average prices	80–100+	90–175	130–250+	180–400+	300+	→
Houses	2b	3b	4b	5b	6/7b	8b
Average prices	250–300+	300–375+	360–575+	500–1m	800–1m+	→

The properties Heart of desirable, residential London: Victorian houses, some earlier ones, large numbers of flats both mansion and converted, plus mews and some new-build. Hardly a bad street in the place.

The market Kensington has never been unfashionable. Today, the settled, prosperous population is joined by international buyers/renters. More domestic than Knightsbridge, more respectable than South Kensington. Local searches: 7 days.

Area Profile

Kensington deserves its 'Royal Borough' title. It owed its origins as a fashionable suburb to the presence of Kensington Palace, and the royal connection continues. It is not many years since the nonagenarian Princess Alice, last surviving granddaughter of Queen Victoria, used to potter around from the Palace to morning service at St Mary Abbots. Prince Charles and Princess Diana have their London home at the Palace, so does Princess Margaret. Embassies and consulates occupy an increasing number of Kensington's grand houses.

Kensington began as a roadside hamlet, but real development began after 1689 when King William III moved his court to Kensington Palace, drawing people of rank to the area. However, the main boom came during the second half of the 19th century, immediately after the Great Exhibition. The result is a rich mix of Georgian and Victorian terraces, grand stucco villas, attractive cobbled mews, tall red brick mansion blocks and eccentric studio houses.

Most streets are within easy walking distance of either of the two main shopping/entertainment centres of *Kensington High St* and *Notting Hill Gate*. Between them they boast three cinemas, clubs, pubs, good restaurants and a wide range of shops. Several leading department stores line *Kensington High St* which is currently undergoing a £400,000 facelift to improve its appearance and attract more shoppers. Another of the area's attractions is the vast amount of public open space in the shape of Kensington Gardens (riding and swimming) and Holland Park. This chapter deals with Kensington proper: Holland Park has its own chapter, as do North and South Kensington.

K

Campden Hill

Campden Hill Rd climbs sedately uphill from *Kensington High St* and down again to *Notting Hill Gate*. A through route between the two main shopping streets, it is lined by a wide range of period and modern homes, merging with pubs, shops and restaurants at its N end.

King's College's Kensington campus lies hidden away behind a tall brick wall and trees on the corner with *Duchess of Bedford's Walk*. Opposite stands Campden Hill Court, a red brick and stone gabled mansion block with elaborate towers, turrets and domes. The Uruguayan Embassy and the securely-walled South African ambassador's residence lie just beyond here, down the hill on the W side. A short distance away in *Airlie Gardens* is Holland Park comprehensive school. A series of large modern flats blocks extend between *Airlie Gardens* and *Notting Hill Gate*. Many have superb views E across London.

Turn W into *Aubrey Walk*, a surprisingly quiet leafy backwater sitting on the hilltop. Brick and stucco terraces, 20th century Dutch-style houses and some highly individual studio houses line the S side facing the water works opposite. On top of the covered reservoirs are Campden Hill Tennis Club's courts.

The large houses around the corner in *Aubrey Rd* slope downhill to *Holland Park Avenue*. Halfway down *Aubrey Rd* is the entrance to select *Campden Hill Square*. The main terrace of this three-sided Regency square perches near the brow of the hill above the private central gardens. The remaining two terraces are stepped down on either side of the tree-lined gardens. Street trees add to the summer canopy of greenery. The houses also have leafy front gardens. The houses and painted cottages in *Hillsleigh Rd*, E of the square, also slope down to *Holland Park Avenue*.

East across *Campden Hill Rd* is Hillgate Village, an extremely popular enclave of pretty painted former artisans' cottages. The village is bounded by *Notting Hill Gate* N, *Campden St* S, *Campden Hill Rd* W and *Kensington Church St* E. Best examples of the gaily-coloured all-cottage streets are *Jameson*, *Calcott* and *Farmer Sts*, *Hillgate Place* and tree-lined *Farm Place*.

Kensington Place has long terraces of attractive 2-storey and basement stucco/brick cottages N, mostly built in the 1850s, as in the previously-mentioned streets. On the opposite side is Fox primary school and a 1970s red brick development of 3-storey townhouses lying between two tall blocks of flats set back from the road. *Peel* and *Campden Sts* are more mixed. The latter has terraces of 2/3-storey period/modern cottages and houses. More painted/ brick and stucco cottages are found in *Peel St*, where half of the N side is taken up by the tall red and grey brick blocks of Campden Houses. *Bedford Gardens* to the S is a particularly leafy street with mainly 3-storey houses.

Terraces of mainly 3-storey white stucco houses and some big villas stand on the N side of *Sheffield Terrace*. (Poet and novelist G K Chesterton lived at No 32). By contrast, most of the S side is lined by a long row of matching 4-storey and basement red brick gabled buildings with white stucco and striped entrances. Another 5-storey and basement red brick and stone block, Campden House, lies at the corner of *Hornton St*. Hidden away behind the S side of *Sheffield Terrace* is a two and a half acre private communal garden. Residents of properties in *Hornton St* and *Gloucester Walk* also have access. *Gloucester Walk* has a mix of modern flats and red brick gabled mansions as well as 3/4-storey brick and stucco houses.

Tucked away off the N-W end of *Hornton St* opposite *Gloucester Walk* is *Campden House Close*. A narrow lane leads to a group of 2-storey cottages set around a pleasant spacious courtyard. Varying styles of houses and flats stretch down *Hornton St*, including some large semi-detached paired stucco properties. An eye-catching terrace of brown brick and white striped Victorian buildings with elaborate stucco decoration is stepped down the W side as far as *Holland St*. The style continues into *Observatory Gardens* with its red brick and stone striped 3-storey houses. An attractive terrace of 20th century Dutch-style houses extends down *Hornton St* opposite the Town Hall.

Cutting across *Hornton St* is *Holland St*, a popular narrow road where properties nudge the £1 million mark. Detached stucco houses and Georgian-style terraces are interspersed with a handful of speciality shops and restaurants. An undistinguished terrace of 20th century houses lies on the S side. Halfway along *Holland St* is *Gordon Place*. The S end forms a pretty, overgrown walkway, set back from the road and looking like a country lane. Hidden behind the trees and mature front gardens are two terraces of Georgian-style houses turned sideways on to *Holland St*. Just N of the E end of *Holland St*, through a gateway off *Kensington Church St*, is Bullingham Mansions. This yellow and red brick and stone Dutch-style block is built around a landscaped fountain courtyard guarded by some impressive stone lions.

Dominating the S-E corner of the neighbourhood is Kensington's parish church, St Mary Abbots, with its dramatic 250 foot spire, the tallest in London.

Kensington Palace

As its name suggests, the focal point of the neighbourhood is Kensington Palace. The Renaissance-style palace, rebuilt in the late 17th century by Sir

Christopher Wren, is set in Kensington Gardens. Once the main royal residence, these days it is the London home of the Prince and Princess of Wales, Princess Margaret and various other members of the Royal Family.

The next most exclusive address in the neighbourhood is *Kensington Palace Gardens*, a long tree-lined avenue running N/S past the palace and gardens. Stately mansions with sweeping driveways and landscaped grounds line this prestigious private road. Although known as 'Millionaire's Row', most of the once private residences have now been taken over by embassies. The road is guarded by gates and gatekeepers at both ends. At the S-W end, overlooking Kensington Palace, lies the vacant Kensington Barracks site. Regalian Properties is building Britain's most expensive flats. The ultra-exclusive £90 million development of vast luxury apart-ments with separate guest or staff suites cost from £2 million up to £10 million for each of three penthouses. Building should be completed by spring 1990, but flats are already being marketed. Prince Charles raised objections to the ori-ginal scheme: the flats will overlook the Palace.

Alongside the Barracks site in *York House Place*, a narrow passageway leads to York House, a prestigious Victorian mansion block. The 7-storey red brick and stone block with red and white striped gables stands in a relatively quiet cul-de-sac with an ornamental water garden in the mid-dle, creating a courtyard.

The passageway continues into *Kensington Church St*. From here the streets wend their way gradually uphill to *Notting Hill Gate*. *Church Close*, opposite the Carmelite Church in *Kensington Church St* is a 3-storey red brick and stone Tudor-style com-plex, set around an inner garden courtyard.

K

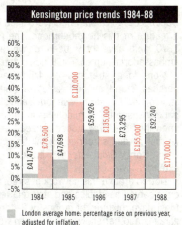

Kensington price trends 1984-88

■ London average home: percentage rise on previous year, adjusted for inflation.

■ Typical home in this area, percentage rise on previous year, adjusted for inflation.

Two-bed flat in the Marloes Road area, price change compared to London-wide average home. As with other prestige areas, Kensington did its racing ahead in '84 and '85. In 1988 its high starting price meant it barely beat inflation, but easy resales in this prestige area make such homes safe if not spectacular investments.

The scale suddenly changes where *Vicarage Gate* branches off *Kensington Church St*. Two 8-storey 1930s flats blocks, Winchester Court (W) and Vicarage Court (E) spread along each side of the street. The side of the latter block also occupies most of the S side of the E arm of *Vicarage Gate*. A Victorian brick and stucco terrace with polished marble porch columns stands on the N side. St Marys Abbot's modern vicarage is set in a private courtyard at the end of the street, forming a cul-de-sac. *Vicarage Gate* N contains a jumble of tall houses in varying styles. It leads to *Vicarage Gardens*, lined by terraces of white stucco properties N and brick and stuccos. A barrier of trees and shrubs separates *Vicarage Gate* from *Inverness Gardens*, a semi-circular sweep of 3-storey white stucco houses. More terraces of 3-storey and basement white stucco houses, some split into flats, are found in *Brunswick* and *Berkeley Gardens*.

The white paint continues in tree-lined *Palace Gardens Terrace* – 3-storey basement terraces on the E side and 4-storey and basement houses with elaborate Greek-style columned porches W. *Strathmore Gardens*, lying off the W side of the street, is a short cul-de-sac of 4-storey and basement stucco terraces. Just beyond here, *Palace Gardens Terrace* becomes part of a district one-way traffic system linking *Notting Hill Gate* with *Kensington Church St.*

Kensington Church St, a residential/shopping street lined by pubs, antique shops, galleries, and jewellers, among others, is a main N-S traffic route running between *Notting Hill Gate* and *Kensington High St.*

Queen's Gate

Queen's Gate is a busy boulevard lined by the grand stucco terraces which are a feature of this neighbourhood. The majority were built between 1850 and 1870 and have now been converted into flats, hotels, embassies and ambassadorial homes. The E side of the street is the boundary.

More long stretches of 4/5-storey Victorian terraces, with columned porches, stand on both sides of *Queen's Gate Terrace* (white and cream stucco) and *Elvaston Place* (brick and stucco). Both are wide streets with extra parking space in the middle, as in *Queen's Gate*. In *Queen's Gate Gardens*, the imposing 5/6-storey stucco terraces are set around three sides of a large leafy central garden screened by tall trees. A 1960s flats block, Campbell Court, which fronts *Gloucester Rd*, backs on to the W side of the garden with its extensive lawns.

Dotted around this network of streets is a series of small-scale mews, which once served as stables and staff quarters for the large houses they lie behind. Most have mixtures of groups of 2-storey brick/painted cottages and working garages and car showrooms. *Queen's Gate Mews*, lying just off *Queen's Gate Terrace* at a right angle to *Gloucester Rd*, has the added attraction of its own pub, the Queen's Arms. Facing the pub is an old-fashioned three pump petrol station opposite a vintage car showroom, boasting Bugattis and Bentleys among other top makes. Impressive classical-style stone arches lead into *Elvaston Mews* and *Queen's Gate Place Mews*. The latter sits behind more 5-storey brick and stucco terraces in *Queen's Gate Place*. It is wider than the other mews, leaving room for cobbled forecourts in front of the varied modern and period 2-storey cottages.

The tall brick and stucco terraces reappear in *Gloucester Rd*, a busy district road and shopping centre. They have been turned into hotels, offices or flats, usually with shops on the ground floor. *Gloucester Rd* merges into *Palace Gate*, which is lined mainly by a collection of highly individual stone, or red brick and stone, period buildings, occupied by embassies, offices and flats.

Exclusive *Kensington Gate* lies to the E at the point where *Palace Gate* and *Gloucester Rd* meet. Two grand terraces of richly-ornamented 3/4-storey white stucco Victorian houses stretch along a narrow strip of garden with tall trees and well-kept flower beds. At each end of the terraces stand paired 'tower' houses, looking like iced wedding cakes. *Kensington Gate* and *Hyde Park Gate* to the N still have high proportions of single family houses.

The E leg of *Hyde Park Gate* contains a mix of period/modern houses and flats, plus some large 'one-off' houses such as number 28, where Sir Winston Churchill lived and died. Tall red brick and stone mansions and an 11-storey 1960s red brick flats block, Broadwalk House, stand on either side of the entrance to the more exclusive W leg of the street. Beyond here, the street opens out into a circle with a central garden. A handful of elegant detached villas with their own large gardens sit around the circle. Halfway along the street off to the W is *Reston Place*, a charming little enclave of 2-storey white-painted cottages set around a secluded courtyard.

The *Kensington Rd* frontage of the neighbourhood is dominated by the huge modern 11-storey red brick Thorney Court flats block, and Broadwalk House, which overlook Kensington Gardens. In common with the other period/modern properties lining the N boundary (flats, embassies and offices), they are set back from the road behind driveways and screens of trees.

De Vere/Cornwall

West of *Gloucester Rd* is a neighbourhood that in many ways is the heart of Kensington. It runs S from the centuries-old *Kensington Square* in a series of quiet, leafy streets.

Gloucester Rd is a busy road lined by a mix of residential and commercial properties and shops. It has a tube station. The main residential grouping is the 4/5-storey Edwardian red brick and stone mansion block of St George's Court, which has a row of shops on the ground floor.

Behind St Stephen's Church at the S-W end of *Gloucester Rd* is *Emperor's Gate*. This almost triangular-shaped street has a tiny triangle of green in the middle and a central block of painted stucco terraced properties sitting on a similarly shaped site. A terrace of late Victorian red brick and stucco buildings with ornate columned porches stands on the W side and a terrace of 5-storey and basement brick and stucco prop-

K

It may look 18th century – but it is modern. A clever pastiche of the Kensington town house style, with 'Georgian' fanlight, panelled door with windows either side – even the ivy is authentic. For the real thing in Kensington, visit Kensington Square, which grew up as homes for Palace courtiers and has some beautiful Queen Anne and early Georgian houses.

erties on the E. Most are split into flats. Concealed behind a red brick and stone arch in the N-E corner of the street is *Osten Mews*, a looped cobbled mews of 2-storey painted cottages.

The view here is dominated by the towering shape of Point West, a luxury apartment block on the site of the former West London Air Terminal fronting *Cromwell Rd*. Many of the 400-plus flats were initially sold off-plan and have risen in price by about 10 per cent in a year. Many resales starting at £130,000 for a studio flat, increasing to £1 million for penthouses. Thirty penthouses to be launched this summer. Special features are a health club, restaurant, shops, business meeting suites and secretarial services. Developers are Berkley House.

On either side of *Grenville Place* (brick and stucco terraces), lies pretty *Cornwall Mews South* with a mix of 2-storey period/modern brick and painted cottages. Just up the road, the scale changes dramatically in *Cornwall Gardens* with its tall cliffs of white stucco. Terraces of mid-19th century Italianate houses with columned porches stretch along both sides of three large private gardens. The trees match the height of the 5-storey and basement houses, long ago divided into flats of various sizes and conditions. Some flats are very large.

Launceston Place to the N signals the beginning of an enclave of highly-desirable, quiet steets lying in the heart of the neighbourhood. The group is bounded by *Launceston Place* itself and *Victoria Grove* E, *Stanford Rd* W, *Albert Place* N and *Kynance Mews* S.

Picturesque *Kynance Mews* must rate as the most attractive mews in the whole of Kensington and Chelsea. Divided in two by *Launceston Place*, the shorter E section is lined by 2/3-storey white/cream painted cottages and has a splendid view of Queen's Tower. The W and most delightful section is full of charming vine-covered 2-storey cottages of different styles. A profusion of flowers and shrubs spread along the mews in tubs and urns. Part of the N side backs on to the walled gardens of houses in *Eldon Rd* and the prize-winning gardens of Christ Church in *Victoria Rd*, giving the mews a particularly leafy look at this point.

Halfway along the mews, a set of steps leads past the Pooh Corner Montessori Nursery School to *Victoria Rd*. Small groups of semi-detached stucco/brick and stucco villas with leafy front gardens line the most desirable stretch of the street S of *Cambridge Place*, where homes can fetch over £1 million. North of here, the road is flanked by the backs of hotels fronting adjoining streets.

More 2-storey semi-detached Victorian villas are found in *Launceston Place*, running parallel. The black and white colour scheme is accentuated by the black window canopies remaining on the houses on the W side of the street. *Eldon Rd* is a particularly attractive street with terraces of pastel-painted 3-storey stucco houses adjoining Christ Church on the corner of *Victoria Rd*. Groups of highly individual brick/stucco houses stand on the N side. Tree-lined *Cottesmore Gardens* to the N has paired 3-storey stucco villas and more big individual houses.

The W end of the street runs into *Stanford Rd*, lined by detached brick and stucco villas, paired stucco/brick and stucco houses and simple brick and stucco terraces. Standing in their midst is Cottesmore Court, a tall 1930s brown brick flats block, which spreads around into *Kelso Place*. The S arm of this T-shaped street has rows of 2/3-storey brick terraced houses backing onto St Mary Abbots Hospital on the W side. The hospital site is earmarked for redevelopment as there are plans to merge St Mary Abbots with another hospital. Nearly nine acres of this choice site is expected to be sold off for a 'grand scale' residential development. A modern brown brick townhouse development lies in a private cul-de-sac at the end of the W arm of *Kelso Place*, which flanks the underground line (above ground at this point).

Running across the N end of *Stanford Rd* is *St Alban's Grove*. More brick and stucco detached houses and stucco paired houses can be found on the S side opposite Richmond College, the American international college of London. Next to it is the red brick and stucco block of St Alban's Mansions. The W end of the street culminates in a small local shopping centre, a feature of which is the famous Leith School of Food and Wine. A bunch of grapes and a knife and fork have been wittily worked into the brickwork of the gabled building. Just around the corner to the S, hidden from the street, are the vine-covered St

Alban's Studios, set around a neo-Tudor courtyard.

The E end of the street also forms a pleasant villagy shopping centre at its junction with *Victoria Grove*. A terrace of 1840s stucco houses with a continuous black first-floor canopy and unusual decorative ironwork columns stretches along the N side. It joins up with more shops spilling around the corner from *Gloucester Rd*.

Canning Place just to the N is a pleasant, leafy street with pairs of linked stucco villas and a terrace of 2/3-storey and basement stucco houses. On the N side are the entrances to two converted mews developments, *De Vere Cottages* and *De Vere Mews*. Both have white cottages with black detailing set around private courtyards. *De Vere Gardens* off to the N is lined mainly by tall brick and stucco terraces converted into flats with hotels at its N end.

Canning Passage, a pedestrian walkway, runs through to *Victoria Rd*. Off this road is a series of three leafy cul-de-sacs – *Albert*, *Cambridge* and *Douro Places*. The first two have early Victorian stucco villas. Much of *Douro Place* was completely rebuilt following war damage, resulting in modern and period houses standing side by side. The cul-de-sac here is created by the rear of the flats in Kensington Court.

Kensington Court is both the name of the street and the red-brick Dutch-style development which dominates this seven acre triangular site S of *Kensington High St*. A series of mansion blocks and terraces of gabled houses of differing heights and degrees of ornamentation make up the development. Built between 1880-1900, Kensington Court was the first group of buildings in London to be lighted by electricity. At the S end of *Kensington Court* is *Kensington Court Mews*, an unusual late Victorian multi-storey stable block, which now has two tiers of flats above ground floor garages. Another 5/6-storey red-brick block, Kensington Court Gardens, stands on the E side of *Kensington Court Place*, dwarfing the terrace of early 19th century cottages opposite.

K

Beyond *Thackeray St* with its parade of shops is *Kensington Square*. This is one of London's oldest squares, dating back to 1685, when it was built to house Palace courtiers. Blue plaques dotted around the square with its large central gardens give a clue to its former distinguished residents, including Edward Burne-Jones, Mrs Patrick Campbell and John Stuart Mill. Some of the buildings, which range from Jacobean and Georgian to 1900s developments, remain as houses. Others have been converted into offices. House of Fraser plan 22 flats in a new-build/conversion scheme behind the Square.

Scarsdale/Abingdon

The Circle Line in its deep cutting and the St Mary Abbots hospital divide this neighbourhood from *Kensington Square* to the E.

Wright's Lane is the entry point from *Kensington High St*. The street, with its mix of modern shops and office blocks, opens out at its S end to form a wide service area for the big London Tara and Kensington Close Hotels. On the W side of the street, not far from its junction with *Kensington High St*, stand two of the late Victorian mansion blocks which make up Iverna Court. Iverna Court is a set piece development of 5/7/8-storey and basement red brick and stone mansion blocks with elaborate stucco entrances and black cast iron balconies. The blocks spread around the corner into *Iverna Gardens*, stetching almost to its junction with *Abingdon Villas*. Flats in the square at the N end of the street overlook the unusual white marble St Sarkis Armenian Church, which sits in the middle, behind a rectangular strip of tall trees and shrubs.

More tall brick and stone mansions, including the popular Zetland House, line the E side of busy *Marloes Rd* as far as St Mary Abbots Hospital (see above). The rest of the street has terraces of 3/4-storey and basement brick and stucco properties, some with shops and offices on the ground floors. The large grey concrete and blue glass building at the S junction with *Cromwell Rd* is the private Cromwell Hospital. It fronts the length of *Cromwell Rd* between here and *Lexham Gardens*.

Lexham Gardens stretches right across the neighbourhood, changing in character as it goes. The S crescent, which curves N from *Cromwell Rd*, contains mainly hotels, presumably remnants from the days when the West London Air Terminal stood behind the street. The rest of the brick and stucco terraced properties here have been converted into flats. Leading off the N end of the crescent is *Lexham Walk*, a pleasant passageway lined by white 2-storey cottages. It crosses into the De Vere/Cornwall neighbourhood to the E. *Lexham Gardens* E of *Marloes Rd* is made up of 4/5-storey and basement brick and stucco terraced houses of varying quality set around narrow central gardens. The houses in the W arm across *Marloes Rd* are built in the same style but generally of better quality. As in the E arm, most have been split into flats.

Tucked away behind *Lexham Gardens* are *Lexham* and *Radley Mews*, which join together at the S end of *Allen St*. The long cobbled mews has mostly 2-storey period/rebuilt brick/painted cottages with some garages and other light industrial uses. Emerge from the mews into *Stratford Rd* with its upmarket village shopping centre and terraces of 3-storey and basement brick and stucco houses, some with small front gardens and forecourt parking.

Lying off the N side of *Stratford Rd* around the corner from the parade of shops is *Blithfield St*, an appealing tree-lined cul-de-sac of colourfully-painted 3-storey terraced houses dating back to the 1860s. *Sunningdale Gardens* stands on the S side of *Stratford Rd* at the junction with *Abingdon Rd*. Here the terraces turn sideways on to form an attractive enclave of 3-storey and basement brick and stucco houses on two sides of a small central garden with trees in the middle.

Tucked well behind the houses on the N side of *Stratford Rd* near its junction with *Earls Court Rd* is *Shaftesbury Mews*, a development of modern 4-storey brown brick houses with garages. *Scarsdale Studios*, off *Stratford Rd*, is an enclave of nine artists' studios bult in the 1890s around a private courtyard. One was marketed last summer for £265,000.

Scarsdale Villas, another tree-lined street, has Victorian terraces of 3-storey and basement stucco, or brick and stucco houses up to *Allen St*. East of here, they become paired 3-storey and basement stucco-fronted villas N and similar style houses in groups of four S. In tree-lined *Abingdon Villas*, a mix of Victorian terraces of 3-storey and basement painted stucco, or brick and stucco terraced houses stand alongside tall red brick and stone mansion blocks. *Abingdon Court* N, which stretches from *Iverna Gardens* to *Allen St*, is a late Victorian block, and *Abingdon Gardens* S is Edwardian.

Allen St and *Abingdon Rd*, which runs N/S from *Kensington High St* to *Stratford Rd*, combine a mix of residential and commercial uses. Shops and restaurants spill around the corner from the high street into both. A short distance S of the high street in *Allen St* is *Wynnstay Gardens*, a development of 4/5-storey red brick and stucco flats blocks. One group fronts *Allen St* while further blocks are tucked away behind, lining a private road. Allen House, a red brick gabled block of timeshare flats, stands on the opposite side of the street near the listed Kensington Chapel, built in 1855 and noted for its classical facade. More mansion flats and 3-storey brick and stucco terraces lie to the S.

Beside the chapel is one of two entrances to *Adam and Eve Mews*. (The other is in *Kensington High St.*) The mews contain 2/3-storey modern/period houses, some garages and offices. *Eden Close* at the N-W end is a new red brick development where a mews has been created within a mews.

Abingdon Rd is lined by 2/3-storey brick and stucco/painted terraced houses of varying styles. The brown and red brick late Victorian flats in *Pater St* to the W spread around the corner into the N end of the street, merging with the shop and restaurants which lead to the high street.

Earls Court Rd on the W boundary of the neighbourhood is a two-way street as far S as *Stratford Rd* where it joins the notorious West London one-way traffic system. The most attractive residential section – a terrace of 4-storey and basement stucco fronted houses – lies between *Stratford Rd* and *Scarsdale Villas*. The unusual new cream and brown stone, brick and glass development at the junction of *Earls Court Rd* and *Kensington High St* is a flats and offices block, topped by a penthouse overlooking Holland Park. Monarch House has luxury flats to let, aimed at businessmen and expatriates, with hotel-style amenities.

K

Pembrokes/Edwardes Square

Although bounded by some of the busiest and noisiest roads in the borough this desirable neighbourhood contains some of the earliest and choicest properties in Kensington. The first surprise lies at the end of an unpromising lane off the N end of bustling *Earls Court Rd*, behind the Odeon cinema. Turn the corner to find *Pembroke Place*, an oasis of pretty painted 3-storey Victorian houses set around a courtyard with trees in the middle. The 3-storey brick and stucco terrace on the E side is a modern rebuild. Plans are in the pipeline to demolish the Odeon to make way for a new cinema, offices and flats complex. The 47 1-3 bed flats fronting *Kensington High St* and set around a grassed courtyard at the rear of the site are expected to cost around £100-£300,000. Developers Merivale Moore and the Prudential intend to start work Spring 1989, depending on planning consent.

Tucked away behind Kensington police station immediately to the S is *Pembroke Mews*. The mostly 2-storey brick/painted brick and stucco cottages vary widely in quality and condition but a noticeable amount of rebuilding is under way as buyers discover the charm and location.

Within yards of *Earls Court Rd* with its mix of residential/commercial properties is *Pembroke Square*. This Georgian square is neatly shielded from the main road by Rassells garden centre and the flower-bedecked Hansom Cab pub. Two terraces of 3-storey and basement mellow brick terraced houses with stucco-faced ground floors line a long private central garden. The garden has its own tennis court and even a daily weather chart posted on the gate. The W end of the square becomes *Pembroke Villas* to the S, an attractive colony of 3-storey paired stucco or brick and stucco villas set in gardens with tall trees overhanging the street.

Pembroke Walk, an easily missed cul-de-sac tucked away off the E side of the street, is a narrow lane with unusual, nay eccentric, 2/3-storey period and modern houses/studios. North of *Pembroke Square*, past the pretty Scarsdale pub with its profusion of hanging baskets, stands *Edwardes Square*, the gem of the neighbourhood. This fine late Georgian square was built in 1811-20. Immaculate terraces of beautiful 3-storey and basement brick houses with stucco ground floors stretch along the W and E sides of mature central gardens. Front gardens, vine-covered houses, hedges and overhanging trees contribute to the leafy look of the square, only a short walk from the shops and restaurants of *Kensington High St*. Green Victorian street lamps, original cast iron fanlights and black cast iron railings with unusual pineapple kingheads add to the period character.

The N side of the square is bounded by a long brick wall and mass of trees in the rear gardens of *Earls Terrace*, which fronts *Kensington High St*. Here a long uniform Georgian terrace of 4-storey and basement houses is set back from the main road behind a carriageway and trees. A matching terrace stands in nearby *Edwardes Place*, separated from the high street by a private passageway, iron gates and a screen of shrubs and trees.

The S arm of *Edwardes Square* feels like a separate street, being a complete contrast to the Georgian terraces. It has mostly studio houses (Annigoni lived here) alongside 1930s Pembroke Court, a 5-storey brick and stone flats block. These buildings face the white 'Temple', a listed gardener's cottage in the square garden designed to look like a Grecian temple. Lying just to the S of the square at its W end is *Pembroke Gardens Close*, a private landscaped cul-de-sac of very desirable 2-storey brick houses. This exceptional enclave has the peaceful air of a village green.

Pembroke Gardens (the name derives from the Welsh estates of Lord Kensington's family) is split into two arms. A feature of the N arm is *Pembroke Studios*, a complex of 2-storey red and brown brick Victorian houses looking like a group of 19th century almshouses. The studios are set around a central courtyard and the complex itself is separated from the street by a garden and large cast iron gates. The rest of the leafy street has a mix of brick and stucco paired houses, 1920s Dutch gabled houses, modern brick terraces and Victorian brick and stucco terraces.

Pembroke Rd is cut in two by the heavily-trafficked Earls Court one-way system, which runs southbound along the E stretch to join *Earls Court Rd*. Two large flats blocks – Chatsworth and Marlborough Courts – dominate the S side of the E arm. Painted brick, or stucco and brick, paired/detached stucco houses line the rest of the S and N sides.

A new red brick apartment block, Pembroke Heights, stands at the junction of *Pembroke Rd* and *Cromwell Crescent*. The development of 80 1-to-3-bed flats stretches to the council's central works depot on the corner with *Warwick Rd* W.

Although *Warwick Gardens* forms the S-bound section of the Earls Court one-way system, it is a relatively pleasant tree-lined street. Pairs of large Victorian stucco houses with columned porches and terraces of 3-storey and basement brick and stucco houses predominate. St Mary Abbots Court is a group of three large 7-storey brick and stone flats blocks which congregate at the N-W end of *Warwick Gardens*.

Warwick Rd is a major route on the N-bound section of the one-way system. The council's central works depot with a modern housing estate perched on top dominates the E side of the road. On the W side, public car and lorry parks, a petrol station, a Sainsbury's Homebase DIY centre and the West Kensington telephone exchange lie between the road and railway line. The proposed

Western Environmental Improvement Route (WEIR) will run beside the railway. See the borough profile and 'Transport' chapters for more details: this road, if built, will have a considerable effect on Kensington.

Phillimore Estate

Substantial Victorian houses and villas predominate in this salubrious, leafy neighbourhood where properties consistently change hands for £1 million plus. The streets climb gently uphill and are remarkably peaceful considering their proximity to busy *Kensington High St*.

Most of the big white stucco detached villas and 4/5-storey stucco/brick and stucco terraced houses on the W side of *Phillimore Gardens* have the added advantage of rear gardens backing on to Holland Park. More large detached houses stand on the E side, alongside 3-storey and basement brick and stucco semi-detached paired houses. Some have front gardens, others patios with tubs and urns of flowers.

A pedestrian passageway leads into Holland Park from the N side of the street where it joins *Duchess of Bedford's Walk* at the top of the hill. Plane Tree House, an award-winning 7-storey 1960s flats development, stands in the N corner overlooking the park. A series of Edwardian flats blocks, including the prestigious Duchess of Bedford House, spread along the rest of this tree-lined street, adjoining the campus of King's College on the E corner. The 7-storey brown brick and stone blocks stand in beautifully-kept landscaped grounds, set back behind neatly-clipped hedges.

They overlook the walled back gardens of houses in *Upper Phillimore Gardens*. This street is lined by large white stucco linked houses and smaller brick and stucco terraced homes, all with front gardens, hedges and doorstep urns full of roses and shrubs and bushes. Tall trees add to the street's charm. *Phillimore Place*, a one-way street, and *Essex Villas* have mainly 3-storey and basement brick and stucco terraced houses. The exception is a group of Tudor Gothic houses in the former. Taller, more ornate, brick and stucco terraces are found in *Stafford Terrace*.

The scene changes completely in *Phillimore Walk*, which is overshadowed by the back of Stafford Court, a big early 20th century brown brick and stone flats block. It fronts *Kensington High St* and takes up the whole block between *Phillimore Gardens* and *Argyll Rd*. More large semi-detached houses and white stucco terraces with front gardens line *Argyll Rd*.

The S end of *Campden Hill Rd*, which forms the neighbourhood's E boundary, also has big white stucco houses and brick and stucco terraces. They look across to the modern red brick Kensington Town Hall on the E side of the street.

Among those estate agents active in this area are:

- Alex Neil
- Allsops
- Aylesfords
- Jackson-Stops & Staff
- John D Wood
- Keith Cardale Groves
- Knight Frank & Rutley
- Marsh & Parsons
- Prudential Property Services
- Savills
- W A Ellis
- Cluttons

K

Kentish Town and Tufnell Park

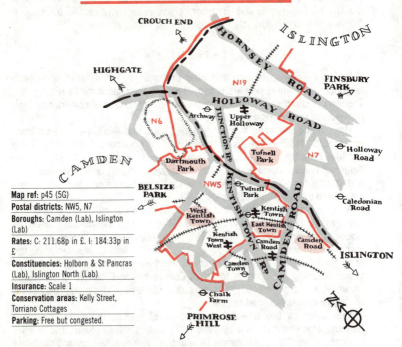

Map ref: p45 (5G)

Postal districts: NW5, N7

Boroughs: Camden (Lab), Islington (Lab)

Rates: C: 211.68p in £. I: 184.33p in £

Constituencies: Holborn & St Pancras (Lab), Islington North (Lab)

Insurance: Scale 1

Conservation areas: Kelly Street, Torriano Cottages

Parking: Free but congested.

Transport   Tubes: Kentish Town, Tufnell Park (zone 2, Northern). From Tufnell Park: Oxford Circus 20 min (1 change); City 15 min; Heathrow 55 min (1 change). British Rail: Kentish Town (to St Pancras); Gospel Oak, Kentish Town West, Camden Rd (North London Line).

Convenient for   Hampstead Heath, road links to North. Miles from centre: 3.

Schools   ILEA Divisions 2/3: Acland Burghley, Parliament Hill, Jewish Free School, Camden School for Girls, William Ellis (b), La Sainte Union Convent (g).

Flats	S	1b	2b	3b	4b	5b
Average prices	55–65	70–95	80–120	120–150+	150+	–
Houses	2b	3b	4b	5b	6/7b	8b
Average prices	130–180	130–190	190–275+	280+	300+	–

The properties   Largely 1840s onwards, mostly terraced, many houses now flats. Some streets of Hampstead quality, other parts disrupted by council building good and bad. Grander terraces and squares on Camden borders.

The market   Brisk conversion/renovation activity in this convenient if mixed area. The closer to tubes and the further from main through-routes, the higher the price. An area that will increase in status. Local searches: Camden 12 weeks, Islington 2 weeks.

Area Profile

The Kentish Town area was one this guide tipped for 1988, and indeed it is moving briskly up the status scale. We draw your attention to the North London Line, which goes direct to the City Airport – thus making Gospel Oak Station 2 hours 10 minutes from Paris.

The first mentions of 'Kentystown', 'Kentisshton' and 'Kentissetone' begin to be found in documents dating from as early as the 13th century when it probably started life as a cluster of houses around an inn – a welcome refuge on what was one of the few roads leading north from the city through the forbidding Forest of Middlesex.

The village grew as the area around became important farming land, but the real population explosion came in the 1840s when large-scale development began – catering for middle-class families with servants, but not being able to compete with its illustrious northern neighbours, Hampstead and Highgate, for really wealthy inhabitants.

The area passed through ups and downs, becoming first a rather pretty and fashionable place, but then falling into a long and steady decline which lasted until the 1960s when two important things happened. The first was the dramatic acceleration of large council housing development schemes started by St Pancras Council and then, more importantly, by the newly-formed larger Borough of Camden, which changed the face of Kentish Town, particularly in the west. The second was that Kentish Town began to benefit as an overflow area into which trickled those who just couldn't quite afford to buy property in Hampstead or Highgate. This factor is still the dominant feature of the property market in the area.

K

There is still a steady stream of small and medium-sized houses coming onto the market – and prices for these have gone up relatively more quickly than in other parts of London, particularly since the late '70s and early '80s when unrepeatable bargains were to be had.

There is also an increasingly large volume of converted flats – particularly 1- and 2-bedroom units – coming on stream, with many more in the pipeline. But the conversion frenzy has assumed nothing like the extent of what happened in recent years in places like Little Venice, Maida Vale and West Hampstead.

Dartmouth Park

This is the area where people first realised that Kentish Town had streets to offer that were every bit as nice as in Hampstead, *and* just as close to Hampstead Heath *and* with all the same advantages of good transport links (see above) *and* being close to the West End – but where prices were, and still are, significantly lower.

Formerly owned by the Earl of Dartmouth and developed in the 1870s, the area lies between *Dartmouth Park Hill* in the E to *Highgate Rd* in the W, and from Highgate's Holly Lodge Estate and the famous cemetery down to heavily trafficked *Chetwynd Rd*.

Particularly popular are *Dartmouth Park Rd* and *Dartmouth Park Avenue* with their large terraced houses in blocks of three, many of which have been converted, as well as *Boscastle Rd* which is literally a stone's throw from the Heath across *Highgate Rd*. *Coutts Crescent*, a development of 11 4-bed houses, is off *St Alban's Rd*. Prices last autumn were £420-475,000.

These streets can get a bit choked with traffic during the morning rush hour as motorists desperately search for alternative ways through the Kentish Town bottleneck, but the myriad attractions (including four excellent state secondary schools virtually on the doorstep – William Ellis, Parliament Hill and Acland Burghley comprehensives, as well as La Sainte Union convent school) heavily outweigh the disadvantages. Camden Council is also considering a number of measures to stop rush-hour through traffic from using the area.

There are also hidden delights, such as the sports ground, tennis courts and bowling club tucked away off *Croftdown Rd*, and the sudden views W and S from some of the houses in the higher streets.

Perhaps the most elegant (and pricy) homes in Kentish Town are the splendid terrace of deceptively large houses in *Grove Terrace* off *Highgate Rd*, which significantly pre-date the rest of the area, having been built in the late 18th century.

West Kentish Town

This is the area of Kentish Town (W of the busy Kentish Town Road shopping centre) most dominated by huge council estates which have swallowed up dozens of Victorian streetscapes. They range from some of the worst of municipal mistakes to shining showpieces of successful modern urban development. But in amongst the large estates and tower blocks there are still some pleasant streets and still some opportunities to buy unmodernised properties in roads that are steadily improving and may well prove to be bargains in the long run.

There are interesting terraces in Maitland Park, on the W edge of the neighbourhood, and also at the S-W end of *Queen's Crescent*, the eastern end of which becomes a bustling street market on some days and was the site of the opening of the second-ever Sainsburys shop in 1876 ... . Also worth looking at are the interesting set of little cul-de-sacs off *Queen's Crescent*, including *St Thomas's Gardens*, *Baptist Gardens*, *St Ann's Gardens* and *Modbury Gardens*. Permission has been given for a small development of flats and houses in Highgate Rd.

Pockets of good properties can also be found in the S, towards Chalk Farm, in streets around *Castlehaven Rd* in the area S of *Prince of Wales Rd*. There is a positively delightful group of streets including *Healey St*, *Grafton Crescent* and the northern end of *Hadley St* containing cheerful and exquisitely preserved 2-storey terraces which are part of the Kelly Street Conservation Area, the only one in Kentish Town proper.

East Kentish Town

The triangle bounded by *Kentish Town Rd*, *Camden Rd* and *Brecknock Rd* contains the heartland of Kentish Town – and is largely unvandalised by the council, with the exception of some crumbling pre-war estates in the *Islip St* area, which should be avoided.

Otherwise the area is awash with fast-improving streets, most of which are still far short of their potential. And although prices are rising in line with the improvement, there is still a good supply of (smaller) family houses, and an increasing supply of flat conversions and lots of rather run-down properties to be had – if you can get there before the developers.

There is also a great deal of charm and elegance, particularly in roads like

Patshull Rd, *Bartholomew Rd*, *Lawford Rd* and *Bartholomew Villas* (which contains the well-known Kentish Town Community Health Centre), most of which have attractive 3-storey terraces, with pleasing architectural features such as cast-iron balconies.

North of the rather narrow and busy *Leighton Rd* there are more rewards and surprises. The main surprise is *Lady Margaret Rd*, built in the early 1860s, which is almost twice as wide and gracious as any other residential street in the area. Leading off it are the rewards, traditionally narrow streets that are among the most intensively gentrified in London, including *Falkland Rd*, *Ascham St*, *Dunollie Rd*, *Leverton St*, *Ravely St*, *Countess Rd* and *Montpelier Grove*, all with 2- and 3-storey terraces and semi-detached rows.

Tufnell Park

Mainly in the Borough of Islington, this area, bounded by *Camden Rd*, *Brecknock Rd* and *Holloway Rd*, was almost completely ignored by buyers and even estate agents until about 10 years ago, and it is still much more blighted by its rather down-market reputation – and association with the Holloway area – than it deserves. In reality it contains a nest of extremely pleasant streets which, although bordered by some polluted and juggernaut-dominated trunk roads, are themselves quiet, charming and relatively free of through traffic. Flat conversions have proliferated.

K

There are some large council estates in the southern part (as well as the famous Holloway Prison for women), but closer to the tube station in the W there are increasingly popular roads such as *Hugo R*d and *Corinne Rd* with attractive 2-storey terraces.

North of *Tufnell Park Rd* itself there is the very pleasant *Huddleston Rd* cul-de-sac, and the group of roads around *Tytherton Rd* which include *Mercers Rd* (convenient for open playing fields), *Yerbury Rd*, *Beversbrook Rd*, *Campdale Rd* and *Foxham Rd* with its unusually pleasing development of modern council houses together with communal gardens and children's playground.

In Tufnell Park, the rule of thumb is: avoid *Holloway Rd*. But at the same time it is interesting to see just how close one can get to that road before it starts impinging on the neighbouring properties.

King's Cross Borders

The southernmost part of Kentish Town is destined dramatically to feel the effects of the giant King's Cross Railway Lands development due to get under way in a few years' time. Streets closest to the vast site will no doubt suffer the inconvenience of being near what will be the largest single development in Europe, but eventually proximity to it, with its envisaged housing, new park and huge commercial centre, can only have a beneficial effect on prices. Values in the immediate area of the site have already shot up.

Camden Road Borders

Strictly speaking part of Camden Town (which also see) and in the NW1 postal district, the Camden Square Conservation Area is in essence very much part of the eastern section of Kentish Town. The houses are larger here, though, and more splendid, particularly the terraced and semi-detached examples in

Camden Square itself (with its children's playground), *Cantelowes Rd*, *St Augustine's Rd*, *North Villas*, *South Villas* and *Murray St*. There are also attractive houses in *Camden Mews* and smaller, 2-storey terraces in *Marquis Rd*. These roads are protected from through-traffic by a series of road closures.

Across *York Way* and NE of a large council estate, there are roads off *Hillmarton Rd* which have large rather grand houses now mostly flats. These streets too are well blocked off to through-traffic and are convenient for Caledonian Road tube on the Piccadilly Line. On the Islington borders, on old railway sidings off *Stock Orchard St*, Laing are building 34 3 and 4-bed houses and 100 1 and 2-bed flats. Prices from £95,000.

Archway Borders

On the Camden (W) side, this area is sometimes known as Highgate New Town because of its proximity to the rather superior examples of council housing built by Camden at the northern end. But between *Junction Rd* and *Dartmouth Park Hill* there are some streets full of character such as *Bickerton Rd* and *Tremlett Grove*, which also adjoin a little-known and un-named park around a covered reservoir.

On the Islington side, and E of *Archway Rd*, which is virtually a motorway at this point, there is a surprisingly secluded set of roads which have become very popular in recent years. North of the huge GLC-built council estate blocks in *St John's Way*, these streets include the Whitehall Park Conservation Area, comprising *Whitehall Park*, *Gladsmuir Rd* and *Haberton Rd*, a relatively well-preserved Victorian estate ranging from grand semis to modest 2-storey terraces, but all with attractive architectural features. Other streets in this area well worth a long second look include *Gresley Rd*, *Dresden Rd*, *Cheverton Rd* and *Parolles Rd*.

Among those estate agents active in this area are:
- Brian Lack
- Benham & Reeves
- Dillons
- Ellis & Co
- Lloyds
- McHugh & Co
- Salter Rex
- Folkard & Hayward

Kew and Sheen

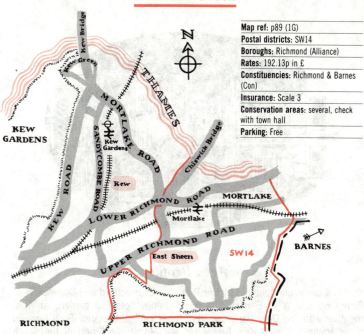

Map ref:	p89 (1G)
Postal districts:	SW14
Boroughs:	Richmond (Alliance)
Rates:	192.13p in £
Constituencies:	Richmond & Barnes (Con)
Insurance:	Scale 3
Conservation areas:	several, check with town hall
Parking:	Free

K

Transport	Tubes: Kew Gardens (zone 3a/b District).To Oxford Circus: 32 min (1 change), City 37 min (1 change), Heathrow 43 min (1 change). British Rail: Kew Gardens (North London Line), Mortlake to Waterloo 20 min.
Convenient for	Kew Gardens, Richmond Park; M4 to Heathrow and West; M3, M25.
Schools	Richmond Education Authority: Shene School.

Flats	S	1b	2b	3b	4b	5b
Average prices	58–75	70–95	85–125	115–145	–	–
Houses	2b	3b	4b	5b	6/7b	8b
Average prices	125–160	150–275+	185–400+	250–600	400–850	→

The properties	Kew boasts Victorian villas and gracious Georgiana (premier site around the Green), plus rows of pretty cottages, and some modern blocks of flats. Many flat conversions. There are a few 1930s semis, like those which proliferate in East Sheen. Some Sheen surprises are older cottages and Edwardian terraces. Its grandest homes (Fife Rd) can reach £800,000 or more.
The market	This area is attracting younger families these days. The professionals and those who are 'something in the City' find family homes from servicable semis upwards at prices less expensive than Barnes/Richmond. Georgian splendour commands half a million and more. Local searches: 3+4 weeks.

Area Profile

Kew is a peninsula bounded by the Thames S of Brentford and Chiswick, N of Richmond and W of Barnes. The world-famous botanical gardens at Kew, together with Old Deer Park, take up 50 per cent of the area. Busy *Kew Rd* bears traffic SW from *Kew Bridge Rd* and *Mortlake Rd*, part of the South Circular forks SE. Between these roads is the bulk of the area's housing. The Kew Garden side of *Sandycombe Rd* is sought after, with the eastern side increasing in desirability.

Despite its historic importance, Kew has only recently shrugged off its fuddy-duddy image. Ten years ago it was considered an old people's area but recent pressures for spacious houses near open spaces and good schools has seen an influx of young families.

Kew Green and Gardens

The most prestigious property is found around *Kew Green*, where gracious Georgian houses and cottages, surrounded by mature trees, decked with wisteria and backing onto the river can scrape the £750,000 mark. To the E of the *Green*, *Bushwood*, *Priory*, and *Maze Rds* are leafy Victorian/Edwardian 3-bed terraces which can command prices of up to £350,000. Close to the bridge, *Thetis Terrace* and *Cambridge* and *Watcombe Cottages* (2 beds) fetch prices of £150,000 for their 2-bed cottages. A row of cottages (slightly sunken) overlooking the Thames and Strand on the Green and fronted with green lawns can cost around £200,000.

South into *Kew Rd* from the *Green*, there is a clutch of interesting houses on the left hand side ranging from *Hanover Place* (early 18th century) to later styles with Regency bow windows. These give way to large Victorian villas interspersed with modern blocks of mansion flats: if high enough they can have views over the Gardens. Past Newens (the traditional English tea shop serving Maid of Honour tarts), *Kew Gardens Rd* dog-legs around towards *Station*

Approach. Large 3-storey Victorian houses dominate; some flats, some spacious family houses.

Station Approach and *Station Parade* join at Kew Gardens station (District Line). Pretty little shops – aimed mostly at tourists – are beginning to also supply day to day foodstuffs for locals, but residents say there is room for improvement. The only other shopping area is *Sandycombe Rd* which has an odd mish-mash of junk shops, and the little shops dotted around the Green.

Popular *Lichfield* and *Ennerdale Rd* join *Kew Rd* and *Sandycombe Rd*. Here the large Victorian family houses with 5 bedrooms (some converted into desirable flats) cost £450,000-500,000+ *Ennerdale Rd* (transversed by *The Avenue*) stretches down to *Stanmore Gardens* and the Victorian houses are interspersed with solid '30s styles. Turning E into *Gainsborough Rd* there is a recent development of neo-Georgian houses on the site of a school; opposite some little council houses. On *Kew Road*, between *Lichfield Rd* and *Hatherley Rd*, are two new flats developments. Charles Church aims to finish 16 1-and 2-bed flats in a Georgian-style block by August. Prices range from £114-170,000. Bewlay Homes have just finished 11 flats nearby.

On the E side of *Sandycombe Rd*, past the shops, there are pretty 2-bed cottages which are fetching over £110-130,000; to the W of *Sandycombe Rd* there are *Victoria Cottages* and *Elizabeth Cottages*, which fetch a little more because they do not back onto the railway.

East of *Sandycombe Rd*, towards *Mortlake Rd* are *Atwood Avenue*, *Marksbury Avenue* and *Chelwood Gardens* where large '30s houses have been renovated to provide solid family homes. They are now commanding prices of around £210-250,000 for a well-maintained 4-bed house. Gardens on this side of Kew are supposed to be more spacious. For bargain 3-bed houses (Victorian/Edwardian) look towards *Dancer*, *Darell* and *Raleigh Rds* where they can be picked up for around £125-150,000, although they do run down to a particularly soulless stretch of the *Lower Richmond Rd*.

The Kew riverside, between Kew rail bridge and Chiswick road bridge, is currently the subject of plans by Kew Riverside Developments Ltd. Whether it will definitely involve housing was not known at the time of writing, but a riverside view and a Richmond postal address makes it highly likely.

Sheen

East Sheen lies either side of the *Upper Richmond Rd*; S of Mortlake and Barnes and E of Richmond. Its boundaries are *South Worple Way* (N), Sheen and Palewell Common (S); with *Clifford Avenue* and *Stanley Rd* to the west.

Richmond was once called Sheen until Henry VII built a palace there and named it after his Yorkshire estates. East Sheen – a hamlet until the turn of the century – hangs on to the name. It is Saxon for 'bright and shining place'.

There is nothing bright and shining about the *Upper Richmond Rd*. It comprises a sprawl of '30s shops typical of any English suburb, with excellent supermarkets and restaurants attracting people from Richmond and Barnes. However, there are stunning houses on the fringes of Richmond Park (with prices to match) and bargain surprises on the Mortlake side. Parts of Sheen may not be as fashionable an address as Barnes or Richmond, but it attracts young families and first time buyers who enjoy much the same facilities and lower prices.

Between *South Worple Way* and *Upper Richmond Rd West* lie *Trehern*, *Lewin*,

Kings and *Queens Rds* (sometimes referred to as The Royals). These are 2-bed cottages which mirror those found in Little Chelsea, Barnes. At around £130-140,000, they are slightly cheaper and some seem a little larger. A pretty 2-bed cottage along *South Worple Way* may cost less, but all the houses face a main Southern Region railway line which runs along the N side.

Further along where *Vernon Rd* joins *Portman Avenue* and *Thornton Rd* is an area of 3/4-bed Edwardian property. Across *Sheen Lane* (small shops) is *St Leonards Rd* which parallels the *Upper Richmond Rd* and finally swings into a curve before meeting *Clifford Avenue*. At the *Sheen Lane* end there are some lovely 3-storey, flat-fronted houses painted in pastel shades. Behind *St Leonards* and *Elm Rd* there is a pathway called *Model Cottages*.

These semi-detached cottages were built for poor labourers in the 1850s and have pretty front gardens with fruit trees and lavender bushes. Many have been extended to provide garages or extra room. Expect to pay over £250,000. A recently tarmaced road provides car access which makes them more desirable than similar cottages found in *Wrights Walk* Mortlake.

The western curve of *St Leonards Rd* is treelined and has large semi-detached Edwardian houses. Despite the railway it is surprisingly quiet.

Graemsdyke Avenue has quite plain Edwardian terraced houses made pretty by tiny bay windows. *Holmesdale Avenue* has unusual Edwardian cottages (with Dutch style gables) and facing doorways slightly at a slant. *Ormonde Rd* and *Carlton Rd* have grey houses with white wooden fences. A 3-bed house here can cost around £180,000. Converted flats are scattered throughout this area but particularly along *Elm Rd* and *St Leonards Rd*.

Parkside

South of the *Upper Richmond Rd* between *Stanley Rd* (with pretty cottages at the common end) and *Hertford Avenue* a number of roads snake up to the common. *Stanley*, *Derby*, *Deanhill* and *Coval Rds* begin with tight terraced Edwardian houses which gradually ease out into more space. Prices range from £195-210,000 in lower Parkside for 3/4-bed houses with a garden, but climb as the houses grow in size towards the common. There is a feeling of space, the roads are wide and curving and houses are either semi-detached or detached with driveways. Around *Vicarage Rd*, *Stonehill Rd* and *Hood Avenue* large postwar family houses enjoy the kind of space associated with the Surrey suburbs and yet East Sheen is less than seven miles from London. The largest and most prestigious houses are found along *Fife Rd* (around £800,000) and *Christ Church Rd*. One early 1930s property with swimming pool in Fife Rd was on the market last December at £1.25 million. There's a mix of Victorian/Thirties/postwar houses of 6-bed plus in the kind of individual architecture that money can buy.

There are two pretty pubs in the area, the Victoria (*West Temple Sheen Rd*) has a garden and the Plough Inn which is flanked by pretty cottages and faces Percy Lodge (Georgian), in *Christ Church Rd*. There are few disadvantages of the area. The closer to the common the further away you are from public transport and there are no corner shops. It is a good 10-15 minute walk to the *Upper Richmond Rd* (shops and buses) and 15-20 minutes to Mortlake station.

Among those estate agents active in this area are:
- Barnard Marcus
- Mann & Co
- W Hallett & Co
- Prudential
- Hamptons Dixon Porter
- Victor Lown

Kilburn and Kensal Rise

Map ref: p59 (2J)
Postal districts: NW6, W10
Boroughs: Brent (Lab) Westminster (Con
Rates: B:261.1p in £. W:136. 4p in £
Constituencies: Brent East (Lab), Westminster North (Con)
Insurance: Scale 1
Conservation areas: Queen's Park
Parking: Free

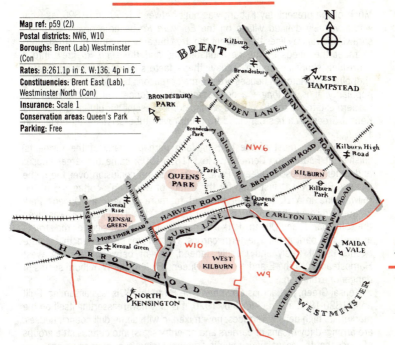

Transport — Tubes: Kilburn (zone 2, Jubilee) Queen's Park, Kensal Green, Kilburn Park (zone 2, Bakerloo) . From Kilburn: Oxford Circus 20 min (1 change), City 25 min (1 change), Heathrow 1hr 10min (2 changes). British Rail: Brondesbury 35 min to Liverpool St; Kilburn High Road 8 min to Euston, 30 min to Liverpool St. Others see map.

Convenient for — M1, North Circular Rd. A40 West End. Miles from centre: 4.

Schools — Brent Education Authority and ILEA zone 2: Brondesbury & Kilburn School, Aylestone Community School, South Kilburn Community School, St Augustine's C of E, St George's RC.

Flats	S	1b	2b	3b	4b	5b
Average prices	–	68–80	80–120	100+	–	–
Houses	2b	3b	4b	5b	6/7b	8b
Average prices	110–130	140–220	180–280+	180–300+	→	–

The properties — Terraces of small Victorian homes give way, round Queen's Park, to large Edwardian ones in broader streets. High rates in Brent.

The market — Prices are starting to reflect the area's good transport links and the growing popularity of next-door West Hampstead and Maida Vale. Good hunting-ground for first-time buyers of flats and small houses; Queen's Park area's family homes command up to £400,000. Local searches: Brent 5–6 weeks, Westminster 1 week.

Area Profile

Much of the present-day Kilburn was built between 1860 and 1890, as what was a vaguely defined village on the *Edgware Rd* became organised urban sprawl. The railway lines that dissect the area became punctuated with stations to meet the needs of the new inhabitants, and the *High Rd* grew into a flourishing shopping centre. Today, these factors of good transport, good shopping and Victorian houses are the major reasons behind Kilburn's growing popularity. It is no longer a down-market area (once you look beyond the modern estates to the S), but the up-and-coming neighbour of Maida Vale. The Kensal Green area has benefited from improved tube services, introduced in 1988.

Up to 1890, most of the housing (and perhaps many of the residents) finished at Paddington Cemetery. Next (1895-1905) came the larger houses and wider avenues of Queens Park. There is some confusion over the name Queens Park: it was first used for the estate of workmen's cottages S of the railway line in W10 (hereafter referred to more properly as Queens Park Estate). However, the 30-acre park N of *Harvist Rd*, laid out in 1886, was given the same name, and Queens Park as a neighbourhood now signifies the streets around the park itself. The term carries a premium: be warned that estate agents use it freely and loosely. Indeed, caught between creeping West Hampsteaditis to the E and a swollen Queens Park to the W, Kilburn seems in danger of extinction.

Kensal Green, just across *Chamberlayne Rd* to the W, is less assuming. Built up in 1880-1900 and run down by 1920, it is only now reasserting itself on the market. Its high-density terraces, now mixed in with some dull council houses, are arranged (by means of barriers and no-entry signs) into curious little groups of roads that the casual house-hunting motorist may never happen across.

Another neighbourhood that must be treated separately is West Kilburn, S of *Kilburn Lane*, not least because it is in Westminister where the rates are considerably lower than in Brent. Apart from the unspoilt Queens Park Estate, it is an area undergoing much change, with almost entire streets up for development and brand new flats fitted snugly in Victorian terraces.

For the area as a whole the police consider the crime rate high but this only really applies to particular estates. Pubs, for all Kilburn's reputation, are cavernous rather than numerous and are concentrated in the main shopping streets. Estate agents assert that schools are not an issue, as it is largely first-time buyers, joint mortgagees and young couples who are moving in, to replace those seeking a more fashionable postcode. New conversions can be snapped up as developers, eager to see some return on their investment, undercut market prices. Professional people with families continue to buy into leafy Queens Park.

Kilburn

The *High Rd*, with its shops, chain stores, pubs and stations (Kilburn tube, Brondesbury and High Rd BR) is the main artery rather than the heart of Kilburn; just about everything to the E of it is claimed by West Hampstead. A baroque 4-storey terrace on *Kilburn Priory* and four Georgian town houses on *Springfield Lane* stand out from the surrounding Abbey and Kilburn Vale estates. The latter includes attractive new mews-type homes over garages on *Mutrix Rd* and *Bransdale Close*. *West End Lane* here has some purpose-built blocks, both private and council; *Birchington Rd* has 4-storey terraces with imposing porches. North of *Quex Rd*, which has the main Catholic church are the ornate terraces of *Mazenod Avenue,* while *Kingsgate Rd* has a mixture of terraces with basement flats, council blocks and flats over shops. The terraces of *Messina Avenue* stand opposite a school and a small park, N of which is more council housing up to the railway line.

Across the *High Rd* and N of *Willesden Lane, Dyne Rd* has some large square-fronted houses, not all flats, that look like semis but which are joined at the back. *Torbay Rd* has smaller terraces while *Plympton* and *Buckley Rds* have 3-storey terraces – all bright and cheerful houses on quiet streets. *Willesden Lane*, with its small shops, mansion blocks, junior school, filling stations and even a cinema, is the border of a tract of more modest terraces S to *Glengall Rd. Tennyson Rd*, for example. has an unbroken terrace along the W side incorporating a dozen minor variations on, and later amendments to, its Victorian artisan theme. The houses on *Donaldson, Victoria* and *Hartland Rds* display a touching homogeneity: nearly all highlight the decorative panels on the 2-storey bays.

Brondesbury Rd runs the gamut from council tower blocks at *Kilburn Square*, through large red-brick 3-storey terraces – some ornate, some Italianate, but nearly all flats – to some very suburban semis near Queens Park station. *Brondesbury Villas* echoes its namesake for much of its length, but has some particularly ornate large houses, now luxury flats. The fact that it backs on to the railway line, and that basements were subject to flooding until 1986, does nothing to lower prices; a sought-after address.

South of the railway is largely sprawling council estates on either side of *Carlton Vale* and surrounding the 1860s James Bailey villas of *Cambridge Avenue*, *Chichester*, *Cambridge* and *Oxford Rds* near Kilburn Park station. These look splendid when restored, but sadly most look tattier than surrounding estates. The modest terraces of the *Fernhead Rd, Saltram Crescent* area are a less expensive corner in a mixed council/private area.

West Kilburn

West Kilburn is between *Harrow Rd* on the S and *Kilburn Lane* on the N, the E boundary with Maida Vale running along *Fernhead, Shirland* and *Walterton Rds*. The battle of *Fernhead* and *Walterton Rds* – fought between tenants and developers, the one pasting posters on houses the other boarded up – seems to have settled down, with the developers coming out on top. There are several new flats developments around here and many of the Victorian houses are being converted and put on the market. A modern estate separates these streets from the private terraces of *Bravington, Portnall* and *Ashmore Rds*: there are many rented flats here. Next is the Mozart Estate, a jumble of red-brick blocks and aerial walkways, which boasts a sports centre on *Caird St. Beethoven St* has a few private houses, some light industry and schools.

South of *Kilburn Lane*, which has some shops and terraces, is the placid Queens Park Estate of charming terraced cottages (1870s-80s), many with almost Gothic porches suggesting benign ecclesiastical origins, despite the rationalism of the *First* to *Sixth Avenue* names. Now a conservation area, the estate passed through council hands but now the houses are privately owned. From E, *Harrow Rd* has shops and pubs near junction with *Great Western Rd*, then has modern council housing below Queens Park Estate opposite the

K

canal, up to the junction with *Ladbroke Grove*. This part of the *Harrow Rd* is a very busy thoroughfare.

Kensal Green

The small triangle (bounded by *Chamberlayne Rd*, *Harrow Rd* and the North London line), is Kensal Green. This area is in Brent. *Harrow Rd* here has cemeteries to S, offices etc on N, behind which are 3-storey terraces giving way to smaller ones in the quiet area of *Wakemen, Pember* and *Rainham Rds*. *College Rd* passes Kensal Green station (BR and tube), and divides larger terraces of *Ashburnam* and *Mortimer Rds* from smaller homes (including some council) S of *Purves Rd*; still many houses here not converted to flats, also much rented property. Similarly terraces of *Napier* and *Victor Rds*, tucked away behind and very easy to miss from *Harrow Rd*, which here has shops and some flats above; note terraced cottages next to *Alma Place*. *Purves Rd*, running back E, leads to the shops of *Station Terrace* below Kensal Rise station, and a mansion block. Here are the shops of busy and steep *Chamberlayne Rd*.

Queens Park

Across *Chamberlayne Rd* are the putative beginnings of desirable Queens Park, marked by the monkey puzzle trees of *Chevening Rd*; this runs E with its huge semis, mostly flats, and large terraces, those above *Dunmore Rd* having garages at rear. But Queens Park proper, the conservation area with its rich mixture of late Victorian and Edwardian styles, begins only at *Peploe Rd* (and continues between the railway lines as far as *Salusbury Rd*). On roads that cross this W border, such as *Kempe* and *Keslake*, both house prices and flights of architectural fancy can soar as one nears the park. Even within the conservation area, prices can vary considerably for houses of similar size, depending on style and situation – compare the decorative *Kingswood Avenue* with the plainer *Milman Rd* directly across the park.

The smaller terraces of the avenues behind *Kingswood* are popular but *Montrose* and *Hopefield* are marred by some drab modern houses which detract from the essentially gracious tone of Queens Park. *Harvist Rd* has a variety of 3-storey terraces (note the Dutch touches of Nos 10-16) to *Salusbury Rd*. This runs between Brondesbury Park and Queens Park stations, and furnishes the locals with schools, shops, churches, constabulary and a library.

Among those estate agents active in this area are:

- Bancroft
- Casa
- Dutch & Dutch
- Greene & Co
- Jackson Property Services
- Plaza Estates

Knightsbridge

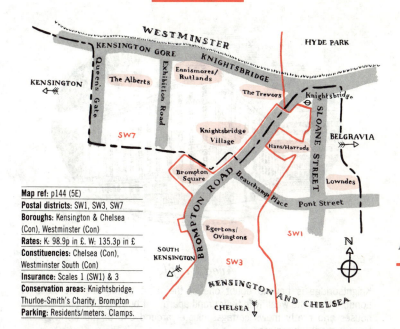

Map ref: p144 (5E)
Postal districts: SW1, SW3, SW7
Boroughs: Kensington & Chelsea (Con), Westminster (Con)
Rates: K: 98.9p in £. W: 135.3p in £
Constituencies: Chelsea (Con), Westminster South (Con)
Insurance: Scales 1 (SW1) & 3
Conservation areas: Knightsbridge, Thurloe-Smith's Charity, Brompton
Parking: Residents/meters. Clamps.

Transport | Tubes: Both zone 1, Knightsbridge (Piccadilly), South Kensington (Piccadilly, Circle, District). From Knightsbridge: Oxford Circus 10 min (1 change), City 22min (1 change), Heathrow 42 min.

Convenient for | Hyde Park, Harrods, West End, Heathrow. Miles from centre: 1.5

Schools | ILEA zone 1: Holland Park, Cardinal Manning RC (b), Cardinal Vaughan RC (b), St Thomas More RC, Sion Manning RC (g). Private: St James' Independent (b) (g), Falkner House (g), Queen's Gate (g).

Flats	S	1b	2b	3b	4b	5b
Average prices	100+	175–230	250–350+	315–600+	500+	850–1m+
Houses	2b	3b	4b	5b	6/7b	8b
Average prices	350	350–500+	500+	750–1.5m+	→	→

The properties | The scale ranges from tiny mews via elegant 18th/19th century squares and terraces to lofty apartment blocks in stone or the redbrick, gabled style widely known as 'Pont St Dutch'.

The market | The wealthy market for these coveted homes, whether true-blue British or international jet-set, are as one in considering this the hub of London. Large homes are scarce and at a premium. Flats reign, with companies buying the short-lease ones as London bases. Prices vary widely according to degree of luxury/lease length/views of Park. Local searches: 7 days.

Area Profile

Knightsbridge is beyond doubt one of the most prestigious addresses in London. Here the wealthy in their grand apartment buildings, elegant terraced houses and pretty mews cottages cluster around one of the world's most famous shopping centres.

The area lies S of Hyde Park, which is fringed by the road variously named *Kensington Gore/Kensington Rd/Knightsbridge*. To the S the boundary is *Walton St/Pont St*. In the W, the museums and colleges cut Knightsbridge off from Kensington, while Belgravia is on the E.

The old hamlet of Knightsbridge was originally part of a large forest around London, of which Hyde Park and Kensington Gardens are surviving open remnants. The parks are the areas's biggest asset. They provide a 600-acre playground, and some fine views: properties overlooking the parks can command £1.5 million plus.

The other big draw is the 'top people's store', Harrods. This famous turn-of-the-century department store in *Brompton Rd*, with its distinctive green and gold canopies and royal warrants, sets the tone for the high-class shops in the area, where the 'by appointment' sign is a familiar sight. Gold-braided commissionaires, chauffeur-driven limousines and security cameras over the doorways are also essentials of the Knightsbridge streetscape.

Like Harrods, the Royal Albert Hall and the other establishments within it, Knightsbridge is itself an institution. As one estate agent put it: 'You have the confidence that the market is never really going to collapse because there is too much to go down with it.' This is, of course, to take the long view: what's the odd stock market dive to the Old Money of Knightsbridge?

About 80 per cent of Knightsbridge residents own their homes. The area is favoured by bankers, both British and international, and diplomats. Several embassies and foreign cultural centres are located here.

Every urban taste in homes is catered for, from the tall late Victorian red brick gabled buildings in the *Hans/Egerton Gardens* neighbourhoods to the grand Portland stone blocks in *Ennismore Gardens*. Bijou mews cottages and 19th century terraced houses are spread throughout the area in some particularly pretty streets and cobbled mews .

Most homes are flats and leases are often short. This means they do not qualify for a mortgage and buyers have to be able to pay cash. Strict maintenance conditions are contained in many leases to keep up the tone of the area by preventing properties slipping into disrepair. Service charges vary widely but you usually get what you pay for, according to local estate agents.

A peculiarity of the area is that it falls within two boroughs. All of the area N of *Brompton Rd* (with the exception of *Brompton Square, Cottage Place*, the Oratory, Holy Trinity Church, *Cheval Place, Rutland* and *Fairholt Sts* and *Rutland Mews South*) is in the City of Westminster. The rest is in Kensington.

Brompton Rd is the main shopping street, lined by a jumble of period and modern flats blocks and offices with shops beneath. These range from fashion and shoe shops to jewellers, antique shops, galleries, banks, restaurants and pubs. *Knightsbridge* and its continuation *Kensington Rd* is a busy main route running alongside the parks W to Kensington and E to the West End. It is flanked by a combination of tall apartment buildings and embassies.

K

Lowndes

Lowndes Square forms the heart of the neighbourhood, which is bounded to the W by *Sloane St*. It differs from other garden squares in Kensington and Chelsea in that it is dominated by huge 1900s flats blocks. The 6/7-storey brown brick buildings spread along whole blocks of the square and loom over its narrow central garden. Some earlier properties remain, mostly 5-storey and basement stucco-fronted terraced houses, many split into flats. But overall, the atmosphere is of a square of hotels. This impression is heightened by the appearance at the N end of the Sheraton Park Tower Hotel, which fronts *Knightsbridge*. The existing appeal of *Lowndes Square*, particularly popular with foreign buyers, will be enhanced by the ultra-luxurious Lowndes Court development, due for completion in August/September. The 25 flats will start at about £650,000 for 2 beds, rising to £2.1 million for a 4-bed apartment and £3.2 million for the two 6/7-bed duplex penthouses.

Lowndes St, a continuation of the square's E leg, contains more flats, shops, galleries and banks. Terraces of 4-storey stucco-fronted houses stand on both sides of the S end of the street. Another 1900s flats block, Chelsea House, provides visual interest as it curves around the corner of *Lowndes St* into *Cadogan Place*. A collection of period and modern houses and flats at the N end of *Cadogan Place* overlook its large tree-lined landscaped gardens. The prettily-named *Harriet Walk* is gaining seven new mews houses and two commercial studios. *Sloane St* on the neighbourhood's W boundary serves as both the main road to Chelsea and a smart shopping street.

Hans/Harrods

This neighbourhood is dominated by Harrods, one of the most famous department stores in the world. The baroque-style building with its ornate dome and turrets covers 4½ acres of one of the choicest parts of London.

Harrods is surrounded by tall red brick and stone gabled blocks of flats in *Hans Crescent, Hans Rd* and *Basil St*. The most ornate can be found in *Basil St* alongside a mix of hotels, restaurants, shops and Knightsbridge fire station. *Hans Crescent* is another shopping street and home of Knightsbridge Crown Court. It links up with *Herbert Crescent*, where a group of large mock Tudor houses stand out among the prevailing blocks of ornate red-brick mansions.

The crescent leads into *Hans Place*, a very popular garden square where largely red brick Dutch-style buildings, converted into flats, encircle the private central gardens. Prince Charles' old prep school, Hill House, stands in the SE corner of this relatively quiet square. Just beyond the N-W entrance to the square, the red-bricks are replaced by terraces of mid-19th century white stucco houses in *Walton Place*. At the S end of this attractive street is the brick Gothic-style St Saviour's Church, providing a striking contrast to the white stucco. A drawback here is the amount of traffic taking short cuts through the street. Queues of lorries also form at the junction with *Hans Rd* and *Basil St*, waiting their turn to make deliveries to Harrods. To the E of *Walton Place* through a pointed red-brick arch lies *Pont St Mews*, a collection of 2-bed gabled cottages. *Brompton Place* to the W is a narrow private road, choked in the daytime with cars waiting for a place in Harrods' car park at the end of the street. The House of Fraser has plans to develop their four-acre site on the *Brompton Rd*. This should provide 10 rebuilt mews houses and 22 new flats as well as the Harrods car park.

Beaufort Gardens, until now the odd street out in the neighbourhood, is improving rapidly as a number of hotels are converted into luxury flats. Many of the tall brick and stucco Victorian terraced properties have been completely refurbished or smartened up. An unusual feature of this wide street is the line of trees down the middle with car parking on each side. The street is closed off at its S end by a stucco balustrade and the backs of the houses in *Walton St*. *Beauchamp Place* at the W edge of the neighbourhood is a high class shopping street, containing some of the area's top shops and restaurants.

Egertons/Ovingtons

This corner, enclosed by *Brompton Rd* to the N and W, has several streets and squares of handsome houses. *Ovington Square* contains good examples of the 'Kensington Italianate' style – tall narrow white stucco terraced houses with rich detailing. The 4-storey and basement houses, built in the 1840/50s, are set around narrow private gardens. The *Square* and *Ovington Gardens* to the N are both relatively busy roads because they are used as a short cut by through traffic from *Brompton Rd* and *Walton St. Ovington Gardens* has 3/4-storey stucco-fronted or brick and stucco terraced houses. Tucked away at right angles to the E side of the street is *Ovington Mews*. Pretty 2-storey painted cottages line this pleasant little backwater. Tubs of flowers and window boxes add extra colour. *Yeoman's Row*, just one street away, is different again. A short terrace of 2-storey Georgian cottages remain on the E side of this small-scale street. Further along the same side is an attractive group of paired brick houses with stucco entrances and leafy front gardens. Pass by a handful of cottages in *Egerton Garden Mews* through a red-brick arch, which marks another sudden change of scene.

Rows of tall late Victorian red-brick gabled buildings congregate around rear communal gardens in *Egerton Gardens* and the N end of *Egerton Terrace*. The blocks, built in the 1880s/90s, form the main concentration of flats in the neighbourhood. Cross the road to the two most exclusive streets in

Knightsbridge – *Egerton Crescent* and the S end of *Egerton Terrace*. A curved terrace of elegant early Victorian white stucco houses sweeps around *Egerton Crescent*. The 3/4-storey houses are screened from the road by a semi-circular private garden with tall trees. Green Victorian lamps line the crescent and tubs of trees and shrubs on the first floor balconies emphasise the striking green and white colour scheme. In *Egerton Terrace*, pairs of mid 19th century white stucco houses have the advantage of large leafy front gardens. The street is closed off at its S end by a balustrade and trees.

Brompton Square

Brompton Square, to the N of *Brompton Rd*, is a distinct neighbourhood to itself. Terraces of 3/4-storey early 19th century houses stretch along narrow central gardens. Virtually all the houses in the square, built between 1824-39, are Grade II listed buildings. A few have been converted into flats. The gardens are also listed as being of architectural or historic interest.

To the W is one of Knightsbridge's most important landmarks, the Oratory Catholic Church. This Renaissance style church with its impressive white stone facade and dome is the focal point of this end of *Brompton Rd*. Behind the Oratory sits Holy Trinity Church. Its large tree-lined graveyard provides welcome fresh air and a leafy open space and outlook for adjoining properties in the Ennismores and a playground for inner-city squirrels.

Knightsbridge has several enticing corners of mews cottages, which have evolved a long way from their earthy origins to become a style of home all their own. Many are cul-de-sacs, tucked away from the busy streets. Mansard roof extensions are popular, as are shutters and flower tubs beside the doors. The most prized are those with a surviving garage: parking around here is impossible.

Ennismores/Rutlands

N of *Brompton Square* as far as the Park stretches a quiet, cut-off neighbourhood of mews and squares. L-shaped *Ennismore Gardens Mews* is a delightful long cobbled mews lined by gaily-coloured 2-storey cottages. Tubs of flowers and window boxes add a picturesque touch. The cottages in the S leg of the mews overlook the peaceful tree-lined graveyard of Holy Trinity Church. An imposing stone arch of Greek-style columns at the entrance to the mews is a hint of things to come in *Ennismore Gardens*. Here grand 5-storey Portland stone terraces with double columned porches and ornate black iron balconies are set around a large private garden. One of the blocks has just been completely rebuilt behind the facade to provide 11 luxury flats. The £5 million development of 1-to 4-bed flats includes a fully-equipped gym and a gold-braided porter. The more traditional stucco-fronted terraces reappear in the E arm of the square, and further stucco terraces can be found in *Princess*

K

Gardens. Spreading along the W-E section of *Ennismore Gardens* is the highly-rated Kingston House flats complex, which stretches right back to *Kensington Rd*. Around the corner, on the W side of the N leg of *Ennismore Gardens*, is *Bolney Gate*, a development of modern 5-storey brick and stone town houses, which sell for more than £1 million each. On the E side of the road stand, in quirky juxtaposition, the Russian Orthodox Church and the Omani Embassy. S of the church is *Ennismore Mews*, an exceptional example of its type with often large 2-storey painted/brick houses. Window boxes, flower tubs and Victorian street lamps abound. Another attractive feature is the Ennismore Arms pub at the corner with *Ennismore St*. *Ennismore St*. leads into *Rutland Gate*, which is made up of two separate garden squares. Terraces of brick and stucco houses line the N square, just off *Knightsbridge*, and cream and white stucco-fronted houses are set around the more desirable S square. The properties have mostly been converted into flats or house foreign cultural institutes and other organisations. A large brick mansion block – Eresby House – stands at the point where the two squares meet.

Rutland Gardens and its tiny mews contain a mix of interesting houses, cottages and flats of very different sizes and styles, but the dominant view here is of the tower of Knightsbridge Barracks, consistently voted one of London's biggest eyesores in public opinion polls. S of *Rutland Gate* lie more small mews, including *Rutland Mews* W, no more than a tiny group of white stucco cottages clustered around a cobbled courtyard. *Rutland* and *Fairholt Sts* are two more small-scale streets. They have mainly 2-storey stucco/brick and stucco/painted houses.

Knightsbridge Village

Exclusive *Montpelier Square* is the centrepiece of this neighbourhood of predominantly single family houses. The 19th century brick and stucco/painted stucco houses in the square face on to mature private gardens. One house here was on the market for £1.4 million in the autumn, and an unmodernised property for £1.1 million.

Narrow *Montpelier Walk* is a mix of painted brick/stucco houses. It leads to *Cheval Place*, where the 2/3-storey painted cottages stand alongside modern flats blocks, smart shops, restaurants and the Aston Martin salesroom. *Montpelier Place* is a pleasant street of 3-storey brick and stucco/stucco-fronted houses with two flower-bedecked pubs, one right next to the German Evangelist Church. *Montpelier St* to the E is the main street of the village, lined with a mix of 3/4-storey brick and stucco terraced houses, pubs, restaurants, shops, galleries and auction rooms. There is no route for traffic W from the village to the adjoining *Rutland Gate*, thus traffic is relatively light. A footpath, leading through a gap in an old brick wall, allows pedestrians to cut through to *Rutland Mews* and on, under a grand archway, along *Ennismore Gardens Mews* to *Prince's Gate Mews* and the museum/university quarter of South Kensington: one of the most charming walks in London.

The Trevors

East of Knightsbridge Village come the streets around *Trevor Square*, dominated by 3/4-storey 19th century terraced houses. In *Trevor Square*, they are set on two sides of a long narrow private garden. A stretch of modern flats can be found at the N-W end of *Trevor Place*, a quite busy road taking traffic to Harrods despatch depot S of *Trevor Square* and through to *Brompton Rd*. In *Lancelot Place*, a row of 2-storey brick cottages stands opposite the post office. Turn E into *Raphael St*, which links up with *Knightsbridge Green*, a pedestrian passageway lined with small shops, cafés and restaurants. Standing alongside the passageway is Park Mansions, a large red brick and stone block fronting *Knightsbridge* and stretching to *Scotch Corner*. The Knight's Arcade of luxury shops runs beneath the mansions at ground floor and basement level through to *Brompton Rd*.

The Alberts

The Royal Albert Hall is the focal point of the neighbourhood from which the main residential complexes take their names. They are Albert Hall Mansions – five large blocks of flats on the E side of the famous concert hall – and Albert Court to the rear in *Prince Consort Rd*. The tall red brick and stone Norman Shaw blocks, the very first to be built in the Dutch style, contain 80 flats each, including some of the largest family apartments left in Knightsbridge. They were built in the 1880s/90s by the Commissioners for the Great Exhibition of 1851, who remain the freeholders to this day. The flats are popular with wealthy overseas buyers, particularly from the Middle East, India and Pakistan. They are also used as a base for international companies and business people. Very few are let out. Some have been modernised, others still have the original panelled walls, staff quarters – even wine cellars. A typical 3/4-bed apartment in Albert Hall Mansions costs from £375,000-£450,000. Prices rise to £1.5 million for apartments with breathtaking views of Kensington Gardens and Hyde Park.

Albert Court has a vast hall which was once a carriageway through which coaches drove. A 4-bed flat here can cost between £525,000 and £1.5 million depending on its position, its condition and whether it is on one or two floors. The two blocks lie midway between the main shopping centres of Knightsbridge and Kensington. They are just a short stroll away from the major museums in South Kensington and the neighbouring colleges of art, music and science (Imperial College).

Among those estate agents active in this area are:

- Allsops
- Cluttons
- Farleys
- Druce
- Farrar Stead & Glyn
- Foxtons
- Hamptons
- Hobart Slater
- John D Wood
- Friend and Falcke
- Strutt & Parker
- Stickley & Kent
- Callander Wright
- Read Cunningham
- Chesterfield
- Mistral
- Jackson-Stops & Staff
- Knight Frank & Rutley
- Keith Cardale Groves
- Prudential Property Services
- Savills
- Winkworths
- W A Ellis
- Ellis & Co
- Barnard Marcus
- Bensons
- De Groot Collis
- Stuart Wilson
- Marsh & Parsons
- Russel Simpson

K

Lewisham

Map ref: p96 (3D)	
Postal districts: SE4, SE13, SE6, SE8	
Boroughs: Lewisham (Lab)	
Rates: 226.44p in £	
Constituencies: Lewisham E (Con), Deptford (Lab)	
Insurance: Scale 1	
Conservation areas: Brockley, St John's	
Parking: Free; residents/meters in centre	

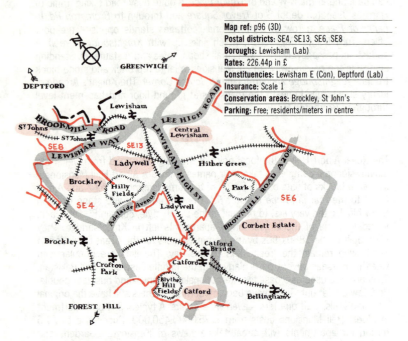

Transport	British Rail: St Johns, Lewisham (Blackfriars/Charing Cross 20 min, Victoria/Holborn 21 min), Ladywell, Catford, Catford Bridge.	
Convenient for	Docklands, City via riverboat from Greenwich, Kent. Miles from centre: 6.	
Schools	ILEA zone 7: Crofton, Prendergast (g), Addey & Stanhope. Private: Blackheath High School (g), St Dunstan's College (b)	

Flats	S	1b	2b	3b	4b	5b
Average prices	46–55	55–65	62–75	70–80	–	–
Houses	2b	3b	4b	5b	6/7b	8b
Average prices	70–80	80–110	95–125+	120–165	160–240	–

The properties	Mainly Victorian, from tiny workers' homes through larger terraces to grander villas with conservatories. Interspaced with '20s/'30s suburban houses. Catford has well-preserved estate of 3–6 bed 1880s houses, many now flats, plus '30s semis in large gardens.
The market	The Lewisham area, once hardly considered London, is now firmly on the central London workers' list of possibles. Prices still seem modest considering the City's proximity. Fertile first-home hunting-ground. Local searches: 6–7 weeks.

Area Profile

Lewisham, lying to the SW of historic Greenwich, also has its roots in the past: a large village was already established there in Domesday times, but the area hardly grew until the 1840s, when the railway arrived and turned it into a new centre for commuting. By the start of the 20th century virtually all the available land had been built over. The area is ringed with convenient little stations – and criss-crossed with less than convenient railway lines, which carry fast through-trains as well as local traffic. Those allergic to noise should check maps carefully when house-hunting.

Today, the area has a surprising number of parks and open spaces. Some, like Ladywell, have tennis courts, a running track and warming-up equipment. Fitness enthusiasts are well catered for: there are health clubs in most neighbourhoods. Lewisham has a bowling alley, but there are few good pubs or restaurants and the nearest cinema and theatre are in Catford.

Central Lewisham

The best bits of Lewisham are those closest to the southern tip of Blackheath. From Blackheath Village turn W into *Lee Terrace* and explore the roads to your left bearing the SE13 postal address. Some of Lewisham's best buildings were destroyed by the heavy bombing which the borough suffered during World War 2, but happily roads such as *Dacre Park*, *Quentin Rd* and *Eton Grove* escaped untouched. These 4-storey mansions with their grand sash windows and huge back gardens are extremely well kept and would not be out of place in Kensington. Most have been converted into flats, but some remain as superb family homes. The nearby parish church of St Margarets and little back-street pubs all add to the quiet, country feel, although the atmosphere is broken by modern low-rise council housing in the roads leading directly off *Lee High Rd*.

Lee High Rd joins *Lewisham High St*, recognised as the biggest shopping centre in SE London. It is, consequently, notoriously congested, but includes a massive indoor shopping complex and most well-known chain stores – and the council is planning to pedestrianise the *High St* in 1992. Roads to the E mostly contain Victorian town houses – some undergoing conversion work after years of neglect. *Limes Grove* with its 3-storey pitched roofs and sash windows is a prime example of this process, as are *Clarendon Rise* and *Gilmore Rd* which sport terraces with steps to the front door and black wrought-iron balustrades. Opposite stands a beautiful 10-15 year old development of council housing in red-brick terraces. Each has its own garden and there's a small park at the centre. Many tenants have already bought their homes and some are now selling. A good area for children as the streets are paved over and can be played in without fear of traffic; however inside the houses are tight for space compared with Victorian counterparts opposite.

St John's

Next, explore St John's – which you'll find by following road signs for Deptford. St Johns village consists of the streets leading off *Brookmill Rd* such as *Friendly St*, *St John's Vale* and *Albyn Rd*, and is made up of neatly kept close-packed 2-bed workmen's cottages. Some streets are sealed to traffic by ornamental bollards, and the rows of neat yellow-brick terraces and 'Coronation Street' style shops and pubs remain quiet. The area has its own station but rail commuters should beware of the extremely patchy service offered by BR. Hundreds of trains pass through the station daily – but very few stop! Another point worth noting is that a men's hostel lies at the end of *Brookmill Rd* – but this is to close next year and will become flats. The SE8 postal address is usually associated with Deptford (currently getting a face-lift), but this corner is well worth a look.

Travelling up hill to *Loampit Vale* the small two-up, two-downs are replaced by grander 4-storey homes, now converted into flats but still neatly kept with window boxes and many with new roofs.

From here turn right into *Shell Rd* and its surrounding streets dominated by 3- and 4-storey houses with outrageous Gothic style turrets, ornate porches and high pitched roofs. Cognoscenti of this period will find fine examples of decorative plaster mouldings – often a shell motif echoes the street name.

Brockley

On reaching the Hilly Fields park where '30s-style semis are dotted among the Victorian conversions, turn back towards New Cross and the fast improving – and charming – Brockley conservation area. You will not find many young upwardly-mobile professionals in down-town Lewisham, but in these quiet tree-lined avenues they have already arrived. The area's large spacious flats have become increasingly sought-after in the past few years, but buyers should beware: Brockley's charms are contained almost exclusively within its conservation area. Land to the W of *Brockley Rd* and the railway line is still widely regarded as being on the wrong side of the tracks, say estate agents.

Instead, first check out the area boundary, marked by *Tressillian* and *Tyrwhitt Rds* to the E, *Lewisham Way* to the N, *Upper Brockley Rd* to the W and *Brockley Rd* to the S. These streets are largely filled with 3- and 4-storey houses, mostly – but not entirely – converted into flats. Some have huge 150 foot gardens and there are panoramic views across to St Paul's for people with attic bedrooms. Inside the grand-looking yellow brick mansions the rooms are large with high ceilings. Flats here held their appeal even in the quiet winter market. Conversion work is continuing although some builders are spoiling the splendour by squeezing too many flats into too small a space.

Agents report massive interest in this area, with flats in *Manor Avenue*, *Breakspears* and *Tressillian Rds* particularly sought-after. However, there are still some relative bargains to be had since its charms are not yet widely known. Look out, too, for some original mews houses here.

Ladywell

From Brockley travel on to the nearby Hilly Fields playing area, mostly surrounded by post-war 2-storey family homes, some with balconies. From *Vicars Hill* look out for *Adelaide Avenue's* ornate terrace fronting the park, sadly blighted in parts by squatters.

Then head down the hill into Ladywell village, perhaps more of an invention of local estate agents than a real village, but still worth examining. There is a good selection of shops in the 'village' centre on *Ladywell Rd* – and yet another BR station within a few minutes' walk. The impressive and huge Ladywell Baths swimming pool and the bigger shops of *Lewisham High St* are also just round the corner. 'Village' properties are largely Victorian conversions of 2- and

3-storeys – some with huge gardens – although there are some '30s semis to provide a contrast, notably in *Veda* and *Ermine Rds*.

Catford and the Corbett Estate

Catford, like the rest of the area, was rapidly developed towards the end of the 19th century, but unlike Lewisham owes much of its housing character to a single man – Archibald Corbett. This canny Scot bought nearly 300 acres of then virgin land and proceeded to build thousands of houses, laying out the roads in a strict grid pattern. Catford today has its own shopping centre, two BR stations and even its own dog track but it is best known for the massive Corbett Estate and its distinct lack of pubs – Archibald Corbett was teetotal. Many of the street names have a Scottish flavour – *Arngask* and *Glenfarg Rds*, for example. The boundary roads are *Wellmeadow* to the E, *Hazelbank* to the S, *Brownhill* to the N and *Muirkirk* to the W.

The area comprises of 3- to 6-bedroom houses, all solidly built, with large spacious rooms. Many of the bigger properties have now been converted into flats, but the estate still retains its prim and proper identity. All the houses have their own front garden and most have 80 foot rear gardens. The smaller, single-fronted Corbett houses are almost exactly half the size of the double fronted ones, which are slightly more ornate. The area remains very quiet, very respectable. Visitors will need a map: every road really does look the same!

A similar estate lies close by, this time made up of '30s-style semis and bounded by *Bellingham Rd* to the S, *Thornsbeach* to the E, *Bromley Rd* to the W and *Culverley Rd* to the N. Homes here boast extremely wide roads, 3 and 4 bedrooms and large gardens – one or two even have swimming pools.

From here head into central Catford. Note that a £12 million scheme to improve the South Circular by taking traffic out of Catford is in the current transport ministry programme for the 1990s. . . . See 'Transport' chapter. There are some down-market streets surrounding the stations, but the popular St Dunstan's College lies on *Stanstead Rd* to the right and is backed by the open space of Blythe Hill Fields and attractive 3-storey Victorian family homes in roads such as *Ravensbourne* and *Montem Rds*.

Bordering areas

Hither Green is a fertile hunting ground for first-time buyers seeking inexpensive flat conversions or terraced cottages. The area is bordered by Lewisham, Lee Green and Blackheath; it has its own well-served BR station.

To the W leafy Forest Hill (which see) has a mixture of Victoriana and '30s semis in peaceful roads, but also has many flat conversions and a good cache of cheapish properties for first-time buyers. Crofton Park, sandwiched between Brockley and Catford, consists mainly of terraced streets which some will probably find too drab. Near Crofton Park station, however, Barratt's Crofton Gate in *Buckthorne Rd* has new flats and 1-, 2- and 3-bed houses from £99-295,000.

Among those estate agents active in this area are:
- Ellis & Co
- Rocodells
- Woolwich Property Services
- Hamptons Levens
- Oak Estates
- Winkworths

L

Leyton and Walthamstow

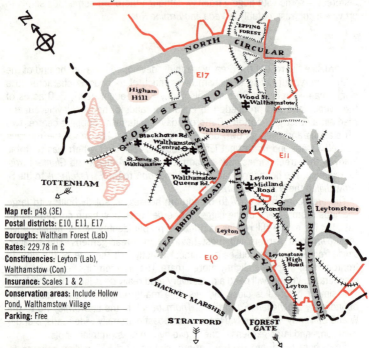

Map ref: p48 (3E)	
Postal districts: E10, E11, E17	
Boroughs: Waltham Forest (Lab)	
Rates: 229.78 in £	
Constituencies: Leyton (Lab), Walthamstow (Con)	
Insurance: Scales 1 & 2	
Conservation areas: Include Hollow Pond, Walthamstow Village	
Parking: Free	

Transport Tubes: Leyton, Leytonstone (zone 3a, Central) Walthamstow Central, Blackhorse Road (zone 3a, Victoria). From Walthamstow Central: Oxford Circus 35 min, City 1 hr (1 change), Heathrow 1hr 20 min (1 change). British Rail: Liverpool St 15 min.

Convenient for Transport to City, West End, Epping Forest, Lea Valley, M11 to Cambridge, M25; tubes/trains into town. Miles to centre: 7.

Schools Waltham Forest Education Authority: Leytonstone School, McEntee Secondary School, Walthamstow Girl's. Private: Forest School.

Flats	S	1b	2b	3b	4b	5b
Average prices	50–60	57–60	60–70	68–72	–	–
Houses	2b	3b	4b	5b	6/7b	8b
Average prices	73–80	80–110	90–115	110–125	135–150	–

The properties Largely 1900s terraces of 2/3 bedroom homes and p/b flats. Upper Walthamstow boasts some large detached houses; bigger ones, too, in Leyton's Barclay estate. Flats, converted and p/b, abound.

The market Good transport links and cheap first homes provide a stepping stone for buyers from a lot further afield than the East End. As young City secretaries move in, the elderly, say agents, are taking advantage of the rise in value of their homes and retiring to Wales or Clacton. N Circular being improved at Crooked Billet. Local searches: 5 weeks.

Area Profile

Mention the name Walthamstow and people will think either of greyhound racing at the track in *Chingford Rd*, or of the busy street market which brings the *High St* to life three days a week. Nearby, however, there is now a brand new under-cover shopping centre, and a new swimming pool and athletics track by Lloyds Park. Walthamstow, and neighbouring Leyton and Leytonstone, are changing. Many young people find their first home here, among the affordable flats and little houses of the neat rows of Victorian terraces with their good transport links into town. By the same token, older inhabitants have been selling to these newcomers and moving to the coast.

Walthamstow may not be one of London's most elegant corners, but it is probably one of its liveliest and it holds a surprise for property seekers – Walthamstow Village, a conservation area, where prices are high and street names are ecclesiastical. A lot of conversions are taking place here.

Walthamstow, Leyton and Leytonstone lie in the borough of Waltham Forest – which in 1987 boasted the highest rates in London. But last year, much to everyone's relief, they went down by nearly 30 per cent.

Even though they are separated from neighbouring Tottenham and Hackney by reservoirs and marshland, Walthamstow and Leyton are not cut off. Both areas are eminently accessible and between them have no fewer than 11 stations (tube and BR). Local bus services are excellent too.

A new road linking the Blackwall Tunnel approach motorway, the A102M, and the North Circular will thrust right through Leyton, Leytonstone and Wanstead. Neither exact alignment nor construction date are fixed, but the road seems to be a key part of the plans to make access to Docklands easier.

On the fringes of Leyton, the big Stratford Goods Yard has been earmarked as a possible site for major homes development. And at Temple Mills the new Spitalfields market should start operation this year.

Walthamstow

A pleasant tradition says that the name comes from the Old English 'wilcumestou', meaning a welcoming place. Walthamstow lies six and a half miles NE of the City of London, between the River Lea and Essex's beautiful Epping Forest. To the N is Chingford, to the E are Woodford and Wanstead and to the S Leyton.

Most of the homes here are terraced houses built in late Victorian and Edwardian times but there are also purpose-built blocks of flats, small cottages behind the Vestry museum in the Village and large detached houses in the area known as Upper Walthamstow.

The terraced houses tend to be found in the *St James St* corner of Walthamstow, and property here tends to be cheaper than in other parts, though it is convenient for the BR station at St James St and for the tube and BR station at *Blackhorse Road*. There's a new development of flats in *Markhouse St*.

Heading E, there are also many reasonably priced 2- and 3- bedroom houses in the area off *Hoe St* near Walthamstow Central BR/tube stations.

The jewel in Walthamstow's gilt crown is a small area known as 'Walthamstow Village' a little further E but still near Walthamstow Central stations. These few streets contain houses and quaint cottages which command higher than average prices when they come onto the market. Two of the best roads here are *Eden Grove* and *Maynard Road*. In *Wood St* – again a road with its own BR station – Fairview have added a new development of 1- and 2-bed flats to the area.

Upper Walthamstow is the most expensive part of the area. The tree-lined roads boast many large detached houses, often with 5 or more bedrooms. Prices here can reach £150,000 for the large 1930s type properties.

West of the *Chingford Rd*, the area surrounding *Lloyd Park* and *Higham Hill* are very popular with first-time buyers and have a mixture of houses and purpose-built flats. They are quiet areas and offer a large number of 2- and 3-bedroomed houses. *William Morris Close* here recalls Walthamstow's most famous resident who lived in Water House on *Forest Rd*. There's a museum dedicated to his work. As you head along the *Chingford Rd* you approach Chingford itself which offers larger and more expensive property, including a number of large detached houses and also well-built, smart flats.

With the influx of young professional people, Walthamstow is becoming, relatively, a more expensive place to buy but many areas are still in the reach of the first-time buyer and developments are being built with them in mind.

Leyton and Leytonstone

Leyton and Leytonstone lie between Hackney Marsh and Wanstead Flats in E10 and E11. Well situated, it takes just 20 minutes to get to the West End and is equally near Epping Forest heading out to Essex. Here is some of the cheapest property this close to the City and West End.

Most of the property here is terraced houses built in the early 1900s, though some dates back to the 1880s. 3-bedroom terraced houses are the most common and homes with more than 4- or 5-bedrooms are very difficult to find. Many conversions are available and these can still be purchased quite cheaply, though the council are likely to limit the rash of new ones in an attempt to avert parking problems. Developers are adding to the so far small stock of purpose-built blocks. There is also scope to buy cheaper and unrepaired property.

Look, too, for the terraces of little houses built as two flats. Sometimes these provide an interesting phenomenon; first-floor flats with gardens. Your front door opens on to the stairs to your flat, and another narrow stairway at the back leads down to an (also narrow, but welcome) little garden.

Leytonstone is well served by both the tube and bus and close to its underground station are some of the larger properties in the area known as Upper Leytonstone. *Forest Drive East* and *Forest Drive West*, and the surrounding areas offer large double-fronted houses in tree-lined streets.

Avondale Court, a smart, purpose-built block, is on the corner by the underground station; Fairview have built new studios, 1- and 2-bed flats in the *High Rd*. On the borders of Upper Leytonstone is the area known as the Barclay Estate which contains some of the best houses in Leyton. These lie at the back of Leyton Midland BR station and the roads are quieter and pleasanter in appearance, with more trees than is common in the area.

A cache of good-value, and equally convenient, terraces include roads like *Colchester*, *Nottingham*, *Canterbury*, *Ely*, *Epsom*, *Cromer*, *Essex* and *Sandringham*.

Grove Green Rd stretches from Leytonstone to Leyton, and the streets which lie off it are plentiful with terraced house and flat conversions, though there are also many run down properties.

The roads surrounding Leyton Orient football club also offer an abundance of terraced houses at reasonable prices, and are close to Leyton tube station.

There are few blocks of flats in the area, save for some council blocks, and the majority of flats are conversions. However, there is a large purpose-built block on the corner of *Francis Rd*. This and the properties near the station and football ground are well served by the shops in *High Road Leyton*.

A 6-acre site in *Church Rd* is being developed by Kentish Homes partly as light industrial, partly as homes/workspaces. This combination of small home with its own studio/workspace is provoking great interest.

The area along *Leyton High Rd* is residential, and purpose-built flats are a feature here; Leytonstone Court – 1- and 2-bedroom flats, is towards the Stratford end of the *High Rd*. *Buckland Rd*, which runs parallel, now boasts 19 new 1-bed flats; *Ruckholt Rd* too has sprouted smart 1- and 2-bed apartments.

In the opposite direction to the *High Rd*, towards Wanstead and Whipps Cross, is the area known as Bushwood. Here are some of the largest properties in the area and are less cramped than properties in the heart of Leytonstone. Prices tend to be quite high.

At the roundabout of *Leytonstone High Rd*, and close to Leytonstone itself is Wanstead. Prices in Wanstead are higher and larger properties can be found in roads running off *Overton Drive*. There are also more flats to be found here.

The area is coming up and is regarded as an ideal place for the first time buyer, being cheaper than nearby Redbridge, but just as well placed in London.

L

Borders

Heading E from Wanstead is Redbridge. There are many houses, and blocks of flats. It is a typically middle-class area, and the houses are of good appearance. Well served by Redbridge tube. Same prices as found in Wanstead.

Running alongside Wanstead are Snaresbrook and South Woodford. Both are smart areas with a lot of tree-lined streets, quiet, offering all sizes of houses and some of the best roads in that part of Redbridge borough. Many blocks of purpose-built flats, all of which are quite expensive. Straight on to South Woodford, again similar to Snaresbrook, with many flats and large houses. Well served by tube, direct to London, and sited on the edge of Epping Forest. Southwards from Leyton lies Forest Gate, whose BR station direct to the City makes homes here an inexpensive convenient alternative to central London. For details see Newham.

Among those estate agents active in this area are:
- A Kennedy
- Hunters
- Land & Co
- Guardians
- Jackson Reed Estates
- Leyton Estates
- Douglas Allen Spiro

Maida Vale

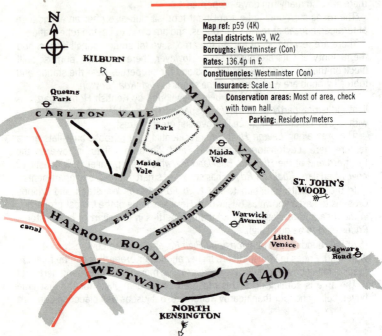

Map ref: p59 (4K)	
Postal districts: W9, W2	
Boroughs: Westminster (Con)	
Rates: 136.4p in £	
Constituencies: Westminster (Con)	
Insurance: Scale 1	
Conservation areas: Most of area, check with town hall.	
Parking: Residents/meters	

Transport	Tubes: Maida Vale, Warwick Avenue (zone 2, Bakerloo): Oxford Circus 10 min, City 20 min (1 change), Heathrow 1 hr (1 change).
Convenient for	Paddington, roads to W and N, West End. Miles from centre: 3.
Schools	ILEA zone 2: St George's RC, North Westminster. Private: American.

Flats	S	1b	2b	3b	4b	5b
Average prices	70–80	80–125	100–250	120–250+	200–300+	–
Houses	2b	3b	4b	5b	6/7b	8b
Average prices	125–200	190–300	225–500	350–800	→	→1.2m+

The properties	Gracious white stucco terraces and villas, rows of neat red-brick mansion flats, some modern mews/town houses. Flats reign: mainly mansion or period conversions. These can be large. Small houses rare; the garden maisonette replaces, and can be lovely. Few houses: best canal-side ones now over £1 million.
The market	Flats fall into three bands: redbrick mansion (cheapest, but watch service charges), period conversions (top-floor flats good value), loads of new luxury (make developers an offer). Large flats common here. Over-supply of smart flats, but the Vale's location makes it a good long-term bet. Buy before area's unique 'hidden gardens' are known to all. Local searches: 1 week.

M

Area Profile

Maida Vale is a wholly residential district, spacious, well placed and increasingly popular. The area is N of *Harrow Rd*, W of *Maida Vale* (the road), which is the continuation to N of *Edgware Rd*. Strategically placed for the main routes out of town to the West and North, it will also be boosted by the advent of the fast Paddington–Heathrow link.

Warwick Avenue, running N from the *Harrow Rd* across the Grand Union Canal, set the tone in the 1840s and '50s. The large cream stucco houses here and fronting the canal are still the area's biggest and smartest. The pretty neighbourhood around the canal is known as Little Venice. Later building confirmed the spacious feel: wide avenues, large terraced houses and mansion flats behind whose ramparts are often concealed large (some vast) shared gardens – a secret unsuspected by passers-by. These delightful 'inverted square' gardens are the area's hidden bonus: they can include tennis courts, and ground-floor flats often have direct access through gates at the bottom of their own back gardens: a delight for those with kids.

Maida Vale's character was largely determined by the district's long-time ownership by the Church Commissioners, who planned, built, maintained, laid down the rules for and let the property. This meant very little buying and selling: most homes were let. Only in the 1980s did they start to sell. Tenants who could afford to bought at preferential rates (20% discount), some making large sums by reselling (often immediately in 'back-to-back' deals). Developers moved in wholesale; the houses were converted, prices soared.

The area is now a rich (in both senses) mine of newly-converted flats. However, it lacks houses – in particular small houses. The garden-level maisonette replaces these, and can be bigger and nicer than other areas' narrow Victorian terraces. The spacious lay-out of Maida Vale makes for exceptionally light and pleasant flats with leafy outlooks. Those with access to one of the 'hidden acres' mentioned above are the ones to watch for. The most coveted homes, however, are those nearest to or overlooking the canal: truly a

'Little Venice' – though estate agents now use this more picturesque name for all the Vale's most desirable white stucco streets. These form the heart of the area, and are succeeded by streets of red-brick mansion flats: these can provide a lot of space for your money. The Church land ends to the W at *Shirland Rd*. Next come smaller-scale Victorian terraces, improving. Although the initial flood of unmodernised homes in Maida Vale has slowed to a trickle, they do appear – representing a rare chance these days to do up a central London home to your own taste. But don't look for bargains: it's not unknown for a good unmodernised property actually to command a premium.

Little Venice

Blomfield Rd and *Maida Avenue* residents have homes made magic (and expensive) by the presence of water. The canal runs between the two, widening by the *Warwick Rd* bridge – where it branches – into a young lake with willow-pattern islet and waterside public gardens and walk. The canal ends of adjoining roads also get called Little Venice; non-natives can be startled by narrow boats apparently gliding across the top of the street. A charming, prized corner of London.

From *Paddington Green* to the S (today marooned between the *Westway* and a hospital, '60s college blocks and council towers) *St Mary's Terrace* runs up towards the canal: No 1, in classic double-fronted stucco, sets the tone for the left side. On the other side is Fleming Court (council), then the stately redbrick mansion blocks of Osborne House and St Mary's Mansions, which comprises several blocks around its own courtyard (unmodernised flats are sometimes available). *Porteus Rd* opposite leads to *Hogan Mews*: new mews houses (Martin Grant, 1983) of a quality which ensured quick sales despite their proximity to the *Westway*. The opposite side has council flats. *St Mary's Terrace* becomes *Park Place Villas*, which runs to the canal – and little Venice proper. On the corner with *Maida Avenue*, an enormous Italianate villa has a prime position. Both *Maida Avenue* and *Blomfield Rd* have covetable stucco villas (strictly for millionaires) facing over the water. These give way to later Victoriana towards the *Edgware Rd* end; mansion blocks can provide very large flats.

From *Harrow Rd* bridge westwards, the S bank of the canal is Westminster City's Warwick Estate: pleasant '60s low-rise, now increasingly in private hands as tenants exercise their right to buy and, in some cases, sell. Prices are low for their neighbourhood: well under half an equivalent 'private' home. The canal then dips below the *Harrow Rd*, and between the two the site of St Mary's Hospital is a mass of cranes as the area's biggest development, Carlton Gate, takes shape. It will take till 1992 to complete, with the homes being released in phases. The first 100 sold briskly last year; prices ranging from £100,000 for a studio to £600,000 for penthouses.

Behind *Blomfield Rd*, to the W of *Warwick Avenue* lies villagy *Warwick Place*, with the pleasant Warwick Castle pub, which overlooks Clifton Nurseries (entrance in *Clifton Villas*) one of London's first and best garden centres. More little shops in *Bristol Gardens*, off which is *Bristol Mews* has had to wait for rebirth from its sadly derelict state. Now 15 houses with roof terraces, parking and a swimming pool, are planned: £350,000-plus. Across *Formosa St*, *Elnathan Mews* is already being transformed: 44 traditionally styled mews homes with garages, from 2- to 4-bedroomed. also run down, had at time of writing been sold en bloc. The streets between the canal and *Clifton Gardens* also enjoy the Little Venice premium.

Maida Vale Central

The name really applies to the old Church estate, from Little Venice northward, with *Maida Vale* (the street) forming the E boundary. *Warwick Avenue* runs NW from Little Venice into the heart of the district. It is the Vale's boulevard, with the clean, striking lines of the modern St Saviour's Church (junction with *Clifton Gardens*) as its focal point. The church has matching flats, Manor House Court, behind. The *Avenue* is lined with classical white early 1850s mansions, many still one home.

Clifton Gardens runs NE from St Saviour's to *Maida Vale*. It is a wide street of 1860s stucco terraces. Top-class conversions into luxury flats back, on the N side, onto vast communal gardens. Cumberland House, on the junction with *Warwick Avenue*, is new (1987) despite its handsome 'period' appearance: top-of-the-market apartments. Another such is Europa House in *Randolph Avenue*: it has the handy anachronism of underground parking, and prices of £240-325,000 for roomy 2-bed flats. The car-space is £15,000 extra, and necessary, nowadays. The *Avenue* saw several more luxurious developments last year. *Clifton Gardens* becomes, at E end, *Clifton Rd* – the Vale's 'high street'. *Warrington Crescent* runs N from *Clifton Gardens* to *Sutherland Avenue*, and is mostly more conversions with communal gardens both sides. *Randolph Crescent*, running parallel, ditto.

Castellain Rd, parallel to (and converging with) *Warwick Avenue* on the E, is a long road which crosses *Sutherland Avenue* to reach *Elgin Avenue*. Between these two avenues is Castellain Mansions, a large block of red and grey brick mansion flats: tidy, homogeneous, quite handsome in turn-of-century style. Behind, to E, are communal gardens; to the W, Paddington Bowling and Sports Club offering 'bowls, tennis, squash, social'. In the angle behind *Castellain* and *Sutherland*, the communal gardens boast tennis courts. An old garage site in *Castellain Rd*, has become Katherine Court, whose style handsomely acknowledges its neighbours': 1- to 3-bed flats, £115-290,000. Across the road a large site in *Warrington Gardens* will yield more than 50 new homes.

Sutherland Avenue is classic Maida Vale, wide, tree-lined, parking down the centre, its vista stopped to the E by the '60s Stuart Tower. At the W end (W of *Shirland Rd*), stand ornate stucco houses, with wrought-iron balustrades at the 1st floor. Then come slightly smaller houses, then enormous Victorian redbricks. This is flat-land. Many boards advertising 'luxury conversions' explain why parking is a problem. Note '*The Sutherlands*' – cream Italianate villa by the circus at the E end: now 10 flats, one with a 1st-floor conservatory, plus a house. Or Nos 172/4 where Alfred MacAlpine are rebuilding in original style. *Lauderdale Rd* runs from the E end of *Sutherland* westwards to *Elgin*. More mansion flats, with large gardens behind those on the S side.

Elgin Avenue starts in the E at Maida Vale tube, runs W to cross *Shirland Rd* and into western Maida Vale (see below). Compared with *Sutherland Avenue* it is more anonymous, more of a throughway. Lined with comfortable red-brick mansion blocks. Behind its lovingly restored facade, the new flats of Westside Court are not the usual anonymous rooms. Architect Stewart Moss has put personality (and lovely large windows) into them, and can be forgiven the waterfalls in the foyer.

M

Grantully Rd runs beside Paddington Recreation Ground: hardly scenic, but at least green and open. Facing it are mansion flats; Leith Mansions then Ashworth Mansions: many still let. A quiet corner. *Ashworth Rd*, which crosses the *Avenue*, has mansion flats at the N end. A surprise here: *Ashworth Rd*, S of *Elgin*, suddenly becomes Surrey: low-built between-the-wars pairs of houses joined by garages – the nearest semis to Marble Arch? Low eaves, deep porches, stockbroker-Tudor. . . . *Morshead*, *Wymering* and *Widley Rds*, plus *Essendine*, are red-brick mansions. Views from the *Morshead* ones (Nos 25 on) across the recreation ground. There is a small school (junior mixed primary) in *Essendine*. *Elgin Mews*, N and S, are tucked behind the shops around Maida Vale tube. *Mews* N has been rebuilt: smart town houses. *Mews* S is still original: pretty, un-done-up white-painted brick houses.

Randolph Avenue and *Lanark Rd* run parallel to Maida Vale, with large houses (mostly recent flat conversions) in *Randolph*. The smart new villa-style blocks of flats in *Lanark* were built by Westminster Council in '83 as starter homes. These are now starting to appear on the open market. The S end of *Randolph Avenue* runs down to the canal and enters Little Venice. Big stucco terraces here. Priciest house of 1988, though, was the converted red-brick electricity sub-station in *Randolph Mews*, complete with a conservatory bathroom (one-way glass!). It sold for £1,275,000. At the N end, Nos 171 onwards overlook the recreation ground. The N end of *Lanark* is a council estate with tower blocks.

Maida Vale, a major road, bounds the district. To the E is St John's Wood. The W side starts (from the N) with a Westminster Council estate; then past *Elgin Avenue's* '30s mansions, then more council, then Y-shaped Stuart Tower: private flats, enjoying fine views from upper floors, well-run and very popular: 1-bed flats that three years ago were £30,000 now fetch £95,000 – unmodernised. South of *Sutherland Avenue* are big 1890s mansion blocks such as Blomfield Court and Sandringham Court. Over the canal bridge, *Maida Vale* becomes *Edgware Rd*, scruffy but lively shopping street.

Borders

Vale proper, the developers moved W into a zone which is somewhat of a no-man's-land of council estates and small terraces, many of which have now been converted into flats. The southern part, N of *Harrow Rd* and up towards Queen's Park station, is in Westminster council's patch. The NE corner is in Brent, where rates are considerably higher. Agents report that at one time, people were reluctant to move W of *Shirland Rd*: the first question for an *Elgin* or *Sutherland Avenue* flat was which side of *Shirland* was it? Today, the border of respectability has moved W to around *Fernhead Rd*.

The N part of the borders district is largely sprawling council estates on either side of *Carlton Vale*. South of here, the modest terraces of the *Fernhead Rd*, *Saltram Crescent* area are a good-value corner in a mixed council/private area. *Saltram* was discovered early by converters. The Westminster frontier runs from the S end of *Kilburn Park Rd* up behind *Saltram Crescent*. The streets between *Walterton* and *Fernhead Rds* have been something of a battle-zone between Westminster Council, who have been redeveloping their terraces here, and the Walterton and Elgin Action Group, whose posters decrying council policies claim tenants are being edged out of the area. A modern estate separates these streets from the private terraces of *Bravington*, *Portnall* and *Ashmore Rds*: there are many rented flats here but owner-occupiers are appearing in numbers as buyers relish the value of a 2-bed flat for £85,000 upwards. Next, and into W10 and (fast-eroding) Kensal, is the council's Mozart Estate. West again, Maida Vale has its eye on annexing the placid Queens Park Estate of charming terraced council cottages....

Among those estate agents active in this area are:

- Ashley Milton
- Benham & Reeves
- Brian Lack
- Ellis & Co
- Greens
- Marsh & Parsons
- Plaza Estates
- Prudential Property Services
- Raymond Bushell
- Vickers

M

Marylebone, Lisson Grove, Fitzrovia

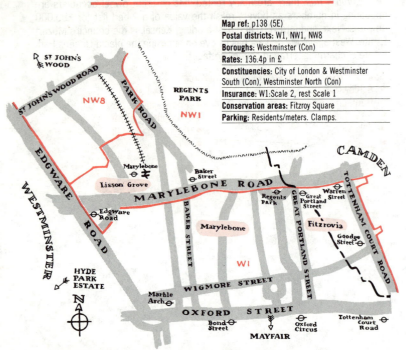

Map ref: p138 (5E)	
Postal districts: W1, NW1, NW8	
Boroughs: Westminster (Con)	
Rates: 136.4p in £	
Constituencies: City of London & Westminster South (Con), Westminster North (Con)	
Insurance: W1:Scale 2, rest Scale 1	
Conservation areas: Fitzroy Square	
Parking: Residents/meters. Clamps.	

Transport Tubes: All zone 1. Baker Street (Jubilee, Circle, Metropolitan, Bakerloo), Oxford Circus (Bakerloo, Victoria, Central), Marylebone (Bakerloo), Marble Arch (Central). Others see map. From Oxford Circus: City 15 min, Heathrow 52 min (1 change).

Convenient for West End, Regent's Park, City. Miles from centre: 1.5.

Schools ILEA zone 2: St Marylebone C of E (g). Private: Queen's College (g), North Westminster School.

Flats	S	1b	2b	3b	4b	5b
Average prices	60–90	85–200	130–300+	160–400+	200–600	–
Houses	2b	3b	4b	5b	6/7b	8b
Average prices	170–300	200–400	250–450+	350–600+	→	–

The properties The cry in the heart of the West End is for flats, from tiny studios to company luxury. Cheaper ones above shops, red-brick mansion blocks, conversions of the gracious period homes. Also mews, and a few surviving family homes. Parking atrocious, garages at premium.

The market Marylebone is long-established, especially the medical district. Fitzrovia is more bohemian but changing. Lisson Grove is the up-and-coming corner. Whole area is mixed residential/commercial, therefore cheaper than other central areas. Ideal for young buyers and businessmen's pied-a-terres. Local searches: 1 week.

Area Profile

The slice of London that lies above Oxford St, sandwiched between that shoppers' mecca and Regent's Park, could hardly be more central. Its homes can range from the 18th century to the present day, from tiny studio apartments through mews cottages to vast family mansions with dining rooms that seat 50. Blue plaques, commemorating famous residents of yesteryear, abound – sometimes more than one on each (very likely listed) building.

And yet, although it contains many most exclusive addresses, as an area it fails to spring instantly to the home-hunter's mind. Mayfair, Belgravia, Kensington – all those are, in fact, further from the hub. But this tract is a diverse one: many of its family homes have been appropriated for shops or offices, its through-routes are busy. People think first of its landmarks, and they are not domestic ones: the BBC's Broadcasting House, the Courtauld Institute, Middlesex Hospital, the Central London Polytechnic ... and of course *Harley St*, heart of the medical profession.

The other shaping influence is the continued ownership by major landlords such as the de Walden and Portman estates. This means few freeholds and, frequently, short leaseholds.

The north-of-Oxford Street area's orderly 18th-century grid of streets and squares is broken by the irrepressible wiggle of Marylebone Lane which, with the High Street (straight for while, but not for long), marks the centre of the original village of Marylebone. Across to the E the grid resumes its orderly progress to Portland Place, a giant boulevard more reminiscent of Paris than London, lined with many a luxurious apartment on its way up towards Regent's Park. Parallel is Great Portland St, and at Cleveland St the grid swings slightly on its axis to mark the borough boundary and the start of Fitzrovia. In the other direction, W of the still-villagy Marylebone Lane, the orderly pattern runs across to the diagonal of the Edgware Rd. To the N, across the Marylebone Rd, W1 gives way to NW8 and Lisson Grove laps the margins of the Park: this is the up-and-coming corner.

As few as three or four years back there were still real bargains, considering the location, among – particularly – the flats to be found above shops or in the less obvious of the mansion or more recent blocks. Prices have been catching up rapidly, but it is still an area well worth a searching look. It best suits single people – no need for a car, the West End on your doorstep – and those unburdened with young children. You have the advantage that a limited number of housethunters even think of looking here; the disadvantage of competition from companies, or businessmen looking for pieds-à-terre.

Buyers will gain all the perks of residing cheek by jowl with a multitude of highly convenient shops of all descriptions, situated not only in *Oxford St*, but also along *Tottenham Court* and *Edgware Rds*, yet without feeling as if they are bang in the midst of an extremely noisy tourist trap. Mysteriously, the shoppers display no curiousity about what lies to the N, E or W of the stores they patronize. Away from the bustle of Mothercare and John Lewis, the hustle of the food, fashion and audio-visual chain stores, lie corners of surprising residential peace and tranquillity.

The population of the West End is not homogeneous, although there is a significant indigenous and European content. Everyone mingles here within an intensely international environment that includes wealthy Middle and Far Easterners, as well as Americans and Africans (the retailers and restaurateurs of *Edgware Rd* have increasingly devoted their energies to Arab needs).

M

One of the advantages of this is that the area is not reliant upon the vicissitudes of the UK economy alone. When things were not going so well here some years back, the foreign market kept property sales brisk with money from oil and other sources abroad.

Most West End buyers are looking either for an investment or a pied-à-terre, which means that there is quite a high level of absenteeism by owners. This is a commercially-based residential market in which investors are tending to seek capital growth rather than incomes from rent. Developers are beginning to respond to the demand for convenient and relatively inexpensive little 1- and 2-bedroomed units; and although many happy families live N of *Oxford St*, they are not typical. Proof of this is offered by estate agents in the area, many of whom say that they have never been asked by anxious parents for advice on local schools.

The most common type of home in the West End is the 3- or 4-bedroomed flat, but there is increasingly less demand for these than for smaller apartments (see above). Only about 10% of West End properties are houses; and nearly all are terraced. There are decreasing numbers of tenanted properties as owner occupation expands (the 'protected tenant' is a dying breed). But freeholds are still hard to come by (see also Who Owns London).

Marylebone

The name 'Marylebone' has always been synonymous with medical excellence, for it is here that the cream of the British medical profession is gathered, crammed into *Harley St* and its immediate environs (*Wimpole St*, for example). This district, which is bordered by the southern margins of Regent's Park, as well as *Edgware Rd* and *Great Portland St*, encompasses street-by-street variations in architecture, general character – and price.

Differences in property prices (one flat can cost double what a seemingly similar flat costs) depend not just upon the quality and location of the property itself, but upon the length of the lease. Private landowners such as the Howard de Walden estate (which owns 120 acres-worth of the freeholds in Marylebone, mostly around the medical area, between *Marylebone High Street* and *Great Portland St*) do not often deal in long leases. A fair amount of this land is also owned by the Crown Estate (for example, parts of *Harley St* and *Park Crescent Mews West*). If landlords like the de Walden estate mean few freeholds, they also make for continuity. Thus the unchanging nature of the medical groves. They are responsible for the lovely Georgian doorways, staircases, rooflines still so much in evidence. These older buildings are supplemented by the redbrick blocks built at the turn of the century and some modern apartments that replaced wartime damage (a purpose-built block in *Wimpole St* is one of the few buildings hereabouts which can offer underground parking). Doctors must still get permission from the estate in order to mount their brass plate on the door of one of their houses. Some developments occur: an example is the 10-flat scheme in *Wimpole St*. In *Crawford St* Regalian have transformed old police flats into Macready House, 84 1- to 3-bed flats starting at £180,000. And Taylor Woodrow have plans for 66 flats in *Old Marylebone Rd*.

There is much to choose from in Marylebone: There is the almost rustic olde worlde charm of Marylebone Village, with its pretty little shops and restaurants (and also the fashionable American College). There is the cheerfully commercialised (busy but not unpleasant) *Baker St*, home of Sherlock Holmes, sleuth of legend. *Baker St* stretches from Regent's Park at one end to the upmarket Selfridges department store at the other; and where it bisects *Marylebone Rd* are the waxworks of Madame Tussaud's and the London Planetarium, each a focus for sightseers and day trippers. There is *Wigmore St*, with its world-renowned concert hall and smart shops, visited by a quite different clientele from the Oxford Street crowds. A major refurbishment of a big former store on the corner with *Welbeck St* has resulted in some smart new flats: 2 beds around £400,000.

Then there is *Portland Place*, the grand, wide-avenued refuge for the BBC's Broadcasting House (moving soon to White City to give way for a hotel and office complex developed by Ladbrokes), the Royal Institute of British Architects and a clutch of embassies. Portland Place homes are likely to be luxurious (discreet luxury, or mirrored, marbled, Jacuzzi'd luxury; but decidedly luxury) apartments in conversions or – more likely – the modern buildings that have superceded Robert Adam's original elegance. This is company, or perhaps top BBC-executive, territory. Many have uniformed porters; a large and elegant block in nearby *Mansfield St* runs to maid service and its own restaurant. At the N end of *Portland Place* is a delight: instead of debouching straight onto the roaring *Marylebone Rd*, the street divides into the two curving arms of Nash's *Park Crescent*, its lovely homes sheltering behind the protective half-moon of its gardens. The rare family home with garage is occasionally to be had in its mews.

M

Indeed, one of the area's special delights is the many and varied mews tucked away behind its main streets. These compact little homes – mainly modernised, but some unrefurbished – are dotted across the area, though many are concentrated in the *Harley St* environs. These, of course, are often the extremely proud possessors of garages, thanks to their original function as stables – some still have rings for tethering the horses. Though if you don't care for history, look to *Richardson's Mews*, just off *Warren St*, for the modern version. Parking in the West End is a real problem, no matter how much you pay for your property; but more and more residents' parking permits are being issued by Westminster Council; and National Car Parks offer residents a reduced rate.

There is the discreet elegance of the various squares, such as *Bryanston* and *Montagu Squares*, with their communal gardens in the centre. These well-kept and railed patches of green are accessible only to residents and are not to be sniffed at in a district where private gardens are almost non-existent, or barely bigger than a suburban household's window box.

Portman Mansions, on the corner of *Chiltern St* and busy *Marylebone Rd*, has sprouted 11 elegant penthouses prices from £265,000. This block is one of many: there is always a good supply of mansion flats, of every standard from scruffy to palatial, in this part of town.

Turn-of-the-century buildings like Bickenhall Mansions, with their high ceilings and coved fireplaces, are particularly popular, as are the huge 9-bedroomed flats in mansion blocks like Orchard Court (*Portman Square*). *Harley St* is, as you might expect, another much-prized address. *Weymouth St* nearby had a rare virtual freehold house for sale over the winter. The 4-bed, 3-bath house was built in the 1930s to the designs of George Gray Warnum, who designed the RIBA headquarters. It was priced at £750,000. A major scheme in *Marylebone Lane* has 80 1- to 3-bed new flats. *Harrowby St*, off *Edgware Rd*, has a redevelopment of 140 flats.

Lisson Grove

The area around Lisson Grove (NWl) remains the least fashionable part of Marylebone. Indeed, *Old Marylebone Rd*, with its noisy traffic and less salubrious surroundings including some rather depressing-looking nearby council estates, has not been very popular with the more discerning residential purchaser. But things are changing: canny developers, out to make a slowish killing, have earmarked Lisson Grove for special attention now and in the near future. Given the exclusive areas which lies to the N and S, growth was inevitable. The Regents Canal runs through the area, conveying hints of neighbouring Little Venice and Regents Park. A house actually straddling the canal was sold last year.

Though it is still much cheaper to buy in Lisson Grove than in somewhere like *Devonshire St* (Wl), relative prices are rising as private landlords invest in conversions. The area is adjacent to the main arteries giving access to the *Ml* and *M4* motorways; and Edgware Road tube station is a five minute walk away. Lisson House, a newly-modernised block containing 1- and 2-bed apartments is a classic example of the kind of property that is coming onto this market. These offer some of the lowest prices for a new scheme to be found in the West End.

The Georgian facades of *Bell St*, which runs from *Edgware Rd* to *Lisson St*, are already attracting a lot of attention. But even more exciting for estate agents is the expected enhancement of the area when Europe's largest permanent, undercover antiques market opens on the junction of *Cosway St* and *Bell Sts*.

Portman Gate in *Lisson Grove* has 114 houses and flats, with more coming available this spring: three £600,000-plus penthouses. There may well also be re-sales from early buyers who bought off-plan.

Fitzrovia

Fitzrovia is the rectangle enclosed by *Euston Rd* to the N, *Oxford St* to the S, *Great Portland St* to the W and *Tottenham Court Rd* to the E. Presiding over the northern end of the neighbourhood named after it is *Fitzroy Square*, a handsome, semi-pedestrianised conservation area, inhabited by commercial concerns and embassies, but also by private residents. Fitzrovia is a quiet, quirky London village with a Bohemian flavour and history – William Blake lived in *Fitzroy Square* and the area as a whole has long attracted artists, writers and aesthetes. 1988 saw a book published on their artistic and alcoholic abilities.

Fitzrovia is packed with interesting period properties (mostly, now Victorian and turn-of-the-century, though Georgiana does survive in the *Square*, *Conway St* and other enclaves). Modernised purpose-built blocks house hundreds of studio and 1-bedroom apartments. Old-style – and increasingly scarce – mansion blocks are being carved up to meet the surging demand for small, compact central London residences. There is a shortage, but developers are not idle. Recent conversions in *Riding House St* were snapped up within a week of completion. But although Fitzrovia is more upmarket than Lisson Grove, there are still relative bargains to be had. Prices are hard to generalize about due to the small number, a clutch of flats and mews houses in *Whitfield St* came on the market last year at between £220,000 (3 beds) and £320,000 (4-bed house).

For this reason, it is very popular with young couples, first-time buyers and people who simply need a 'little place in town' now and then. Westminster Council is forging ahead with ambitious plans to ease the traffic problem and improve the area in general. Westminster controls the W half of Fitzrovia; Camden's patch spreads E from *Cleveland St* and includes *Fitzroy Square* itself. Some might say that the area, with its unique atmosphere, proximity to Regent's Park and first-class restaurants and wine bars, doesn't need much improving outside a general spring-cleaning of the rag trade area around *Great Portland St.*

Fitzrovia divides into three sections of roughly equivalent standards: there is the *Charlotte St/Tottenham Court Rd* slice – a 'fun' area with pedestrian walkways. There is the grandeur of *Fitzroy Square* and its surroundings. Then there are the sections to the W between *Great Portland* and *Great Titchfield Sts*, home of the wholesale fashion industry. The landmark that keeps reappearing – always, somehow, where you least expect it – is, of course, the soaring Telecom Tower.

Among those estate agents active in this area are:

- Debenham, Tewson & Chinnocks
- Druce
- Elliott Son & Boyton
- John D Wood
- Brian Lack

- Gross Fine
- Robert Irving & Burns
- Harrods Estate Offices
- Sweby Cowan
- Hirschfields

Mayfair

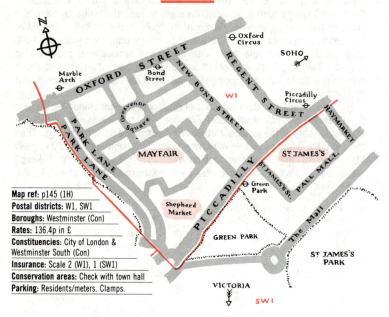

Map ref: p145 (1H)
Postal districts: W1, SW1
Boroughs: Westminster (Con)
Rates: 136.4p in £
Constituencies: City of London &
Westminster South (Con)
Insurance: Scale 2 (W1), 1 (SW1)
Conservation areas: Check with town hall
Parking: Residents/meters. Clamps.

Transport	Tubes all zone 1: Marble Arch, Bond St (Central); Oxford Circus (Victoria, Bakerloo, Central); Piccadilly Circus (Bakerloo, Piccadilly); Green Park (Victoria, Piccadilly). From Green Park: Oxford Circus 2 min, City 10 min (1 change), Heathrow 1 hr.
Convenient for	West End, City, Hyde Park. Miles from centre: 1.
Schools	ILEA zone 2: Westminster City C of E.

Flats	S	1b	2b	3b	4b	5b
Average prices	70–120	100–200	200–350	275–450	450–1m+	→
Houses	2b	3b	4b	5b	6/7b	8b
Average prices	275–350	350–550	550–1m	650+	850+	2m+

The properties	Mostly flats and mostly grand ones, in mansion blocks or conversions of period homes. Some mews cottages and a few lovely Georgian and Victorian houses. Degree of luxury ranges from the ordinary mansion flat to the super-opulent. St James's has fewer homes, but some with lovely park views.
The market	Length of lease and degree of opulence are key price factors. Check service charges in big blocks. Very international area, but signs that rich British are moving back in. In recent years Mayfair's status and thus prices fell behind Belgravia and points west; but now some signs of residential renaissance. Local searches: 1 week.

Area Profile

Mayfair, said an estate agent, has always been for the really rich. How true. Yet only, perhaps, nine-tenths true, when one peels back the facades and checks who really lives there. For a start, Mayfair, and St James's to the south, are still surprisingly residential. This may be the centre of town, crammed with coveted shops and offices, but there are plenty of people around at every hour of the 24. Mayfair even has a thriving residents' association, vigilant in defence of peace and amenity, under the chairmanship of a retired brigadier.

Top people have lived in Mayfair since early Georgian times. Never has it sunk from its position as a centre of fashionable London. Other places – Soho, Bloomsbury, North of the Park – have had their ups and downs but Mayfair has always been a correct address. Until within living memory it was dotted with the very grand houses, palaces really, of dukes and other noblemen. These have gone, to be replaced by great blocks of flats and hotels. Yet many of the smaller Georgian houses survive, providing the less spacious but no less luxurious London homes of today's magnates.

Mayfair is bounded in the N by the great shopping parade of *Oxford St*, in the E by *Regent St*, in the S by *Piccadilly* and in the W by *Park Lane*, the six-lane highway that separates Hyde Park from Mayfair's western rampart of hotels and car showrooms. The NW corner, from Marble Arch down to *Berkeley Square*, is part of the Grosvenor Estate, as is Belgravia. The rest is divided among several landlords. Quite a bit of Mayfair is now offices, but many exist on sufferance, under temporary planning permissions granted after the war when there was a shortage of office space. These permissions are due to expire in 1990, when around 120 buildings should revert to homes. So many extensions were granted over the years that firms such as property giant MEPC were amazed to find they really were to lose the use of their vast *Park Lane* HQ. Some small firms will be genuinely hard-hit, but the result, after the landlords v council negotiations, should be more homes in the residential *South St/Balfour Place/Park St* area.

Mayfair

Mayfair is big, and has its quiet corners and districts of bustle. As a broad generalisation, the further W, the quieter and smarter. In general, the E and S are older than the N and W. The SW corner, Shepherd Market, has an air of its own and is dealt with below. A few controlled-rent flats apart, Mayfair is the province of the mansion block and expensively-converted flat, with a few period houses and rather more mews cottages. No area is without homes, but in some parts they are hard to spot amid the shops, offices and banks. While nothing in Mayfair is cheap, the prices asked for properties can vary widely based on the two variables of length of lease and degree of opulence.

The NE corner, around *Hanover Square*, is among the oldest parts of Mayfair – the *Square* dates from 1715 – but is today mostly commercial, with offices and shops spilling out from *Oxford St. New Bond St*, Mayfair's main shopping street, divides this area from the fashion quarter centred around *South Molton St*, now pedestrianised. *Davies St*, running N-S and dead straight, as so many Mayfair streets are, forms the edge of a more residential district to the W. The shops and crowds of *Oxford St* are a moment away, but here is a more peaceful world of mansion blocks and converted period houses. *Gilbert St*, *Brook St* and *Duke St*, running parallel N-S, contain some attractive red brick

M

mansion blocks with gabled skylines. Many apartments sit above shops. Off *Duke St* is an unusual garden, raised on a plinth over an electricity station. This neglected square with its pavilion is happily being restored. Hereabouts are some early red-brick council homes, now run by the Peabody Trust. Also mansion blocks in what Pevsner calls 'typical Northwest-Mayfair style – red brick and pink terracotta, gables, and much smaller Renaissance detail'.

This is Grosvenor Estate country. Few realise that the northern part of Mayfair includes not only grand houses and flats but also a wide area of low-rent housing. These flats are is tucked away between *Grosvenor Square* and *Oxford St* and are owned by the Grosvenor Estate and run by it in partnership with housing associations. In *Duke's Yard*, off *Duke St*, the site of an old coach house has been developed with 4-bed apartments. These are 2-storey, red brick properties over garages and shops.

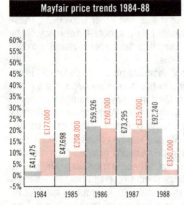

Mayfair price trends 1984-88

London average home: percentage rise on previous year, adjusted for inflation.

Typical home in this area, percentage rise on previous year, adjusted for inflation.

Two-bed, two-bath flat in the Charles Street/Mount Street area, price change compared to London-wide average home. This modest rise gives credence to agents' cries that Mayfair is cheap. But this home beat the London average in each of the preceding five years, except '86 (when it came very close). And 2% of a lot of money is still well worth having.

Further E off *Brook St* is *Avery Row*, a narrow lane with attractive 3-storey stucco and brown brick terraces of flats above shops. Behind Claridges in *Brook St* is *Brook's Mews*. Its brick flat-fronted cottages face an unattractive modern brick development providing 5 storeys of flats. These are achieving high prices as piéds-à-terre. Further up the road a new development will be rented flats for a housing association. At the top of the road are more much-sought-after flats in the grey concrete Grosvenor Hill Court next to an NCP car park. *Mount Row*, to the W of *Davies St*, has brown brick homes with casement windows and leaded glass with mansard roof and attic. On the south side stand red brick mews-style houses with shuttered windows.

Curving round into *Berkeley Square* are red brick and terracotta Dutch gabled blocks above galleries and wine shops. *Berkeley Square* has everything from beautiful early Georgiana to '30s to a modern block with stepped roof line and shops and bank below. On the S side Lansdowne House has been redeveloped as offices for Saatchi and Saatchi. There are handsome stucco and brick houses along the W side.

Travelling down *Fitzmaurice Place* and into *Curzon St*, *Clarges Mews* leads off behind a major development of the Washington Hotel. On *Curzon St* is the Christian Science Church, behind which a courtyard of flats and offices was cunningly inserted. Smart modern blocks like Glendore House punctuate the houses of *Clarges St* and *Half Moon St*. In *Half Moon St* attractive red brick gabled houses line the SW side, on the SE there is a modern block of luxury apartments. The Naval and Military Club is here and the Green Park Hotel, along with some attractive period properties.

Chesterfield Hill contains an attractive row of 5-storey cream stucco and chocolate painted brick period houses with cast iron railings at the front and iron balconies decked with window gardens. This small area of *Hill St* and *Hays Mews* contains some of the most attractive mews and period homes, tucked away in relative peace and quiet. Approaching from *Charles St* you pass plaques commemorating the former residence of King William IV, the sailor king who lived there in 1826. *Hays Mews* is a wide sloping road with pretty mews cottages of brick and painted brick with garages below. Curled around the top of the mews is *Red Lion Yard*, with a pretty pub giving it an 'out of London' atmosphere. Cobblestones lead to more 3-storey brick town houses in the yard itself. The E end of *Hay's Mews* on the opposite side of *Chesterfield Hill* is perhaps less attractive, but has the same wide roadway, a mixture of modern houses and period 2-storey brick cottages and a 5-storey modern brick development of flats, Rosebery Court. *Hill St's* grand period houses can reach £3 million. *South St* is residential, with red-brick conversions and a number of attractive smaller houses, and the St George's primary school.

Waverton St contains Mayfair House, and the imposing brick mansion Garden House, whose name is the only clue to the hidden garden shared (by the houses only) between *South St/South Audley St/Waverton St* and *Hill St*. Travelling up *South Audley St* there are cream stucco period houses and gabled red brick and terracotta mansion flats above pleasant shops. Mayfair library, built in 1984, sits next to a quiet public garden in a cul-de-sac alongside the Grosvenor Chapel. The garden, with rows of benches, is overlooked by red brick mansion blocks. To the W is *Balfour Mews* with more red brick and stucco and red brick and stone houses with balustrades. *Balfour Cottages* are a pair of pretty, painted brick homes with tub trees outside. *Reeves Mews* has brown brick and stone flats opposite a row of mews cottages.

Culross St behind the US Embassy has terraces of period town houses. They are of varying heights and materials, brick, painted brick and stucco fronts. Shutters and tiny steps up to the front door give this road a village feel. *Green St's* red-brick houses, many now flats, hide another concealed garden, shared with *Woods Mews*.

The word 'flat' can sometimes be inadequate in Mayfair: the refurbishment of a Lutyens-design building in *North Row* has yielded 15 house-sized apartments. £600,000 buys four beds, £1.5 million one of three penthouses each with five bedrooms, conservatory, roof terraces – and a summer house.

Park St, the main street of the NW corner of Mayfair, has some large red brick and stone mansion blocks with colonnaded facades and balconies. The whole district is defined by the tall, terracotta and brick houses, once mansions, now often offices or flats. *Park Lane*, on the W edge of Mayfair, used to be lined with grand homes. Only a handful of the period houses survive, having been replaced by monolithic hotels and car showrooms. Some flats, including serviced ones attached to hotels like the Grosvenor House, can be found on busy *Park Lane*. The view from them may be lovely, but noisy.

Grosvenor Square, the largest square in the district at six acres, is best known as the site of the enormous American Embassy. The other sides have some very smart flats, reckoned the most luxurious in Mayfair. The flats on the N side are on 48 or 72 year leases, the E and S side ones, 70-80 years. Few come onto the market: they tend to be held by families, often eminent ones.

The SE corner of Mayfair, towards *Piccadilly Circus*, has fewer homes. *Albany*, the famous warren of presitige 'chambers' off *Piccadilly*, is very exclusive and

M

inhabited by the great, the good and the long-term rich. There are flats above shops, a few mews, and some blocks in streets such as *Hay Hill*.

Shepherd Market

Shepherd Market is an unexpected village of narrow streets and small-scale buildings, incongruous amid Mayfair's grandeur. Once it was frowned upon as being seedy and the haunt of prostitutes. Today the area's image has greatly changed; more streets have been pedestrianised and the pretty cottages to be found there are now some of the most sought-after homes in Mayfair. Nevertheless, there is a variety of properties in the area ranging from modern luxury apartments through period mansion blocks to tiny town houses and mews cottages. Approaching from *Hertford St*, there are mansion flats in brick and stucco blocks and some handsome old houses. A massive 7-storey block, *Carrington St*, with luxury 1- and 2-bed flats for sale. Until recently the flats were rented on short lets and had a high turnover of residents.

Turning into *Shepherd St* there are some attractive cream 2-storey mews period cottages. The brick and painted brick homes over shops are now much in demand. On the other side of the street is a modern red brick block of flats called May Fayre House, developed by Ladbroke's.

The Shepherds Tavern is a red brick building with bow front windows. Its jaunty, floral exterior sets the tone for the pretty village that scatters down *Shepherd St* and round into *Shepherd Market*. On the left of *Shepherd St* is a red brick terrace of flat roofed homes over shops. The market square itself is pedestrianised and a flower stall and pavement bars contribute to the busy atmosphere. More large 3-storey brick and stucco buildings line the continuation of *Hertford St*. Cobblestones take you further up the road towards 3-storey mews-style brick houses. A large block of flats in *Carrington St* has been refurbished; *Down St* has 5/6-storey mansion blocks.

St James's

The best homes in St James's are palaces and are unlikely to be for sale. Non-royals have to hunt hard for a flat, harder for a house. *Cleveland Row*, next-door to St James's Palace, used to be residential but now seems to be offices. *Little St James's St* has some old houses in mixed use, and the development of a giant old mansion is expected to provide some flats. There are some exclusive flats in *St James's Place*, some with wonderful views over Green Park. More flats are found along the park reached from *Arlington St*.

St James's St itself has a mere handful of homes. Some flats are in a corner block next to *Little St James's St*. Further E is *St James's Square*, which was once a dignified assembly of town houses, but now has only one residential building. *Bury St* has some flats in tall buildings, often above shops and offices, as does *Duke of York St*. But living in St James's is hard. It might be easier to marry into the Royal Family.

Among those estate agents active in this area are:

- Harrods Estate Offices
- Beauchamp Estates
- Cluttons
- Hamptons
- Jackson-Stops & Staff
- Keith Cardale Groves
- Knight Frank & Rutley
- Lassmans
- Prudential Property Services
- Savills
- Debenham Tewson
- Radius
- John D Wood
- Hirschfields
- Wetherells

Morden, Mitcham, Colliers Wood

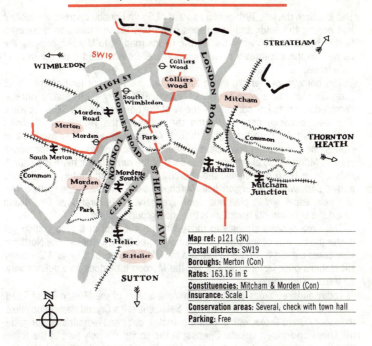

Map ref:	p121 (3K)
Postal districts:	SW19
Boroughs:	Merton (Con)
Rates:	163.16 in £
Constituencies:	Mitcham & Morden (Con)
Insurance:	Scale 1
Conservation areas:	Several, check with town hall
Parking:	Free

Transport Tubes: Collier's Wood, Morden (zones 3a/b Northern). From Morden: Oxford Circus 35 min (1 change), City 40 min, Heathrow 1 hr 30 min (2 changes). British Rail from Mitcham Junction and Mitcham.

Convenient for Tubes to central London, routes South, Wimbledon.

Schools Merton Education Authority: Eastfield High (b), Raynes Park (b), Rutlish (b), Rickards Lodge (g) Willows (g), Rowan (g), Garth, Tamworth Manor, Ursuline Convent (g), Wimbledon College (b).

Flats	S	1b	2b	3b	4b	5b
Average prices	–	60–70	63–80	67–85	–	–
Houses	2b	3b	4b	5b	6/7b	8b
Average prices	78–100	85–160	110–200	140–225	–	–

The properties Behind the busy main roads, all three areas have large estates of 1930s terraces. These generally provide the most common source of converted flats or 2/3- bed homes: 4 or more beds are scarce, and range up to c £170–190,000. Prices above are for top houses beside parks in Mitcham.

The market First-time buyers find good-size, good value flats here. Mitcham prices are held back by lack of a tube, except for best family homes. Inexpensive ex-council homes are now widely available. 3-bed flats are rare: generally ex-council or above shops. Local searches: 4 weeks.

Area Profile

This is where the late 19th-century sprawl of South London came to a reluctant halt among the fields and woodlands of Surrey. Urban expansion received a further boost in 1926 when the Northern Line made it to Morden, bringing the name into the vocabulary of millions of travellers who read it on the front of tube trains.

The borough of Merton, which takes in all this area but for Colliers Wood, gives its name to a wide spread of suburbia of every 20th-century vintage. Wimbledon, on its hill, commands the W of the borough. To the SE is Croydon. The area between centres around the valley of the Wandle, which flows northwards from here through Earlsfield, Wandsworth and other more urban places. Merton itself is an ancient village, but little survives except the parish church. Morden also clings onto what's left of the rural charm: there is a church dating from 1636, and behind the church a pub with 16th century foundations and a park with a Georgian hall. Mitcham is an old place too, with a few survivals, especially in plan and open greenery, of its rural days. Of Colliers Wood the only notable landmark is the underground station.

This area appeals strongly to those who need to get at a tube station yet prefer the charms of suburbia to more congested living further in. The Northern Line takes a good half hour to get into the West End or the City, and the many BR stations offer faster progress. Yet the Morden tube does, in a definite way, tie the area into London.

Today all three areas await the imminent advent of the Merton Relief Road (under construction) and the vast new Savacentre – a Crystal Palace lookalike the size of Brent Cross, with a leisure complex, pubs and restaurants alongside the shops and supermarkets. Opening in the spring, it's only part of the River Wandle development, behind *Merton High St* and alongside *Christchurch Rd*. Plans include revitalising the old mills and adding craft shops and museums.

The council also has plans to smarten up and 'landscape' both Mitcham and Morden town centres, and Mitcham will also gain a pedestrian precinct.

Morden

Morden, until the mid-1920s, was a small agricultural community. The landscape was dramatically changed by a high concentration council house building programme and today can be described as 'Thirties-semi suburbia'.

Morden is at the southern end of the Northern Line tube (Waterloo 30 minutes, City 40 minutes) while Morden South BR station provides good links to London and the south coast via Sutton and Wimbledon. A short drive away, the Reigate-Leatherhead M25 intersection gives easy access to Heathrow and Gatwick airports.

Generally, Morden is a green, leafy, residential area and includes Morden Hall Park (more than 50 acres of National Trust parkland), Morden Park (swimming baths, playing fields) and Cannon Hill Common. Houses facing, or with views of, park areas are never on the market long.

Premier roads include the leafy *Lower Morden Lane* and *Hillcross Avenue* (mainly 1930s 3-bed solid semis, with front/rear gardens and garages).

Flats and bungalows are scarce but Croudace Homes have built 75 1/2-bed flats, some with bay windows, in landscaped gardens at Bordesley Court (*Bordesley Rd*). As building land is scarce, too, Morden is not likely to lose its 'open' qualities; though plans are in hand to develop and landscape the town centre. New shops and offices (some 2,300 sq m, with parking behind) will appear on the site of the old cinema.

The St Helier Estate, built by the LCC in the 1930s and considered advanced for its time, comprises a large area of wide, well-planned roads (*Blanchland Rd* and *Hazelwood Avenue* are typical) of 2/3-bed red-brick semis and terraces with front and rear gardens. These pre-war council-built houses are high quality and popular with first-time buyers – they account for 25% of all sales in the district. Many new owners have added imaginative (and sometimes misplaced) exterior features to their homes.

Many inner-London families (trading down) are moving into the area. Turnover is faster than average (one attractive semi sold last year on the first day it was on the market).

Mitcham

Mitcham, once renowned for its lavender fields and watercress beds, is an odd blend of bustling town, light industry, and country village. Though it has a Surrey postal address, it comes under Merton council.

Determined to retain its rural atmosphere, Mitcham resisted efforts to link it to London's Underground. Consequently, it now presents a problem for commuters. The nearest tube station (Tooting Broadway) is a bus ride away. Mitcham Junction BR station (a mile from the centre of Mitcham) serves Victoria (18 minutes) while Mitcham BR station is on the branch line linking Wimbledon and West Croydon. There is good access to the M23 (Gatwick) and M25 (Heathrow), but the centre of town is congested with through-traffic. Matters should improve with a new road and pedestrianisation from the bot-

M

Mitcham and Morden mushroomed in the 1920s and '30s, after the extension of the Northern Line tube speeded commuting into the City. The result was wide areas of neat, semi-detached homes. Mock-Tudor detailing was popular – this is quite a restrained example. The tile-roofed porch-cum-bay is also typical. After a period of disdain, these houses are now fashionable.

tom of *London Rd* to *Upper Green West*. Work starts in the autumn.

Georgian cottages, manor houses, 18th-century houses and Eagle House, a superb example of Queen Anne architecture, are reminders of Mitcham's rural past. *Commonside East*, facing the Common and pond, has a row of pretty 2-bed Victorian terraced cottages. These, like homes facing Fair Green and Mitcham Park, command good prices (there is a waiting list for *Cricket Green*, for example). Other desirable areas include *Denham Crescent* (off *Bramcote Avenue*) and *The Close*.

Chatsworth Place, off *London Rd*, is a recent development of 1/2-bed flats and 4-bed semis. In *Church Rd*, *Cannons Place* has 2/3/4-bed houses with private gardens and garages/parking. At *Lower Green West*, Mitcham Village Studios is a Georgian schoolhouse conversion of studios and apartments. *Chestnut Grove* has 20 Victorian-style 1/2-bed flats and 2/3-bed houses.

New developments are appearing in the *Western Rd* area, influenced no doubt by the new Savacentre near its Merton end. Laing's 'The Hamiltons' is here, with everything from studios to 3-bed houses. Fifty-three flats and houses are also proposed for a 2-acre site in *Mount Rd*, and more are planned for part of the Athletics Ground site behind Lavender Avenue. In nearby *Lewis Rd*, too, Croudace plan 46 1- and 2-bed flats this year.

'Mitcham', summed up one local estate agent, 'is divided into the good, the bad and definitely the ugly.' The latter includes some hardly scenic tower blocks and council estates on the Colliers Wood borders, and explains a wide range of home prices. A villa on a leafy green effortlessly tops £200,000; a 3-bed flat in a good road can command over £80,000 – while a huge 3-bed flat in one of the tower blocks is worth £25,000 less.

Colliers Wood

Colliers Wood is sandwiched between Merton and Tooting High Streets. Dominated by an ugly grey tower block of offices, it has been dismissed for years as a 'depressed' area. Now its potential is beginning to be recognised.

Everywhere is showing signs of improvement: pubs have smartened up, restaurants and new shops have opened, and (infallible sign) estate agents have moved in. Nearby Wandle Park (part-owned by the National Trust) provides some welcome green space. With direct access to London from Colliers Wood tube station (Northern Line, 25 minutes Waterloo; 35 minutes the City), it's ideal commuter territory. Here, as in Mitcham, agents report that news of the road improvement plans and the extensive shopping and leisure schemes began to increase interest in the area last year. Staff for the vast Savacentre were early on the scene.

The area has a pleasant mix of 1880s, 1930s and 1960s houses with pretty stucco/yellow-brick Edwardian villas, many Victorian terraces (some with bay windows), and some conversion flats.

Few houses have off-street parking, but most have the bonus of long back gardens. The better roads are bordered by *Cavendish Rd* and include *Marlborough*, *Clive*, *Warren Rds*, *Daniel* and *Defoe Closes*, *Norfolk* and *Harewood Rds*. Some have bollards, preventing noisy through-traffic.

Only six years ago a 5-bed house was £50,000; today £160,000 is the going rate. There are still bargains to be had – look out for pockets of as yet run-down late Victorian 2/3-bed terraced houses.

Mead Park, the Wimpey development in the Wandle Valley NW of *Colliers Wood High St* has provided this corner with 160 new homes, from studios to townhouses. Last winter's prices for 1- and 2-bed flats were from £69-87,000.

Merton

The Merton Park Estate is described in the Wimbledon chapter.

Among those estate agents active in this area are:

- Andrews & Partners
- Prudential Property Services
- Mann & co
- Rogers
- Chris James & Partners
- Drury & Cole
- Winkworths
- Mallards

Muswell Hill

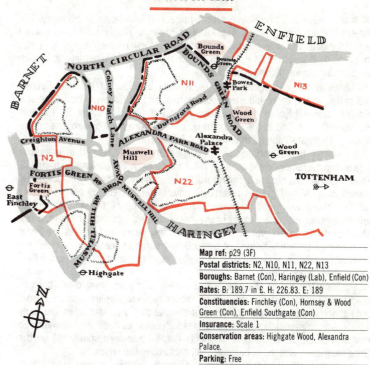

Map ref: p29 (3F)
Postal districts: N2, N10, N11, N22, N13
Boroughs: Barnet (Con), Haringey (Lab), Enfield (Con)
Rates: B: 189.7 in £. H: 226.83. E: 189
Constituencies: Finchley (Con), Hornsey & Wood Green (Con), Enfield Southgate (Con)
Insurance: Scale 1
Conservation areas: Highgate Wood, Alexandra Palace.
Parking: Free

M

Transport   Tubes: Bounds Green, Wood Green (zone 3a/b, Piccadilly); East Finchley, Highgate (zone 3a, Northern). From Highgate to: Oxford Circus 20 min (1 change), City 25 min, Heathrow 1 hr 15 min (1 change). British Rail: Alexandra Palace to City.

Convenient for   Brent Cross Shopping Centre, Wood Green Shopping City. North Circular Rd, A1/M1. Miles from centre: 6.

Schools   Barnet, Haringey and Enfield Education Authorities: Fortismere School. Private: Whittingham, Channing (g), Highgate School.

Flats	S	1b	2b	3b	4b	5b
Average prices	55–62	65–75	80–100+	100–130	–	–
Houses	2b	3b	4b	5b	6/7b	8b
Average prices	100–125	110–165	170–220+	220–260+	→	–

The properties   Solid Edwardian houses, some very large, providing roomy conversions as well as family homes. Also some mansion flats. Smaller houses '20s/30s, but smallest are modern or little Victorian terraces in fringe areas.

The market   Spacious houses attract families – many of media/professional/liberal persuasion – who find value in this green, well-schooled area. Lack of tube keeps prices down. Big jump in quality (and price) from 3 to 4-bed homes. Local searches: Barnet 4 weeks, Haringey 4, Enfield 6.

Area Profile

Muswell Hill is a Conservative salient projecting into Socialist Haringey. The hill-top suburb has grown in popularity as prices in neighbouring Hampstead and Highgate became beyond the reach of many mortals' pockets. It has become re-established as a place in its own right, a hilly, residential district with its own distinctive, dignified character.

The wider area can be defined to the N and E by a loop of the *North Circular Rd*, taking in the more industrial/commercial end of *Colney Hatch Lane* and *Bounds Green* plus its tube, across to Wood Green. To the S, it meets Hornsey/Crouch End at the southern tip of Alexandra Park, and reaches down towards Highgate Tube on the main A1 *Archway Rd*.

It's always had a genteel air. Its homes are mostly ranged in grandiose Edwardian terraces or set in wide leafy roads (with no parking restrictions). They boast almost bizarre architectural features including spires and balconies, heavily ornamented gables, pillastered bays. After the elderly people (whose families had often owned the larger places since they were first built) died, or left for smaller premises, many houses were divided into flats or maisonettes. This trend has been reversed over the past few years, and houses are being reconverted to family homes of up to 6 bedrooms in some cases. Haringey Council frowns on conversions, and is also against the building of small flats rather than family homes.

Although the actual Muswell, with its early monastic links, dates back to mediaeval times, little was built here except the odd elegant country retreat until the mid-Victorian period. Most of the building was started in the early 1900s, in large estates of varying-sized houses as well as many-storied mansion blocks of bachelor apartments (large by today's standards) on the *Broadway* itself, and those purpose-built flats above the shops.

Shopping in the *Broadway* is small and friendly, with everything you need for immediate purposes; Greek delicatessens abound and there are several useful late-opening small supermarkets. The last year has seen more restaurants, wine bars and art shops. The necessary wider choice and departmental-store type shopping is supplied by the nearby Brent Cross Shopping Centre – London's first major edge-of-town centre – and also the centre at Wood Green. And now, closer to home, a big new Tesco superstore on the N Circular (junction with *Colney Hatch Lane*) has just opened. There are several different restaurants, a cinema and two swimming pools in the area, as well as the golf course and the amenities of Alexandra Palace, which has been restored for arts, leisure and other uses. Interestingly, as the main estates were built on Methodist Church land, there are few original pubs, but this has been rectified of late with new additions on the *Broadway* drag.

Another drawback is the lack of a nearby tube. Highgate and Bounds Green are a 10-minute bus (if it arrives) ride away, and Finsbury Park's a good 15 minutes. There are several bus routes to the West End and the City, as well as a BR line at Alexandra Palace to Moorgate. This is a car-driver's area and a good number of households have two. Luckily, streets tend to be wide and parking is not the nightmare it is in denser-packed suburbs.

But the number of people using their cars to get to work or schools is reflected on the frustrating bottleneck at the main Muswell Hill Roundabout. On the whole, the sort of people buying and living in this area are middleclass, dual-income families, many in the media-type industries or smart *Guardian*-reading high income professionals. Stemming from this, the local schools have a good reputation as they are well supported by aware parent groups, who do not only donate money, but a great deal of time and energy to their children's education. There is consequently an obvious requirement for houses/flats in the 'right' catchment area. As a consequence of its family inhabitants, Muswell Hill has a very high density of au pair girls.

Muswell Hill

The little town, with the *Broadway* as its high street, is set in a unique position on one of the highest hills in North London, giving long, long views over the City and West End: St Paul's and British Telecom Tower can be seen on clear days. There is a sense of being a place apart, a slight but definite distancing from the main thrust of London... the eccentric architecture of the Hill sailing red-bricked above the more polluted air of lower domains. Indeed, the air is purer (and some say colder) than that of its lower neighbours, not only thanks to physical height, but surely because of the many acres of woods at the end of *Muswell Hill Rd* and the extensive parkland surrounding Alexandra Palace. There are, indeed, many other smaller pockets of parkland, complete with bowling greens and tennis courts, which invoke the leisurely Edwardian era of the suburb's flowering.

Coveted areas are those Edwardian enclaves off *Dukes Avenue* behind *The Broadway*, stretching north-eastwards across to encircling *Alexandra Park Rd*. The peaceful streets are treelined and wide enough to take four cars side by side (no parking restrictions as yet). The houses are mostly large – and some double-fronted – with anything from 3-6 or even 8 bedrooms, longish gardens, and festooned with the 'original features' so beloved of estate agents.

There are other, plainer Edwardian estates stretching from the far side of *Alexandra Park Rd*: the 'lake' roads – *Windermere Rd, Grasmere Rd* – across to *Sutton, Wilton* and *Greenham Rds* off the W side of *Colney Hatch Lane*, but here the streets are narrower, and the houses do not have quite the same dignified air. However, they still boast interiors which command a good price, plenty of space, and are still not far away from the main shopping area.

Less sought-after areas, commensurately cheaper in price, lie to the N up towards the *North Circular Rd*. Between *Colney Hatch Lane*, the *North Circular* and *Alexandra* and *Wetherill Rds* are some Edwardian homes mixed with smaller Victorian ones. The tenor gets decidedly more commercial (*Hampden Road* Bus Terminus and even a tattoo shop are to be found here), but this corner, nevertheless, has been catching up fast: prices, and new developments, have arisen. 'Cambridge Gardens' is a cul-de-sac of new houses off *Sydney Rd*; 'Mayfair Lodge' has 18 retirement flats (from £65,000) in *Wetherill Rd*. Plans, too, for an 11-flat development in *Bedford Close*. Houses off *Coppetts Rd* to the W, although in leafy streets, are generally less popular, there being '60s blocks of flats and a fairly large council estate of indifferent architectural value there. The Rialto development, two years old, on the other side of the *North Circular Rd*, is neat and quiet. All these convenient for the new Tesco Superstore.

At the other end of the area, and the other end of the scale, lie Muswell Hill's choicest homes. The select street to the S, on the edge of Highgate and Queens Woods, also have the advantage of lying nearest to Highgate Tube. These roads – *Onslow Gardens, Woodland Rise, Woodland Gardens* – and those roads off to *Wood Vale*, as well as the main *Muswell Hill Rd*, are lined with very large houses, sometimes with balconies and basement areas (easily converted to utility rooms) which are definite assets. Often set further back, or higher up, from the road, probably with a car port, these houses command high prices (sometimes up to £300,000) for the most luxurious. Parking can be a problem here as many of these homes have two or three cars apiece, and some agents are now advocating the similar roads, convenient for East Finchley tube, around Fortis Green as being the better bet for size:cost ratio. *Grand*, *Collingwood*, *Leaside*, *Fortismere* and *Birchwood Avenues* are very popular – but expensive. Cheaper but not so large and grand are those off nearby *East Finchley High Rd* itself – smaller-scale versions intermingled with 1930s semis; much more everyday roads, but highly convenient for the tube and only an extra five minutes' tube journey (above-ground at this point) to town.

Newer parts of Muswell Hill regarded favourably are the 1920s Collins-built private estate off the main Hill (the road which runs up to the *Broadway* from the S tip of Alexandra Park) itself. The Rookfield estate has neat houses set in privately maintained roads – with five barriers to disallow through traffic. A decade later came the 1930s bay-fronted houses of *Creighton Avenue* and *Pages Lane*, as well as those lining *Alexandra Park Rd*, in a broad sweep across the area. These are typical of their kind; since they often have garages, they fetch high prices. So, too, do those in *Cranley Gardens* on the Muswell Hill/Hornsey borders. For flats hereabouts, watch the Baptist Church Hall off *Creighton Avenue*: there are plans to develop the site with 13 new homes. Apart from the Rookfield Estate, these roads are all quite busy so more traffic noise is likely here.

Bounds Green and Wood Green

If you are not willing or able to invest the larger sum required for Muswell Hill proper, the surrounding areas may be the answer. Bounds Green, perhaps the best investment now, has the same sort of houses – not such elegant roads, but close to the tube, and therefore a good compromise for those requiring space and convenience. Some smaller Victorian 'artisan dwellings' around Bowes Park are still affordable, and there is a general air of 'gentrification' which bodes well for investment.

The triangle between *Durnsford Rd*, *Victoria Rd*, and the railway line has become popular recently with prices rising fast. There are more flats here, and solid houses, but part of *Crescent Rise* and *Dagmar Rd* back onto the railway. Over this line to Wood Green the desirability wanes: the areas around *Truro Road* and the *High Rd* are not likely to be an 'investment', but would be cheaper for first-time buyers on their way up the ladder. However, the little pocket between *Park Avenue* and *Station Rd* with its little 2-storey Victorian houses is proving popular with single professionals, who can get into the city quickly on the BR line nearby. Wood Green has its shopping city which has many amenities, but is less select, with a very much more urban, bustling, multi-cultural atmosphere, than the tranquil climes of Muswell Hill.

Among those estate agents active in this area are:
- Batty Stevens & Good
- Nicholas Shepherd
- Holden Matthews
- Prickett & Ellis
- Martyn Gerrard
- Bairstow Eves

New Cross and Deptford

Map ref: p80 (6A)
Postal districts: SE14, SE8
Boroughs: Lewisham
Rates: 226.44p in £
Constituencies: Deptford (Lab)
Insurance: Scale 1
Conservation areas: Telegraph Hill, Album St.
Parking: Free

Transport Tubes: New Cross Gate, New Cross (East London) to: Oxford Circus 30 min (2 changes), City 20 min (2 changes), Heathrow 90 min (2 changes). BR: New Cross/Gate (London Br, Charing X, Cannon St).

Convenient for Greenwich, City, Docklands. Miles from centre: 4.5.

Schools ILEA zone 7: Haberdashers' Aske's, Hatcham (b) (g), South East London Secondary School.

Flats	S	1b	2b	3b	4b	5b
Average prices	45–52	53–65	57–75	75–85	–	–
Houses	2b	3b	4b	5b	6/7b	8b
Average prices	80	75–95+	88–110	110–150	140–170	–

The properties Deptford's small stock of homes for sale (most housing is council) include some unmodernised 3-bed Victorian terraces. New developments appearing (3-bed hse: c £145,000). New Cross is full of large 19th century terraces, converted into flats; stately in Telegraph Hill (flats or 4/5 bed houses), run-down on the main roads.

The market Cheap, convenient (only tubes for miles) homes are attracting first-time buyers unable to aspire to nearby Docks, Greenwich. Prices rose, then steadied as over-eager sellers found their prices not being realised. Most popular properties are 2-bed flats/houses sought by mortgage sharers. Local searches: 6 weeks.

Area Profile

'Deptford', said an inhabitant, is '*local*'. This was the closest she could get to explaining why this untidy, unkempt corner of town, cheerfully grimy in some places, plain grim in others, nevertheless feels like a proper place, unlike many a politer but more faceless tract of South London.

Local it so far remains: both Deptford and New Cross to the S are still largely (but not entirely: see below) undiscovered by outwardly-questing young City types. Both have their rough areas, both their surprises. Both, too, have illustrious, entertaining pasts. And the future? Robust communities are making full use of the spirit of regeneration and renewal around now. The long period of demoralisation that set in as London's docks shut down, taking the traditional employment with them, is fading. There are plans for a major residential, leisure and industrial waterside development of Deptford Creek and Deptford Power Station in the near future, which will hopefully be served by river bus and the Light Railway. Gracious Greenwich lies on one side, the renascent Surrey Docks area on the other, and improved transport link plans for SE London include the exciting possibility of extending the Docklands Light Railway across to Lewisham. Already Surrey Docks has gained the 'giant' Surrey Quays shopping centre and now a marina, no less, is planned.

Both Deptford and New Cross are served by the overground British Rail, but New Cross and New Cross Gate have the inestimable advantage of a tube – the only one for miles – which reaches the City in under 10 minutes and at present runs four times an hour. BR trains run six an hour from New Cross Gate and New Cross into London Bridge and four an hour into Charing Cross. Deptford has a service into Charing Cross that takes 13 minutes twice an hour.

Many of Deptford's homes are local authority-owned, but the stock of private houses still includes unmodernised ones: inexpensive and un-messed about homes beginning to attract the attention of young City secretaries and the like, in search of cheap first homes and not able to afford the sky-high prices of the Docklands developments north of the river. And now, new chi-chi 'mews' developments have appeared, and more and bigger ones (many on ex-BR land) are scheduled. The larger, once grand terraces of New Cross make for conversions; though the centre is largely no more than a busy road system, the Telegraph Hill area at the southern end is a pleasant and surprising corner now discovered by property writers. The redevelopment of the New Cross hospital site will ensure a rise in popularity around the Hatcham Park area.

Deptford

Deptford lies on the river in SE London, between Greenwich, New Cross and Surrey Docks. Its main industry was the docks, and consequently there is today a high level of unemployment in the area. In Tudor and Stuart times, Deptford Strand was an important boarding place for ships to the continent and the scene of events as disparate as the knighting of Walter Raleigh and the murder of Christopher Marlowe in a riverside tavern.

The Royal Naval Yard, royal no longer but which once built the ships of Henry VIII's fleet, is still to be found so labelled on maps. Georgian Deptford gave way to Victorian, and what remained largely succumbed to wartime bombing raids or the ministrations of the GLC.

The look and feel of Deptford is to a certain extent still industrial. However, this is changing as massive investments are being made in the High St and surrounding area, and there is evidence of much rebuilding and refurbishment. The High St itself won an award some years back as the 'most authentic in London', and the Deptford Enterprise Board is encouraging small businesses, with new restaurants and shops opening every month. (Deptford and New Cross run to small grocers rather than large supermarkets: both use Lewisham or Surrey Quays as their shopping centre.) There is now a wine bar in the High St, no less, and an excellent theatre/community centre, The Albany Empire in Douglas Way. A note should be made here of part of the historical and cultural life of Deptford: the Dog and Bell. Set in *Prince St*, a quiet cobbled backstreet five minutes' walk from the *High St*, this estimable hostelry used to be called the Royal Marine and was, in the Napoleonic Wars, a notorious press-gang pub.

St Paul's Church, another pointer to Deptford's past status, lies between the *High St* and *Church Street*. This magnificent Baroque building was erected for the people of Deptford in the 1720s, after their request for a 'grand church' – they got it. The crypt of the church is used as a nightclub. There is easy access from Deptford to Greenwich and Lewisham, and excellent shopping in Lewisham and the brand new Surrey Quays shopping centre. Deptford market is fairly comprehensive and very cheap (and, with the recent part-pedestrianisation of the High St, has expanded), the best days being Wednesday and Saturday when the *High St* is closed to traffic and given over to the stallholders. There is also a food market in Lewisham, open every day.

Due to heavy wartime bombing, many of the older houses were destroyed and replaced with modern council blocks; however, the older properties that are left are a good bet: many are in need of modernisation, and so can be bought at un-chi-chi'd prices and done to your own taste. Look for these around the evocatively-named *Friendly St*, whose buildings range from artisan cottages to a large men's hostel, and among the turn-of-the-century houses around *St John's Vale* and mid-19th century ones in *Florence Rd*.

Albury St is a cobbled Georgian street that escaped the bombing but not years of waiting for the GLC, who had emptied the houses to restore them. However, those of its terraced 1780/90s cottages still standing are now at last being renovated to English Heritage standards.

There are also several streets of Victorian 3-bedroom terraced homes around the Deptford Park area, up towards Surrey Docks, and housing developments in *Trundley's Rd* and *Sanford St*. These upmarket schemes are indicative of the way Deptford is going but most sites are ex British Rail and therefore back onto the railway. New flats, too, have appeared on the *High St* near the station and another development of houses and flats runs between *Clyde* and *Edward Sts*.

The houses lucky enough to face onto Deptford Park itself fetch prices around £100,000. These streets are about ten minutes' walk from the river. Between *Evelyn St* and the river lies the Pepys Estate, a '60s council scheme: 16-storey concrete towers and low-rise blocks built on a bomb-site which destroyed rows of Georgian merchants' terraces ... but look in your A-Z map for *Deptford Strand* and, at right angles to it, *The Terrace*, along *Longshore*. Here are the remains of that Georgian heritage: houses in *The Terrace*, and what were waterside warehouses (now converted into flats and a library for the estate). The estate, nevertheless, is brilliantly designed of its type: a model estate in the '60s, it won a clutch of design awards. The towers have stunning views, as estate agents would say, over the river and central London (there being nothing very high in the Surrey Docks to get in the way). Inside the blocks are split-level flats with the sort of lay-out that costs serious money in the private sector. Tenants, not surprisingly, are 'right-to-buy'-ing. . . .

The same cannot be said of the grimmer blocks of Milton Court, another council estate which runs between *Milton Court Rd* and *Sanford St*, in the angle between two railway lines. This is not the place for your evening stroll.

The area to the NW, on the borders with Rotherhithe and the Surrey Docks, is improving due to the spillover effect from Docklands. Surrey Docks tube is on the same line as New Cross and New Cross Gate. There are vast areas of new housing in Surrey Docks: see Docklands chapter.

New Cross

New Cross, apparently, used to be a pretty little village until it started being used as a coaching point to avoid taking tired horses over Blackheath, which was then a notorious haunt of highwaymen on the *Dover Rd*. This proved to be its eventual downfall, as its high street evolved into the main road which effectively sliced the place in half. New Cross thus has once-grand terraces (whose potential depends on distance from the road) extremely convenient for BR and tube – but feels somewhat transient, with the large amount of traffic travelling through, compared to Deptford's far more of a village feel.

Central New Cross is unlovely, but any houses that have a one-way system running ten feet from their doors are almost bound to look depressed. This despite the fact that the buildings theselves are – or rather, were – dignified early Victorian terraces. However, new and smarter shops have appeared in the last year: a general tidy-up seems to have begun.

Many of the tall houses along *Lewisham Way* and *New Cross Rd* are now being converted into flats; these 5-storey houses near Goldsmiths' College are set comparatively far back from the road. There are also some 3-bed flats – mostly over shops.

But go S from the from the two stations and you come to a neighbourhood with an identity all its own. These are the large boulevards, lined by trees and flanked by huge Victorian mansions, surrounding Telegraph Hill. This corner was developed by the Haberdashers' Company, and this quiet, pleasant area is becoming increasingly popular: the houses yield nice flat conversions and there are also some 4-bed purpose built Victorian mansion flats. *Pepys Rd*, *Kitto Rd* and *Vesta Rd* also have magnificent, panoramic views over central London. The telegraph station which gave the hill its name passed the news of Waterloo.

Almost directly opposite *Telegraph Hill*, across *New Cross Rd, is the Hatcham Park* area. There are many houses in need of refurbishment – good hunting ground for the (adventurous) first time buyer. *Billington Rd*, *Camplin St* and *Hatcham Park Rd* and *Mews*. Nearly all these properties have gardens and are fetching sensible prices for 3-bed terraced homes. Many homes here were also part of the Haberdashers' estate: bought through its own 'right to buy' scheme, these are now appearing on the open market for the first time. Many owners delayed selling until the fate of the New Cross hospital site was decided: it's being transformed by Barratt into 'Avonley Village'. (All sizes from studios to 3-bed houses; selling now started at £52-145,000).

Among those estate agents active in this area are:
- Burnett, Ware & Graves
- Housemasters Property Service
- Jacksons Property Service
- Docklands Estates

Newham

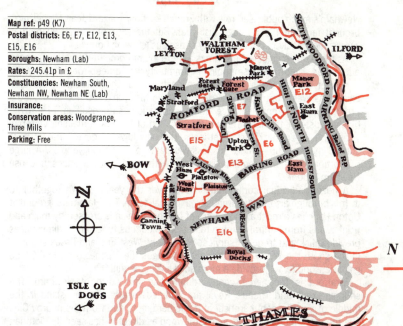

Map ref: p49 (K7)	
Postal districts: E6, E7, E12, E13, E15, E16	
Boroughs: Newham (Lab)	
Rates: 245.41p in £	
Constituencies: Newham South, Newham NW, Newham NE (Lab)	
Insurance:	
Conservation areas: Woodgrange, Three Mills	
Parking: Free	

Transport Tubes: Stratford (Central), West Ham, Plaistow, East Ham (District). From Stratford: Oxford Circus 30 min, City 12 min, Heathrow 90 min (1 change). Docklands Light Railway: Stratford to Tower, Isle of Dogs. BR: Stratford (Liverpool St 8 min), others see map.

Convenient for City, Docklands, City Airport; Epping Forest, M11; A12, A13 for M25. Miles from centre: 7

Schools Brampton Manor, Cumberland, Eastlea, Forest Gate, Langdon, Lister, Little Ilford, Plashet, Rokeby, Sarah Bonnell, Stratford, Trinity, Woodside. St Angela's RC, St Bonaventures RC, St John's RC. Private: Grangewood.

Flats	S	1b	2b	3b	4b	5b
Average prices	50	53	58	67	–	–
Houses	2b	3b	4b	5b	6/7b	8b
Average prices	70	73–85	85–95	110–180+	–	–

The properties Largely 1900s terraces of 2/3-bed homes and p/b flats. Woodgrange Park boasts large period houses, now mostly flats. East Ham's Central Park estate has mainly inter-war family homes.

The market Possibly the last stomping ground for first-time buyers. Where else are there flats below £50,000 just 15 mins from the City? A dying species, but not entirely extinct. Local searches: 12 weeks.

Area Profile

Newham's much publicised row with French keyboard wizard Jean Michel Jarre brought fame to the borough last year. But there's more to Newham than 'Destination Docklands' and a safety-conscious left-wing Council.

As the name suggests Newham is a mere infant compared to other London authorities – yet it's a cosmopolitan community with a deep-rooted past. Over a quarter of Newham's houses were destroyed in the Blitz when the area existed as West Ham and East Ham. The two fused in 1965 and continued a programme of slum clearance and regeneration. The result is 115 tower blocks, post-war terraces, recent gentrification of the few remaining Victorian villas, and a general 70s-clad tattiness. But new low-rise developments have started marching in – more for less-well-paid couples than yuppies. A large proportion of the area remains dilapidated with housing at low prices, because Newham is poor.

A dozen individual communities have, over the years, grown together to form a borough also made famous by a football team. The Hammers' ground at Upton Park lies almost at the centre of Newham which is crossed by main and trunk roads from central London to Essex; ubiquitous tubes and train services provide quick and frequent services to the City, West End and Essex suburbs. In the south the Woolwich ferry service bridges the Thames. And ELRIC, the giant new bridge, will provide a more solid link in the mid-90s.

Stratford is the nerve centre, dominating the north of Newham. The shopping mall and Theatre Royal are huddled together on an island in the middle of a permanent carousel of traffic herding to and from the nearby City. The theatre, which once had Joan Littlewood as director, has seen its Victorian auditorium restored to its former gilded splendour.

Dick Turpin lived in Plaistow and married a girl from East Ham. It's not too hard to imagine Black Bess galloping down the wide thoroughfares of the *Barking Road*, now a monument to the congested 80s. It could take nearly an hour to creep from Canning Town on the western tip of Newham to East Ham on a number 15 bus at rush hour, even though the A13 has offloaded much of the City-bound traffic.

South of the A13 lies Docklands, a diverse and crowded collection of communities including the Royal Docks, the largest group of enclosed docks in the world and once the pride of the Port of London. Now these dinosaurs contain a waterskiing centre and the new City Airport. Great new things are planned for the Royals: see the Docklands chapter. Canning Town and Custom House almost died with the docks: the flood of '53 almost assured them a watery grave. But the community soldiers on, mainly in council tower blocks and terraces – it's bleak here.

A huge sugar factory still dominates Silvertown and North Woolwich. Pubs with romantic names like the Spanish Steps sit beside a lonely little airport motel – will the area ever take off? Beckton certainly did: the 'dream' estate reaches almost to the River Roding and, as Docklands' first concentration of cheap new homes, was a runaway success. It is now well established, but taking a breather from the heady early days.

Follow the River Roding northwards and you eventually hit Little Ilford, sitting to the West of its larger namesake and perched on Newham's NE edge. The Romford Road (A12) takes you back to town through cosmopolitan Manor Park and up-and-coming Forest Gate, past the North East London Polytechnic back to Stratford. To the SW lies West Ham – industrial, terraced and cheap. Notable for the thousands of postmen that spill out of the sorting office onto the nearby tube station, and for houses under £60,000.

Stratford

Maryland Point was a bustling agricultural village in the 17th century; today it marks Stratford's northern tip on the outskirts of Leytonstone. This is where you'll find the real *Albert Square* – an anticlimax of a road that doesn't resemble a square or 'The Square'. Neatly anonymous terraces line this street – and, indeed, most of the area bounded by *Forest Lane* to the South and the Forest Gate area to the East. But don't knock it till you've had a look: new flats are there and they're modestly priced. On the other side of *Leytonstone High Rd* you can pick up a newish 2-bedroomed terrace for £60,000 – a word of warning though: it's pretty isolated here. No tubes or shops, unless you're prepared to walk to Stratford, but it's a handy location if you happen to drive to Hackney to work.

Move further S and the picture brightens – follow *West Ham Lane* past Queen Mary's Square, a spanking new enclave of 1- and 2-bedroomed flats. This Countryside development is part privately owned and part rented to East London Housing Association tenants. Prices were pocket-money, and flats were instantly snapped up because it's so convenient (and next to the police station). The *Portway* is a pleasure, and opposite the surprisingly verdant West Ham Park. Don't stick to the road itself – slip down one of the side streets. *Church Lane North* is definitely mewsy: walk through here and you'll catch a glimpse of what Stratford could be all about. Newly-built townhouses stand elegant in the privacy of this quiet offshoot.

N

Plashet

Plashet has some of Newham's more desirable properties and a highly regarded all-girls' school. Look in *Stopford Rd* for family homes: 3-bed and larger pre-war houses. Prices start around £85,000. The neighbourhood extends N and S along *Plashet Rd* to *Green St* and *High St North*, East Ham. The cluster of streets to the north of *Plashet Rd* is known as Upton – it's perched on Upton Park's shoulder, close to its tube station but not half as seedy.

Huge Edwardian mansions line the *Romford Rd*, heading towards Forest Gate: many have been lucratively converted into B&Bs, others remain run-down – definitely room for gentrification and conversion here. 6/7 bed dilapidated dwellings sell for less than £200,000. But you'd better consider double glazing, and a bus pass, for townhouses and terraces set nearer the road. Traffic charges through day and night, and double yellow lines extend to Ilford. The Bethnal Green bounty-hunters did up their homes – soon these Stratford properties will be sporting stripped-pine front doors. A few 2-bedroomed starter terraces have sprung up in *Vicarage Lane*, which could be worth a visit. But for the more up-market buyer, East Ham and parts of Forest Gate are a better starting point.

Forest Gate

'Up-and-coming' are the enthusiastic words which spring to estate agents' lips when they mention Forest Gate. *Capel Rd* overlooks Wanstead flats, the southernmost outpost of Epping Forest (hence the name Forest Gate). Don't be surprised to see cows wandering off the flats onto this speed-humped street. The refreshingly pleasant Golden Fleece pub makes a good focal point for the road, where houses sell like gold dust. although it has an E7 postcode, Capel Road's £120,000 family-sized terraces face highly sought-after homes across the park in Redbridge. Hats must be raised to those who bought a house for a song here two years ago.

Woodgrange Village isn't really a village but an estate agents' term for the gentrified area bordering less-fashionable Manor Park. Fine for home buyers who prefer more salubrious surroundings and don't mind travelling by British Rail. The conservation area of the Woodgrange Estate instantly 'ups' the price of houses in this part of Forest Gate, even the nearby run-down council blocks are due for a face-lift, so buying here could be a shrewd move: and prices for a 2-bedroomed terrace range between £60-70,000 around the pretty little station.

The Woodgrange Estate itself boasts 1880s villas in leafy streets to the East of *Woodgrange Rd*. Wander down *Richmond Rd, Hampton Rd* or *Windsor Rd* to view these regal residences, which might cost anything from £98-120,000 depending on their condition. Some have front drives and original glass porches extending across the width of the house, fringed with decorative wooden 'teeth'. Stratford is a mere two stops down the track.

Manor Park

Manor Park is largely devoted to resting places. Lacquer-black horse-and-carriage Cockney funerals regularly plod to the huge City of London Cemetery and Manor Park's own smaller graveyard. But the area's far from dead; it's brash, bustling and cosmopolitan, especially in the area around the Romford Road which lies just S of the railway track, a useful natural boundary. The new South Woodford to Barking Relief Road forms the eastern boundary. *High St* the western, and East Ham's tube line cuts across to the S.

The neighbourhood of Little Ilford provides a quiet backwater, and the parks and playing fields in the W of Manor Park form a welcome break from the row upon row of terraced housing. The heart of Manor Park is a comparatively sleepy area centring around poetic-sounding streets – *Browning Rd, Coleridge Avenue, Shakespeare Crescent* and *Shelley Avenue* live here. 3-bed terraces fetch around £85,000 (for a large one). £75-80,000 could buy a modern 'estate' type 3-bed terraced house. £68,000 is a reasonable price to pay for a 2-bed Victorian terrace. Flats conversions abound; £60,000 buys a large two-bed flat and £55,000 is the going rate for a 1-bed period conversion. Yes, compared to the rest of London it's dirt cheap, but entertainment-wise there's not much to recommend it, unless you fancy a trip to nearby Ilford for a taste of nightclubbing. But it is near East Ham tube station, Woodgrange Park and Manor Park BR stations, and the area boasts some marvellous Indian restaurants.

Capel Manor is the jewel in Manor Park's crown. A Grade II listed manor house has been carefully converted into luxury flats, with newly built townhouses neatly attached to its flanks. Prices match the style: flats range from £92-140,000 and houses cost between £150-165,000. Sumptuous these homes may be, starter homes they are not. Visit Plaistow for more affordable accommodation.

Plaistow and West Ham

Plaistow is deceptively large, running from the station along the *High St*, down *Greengate St* and *Prince Regent Lane* to the A13. To the east it extends to the Abbey Arms pub on the *Barking Rd*, continuing to *Green St* which marks the Boleyn neighbourhood of Upton Park. Scattered between the stock terraces are new purpose-built flats. A Wimpey development of such flats lies tucked away behind the Memorial Recreation Ground (the birth place of West Ham Football Club). Rowan Court in the *Broadway* and flats in *Plaistow Park Rd* offer a similar style.

For something slightly cheaper, larger and older look in *Balaam St* (pronounced Bale-am) which emerges at the Abbey Arms. *Balaam St* now boasts the Phoenix and Firkin pub, undoubted sign of the advancing young professionals. Equally palatable is the Black Lion in the *Broadway*; Beamish Irish Stout is served to a packed house of art students, teachers and locals. Behind the pub stands a monument to East End culture – West Ham Boy's Boxing Club. Another local tradition is pie, mash and liquor – heartwarming stuff on a cold winter's day and heartily served in Plaistow's Pie and Mash shop on the *High St*. The shop may look spartan but it's reckoned the best for miles around.

Plaistow literally means a place where people gather to play, and if you're sports-mad a house near the Terrance Macmillan Stadium in *Prince Regent Lane* would be ideal. To the E of the road lies a spacious neighbourhood. Houses in *Holborn Rd*, *Botha Rd* and *Denmark St* have more breathing space, but they are treacherously near the A13, which can only become even busier with the opening of the East London River Crossing. And you're a fair walk from the tube station here.

West Ham must be the cheapest end of the borough to live, and it is the closest Newham neighbourhood to the City. Much of West Ham's housing is owned by Newham Council, and the rest is small and terraced. West Ham can seem like an industrial wasteland to the uninitiated. Don't be fooled by the A-Z – West Ham is considered by locals to be the area around the tube station, nowhere near West Ham Park, Stratford. This confusion arises from the days before Newham when the Borough existed as East and West Ham. For example West Ham Town Hall is in the middle of Stratford. West Ham itself is a small area, roughly consisting of the streets off *Manor Rd*, where a 2-bed terrace can cost under £60,000, with or without spray-canned tagging on its exterior walls.

Upton Park and East Ham

Upton Park is a fairly small neighbourhood, stretching from the tube station in *Green St* to the Boleyn Pub on the *Barking Rd* and Upton Park also extending eastward to *Katherine Rd*. Purpose-built flats and new terraces are scattered in the streets around the football ground. The recently re-vamped Boleyn is a landmark which has lost favour with locals. The brewery put 40 pence on the price of a pint after refurbishment, undoubtedly in a bid to keep destructive elements out. *Inniskilling Rd* typifies the older-style streets crammed with 2-bed terraces which go for around £60,000. East Ham's better for shopping, but beware of Upton Park's Queens Market, a local muggers' hiding ground.

East Ham is considered to be the best part of Newham. House prices reflect this. Central Park is a popular inter-war terraced estate. *Cotswold Gardens* contains the only line of semis on the estate; they sell for £110,000 plus. *Lonsdale Rd*, *Henniker Gardens*, *Haldane Rd* and most of the other streets contain 2-bed '30s terraces – some with ground-floor bathrooms. All have neat gardens at the rear which are secluded and much cherished. £73,000 seems to be the fashionable bench-mark set for such properties. *Central Park Rd* and its offshoots contain larger, often pebble-dashed versions. Houses in this area boast 3 double bedrooms and go on the market for £85,000.

For convenience, investigate the streets on the E side of *High St North*. Streets like *Lathom Rd*, *Caulfield Rd*, *Clements Rd* and *Skeffington Rd* are within easy reach of the tube and close to the shops. Apart from the usual High Street stores East Ham has the covered market, an Aladdin's cave of goodies at knock-down (possibly knocked-off?) prices. It's 'onest East End round here: just go into one of the cafes and listen to the tales. And you won't have to pay £2 for a dainty sandwich – bacon/eggs/sausage and fried slice are more the menu.

Burges Rd, *Leigh Rd* and *Watson Rd* are situated close to the new South Woodford to Barking Relief Road. But don't worry, these rat-runs have just been blocked off, leaving a quiet, respectable neighbourhood to clock up the house prices. £80-87,000 for a 3-bed house round here. Pockets of select 4-bed dwellings can be found in this corner of East Ham – definitely one to watch. But there's a big difference between East Ham's *High St South* and *High St North*, look to the east of *High St South* and you'll see suburbs mirroring those in Central Park but a fraction cheaper. The huge minareted town hall divides the 'posher' south and the less well favoured north of East Ham.

Borders

Newham extends from a long southern boundary formed by the River Thames, northwards to a boundary with Waltham Forest and the southernmost extremities of Epping Forest; to the W the line of Bow Creek and the River Lea separate it from Tower Hamlets and Hackney; it's eastern boundary is a river too – the Roding, beyond which are the boroughs of Redbridge and Barking.

Among the estate agents active in this area are:
- Douglas Allen Spiro
- Guardian Estates
- Hooper
- Bairstow Eves
- Jacksons
- Falconer Wimborne

Notting Hill and North Kensington

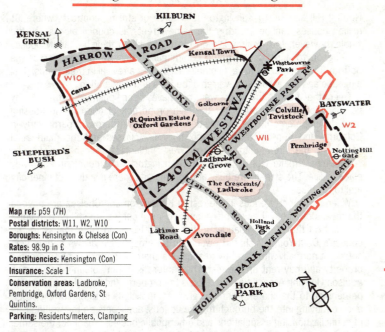

Map ref: p59 (7H)
Postal districts: W11, W2, W10
Boroughs: Kensington & Chelsea (Con)
Rates: 98.9p in £
Constituencies: Kensington (Con)
Insurance: Scale 1
Conservation areas: Ladbroke, Pembridge, Oxford Gardens, St Quintins.
Parking: Residents/meters, Clamping

Transport	Tubes: All zone 2. Notting Hill Gate (Central, District, Circle), Holland Park (Central), Latimer Road, Ladbroke Grove, Westbourne Park (Metropolitan). From Notting Hill Gate: Oxford Circus 10 min, City 20 min, Heathrow 42 min (1 change). British Rail: Kensal Green 30 min Broad St.	
Convenient for	Kensington Gardens, West End, City, A40 to West, Paddington BR. Miles from centre: 3.5.	
Schools	ILEA zone 1. Sion Manning RC (g), Cardinal Manning RC (b).	

Flats	S	1b	2b	3b	4b	5b
Average prices	70–80	80–120	90–180	140–300+	180–400+	→
Houses	2b	3b	4b	5b	6/7b	8b
Average prices	150–200	160–300+	175–400+	350–750	500–800+	1m+

The properties Handsome Victorian terraces and paired villas characterise the area, from the grand white crescents and rows at the Hill's top, smaller brick/stucco streets, to the as-yet un-done-up roads down the Hill and in North Ken, punctuated by council blocks.

The market Inhabitants are as mixed as the area: at one end young people find shared-ownership schemes, at the other Hong Kong expats buying for investment. A cheap, cheerful area no longer. Flats, mainly converted are the market staple. Local searches 7 days

Area Profile

Notting Hill and North Kensington is an area of striking contrasts where £1 million houses can be found in the same streets as council blocks. On the whole, however, the wealthy live on top of the hill in their big family houses backing on to acres of delightful communal gardens, and the poor at the bottom. The big houses have, in many cases, seen a revival in their status: until a decade ago the area was a warren of bed-sits and dilapidation.

Over the years, the less well off have been pushed further N by gentrification. This accounts for the high proportion of council and housing trust developments in the socially-deprived N of the borough, particularly in Golborne and Kensal Town. The mix of social classes and the multi-racial nature of the area, with its large West Indian, Moroccan and Filipino communities, make Notting Hill/North Kensington a cosmopolitan and lively place to live. The streets are busy at midnight, and there is a distinct inner-city feel to the place.

Whereas property prices in the rest of Kensington and Chelsea are beyond the means of all but the well-off, people on low incomes are still able to get a foothold on the property ladder in this area. This is possible thanks to the council's Do-It-Yourself shared ownership scheme, which allows people who could not normally afford to buy to acquire a share of 25 per cent or more in a property and pay rent on the rest. The venture is run in conjunction with the Addison Housing Association which buys the property and sells the appropriate percentage to the sharer. Priority is given to applicants in the following order: people moving into the borough to take up jobs; applicants on the waiting lists of councils, housing associations and other public bodies; tenants of the same; and single people in urgent need of housing, particularly single parents. The catch is that the value of the property must not exceed £73,000 (up from £58,000 in 1987), which is very low considering prices in this area. However, the council is urging the Department of the Environment to raise the limit again to give more low-income households the chance to become owner-occupiers.

At the same time, the well-off get better value for money than in other parts of Kensington and Chelsea. Houses are generally cheaper, there are probably more communal gardens than anywhere else in London and the area is well placed with direct underground links to the City.

One unusual feature of the housing scene here is the domination by housing trusts. These own very large amounts of property, usually homes they have bought up and converted, though some are new-build. Unlike council properties, these homes are dotted around in otherwise owner-occupied streets. And once in housing association hands they stay that way, never being re-sold. This 'freezes' whole sections of streets and reduces the number of homes on the open market.

Two major street events also shape the character of the area – the internationally famous *Portobello Rd* market (Saturdays) and the annual Notting Hill Carnival, Europe's biggest street festival. It draws enormous crowds to the area every August Bank Holiday weekend. The festivities are usually concentrated in the Colville/Tavistock and Golborne neighbourhoods. For two days, the streets are alive with pulsating rhythms and superbly colourful floats. Residents either love it or hate it. The 1988 Carnival was notably more peaceful than in previous years, and noisy road-side sound systems were banned. Despite this, many locals plan to leave town for the Bank Holiday weekend.

Portobello Rd has had a market since the 1860s when it was known as The Lane. Antiques, bric-a-brac, fruit and vegetable and clothing stalls spread for two-thirds of a mile along the road from *Chepstow Villas* to *Golborne Rd*, with the antiques concentrated at the S end. The market is a major tourist attraction drawing thousands of visitors to the street every Saturday.

The social N-S divide in the area is accentuated by the physical barrier of the *Westway* elevated motorway. Built in the mid-'60s, it creates a vacuum between streets N and S of *Cambridge Gardens* and *Acklam Rd*. That vacuum has been filled to some extent by the bays built under *Westway* to accommodate everything from an ambulance station and community laundry to an advice and information centre and the Portobello Green complex of trendy clothing and jewellery shops/workshops.

Ladbroke Grove is the area's main traffic artery, stretching from the desirable leafy S boundary of the neighbourhood to the rundown N border. The main shopping centre for the area is *Notting Hill Gate* to the S, the westward continuation of *Holland Park Avenue*. The *Gate* also boasts two cinemas and a number of popular restaurants and pubs.

Notting Hill price trends 1984-88

London average home: percentage rise on previous year, adjusted for inflation.

Typical home in this area, percentage rise on previous year, adjusted for inflation.

Two-bed flat on the W2 side of the area, price change compared to London-wide average home. The relatively low rise here is in line with other central areas, but it follows rapid gains against the average in '84, '85 and '87. And flats in this area are slowly lessening the gap with Kensington proper, which see.

Pembridge

Pembridge stretches north from *Notting Hill Gate* as far as *Westbourne Grove*, bounded on the W by *Kensington Park Rd* and on the E by *Chepstow Place/Ossington St*. Pembridge Rd*, the south half of the main route between the *Gate* and *Westbourne Grove*, leads into the heart of this sedate and leafy neighbourhood. To the E lies *Pembridge Square*, the only one in the borough lined by large detached villas. The 4-storey ornamental stucco houses overlook narrow private central gardens. Some remain in single occupation but most have been converted, a few into hotels and schools. Prince William's school, Wetherby, is on the S side of the square. The E side of the square is across the borough boundary in Westminster.

South of the square, a short walk from bustling Notting Hill Gate, are the cul-de-sacs of *Linden* and *Clanricarde Gardens*. Tall ornate stucco terraces characterise both streets. In *Clanridarde Gardens*, the large houses of bedsits are gradually being converted into top of the market flats, with revamped studios going for as much as £95,000.

The scale changes in *Ossington St* on the E edge of the neighbourhood. Here terraces of smaller stucco houses face the backs of buildings fronting Palace Court in Westminster. More large houses are found N of *Pembridge Square* in leafy *Pembridge* and *Dawson Places*. Both are lined by paired stucco villas with front gardens. *Dawson Place* also has detached villas, some with the same decorative cast iron and glass entrance canopies as the imposing Victorian mansions in Holland Park. Groups and pairs of stucco/brick and stucco villas curve around *Pembridge Villas*, the N half of the main route through the neighbourhood. Leading off to the NW, *Pembridge Crescent* has more groups and pairs of stucco villas. These contrast with the 2-storey painted cottages in *Pembridge Mews*.

Chepstow Crescent, which has mainly 3/4-storey brick and stucco terraces and a couple of hideous post-war flats blocks, leads into tree-lined *Chepstow Villas*, considered the most prestigious address in the neighbourhood. About half of the elegant paired stucco/brick and stucco villas remain as family houses. A £2 million development of 2-, 3- and 4-bed flats is planned for the street. Leading N from here into the Colville/Tavistock neighbourhood is *Ledbury Rd*, a pleasant street of 3-storey stucco houses with antique shops and galleries on street level. There were plans for new luxury flats on the Sion Convent site, but these seem to be in abeyance. *Denbigh Rd* has a mix of properties ranging from Longlands Court council estate to low-rise modern brick properties and painted stucco houses. A winged stucco arch halfway along the E side leads through to *Penscombe Mews*, a group of modern 3-storey brick houses.

The W side of the neighbourhood is dominated by *Portobello Rd*, although only part of the internationally famous market falls within its boundaries. S of Chepstow Villas stands a row of charming 2-storey gaily-painted stucco cottages with front gardens. Street trees add to the leafy look. They face the backs of the big red brick and stone 1900's flats blocks fronting *Kensington Park Rd*. Lying at the rear of the cottages is Simon Close, a small cul-de-sac of modern 2-storey town houses.

Although this stretch of *Portobello Rd* is quiet during the week, on Saturdays it is invaded by thousands of tourists from all over the world heading for the market, which begins just beyond Chepstow Villas. Antique stalls spread along both sides of the street, spilling around into Denbigh Close, a pleasant cobbled cul-de-sac of mews cottages, some with roof terraces. *Denbigh Terrace*, one street away, has an attractive stucco terrace of 2/3-storey and basement family houses S, looking across to Longlands Court council estate. A plan for 24 flats and 4 mews houses, comprising homes above and an antique market below, has been approved for *139-151 Portobello Rd*.

The Crescents/Ladbroke

This is the most prosperous and elegant part of the area, set on the highest ground and benefitting from an expansive street plan of crescents and gardens. The area dates from the mid-Victorian age and many large houses survive. *Clarendon Rd* on the W edge of the neighbourhood sets the tone for this highly desirable area. The best stretch, between *Lansdowne Walk* and the smart *Clarendon Cross* shops, has big paired brick and stucco villas with front gardens. South of here are terraces of 3-storey and basement Victorian houses, modern townhouses and flats. North of the junction with *Elgin Crescent*, the street becomes more mixed and less attractive with the appearance of council blocks and a tatty parade of shops. However, a terrace of 4-storey houses on the E side has the advantage of backing on to the beautiful communal gardens between *Elgin* and *Blenheim Crescents*.

Terraces of 3-storey plus semi-basement houses line both sides of tree-lined *Blenheim Crescent*. Properties on the S side back on to the communal gardens. *Blenheim Crescent* is like a different street to the E across *Ladbroke Grove*, combining a mix of private (S), council and housing trust properties (N), which merge with the shops, pubs and cafés in the stretch between *Kensington Park Rd* and *Portobello Rd*.

Leafy *Elgin Crescent*, more salubrious and sought-after than *Blenheim*, has terraces of mainly 3-storey painted stucco houses with basements and attic windows. Huge communal gardens lie at the rear on both sides of the street. As with *Blenheim Crescent*, many houses have been converted into flats.

South of *Elgin Crescent*, the streets climb uphill. *Arundel Gardens* has mainly 4-storey brick and stucco terraces, while *Ladbroke Gardens* is lined by ornate stucco terraces with attic windows. *Ladbroke Gardens* leads into *Stanley Crescent* with its huge 6-storey brick and stucco paired villas at the bottom of the hill, and a terrace of 4 and 5-storey ornate painted stucco houses at the top. Interesting gaps and intriguing arches between the houses give glimpses of the sky, trees and gardens at the rear. The houses overlook communal gardens between *Stanley* and *Kensington Park Gardens*.

N

Stucco is the trademark of the Ladbroke area. The pillared porch, the rusticated stucco around the ground-floor window, the steps, the railings, the balcony, all are typical of these large houses. Many are now flats, which benefit from the lofty rooms. Many of these houses back onto communal gardens: the area was planned as one estate, though built over quite a long period.

The summit of the hill was developed in the form of an oval cut in two by *Ladbroke Grove*. *Stanley Crescent* forms one half of the oval, and across the *Grove* to the W is the complementary *Lansdowne Crescent*. An elegant white 'iced wedding cake' terrace curves half-way round the semi-circle to the N. The richly-decorated houses have distinctive rounded facades and corinthian-columned entrance porches. Big paired brick and stucco villas, stone-gabled houses and some modern brick townhouses spread around the rest of the crescent.

More extensive communal gardens lie behind *Lansdowne Crescent* and *Lansdowne Rd*, another choice residential street, lined with trees taller than the buildings. Terraces of 3-storey and basement stucco painted houses, some gabled, wind around the hill, merging with pairs of villas where the street drops down again to *Holland Park Avenue*. *Lansdowne Walk* has groups of handsome stucco and brick and stucco houses. On the NE corner of the street, set back from *Ladbroke Grove*, is Bartok House, considered one of the best blocks of flats in the Notting Hill area. The modern brown-brick development with its own communal gardens joins up with a terrace of brick and stucco houses (split into flats) and another modern flats block. These flats face *Ladbroke Grove* but are separated from the road by a private driveway and screen of trees and lawn.

Tall trees in the gardens surrounding St John's Church on the hilltop add to the leafy outlook. The church spire can be seen from miles around rising above the treetops. This stretch of *Ladbroke Grove* and the leg between *Ladbroke Square* and *Ladbroke Rd* (attractive 4-storey wide-fronted painted stucco houses), are the best sections of this long road.

Lying between the houses in *Kensington Park Gardens* and *Ladbroke Square* are the largest private gardens in the borough. Despite its name *Ladbroke Square* is, in fact, made up of a long terrace of 4 and 5-storey brick and stucco houses on one side of the street, facing the gardens. Most are divided into flats. The gardens are enclosed by tall trees and hedges, and street trees stretch along adjoining roads as far as the eye can see.

Ladbroke Rd, a relatively busy but pleasant local road, has a mix of smaller brick and stucco terraces, big detached houses and a 5-floored 1900s flats block. Notting Hill police station stands on the corner with *Ladbroke Grove* and the Kensington Temple at the E junction with *Pembridge Rd*. Leading off here are a series of small streets and cobbled mews including *Wilby Mews*. The mews, tucked in behind the flower-bedecked Ladbroke Arms pub, has a mix of little 2- and 3-storey brick cottages set around a wide inner courtyard. More low painted Victorian cottages are found in *Horbury Mews*. *Horbury Crescent* has curving terraces of larger brick and stucco properties in varying states of repair. Hidden away behind the houses at the SE end of *Ladbroke Rd* and the shops in *Pembridge Rd/Notting Hill Gate* is *Bulmer Mews*, a development of 2-storey brown brick houses with garages (1987).

Forming the E border of the neighbourhood is *Kensington Park Rd*, a busy bus route. Terraces of 3-storey brick and stucco buildings with shops, restaurants and wine bars on the lower floors line the N end of the street. They give way to terraces on the W side, broken up by stretches of the area's splendid communal gardens.

Avondale

Newly-created private squares and mews stand amid large council estates and housing association developments in this very mixed neighbourhood in the W of the area. It is on the border with Hammersmith borough, and is cut off to the W and N by motorways.

The W end of *Lancaster Rd*, a short walk from Ladbroke Grove Station and the shops clustered around it, combines residential, educational, health and light industrial uses. A terrace of 3-storey and basement brick and stucco houses, many split into flats, lines the NE arm of the street. Opposite stands the imaginative Royalty Studios, a new complex of studios/workshops. Next door is the London Lighthouse AIDS hospice and support centre. The first of its kind in Britain, it cares for sufferers of the disease 'from diagnosis to death'. Standing alongside is the large brick Paddington College annexe. Thomas Jones Primary School is tucked in behind.

Back on the N side of the street lie *St Andrew's* and *Wesley Squares*, modern developments of 3-storey terraced houses and flats (late 1970s) set around pleasant communal gardens. Properties are shielded from *Lancaster Rd* by a high brick wall, adding to the sense of enclosure and privacy. Beyond Notting Hill Methodist Church, the road comes to a dead end, opening out into a large car parking area. This acts as a barrier between this side of the neighbourhood and the sprawling Lancaster West council estate beside the railway line. The estate spreads through *Verity Close* where it becomes a cul-de-sac of modern 2/3-storey red brick terraced properties with small gardens. Some council houses are now coming on the market. The remainder of the estate stretches along the N side of *Cornwall Crescent*, where it joins up with more council flats. A tatty looking Victorian terrace stands on the S side.

More Victorian terraces are found to the N in *Ladbroke Crescent* – 3-storey, basement and attic painted stucco houses converted into flats. At the NW end of *Walmer Rd* is Kensington Sports Centre with swimming and many other sports. More brick council blocks extend S along the street, leading to the smart and pricey *Hippodrome Mews* development. Here 3-storey brown brick townhouses line two private mews overlooking Avondale Park. Terraces of modern brick low-rise housing association properties are found in *Wilsham St* and *Kenley Walk* S of the park and *Runcorn* and *Hesketh Places* to the N.

Private residential property in the SW corner of the neighbourhood is concentrated in *Avondale Park Rd*, *Mary Place*, *Sirdar Rd*, *Stoneleigh Place* and *St*, *Treadgold St* and *Grenfell Rd*. Many of the 2/3-storey brick terraced houses found here are split into flats. Tucked away in the middle of this group is *Avondale Park Gardens*, a pleasant square of 2-storey brick artisan cottages with walled front gardens set around a small central green with trees. The cottages, which were built by the former LCC after the First World War, passed on to the council, which is gradually selling them off. Bordering this chunk of private property is the big Henry Dickens council estate, fronting *St Ann's Villas*.

N

Colville/Tavistock

This is the heart of the 'other' Notting Hill, down the slope and a world away from the stucco crescents of Ladbroke. *Westbourne Grove* with its proliferation of antique shops is a main W-E route between Notting Hill and Bayswater. On Saturdays antique and bric-a-brac stalls spill around the corner into the NW arm of the street from the famous *Portobello Rd* market. Stucco/brick terraces line this end of the *Grove*, many with shops on the ground floor. Around the corner on the E side of *Kensington Park Rd* is an attractive terrace of 3-storey and basement painted houses with front gardens. More antique shops are found at the S end of *Ledbury Rd*, beneath the 3/4-storey brick and stucco properties which stretch along the W side. The E side is in Westminster.

Off to the W is tree-lined *Lonsdale Rd*, probably the nicest street in the neighbourhood together with the S end of *Colville Rd*. Attractive terraces of 3-storey painted stucco houses stand in the former, E of the brown brick Portobello Court council estate, which spreads back to *Westbourne Grove*. Taller stucco terraces line the E side of *Colville Rd* and 4-storey semi-detached stucco painted/brick and stucco villas the W. *Colville Terrace* has 4/5-storey painted stucco houses, mostly converted into flats.

Powis Square to the N has a mix of private 4-storey stucco terraced houses to the W and a long modern terrace of 4-storey brick council flats E. They lie on either side of a public garden with a children's playground in the middle. This is a popular street for DIY co-ownership schemes (see area profile). Standing at the N end of the square is the Tabernacle community centre.

Another public garden and playground lies to the W in *Colville Square*. Backing on to the E side of the garden is the 5-storey and basement Pinehurst Court flats block (painted stucco), which actually fronts *Colville Gardens*. It is set back off the road behind railings, lawn and trees. Overlooking the W side of *Colville Square* are more 4-storey and basement stucco terraces. Lining the W side of the square in *Talbot Rd* are a series of tall modern red brick housing trust flats blocks, including Daley Thompson House. The former Olympic decathlon champion was brought up in the area.

Westbourne Park Rd, another busy W-E road, has mainly brick and stucco terraces with clusters of shops on the ground floor. The council's Covent Gardens estate and a modern housing trust development take up the S side of the street from *Ladbroke Grove* to *Kensington Park Rd*. Off to the N is *All Saint's Rd*, notorious for drug dealing and street robberies. In 1987 police launched a massive clampdown to drive the pushers out of the area and have followed up with regular raids to show they remain vigilant. Property is not cheap, despite the neighbourhood's reputation. Prices for those few homes in *All Saint's Rd* and the immediate streets not owned by trusts have been rising steadily. Most properties are 3/4-storey brick and stucco buildings with shops below, a high proportion being owned by housing associations. Standing at the SE end of the street is the Mangrove Community Association and restaurant, a traditional focal point for the local West Indian community. *All Saint's Rd* also lies in the heart of Carnival territory. The two-day Notting Hill Carnival is concentrated in the streets around here (see area profile).

McGregor Rd off the E side of *All Saint's Rd* is lined by 3-storey and basement Victorian brick and stucco terraces. It is a designated play street from 8am to sunset. Traffic is banned during these hours except for access.

Long stepped terraces of modern yellow brick housing trust co-ownership flats stretch along *Tavistock Crescent*. It runs into *Tavistock Rd* (3-storey brick and stucco terraces), which is pedestrianised at its W junction with *Portobello Rd*. This stretch of *Portobello Rd* takes in the heart of the market. Antique and bric-a-brac stalls line the section between *Westbourne Grove* and *Elgin Crescent* (Saturdays only). Fruit and veg stalls (Mon-Sats), take over between here and the covered market under *Westway* – bric a brac, new and secondhand clothing (Sats). From *Acklam Rd* to *Golborne Rd* there is a junk market on Friday morning and Saturday.

Several small mews off the E side of *Portobello Rd* are used by market traders to store their barrows and stock. But *Alba Place*, a short cul-de-sac between *Lancaster* and *Westbourne Park Rds*, also has gaily-painted 2/3-storey cottages, some with roof terraces, at its E end. An upmarket development of new red brick cottages stands in *Dunworth Mews* between *Westbourne Park* and *Talbot Rds*.

Lancaster Rd, which leads W to *Ladbroke Grove*, has mainly 3-storey terraces and paired villas in varying states of repair, divided into flats. The Serbian Orthodox Church and community centre stands on the S side near the junction with *Ladbroke Grove* across the road from the Lancaster Youth Club. This is another street where a number of properties have been bought through DIY co-ownership schemes. The council library stands on the corner of *Ladbroke Grove* and *Lancaster Rd*. Next door to St Sava's Church is the Campden Technical Institute (built and owned by Campden charities), which had yet to decide the fate of the site at the time of writing.

Golborne

Golborne is tucked into the NE corner of the area, bounded by the BR Western

Region railway line to the N & E and the *Westway.* to the S. Most of the Golborne area is dominated by council and housing trust/association developments, mainly low-rise lookalike modern brick dwellings. They are concentrated in *Bevington, Swinbrook, Acklam, Wornington* and *St Ervan's Rds.*

The main chunk of private residential property is found in *Portobello* and *Golborne Rds*, typically flats above ground floor shops. Both streets are being gentrified slowly as evidenced by the number of pine and fireplace shops/art galleries opening up. This stretch of *Portobello Rd* N of the *Westway* flyover is on the fringe of the famous street market. It is given over to stalls selling mainly second-hand clothing and household goods. More stalls spread along *Golborne Rd*, a bustling local shopping centre in its own right.

The area lacks public open space, the only park being Portobello Green alongside the flyover. But it boasts a wide range of amenities for the neighbourhood's younger residents including the Royal Court's Young People's Theatre (corner of *Portobello* and *Raddington Rds*), the Venture Centre community centre and adventure playground (*Wornington Rd* N), and the Acklam Play Centre and adventure playground (under *Westway*).

Kensal Town

N

In the far north of the area, and about as far in atmosphere from the lush Kensington heartlands, is Kensal Town. Crossing *Golborne Rd* railway bridge into Kensal Town is like entering another world. Grim concrete council blocks scar the landscape on the E side of this socially-deprived neighbourhood lying between the railway line in the S and the Grand Union Canal in the N. Dominating the skyline at the gateway to Kensal Town is 30-storey Trellick Tower. This grey concrete 1970s council tower block is regularly singled out in opinion polls as one of the capital's biggest eyesores.

Most of the homes here are council or housing trust. The rest of Kensal is taken up by trading estates, workshops and industrial uses, mainly concentrated in *Kensal Rd*, with only a handful of private residential properties scattered about the neighbourhood.

On the W side of *Ladbroke Grove* alongside the railway line is the 1930s Kensal House complex. A big new Sainsbury's supermarket stands immediately to the N. *Ladbroke Grove* is to be widened between here (canal bridge), and the junction with *Harrow Rd*. Behind the supermarket site, between the railway line and the canal, is the seven acre Gas Works site, which has lain vacant for 10 years. On the other side of the canal in the NW corner of the neighbourhood is Kensal Green Cemetery, a favourite haunt of wildlife enthusiasts.

St Quintin Estate/Oxford Gardens

This neighbourhood, cut off to the S by the flyover, is as distinct in its way as Golborne to the E. Immediately N of the *Westway* flyover lies the main concentration of family houses in this neighbourhood. Hundreds of 2-storey red brick terraced houses, built in 1905, dominate the SW corner in *Oxford Gardens* W, *Highlever, Balliol, Finstock* and *Kingsbridge Rds, Kelfield* and *St Helen's Gardens, Wallingford Avenue* and *Barlby Rd* W. Most have reasonably-sized front and rear gardens and many of the streets are lined with trees. A mix of 3- and 4-bedroom houses, they represent good value for money and are still cheap in Kensington terms. Prices are rising rapidly, however. A 3-bedroomed property in *Highlever Rd* was fetching £250,000 at the time of writing and one in *Wallingford Avenue* £230,000. Properties are cheaper towards the less accessible north and at the W end of *Oxford Gardens* where they back on to the flyover.

Cutting W-E through this enclave is *St Quintin Avenue*, a pleasant, up-and-coming tree-lined street despite being a main through route between Hammersmith and *Ladbroke Grove*. Pairs of semi-detached brick and pebbledash/red brick and stucco houses stretch along the avenue from the local shopping centre in *North Pole Rd*. Halfway along on the N side is St Quintin health centre and Princess Louise Hospital for the elderly. Behind the hospital lies Kensington Memorial Park, five acres of public open space. *Oakworth*, *Hill Farm* and *Methwold Rds* N of the park are given over to inter-war council dwellings comprising 2-storey brick houses and flats. Tucked away behind the houses in *Pangbourne Avenue* W and *Highlever Rd* E is the West London Bowling Club and green.

Late Victorian 3-storey and basement brick and stucco terraces and 2-storey brick and painted pebbledash houses with timber porches appear in the N end of tree-lined *Highlever Rd*. More 2-storey pebbledash/brick adn pebbledash houses stretch along the W end of *Barbly Rd* into *Dalgarno Gardens* and *Pangbourne Avenue*. A small parade of local shops lies at the junction of *Dalgarno Gardens* and *Barlby Rd*.

The NW corner of the neighbourhood is dominated by the Peabody Trust flats blocks in *Dalgarno Way* and Sutton Dwellings in *Sutton Way*. The latter flanks Little Wormwood Scrubs, a 22-acre recreation ground just over the borough border in Hammersmith. Most of the rest of the N boundary is taken up by warehouses/industrial uses and *Barlby Rd* railway sidings. BR plans to use the sidings for Channel Tunnel trains (see Major Developments). Between here and the car and lorry park at the NE end of *Barlby Rd* is *Barlby Gardens*, a small enclave of 2-storey brick and pebbledash houses set back off the road around a tiny green. On the S side of the road is Barlby Primary School.

South of the school, between *Ladbroke Grove* and *Exmoor St*, are the council's Treverton and Balfour/Burleigh Estates, built to house returning servicemen from the Second World War. The estate is one of the most popular in North Kensington with a long-standing close-knit community. *Exmoor* and *Hewer Sts*, between the two estates, have 2-storey late Victorian houses, mainly 3-bedroom. They go cheaply because of the warehousing in the area and proximity to St Charles Hospital, Kensington's general hospital.

The main entrance to the hospital is in *St Charles Square*, which is half made up of private homes and half housing association: 3-storey and basement brick and stucco semi-detached houses converted into flats. Clustered around the square are a Carmelite Monastery, the RC Sion-Manning girls' school and Cardinal Manning boys' school plus St Pius X Church.

The most sought-after properties in the neighbourhood lie S of the square in *Chesterton Rd* W, *Bassett Rd* and *Oxford Gardens* (between *St Helen's Gardens* and *Ladbroke Grove*). These were designed for the first railway commuters when the Metropolitan Railway opened up North Kensington in the 1860's, linking it to the City. Both sides of *Chesterton Rd* are lined by 3-storey Victorian terraced houses. The more expensive, leafier *Bassett Rd* has big 3-storey paired and detached brick and stucco houses with front gardens. More large semi-detached paired brick and stucco houses, mostly split into flats and bedsits, are found in *Oxford* and *Cambridge Gardens*. Properties have front gardens and cherry trees line the former, bursting into a cascade of white blossom between April and May. This is the best stretch of *Oxford Gardens*, where houses fetch up to £500,000. The E arms of both streets across *Ladbroke Grove* are more mixed with a number of council and housing trust properties.

A handful of streets across to the E of *Ladbroke Grove* link architecturally with the neighbourhood but have little garden space. *Bonchurch St* and *St Michael's Gardens* S are both lined by 3-storey and basement brick and stucco houses converted into flats. The Romanesque-style St Michael of All Angels Church stretches along the N side of the latter, fronting *Ladbroke Grove*. *St Lawrence Terrace* features high Victorian terraces, notably 3-storey and basement brick and stucco houses with bands of stucco to give a striped effect. About 70 per cent of the properties are still unconverted. As the street is designated a general improvement area, discretionary improvement grants are available from the council.

Among those estate agents active in this area are:
- Barnard Marcus
- Brian Lack & Co
- Browne Beck & Findall
- Foxtons
- John Wilcox
- Callander Wright
- Savills
- Marsh & Parsons
- Prudential Property Services
- Willmotts
- Winkworths
- Jacksons
- John D Wood

N

Peckham

Map ref: p95 (2H)
Postal districts: SE15, SE22
Boroughs: Southwark (Lab)
Rates: 195.68p in £
Constituencies: Peckham (Lab), Dulwich (Con)
Insurance: Scale 1
Conservation areas: Several, check with town hall
Parking: Residents/meters

Transport   British Rail: Queen's Road (Peckham), Peckham Rye, Nunhead to London Bridge, Victoria, Holborn Viaduct.

Convenient for   Dulwich, South Circular Rd. Tubes at Kennington, Oval, Brixton, New Cross. Miles from centre: 3.

Schools   ILEA zone 8: Warwick Park, St Thomas the Apostle RC (b). Private: Alleyn's.

Flats	S	1b	2b	3b	4b	5b
Average prices	48–52	55–63	65–75	75–82	–	–
Houses	2b	3b	4b	5b	6/7b	8b
Average prices	80–95	85–115	95–145	110–180+	–	–

The properties   Peckham Rye has pleasant Victorian/Edwardian (a few earlier) terraces and larger family homes focused on the little green and the common. Flats are mainly conversions. New homes being built, generally near rail lines. North Peckham is more mixed: large council estates, some older terraces.

The market   Peckham, in common with other SE areas, has surprising nice corners of good homes at some of London's most reasonable prices. Now that the N Peckham estates are to get major facelift, and it finally seems that a tube will arrive to join the good BR links, values are likely to rise even faster. Local searches: 12 weeks.

Area Profile

Peckham's notoriety as the site of a traffic jam on the Dover road conceals its admittedly shyly worn attractions as a place to live. Behind the grime of the main road, it divides into two very different neighbourhoods, Peckham and Peckham Rye. Built as one of the original London suburbs for rail-commuting clerical workers, the area used to consist of many small streets of late Georgian and Victorian terraced houses. Not any more. Much of the north of the area has been rebuilt following war damage and slum clearance. This rebuilding is at the root of the sharp contrast between the north and south of Peckham: the southern bit, Peckham Rye, survived. The north did not. Although there are several potentially desirable properties north of *Peckham High St* the area is mostly council housing of the least inspired period. Some parts, such as the North Peckham estate, have an unenviable reputation. However, there are serious plans to give the place a facelift in the hope that the estate will become attractive enough for some tenants to buy their flats. The government has set aside a sum of £2 million to improve the area. However that is in the future. For the present, North Peckham is a place more people are trying to get out of than get into.

By contrast Peckham Rye, S of the *High St* and more so S of the railway, is a surprise: a mature Victorian suburb grouped around a pleasant park. There is a little green complete with antique shops, almost like a Surrey town. Respectable streets of solid homes have much more in common with Dulwich and Forest Hill, their neighbours to the S, than they ever do with Peckham proper on the other side of the tracks. That said, North Peckham is very close to Docklands and to central London. It will require a major shift of social and financial geography before North Peckham becomes desirable, but respectability is creeping in at the edges . . .

Transport is a Peckham plus if you can clear your mind of the thought of tubes. Peckham Queens Rd station has a fast and regular service into London Bridge (every five minutes at peak time, every 30 minutes off-peak). Halfway up *Rye Lane* there is Peckham Rye station. The trains run with the same frequency into London Bridge station as from Peckham Queens Rd and there is also a less frequent service into Victoria. There is an excellent bus service to practically all areas – the number 12 bus runs to Oxford St and through to Willesden: on a good day the journey from *Rye Lane* into Oxford St can take as little as 25 minutes. The parking in central Peckham and Peckham Rye is metered and costs 20p for 20 minutes. Meters and car parks are plentiful (as are the wardens). Residents' parking permits are easily obtained from the council offices in *Larcom St*, off the *Walworth Rd* and cost about £20 per year. It should be mentioned that the local one-way systems can be a nightmare to navigate without detailed local knowledge.

Peckham North

The traffic grumbles along Peckham High Street in a vain attempt to reach the Dover road (laughing at bemused foreign drivers is a local sport). On either side, Peckham extends to the *Old Kent Rd* to the NE, the old Canal to the N, *Pomeroy St* to the E and *Southampton Way* to the W.

The council estate that dominates the neighbourhood is so enormous that it is hard to believe other kinds of homes exists. Yet they do. N of *Queens Rd* are some streets of small terraced houses, such as *Asylum Rd* which runs from the *Old Kent Rd* to the Queens Rd Station and which has some old almshouses in it, built for retired Licensed Victuallers (almshouses, especially with alcoholic connections, are a feature of Peckham). The streets between *Asylum Rd* and *Meeting House Lane* are similar, with houses and converted flats. *Kings Grove* has some spacious 3-floored flat-fronted houses. Further W, *Friary Rd* has some surviving late Georgian town houses and to the N *Glengall Rd* has its flat-fronted, semi-basemented houses. To the N of the *Old Kent Rd*, a few streets have terraced homes which can be very good value. A 3-bed house in *Ethnard Rd*, for instance, was on the market last autumn for £85,000. The E borders of Peckham, beyond Queens Rd station, have some quiet if unexciting streets of Victorian terraces such as *Dayton Grove* and *Astbury Rd*. Useful properties, good value (houses from £75,000) in a convenient corner, and one that has decidedly started to get smarter – if not yet 'the next Clapham or Battersea' as local agents hopefully claim.

The N part of the neighbourhood has the unexpected amenity of Burgess Park, a large green space, complete with lake, carved out of the slum streets by Southwark Council over the last quarter of a century. A few good 19th-century houses survive in the park. They were scheduled for demolition in sterner days but now seem likely to survive.

Peckham High St, at its junction with *Rye Lane*, is the main shopping centre. There are all the usual high street shops here: Marks & Spencer, Woolworths, British Home Stores and Sainsbury's. There is a newly-completed shopping arcade called The Aylsham Centre and a sports centre at the northern end of *Rye Lane*.

To the W of the shopping centre there is a maze of streets which make up the most interesting residential corners in this district. There are roads of Victorian terraced houses and some large detached town houses in the conservation areas of *Holly Grove*, *Elm Grove*, *Highshore Rd*, *Bellenden Rd* (handsome flat-fronted cottages) and *Lyndhurst Rd*. *Lyndhurst Square* is an interesting 1840s cul-de-sac of gabled, large-gardened houses on the Camberwell borders. *Denman Rd*, to the W, shares the same leafy environment but has later-Victorian purpose-built maisonettes.

The railway line cutting across *Rye Lane* forms the most widely accepted frontier with Peckham Rye to the S.

Peckham Rye

Choumert Square, tucked away W of *Rye Lane* close to the station, contains some of the most desirable homes in Peckham Rye. The immaculately tended trellis rose gardens won a best-kept square award recently. Nearby *Choumert Rd* has yet more almshouses, while *Blenheim Rd*, conveniently, if noisily, close to the station, has some newly-converted 1-bed flats. These went on the market late last year for a shade under £60,000. Look, too, at the charming little 2-bed early Victorian cottages at this end of neighbouring Chadwick Rd.

Going S, *Rye Lane* suddenly widens and, there, for all the world like some small market town, is a little green surrounded by a cluster of antique shops. The triangular tip of Peckham Rye Common holds a swimming pool; across the *East Dulwich Rd*, Peckham Rye Common and Park open out in a sweep uphill to the S. Mile for mile, the areas of Peckham, Peckham Rye and Dulwich have more green spaces than many another more well-thought-of area of London. Apart from park and common the green spaces include Warwick Gardens, behind *Lyndhurst Grove*, the gardens in *Holly Grove* and the gardens in *Elm Grove*.

The houses that flank Peckham Rye Common are large 3-4 storey family homes, many of which have been converted into flats although this trend is slowing up. A noteworthy road is *Colyton Rd* which faces north over the park and has a big variety of properties varying from Victorian to 1920/30s. This is a road of impeccable suburban style. *Peckham Rye* itself, which runs down the common on the E side, has some of the area's very few 1930s purpose built flats as well as conversions. Here, too, a little Georgiana has survived intact: one, with a 100 ft garden to supplement the sweeping expanse of common it overlooks, commanded an asking price of £275,000 last summer. The common itself has some immaculately cared for gardens in the centre, including a water garden, rockeries, a beautiful trellised rose garden and a bowling green and duck pond.

West of *Peckham Rye* and N of *East Dulwich Rd* is a district of small terraced houses with streets including *Nutbrook St*, *Maxted* and *Bellenden Rds*, *Amott St* and *Adys Rd*. ('Decidedly up-and-coming', say local agents). Some houses in the latter are bigger than they look, having 5 bedrooms, and are good value at under £120,000 (late '88). The houses in *Fenwick Rd* are larger still, 3 storeys with big bays. Many are flats. In this district, it is worth watching out for new homes being built, on the expanses of land that fringe the many railways. To the W this district shades into East Dulwich (the cheaper end of that select suburb: see the Dulwich chapter and search here, too).

South of *East Dulwich Rd* and W of the common is the wide tract of respectable Victorian and Edwardian housing that forms the residential core of Peckham Rye. The ground slopes up towards Dulwich, adding interest to the long straight streets such as *Barry Rd*. *Crystal Palace Rd*, misleadingly named because it is miles from the place, has flat-fronted cottages which make good small houses or pretty flat conversions. *Barry Rd* and *Upland Rd* have larger houses, many with good views as the land rises. The summit, at *Overhill Rd*, is crowned with a large block of council flats which must be much nicer to look out of than at. Barratts have built some smart new flats here in a neighbourhood which is perhaps more East Dulwich than Peckham. The S end of this neighbourhood has spacious Dulwich Park as well as the Rye common to play with.

A mention here should be made of Goose Green. This is an area at the W end of Peckham Rye where it meets with Dulwich. It consists of a wide strip of grass with *East Dulwich Rd* on one side and large Victorian houses on the other. Many of these houses have been converted into flats. A new mews and some refurbished flats have joined the pleasant houses overlooking the Green. Transport is good, being situated very close to East Dulwich station and car parking is unrestricted.

East of the common there are neat flat-fronted terraced houses in streets such as *Somerton Rd*. Prices here are lower than on the W side of the common, which is closer to Dulwich.

Nunhead

Nunhead is the neighbourhood to the E of Peckham Rye. It is an area of small residential roads of small 2-3 bedroom houses that run off *Nunhead Lane* and *Evelina Rd*, the latter of the two providing the main shopping street. As with Dulwich and Peckham, there is no underground service; however it too has its own BR station. There is unrestricted parking off the main street and the main

P

shopping street has all the shops necessary for day-to-day living including what locals say is the best bakers and confectioners in the area (Ayre's) and a very good, very large wet fish stall.

The better properties are found S of *Evelina Rd*, in particular the houses on *Tresco Rd* and the Victorian square-bayed terraces of *Carden Rd* (houses c£125,000). *Somerton Rd* and *Waveney Avenue* are similar. *St Mary's Rd* is another noteworthy road with early Victorian 3-bedroom houses on one side and larger Victoriana on the other. *Howbury Rd* has tidy flat-fronted 19-century cottages which were on the market for less than £90,000 late last year. Nunhead also has a fair turnover of ex-council houses, as many former tenants have found it worth their while to buy. *Seldon Rd*, for instance, has unpretentious '60s terraced houses with the benefit of a parking space. Three beds for £80,000 (end '88), a price which looks even better value than the £65,000 of 12 months before. Like its neighbour Peckham, Nunhead has very few purpose built flats. However, most of the larger period houses have been made into flats.

The Nunhead Estate of council flats (1930s brick blocks) overlooks the Common. The Rye Estate further up the hill, on *Peckham Rye*, is similar. *Rye Hill Park* has '60s council towers, *Torridge Gardens* and adjoining *Limes Walk* have low-rise council houses. Roy Brooks, in offering a 3-bed house in the latter, comments on the 'particularly well-designed development'. A particularly canny buyer could, last winter, buy this extremely spacious 3-bed (one is 19 ft x 10 ft) modern house for £80,000.

The expanse of Water Board land abuts the cemetery and the allotments which blanket the slopes of a considerable little hill. In *Stuart Rd* a block of 6 flats has been done up. The triangle of streets E from here towards Brockley has several peaceful corners: *Limesford* and *Harlescott Rds* are late-Victorian cottages, *Lanbury* has '30s cottage-style council homes. The *Ivydale Rd/Kelvington Rd* corner has more of these. Here, too, more water works – and a golf course. *Brenchley Gardens* bounds the area, from One Tree Hill up towards Brockley with more council homes in a green setting. In a leafy corner at the end of *Brockley Way* behind Camberwell New Cemetery, and (well) above a railway, are 19 new mews houses by Whelan Homes.

A point some people may find interesting is the Nunhead cemetery. This large and rather overgrown Victorian cemetery is as renowned as the Highgate one and like Highgate offers tours at certain times of the year.

Among those estate agents active in this area are:

- Roy Brooks
- Burnet Ware & Graves
- Harvey & Wheeler
- Mortimer & Hutchinson
- Morgan Gillie
- The Property Spot
- Winkworths

Pimlico and Westminster

Map ref: p77 (5G)	
Postal districts: SW1	
Boroughs: Westminster (Con)	
Rates: 136.4p in £	
Constituencies: City of London & Westminster South (Con)	
Insurance: Scale 1	
Conservation areas: Several, check with town hall	
Parking: Residents/meters	

P

Transport Tubes: All zone 1, Pimlico (Victoria), Victoria (Victoria, District, Circle); Westminster, St James's Park (Circle, District). From Victoria to: Oxford Circus (5 min), City 20 min, Heathrow 1 hr (1 change).

Convenient for West End. Gatwick Airport (express from Victoria BR). Tate Gallery. Miles from centre: 1.5.

Schools ILEA zone 2: Pimlico School, Grey Coat Hospital C of E (g). Private: Francis Holland (g), Westminster School (b), Southbank – The American International School.

Flats	S	1b	2b	3b	4b	5b
Average prices	60–100	95–145	125–240	180–270	300–400+	–
Houses	2b	3b	4b	5b	6/7b	8b
Average prices	195–250	280–400	300–500	375–600	→	–

The properties Regency stucco terraces, many now flats, plus mews cottages and p/b flats in Dolphin Square, ultra-mod or repro schemes, and council blocks. Westminster has mainly mansion flats (some very large), plus a few 19th century and Georgian houses.

The market Constant supply of new conversions of Pimlico's stucco houses into flats. Quality, however, varies widely depending on vintage: Pimlico's rise from bed-sit land to fashion is recent. Buyers include MPs and pied-a-terre seekers. Local searches: 1 week.

Area profile

Westminster, hub of Church and State, is known far more for its grand buildings than its homes, although the Georgian front door of its most famous residence, 10 Downing Street, gets more TV coverage than most. It is possible to live in Westminster without being Prime Minister, as many MPs and officials have discovered. Pimlico, which shares the SW1 postcode, is conversely almost entirely residential; its long white terraces once more established as a hunting-ground for centrally-placed flats and houses.

Both areas have their own individual presence and charm. While being very much at the centre of things, they have the river and the Royal Parks to bring air and perspective into the city streets. And, outside working hours, the residential corners are surprisingly peaceful. Both areas fall within the City of Westminster and are run from City Hall in Victoria Street – or Oil Street, as rude residents call it after the number of oil company office tower blocks which line it. Victoria Street is a canyon of bustling commerce, yet but a few hundred yards away is the quiet of Vincent Square, with period houses overlooking a public school's cricket pitch. And a few streets away from Victoria Station are the stucco terraces and squares of Pimlico, almost as handsome as Belgravia and an awful lot less expensive.

Pimlico

Bordered by plush Belgravia and august Westminster, Pimlico, tucked into a bend in the river, remained for a long time remarkably unknown. The social mix of the community is now changing as a tenanted and rather run-down district becomes a place of converted flats and smart developments.

This is MP's land, full of politicians' pieds-à-terre or main homes within the division bell boundary – the zone close enough to the House for them to rush from dinner, or whatever, to be counted through the lobbies. If you live in one of the streets known for a high political population, watch out for the regular stampede when there's a vote in the House. *Cambridge Street* is a typical 'little Westminster' – 25 MPs have homes there.

Pimlico used to be part of the Grosvenor Estate, like Belgravia. Thomas Cubitt, the Estate's architect and builder, laid out the straight streets and regular squares. The land was open, rather marshy and used for market gardens and pasture. In order to raise the level above the Thames floods, Cubitt with typical ingenuity brought thousands of tons of gravel and earth up by barge from the St Katharine's Dock, which he was excavating at the same time. If your Pimlico cellar is damp, remember that it's sitting at original marsh level. Pimlico may look superficially like Belgravia – lots of Regency stucco, classical detailing and regularity – but it has never been quite as smart. During most of this century it has been the province of the small hotel, the house clumsily divided into bedsits, the shared bathroom. The Grosvenor Estate sold the whole area in the 1950s, preferring to concentrate on Belgravia and Mayfair. It was only in the 1972/3 property boom, which coincided with the opening of Pimlico's Victoria Line tube station, that Pimlico began to be 'discovered'. The big old houses began to be converted into smarter flats, the MPs and busy people of all sorts found out how close it is to everything, and Pimlico began to change. The process was helped (though some would claim hindered) by the council's early scheme to ban through traffic. The place is a maze of one-way streets, blocked-off cul-de-sacs and residents' parking bays, and thus remains remarkably peaceful, a place apart, despite being central.

An average Pimlico property today is a big Cubitt town house split into flats. They are of varying sizes but a good number are small, aimed at single people or pied-à-terre owners. Family houses exist, but this is primarily flat-land. The network of streets at the heart of Pimlico are predominantly Cubitt terraces: *Clarendon, Cambridge, Alderney* and *Sutherland Sts* for example, and *Gloucester, Winchester, Sussex,* the *Moretons* and the *Westmorelands.* But even here there are gaps in the stucco and brick, often caused by wartime bombing, which have been at various times filled by small, often inappropriate, blocks of flats. These are less admired ('quite unpleasant', remarked one local agent) than the period conversions. Other exceptions to the rule are the mews cottages both behind the squares and terraces and, occasionally, on the main roads: *Clarendon St* has a few such. Look for the cobbled, sloping charm of *Warwick Square Mews. St George's Square* also has its mews, and *Moreton Terrace* boasts two, *North* and *South.* New mews houses in Charlotte Place, off *Wilton Rd,* were priced at £285,000 last winter. Some houses have survived the mania for conversion: try *Cambridge* and *Alderney Sts* and *Westmoreland Terrace.* A house in *Denbigh St,* with 3 terraces and 5 bedrooms, was priced in January at £560,000.

Pimlico is short of open space, though there's Ranelagh Gardens over on the Chelsea side and the splendid (if rather more public) St James's Park on the other. So the three large garden squares have long been its most desirable addresses – apart from the riverside flats. The big houses in the squares convert readily into spacious flats. *St George's Square* has some interesting recent conversions, and one tall house in this square offers 8 flats (ready this spring) from £125,000-£225,000.

The elegant stucco terraces surrounding the gardens make *Eccleston Square, Warwick Square* and *St George's Square* hugely attractive – in that order. With an eye to the lack of parks, while the first two have private gardens those of *St Georges* and *Bessborough Gardens,* are both open to the public. The only new London square to be created since the war, *Bessborough Gardens* is part of the Crown's Millbank Estate. The gardens (locked at night) have a fountain in honour of the Queen Mother's 80th birthday. The L-shaped terrace surrounding the garden on two sides is classic Cubitt: the smooth stucco finish, decorative ironwork balconies, the mouldings of windows and pillared doorways. Or so you might think: but these rows didn't exist two years ago. The Wimpey-built replacements of war- and flood-damaged terraces for the Crown Estate have provided a cache of new flats and penthouses, from studio to 3-bedroomed. The detailing inside matches the exterior and on occasion the sales team have had trouble convincing buyers that the apartments really are new. The few remaining homes are now on the market for £250-£460,000, though re-sales are increasingly found on local agents' lists. The next development on the Crown Estate, next-door to *Bessborough Gardens,* and sharing its entrance, is *Lindsay Square* which has 29 new town houses. They will be ready this summer and priced from £365-£675,000.

The main road along the river side is *Grosvenor Rd*; it does not hug the embankment, however, and wherever it bends slightly inland a waterside development has been squeezed in. The most successful of these is Crown Reach, which lies just W of Vauxhall Bridge, past an office block and an undistinguished earlier flats block. Its jutting, staggered riverside floors give the maximum light, privacy and unimpeded views to its apartments and their

P

balconies, while the landward side's sweeping gull's-wing roofs have become a landmark. Other plush and pricy waterfront blocks include River Lodge, parked on a narrow site almost in front of Dolphin Square. St George's Wharf will have 13 new riverside homes this year or next.

Lupus St runs E-W, a wide busy road paralleling *Warwick Way*, the other main cross-route to the N. On the S side the splendidly uncompromising modern lines of Pimlico School are reticent in one thing only: the mass of the 'glass school', as it is generally known, stands, amid its playgrounds, considerably below the level of the surrounding streets. A big new development in *Gloucester St* will add 94 flats – and 122 car parking spaces – to the area. Completion is scheduled for late this year.

Pimlico price trends 1984-88

London average home: percentage rise on previous year, adjusted for inflation.

Typical home in this area, percentage rise on previous year, adjusted for inflation.

Two-bed flat in Warwick Square, price change compared to London-wide average home. Prices virtually stood still here in '88: agents say that the mortgage relief boom passed Pimlico by: homes are too expensive, and the typical pied a terre buyer is unworried about tax relief. Contrast with '87: City gloom, perhaps, lessening demand?

Beyond the school rises the river-side, red-brick mass of *Dolphin Square*. A huge '30s flats development, it was at the time of its building the biggest in Europe. Its 1,200 flats surrounding a private courtyard are half rented, half privately owned (on fairly short leases). It is large enough to form a complete community, with its own shops, garage, pub and restaurant: the latter, open to non-residents, overlooks the indoor pool. Not surprisingly, there is a long waiting list for homes here.

South of *Lupus Street* are some of the most desirable council homes in London, the riverside towers of the Churchill Gardens estate. To the E along *Vauxhall Bridge Rd*, in contrast is the red-brick of Lillington Gardens, with its roof-gardens, third-storey trees and terraces. Tenants on both estates are buying their homes and they are starting to appear on the resale market – far cheaper, in these initial stages, than any other Pimlico properties. On *Peabody Avenue* and the wonderfully named *Turpentine Lane*, and further E towards *Vauxhall Bridge Rd* are two Peabody estates of red-brick rented flats run by a charitable trust.

Behind *Lillington Gardens*, the irregular meander taken by *Tachbrook St*, contrasting with Cubitt's orderly grid, betrays its earlier origins. This is Pimlico's village high street, complete with not only shops but a thriving, much-prized street market, now being tidied up somewhat. To the N it joins *Warwick Way*, (once a track through the marshes) and to its W lies *Belgrave Rd*: largely unreconstructed Pimlico, this. It is a main through-route to Victoria and is still full of cheap hotels.

The last year has seen a quickening of the pace of change in *Belgrave Rd* as converted flats succeed hotels. There are plans for 48 new homes, including 6 houses to be built on land which once housed a furniture depository near Victoria Station.

Westminster

Westminster seems to be climbing the scale of desirability, and visibility, as a place to own a home. Some big blocks have been done up, and one or two major developments are in the offing. That said, it is still true that homes are a secondary matter here: Westminster is first and foremost the home of Parliament and the Civil Service. Tucked away in side roads, though, are homes that can be surprisingly peaceful, considering their centre-hub position; the most obvious, and plentiful, are the imposing mansion blocks whose brickwork echoes the Roman Catholic Cathedral. But there are also, by contrast, modern flats, a few neat terraced homes and a little cache of unsuspected Georgiana.

Westminster the place – as opposed to the Borough – starts across the *Vauxhall Bridge Rd* from Pimlico and runs up to St James's Park in the N. The stretch between the Park and the river is home mainly to the Ministries of this or that along Whitehall. *Downing St* boasts only temporary accommodation, sheltering, strictly for their term of office, the Prime Minister and the Chancellor of the Exchequer. The riverside holds the only other exception: the fantastical turrets of *Whitehall Court*, where you can pay a small fortune for a very short lease: views river and Changing of the Guard... An enormous 5-bed example was on the market recently at £575,000.

Mansion flats are the staple form of what homes there are between the main through-road, *Victoria St*, and St James's Park. Vandon Court in *Petty France* offers flats including studios for under £80,000. This corner has hidden delights, though: glorious *Queen Anne's Gate*, where the stately houses do indeed date from the reign of that monarch and are wasted as offices, even if one is the headquarters of the National Trust. At the Victoria end lies the tiny, hidden *Victoria Square*, a stuccoed out-post of houses built in 1838.

But the bulk of Westminster's homes lie S of *Victoria St*. Again at the end nearest Victoria Station, grand Edwardian mansion flats are the norm. Though a new block of ultra-smart flats has recently been finished in *Artillery Row*. Flats built, as these are, above offices, are often uninteresting if convenient; however developers Warwick Balfour have a background in stylish homes, and it shows. *Morpeth Terrace* and *Carlisle Place* are typical, both lined with similar blocks. Inside, the apartments are impressive, with large rooms and high ceilings; their entrance halls have an old-world feel, with shining wood panelling and crusty porters in traditional uniform.

Though tree-lined, street succeeds street until, crossing *Rochester Row*, the vast green rectangle of *Vincent Square* surprisingly opens up. Some houses are lucky enough to overlook this open space, larger than *Belgrave Square*, used as a playing-field by the boys of Westminster School. The school forms part of the precincts of Westminster Abbey, and it is in that corner of Westminster that the oldest buildings are found. This includes the Georgian houses of *Smith Square* and surrounding streets. Some have been lost, some serve other purposes (such as the Conservative Central Office), but some are still enviable homes. Between *Vincent Square* and *Horseferry Rd* is *Maunsel St*, a pretty terrace of brick cottages with gardens. A 2-bed one would set you back around £350,000. Rowan House and Stockton Court are two recent blocks of 2-bed flats in *Greycoat St*: prices are around £240,000. A big (2-acre) site in *Horseferry Rd*, vacated by the Post Office, is to be developed with homes and offices. And Bovis are building 67 1-and 2-bed flats on the site of a council depot in *Monck St*. Marketing this spring, completion this summer.

Some of the Edwardian blocks in Westminster are being refurbished, and

P

other blocks are moving from rental to sale. Gladstone Court in *Regency St* is four red-brick blocks surrounding a central inner courtyard. Regalian's 1988 conversion resulted in 52 luxury apartments sharing a fitness complex. Alice House in *Douglas St* was another block to get the 5-star treatment in 1987 from developers Great Gable. Back in *Regency St*, Lucas House will be a 6-storey block with 20 flats and basement parking.

The other source of Westminster homes can be found in the southernmost corner, towards Vauxhall Bridge. En route, in *John Islip St*, is Millbank Court, built in the '60s. These convenient flats are popular and competitively priced, even for the higher ones with views to the river. The far end of *John Islip St* and the streets surrounding it in the angle of the river and *Vauxhall Bridge Rd*, form the Westminster side of the Crown's Millbank Estate. There are neat terraced houses in *Ponsonby Place* and *Ponsonby Terrace*, and beautiful converted apartments in the river-facing white stucco *Millbank* terraces (the stretch culminating in the Paolozzi leaping dancer statue has been painstakingly restored and converted by Rosehaugh). The Crown's houses are a mixture of fair-rent homes and others available, when they come up, on long leases.

Among those estate agents active in this area are:

- Barnard Marcus
- Clarendons
- Dauntons
- Prudential Property Services
- Ellis & Co
- Chesterfields
- Bensons
- Cobdens
- Jacksons
- Tuckermans
- Cluttons
- Winkworths

Poplar

Map ref: p64 (6D)	
Postal district: E14	
Borough: Tower Hamlets (Lib)	
Rates: 217.89p in £	
Constituency: Bow and Poplar (Lab)	
Insurance: Scale 1	
Conservation areas: include York Square, Naval Row.	
Parking: Free	

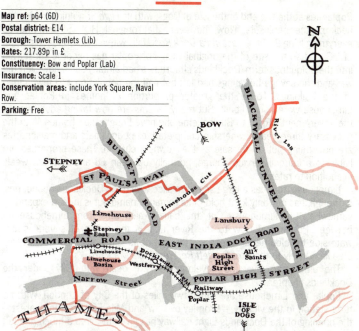

Flats	S	1b	2b	3b	4b	5b
Average prices	50–60	50–70	55–90+	75–100	–	–
Houses	2b	3b	4b	5b	6/7b	8b
Average prices	90–110	100–140	125–160+	→200	–	–

Transport   Docklands Light Railway: Limehouse, Westferry, Poplar, All Saints. British Rail: Stepney East.

Convenient for   BR at Stratford, Fenchurch St; Docklands, City. Routes east. Blackwall tunnel to south. Miles from centre: 4.5.

Schools   ILEA Zone 5: Langton Park, St Paul's Way, St Philip Howard RC.

The property   Docklands-style warehouse conversions and work-homes mushrooming along Limehouse Cut: prices below Docks, but well above local homes, which are largely 2/3-bed flats and maisonettes, many of them ex-council. Studios, big houses scarce. Owner occupation: as yet extremely low (90 percent council-owned).

The market   The lower end of the flats scale represents ex-council sales; other 2-bed flats will range c £70–90). Exceptions at the top end are the new canalside schemes (2-bed duplex: £165,000) and the occasional listed home around Salmon St: up to £200,000. Riverside Narrow St, annexed by Docklands (which see) is not included here. Local searches: 4 weeks.

P

Area Profile

Poplar lies at the top end of the Isle of Dogs, with its *High St* running across the neck of the peninsula. Now, however, that original High St and indeed everything lying S of the *East India Dock Road* falls within the boundaries of the LDDC, and so the site of the original village of Poplar has become subsumed into the ubiquitous term 'Docklands'. It fortunes had already sunk, however: the war and the savage bombings had left but half the population and few indeed of the buildings. Today the greater proportion of homes in Poplar and Limehouse were council-built. But many tenants are now taking advantage of the government's Right to Buy scheme and have bought their homes. With the necessary three years ownership completed, ex-council flats and maisonettes are now being put up for sale as their owners cash in. These properties are liable to a council service charge, normally between £8 and £15 per week, in addition to rates.

Limehouse, too, has a large southern slice within the Docklands boundaries. It, though, has not only kept hold of its romantic name but is indeed expanding somewhat: the Limehouse Cut, the canal which runs from Limehouse up between Poplar and Bow to the River Lea, is the scene of several smart waterside developments. These are thought of as Limehouse, but the original area lies largely to the W of *Burdett Rd/West India Dock Rd*.

The ultra-smart riverside developments are dealt with fully under the Docklands chapter.

Poplar and Limehouse are within two miles of the City of London. With no tube station in the vicinity – Bromley-by-Bow and Mile End are the nearest – the opening of the Docklands Light Railway has given the area a much-needed boost. Poplar and Limehouse stations now provide a regular service to Stratford (British Rail and tube) and Tower Gateway which is near Tower Hill (tube). The DLR will eventually be extended E to the neighbouring borough of Newham, and in 1990 W as far as Bank. Limehouse BR is one stop into Fenchurch St.

Poplar and Limehouse are bordered by the Isle of Dogs to the S, Bow to the N and Stepney to the W. To the E of Poplar is the Blackwall Tunnel Northern Approach motorway which gives easy access to South London, via Blackwall Tunnel, and Hackney and Leyton to the N. *East India Dock Rd* is the area's main thoroughfare and this extremely busy road leads to the City in the W and E to Essex, via Newham.

Many local men worked in the West India and East India docks before their decline and unemployment in the area is now very high. The docks are part of the fascinating history of Poplar and Limehouse and the area includes six conservation areas – *York Square* close to the border with Stepney, St Anne's Church, St Matthias Church, All Saints Church, *Naval Row* and *Narrow St*. There are also numerous well-known pubs and Langdon Park Sports Centre in *Byron St* provides evening and weekend facilities for squash, tennis, football, volleyball, karate and badminton.

One of Poplar's attractions is *Chrisp St* market, one of the few remaining East End street markets, but the area has a shortage of big stores. The market, which is part of the Lansbury Estate, named after Labour Party stalwart George Lansbury, is one of the more appealing parts of Poplar.

Limehouse is the scene of a major road scheme, the Limehouse Link, a four-lane tunnel which will form the main route into Canary Wharf. It will drive under Limehouse Basin, a large dock scheduled for development. *West India*

Dock Rd and its surrounding streets were once known as Chinatown as a number of Chinese immigrants settled there. Many Chinese restaurants still survive – some exceptionally good.

Poplar

The Lansbury Estate, which includes *Chrisp St* market, is one of Poplar's more attractive parts. The estate, built in the early '50s, comprises much of the property to the N of the busy *East India Dock Rd. Duff St, Grundy St, Susannah St* and *Ida St* have much-improved terraced ex-council houses. Houses in *Bygrove St*, N of *Grundy St*, are split into maisonettes and flats with delightful roof gardens. Some of the newer town houses and terraced houses in *Brabazon St, Carmen St* and at the N end of *Chrisp St* have been purchased from the council by their owners and tastefully improved. So too have smart terraced houses in *Giraud St* and flats and maisonettes in *Hobday St* and *Cordelia St*, which has Poplar Boys Club on its corner next to the Young Prince pub and Susan Lawrence Primary School halfway down.

To the W of the Lansbury Estate, the towering St Mary's and St Michael's Roman Catholic Church, opposite Mayflower Primary School, is flanked by more smart terraced ex-council houses in *Canton St* and *Pekin Close* which take their names from the nearby area once known as Chinatown. N of *Canton St*, with its neat rose-filled gardens, is St Philip Howard Roman Catholic Mixed Comprehensive School and then the Sabbarton Arms, the Poplar Royal British Legion club in *Arcadia St* and Bartlett Park, a rare stretch of greenery. Opposite the S end of *Chrisp St*, on the S side of *East India Dock Rd*, is the recently-opened Docklands Light Railway station of Poplar, providing a link to Stratford and Tower Hill. The station sits between the two London Docklands Development Corporation conservation areas of All Saints Church and St Matthias Church.

The grounds of All Saints Church are adjacent to some of Poplar's most desirable private homes, imposing 3- and even 4-storey Victorian terraced houses in *Newby Place* and *Mountague Place*. Similar houses can be found to the W in *Woodstock Terrace* facing Poplar Recreation Ground which houses Poplar Bowls Club's green and the entrance to St Matthias Church. S of *Woodstock Terrace* and *Newby Place* is *Poplar High St* – council flats on each side – which leads eastwards to *Naval Row*, another LDCC conservation area.

Past The Steamship, yet another pub, pre-war flats in *Naval Row* have been converted into centrally-heated blocks with video entryphone system. New leases on the 2-bed flats were marketed after conversion. The old Poplar Power Station signals the end of *Naval Row* and the unattractive exterior view of *Robin Hood Gardens* maisonettes is a local eyesore before the northern entrance to Blackwall Tunnel, leading south of the Thames. Blackwall Tunnel Northern Approach motorway is flanked to the west by the run-down Teviot Estate although *Daniel Bolt Close*, with its '60s-built 3-storey terraced houses, is popular with buyers. *Bright St, Byron St, Burcham St* and *Hay Currie St* are dominated by Langdon Park school, sports centre and social club. *Byron St* also includes the Duke of Wellington pub, known locally as The Germans.

East of the motorway are some of Poplar's worst properties with flats in Oban house, *Oban St*, particularly bad. Canning Town Bridge over Bow Creek provides Poplar's eastern boundary with Newham.

St Paul's Way is the northern boundary with Bow. Burdett Estate, another

P

run-down council estate which includes Stebon Primary School, stretches S to Limehouse Cut through *Wallwood St, Burgess St, Selsey St* and *Thomas Rd* where small industrial units can be found on the S side. S of Limehouse Cut is *Dod St* with its Charlesworth House council flats and Poplar Department of Health and Social Security.

Limehouse

Limehouse dates back to Elizabethan times and has always been a place closely linked to the river. Seamen and dockers were its inhabitants for centuries until the closure of the docks brought the tradition to an abrupt end. As well as its old established Chinese restaurants, *West India Dock Rd* includes Limehouse Police Station and two famous pubs, Charlie Brown's and The Blue Post, just outside the old dock gates. Charlie Brown's is on the corner of *Garford St* which has a Salvation Army hostel halfway down.

The N end of *West India Dock Rd* is flanked by Barley Mow council estate and there is a stark contrast as the estate sweeps down to very expensive *Narrow St* where the Social Democratic Party was formed in Doctor David Owen's house. This is a conservation area and is covered in greater detail in the Docklands chapter. W leads to *The Highway* and Tower of London.

West India Dock Rd continues to the N across *East India Dock Rd* into *Burdett Rd* where some of the larger properties on either side have been converted into split level flats. W of *Burdett Rd* are the council homes of *Turners Rd, Clemence St, Dora St* and *Norbiton Rd* which all lead into *Salmon Lane* where some delightful Victorian terrace houses can be found on either side at the W end (Mercers Estate). Similarly attractive properties are S of *Salmon Lane* in *Barnes St* and *York Square*, a conservation area, as well as *Flamborough St* which includes the Queen's Head pub. The Grade II listed houses in *Barnes St* command premium prices.

The S end of *Barnes St* leads into busy *Commercial Rd*, almost opposite the new Docklands Light Railway station of Limehouse. Further E along *Commercial Rd* is St Anne's Church, another conservation area. *Aston St* is Limehouse's western boundary with Stepney while the northern boundary with Bow is *Rhodeswell Rd*, which includes East London Stadium with its football pitch and athletics track.

Where Limehouse Cut canal passes under *Burdett Rd*, a new canalside development is planned in *Dod St* with 50 homes and 50 commercial units. Work was due to start this spring. Further along the canal, Enterprise Works in *Hawgood St* uses the Limehouse name despite being in E3. The courtyard development consists of work/homes, ranging from 4-storey houses to 1-bed flats. The first inhabitants here include two nursery schools, architects and marine engineers. And further east at the *Morris Rd* bridge, a big 4-phase conversion of warehouses into work/homes, priced from £51,000 and sold in shell finish. The whole 'village' goes by the name 'The Limehouse Cut'.

Among those estate agents active in this area are:
- Alan Selby & Ptnrs
- Essex Estates
- John Barber & Mrs Jones
- Land & Co

Putney

Map ref: p91 (4G)
Postal districts: SW15
Boroughs: Wandsworth (Con)
Rates: 130.8p in £
Constituencies: Putney (Con)
Insurance: Scale 1
Conservation areas: Include Doverhouse Estate, Putney Embankment, Parkfields.
Parking: Residents/meters

Transport Tubes: East Putney (zones 2/3a, District) to: Oxford Circus 25 min (1 change), City 25 min, Heathrow 50 min (1 change). British Rail: Putney, Barnes to Waterloo.

Convenient for Common and Heath, Richmond Park, the Thames. Routes to the SW and W. Miles from centre: 5.

Schools ILEA zone 10: Burntwood (g), Elliott. Private: Ibstock Place, Willington (b), Putney High (g), Putney Park (g).

Flats	S	1b	2b	3b	4b	5b
Average prices	60–70	75–85	90–120	125–150	150–175+	180+
Houses	2b	3b	4b	5b	6/7b	8b
Average prices	140–160	170–190	180–270+	250–500+	350–700+	–

The properties Family houses, some large, and many p/b flats. Riverside, Heath and Common locations attract premiums. Smaller Victorian cottages near centre and river. Putney Hill is E-W divide: W is best.

The market East Putney is cheaper: flats, small terraces. Then in price order comes smarter cottages W of the High St, smart inter-war and modern flats on Putney Hill and spacious family homes near the Heath. Mansions with grounds, rather than mere gardens, range up to a million. Families tend to stay put: schools are good and gardens large. Local searches: 1 week.

Area Profile

Bordered by Richmond Park, Putney Heath and Putney and Wimbledon Commons, and with more than its share of tree-lined streets and avenues, it is not for nothing that Putney is known as 'leafy Putney'.

Perhaps, though, a better description would be 'respectable Putney'. The majority of Putney houses are substantial late Victorian and Edwardian properties built for the middle classes and those who aspired to that status. Their descendants still live here: a mix of lawyers, medical consultants, circuit judges and respectable company directors enlivened by a sprinkling of media types who nest in the (slightly) smaller houses of East Putney and Thamesfield. Porsches are fairly rare but there are huge numbers of Volvo Estates (for the school run), company BMWs and Golfs.

There are a number of fairly large council estates scattered around Putney. But as Labour found to their cost at the last General Election, when Tory MP David Mellor increased his 1983-acquired majority, the tenants have been busily buying their homes: Austrian blinds and new front doors are proliferating.

Putney people are sworn enemies of property developers and people who cut down trees or build unsuitable extensions to their homes. As a result, the machinations of those trying to get onto committees of the astonishingly active Putney Society, an 'illegal' tree-felling, or the council's latest bid to solve the area's traffic problems are major topics of conversation. Concerns in Putney in 1989 are the pressure of the car and the activities of developers. Parking congestion is leading to pressure on the council to ban further conversions of houses to flats. Developers, frustrated by lack of sizeable sites, are looking hungrily at the large back gardens of West Putney: a trend councillors and locals deplore. Whitehall road schemes would affect the area seriously if they came to pass (see 'Transport' chapter). The problem of getting a daughter into Putney High School also provides a fruitful source of local debate.

Because so many large houses have escaped the attentions of property developers, the area is especially popular with families. Five- and 6-bedroom houses are, if not the norm, then certainly not unusual, particularly in West Putney, which has one of the biggest concentrations in London. Flat dwellers are better catered for than in many areas of London, with an enormous range of purpose built mansion flats – some exceptionally large – as well as conversions. Mansion flat developments such as *Highlands Heath* (Putney Heath) and Manorfields on *Putney Hill* are hugely sought after – with prices which reflect their popularity. Many of the older 1930s blocks, however, notably on *Upper Richmond Rd*, are suffering from the effects of high service and repair charges.

Most Putney residents pay a Commons Rate (seldom more than £10-15 a year) towards maintenance of Putney Common, Putney Heath and Wimbledon Common. Each of these commons has its own special character. The Heath is wild and much is heavily wooded while Putney Lower Common is old meadow land with a few spinneys and hosts the annual 'country' Putney Show each summer. Richmond Park, which marks the borough boundary, offers fine walking and horse-riding with livery and riding stables at Roehampton Gate and Robin Hood Gate.

At the heart of Putney is the traffic-choked *High St* which boasts some surprisingly good shopping, including multiples like Sainsbury's, British Home Stores and Marks & Spencer. Facilities are set to improve still further on completion this year of the massive Guardian Royal Exchange shopping development. There is even a cinema (Cannon) at the junction of the *High St* and *Putney Bridge Rd*. It must be assumed however that Putney people buy their wine in bulk and drink it at home for there are surprisingly few wine bars.

Every area in London has its own special problem. In Putney, that problem is the motor car. *Putney Bridge* and *Upper Richmond Rd* seem to act as a magnet for commuters from across the whole of South and West London and the result is monumental traffic jams during rush-hours. Traffic jams mean rat-running. But the problem has eased thanks to a new road system of even more fiendish complexity than the one which preceded it.

Rail commuters are well catered for with tube transport via Putney Bridge (District Line) on the Fulham side of the river, or East Putney (*Upper Richmond Rd*); British Rail from Putney (*High St*) or from Barnes stations.

Anybody considering buying a house in Putney – especially in West Putney or Thamesfield – should first read Jilly Cooper's The Common Years. The book caused severe offence to a number of Putney notables (not to mention those who walked their dogs with Mrs Cooper) but it remains a remarkably accurate reflection on life in Putney . . . a sort of conservative Hampstead.

Thamesfield

P

This little wedge-shaped area lies between the river and the *Lower Richmond Rd* to the W of *Putney Bridge*, running westwards to Putney Hospital and the common. Generally, prices here are slightly less expensive than in West Putney, with smaller, cottage-style, late-Victorian terraces predominant. There are also pockets of older Regency and early Victorian houses – and a few exceptionally large houses around Putney Common.

Lower Richmond Rd runs from *Putney High St* along the length of Thamesfield to Putney Common where it meets *Queens Ride*. There are small parades of shops sufficient for day-to-day needs strung along it, although it is fast becoming easier to buy an oil-painting, smart curtain fabric, a doubtful antique or a good cheese board than a 13-amp fuse or fresh sliced white. The road carries through-traffic from Richmond and Barnes but does not suffer as severely as *Upper Richmond Rd* – which forms part of the South Circular. Mainly terraced houses on *Lower Richmond Rd* although there are some Victorian detached and semi-detached villas set well back: notably attractive are Nos 139-144.

West from *Putney High St* are three large Victorian mansion blocks – Star and Garter Mansions, Kenilworth Court and University Mansions. Most but not all of the flats have river views although you may need to crane your neck. Kenilworth Court has a reputation for good management and University Mansions was recently refurbished. Some flats in Star and Garter Mansions and Kenilworth Court may suffer noise from the nearby pub – those with sensitive ears, beware!

The roads leading off *Lower Richmond Rd* towards the river tend, in the main, to be smaller mid- and late-Victorian terraced cottages, some purpose built maisonettes and flats. *Ruvigny Gardens* features larger 3-storey Victorian terraced houses; some now converted to flats, some with river views. Don't skimp on surveys close to a river: problems with settlement have been reported among properties in Putney which stand very near the Thames. In *Ruvigny Gardens*, a modernised 5-bed house with river views (just) sold last autumn at £475,000.

Festing Rd is one of the most popular streets in this area. Some of its houses are in fact purpose built Victorian flats and maisonettes. It runs down to *Putney Embankment* and its boathouses. By the junction is Leaders Gardens, a small, attractive park with public tennis courts. Popular *Ashlone Rd*, a street of mid-Victorian terraces, also leads down to Leaders Gardens. Adjoining *Ashlone Rd* is *Stockhurst Close*, a small council development of flats, some with river views. *Pentlow St* features attractive Victorian houses, mainly 3-bed houses, some semi-detached. A commercial laundry at the end of the road does not appear to affect popularity, with prices around £180,000. *Sefton St* offers small Victorian terraces leading to *Home Way*, inter-war blocks of council flats backing onto sports grounds. *Commondale*, overlooking Putney Hospital and Common, is a row of little 2-bed cottages, some flat-fronted. The prettiest ones were built in the 1870s to house the 'deserving poor' with money provided by Putney Pest House, no less, and wealthy local benefactors: these characterful houses are rarely on the market for long. Round the corner in *Danemere St* there are plans for an infill development – yet to receive Council permission.

Putney Embankment itself has few houses available – they are generally tied to the boat houses and rowing clubs which line the embankment. Ruvigny Mansions, a small Victorian block, has spacious flats, most with river views. It is inadvisable to leave cars parked on the Embankment owing to the tide's unfortunate habit of rising above embankment level. This is however popular with local garages called upon to repair the damage.

Lower Richmond Rd to Upper Richmond Rd

On the other (S) side of *Lower Richmond Rd* from *Commondale* is *Putney Common*, a tiny no-through-road used as a turn-around point for the No 22 bus, which terminates here. Past the pub on the corner of *Lower Richmond Rd* are cottages, then late '60s private flats (Commonview) backed by a builders' merchant's yard, then a primary school and Victorian church. Rumours continue of a development of the builders' yard. A path leads through into *Egliston Mews* and *Egliston Rd*.

Lower Common South is a road of huge detached houses, mainly 1870s-80s, mainly red brick and wonderfully ornate, set well back from the road and overlooking Putney Common – this is one of the very rare 'common' views not to be spoiled by heavy traffic. Residents should stay away one weekend a year – during the Putney Show. These homes are very, very rarely for sale and consequently appear from around £600,000 for a 6-bed detached house, £475,000 for a 4-bed semi. *Chester Close* and *Sherwood Court*, off *Lower Common South*, have small, attractive, late '70s 'traditional' 3-bed town houses (style is half 'Georgian', half clever-architect).

Egliston Rd (Jilly Cooperland), has vast mid- and late-Victorian detached houses with a handful of almost as large semi-detached early Edwardian houses; virtually all have substantial off-street parking and very large gardens. *Egliston Mews*, at the junction of *Egliston Rd* and *Lower Common South* is a smart development of flat-fronted 4-bedroom, 2-bathroom town houses, in 'developers Georgian' style, with £400,000-plus price tags. Red-brick Dryburgh Mansions occupies a large corner site on *Dryburgh Rd* and *Egliston Rd*. Unfortunately, the lovely, big, roomy flats have only 13-year leases available. The main part of *Dryburgh Rd* runs parallel to the Barnes to Putney railway line. Late Victorian/early Edwardian houses, mainly semi-detached, some detached.

Odd numbers back onto the railway but have reasonable-sizes gardens as barriers. Hidden at the end of the road is tiny *Beauchamp Terrace* with Victorian cottages waiting to be loved. The low numbers are nearer the railway.

Erpingham Rd runs between *Dryburgh Rd* and *Lower Richmond Rd*, with 3-storey early Edwardian semi-detached and terraced houses and there are some unusually large conversion flats. Rat-running is still a problem although *Dryburgh Rd* is closed to traffic at *Upper Richmond Rd* junction during the morning rush-hour. *Felsham Rd*, with its late Victorian mainly red-brick terraced houses, runs from *Erpingham Rd* through to *Putney High St* but council traffic engineers have reduced traffice problems from previous unacceptable levels to simply an occasional nuisance. Roads running off on either side are generally unexcep-tional South London late Victorian/ Edwardian terraces.

Stanbridge Rd, which crosses *Felsham Rd,* has some pleasant semi-basement flat-fronted mid-Victorian houses, while *Westhorpe Rd* attracts such exalted residents as MPs and the like. Houses in *Roskell Rd* are slightly larger 2- and 3-storey Victor-iana, some semi-detached. By the mid-100s *Felsham Rd* houses are larger, mainly 3-storeys. In *Henry Jackson Rd* is a council infill develop-ment of low-rise homes. Thereafter more small council blocks and St Mary's Church of England Primary school with Putney St Mary's Youth Club (which has a good local reputa-tion) opposite. *Bemish Rd* includes some flat-fronted Victorian cottages and larger Edwardian houses but suffers from traffic using it as a short-cut from *Lower Richmond Rd* to *Putney High St.*

P

Elaborate Edwardian is the hallmark of suburban Putney. These homes, solid and spacious, are eclectic in style. This one has copious 'Tudor' detailing in the heavy gable, the stuck-on 'timbers' and the tall chimneys. Other styles to be found – frequently in the same house – are Queen Anne and gothic. However mongrel their architecture, they find favour with families.

Charlwood Rd provides a welcome release from red-brick Edwardiana with Georgian/Regency semi-detached flat-fronted cottages and larger de-tached houses set well back from the lane running from *Felsham Rd,* across *Hotham Rd* to *Clarendon Drive.* (A 2-bed semi-detached cottage was recently on the market at £280,000 'in need of work'.) Perhaps the prettiest houses are between *Felsham* and *Hotham Rds:* this is rightly a conservation area.

Much of *Lacy Rd* is set to be altered beyond recognition by the massive Guardian Royal Exchange shopping development about to get under way. Otherwise 2- and 3-storey Victorian terraces, some small Victorian cottages, a public house and some council infill development. *Modder Place* has nice plain flat-fronted 2-bed cottages and looks directly onto unprepossessing '60s council flats, which is why they can be less expensive than neighbouring roads – not because the estate agent made a mistake with the valuation. West from *Lacy Rd, Hotham Rd* is mainly Edwardian 2- and 3-storey houses, most semi-detached (just) with an adult education centre and primary school at the junction with *Charlwood Rd*. Most houses here have 4 or more bedrooms. A good 5-bed, 2-bath house in *Hotham Rd* recently made £310,000.

Clarendon Drive features more 2- and 3-storey late Edwardian and '20s semi-detached houses. Houses on the S side of the road back onto the railway line but have gardens of up to 100 feet to keep it at bay. *Charlwood* and *Clarendon* are however affected by new road proposals. *Norroy Rd* and parallel *Chelverton Rd* with its good-sized late Victorian family houses, are both convenient for Putney BR station. *Spencer Walk*, to the W off *Charlwood Rd*, has pretty, early Victorian, flat-fronted 3-storey houses with semi-basements and some modern infill town houses. Some train noise is possible here, as is noise from the popular Quill pub, but problems are unlikely as it is the 'local' for detectives and senior officers from Putney police station in *Upper Richmond Rd*. Current problems of rat-running in *Clarendon Drive*, *Felsham Rd* and *Lacy Rd* are likely to be eased with *Felsham* and *Lacy Rds* set to be closed to through traffic.

Upper Richmond Rd is a major trunk road carrying traffic not only from Richmond but also from the M3 and M25 and is busy at all times. The road is among those currently under scrutiny by Department of Transport consultants (West London road assessment studies). However, the majority of houses on the road are set well back. From the junction with *Putney Hill* it becomes increasingly commercial. Thereafter increasing numbers of '30s and more modern mansion blocks as the road heads E towards Wandsworth. Off-street parking is essential. The western section of the road features many blocks of flats ranging from early '20s to fairly new. Brittany House has gained new penthouses in a total refurbishment. Maintenance charges on the older blocks are beginning to be off-putting to some buyers. Among the best-known blocks close to *Putney High St* are old-style Ormonde Court and '30s-built Belvedere Court at the junction with *Dryburgh Rd*, overlooking Putney swimming baths and convenient for early morning swims. All properties on this side of *Upper Richmond Rd* back onto railway lines although the majority have large gardens to cut noise levels. Harwood Court (opposite *Colinette Rd*) is another '30s-style block while *Isis Close* is a modern '60s-built development. Wellwood Court is next, then *Breasley Close* a council infill of flats and houses; *Fairfield Gardens* is a small town-house development. Northumberland Row in *Dyers Lane* (a no-through-road) is a small terrace of mid-Victorian cottages, some flat-fronted, overlooking small modern council homes. A small scheme of 9 flats and 4 houses is planned near *Dryburgh Rd*.

Probably the best-known houses in *Upper Richmond Rd* are the 'Nelson Houses' a row of half-a-dozen lovely late Georgian/early Victorian detached houses supposedly built for Nelson's sea captains. The houses are set well back from the road with gravel sweeps and Regency iron-work canopies.

East Putney

Popular with people moving into the area who cannot yet afford to live in Thamesfield or West Putney but choose not to live in Wandsworth or Earlsfield and are determined to have SW15 on their headed writing paper. Prices for the late Victorian/early Edwardian terraced houses are generally below those in Thamesfield, even though transport and shopping facilities are better, with the BR station in *Putney High St*, East Putney District Line tube in *Upper Richmond*

Rd and Putney Bridge tube just over the river. Off *Upper Richmond Rd* is Woodlawns, a new development of small town houses from £199,000. Although not large, they do have garages.

Putney Bridge Rd runs parallel to the river from *Putney High St* to Wandsworth, meaning very heavy traffic at times. Wandsworth Park runs most of the length of *Putney Bridge Rd* so many of the late Victorian terraces of 2- and 3-storey houses and purpose built flats have views across the greenery to the river and Hurlingham beyond. Few of the houses are very special with the exception of Park Lodge at the junction with *Atney Rd*: an early Victorian detached house followed by the single-storey Sir Abraham Dawes Almshouses.

Fawe Park Rd, with its early Edwardian terraces, also suffers some rat-running, and even numbers back onto the railway line. Terraced houses in *Skelgill Rd* overlook Brandlehow Primary School playground, while the 3-bed houses in *Brandlehow Rd* overlook the front of the school. *Bective Rd* is a popular mix of flat-fronted mid-Victorian cottages and bay-windowed late Victorian terraces. Disraeli Gardens is a large Victorian mansion block on the corner of *Bective Rd* and *Fawe Park Rd*. *Wadham Rd* has a very popular mix of small, pretty, late-Victorian cottages, many flat-fronted (about £125,000 for 2-beds); some 3-storey flat-fronted Victorian (c £170,000 for 4-beds). But the tube line runs at roof level behind.

Oxford Rd runs between *Upper Richmond Rd* and *Putney Bridge Rd*. 'Sleeping Policemen' have reduced the speed of the rat-runners, but not the numbers. There are some large detached mid-Victorian houses with porticoed entrances (mainly odd numbers). The remainder are Edwardian semi-detached with some modern (council) infill. *Montserrat, Werter, Disraeli Rds* run from *Oxford Rd* to *Putney High St* with a range of large Victorian houses, many now converted into flats. The roads are all one-way, either to or from *Putney High St*, and suffer from frustrated hopelessly lost rat-runners.

Deodar Rd off *Putney Bridge Rd* is the most popular (and expensive) street in East Putney: odd numbers overlook the river and are the last houses before Central London to have private moorings at the end of their big gardens. They are large 3-storey semi-detached houses: a river-front house sold for £475,000 in the autumn. To E of *Deodar Rd* is a new commercial development of workshops with studio accommodation above. There are drawbacks of course – the District Line bisects *Deodar Rd* (at roof level).

Oakhill Rd links *Upper Richmond Rd* (and the rat-runners) to *Putney Bridge Rd*. The street is first Victorian and more recent mansion flats, then detached double-fronted mid-Victorian, then later, smaller red-brick terraces. Roads running between *Oakhill Rd* and *West Hill* – Schubert, Galveston, Mexfield, Cromford, Santos – are generally substantial Edwardian terraces, with an increasing number converted to flats causing some parking problems. Convenient for East Putney tube. The least known corner is *Point Pleasant*, tiny terraced flat-fronted Victorian cottages hidden off *Putney Bridge Rd* with 'scope for improvement . . . '. Railway at head of terrace, river at foot.

Putney Heath and Putney Heights

Putney Heath is wild and heavily wooded and walkers can get to the neighbouring Wimbledon Common by an underpass under the A3. *Portsmouth Rd* runs across the heath to the junction with *Telegraph Rd*, where there is the Telegraph pub. Next door is unusual 1930s Wildecroft Manor mansion flats, built in mock-Tudor style with exposed beams, with large 3- and 4-bedroom flats. Many go to overseas buyers who are unworried by hefty service charges. Then comes Highlands Heath, also '30s mansion flats with slightly smaller homes, lower service charges and tennis and squash courts. Both blocks back onto the heath. Prices start at around £117,000 (2-bed, un-mod).

Heathview Gardens and Bristol Gardens have among the most popular – and pricey – houses in the area. Vast 6/7/8-bedroom Edwardian detached houses in quiet tree-lined roads with large gardens, some running onto the heath. Virtually all remain in single occupation. One was recently for sale with 8 bedrooms at £700,000. Bensbury Close has small flat-fronted mews cottages, 2- to 4-bed houses. Portsmouth Rd: small (in comparison with Heathview Gardens) detached houses overlooking the heath, including Bowling Green Cottage, a flat-fronted, white-washed country cottage thought to date back to the early 18th century. Bowling Green Close is a private development of extraordinary large 1930s Art Deco detached houses very rarely on the market.

Lynden Gate is 'Developers' Regency': 3-storey semi-basement stuccoed townhouses, 2- and 3-bedroom in a high-security development surrounded on three sides by the heath and woodland. Second and third bedrooms of these houses seem on the compact side given the £350,000 price tags.

Putney Heath (the road) runs from Roehampton to Putney Hill and suffers serious rat-running at rush-hours with traffic out to beat the Roehampton Lane/A3 junction lights. Mainly council developments (increasingly owner-occupied) along the heath, then Exeter House, large 1930s mansion block development in its own large grounds. Many, but not all, the flats have views over the Heath. 2-bed flats recently fetching about £125,000. Manorfields is a huge 1930s mansion flat development of nine-plus acres on the corner site between Putney Heath and Westleigh Avenue. Newnham House (demolished in a gas blast five years ago) has now been built. Superb 2-, 3- and 4-bed flats, all with good views of beautifully kept landscaped grounds with specimen trees and ponds. Service charges are high but full-time gardeners and porterage explain the charges. Probably the most sought-after development of its kind in Putney.

The triangle bordered by Putney Hill, West Hill and Upper Richmond Rd offers the largest choice of modern purpose-built flats in Putney, although there is also a wide selection of older Victorian and Edwardian houses. Putney Hill is a busy through-road but flats in the blocks on either side of the road remain popular. Properties include some substantial double-fronted mid-Victorian houses still in single occupation. But the most fantastic, a Gothic revival monster at 76 Putney Hill, is now a council residential hostel. Last year a large detached house with ballroom on the Hill was for sale for £1m. By the winter, no millionaire had snapped it up. Some popular, mainly '30s and '50s blocks of flats, while Fairhaven is a Victorian detached mansion now converted to flats. Putney High School for Girls (fee-paying) fronts onto Putney Hill between Carlton Drive and Lytton Grove. Radcliffe Square, between Lytton Grove and Kersfield Rd is a '70s flats development.

At the top of Putney Hill is a no-through road spur of Putney Heath Lane with two mansion blocks including Ross Court, which is popular for its large flats with big rooms.

St John's Avenue is probably the best road for (well-heeled) flat buyers in Putney, with some of the best modern blocks in the area – Downside, Claremont, Marlin House, all well-maintained with indoor swimming pools and five minutes' walk to East Putney tube. *Carlton Drive* is also lined with modern '60s blocks of flats but is slightly less popular. Neither road is, however, the prettiest in Putney.

Lytton Grove is a mixture of good-sized late Victorian detached and semi-detached houses with some '30s and modern infill. Some of the houses are now converted to (fairly spacious) flats. The road suffers from bad rat-running, especially in peak hours. Houses on the S side of the road between the junctions with *Holmbush* and *Rushholme Rds* back onto the tube line but sidings between rails and gardens cut noise.

Kersfield Estate by the junction with *Putney Hill* is a development of '60s council flats and houses. *Tintern Close* and *Arlesey Close* feature small modern town-houses, then a mix of late Victorian/Edwardian detached and semi-detached houses and the Royal Green Jackets Territorial Army HQ. *Chepstow Close*, a good modern town-house development (flat-fronted, 3-storeys with garages), backs onto tube lines.

Kersfield Rd is mainly modern early '60s blocks of flats with some late '30s flats (private) although *Littleton Close* is council built. Blocks include Heath Royal, Garden Royal, Heath Rise, a series of modern-style blocks close to *Putney Hill* with well-kept gardens. Flats range from 1- to 4-beds with recent prices from £75-295,000. Council blocks in the area are of reasonable quality, built during the same period and in similar style to many of the private blocks – spot the difference. *Putney Heath Lane* – a mix of good sized 2- and 3-storey early Edwardian semi detached and terraced houses interspersed with modern mansion flat developments. Some houses are detached (just). There are plans for 18 new flats and 6 houses. *Van Dyke Close* is town houses and flats. Behind is *Lavington Stables* – a tiny mews too small to find in the A-Z. *Rusholme Rd* has flats at the junction with *Putney Heath Lane*, thereafter late Victorian red-brick detached and semi-detached houses, an increasing number now conversion flats. Modern flats at the junction with *Holmbush Rd* overlook an open area.

Keswick Rd runs between *Upper Richmond Rd* and *West Hill* and like *Lytton Grove* suffers badly from rat-running. Some potential buyers may also be put off by the (above ground) tube-line running behind, but gardens and large grassy sidings cut noise levels. Some exceptional large early Victorian houses, typically 5-bed, 3-reception and half a million, with large gardens. Cavalry Gardens is a sybaritic complex of houses and flats, both new and converted, with its own pool and sauna, off *Upper Richmond Rd*. From £100,000 to £330,000. *Portinscale Rd* off *Keswick Rd* features some large detached Victorian houses and '20s and '30s infill of Tudor-style herringbone brick. The road suffers some rat-running. By the junction with *West Hill* is Burntwood School and Portinscale Estate (modern houses/low rise flats). Opposite are large '70s flats.

West Hill – a continuation of the A3 – is exceptionally busy at all times. The safest time to cross is during rush hour when the traffic is generally stationary. From *Tibbett's Corner* underpass is *Colebrook Close*, off *West Hill*, an extraordinary 'Spanish Hacienda' style development of houses and maisonettes built in the '30s by a film company for stars and starlets visiting Britain for filming. A 3-bed flat was recently on offer at £139,000.

Thereafter large, mainly late Victorian houses most, fortunately, set well back from the road with essential off-street parking and for the most part converted to spacious flats.

P

West Putney

This is where you live when you have made it in life and have chosen not to commute into London each day from Berkshire or Hampshire. There are some small houses, flats, even council estates. But the vast detached late Victorian houses in wide tree-lined avenues are the Putney properties of popular imagination. They house three-car families with daughters at Putney High or St Pauls, sons at a good boarding school and a husband with a secure seat on the Board and a useful handful of non-executive directorships.

West Putney is bordered by *Upper Richmond Rd* to the N, *Putney Heath* to the S, *Putney Park Lane* and *Putney Hill*. It is a wholly residential area save for the shops and offices of the *Upper Richmond Rd* and is a conservation area.

The area is laid out on a grid pattern with four roads – *Westleigh Avenue*, *Chartfield Avenue*; *Hazlewell Rd* and *Howard's Lane* – running parallel to the *Upper Richmond Rd*. Cutting between and across are avenues such as *Larpent*, *Castello* and *St Simon's* which run parallel to *Putney Hill*. Major building started in the 1870s and houses range from huge detached Victorian and early Edwardian through to mid-'20s architect-designed flights of fancy with some '50s and early '60s infill. The area is exceptional in the number of large detached or generous semi-detached houses on offer.

Westleigh Avenue running W from *Putney Hill* starts with low-rise council homes then there is a mix of Victorian, Edwardian and newer detached houses all well set back from the road. From the junction with *Pullman Gardens*, council houses and small blocks of flats back onto a '50s and '60s council estate (the mainly low-rise flats, houses and maisonettes of *Cortis Rd*, *Pullman Rd* and *Heyward Gardens*.) Houses on the S side of *Westleigh Avenue* between *Cotman Close* and *Pullman Gardens* back onto Elliot secondary school in *Pullman Gardens*. By the junction with *Granard Avenue* is Granard primary school (which produces demon seven-year-old chess players), then small council houses. Leading off *Westleigh Avenue*, *Genoa Avenue* is mainly late Victorian 3-storey semi-detached with some '20s houses and small council infill. *Solna Avenue* has small modern council houses, most now owner-occupied. At the junction with *Westleigh Avenue*, *Granard Avenue* is small neat council houses then substantial detached – many '20s, '30s, and '50s double-fronted with fine views. (Recently on offer, a 4-bed house at £329,000.)

Chartfield Avenue is a mixture of late Victorian/Edwardian detached houses set back from the road with some substantial inter-war stockbroker-Tudor homes. As with *Westleigh Avenue* substantial amounts of council property with the Asburton Estate between *Putney Hill* and *Genoa Avenue*. Some of the largest Victorian detached double-fronted houses are now converted to vast flats: 3-bedroom, garden, two reception rooms not unusual. Roads leading off *Chartfield Avenue* from *Putney Hill*. *Chartfield Square* and *Cherryfield Drive* are undistinguished modern town houses, the former overlooked by an ugly '60s office block on *Putney Hill*. (Four-bed house in *Chartfield Square* recently offered at £173,000.) Late '60s council flats (not high rise) and houses opposite in *Winchelsea Close*.

Gwendolen Avenue:- popular large 1880s detached and semi-detached houses and some small council houses (suffering structural faults and likely to be demolished). Site Developments have built large 5-bed Victorian-style semi-detached houses; another scheme for 3 4-bed houses is pending. *St Simons Avenue* features more very large detached houses and a church at the junction with *Hazlewell Rd*. *Genoa* and *Castello Avenues* are smaller (but large by any other standards) turn-of-century 2/3-storey semi-detached and detached red brick houses. *Larpent Avenue* has some modern infill but generally substantial late Victorian detached and semi detached 2- and 3-storey houses. Some houses (the low even numbers) have extraordinary domes on the front elevations – Turkish architect perhaps? *Luttrell Avenue* – late Victorian/early Edwardian semi and detached houses.

Hazlewell Rd, mainly 2- and 3-storey late Victorian and early Edwardian detached and semi-detached houses. Some smaller modern infill houses (also detached). The road suffers occasional rat-running. *St John's Avenue* runs between *Hazlewell Rd* and *Putney Hill* with very large 1880s 3-storey semi-detached and detached homes. *Ravenna* and *Burston Rds*, large semi-detached and detached, also convenient for Putney Station. *Tideswell Rd*, 3-storey Edwardian semi-detached; *Holroyd Rd* is Edwardian 2- and 3-storey semi-detached houses. *Coalecroft Rd* (a conservation area within the West Putney conservation area): even numbers are very pretty flat-fronted early Victorian cottages, mainly 3-bedrooms (a 2-bed one sold recently for £235,000). Odd numbers are good-sized Edwardian semi-detached.

Howards Lane is a wonderfully esoteric blend of house styles ranging from vast mid- and late-Victorian and early Edwardian to stunning early '20s architect-designed – with a few Victorian and modern terraces thrown in for good measure. The road includes one of the most desirable houses in Putney at *115 Howards Lane*: a detached art deco flight of fancy with a vast red dragon weather vane. *Howard's Lane* houses start off in the E as small (for West Putney) terraced and semi-detached mainly 4-bed houses. Nos *50-60 Howard's Lane* are a nice-looking town house development with integral garages, then mainly larger late-Victorian detached and semi-detached houses. *Kingslawn Close* at the junction with *Woodborough Rd* is an attractive town house and flat development with communal gardens including tennis courts. Leading off Howards Lane to the N are *Carmalt* and *Balmuir Gardens*, turn-of-century, 4-bed semi detached (just) houses. Some *Balmuir Gardens* houses back onto Putney Tennis Club. *Tideswell* and *Enmore Rds* are similar but slightly larger. *Parkfields* is a narrow, hidden lane concealing enchanting Georgian and early Victorian cottages and some larger Georgian houses. It is a conservation area with original, restored lamp posts in the road. Convenient for a small parade of similar period shops in *Upper Richmond Rd*. *Dealtry*, *Colinette* and *Campion Rds* all have 3-storey Edwardian terraced and semi detached homes.

The area between *Woodborough Rd*, *Malbrook Rd* and *Upper Richmond Rd* boasts some of the biggest and most popular houses in Putney. Two- and 3-storey ornate mid- and late-Victorian detached houses with 5 or 6 bedrooms (and many with more), drives and huge gardens. There is a small council infill block half-way up *Woodborough Rd*.

At the junction of *Woodborough Rd* and *Upper Richmond Rd* are private flats: The Briars, Somerset Lodge, and also private modern flats at the junction with *Briar Walk*. Pear Tree Court which is similar, is at the junction of *Malbrooke Rd* with *Upper Richmond Rd*.

West of here is considered to be in Roehampton, though the transformation is a subtle one. The boundary is *Putney Park Lane*, not a road but rather a woodland track marooned in suburbia, running N-S between the houses and past the bottoms of gardens.

P

Roehampton

Drive up the *A3 Kingston Vale* towards Putney and to your left you will see what anywhere else would be a series of luxury blocks of flats overlooking the green acres of Richmond Park. They are, in fact, the 'point' blocks of the vast Alton Estate built in the '50s and early '60s by the GLC, now owned and managed by Wandsworth Council. The views from them must be terrific – and the views *of* them, when seen across the park, gives an inkling of what was in the minds of tower-block architects.

Roehampton is bordered by Richmond Park and Richmond Golf Course to the S and W, *Upper Richmond Rd* to the N and by enchanting rural *Putney Park Lane* to the E. It is an area of contrasts – it is just a five-minute walk from the modern towers of the Alton Estate to the small Victorian terraces of *Medfield St* or to the three-quarter million houses of *Roedean Crescent*.

The area bordered by Richmond Park, *Clarence Lane*, *Roehampton Lane* and the *A3 Kingston Road* is mainly council-built properties known under the generic name of Alton but in fact a number of different estates. Low-rise blocks and houses are increasingly owner-occupied, and tower flats with views over the park are becoming popular. As elsewhere in the borough prices are lower than for privately built properties, for example 3-bed maisonettes in roads like *Harbridge Avenue* without park views are making around £88,000. Tower-block flats go for £70-75,000 for 2 beds. *Laverstoke Gardens* and *Holybourne Avenue* back onto listed Manresa House, a Jesuit training college, and a convent. As usual the planners forgot about the transport and shopping needs of inhabitants: the only shops of note are a tatty parade in *Danebury Avenue*. Nor is there a lot for youngsters to do in the evenings with the result that residents complain about roving gangs of bored youths.

Roehampton Village, just across *Roehampton Lane*, could not be more different. *Roehampton High St* has pretty early and mid-Victorian houses and small 'village' shops. Most, but not all, of *Medfield St* overlooks Putney Heath and comprises 2- and 3-bedroom mid-Victorian terraced cottages and a row of larger red-brick terraced houses (late Victorian) with tall chimneys, some semi-basements. The road is a bus route and suffers congested traffic during rush-hours. *Ponsonby Rd*, running off *Medfield St* back to *Roehampton Lane* S has small flat-fronted Georgian semi-detached cottages overlooking the Heath, then beautiful Roehampton Church and Roehampton Church School (primary).

On the other side of *Roehampton High St*, *Nepean*, *Akehurst* and *Umbria Sts* form a quiet enclave of semi-detached and detached houses ranging from Edwardian through to early '30s (some modern infill), many now flat conversions. Large gardens and generally very quiet, tree-lined roads. *Rodway Rd* however, suffers occasional rat-running problems.

From Putney Heath, *Dover House Rd* leads down to the *Upper Richmond Rd* and passes through the Dover House estate, built, like the Magdalen Park Estate in Earlsfield (which see) as a 'cottage' estate. Its borders run from *Crestway* down *Dover Park Rd* to *Upper Richmond Rd* with *Huntingfield* and *Swinburne Rds* the borders to the W and peaceful *Putney Park Lane* to the E. The houses are a mix of inter-war chalet style semi-detached and terraced with steeply inclined roofs and dormer windows, and pretty flat-fronted terraced and semi-detached. The estate is now a conservation area but too late for some houses, where new owners have pebble-dashed, rendered or fake-stone-clad. The area is now well-known to postal-zone-conscious buyers without the cash for Putney proper and the well-modernised houses now fetch up to £110,000. The estate is quiet (with the exception of *Dover House Rd* which suffers some through traffic), with 'village' greens and open spaces. Among those most in demand are houses backing onto *Putney Park Lane*, an unmade-up tree-lined lane running between Putney Heath and *Upper Richmond Rd.*

Roads leading down to the estate from Putney Heath such as *Dover Park Drive*, and *Longwood Drive* feature large, mainly detached family houses, most built in traditional styles in the '30s and '50s. *Coppice Drive* backs onto playing fields behind Queen Mary's Hospital.

Off *Upper Richmond Rd* are mainly late Edwardian and early '20s homes with some modern private developments. *Putney Park Avenue* is a private unmade-up, tree-lined road which features lethal speed humps and a mix of Edwardian and newer houses with a small modern flat development at the top of the avenue: a very quiet road. *Marrick Close* has a small development of modern town houses. *Dungarvan* and *Langside Avenues* of substantial '20s semi-detached houses could suffer rat-running. Cornerways is modern flats on the corner of *Daylesford Avenue* and *Upper Richmond Rd.* A useful small parade of shops stands on either side of the *Dover House Rd* junction.

Roehampton Lane (A306) is at all hours of the day an exceptionally busy road, used as a route by traffic from Richmond, Barnes and Hammersmith to the A3 and Kingston. A 5-bed semi-detached with big garden sold in the winter for £260,000. The best houses are set back from the road behind high walls or in private closes and some are exceptionally large and aspire to half a million. *Roehampton Close* has '20s and '30s mansion blocks set in large private grounds well away from *Roehampton Lane*, with easy access to Barnes station and the A3. *Eliot Gardens*, a newly built development of 3-storey town houses with garages, is set back off *Roehampton Lane*. Upper numbers of *Roehampton Lane* towards Roehampton proper are mainly '30s terraced and semi-detached homes set rather close to the road.

On the edge of Richmond Park and bordered by playing fields and Roehampton Golf Course, *Roedean Crescent* features large detached double-fronted houses, mainly '30s and '50s, built in traditional styles with vast gardens at front and back and most with in-and-out drives. Neighbouring *Roehampton Gate* is also quiet and has smaller, detached pre-war houses also popular, but fetching lower prices. Prices of the detached houses in *Priory Lane* by *Roehampton Gate* tend to be kept down because of the volume of traffic from Richmond Park. At the northern (Barnes Common) end of *Priory Lane* is a small council estate to the W and Rosslyn Park rugby football club to the E.

Among those estate agents active in this area are:

- Allan Fuller
- Barnard Marcus
- Kinleigh
- Scotts
- Hugh Henry
- Sturgis
- Hamptons Dixon Porter
- Warrens
- Winkworths

P

Regents Park

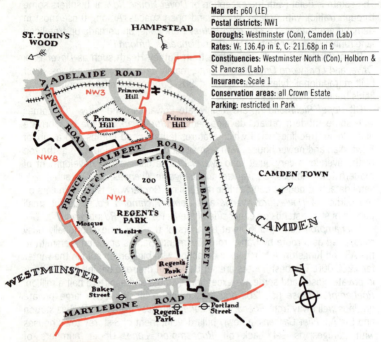

Map ref: p60 (1E)
Postal districts: NW1
Boroughs: Westminster (Con), Camden (Lab)
Rates: W: 136.4p in £, C: 211.68p in £
Constituencies: Westminster North (Con), Holborn & St Pancras (Lab)
Insurance: Scale 1
Conservation areas: all Crown Estate
Parking: restricted in Park

Transport	Tubes: Regents Park (Bakerloo), Baker Street (Metropolitan, Bakerloo, Circle). From Regents Park: Oxford Circus 3 min, City 20 min (1 change), Heathrow 55 min (1 change).
Convenient for	West End, City. Euston, King's Cross and St Pancras BR. Roads to West and North. Miles from centre: 1.5
Schools	ILEA zone 2. Haverstock School, Maria Fidelis Convent RC, St Marylebone C of E. Private: Cavendish School (g), Francis Holland School (g)

Flats	S	1b	2b	3b	4b	5b
Average prices	–	150–300	250–450+	325–650	600–1m	→
Houses	2b	3b	4b	5b	6/7b	8b
Average prices	250–400	→	400–500+	950–1m+	1.3m+	9m

The properties	Enclave of top-quality homes for millionaires: no-expense-spared conversions of Regency terraces into houses and apartments. Luxury 20th-century flats on Prince Albert and Park Rds, and mews behind terraces. A handful of London's finest mansions.
The market	Crown Estate leases are typically 60 years; strict conditions on upkeep and use: no sub-letting. Steady demand from foreign and British buyers for some of London's smartest homes. Local searches: Westminster 1 week, Camden 12 weeks

Area Profile

London, on the whole, is not a planned city. Centuries of piecemeal expansion and a strong sense of the sanctity of individuals' property have left it without the grand boulevards and squares of Continental cities. The one exception is Regent's Park. As its name implies, the graceful terraces and villas were planned during the Regency. Nash, with the backing of the Prince Regent, conceived the startling scheme, making each terrace of houses appear a single, classical palace, set in a sylvan landscape; the gleaming white facades accentuating the difference between London's town streets and this idealised countryside. Regent's Park still forms part of the Crown Estate, and benefits from its careful management and long-term planning, which has led to the restoration of nearly all the great terraces since the war. A common policy has been to sell individual houses in the terraces on relatively long leases – 60 years is typical – on the condition that the leaseholder completely restores the house. The estate stipulates the architect, has a veto over the plans and retains control over the exterior. When a lease on St. John's Lodge came up for sale, the Estate told would-be buyers that it, the Crown, would also choose the interior decorator and the landscape designer. All the buyer had to do, of course, was to pay their fees.

R

The grand sweep of *Portland Place* leads triumphally up to the Park, dividing at the end into the graceful double curve of *Park Crescent* (see *Marylebone*). The six-lane *Marylebone Rd* is decently shielded from view by the curve of its garden. N of the main road is more greenery, *Park Square*, with its two facing rows of Nash houses forming an entrance to the Park.

Going clockwise around the *Outer Circle*, row succeeds row, each terrace having a distinguishing feature within the overall classical style. The short *Ulster Terrace* has pairs of bow-fronted windows at either end, then come the gardens of *York Terrace East* and *West*, flanking *York Gate*: these houses face onto their own private roads, while their backs look N over the Park. The east stretch is original, and is offices and apartments: it is considered the more exclusive of the two. The west terrace was rebuilt behind the facade and has good, popular flats on 75-year leases complete with underground garage and security. *Cornwall Terrace* is the earliest of the park terraces, dating from 1820 and designed by Decimus Burton. Some of the 19 houses are offices. Again, bow windows at either end and three great, full-height porticoes with classical columns. The Crown Estate is redeveloping *Cornwall Terrace Mews* at the moment. Clarence Gate leads out to the top of *Baker St*, small, elegant *Clarence Terrace* with 2- to 4-bed flats is next in line.

Next comes *Sussex Place*, curving round behind its own garden and served by a private road. Its astonishing row of five pairs of Saracen's-helmet shaped cupolas give it a unique, exotic air. The graceful facade is original, but behind it is a modern re-building carried out for the London Business School, whose principal has a particularly enviable private residence. The next building along, *Hanover Terrace*, is set back behind a garden, its insubstantial-looking statues still adorning its blue-painted portico. This sweep has been completely restored following the Crown's sale of 20 refurbishment leases. These enviable homes have private, west-facing gardens and their own mews houses behind. One recently sold at (and another was on the market for) £1.75 million.

The astonishing London Central Mosque with its gold dome stands on the western edge of the Park: a splendid building whose outlines somehow marry well with Nash's classical. From here on, the Canal curves around the northern edge of the Park. Between it and the *Outer Circle* is Hanover Lodge, the fourth of the splendid Park 'villas' to revert from institution to private home. The leather-bound particulars went out in November to those seeking an £8.25 million home – unrestored. A '60s extension has been demolished, and six new detached villas by architect Quinlan Terry are emerging: the first should be ready next year. Opposite, within the Park, is vast Winfield House, the American ambassadorial residence. The Zoo takes up the N corner of the Park, its muted roars and trumpetings carried on the summer nights' breezes.

On the E side the terraces take up the tale once more: *Gloucester Gate's* houses are the latest for no-expense-spared refurbishment. The vast colonnaded central mansion has sold already for £6 million – a million a pillar; a record price for a terraced house. The smallest is a modest £1.4 million, the beautiful show house seems cheap at £2.65m – and all seven boast mews houses with garages. *Cumberland Terrace*, large, solid and square-bayed, with arches linking its three sweeps was rebuilt behind the facade after the war as houses and flats. The leases here can range from 35 to 60 years, with correspondingly varying prices. *Cumberland Place* boasts a lovely, large classical villa, bow-windowed at either end. *Chester Terrace* is a long row of 42 more normal-sized houses which remain as individual homes. They were completely rebuilt behind the facade 25 years ago, so allied to their Regency proportions are such modern facilities as lifts and integral garages. Recent examples on the market have averaged between £1-£1.2 million for a 72-year lease. The self-contained wings set forward at either end are linked to the main terrace behind them by flying buttress-like archways. *Cambridge Terrace*, with its Georgian curved-top windows, now has flats, maisonettes and houses plus 30,000 sq ft of offices. This is the last terrace to be modernised in the Crown Estate's current refurbishment programme. The next block, *Cambridge Gate*, was built half a century later than its Regency neighbours in sandy stone, and has an ornate and overdecorated air beside their white stucco. On past the uncompromising modern lines of the Royal College of Physicians, and the little Regency cul-de-sac of *St Andrew's Place*, you return to *Park Square*, overlooking its private square gardens, having completed the circuit.

Within the Park, around the *Inner Circle*, are the enchanted Open Air Theatre and a handful of scattered 'villas'. Most had dwindled into institutional use, but now some, like Hanover Lodge above, are homes again: among London's finest. New Crown leases have been sold on The Holme, Nuffield Lodge and St John's Lodge, with stringent clauses about renovation and upkeep. The Holme was the first, in a splendid position beside the lake: it has its own section of water, out to the island, roped off. St John's Lodge sold for around £9 million a year ago. Rumours that The Holme was again for sale for £30 million (six times its 1984 price) were denied by the owners.

Albany St runs parallel with the E edge of the Park. At the S end, the Crown Estate with Greycoat PLC have refurbished Prince Regent's Terrace, a row of flat-fronted brick houses. The resulting duplexes could be bought singly or as pairs to make a house. To the rear, in *Peto Place*, five mews houses are to be built. The Crown Estate plans refurbishment on *Park Square East* and *Albany Terrace*, which faces busy *Marylebone Rd*. Further N, several rows of mews belonging to the Park terraces open off from *Albany Rd*. There is also some recent housing in brick-and-stucco style. To the right is the *Cumberland Market* estate, a complex of serviceable brick buildings let by the Crown Estate as fair rent housing. The 500 flats have all been recently renovated.

Park Village West is an oddity, a curving lane off *Albany Rd* where the Regency style reappears laced with gothic in a surprising collection of little Nash country cottages. *Park Village East*, which lies behind, suffered when the houses on the E side were demolished to widen the Euston railway.

Prince Albert Rd runs in a sweep along the N bank of the canal, its grand parade of flats, from turn-of-the-century to modern luxurious, attracting top prices with their splendid Park views. At the E end are some surviving pairs of 1850s villas. Nos 6 to 15, which are in pairs, have been expensively reconstructed: one was sold last year for £1.6m: it boasts 6 beds, 4 baths, 3/4 reception rooms and an indoor swimming pool. These houses are being sold on 99 year leases: long for the Crown Estate. What is more, the normal sub-letting prohibition does not apply. The final pair will be released early this year – one boasts a swimming pool pavilion overlooking the Regent's Canal.

St Mark's Square has mid-19th century houses and links with the Primrose Hill neighbourhood. The green sweep of the Hill rises up to the right, then the blocks of mansion flats begin. Prince Albert Court is dark purply-grey brick, St James's Close is red-brick 1930s. Park St James, set back on *St James's Terrace*, was the first new block for some 15 years when built in 1984. Half of its 20 apartments and penthouses were sold off-plan at full market prices, then an unusual occurence. Stockleigh Hall is 1920s, stucco and red brick. Viceroy Court is also '20s with inset balconies and curving ends. Bentinck Close is more '30s, then 1920s Oslo Court. These blocks are a good hunting ground for a decent-sized 3/4 bed flat, which will cost c £350-500,000.

Avenue Rd runs down from the heart of St John's Wood. On the corner, luxurious 2 Avenue Road has large projecting balconies; facing it is a white stone balconied block, Imperial Court. The pair are well-established modern blocks, 12-15 years old, and flats here command premium prices. A 3-bed 3-bath apartment in 2 Avenue Rd would cost c £600-800,000. In Imperial Court, depending on floor and view, prices run from £400,000 for a 2-bed to £650,000-£1 million for a 4-bed. Penthouses can be £2 million. Then comes Edwardian splendour: the red and white mansion blocks of Northgate which run as far as *St John's Wood High St*. These are elegant, well-proportioned, well-thought-of flats, commanding around £600,000 for 4 beds.

Park Rd runs along the western edge of the Park, a fertile ground for ever more flats schemes. Another 55-flat block is planned. The year-old Beverly House is a U-shaped building on a rather cramped site, with windows eyeball to eyeball across a courtyard. The places to live here are the truly vast penthouses: 6,000 sq ft over two floors.

Crown Court by Rosehaugh has just 23 flats of from 1 to 5 bedrooms in its seven floors. The entrance is via an enormous foyer behind an arched brick colonnade, guarded by uniformed porters. The flats each have balconies or roof gardens, reached through more arches. Abbey Lodge, '20s mansion blocks, backs onto the Nash terraces, which resume with *Kent Terrace*. This, being tucked behind *Hanover Terrace*, is one of the few not to overlook the Park. At the S end of *Park Rd* are some pretty early 19th century houses.

R

Among those estate agents active in this area are:
- Anscombe & Ringland
- Chalcots
- Druce
- Hamptons
- John D Wood
- Knight Frank & Rutley
- Lassmans
- Phillips, Kay & Lewis
- Hirschfields
- Stickley & Kent
- Cluttons
- Ashton Chase

Richmond and Twickenham

Map ref: p88 (5D)	
Postal districts: –	
Boroughs: Richmond upon Thames	
Rates: 192.13p in £	
Constituencies: Richmond & Barnes (Con), Twickenham (Con)	
Insurance: Scale 4 (TW17: 7)	
Conservation areas: Include Richmond town, riverside & Green, Twickenham riverside. St Margarets.	
Parking: Residents/meters in centre.	

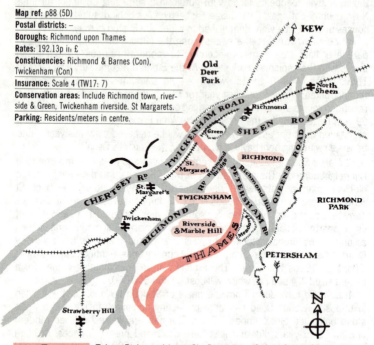

Transport — Tubes: Richmond (zone 3b, District) to: Oxford Circus 35 min (1 change), City 40 min, Heathrow 45 min (1 change). British Rail: Richmond (Waterloo 16 min), Twickenham, St Margarets.

Convenient for — Heathrow, M3/M4 for South and West. Miles from centre: 8.

Schools — Richmond Education Authority: Christ's School, Grey Court, Orleans Park, Rectory School, Shene School. Private: St Catherine's Convent School (g), Hampton School (b), Lady Eleanor Holles (g).

Flats	S	1b	2b	3b	4b	5b
Average prices	60–90	70–120+	80–165+	90–220+	140+	–
Houses	2b	3b	4b	5b	6/7b	8b
Average prices	90–190	105–225	165–400+	230–400+	300–800+	→

The properties — Wide range of desirable houses from early Georgian through mid-Victorian (the majority) to modern, plus mansion flats and conversions. Twickenham is more suburban, with pleasant Victorian and inter-wars family homes and a range of flats. River and parkside locations among the most charming in London. New riverside development has very expensive flats.

The market — Big premiums paid for best locations on Hill and riverside. Twickenham made great gains in '88. English and foreign families find area gives happy mix of London and country. Searches: 3 weeks.

Area Profile

Richmond is a town. It is in no real sense a suburb of London, cut off as it is by its enormous Park. The Thames and the tube link Richmond, just, to London, but the people who live here see themselves, perhaps more than any other inhabitants of areas in this book, as citizens of Richmond rather than the wider city. And who can blame them for keeping the place to themselves? It has a river front, 2,000 acres of primaeval English landscape – oaks and deer-dotted rolling grassland – in its Park, and beautiful buildings. Vulgar commerce may take Richmond people by train or tube into Town, and they vehemently claim that the West End theatres are just as accessible as their own Edwardian gem on the Green, but their heart remains in the Borough.

Politically, Richmond takes in Twickenham, Kew and a wide swathe to the W down to Hampton Court. The Thames, meandering beneath Richmond Hill and past Kew Gardens, links all these places. Here we cover just Twickenham and Richmond as being those areas most involved with London. Within its boundaries Richmond has palaces, wide parks, miles of river bank and no less than 40 conservation areas. It is nine miles SW of London.

Originally it was called Sheen meaning (it's alleged) 'bright and shining place'. Henry VII renamed the town after his earldom in Richmond, Yorkshire. He built a palace S of Richmond Green (the remains of which can be seen as Palace Gate) making the town a fashionable royal resort until Charles II moved to Windsor and Sheen Palace fell into disrepair. Richmond continued to attract noble visitors, (as is evident from the villas along Petersham Rd), artists and writers. The Old Deer Park (N), Richmond Park (E) and Thames-side walks still draw families and frazzled commuters who can shake off the city dust (Waterloo 13 minutes by express train). There is a wealth of good prep schools and church schools. The German School at Ham attracts diplomats. Australian/American expatriates like the quintessential Englishness; the Japanese come for the golf courses (Old Deer Park/Fulwell/Sudbrook Park) and the proximity to the Japanese School in Acton.

Prices are high and this is not the area for a first-time buyer on a budget. There is a fair supply of 1-bed flats but in prime areas near the river, Hill and Green, they can cost more than £125,000. A 2-bed flat may be as much as £230,000 if it has good views and a roof terrace. Most 3-bed flats are found in mansion blocks which may cost around £150,000 towards the *Twickenham Rd* but will start to rise to £220,000+ approaching central Richmond.

Richmond

Richmond is squeezed between the river, its park, the Old Deer Park and the open fields of Petersham. Most of it was built up in or before Victorian times: there is very little modern housing. The fact that Richmond town is a conservation area means that there are few unpleasant areas. A busy railway line passing behind *Pembroke Villas* and *Old Palace Yard* will make no difference to the price of property because the substantial houses and early 19th century cottages have such lovely outlooks onto the Green. Indeed, demand is high. The 6-bedroomed Tudor house which stands at the entrance to Old Palace Yard was for sale last winter for £895,000. Shopping is pleasant south of the Green around *George St*. There are supermarkets, two small department stores and a range of tasteful dress shops. Alleyways lead off *George St*, with delicatessens, coffee shops, restaurants, bookshops and craft shops. *Church Walk*, one of these alleyways, opens onto Richmond Church. Behind *Old Palace Yard* and *The Wardrobe*, where three surviving houses are the remains of Sheen Palace, is *Maids of Honour Row* (1724) which was built for the maids of George II's wife. Next is the Old Court House, Wentworth House, and *Garrick Close*, which offers a collection of neo-Georgian town houses. *Friars Lane* runs close to *Maids of Honour Row*; it curves down to the River where it joins *Cholmondeley Walk* past Queensbury House, with its neat '30s flats, and a row of pretty Georgian houses which fetch around £315,000. The restored Palladian villa, Asgill House, is situated at the northern end of the riverside *Cholmondeley Walk*. Here is the south facade of Trumpeter's House (now converted into flats), with its classical portico, and the early 19th century *St Helena's Terrace*, a handsome row of houses built above their own boat houses.

Tucked away next to Richmond British Rail station is a sheltered complex for retired people which was completed in the summer by Cussen Green Properties. Included in "Northumbria Court" are 1- and 2-bed flats ranging from £97,500 to £132,000.

Further South, beside the river walkway which leds to Richmond Bridge, is the £25m Riverside Development which was opened in October 1988 by the Queen. Designed by Quinlan Terry, and developed by Haslemere Estates, the scheme is one of the most argued-over pieces of architecture of the decade, pitting neo-classicists against modernists in a bitter professional row. Quinlan use what he claims are a variety of classical genres to produce neo-classical facades which hide offices, shops, restaurants and a car park. Unrivalled views of the river are a plus for the studios, 1- and 2-bed flats, maisonettes and a penthouse. Last winter's prices: 1-bed flat £145,000; 3-bed maisonette £300,000.

Favourite roads for 5-bed Victorian houses on the Hill are *Mount Ararat*, *Grosvenor Rd*, *Montague Rd* and *Rosemont Rd* – all E of *Richmond Hill*. However, all hill locations are desirable. *The Vineyard*, which crosses *Mount*

Ararat Rd, is one of the prettiest features of *Richmond Hill*. It comprises houses from late 17th to early 19th centuries, including almshouses all clustered around St Elizabeth of Portugal RC Church. Further E between *Albert Rd* and *Princes Rd* is an area of tiny cottages called *The Alberts*, property here currently fetches between £130,000 and £150,000.

At the top of *Richmond Hill* there is a mixture of prized 18th and 19th century houses which enjoy a view of the Thames painted by J M Turner and Reynolds. Turn E into *Queen's Rd*, which hugs Richmond Park, and on the left are a range of enormous houses – a mix of flats and hotels. On the right hand side there are some pretty roads offering a blend of early Victorian 3-storey houses and 2-bed cottages. Further down there is a new development called *King George's Square*. The scheme has incorporated the facade of Richmond poorhouse, which is now a complex of luxury flats.

North of the junction of *Queen's Rd* and *Sheen Rd* in *Dunstable Rd*, *Sheen Park*, *Townshend Terrace* and *St Mary's Grove* there are Victorian and Regency cottages and large 3-storey houses, some of which have been converted into flats. Houses here may be cheaper than those on the Hill, but the disadvantage is that some back onto the railway line.

Between *Sheen Rd* and *Lower Mortlake Rd* is a grid of roads with 2/3-bed cottages which are in the process of being renovated. The old council depot site in *Cedar Terrace*, *Lower Mortlake Rd* is being redeveloped by Charles Church with 90 homes. In the same road, Fairbriar Homes have plans for 24 flats. *Sheendale Rd* has beautiful Regency cottages. *St George's Rd*, *Bardolph Rd* and *Trinity Cottages* are pretty but they face a small industrial development and are in the shadow of the gasworks which is illuminated at night. Either side of the *Lower Richmond Rd* are Victorian terraced cottages which overlook a very busy road and fetch around £120,000. East of *Manor Rd*, which joins *Sheen Rd* and *Lower Richmond Rd*, there are council house developments on *Kings Farm Avenue* and *Carrington Rd*. Roads between *Sheen Court Rd*, *Tanier Rd* and *Warren Rd* offer '30s-built 3/4-bed houses, some fetching as much as £185,000. South of *Upper Richmond Rd* post-war houses are to be found, particularly on *Berwyn Rd*, *Orchard Rise* and *Sheen Common Drive*. These houses fetch £350,000 because of their prime location.

R

Twickenham

Twickenham is situated on the Middlesex side of the Thames, opposite Richmond. It is bounded by the river in the E, the busy *Chertsey Rd* (A316) in the N and *Staines/Sixth Cross Rd* in the S. During the 13th century Twickenham formed a large park but over the years it was gradually broken up to provide large estates with riverside villas for the wealthy. Many were demolished at the turn of the century to make room for domestic housing for London's spreading suburbia, but the former mansions and their residents live on as street names – *St Margarets*, *Cambridge Park*, *Ravensbourne*, *Riverdale*, *Orleans* and *Coley*. Now the area's character ranges from rural riverside grandeur to small '30s semis overlooking a dual carriageway.

Best known as the home of international rugby (although the ground is in Whitton), Twickenham lacked the kudos of Richmond until recently, though Twickenham people feel as though they have the best worlds. Homes cost substantially less than those on the other side of the River in Richmond, but residents can still enjoy Richmond's amenities. Research carried out by the local branch of a London-wide estate agent in the middle of 1988 showed Twickenham to be the fastest growing area in London with house prices increasing by 2.5% per week. The area has pleasant Thames-side walks with views of Richmond and Petersham Meadows and fewer parking restrictions. Twickenham is under 10 miles from London and travel in is almost as quick as from Richmond. A good range of state schools (Orleans Park/Waldegrave Girls Comprehensive and St Mary's Girl Convent School) attracts families, as do St Paul's (Girls and Boys) Public Schools in Barnes and Hammersmith.

There is a wide range of property available. People with around £500,000+ can afford an 18th century riverside mansion, but there is quite a selection of good family houses around £200,000 in pleasant locations. Two-bed cottages which are dotted throughout Twickenham, can cost under £105,000. Flats abound in the St Margarets area (small purpose built, small conversions and renovated mansion) and depending on the location a 1-bed flat can cost from £78,000 to £110,000. Bargain hunters should look around the St Margarets/Twickenham railway line area or close to the *Chertsey/Staines Rds* where a 3-bed 30s semi can cost £135,000.

East Twickenham/St Margarets

South of Richmond Bridge, *Richmond Rd* is flanked by red brick mansion flats which overlook gardens leading down to the Thames, and by small shops which are open late and have flats above them. Left into *Cresswell Rd* semi-detached Victorian houses with huge bay windows are to be found. Neighbouring *Morley Rd* and *Denton Rd* carry on the style on a smaller scale. A 3-bed house with a garden costs £220,000, but these houses have large, airy rooms with plaster mouldings around their ceilings. The Ice Rink on the riverside may be redeveloped with 250 new homes if the owners, London and Edinburgh Trust, have their way. Council planners were considering this at the time of writing. Nearby, at Richmond Slipways in *Ducks Walk*, flats are planned.

Further S *Cambridge Park* curves around Marble Hill Park to the river. Here large double-fronted mansions (mostly flats) are mixed with small modern developments set back from the road behind mature trees. Behind is *St Stephens Gardens* with a row of 3-storey semi-detached Victorian houses (mostly flats) overlooking a bowling green.

Richmond Rd swings SW towards the heart of Twickenham. To the S is Marble Hill Park, with the cool cream symmetry of the Palladian Marble Hill House, leading down to the river. *Marble Hill Close*, situated close to the park, has neat 3-bed '30s semis priced around £190,000. *Crown Rd* and *Sandycombe Rd* stretch N to *St Margarets Rd* and offer a mix of 2-bed cottages and pleasant 3/4-bed red brick family houses. *Sandycombe Rd* captures the former market garden atmosphere of the area and Sandycombe Lodge (N end), designed by J W Turner as his country retreat, is still a house.

Where *Crown Rd* joins *St Margarets Rd*, *The Barons* curves down past Twickenham Film Studios into a semi-circle. Here large 3-storey houses with pillared porticos cluster around what may once have been a private communal garden but where there is now a block of post war low-rise flats. To the E is *Rosslyn Rd*, with enormous double-fronted Victorian houses, mostly flats.

North of *Rosslyn Rd* is *Riverdale Rd* where the 1870 free standing gothic mansions, shaded by trees, give a touch of the Sir Walter Scott's. This is a fine example of a Victorian suburb, although the great houses are now splendid flats. On the right hand side of the road is a remarkable double-fronted house, wreathed in vines with a colonial-style verandah. Further N is *Ravensbourne Rd* with its half timbered post-war houses, and swinging left into *Park House Gardens* fine whitewashed art deco semi-detached houses run down to the river. Here is *Duck's Walk* where prime properties with mooring spaces face the river. From this point across *The Avenue* a pentangle of roads – *St Margarets Drive*, *Ranelagh Rd* linked by *St Peters Rd*, *St Georges Rd* and *Ailsa Rd*, form an exclusive area known as 'The Grounds'. Mansions either face grandly onto the road or are hidden by high walls. They all back onto secret private parkland where owners's children play contentedly and summer barbecues are held. The price of membership is high, starting around £600,000+.

Winchester Rd leads onto the crossroads of *The Avenue*, *Chertsey Rd* and *St Margarets Rd* and has Victorian/Edwardian flat-fronted houses. Nearby *St Margarets Grove* and *Brook Rd* offer pretty 2-bed cottages, property here fetches around £140,000. some cottages in *Brook Rd* have gardens that back onto the River Crane. On the E side of Cole Park (near *London Rd*) *Cole Park Rd* twists up to *Twickenham Rd* and is lined with detached double-fronted Edwardian, '30s and modern houses priced around £400,000. *Amyand Park Rd*, near *London Rd* and close to Twickenham BR station, hugs the railway up to *St Margarets Rd*. A mixed bag of grand 3-storey houses with basements (now flats) and plain red brick cottages (£130,000 with garden) are to be found, though some unfortunately face the railway.

Riverside and Marble Hill

The prestige property of Twickenham can be found S of *Richmond Rd*. *Montpelier Row* (1724) skirts the W side of Marble Hill Park. Here is a fine example of a Georgian terrace (Walter de la Mare and Alfred Lord Tennyson once lived here). *Chapel Rd* with its cottages joins *Montpelier Row* to *Orleans Rd* where the road, shaded by huge horse chestnuts, swings around Orleans House Gallery into the pretty *Riverside* winding up to The White Swan past some spectacular late 18th century white and pastel-coloured houses. N of *Riverside* is *Lebanon Park* where you can expect to pay £360,000 for a 3/4-bed, red brick Edwardian family house. *Lebanon Park* runs parallel with *Sion Rd* where a terrace of 12 houses runs down to the river.

South of *Heath Rd* is a network of roads (*Popes Grove*, *Grotto Rd*, *Cross Deep Gardens*) comprising a mix of Victorian houses with basements, harsh red brick cottages and pleasant Edwardian family houses. Prices range from £240,000 to £360,000. *Cross Deep* also has houses with lawns which lead down to the river and penthouse flats, these force house prices up to £625,000.

Further E *Heath Rd* feeds into *The Green*, a tree-lined triangle with large white 18th century cottages to the S which give way to modern flat developments. There are pretty 18th century cottages to the W of the green and a row of shops to the N which show signs of improvement. *May Rd*, *Knowle Rd* and *Colne Rd* have a mix of doll-sized cottages and modern houses.

Among those estate agents active in this area are:
- Winkworth
- Barnard Marcus
- Prudential
- Caddick & Co
- Nightingale Chancellors
- Mann & Co
- G A Property Services
- Hampton Dixon Porter
- Jardine & Co
- Sturgis

Shepherd's Bush

Map ref: p58 (7D)
Postal districts: W12
Boroughs: Hammersmith & Fulham (Lab)
Rates: 228p in £
Constituencies: Hammersmith (Lab)
Insurance: Scale 2
Conservation areas: –
Parking: Free

Transport	Tubes: all zone 2: Shepherd's Bush (Central, Metropolitan); White City, East Acton (Central); Goldhawk Rd (zone 2, Metropolitan). From Shepherd's Bush: Oxford Circus 15 min; City 25 min; Heathrow 1hr.
Convenient for	BBC TV Centre, Heathrow, M4/M40 to West. Miles from centre: 4.5.
Schools	ILEA zone 1: Burlington Danes School, Hammersmith School.

Flats	S	1b	2b	3b	4b	5b
Average prices	57–65	70–85	85–125	100–140	–	–
Houses	2b	3b	4b	5b	6/7b	8b
Average prices	115–140	140–180	170–250	200–270+	300–350	–

The properties — Victorian terraces are the staple: smaller 2-storey ones as single homes, taller ones converted to satisfy demand for 1/2-bed flats. Some larger family homes near Hammersmith borders. Also pockets of Edwardian p/b maisonettes; some roomier inter-war houses. Cheaper: ex-council; cottages, eg 'flower' estate, esp. popular. Un-done-up homes still to be found.

The market — Young buyers find the Bush cheaper than Hammersmith, with transport to town as good. BBC TV, already with studios here, will open new HQ soon: staff are chasing property now. Singles in studios become couples in flats, but children usually presage move to more family area. Local searches: 2 weeks.

Area Profile

Good communications and the presence of the BBC are the factors behind the rise of Shepherd's Bush. When the BBC's giant centre at White City is complete, 6,000 people will work there, causing (hope local estate agents) a further influx of buyers.

Until the end of the 18th century it was just another area of countryside around London. But buildings shot up during the 19th century as the capital expanded rapidly and Shepherd's Bush, well placed on a main route from the W, soon became a centre. Its triangular Green became a focus for travelling traders on their way to market.

The origins of the quirky name remain a mystery although various theories have emerged over the years. Some say the area was named after a famous land owner. Others insist that the body of a murdered shepherd was found in bushes on the Green several centuries ago. But by far the most popular explanation springs from its position on a major droving route. It is likely that shepherds rested their flocks on the Green before the final hike up to Smithfield Market. The only sheep there today are the ones painted on the Central Line tube station.

Most houses here are of the solid little workaday terraced variety, built around the turn of the century, and Shepherd's Bush changed very little until the second half of this century when council blocks, motorways and shopping precincts arrived.

Apart from the major roundabout system near the Green, built to accommodate a link with the *A40(M)*, the character of Shepherd's Bush has survived relatively unscathed and much of the dominant Victorian and Edwardian architecture is still intact after a century.

Today bustling Shepherd's Bush is BBC land. The corporation has centres in *Wood Lane*, *Lime Grove*, *Richmond Way* and on the Green. A brand new complex on the old White City Stadium site is building. It should open early in the 1990s and will push property prices even higher in the area. New firms of estate agents are already moving into the area in anticipation, though the BBC tribe has already joined the cheerful cosmopolitan mix of Asians, Irish, West Indians, Poles and representatives of most other London groups.

Shepherd's Bush is ideally situated for public transport and major routes in and out of London. It is on both the Central and Metropolitan tube lines and midway between the *A40* Oxford road in the N and the *A4* – gateway to the W country. The number 12 and 88 buses take shoppers direct to the West End.

But, like many other central parts of London, Shepherd's Bush lacks open spaces and there is a shortage of trees and greenery and of family houses with large gardens.

Facilities are not superb but the shops have improved in recent years and the shopping mall on *Shepherd's Bush Green* is to be redeveloped with a smart new centre. There is a colourful market off the *Uxbridge Rd* under the railway bridge, and there is talk of improving shopping too. BBC clientele keeps a range of local restaurants going, and the Bush Theatre on the Green is well known.

Hammersmith council has just introduced the first residents' parking zones – and towaway trucks. The southern part of Shepherd's Bush, towards Brook Green, is the first to be affected. The boom in flat conversions brings car parking problems to an increasing number of streets.

Shepherd's Bush is very much a first-time buyers' market. More and more of the tall Victorian terraces are being converted into 1- and 2-bedroom flats. The population is relatively transient and young professionals use it as a stepping stone area – staying about a year before moving into the house market further out of London. – or further in, if they do particularly well. There is still a lot of rented property, and many streets are relatively undeveloped. This is changing, and some parts, especially N of *Uxbridge Rd*, are tipped for rapid trans-formation. The area just E of *Askew Rd* is another to consider.

The White City area near the motorway junction is on the short-list for one of London's Channel Tunnel termini. The plan, which the council calls 'a disaster for the area', should be decided this year. It may be that freight only will use the proposed depot, with passenger trains going to King's Cross. And beware too the WEIR road running S from the Shepherd's Bush roundabout.

An essentially Victorian area, Shepherd's Bush shows every variation of the Victorian pattern-book builder's craft. Builders took house plans and details 'off the shelf', resulting in ornamentation like this bay, with its sash windows, stone, or perhaps stucco, parapet and decoration around the tops of the pillars. The house is built of London Stock brick, which when clean contrasts well with the stucco.

Family houses are in the minority, although there are a few near *Goldhawk Rd* on the Hammersmith borders. Most of their owners bought into the area many years ago and now have grown-up children.

Shepherd's Bush does not have neighbourhoods as recognizably self-contained as Brook Green in next-door Hammersmith, but properties of a similar type do tend to form neighbourhoods.

The most sought-after areas lie between the *Uxbridge* and *Goldhawk Rds*. Newer 1930s-style houses can be found near Wendell Park, and the district N of *Cobbold Rd* is a mixture of purpose-built Edwardian mais-onettes and Victorian terraces.

Large family houses lie S-W of *Askew Rd* around *Rylett Rd* and *Ashchurch Park Villas*.

Moving E, Cathnor Park has a village atmosphere which disappears beyond *Boscombe Rd* – home of the 4-storey Victorian terraces, largely converted into flats. North of the *Uxbridge Rd*, properties are generally smaller, although tall houses continue between *Wood Lane* and *Loftus Rd*. West to *Wormholt Rd* sees a mixture of purpose-built Edwardian maisonettes and solid 2-storey Victorian terraces. A selection of larger 1930s semis border the Cleverley and Flower council estates E of *Old Oak Rd*.

North of *Sawley Rd* council property is the norm although much of the stock E of *Bloemfontein Rd* is being sold off. Out E towards *Wood Lane* lies the sprawling White City estate with very few privately owned flats and a rough reputation.

Council housing, in the form of the Old Oak Estate, continues N of the *Westway* near East Acton tube station. These pleasant cottage-style homes, which are in a conservation area, are beginning to be sold privately.

Two small but distinct neighbourhoods complete the overall picture of

Shepherd's Bush today. The first, just N of the *Westway* in *Scrubs Lane*, offers a mixture of Edwardian terraces and purpose-built maisonettes. The second is known as Caxton Village, off *Uxbridge Rd* at the Green; it is a quaint network of Victorian terrace streets bordering the busy *M41* out E.

Wendell Park

Looking E from *Emlyn Rd* S of *Cobbold Rd* on the Acton border lies Wendell Park. *Wendell Rd* is a wide tree-lined street largely made up of 1930s terraces. The delightful park and nearby tennis courts are advantages which give the affluent area a sense of space.

The Ryletts and *Ashchurch Park Villas* to the E contain some of the most expensive properties in Shepherd's Bush. Many of the large family houses are still intact despite the recent conversion blitz. Some are double-fronted well proportioned homes, others 3- or 4-storey Victorian terraces. They ooze classic style with their ornate pillars and regal front door steps.

Roads in this district including *Binden* and *Bassein* are wide with plenty of trees and ornate shrubs. Lovely Ravenscourt Park is just a stone's throw away, with Stamford Brook tube a short step S along the *Goldhawk Rd*.

Purpose-built Edwardian maisonettes can be found W of *Askew Rd* towards the *Uxbridge Rd*. The attractive red-brick houses are particularly plentiful in *Cobbold Rd*. Further N in *St Elmo Rd* Victorian terraces dominate. Many have been converted into flats but it is still possible to purchase a whole house in this popular area.

S

Cathnor Park

Similar style continues E of *Askew Rd*. Most are 2-storey although elegant 3-storey versions have been converted successfully in *Westville Rd*.

Ellingham Rd is one of the prime spots in this district. Closed at one end, this peaceful tree-lined street has mainly 2-storey Victorian terraces with attractively wide windows and well proportioned rooms.

Wedged between two bustling districts is Cathnor Park. *Melina Rd*, a particularly pretty corner of this villagy area, has some of the rare cottage-style houses in Shepherd's Bush. Others in the road are 3-storey terraces with basements and front door steps. The *Percy St* area has potential, say agents.

Central Shepherd's Bush

Moving E beyond *Coningham Rd* the houses are taller and divided into smaller units. This is the heart of flat-land. Nearly all of the elegant properties have been converted for the young professional first-time buyers.

The seven or so roads W of the Green are among the most popular in Shepherd's Bush. They are ideally situated for two Metropolitan Line tube stations as well as regular buses on the *Goldhawk* and *Uxbridge Rds*.

Coningham is one of the busier, traffic-wise. For a quieter life try *Hetley*, *St Stephens Avenue* or *Godolphin Rd*. Many of the streets are one-way – others are closed in the middle as a guard against rat-runs between *Uxbridge* and *Goldhawk Rds*.

The flats have classic elegance, sash windows and high ceilings. Outside the roads are wide, light and tree-lined.

Moving N of the *Uxbridge Rd* properties are generally smaller although W of *Wood Lane* to *Loftus Rd* houses are similar to the S.

Stanlake Road is a prime example. Big flat-fronted 4-storey houses with huge basements. However, nearby *Tunis Rd* has a completely different character. Its Victorian terraces are still in one piece on the whole, as are those in neighbouring *Abdale Rd*. This corner is tipped as prime BBC-land.

Loftus Rd – an attractive tree-lined street and conservation area – has one major drawback: Queen's Park Rangers football club which lies at the northern end. This normally quiet road turns into a sea of football fans at the weekend so homes here could be hard to sell.

West of *Loftus* lies an area of Victorian terraces and purpose-built Edwardian maisonettes. *Bloemfontein Rd* runs straight through the neighbourhood and can be busy. Drivers are inclined to use it as a cut-through from the busy *Westway* in the N to the *Uxbridge Rd*.

Nearby is Hammersmith Park, all that is left of the Franco-British Exhibition of 1908, with ornamental gardens, pavillions and pools. The White City pool at Wormholt Park on *Bloemfontein Rd* is also popular and a stone's throw from the notorious White City estate. West of *Wormholt Rd* to *Old Oak Rd* the houses are newer – 1930s mostly. The neighbourhood is pleasant; it borders the Cleverley and the cottage "flower" council estates to the N.

The area above *Sawley Rd* to the *Westway* and E of *Old Oak Rd* to *Wood Lane* is another model-village, again originally council built and known as the Wormholt Estate. This is the 'flower estate', so-called because street names include *Daffodil, Clematis* and *Lilac*: pleasant and varied in style. Much of the stock is privately owned and the neighbourhood looks well cared for. *Milfoil St* to the N is particularly attractive. Flat-fronted grey brick homes with arched doors. The estate's cosy village atmosphere changes dramatically E of *Bloemfontein Rd*.

The White City estate, five roads arranged in a criss cross pattern, houses council tenants in huge blocks of oppressive red brick. *South Africa Rd* to the S runs parallel to Queen's Park Rangers FC and can be used as a cut through to *Wood Lane* around the back of the former White City Stadium – now a major building site which when complete is to house a large section of the BBC: house prices are already beginning to reflect this move both around the Bush and in neighbouring areas.

North of the *Westway* is also council housing. *Du Cane Rd* runs between *Scrubs Lane* and *Old Oak Lane* in Acton past Hammersmith Hospital and Wormwood Scrubs Prison. The area is dominated by the huge prison compound which looks out over the common towards Willesden Junction and Brent in the distance.

The area near the Hammersmith Hospital on *Du Cane Rd* is tipped for revival; more ex-council homes on the 'flower estate' pattern.

Old Oak

This no man's land area is depressing and lacks identity. But a little farther down *Du Cane Rd* towards East Acton tube station is the Old Oak estate with a strong community atmosphere. The estate is isolated from the rest of the area by the railway line. To the NE is the open space of Wormwood Scrubs, to the E the prison. W of the railway is similar estate housing, bounded to the S by the busy six lane Western Avenue.

Braybrook St on the edge of Old Oak Common has attractive flat-fronted terrace houses with sash windows and stone coloured brick. Sadly the pleasant village feel is marred by a sinister view of the imposing prison walls, bright flood lights and watch towers.

Caxton Village

Finally Caxton Village, possibly the most convenient spot in the whole of Shepherd's Bush. Off the *Uxbridge Rd* on the Green this select neighbourhood of Victorian terraces is walking distance from three tube stations, two on the Metropolitan line and Shepherds Bush on the Central. The bus station at the top of *Caxton Rd* can be a problem traffic-wise but the streets are generally quiet and peaceful.

The exclusive Vanderbilt Raquet Club, haunt of Princess Diana, lies to the E of Caxton Village near the *M41*. This top people's tennis club will keep you star-spotting for months.

Borders

Just N of the *Westway* in *Wood Lane* is a quaint collection of roads on the Kensington and Chelsea border. The streets running off *Eynham Rd* are a mixture of purpose-built Edwardian maisonettes and tall terraces converted into flats. The roads are surprisingly quiet considering their close proximity to the *Westway* junction with the *M41* from Shepherd's Bush Green.

Among those estate agents active in this area are:
- Barnard Marcus
- Duncan Gray
- Dunphys
- Foxtons
- Anscombe & Ringland
- Gavels
- Marsh & Parsons
- Winkworths
- Ellis & Co
- Prudential Property Services

S

Soho and Covent Garden

Map ref: p140 (8A)	
Postal districts: W1, WC2	
Boroughs: Westminster (Con), Camden (Lab)	
Rates: W: 136.4p in £. C: 211.68p in £	
Constituencies: City of London & Westminster South (Con), Holborn & St Pancras (Lab)	
Insurance: Scale 1/2	
Conservation areas: Whole area.	
Parking: Residents/meters. Clamps	

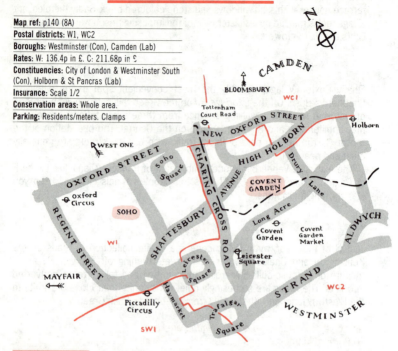

Transport	Tubes: Leicester Square (zone 1, Piccadilly, Northern); Covent Garden (zone 1, Piccadilly). From Leicester Square: Oxford Circus, 10 min (1 change); City, 15 min (1 change); Heathrow 1 hr. British Rail: Charing Cross.
Convenient for	West End entertainment and shopping. City.
Schools	ILEA Division 2: Westminster City C of E (b), Grey Coat Hospital C of E (g).

Flats	S	1b	2b	3b	4b	5b
Average prices	80–100	115–150	180–225+	250–300	–	–
Houses	2b	3b	4b	5b	6/7b	8b
Average prices	–	500+	→	–	–	–

The properties	Pressure from commercial uses means very few buildings are homes. These include rare, lovely pre-Victorian houses, flats above shops, conversions of warehouses etc, and some stylish, extremely expensive new-build. An exciting, if noisy, place to live.
The market	Restricted supply and growing demand as area was cleaned up sent prices rocketing. Covent Garden established since Market transformation; Soho catching up fast as businessmen join the indigenous Italians and Chinese. Local searches: Westminster 1 week, Camden 12 weeks.

Area Profile

Soho and Covent Garden are in the very heart of London. They are, these days, largely business and entertainment centres, attracting many tourists and Londoners to their theatres, clubs and restaurants. The two areas are very different, with distinct characters: Covent Garden's a mixture of theatrical spaciousness, earthy market bustle and bohemianism. Soho has long been London's 'foreign' quarter, the place where daring Englishmen ventured for a little Continental naughtiness and a good meal. It's still true, though the food may be Chinese or Indonesian and the naughtiness these days is well under control. Both areas are very fashionable places to work as well as live: much of London's film industry, many of its most creative advertising agencies, design firms and publishers are found here. ('Creative' is a key Soho/Covent Garden word.) And both areas are zealously conserved, with many historic buildings under preservation orders.

Consequently the pressure on space is intense. Everyone wants their office, shop, market stall or restaurant here. And in the last three or four years the area has been rediscovered as a place to live. Stories of cheap Soho flats above shops, or old banana warehouses in Covent Garden, are now as much wistful legends as the tales of affordable Docklands warehouses.

What homes there are in Soho and Covent Garden are not immediately apparent, often being tucked away behind the scenes in odd corners off commercial streets, or above the ground-floor shops and first-floor offices. What homes there are are mainly 1- and 2-bedroom flats. There are probably only a dozen whole houses in the whole area. The only alternative is the upper floors of a shop or restaurant forming a 3/4-bedroom maisonette. There are no gardens; balconies and patios, occasionally found in new properties, add greatly to prices. They are rare in conversions. Only a handful of flats are available at any one time with huge demand. New developments are usually snapped up on release. The clean-up in Soho is releasing upper parts of shops for conversion. In residential terms, Covent Garden is improved, Soho is still rising. Many properties are purchased as pieds-à-terre and can be easily let if not required all year round.

An obvious advantage of the area is location. It is within easy strolling distance of West End shops and theatres. The City is a 10-minute tube ride away. The main demand for homes seems to come from bankers and brokers who work in the City and from people with businesses in the West End – the bachelors of both species. In Soho one finds prosperous young single people who enjoy the night-life and may work in the advertising or film industries. In Covent Garden, people with a country home who want a pied-à-terre in town. Quite a few homes are owned by companies for the use of their top people. Others are held as investments and rented out to companies.

Before these folk discovered the area, people lived here. And they still do. The original population is more mixed, made up of elderly people and families who work in the traditional local industries – theatre, shops and restaurants – and who live mainly in rented homes.

Both areas are entirely jumbled: shops, offices, theatres, restaurants, pubs and homes often occur in the same street. These amenities provide the plus side to living here but also cause the disadvantages of congestion, both traffic and pedestrian, noise and extreme difficulty in parking. A less tangible benefit is atmosphere. Old-timers say Covent Garden is past its best – Peter York's 'theme park' tag for the restored Garden is uncomfortably accurate – but Soho

S

still preserves a raffish, villagy feel. It's a great place to live and to work, but a wonderful one to live in if you don't have to work. Nowhere in London is idleness more fun.

Soho

Soho is the area S of *Oxford St*, N of *Leicester Square* and E of *Regent St*. *Charing Cross Rd* divides it from Covent Garden to the W.

In the 16th century Soho was a Royal Park where hunting took place – 'So-ho!', an ancient hunting cry, being the presumed origin of the name. It was developed with grand houses in the 17th century and later settled by the Huguenots, giving the area its abiding continental character. The population increased rapidly in overcrowded houses until a serious outbreak of cholera in 1854 after which aristocratic residents moved out and prostitutes moved in. At the turn of the century new theatres were built along *Shaftesbury Avenue* and *Charing Cross Rd*. Restaurants, invariably started by foreigners, gave the area a gastronomic repuation. One famous French restaurant was typically started by a French family in answer to desperate pleas by visiting compatriots for something decent to eat. After the Second World War strip clubs and clip joints increased and the residential population declined rapidly. This exodus of residents has now stopped and due to a massive clean up campaign mounted by Westminster City council after pressure from the Soho Society, the number of sex clubs has been reduced from 164 to less than 50. The aim is a total of 12 strictly licensed establishments. The area is now famous for its restaurants, specialist shops, and some remaining old-fashioned workshops.

Residential Soho has seen a renaissance in recent years; the second half of 1988 saw the first levelling off in residential property prices in five years. Prices, report agents, have hit levels found in other prime central London areas and they are likely to appreciate in line with Kensington, Knightsbridge and Covent Garden. Crown Estates properties are to be had in Soho; in addition to the usual home-buying obstacles, the Estate's approval must be given to prospective owners.

Soho is still a maze of narrow streets and alleys and forms a conservation area. Many 18th-century and early 19th-century buildings remain, interspersed with later infill developments of varying styles. Homes exist mainly in the form of converted flats above shops or more modern, purpose-built infill developments, again usually over commercial property at ground and possibly first-floor level.

South of *Shaftesbury Avenue*, *Wardour St*, *Gerrard St* (pedestrianised) and *Lisle St* form the core of China Town, a tighly-knit neighbourhood characterised by many excellent restaurants, supermarkets and bakeries. Property here is largely owned by the Chinese community and as yet flats are not being converted for sale. However, if council plans for a Housing Improvement Zone in the area come to fruition, this situation may change. There is also evidence of non-Chinese investment in local property. Shaftesbury PLC own an increasing number of buildings. St John's Hospital in *Lisle St* is still up for sale.

North of *Shaftesbury Avenue*, the area where *Brewer St*, *Berwick St*, *Wardour St* and *Old Compton St* meet is the scruffier part of Soho. But such is demand, prices here are only relatively cheaper. These streets still house the largest share of the sex industry (include *Great Windmill St*, *Archer St*, *Tisbury Court* and *Walkers Court*) and there are few flats, although a refurbished building offering 'character conversions' was available last winter in *Brewer St*; prices are £89,950 for a studio, £225,000 for a 2-bed flat and £350,000 for a penthouse with 2 balconies. In nearby *Rupert St*, Consolidated Property are refurbishing and converting houses for use as four shops and 20 flats. On completion late this year, studios will be around £110,000 and 1-bed flats in the region of £140,000. Consolidated Property are major freeholders in the Soho and Covent Garden areas. Several renowned Italian delicatessens and cafés are also in these streets and further along *Old Compton St*, now much improved due to the council clean up, there are one or two small infill developments. The council is pedestrianising the cul-de-sac courts around here which should enhance the popularity of these streets. *Golden Square* and surrounding roads, *Upper* and *Lower St James St* and *John St* and *Great Pulteney St* are more 'respectable' and quieter, but again few homes are available as this is more of a business district. However the former Ear, Nose & Throat Hospital in *Golden Square* itself is being redeveloped by Greycoat who are including 14 flats, which seem to have been well-planned, with car parking spaces. these should be available around April 1989.

S

On the W fringe of Soho, towards *Regent St*, *Kingly St*, the famous *Carnaby St* and *Fouberts Place* are largely shopping areas – becoming more fashionable again – and the occasional flat may come on to the market. However, close by in *Marshall St* is Marshall House, a block of 14 1-bedroom and nine 2-bedroom flats, completed last September. All were sold off-plan but many have come back on the market. A 1-bed was £140,000 last winter, while a large 2-bed was being offered at

Behind the shopfronts and the neon, much of Soho is old. It was a fashionable suburb in the late 17th and 18th centuries, and some houses still survive from these periods. These, in Meard Street, have recently been restored after falling into disrepair. Door, elaborate doorcase and railings are all perfect examples of their period.

£215,000. A 3-storey Victorian building with a basement, unmodernised and gutted, was on the market in the street last winter: over £400,000 was being asked. *Newburgh* and *Marshall Sts* have recently been recobbled and the public swimming pool in *Marshall St* has been refurbished. *Fouberts Place* is due to be repaved as well. Sandringham Court in *Dufours Place* is a popular development, completed by Barratts in 1987; resales do come up occasionally, a studio was being offered at the end of '88 for £125,000. For £285,000, a 2-bedroom maisonette may be had in a Georgian terrace house in *Lexington St*, in fine condition and over a shirtmaker's shop.

Great Marlborough St, *Noel St* and N of here is unlikely to be fruitful for homes, being more of a business/office area. *Poland St*, *Broadwick St* with its Georgian terraces and *D'Arblay St* are more popular and more expensive. *Poland St* has a modern mixed block of offices and flats; a 1-bed flat was marketed last winter at £135,000. There are popular developments at *15 Hollen St* and *68 Broadwick St* but resales are rarely available. A small block of eight flats on the corner of *Poland St/Broadwick St* produces the occasional resale.

Berwick St, S of *Broadwick St*, houses the well-known fruit and vegetable market and is therefore very noisy and delightfully messy during the day. The council is to pedestrianise this part of the street and provide permanent stalls down the centre in 1989.

Meard St is unique in having a splendid terrace of early 18th century houses (grade II listed) a few of which are still in single occupation, most having been split into flats. Tenanted until 1987, the estate has now been auctioned and split up so resales are likely in the future. Prices tend to be high to reflect the scarcity of this kind of period house. One of the two remaining intact houses in the street fetched close to £½ million last summer and an unmodernised 1-bed flat was available at the end of 1988 for £145,000. This is a pedestrian through-way – but beware cycle couriers – newly cobbled at the end of 1988.

The streets leading N from *Shaftesbury Avenue* to *Soho Square* are grander. *Dean St*, *Frith St* and *Greek St* are prestigious addresses. There are several fine restaurants and famous clubs. Many upper storeys to restaurants were purchased for refurbishment in '88 and should be appearing on the market during '89. At the northern end of these streets one or two Georgian houses may remain intact. There are some houses in *Frith St*, for instance: one has become an hotel, another has been expensively restored as a home or office. Flats in these streets will all be pricy and in the *Square* itself, the most expensive of all. Kings House, a modern block in the NE corner of the Square, houses 10 flats. The whole building is for sale for around £1.5 million. Townsend House in *Dean St* is a 1950s block; at the time of writing, a studio was available for £105,000, a 1-bed flat for £130,000, and a 2-bed for £169,000. Busy *Wardour St* is famous for the film industry but there is little scope for accommodation (except some company lets at £200-300 per week). On the edge of Soho is Centrepoint House, an 8-storey block next to the famous office tower on *St Giles High St*. The 36 refurbished 2-bed maisonettes range from £135,000-£145,000, depending on the view. They are being sold with 35 year leases.

Unmodernised flats (or whole upper parts) are occasionally available at lower prices but this situation is unlikely to continue for long; in the last year, unmodernised properties have become very scarce. At *Cambridge Circus*, on a site between *Old Compton St* and *Moor St*, Consolidated Property hope to start work late this year on a large mixed development of homes, shops and offices.

Covent Garden

The area S of *High Holborn*, E of *Kingsway* and N of *The Strand* takes its name from the development, in the early 17th century, of a former convent garden to form an Italian-style piazza laid to an Inigo Jones design. The original fashionable residents moved west and by the middle of the century a fruit and vegetable market had started and grew rapidly. In the 18th century it became an area of seedy lodging houses and brothels. By early 19th century the neighbourhood had been transformed by the market which had expanded and been taken over by traders in all manner of goods. In 1830, the Duke of Bedford organised the construction of the market building in an attempt to restore order. The market remained, in greater or lesser degrees of picturesque confusion, until 1974. Londoners grew to love the fruit, vegetable and flower stalls, the ribaldry of the market traders – and the pubs which opened at six in the morning to cater for them. Covent Garden became a unique mixture of market traders and actors, banana wholesalers and ballet dancers.

When the market finally moved out, an epic row began about the area's fate. A giant scheme to knock most of it down was thwarted by an energetic local campaign and the GLC converted the central market building into a specialist shopping centre which has become a hugely successful tourist attraction. This started the transformation of the area around the market which originally comprised many fruit and vegetable warehouses, hardware stores and workshops of various kinds. Once plans for wholescale redevelopment for offices were successfully opposed, the piecemeal regeneration of the area began which has resulted in warehouses being converted into flats, the retention of small shops and the pedestrianisation of many courts.

Houses are very scarce, a few remaining around *Mercer St* and *Shorts Gardens* (likely to sell in excess of £½ million). Most accommodation is flats above shops and restaurants or in a selection of prestigious purpose-built developments, mainly recent, and again usually with commercial uses at ground floor level.

S

About 35% of home-buyers come from within the area, not families – there are very few – but couples and businessmen who appreciate the life and geography of Covent Garden. Period properties, on the whole, are small; conversions must fit in to these dimensions. Few flats have balconies, let alone terraces. Space for development in Covent Garden and Soho is clearly limited; such is the pressure that recently Phoenix Gardens, one of the few open, public spaces in Covent Garden, has come under threat. A proposal for future development was vigorously opposed by local residents.

Houses are very scarce, a few remaining around *Mercer St* and *Shorts Gardens*; a house in *Mercer St* made £475,000 last summer and, at the time of writing, another is for sale for £550,000. This is one of six freehold houses in Covent Garden. Most accommodation is flats above shops and restaurants or in a selection of prestigious purpose-built developments, mainly recent, and again usually with commercial uses at ground floor level.

The borough boundary between Camden and Westminster runs along *Shelton St*. To the north is Seven Dials (*Monmouth St, Shorts Gardens, Earlham St, Mercer St*) which is a very popular place to live, together with *Neal St* and *Neal's Yard*, now both pedestrianised, the latter packed with wholefood cafés and organic farm produce. One particularly sought-after development is *Seven Dials Court*, built around an attractive landscaped courtyard at first floor level and approached from *Shorts Gardens* leading through to *Neals Yard*. *Mathews Yard* off *Shorts Gardens* is on the market, a new development of 3 houses, three 1/2-bed flats and three 4-bed maisonettes. Period conversions in *Monmouth St* are popular, while 15 new flats are being built by Taylor Woodrow on the Texaco Garage site in *Monmouth St*. The two penthouses will have terraces, the rest of the flats will be 1/2-bed. There will also be four shops. Late '89, early '90 should see completion. At *19 Mercer St* is another recently completed development in the Comyn Ching triangle. These seven luxury flats have balconies or roof terraces. One flat was resold in mid '88, a 3-bedroom maisonette with 2 patios, for £265,000.

Moving over to *Endell St* (still in Camden), is a noisier, so somewhat cheaper, corner. Conversions can be found in *Betterton St*. *Drury Lane* is again a rather busy street – especially around theatre-time – but a number of developments are under way or planned. *46 Drury Lane*, at the end of *Broad Court*, will comprise 18 flats and a 4th floor penthouse with three terraces. The red-brick style is in keeping with the local architecture and should be completed in March '89. The refurbishment and conversion of nos 158 and 159, 5-storey buildings, should be completed around February '89. There will be two 1-bed, one with a balcony, the other with a terrace, and three 2-bed maisonettes, all with 25 year leases. A shop and wine bar/restaurant will occupy the ground floor. Bruce House, a grade II listed building owned by Westminster council, now a hostel, is due to be developed. A new purpose-built hostel for about 60 people will be built behind the existing façade, the rest of the site being put to further residential and perhaps retail use. Bucklesway Developers have been asked to submit plans. Market House in *Parker St* was completed in May '88. The 4 3-bedroom maisonettes have some outside space; two remain at time of writing. There are also six 1/3-bed flats.

In general the higher rates in Camden do not put purchasers off as there is a huge shortage of property. High service charges are much more likely to deter purchasers.

On the corner of *Upper St Martin's Lane* and *West St* is the Thorn EMI office skyscraper – and refurbishment proposals for it are said to include 14 flats. Otherwise, theatres, clubs, restaurants and offices occupy this street. *Long Acre* is largely shops and offices but the quieter *Floral St* has a couple of extremely popular developments – about 20 flats at Nos 16 and 30, where resales have proved infrequent since they were first sold three years ago.

All streets close to the Piazza are very much coveted, although most of the buildings which overlook the market – and the buskers performing in front of the portico of St James' Church – are in commercial use. Period conversions may be available occasionally in *King St*, *Henrietta St*, *Maiden Lane* and *New Row*. A development at *35 King St* is due for completion in March 1990. The new building behind the existing façade will have office space, two shops and 10 1- and 2-bed flats, with access from *Floral St*. The council are pedestrianising parts of *Floral St*, towards *Garrick St*. The Moss Bros building in *Bedford St* is to go and the replacement will have 7 homes as well as offices and shops. Completion 1990. Off *Bedford St*, behind the Coliseum in *Bedford Court*, is a development of 10 flats with private balconies – more resales have occurred here. Peabody plan further development for *Bedford Court*. Following an appeal, permission was given for office and residential use, but a local covenant reserving the land for artisans' dwellings must be waived before building commences. Work is in progress on phase 3 of the new Charing Cross Police Station on *William IV St* and *Agar St*.

The Royal Opera House fronting onto *Bow St* is due to undertake a massive redevelopment scheme involving properties in *Russell St*, *James St* and *Long Acre*. Uncertainty may affect sales of some properties adjoining or overlooking the proposed site. The redevelopment may include some housing. *Hanover Place* has some converted warehouse buildings. 'Period' conversions may be available in *Russell St*, *Tavistock St* and *Wellington St*.

Some council flat resales are becoming available in Covent Garden as the Right to Buy three-year period comes to an end. These are likely to be up to 30% cheaper than equivalent private homes if they are in municipal blocks rather than conversions. The £110,000 being asked for a 1-bed, ex-council flat in *Betterton St* is £30-40,000 less than average prices.

Residential letting is common in Covent Garden. Last winter, a furnished studio could be had for £150-175 a week, a 1-bed from £200 and a 2-bed from £300 up. *21 Mercer St*, a 3-bedroom house with modern interior, was available for £650 a week. Marketed property is often advertised as suitable for owner occupation or for residential letting, which is the case for three unmodernised flats in a property in *Endell St*.

Strand

Just beyond Covent Garden, between *The Strand* and *Embankment*, Tarmac are refurbishing houses in *Craven St* as part of the Charing Cross Redevelopment Scheme. They will probably become offices as well as homes. Independent of this project, a grade II listed Georgian house is for sale in the street for £775,000. Modern luxuries, such as a sauna, supplement original features. South of *The Strand* in *Buckingham St*, a handsome Georgian house has been modernised to provide 6 flats on the third and fourth floors. On release last year, asking prices for the 1-bed flats ranged from £160,000 to £225,000. Most of the quiet, pleasant area south of *The Strand* is commercial, but other flats may be found above offices.

S

Among those estate agents active in this area are:
- Bradleys & Eckhardt
- E A Shaw
- Realty (London Property Brokers)
- Sweby Cowan

South Kensington, Earl's Court, West Brompton

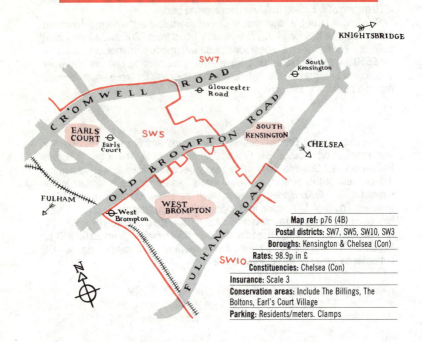

Map ref: p76 (4B)

Postal districts: SW7, SW5, SW10, SW3

Boroughs: Kensington & Chelsea (Con)

Rates: 98.9p in £

Constituencies: Chelsea (Con)

Insurance: Scale 3

Conservation areas: Include The Billings, The Boltons, Earl's Court Village

Parking: Residents/meters. Clamps

Transport   Tubes: South Kensington, Gloucester Rd (zone 1, District, Circle, Piccadilly), Earl's Court (zone 1, District, Piccadilly), West Brompton (zone 2, District). from South Kensington to: Oxford Circus 12 min (1 change), City 21 min (1 change), Heathrow 41 min.

Convenient for   West End. Heathrow by tube or M4. Miles from centre: 2.

Schools   ILEA zone 1: St Thomas More, Holland Park School. Private: Lycee Francaise, Falkner House (g), St James Independent Schools (b)(g).

Flats	S	1b	2b	3b	4b	5b
Average prices	80–110	100–175	130–275+	180–400+	325–450+	–
Houses	2b	3b	4b	5b	6/7b	8b
Average prices	200–325+	250–500+	300–500+	500+	700–1m+	800–1m+

The properties   The peaceful, leafy streets and squares hold large brick and stucco terraces, target of much redevelopment into luxury flats. Flats, converted or p/b, reign, but there are enclaves of mewsy cottages, artists' studios and large villas.

The market   South Kensington saw its share of Big Bang buyers, company or individuals, as homes or for investment. Foreign interest has been strong, too. The huge villas of The Boltons account for the £2 million figure above. Earl's Court is catching up its more salubrious neighbours. Local searches: 7 days.

Area Profile

South Kensington, Earls Court and West Brompton, three diverse areas, form a largely residential, triangular swathe between Chelsea and Kensington proper, narrowing towards the point where the *Cromwell Rd's Thurloe Place* end meets *Brompton Rd*, and Knightsbridge begins.

The enormous (particularly in South Ken and Earl's Court) dignified terraced houses had for many years been hotels or cheap, if seedy, rented flats and bedsits. But no longer. The area is still dotted with concentrations of hotels, be they smart South Kensington establishments or Earls Court B-&-Bs; but the rocketing values have finally made it viable to expend love, care and attention on the tall, decaying houses. Skips, scaffolding and interior decorators abound, classy developers of the Rosehaugh, Residential Holdings, Warwick Balfour ilk are at work. And the property press has been called down to admire the clever (some state-of-the-art) conversions of, it seems, virtually every house in *Evelyn Gardens*, the *Onslows*, the *Cranleys*, the *Courtfields* . . .

The area as a whole lies between *West Cromwell*, *Cromwell*, and *Imperial Institute Rds* to the N, *Fulham Rd* to the S, the West London railway line in the W and *Brompton Rd* and The Oratory church in the E. It contains some of the most expensive homes in London – the handsome £2 million plus villas in *The Boltons* – and some of the most down at heel in Earls Court's bedsitter land.

Two major factors influenced the development of the area, previously covered with market and nursery gardens. The first was the Great Exhibition of 1851 in Hyde Park, profits from which were used to build the major museums complex on the border with Knightsbridge and the two main routes along which they stand, *Cromwell* and *Exhibition Rds*. The second and most important influence was the arrival of the Metropolitan and District railways during the 1860s, which allowed speedy access to central London. Ease of access remains one of the biggest attractions of the area.

With the exception of West Brompton, the rest of the area has three tube lines within walking distance, one being the Piccadilly Line which runs direct to the airport: a big plus for this international area. *Cromwell Rd* also links directly with the M4 to Heathrow, drawing tourists to the hotels in the area and the transitory population which characterises Earls Court in particular. The area is probably the most cosmopolitan in the already various Royal Borough. Earls Court, once known as the Polish Corridor then Kangaroo Valley after successive waves of settlers, is now home to a mini United Nations and is also a favourite haunt of London's gay community. Some Middle Eastern families still remain in South Ken but it is no longer the 'Saudi Ken' of a few years ago. The French have colonised the area around the Lycée Français near the tube.

One thing all the neighbourhoods have in common is leafy garden squares, although there is only one public garden – in *Redcliffe Square*, West Brompton, unless you count Brompton Cemetery, adopted as a de facto park by the locals. Hyde Park is not that far away, though.

The most densely-populated part of the area lies to the N of *Old Brompton Rd*, where red-brick mansion blocks abound and the majority of houses have been converted to flats. The most desirable chunk lies between here and the *Fulham Rd*. Many of the terraces of big brick and stucco houses have been converted into flats but there are still enclaves of single-family houses in small-scale village streets, charming cobbled mews and peaceful cul-de-sacs. Shops are generally clustered around the tube stations and restricted to the main roads bounding the neighbourhoods.

S

Old Brompton Rd, running W-E, a busy boulevard, cuts through the middle of the area. Here the shops, pubs and big brick mansion blocks tend to congregate in groups, the shops near main junctions such as Earl's Court Rd and around South Ken underground station. A string of smarter shops, boutiques, restaurants, pubs, and antique shops stretch along most of Fulham Rd. Cromwell Rd, a wide noisy six-lane highway leading to the M4, has hotels standing side by side with tall terraced houses divided into flats.

Smith's Charity and Thurloe Estates

This strip between Old Brompton Rd to the N and Fulham Rd to the S, extending W to Drayton Gardens, is the heart of residential South Kensington. Most of this district is owned by the Henry Smith's Charity, which has held the land since the 17th century. Consequently, a large proportion of homes in the area remain leasehold and are subject to strict controls designed to keep up the standard and values of the properties. Smith's Charity's holding is concentrated around the Onslows, Cranleys, Evelyn Gardens and the Pelhams. A degree of estate control also applies to the Thurloe Estate (lying between Pelham St S, Thurloe Place N and Brompton Rd E) but here a number of residents have bought their freeholds under the Leasehold Reform Act.

One of the gems of the Smith's Charity Estate is Pelham Crescent. Elegant white stucco terraced houses sweep in a semi-circle around leafy private gardens, which screen the Victorian crescent from Brompton Rd. Stretches of black iron railings, columned porches and green Victorian street lamps complete the scene. Most of the houses are still in single-family occupation. The white stucco continues into Pelham Place, which curves across Pelham St, a feeder road between South Kensington, Knightsbridge and the Fulham Rd. Pelham Place leads to Thurloe Square, one of the area's most exclusive garden squares. Here 4-storey and basement brick and stucco houses (mainly split into flats) stand on three sides of an elongated private garden. Residents in the SE corner of the square enjoy an exceptional view of the entrance to the Victoria & Albert Museum at the top of Thurloe Place with its imposing crown-shaped stone tower.

To the E of the square lies a group of Georgian terraced houses in Alexander Square and neighbouring streets. Despite its name, Alexander Square is a single street of early 19th century 3/4-storey brick and stucco houses, overlooking small private gardens. The gardens act as a barrier between the houses and Brompton Rd as it winds from Knightsbridge to Fulham Rd. Just beyond here, Brompton Rd merges with Fulham Rd at fashionable Brompton Cross with its cluster of ultra-smart shops and restaurants and the newly-revamped art nouveau Michelin Building. Sydney Place combines with the S leg of Onslow Square E to form the main through route from South Kensington to Chelsea.

Onslow Square proper lies to the W of the main road. Immaculate terraces of 4-storey 1846 houses with columned porches overlook award-winning gardens in this choice square. The houses were split into flats during a major conversion programme in the 1960s. White stucco and brick and stucco terraces of varying sizes with the same columned porches are the dominant style in Onslow Gardens (tree-lined communal gardens), Sumner Place, Cranley Place and the N arms of Cranley Gardens. Most of these have already been converted into flats and a noticeable number are now being upgraded to top-of-the-market levels. In Onslow Mews East, what looks like a row of cottages is in fact two handsome 3-bed newly-built houses. At the S end of *Cranley Gardens* and *Evelyn Gardens*, stucco gives way to Victorian red-brick flat blocks. The most attractive examples are the newly-refurbished Dutch-style buildings with unusual brick and white stucco porches which line the S arm of *Evelyn Gardens*. This entire swathe has seen a greater concentration of developers' scaffolding over the past few years than almost any other corner of town.

In contrast to this densely-populated area is a network of small streets just off *Fulham Rd* between *Elm Place* and Brompton Hospital's northern complex. They lie outside Smith's Charity's estate. *Elm Place* (2-storey vine-clad late Georgian cottages with tiny front gardens) and *Selwood Place* (fine Georgian terrace on the N side) are charming, leafy streets. *Selwood Place* is blocked off at its W end by the back of St Peter's Armenian Church in *Cranley Gardens*.

An arched brick entrance and steps on the E side of *Elm Place* leads up to *Regency Terrace*, a group of 3-storey brick and stucco terraced maisonettes above the rear of shops fronting *Fulham Rd*. As the name suggests, the houses line a Regency-style terrace at first floor level, complete with black iron railings and street lamps. They look down on *Lecky Street*, a quiet little private cul-de-sac of white 2-storey houses with columned porches. A number of mews streets are spread throughout the area, by far the most picturesque being *Roland Way*, tucked away off *Roland Gardens*. Pretty painted cottages decorated with hanging baskets and colourful window boxes give this cobbled private street its charm. A row of 24 luxury 3/4-bedroom freehold terraced houses is being

Stucco and the term cottage do not often go together but they coexist happily in this house in Elvaston Place, called a cottage despite its classical rusticated stucco and elegant door surround. The trees hide the lower pair of windows: there are six, set symetrically in the facade. The six-panel door echoes the windows. These features recur on the larger homes.

built jointly by Lovell Homes and Balfour Beatty Homes in the newly-named *Eagle Place* and in *Roland Way* itself. The first nine houses went on the market for between £450-825,000 in autumn 1988 and the remaining 15, which will be priced at around £600,000 each, are to be launched this spring.

The S end of *Roland Way* leads into *Thistle Grove*, a shady pedestrian walkway lined with green Victorian lanterns and trees overhanging the rear walls of *Evelyn Gardens*. Small houses and cottages of varying styles merge with tall brick and stone mansion blocks. *Drayton Gardens*, which forms the W boundary of the area, combines a mix of styles from brick and stucco terraced houses with front gardens (NW) to Dutch-style brick and stone mansion blocks and modern flats. At the S junction with *Fulham Rd* stands the Cannon Cinema and the neighbouring South Kensington Squash Club. The *Fulham Rd* from here back E to Brompton Cross has a high concentration of expensive shops and restaurants, belieing the somewhat scruffy reputation the street held a decade ago. It is now far quieter and smarter than the *King's Rd*. The Fulham Rd is sometimes considered to be in Chelsea, but in this stretch forms a clear boundary between the two districts. The traffic – and parking – in this road is especially problematic.

Museum/Lyceé Area

As its name suggests, the area is dominated by the major museums standing along *Exhibition/Cromwell Rds*. The Science, Natural History, Geological and Victoria & Albert Museums were built following the Great Exhibition of 1851. The museum developments and improved transport links attracted wealthy residents to the area. Nowadays, the neighbourhood is particularly popular with the French, who have established their own colony near the Lyceé Français. The school, together with the French Institute, covers a whole block stretching from *Cromwell Rd* through to *Harrington Rd*.

South Kensington underground station and a number of busy main roads have attracted a mix of shops, hotels and other uses, ranging from the College of Psychic Studies to the British Association of Cancer Research, both in *Queensberry Place*. The Aga Khan's gleaming cultural centre for Ismaili Muslims stands in *Thurloe Place* opposite the V&A Museum. Amid all the hustle and bustle, *Bute St*, with its cluster of small shops, manages to retain a delightfully village-type atmosphere. The busy junction by the tube station is dominated by the red-brick inter-war Melrose Court flats block on the S side. The station site itself is to be redeveloped by Rosehaugh, Tarmac and Amec with a deck across the platforms supporting 142 flats, 50,000 sq ft of offices and 30 shops.

Many of the houses around here are enormous, and they have nearly all been divided into flats at various periods and to various levels of quality. The only exceptions can be found in *Reece Mews*, a pleasant little cobbled street running N-S between *Harrington* and *Old Brompton Rds*. An attractive development of brand new 2-storey brick mews houses fits in well with the older 3-storey painted cottages.

The NW corner of the mews lies empty, forming part of the Iranian Embassy site. The Iranian Government planned to build an embassy on the site, which fronts *Queen's Gate*, in the 1970s but abandoned the idea. Planning consent has now expired and there were no new proposals for the site at the time of writing. Standing next to the empty plot is St Augustine's Church. On the other side of the church, *Manson Place* is a wide cul-de-sac of tall brick and stucco terraces, which has come up noticeably in recent years.

Courtfield

Between *Cromwell Rd* in the N and *Old Brompton Rd* in the S is a varied district which looks to Gloucester Road rather than South Kensington tube as its transport centre. *Queen's Gate*, running N-S is a wide tree-lined boulevard – wide enough for central parking – flanked by tall brick and stucco apartment buildings and hotels. To the W lies *Stanhope Gardens* with its companion mews to the W, E and S, where a number of small-scale development schemes and quality conversions have taken place. *Stanhope Gardens* itself is one of a series of garden squares in the neighbourhood. 4-storey brick and stucco terraced houses line the private gardens, the E arm forming the most attractive stretch.

The mews contain 2/3-storey brick/painted cottages, some with roof terraces and most with their own garages.

Clareville St to the S is a narrow road branching off busy *Gloucester Rd*. Painted houses and cottages stand alongside a handful of offices, the Chanticleer Theatre and the Webber Douglas Academy of Dramatic Art. The street becomes a lane as it runs S past Our Lady of Victories RC School (Fulham and South Kensington adult education institute) and wends its way towards *Old Brompton Rd*. Parallel is tree-lined *Clareville Grove*, a peaceful oasis within easy walking distance of both Gloucester Rd and South Ken tube stations. It is easily the most highly-regarded street in the neighbourhood with its variety of attractive period houses, front gardens and hedges. The street becomes more mixed to the S with the appearance of *Clareville Court*, a modern brick flats block and the PLO's London headquarters near the junction with *Old Brompton Rd*, which stretch back to *Clareville St*. Across *Gloucester Rd*, *Hereford Square* is one of the best preserved garden squares in Kensington. Its three symmetrical terraces of 3/4-storey white stucco houses built in 1848 remain unaltered, except where some parts were rebuilt following war damage. Tucked away behind the square is an opulent, low-level new house, on the market last year for £2½m.

Between the square and *Bolton Gardens* to the W, the streets are dominated by concentrations of red brick Victorian mansion flats. In *Gledhow* and *Bina Gardens* they overlook private gardens. *Wetherby Gardens*, an increasingly popular street, has a mix of styles ranging from brick and stucco paired villas to late 19th century Dutch-style red brick buildings. Exceptional examples of this 'South Ken Dutch' look, with its steep gables, riot of terracotta decoration and tall chimneys, are found in *Harrington* and *Collingham Gardens*. Gilbert of the Gilbert and Sullivan opera partnership lived in *Harrington Gardens*. The houses have since been converted into smaller units or for other purposes. They have rear communal gardens and properties on the E arm of the square also pleasantly overlook private gardens behind houses in *Wetherby Gardens*.

To the N lies *Courtfield Gardens*, another garden square lined with tall Victorian brick and stucco terraces of varying quality. A scheme to turn nos 14 and 15 into 25 flats has received planning permission. The appearance of hotels in the square on the border with Earls Court sets the pattern for the streets between here and *Cromwell Rd*. Hotel signs abound along the often scruffy terraces. The big hotels cluster around Gloucester Rd tube station to the E. A £42 million redevelopment is under way on the vacant site behind the station, including a 12-storey block containing 104 1/3-bedroom flats (Cheval Properties as managing agents for Ashburn Investment Corporation: due for completion May 1991). Dotted among the tall terraces and mansion blocks is a series of mews, mostly residential, such as *Laverton Mews* – a tiny cobbled cul-de-sac – and *Gasper Mews* with its white-painted cottages.

S

Earls Court

When Earls Court was developed in the second half of last century, it was regarded as a favoured residential suburb. The well-to-do moved into the substantial Victorian terraced houses which sprang up around the original Georgian village. Agricultural and service workers lived alongside in modest little cottages. Now, ironically, the situation is reversed. The workers have set up home in the big houses, long since divided up into flats and bedsits, and the prosperous pay high prices to live in the remaining cottages.

The quaint colour-washed cottages lie tucked away in a triangle of streets behind busy *Cromwell* and *Earls Court Rds*, known locally as Kenway Village. Although only a few minutes' walk from the hubbub of *Earls Court Rd*, this pocket of freehold family dwellings retains its villagy character, in sharp contrast to the rest of the area. Properties here are among the most sought after in Earls Court. The enclave, which formed the heart of the original village, gets its name from *Kenway Rd*, its S boundary. Tree-lined *Wallgrave Rd* is the quietest and most popular street, pleasant and leafy with 2-storey and basement brick cottages fronted by black wrought iron railings.

Child's Place and *Child's St* are cul-de-sacs running parallel to each other but noisier because they lie directly off *Earls Court Rd*. The former has mainly 3-storey brick houses and the latter 2-storey cottages with small flowery front gardens. A black wrought iron gate in *Child's St* leads into *Child's Walk*, a charming private passageway of 2-storey cottages lying no more than 10 feet apart. Tubs of flowers, window boxes and benches (complete with large snoozing cat) line the short alleyway, giving the impression of a single patio garden. *Kenway Rd* itself is a mix of 3-storey cottages and houses, rubbing shoulders with shops, restaurants and a rash of travel agents.

North of the village at the busy junction of *Cromwell Rd* with *Earls Court Rd*, is a new apartment block – Cromwell Court – built by Wates. The 80 luxury flats and the eleven townhouses tucked away behind have already pushed up prices in Earls Court. North of the Cromwell Rd, Cromwell Crescent is an enclave of SW5. One pair of houses has just been converted into 10 2-bed flats. S of the village, *Hogarth Rd* marks the NE boundary of the area's hotel land. With *Earls Court Gardens*, it forms a buffer of Victorian terraced buildings between Kenway village and the red-brick gabled, mansion blocks which dominate the rest of the area of *Earls Court Rd*. *Barkston Gardens*, an increasingly fashionable group of red-brick, overlooks a large private garden lined with tall trees and enclosed by hedges and iron railings. Most of the N side is given over to hotels but the rest remains residential. The *Bramham Gardens* blocks are also built around a tree-lined garden square.

Earls Court Rd itself is dirty, noisy and battered by heavy traffic. It forms the southbound leg of the Earls Court one-way traffic system, nicknamed locally 'Juggernaut Alley'. Proposals to build a relief road alongside the West London railway line to take traffic off the *Earls Court Rd* are currently being considered by the Government. If WEIR, as it is called, materialises, *Earls Court Rd* and *Warwick Rd* (the northbound section of the one-way system) would probably revert to two-way traffic. Whether they would be any quieter is another question, but at least the heavy vehicles should diminish.

The character of *Earls Court Rd* has been determined largely by the transitory and tourist population which has gravitated towards the area because of its central location. Fast food shops, restaurants, late night supermarkets, travel agents and newsagents predominate, spreading along both sides of the road from the underground station. W of *Earls Court Rd*, the streets of terraces lying between *Warwick Rd* W and *Penywern Rd* S make up the main chunk of hotel/bedsitter land. *Nevern Square* with its red and brown brick buildings fronting private gardens is primarily residential, however, with only a few hotels sprinkled around the square. One block S at the junction of *Trebovir Rd* and *Warwick Rd* sits Kensington Mansions, a 5-storey and basement 1880s block.

Earls Court Square is the neighbourhood's main square, lined on three sides by 4/5-storey ornate stucco fronted houses, divided into flats. The Poetry Society also has its headquarters here. The buildings look on to mature gardens surrounded by tall trees. By contrast, the S arm of the square comprises 3-storey and basement red-brick and stone gabled buildings. These set the tone for the taller red-brick gabled Wetherby Mansions on both sides of the SE arm of the square. *Warwick Rd* is lined mainly with big late Victorian mansion blocks and undistinguished terraces.

Lying to the W is a series of crescents – *Philbeach Gardens*, *Eardley Crescent* and *Kempsford Gardens*. The condition of properties varies widely but the area is improving, as evidenced by the number of 'luxury' conversion schemes under way.

Tree-lined *Philbeach Gardens* enjoys the advantage of two and a half acres of exceptional landscaped gardens, forming a huge rear communal garden for the properties sweeping around the E curve of the crescent. Styles vary considerably from the heavy brown and red brick buildings at the N entrance to the crescent to the more desirable brick and stucco houses with columned porches at its mid-point.

Eardley Crescent and *Kempsford Gardens*, dubbed Brompton Village by one estate agent, have mainly 3-storey brick and stucco properties, like *Philbeach Gardens*, divided into flats. All three streets suffer from one major drawback. They are choked with traffic trying to park when shows are on at the Earls Court exhibition centre immediately behind. A major expansion scheme is planned for the exhibition centre but a large new car park will be provided to cater for the increased crowds. Properties at the mid-point of the W curve of *Philbeach Gardens* also back onto the railway line and the proposed route of the new road. In addition, *West Cromwell Rd*, the main road lying to the N, has been earmarked as a possible junction for the road. The road plans are starting to appear on searches: the Town Hall will have the latest news. See also 'Transport' chapter.

S

West Brompton

Brompton is one of those London villages which has effectively ceased to exist. Few people, nowadays, would describe themselves as living in Brompton, and this part of SW10, bounded by *Old Brompton Rd* to the N, *Fulham Rd* to the S, and running W from *Drayton Gardens*, is better known as Chelsea SW10 and Kensington SW10. The focal point is *The Boltons*, where handsome white stucco villas are set around an eye-shaped oval garden – unique in London. The huge semi-detached freehold houses with their columned porches and rich ornamentation were built in the 1850-60s to attract the wealthy to the area. They still do. They were originally sold for £1,350 each. Now they fetch around £2 million, more if modernised to the elaborate extent that some are. Some have staff accommodation in the grounds or are still linked to the mews houses at the rear. In the middle of the central gardens is St Mary's Church, with its angel-bedecked spire rising high above the treetops.

The Boltons also gives its name to a network of similarly salubrious streets of big stucco-fronted houses with the same 'villas-in-gardens' character. Leafy *Gilston Rd* has some fine examples with high-walled front gardens. *Milborne Grove* and *Harley Gardens* are desirable small streets with a mix of paired stucco villas and brick and stucco 3/4-storey terraced houses. Houses on the E side of *Harley Gardens* overlook the walled back gardens of properties in *Gilston Rd*, as do the pastel-painted stucco terraced houses in *Priory Walk*.

Large paired brick and stucco villas predominate in *Tregunter Rd*, where properties have the advantage of forecourt parking – a feature of *The Boltons*. *The Little Boltons*, forming the W boundary of the neighbourhood, has more brick and stucco semi-detached houses but is not as grand as *The Boltons*. Caught up in this sea of stucco is cobbled *Cresswell Place*, a charming backwater of 2/3-storey brick cottages. It comes as an unexpected surprise as one turns the corner from *Cresswell Gardens*. No wonder that mistress of the unexpected, Dame Agatha Christie, lived here. To the S lies *Cavaye Place*, a pleasant cul-de-sac of colourful cottages.

Redcliffe Rd a short distance away off *Fulham Rd* is a popular street for rented accommodation. Lined with cherry trees, it is ablaze with blossom in the spring. One street away is *Seymour Walk* – one of the earliest streets in the area, which retains its attractive period character. The oldest terrace in this exclusive cul-de-sac of 2/3-storey houses dates back to 1797. A kink in the road at the S end of the street hides it from *Fulham Rd* and a tree-lined terrace seals off its N end, creating a sense of peaceful seclusion.

Hollywood Rd to the W introduces a commercial note into this predominantly residential area. Smart restaurants, galleries, antique shops and wine bars creep around the corner from *Fulham Rd* into the S end of the street. A new gated mews of 18 town houses and eight flats is being built by LET/Balfour Beatty on the W side of the street on the site of the former Unigate depot. The development should be completed in October/November 1989, marketing May, with prices for 1600 sq ft, 3-bed houses of around £550,000. Larger 4-storey ones with roof garden, conservatory and basement games room/ garage are in the £600,000 region. A similar mews development is planned for nearby. Further N on the opposite side of the street is *Hollywood Mews*, entered through an arch matching the arches of the Hollywood Arms pub (a fringe theatre venue). Modern 2-storey white painted cottages sit around a tiny courtyard with trees in the middle. *Hollywood Rd*, with its mix of brick and stucco homes and red brick flats, merges with *Harcourt Terrace*, a pleasant street of terraced houses, divided into flats.

A surprise lies in store in *Redcliffe Mews*, lying at right angles to *Harcourt Terrace*. The mews was rebuilt in 1987 in traditional style, featuring attractive 2-storey brick cottages with gaily-coloured garages and entrances. Despite its proximity to noisy *Redcliffe Gardens*, the mews is surprisingly quiet thanks to a barrier of big houses separating the two. A short walk away lies *Redcliffe Square*, divided in half by the southbound stretch of the one-way traffic system running between Earls Court and Chelsea. The square is lined by tall ornate brick and stucco terraced houses with French Renaissance-style dormers and polished marble porch columns. Properties on the W side of the square overlook tree-lined gardens occupied by St Luke's Church and those on the E side face the only public gardens in West Brompton. The houses have been converted into flats, as have those in *Redcliffe Gardens*.

Cathcart Rd, *Fawcett St*, *Redcliffe Place*, *Redcliffe St*, *Westgate Terrace* and *Ifield Rd* form another network of streets dominated by 3/4-storey and basement brick and stucco terraced houses split into flats. Cutting a swathe through the area is *Finborough Rd*, the northbound leg of the one-way system. A short distance from the noise and fumes of the main road lies the tranquil haven of Brompton Cemetery, which doubles as a local park. The church hall in

Adrian Mews, backing onto the cemetery, is under threat due to a plan to develop its site with 6 new houses.

The cemetery provides a leafy backdrop for the enclave of pretty artisan cottages in The Billings, just off *Fulham Rd. Billing Place*, *St* and *Rd* form a series of three private cul-de-sacs containing 2-storey and basement terraced cottages. A question mark hangs over The Billings: the proposed relief road, which would run alongside the railway line, could cause the demolition of some homes.

Among those estate agents active in this area are:

- Alex Neil
- Farley & Co
- Allsops
- Cluttons
- W A Ellis
- Stickley & Kent
- Plaza
- Marsh & Parsons
- Farrar Stead & Glyn
- Prudential Property Services
- Jacksons
- Hobart Slater
- Russell Simpson
- Chesterfields
- Winkworths
- Barnard Marcus

S

Southgate and Palmers Green

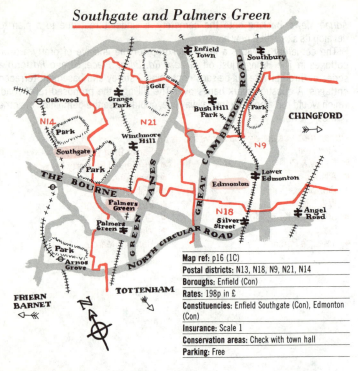

Map ref: p16 (1C)	
Postal districts: N13, N18, N9, N21, N14	
Boroughs: Enfield (Con)	
Rates: 198p in £	
Constituencies: Enfield Southgate (Con), Edmonton (Con)	
Insurance: Scale 1	
Conservation areas: Check with town hall	
Parking: Free	

Transport Tubes: Southgate, Arnos Grove, Oakwood (zones 3a/b, Piccadilly). From Southgate to: Oxford Circus 35 min (1 change), City 30 min (1 change, Heathrow 1hr 15 min. British Rail: Palmers Green, Winchmore Hill to Moorgate, King's Cross; Bush Hill Park, Lower Edmonton to Liverpool St.

Convenient for North Circular, M25. Parks and sports/leisure. Miles from centre: 8.

Schools Enfield Education Authority. Latymer, Alyward, Winchmore, Southgate, St Angela's RC (g). Private: Palmers Green High (g)

Flats	S	1b	2b	3b	4b	5b
Average prices	58–62	63–72	70–80+	80+	90+	–
Houses	2b	3b	4b	5b	6/7b	8b
Average prices	80–125	110–200	125–300+	145–500	160–500+	→

The properties Leafy, suburban homes with gardens in Southgate and Winchmore Hill, including some large expensive ones. Lots of modern houses and flats. Palmers Green has Edwardian 3–4 bed houses, some now flats, Edmonton has smaller terraces and inter-war homes.

The market Commuter country, with trains to City and good access to motorways to attract executives. For junior ranks there are converted flats in cheaper areas; new-build also popular. Local searches 3 weeks.

Area Profile

That part of the *North Circular Rd* which runs between Angel Road BR station and Arnos Grove tube separates two remarkably different areas. Below this dividing line, the northern parts of Tottenham and Wood Green have petered out into a rather colourless hinterland, but head N and as soon as you cross the *North Circular*, the atmosphere begins to change immediately.

The large suburban area beyond the *North Circular Rd*, which comprises Southgate (N14), Palmers Green (N13), Winchmore Hill (N21), and Upper (N18) and Lower (N19) Edmonton, is situated far enough away from the centre of London to be independent of City and West End business, but is still suitable for the commuter – inwards or outwards.

While the journey to the City by British Rail takes around 25-40 minutes from stations like Palmers Green, Lower Edmonton and Winchmore Hill, the potential for inhabitants to work elsewhere is there, thanks to the fact that the *M25, M1, M11* motorways and the *A10* (*Great Cambridge Rd*) are all within reach – if congested.

Edmonton, and also Palmers Green, lying closest to the *North Circular*, are at first similar in style to N Tottenham/Wood Green, with similar shopping facilities serving similar inter-war properties; but already the *feel* of the place is different. Down the wind comes the first whiff of the Alpine North – or, at least, the fresh air from the Green Belt, blowing via a thousand Alpine-plant rock gardens. Indeed, the area changes quite dramatically the further N one travels, becoming more and more green, leafy, suburban and prosperous: with golf clubs, parks, tree-lined streets, huge modern detached houses, and a proliferation of new developments.

The area is populated to a large extent by wealthy, middle-class families and retired (early if possible) couples who moved into the region 20-30 years ago. There is also a large Greek community and, as older couples leave the area to move to smaller houses, more and more properties are being converted into flats – particularly in the southern areas – for younger people, including the ubiquitous young urban professionals. For these, that encircling motorway bracket just over the horizon makes this a good base for a household where one partner may be tied to a local, or Central London, job and the other whose work means travelling to other parts of the country.

Further development and conversion work is now being curtailed thanks to Enfield borough's disinclination to let on-street parking get any more congested. Strict rules apply.

Southgate, Winchmore Hill, Bush Hill Park

This well-off, salubrious area, perched up between the Lea and Barnet villages, holds in the main a wealth of large semis and detached houses set in broad, tree-lined streets. The proximity to Enfield Town and the surrounding green belt is an added advantage. It's served by Enfield Town and Bush Hill BR stations to Liverpool Street; Enfield Chase, Grange Park, and Winchmore Hill BR stations to Kings Cross and Moorgate, and Southgate tube (Piccadilly line to Kings Cross and West End – and on, of course, to Heathrow).

Southgate is a prosperous leafy suburb which falls into three areas: Old Southgate, New Southgate and Winchmore Hill with its village atmosphere. The tube station is Southgate's most surprising landmark: a spirited bit of '30s design, the circular building looks like a spaceship headed for Mars rather than the Underground; it has now been listed. It stands on *Southgate Circus*, where a new flats development is appearing. The road leading down from the Southgate Circus (*High St/Cannon Hill*) is bordered by a technical college and a variety of attractive properties, including little mewsy cottages. The Southgate and District Reform Synagogue now stands on the site of the house belonging to poet Leigh Hunt. Among the neat, untroubled streets of comfortable inter-war houses, new things are appearing – carefully. The recent development off *Fox Lane* is an interesting conversion of an old school house into new apartments, and reflects the policy of preserving the original atmosphere of the area. As well as converting the school, Wimpey have new flats and houses here: prices for the latter can reach £250-300,000.

Churchill Court, consisting of 1- and 2-bedroom retirement apartments and situated to the W of the *A10* on *Church St*, is another example of the many new developments in the area, providing a peaceful alternative to similar schemes closer to Central London.

Going N along *Village Rd* towards Bush Hill Park, the streets become increasingly wider and more tree-lined, with solid 3- and 4-bedroom semis. Just off *Park Avenue* is Laing's recently completed development, Croft Mews, consisting of modern 2-bed flats and houses, and positioned right next to an up-market tennis club. The fact that all the houses were bought before they were even built indicates the popularity of new properties in the area.

A good corner for home hunters, say agents, is currently the triangle made up of *Southbury Rd*, the *West Cambridge Rd* and the Enfield to Bush Hill Park railway line: These streets, they reckon, are more desirable than comparably-priced ones in Edmonton, which 'caught up' in last year's brisk spring market. Agents reckon that the 'Triangle' will regain its lead.

The large homes bordering Bush Hill Park Golf Course continue to be impressively suburban, but it is the village atmosphere of Winchmore Hill, with its neat streets, quaint houses, tidy gardens and attractive pubs, that suggests the prosperity of the area. *Broad Walk*, which leads off the village green with its antique shops, is the Beverley Hills of Southgate/Winchmore Hill. Apparently Rod Stewart once owned one of these vast, recently built properties which have equally vast cars parked in their driveways. £700,000 for a house in this road is cheap.

Broad Walk leads into *The Bourne*, which borders the pleasant Grovelands Park with tennis courts, a putting green, bowling green, and boating lake.

Church Hill leads from Winchmore Hill station to leafy *Eversley Park Rd*, where the new Ashwood Lodge has nine large 2/3-bed, 2-bath flats (fitted kitchens, utility rooms) in the £200,000 bracket.

Palmers Green

To the S lies Palmers Green, a quiet family suburb. In its heyday it was a bastion of Edwardian respectability, whose numerous turn-of-the-century 3- and 4-bed houses, replete with original features, are set along leafy roads. Many of these have been converted into flats, particularly in the *Ulleswater Rd*, *Derwent Rd*, *Lakeside Rd*, *Grovelands Rd*, and *Old Park Rd* ladder. There are good shopping facilities off *Green Lanes* with a number of shops that are open late, but not much in the way of night-life.

During the day, however, and at weekends, residents relax in Broomfield Park which adds numerous sports and leisure facilities to its tranquil lakes.

Transport in the area is not terrific. Nearest tube stations are in Arnos Grove or Bounds Green and the BR service into King's Cross and Moorgate is not all it could be outside of peak hours. However, there is a good bus service into Wood Green and Enfield. Near the station, Pilgrims Close (built by Ideal Homes) is a popular modern development. The studios, 1- and 2-bed flats – some are galleried – fetch between £60-85,000 when they appear for resale. A few streets away, *Windsor Rd* and *Park Avenue* each sport a large Edwardian house being converted to flats. On the borders of Winchmore Hill, Lovell have built 15 1- and 2-bed flats (c £70-80,000) at 'Woodside', *Stonard Rd*.

Perhaps the main point to watch in this area – particularly in Upper Edmonton and Palmers Green – is the projected development of the *North Circular Rd*. Schemes have been drawn up to improve the *North Circular* from *Silver St* to *Upper Fore St* and from *Dysons Rd* to *Hall Lane*, including the building of a fly-over. This is all due to be completed in four years' time.

The development will obviously affect properties bordering the *North Circular*, and house-hunters are already reluctant to buy in this area because of the results of land searches. The development will of course benefit the area in the long run because of the improved transport facilities, but at present it is causing some controversy amongst residents and faint anxiety amongst estate agents.

S

Barratts have recently built 'Arnos Gate': 27 flats and houses in *Arnos Rd*, very close to Arnos Grove tube. On release last year prices were £115-295,000.

Edmonton

Upper Edmonton/Lower Edmonton is bounded by the *A10* to the E, the William Girling Reservoir to the W and the *North Circular* to the S. The area is served by Silver Street and Lower Edmonton BR stations and possesses one of the largest leisure centres in the SE, Picketts Lock.

Edmonton is perhaps the least 'desirable', in estate agents' terms, of the four areas – particularly Lower Edmonton, which is marked by a crop of huge, unsightly high-rise council blocks and a concrete shopping centre which, remarked a local, bears a marked resemblance to a German bunker. Two- to 3-bedroom terraced houses (early 1900s) and inter-war semis, some of which have been converted into flats, are standard in this area, although styles are certainly varied. The Huxley and Westerham estates offer particularly good properties.

Moving W along *Church St* (inter-war semis) the area becomes increasingly attractive with many playing fields and sports grounds providing pleasant backdrops to the houses. Here, the *A10*, bustling importantly off towards Cambridge, runs for a while with allotments bordering both sides of the road.

Among those estate agents active in this area are:
- Adam Kennedy
- Bairstow Eves
- Winkworths
- Ewings
- Meadway
- Prudential Property Services
- Buckinghams
- Craigs

St John's Wood

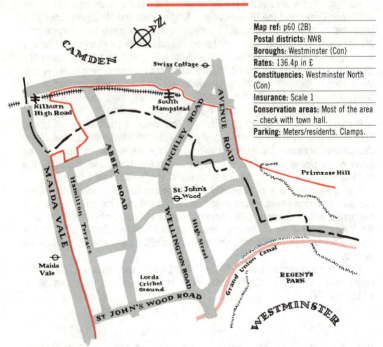

Map ref: p60 (2B)
Postal districts: NW8
Boroughs: Westminster (Con)
Rates: 136.4p in £
Constituencies: Westminster North (Con)
Insurance: Scale 1
Conservation areas: Most of the area – check with town hall.
Parking: Meters/residents. Clamps.

Transport   Tubes: St John's Wood, Swiss Cottage (zone 2, Jubilee); Maida Vale (zone 2, Bakerloo). From St John's Wood: Oxford Circus, 15 min (1 change); City, 30 min (1 change); Heathrow, 1 hr (1 change). British Rail: South Hampstead (direct to Euston).

Convenient for   Lord's Cricket Ground, West End, Regent's Park. Routes to North and West. Miles from centre: 3.5.

Schools   ILEA Division 2: Quintin Kynaston. Private: The American School.

Flats	S	1b	2b	3b	4b	5b
Average prices	70–85	90–125+	150–200+	225–500	375–500	430+
Houses	2b	3b	4b	5b	6/7b	8b
Average prices	200+	250–400	400–500	500–1m	900+	1.5m+

The properties   Smart suburb with big, 19th century villas, plus mansion and modern flats. Flats become luxury-level towards Regents Park (which see) and Lords: London's highest concentration of penthouses. Some expensive new houses.

The market   Cosmopolitan: diplomats, businessmen with families, celebrities all buy here for big family houses and international-standard apartments. Considerable overseas investment/bolt hole-buying. Some house prices held back by 40/50 year leases. Local searches: 1 week.

Area Profile

St John's Wood is London's 'first suburb' – first both in the sense of being just about the foremost and also just about the closest-in.

Primrose Hill and Regents Park lie alongside, and yet the West End is just a mile or so away. Despite this proximity to the bustling heart of town, and despite the many modern blocks which have replaced earlier mansions, the pace and the style of these very select streets are set, it seems, by the lazy, summer sound of wood on willow that drifts across the high walls of Lord's Cricket Ground.

Away from the busy artery of *Wellington Rd* and the hustle and bustle of the *High St*, The Wood's life is conducted at strolling pace – and a very pleasant place to stroll it is. Until Regency times it was still largely a wood – albeit a royal one. Hayfields, whose crops supplied City stables, abounded.

The development which took place here as London spread westward was aimed at the 'carriage people', and was brilliantly successful. Instead of the more economical terraces, large and elegant Regency villas, standing alone or in pairs, with gardens and coach houses, were built – and remain the hallmark of the area.

These set the tone and attracted the 'right' people, a state of affairs which has largely persisted, making St John's Wood one of the capital's prime residential areas. Its inhabitants are undeniably wealthy; business people (often from abroad) and well-established men and women who see a home in St John's Wood as a fair reward for their hard work. Other reasons for the area's appeal include proximity to good shopping along the *Finchley Rd*, the London Central Mosque, a number of synagogues, Lord's and the American School in *Loudoun Rd*. Ambassadors find the area sympathetic.

Property in the area ranges from the studio flats of Grove Hall Court (on the corner of *Hall Rd* and *Grove End Rd*) to the splendid mansions of *Hamilton Terrace*. Demand invariably outstrips supply here.

The earlier history of the area still has a bearing on buying homes here today. After the Priors of St John lost the land at the Reformation it was split up; a long, narrow strip (lying along the *Edgware Rd*) became, eventually, part of the Harrow School estate. A larger section belonged to the Crown, and Charles II used some of this to settle a debt. In 1720, 200 acres of this was bought (for £20,000) by Henry Eyre, a prosperous merchant, whose estate remains largely intact today and is remembered in the name of Eyre Court, a popular block on the corner of the *Finchley Rd* and *Grove End Rd*. Thus many freeholds in the area are owned by Harrow School (a typical lease is around 64 years), the Eyre Estate (shorter leases, around 50 years) and also Eton College, and most property is bought leasehold.

Paradoxically, some of the best houses are on these short leases. This holds down their prices as they are hard to mortgage. There are roads where one side has 47-year leases, the other 70; which explains strange discrepancies in prices. The short leases also explain why these prestigious houses can cost no more than those in Hampstead, further away.

Those who rent, rather than buy, are often representatives of international companies or attached to embassies. They find a ready supply of luxurious flats and houses and wide roads with room to park their Mercedes.

St John's Wood is a fine example of early Victorian suburban development with its large detached and semi-detached houses. There are also some smaller, often older, cottages and later Edwardian and between-the-wars mansions. In the 1920s and '30s a considerable number of mansion blocks were built, and more sprang up in the '60s and '70s on the sites of bomb-damaged streets towards Maida Vale and Swiss Cottage.

The Lord's side

The Lord's side refers, of course, to St John's Wood's most sacred shrine – the cricket ground – which can be viewed from the top of a double decker bus or from the block of flats aptly named Lord's View. However on this, western, side of the *Wellington Rd/Finchley Rd* divide lie most of the area's other religious institutions; churches, synagogues and a mosque.

St John's Wood's southernmost boundary is *St John's Wood Rd*, which cuts off Lord's and St John's Wood from Lisson Grove and Marylebone. On the other side of the cricket ground is *Cavendish Avenue* with some of the largest houses and gardens in St John's Wood attracting buyers such as Paul McCartney. In neighbouring *Wellington Place* stands one of the most expensive private hospitals in London, Humana's Wellington Hospital (South). Nearby *Circus Rd* (whose name reflects an early, but thwarted, plan to develop St John's Wood around a large circus with streets and squares containing pairs of houses) is the site of the Humana Hospital North.

Circus Rd leads W into *Hall Road*, bisected by *Hamilton Terrace*, which runs the length of the area: a wide, tree-lined, prestigious avenue stretching about ¾ mile. Begun in 1820, its variety of semi-detached and detached mansions so large that they now provide the area's best hunting-ground for conversions (at a premium because of the preponderance of purpose-built flats). Many, though, are available only on short leases. When left as single units, houses here range from modest to 'ambassador class'. One on the market in recent years boasted staff quarters, garaging, a 'media room' for the telex, etc, and a control panel by the master's bed to turn on the spotlights in the grounds.

Flats are extremely popular in St John's Wood. Many have superb views overlooking Regents Park and a favoured few can look down on the play at Lords Cricket Ground: premium prices here. Pre-war flats are in evidence in *Scott Ellis Gardens* and *Hall Rd*, while *Abbey Rd* and *Abercorn Place* have good examples of flats built just after the war. On the corner of the two, *38 Abercorn Place* is a new block of eight smart flats, with porter and basement garage. Under its raised roof, a penthouse enjoys the entire top floor, 2- and 3-bed flats here are in the £210-325,000 bracket. Next door is a delight: a Regency artists' studio house designed by Decimus Burton, for sale last year at £610,000.

Grove End Rd, which runs N from *St John's Wood Rd*, is a pleasant road with a mixture of expensive flats and large houses. The St John and St Elizabeth Hospital with its recently converted hospice wards was founded by colleagues of Florence Nightingale and is now run by nuns. It stands opposite St John's Wood United Synagogue, one of the three well-known synagogues in the area. It joins *Wellington Rd* just opposite *Acacia Rd*, on the corner of which is the St John's Wood tube station. A large new scheme in *Wellington Rd* plans 26 new flats here.

Running N from *Grove End Rd* is *Loudon Rd* where you'll find the famous American School and, opposite it, the boy's prep school Arnold House. Running parallel to *Loudon Rd* is *Abbey Rd*, made famous by the Beatles, whose recording studios were here. It, too, is sprouting stylish new homes: at No 20 Rosehaugh Copartnership are building eight houses and 100 apartments. These won't be finished till next year, and a 2-bedroomed flat is expected to be in the £3-400,000 bracket.

S

Off *Abbey Rd* is one of the prettiest corners of St John's Wood. Roads like *Abbey Gardens*, *Blenheim* and *Nugent Terraces* have a smaller-scale village-like atmosphere. There you'll find little rows of shops and small parks like the one in *Violet Hill*. Houses round pretty *Alma Square* have access to its gardens.

On *Finchley Rd* the 1930s Apsley House is being crowned with six luxurious new 2-bedroomed penthouse flats, for sale early spring.

The Park side

Across *Finchley Rd* – which connects St John's Wood with Swiss Cottage – is *Queen's Grove* with its terraced houses boasting large Ionic and Corinthian columns. This quiet, leafy road leads to Primrose Hill. *Norfolk Rd* and *Acacia Rd* are both pretty streets with stuccoed and brick houses, sought after – even fought-over – by those who prefer older style houses. Actress Lily Langtry, King Edward VII's favourite, lived in *Acacia Rd*. A low-built family house on the corner of *Acacia Place* proved how rare, and how popular, are unmodernised homes in top areas in these days of new-build and lavish refurbishment. Such was the interest when it appeared for sale last year that it was auctioned: the reserve was £475,000; it sold for over £600,000.

Woronzow Rd, a learner driver's paradise good for three point turns, contains the slightly less expensive terraced houses. The Woronzow in question was a Russian count who left £500 to build almshouses for the poor. The originals were built round the corner in *St Johns Wood Terrace* in 1827 but were rebuilt block by block from 1960-1963. They are now to undergo improvement and some redevelopment into flats and houses for sale, although 20 flats will remain almshouses.

Newer houses in St John's Wood can be seen further towards Swiss Cottage. *Queensmead* is an estate of 17 town houses and three blocks of flats owned by the Eyre Estate, built 25 years ago. For the first time some of the flats will be for sale this year: 1-, 2- and 3-bedroomed flats are being refurbished and will be released in April/May. *The Marlowes* is another sought-after residential development of town houses which look, comments a local, like flats tipped on their sides. Not to everyone's taste, but desirable because of their location. *St John's Wood Park* also contains other modern housing. *Ordnance Hill* houses the Kings Troop Royal Horse Artillery – a splendid sight to see in the early morning when the horses are exercised.

Running between *Circus Rd* and *Prince Albert Rd* is *St John's Wood High St* with its expensive boutiques, delicatessens and chemists. Outrageous parking here is legendary and cars can be seen daily with big yellow clamps on them. Round the corner is Panzers, St John's Wood's most up-market grocer, and the post office. Council flats (select ones, to match the area) are clearly in evidence behind the *High St*. Some in *Barrow Hill*, *Allitsen Rd* and *Townsend Rd* have already been bought by tenants and many soon will be.

At the end of the *High St* is the roundabout presided over by St John's Wood Church, a large elegant building. *Prince Albert Rd* curves around the N side of the park (see Regent's Park). The Pavillions at 24-26 *Avenue Rd*, a luxurious development of six flats including a sumptuous penthouse and its own swimming pool complex for residents, was completed last summer and was still being actively marketed late last year. Prices range from £1.25 million for a 4-bed flat on the ground floor to £3.5 million for the 5-bed, 5-bathroom penthouse (which also includes a separate staff flat on the ground floor).

Avenue Rd is a grand thoroughfare, highly desirable to the international set: ambassadors from all nations make their homes in the large mansions with landscaped gardens, and overseas business people buy flats.

Primrose Hill

Tucked away between St John's Wood, Regent's Park, Camden and Chalk Farm lies a small public park with soaring hilltop views over London. On its slopes is a picturesque and prosperous enclave whose residents – many of whom are writers, photographers, actors and musicians – take great pride in the area.

The 'village' of Primrose Hill is tucked in between the mainline railway to the E and the hill to the W. Quiet and secluded, it commands high prices and is the most coveted part of the area, being composed mainly of wide, tree-lined streets and elegant stucco-fronted houses. There are few small properties to be had: the majority of Primrose Hill housing is 2- and 3-bed flats in converted period houses, and 3/4-bed houses costing up to £1 million. *Regent's Park Rd*, curving round past the Hill and back to Chalk Farm, forms the W boundary of the 'village' and is a busy thoroughfare for cars and infrequent buses, though its substantial stucco homes, some with views over Primrose Hill, many still family houses, are still highly popular. *Gloucester Avenue* forms an eastern boundary to the area: a wide, tree-lined street with the mainline railway (Euston-bound) behind the homes on the E side – this can lower prices on some houses by as much as 40%, say agents. The period terraces on both sides have for the most part been converted into flats. Unlike many Primrose Hill homes, these come on the market fairly frequently as young couples move on to bigger and better things. The 'village' to the W of the Avenue is a maze of quiet streets, secluded and sleepy. *Chalcot Square* and *Crescent* and *St Marks Crescent* are among the most prestigious addresses: mostly 3-storey stucco fronted houses, nothing below £350,000. *Chalcot Rd, Fitzroy Rd, Princess Rd* have rows of tall period terraces, now mostly flats. The canal, running between *St Mark's Crescent* and *Princess Rd,* makes for attractive back gardens.

Off the N end of *Regent's Park Rd*, where prices are (slightly) lower, *Abinger* and *Oppidans Rds* and *Meadowbank* form a quiet triangle. All three streets have large grey brick-fronted terraces and semis, most divided into flats; in addition, *Oppidans Rd* has Primrose Hill Court (council) a well maintained block, and some large modern town houses. *Primrose Hill Rd* has two big modern blocks overlooking the hill, and the highly desirable period *St George's Terrace* at the bottom, where 1-bedroom flats cost £120,000 minimum.

The area around *King Henry's Rd* has strong links with Eton College and much of the land is still owned by the college: leasehold only here. Most of the elegant, tall grey brick houses have been split into flats with well proportioned rooms; garden flats available here. On the N side, and in the roads leading up to *Adelaide Rd*, are groups of small, modern, 2-storey, white-painted houses.

Harley Rd, Wadham Gardens and *Elsworthy Rd* are the most desirable roads on this northern flank of Primrose Hill, being made up mostly of huge, handsome Edwardian red brick villas, many still in single occupancy.

Among those estate agents active in this area are:

S

- Anscombe & Ringland
- Bargets
- Beauchamp Estates
- Brian Lack
- Cluttons
- Folkard & Hayward
- Hirschfields
- Gillands
- Glentree Estates
- John D Wood
- Knight Frank & Rutley
- Lassmans
- Prudential Property Services
- De Groot Collis

Stepney, Whitechapel

Map ref: p63 (4K)	Postal district: E1
Borough: Tower Hamlets (Lib)	
Rates: 217.89p in £	
Constituency: Bethnal Green & Stepney (Lab)	
Insurance: Scale 1	
Conservation areas: Numerous: contact town hall	
Parking: Meters/yellow lines towards City	

Transport Tubes: Stepney Green, Whitechapel, Aldgate East (Metropolitan, District), Wapping (Metropolitan), Aldgate (Metropolitan, Circle), Tower Hill (Circle, District), Shadwell (Metropolitan). Docklands Light Railway. BR Limehouse. From Stepney Green: Oxford Circus 15 min (1 change), City 10 min (1 change), Heathrow.

Convenient for Docklands, City, Dover. Miles from centre: 3.5.

Schools ILEA Zone 5: Bishop Challoner RC (g), Bow (b), Central Foundation (g), Mulberry (g), Sir John Cass, Stepney Green (b)

Flats	S	1b	2b	3b	4b	5b
Average prices	50–65	55–75	55–95	100+	–	–
Houses	2b	3b	4b	5b	6/7b	8b
Average prices	95–130	100–160	130–200+	→250	→	–

The property Homes here range from ex-council to Grade II listed, from flats to new mews schemes like Hayfield Yard, from Edwardian redbrick to Georgiana on Stepney Green. London Hospital, a major landlord, now selling properties. Some Peabody Estate houses also appearing.

The market Prices reflect the range. Small terraces from c £100,000; larger listed homes reach a quarter million; 7-bedroom Edwardiana can be c £130,000 unconverted, £200,000 done-up. For Wapping riverside and Spitalfields see Docklands and City. Local searches: 4 weeks.

Area Profile

Stepney, Whitechapel and Wapping are a curious mixture of some of London's best and worst housing. The area, defined quite precisely by the E1 postal district, is the heart of the old East End. War and slum clearance brought great changes, and now the ferment in its neighbouring areas brings more. The City's expansion has crossed the border into Stepney while the Docklands boom has brought wealth to riverside Wapping. But some squalor remains, especially around Spitalfields – little more than a stone's throw from the thriving City.

The area has three main roads running from E to W – *The Highway*, *Commercial Rd* and *Whitechapel Rd* which is a continuation of *Mile End Rd*. All three lead to the City and are, therefore, extremely busy. The area is bordered by the Liverpool Street main line cutting it off from Bethnal Green to the N, by Poplar across the canal to the E, by the river to the S and the City to the W. There is convenient access to South London via Rotherhithe Tunnel or Tower Bridge.

This part of London is packed with history, a fact reflected by no fewer than 12 conservation areas. The Tower of London falls within Stepney's boundary while Jack the Ripper once stalked the streets of Whitechapel in search of victims. Whitechapel is dominated by the world-famous London Hospital, directly opposite Whitechapel tube station and *Whitechapel Rd* market, known locally as 'The Waste'. Cultural attractions include the Whitechapel Gallery and the Half Moon Theatre in Stepney's *Mile End Rd*. Bloom's kosher restaurant in the *High St*, with its noted salt beef, is a reminder of the area's connections with the Jewish community.

Apart from the new housing developments in Wapping, (described in the Docklands chapter) some of Stepney's most sought-after properties are in the *Albert Gardens/Arbour Square* conservation area which includes Arbour Square Police Station. Parking here is not such a problem as nearer the City and around the London Hospital. The least desirable housing is in Spitalfields and either side of the W end of *Commercial Rd*. These areas are dominated by the East End 'rag trade' and scores of clothing manufacturers and wholesalers operate. Many of these small businesses are run by Asians. Vehicles loading and unloading in the cramped streets make driving in this area a particular problem. Spitalfields has a high crime rate but, despite its drawbacks includes three conservation areas – *Elder St, Fournier St* and *Artillery Passage*.

Watney Market, S of *Commercial Rd*, is another far from attractive area but it has the asset of a new Docklands Light Railway station of Shadwell. The famous Petticoat Lane market is in *Middlesex St* on Sunday mornings and there is a market throughout the week in nearby *Wentworth St*.

The old centre of Stepney was a thriving village in mediaeval times. All that is left is Stepney Churchyard, surrounding St Dunstan's Church, one of Stepney's most picturesque corners. Nearby, in *Stepney Way*, is Stepping Stones Farm – an unusual sight in such a highly populated area.

One-third of Stepney's homes were destroyed by wartime bombing. The council homes that replaced them are now beginning to change hands as former tenants sell and move out to Essex. Stepney is as convenient for the City as Docklands, if not so chic, and buyers are beginning to find it attractive. And unlike Docklands, Stepney's neighbourhoods have been around for some time and have more in the way of everyday amenities.

Stepney

At the eastern end of the neighbourhood, conveniently close to Stepney Green tube, an enclave of streets is hidden between *Globe* and *Mile End Rds. Portelet Rd, Carlton Square, Holton St, Grantley St, Massingham St* and *Tollet St* are well placed near the Mile End annexe of the London Hospital. These delightful 2-storey Victorian terraced houses, some with semi-basements and steps up to the front door, are also near Tower Hamlets Central Library in *Bancroft Rd* and various Queen Mary College Buildings. Residents in *Grand Walk*, at the E end of *Mile End Rd*, have new terraced houses made magic by the Grand Union Canal which facilitates the occasional houseboat and anglers. A new housing scheme is planned to start soon in *Globe Rd*.

Further along *Mile End Rd*, to the W, is the sprawling, run-down Ocean council estate which includes *Beaumont Square, White Horse Lane, Ben Johnson Rd, Matlock St, Commodore St, Solebay St, Emmott St, Shandy St, Duckett St* and *Harford St* where there are gasworks.

White Horse Lane has 2-storey terraced houses with distinctive open porches and the green of *Beaumont Square* faces the London Independent private hospital. *Maria Terrace*, off *Beaumont Square*, has a row of 10 3-storey Victorian houses. Close by in *Louisa St*, nine 3-bed houses are to be built. And in *Rectory Square*, behind *Stepney Green*, developers are even planning to convert a synagogue into flats and houses.

Stepney Green – not the open, featureless expanse between *Stepney Way/Redman's Rd*, but the street of the same name – is an unexpected gem. Behind the narrow strip of green, enclosed by railings, stand a row of Queen Anne/early 18th century houses, in what is reputed to be the only blue-cobbled street left in south-east England. They are supplemented by some faithful modern copies, and there's wind of 'a few special small new developments soon' in the vicinity. Opposite are the ivy-fronted red-brick Cressy House and Dunstan House and the Stifford Estate (council) which includes *Tinsley Rd, Cressy Place, Redmans Rd, Jamaica St, Stepney Way* and *Smithy St*.

Close to Whitechapel tube and in stark contrast to its busy surroundings in *Mile End Rd* is Trinity Green, a small 1961 Civic Trust award development with beautiful gardens surrounded by railings and wall. Further E along *Mile End Rd* is *Cleveland Way*: smart new housing association flats next to the Golden Eagle pub. Barratt have got permission for 62 flats and work/homes in *Cleveland Way* and *Cleveland Grove*: starting spring. Off *Vallance Rd* on the borders of Bethnal Green, there are plans for 150 flats and houses. Charrington's Anchor House brewery is on the corner of *Cephas Avenue* where attractive 2- and 3-storey Victorian terraced houses, many with steps and railings and some with flat roofs, are in high demand.

Commercial Rd to the S, towards Wapping, lives up to its name with heavy traffic and is dotted on either side with council estates such as Pitsea, Watney Market, Exmouth and Mountmorres. The garden square of *Albert Gardens* is a peaceful haven from the noise of *Commercial Rd*. These desirable 4-storey Victorian terraced houses are part of a conservation area which also includes *Havering St* where 3-storey Victorian houses with railings lead down to a railway arch. Viewed from the rear, the roofs of *Havering St* give an unusual wave effect. To the W, St Mary and St Michael's Roman Catholic Church and primary school are next to the Watney Market council estate which includes *Deancross St, Sidney St, Hainton Path, Hungerford St, Tarling St, Watney St, Dunch St, Bigland St, Timberland Rd* and *Burwell Close*.

From the Watney Market Estate W along *Commercial Rd* to the City, parking starts to become a problem. *Mansell St* and *Leman St*, which includes a police station, are now generally accepted as part of the City itself and are strict no-parking zones. *Aldgate High St*, which houses Sedgwick Sports Centre, is similarly busy. The Exmouth Estate, N of *Commercial Rd*, includes *Clark St, Musbury St, Cornwood Drive, Jubilee St, Exmouth St, Summercourt Rd, Jamaica St, Aylward St, Clovelly Way* and *Clearbrook Way*. To the E of the estate is the *Arbour Square* conservation area where Arbour House council flats are situated alongside 3-storey Victorian terraced houses, some with front steps, facing a garden square. Houses on the S side of the square have a drawback as they back onto far less attractive 4-storey terraced houses in *Commercial Rd*. *Arbour Square* also includes a police station and City and East London College, formerly Raines School.

Further E along *Commercial Rd* is *Bromley St* where railings surround delightful 2-storey Victorian terraced houses, refurbished in 1986, leading to the British Prince pub on the corner and adjoining the Mountmorres council estate. Similar homes are to be found in *Belgrave St*, which includes the Mercers Arms pub and leads down to picturesque St Dunstan's Church, much favoured for local weddings. The church is surrounded by Stepney Churchyard. Facing the churchyard is *Mercers Cottages*, four beautiful terraced homes with a communal front garden.

The *York Square* conservation area, to the SE of the Green, is half in Stepney and half in Limehouse. The Stepney half includes *White Horse Rd* and *Barnes St*. Run-down 3- and 4-storey terraced houses in *White Horse Rd* are on the opposite side to much more attractive 3-storey Victorian terraced properties with railings and hanging baskets of flowers. Similarly attractive 2-storey Victorian terraced houses in *Barnes St* which is on the opposite side of *Commercial Rd* to Limehouse BR and Docklands Light Railway stations.

Names in this area can be confusing as developers annex suddenly-glamorous Limehouse and use it for bits of Stepney and even Bow.

S

Whitechapel and Spitalfields

The world-famous London Hospital is the centre of Whitechapel. The front entrance of the hospital stands in *Whitechapel Rd*, directly opposite Whitechapel tube station and *Whitechapel Rd* market, known locally as 'The Waste'. Some of the Victorian terraced houses at the back of the hospital are owned by the hospital itself, for example in *Philpott St*, and used for research. Other hospital buildings are to be found in *Newark St*, part of the *Sidney Square* conservation area. The conservation area also includes part of *Cavell St*, *Halcrow St*, *Ford Square*, *Ashfield St*, *Sidney Square* and the E end of *Varden St* which houses the Three Feathers Social Club. *Sidney Square* is attractive with 3-storey Victorian terraced houses which have tiny wrought iron balconies on the second floor; but parking is a big problem in this area.

At the junction of *Cavell St*, named after Nurse Edith Cavell, and *Varden St* is a new development of 20 luxury apartments. More 3- and 4-storey Victorian terraced houses, some converted into flats, are found in *Ford Square*. The area's cramped streets also include many Asian-run garment manufacturers and wholesalers. Vans loading and unloading sometimes make access difficult. Whitechapel Bell Foundry, established in 1570, is at the junction of *Fieldgate St* and *Plumber's Row*. The Whitechapel Gallery in the *High St* is a world-famous art venue which balances the cultural with the practical: it's also a well-known local place to eat.

Whitechapel has become a City overspill area, with big office blocks around Aldgate East tube. There are major plans for Whitechapel tube, and speculation that offices will fill in the triangle between *Whitechapel Rd* and *Commercial Rd*. The run-down streets in the corner are mostly occupied by the garment industry.

Truman's *Brick Lane* brewery is one of the few new buildings in run-down Spitalfields, N of *Whitechapel Rd*. The Chicksand Street council estate is particularly depressing and includes *Vallance Rd*, *Old Montague St*, *Daplyn St*, *Deal St*, *Hanbury St*, *Spelman St*, *Chicksand St*, *Greatorex St* and *Davenant St*.

Spitalfields has some beautiful early Georgian houses, of which a handful have been lovingly restored. Pevsner explained their survival by pointing out that Spitalfields, fashionable in the late 16th and early 17th centuries, declined so dramatically that it was not worth anyone's while to rebuild. There are ambitious plans to relocate the wholesale market and redevelop the entire area. This redevelopment will include quite large amounts of housing for the local council, a concession made by the developers in return for permission to build offices. The existing Georgian houses will be kept and may, when the scheme is complete, aquire surroundings in tune with their elegant interiors. As things stand, they are for history addicts only. (There are a lot about, as agents found when they offered an *Elder St* house for £250,000 last year.) The new housing, in position terms at least, could well be equally desirable.

Among those estate agents active in this area are:
- Alan Selby
- Anthony Gover
- Clapshaws
- John Barber & Mrs Jones
- Prevost

Stoke Newington

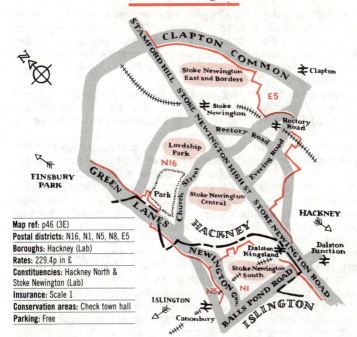

Map ref: p46 (3E)
Postal districts: N16, N1, N5, N8, E5
Boroughs: Hackney (Lab)
Rates: 229.4p in £
Constituencies: Hackney North & Stoke Newington (Lab)
Insurance: Scale 1
Conservation areas: Check town hall
Parking: Free

Transport	British Rail: Stoke Newington, Rectory Rd to Liverpool St. See also map.

Convenient for	City. Buses to tube at Highbury & Islington (Victoria line direct to West End). Miles from centre: 4.5.

Schools	ILEA zone 4: Our Lady's Convent RC, Skinners Senior Girls', King's Lynn Senior Mixed.

Flats	S	1b	2b	3b	4b	5b
Average prices	–	55–70	70–85	83–95	100+	–
Houses	2b	3b	4b	5b	6/7b	8b
Average prices	85–100	100–130	100–140	120–160	130–160+	–

The properties	Mid to late Victorian terraces, many converted to flats, plus a few Georgian ones around Newington Green. Some p/b flats in Victorian and '30s blocks, plus council houses and flats. Some of the open spaces of the reservoirs to north will be developed for new homes.

The market	Council veto on 1-bed flat conversions slowed down the terraced house-into-flats trend. 1/2-bed flats still plentiful and popular, however, as are 3-bed houses. The area south of Church St is the most active; above-average increases in value occur here. Local searches: 16 weeks.

S

Area Profile

Far enough out to feel that you're going home, yet near enough the centre so that you don't feel cut off, Stoke Newington residents – new and old – consider they have the best of both worlds. Many of them are second or third generation Stoke Newington, families who have lived here since the War, and they are faintly amused to see the influx of young media and City types who have moved into the area in recent years.

Largely in N16, Stoke Newington lies N of *Balls Pond Rd*, E of *Green Lanes*, S of *Allerton*, *Fairholt* and *Dunsmure Rds*, and W of *Clapton Common*, with *Brooke* and *Evering Rds*, *Rectory Rd* and *Shacklewell Lane* completing the circle.

Stoke Newington is an amalgam of the old villages of Shacklewell and Stoke Newington itself, the northern points of Kingsland and the southern reaches of Stamford Hill. The villages are Domesday-ancient; the area was popular as a place to retreat from the pestilence-ridden city in the 17th century; thrived in Georgian times; became built-up – as did so many others – in Victoria's reign. Here in the 1830s, Cubitt was sharpening his skills before moving on to create Belgravia and Pimlico. The area prospered until the early 20th century when the more well-to-do moved further out. Much accommodation became tenanted and fell into disrepair. By World War 2 many buildings were in poor condition, and bombs hastened the demise of many sections of the streets.

Post-war redevelopment brought ugly low-rise blocks which Hackney council is currently trying to improve, mainly with surface treatments such as bright paint and the landscaping of open areas, and in the past few years much has been done to restore and renovate streets to an '80s version of Victorian splendour. This work has been carried out by the council, locals and the increasing numbers of young middle-class people who, unable to afford the rocketing prices in Islington, have sought homes half a mile or so north.

Conservation areas now abound, shopping for the basic necessities of life is well served, and restaurants, both fast food and conventional, are numerous, as are pubs. *Church St* has sprouted smart wine bars, delis and restaurants, the *High St* boasts a new jazz bar to add to the jazz cafe on *Newington Green Rd*; all helping to make the distance from Stoke Newington to the West End for evening entertainment seem increasingly irrelevant.

The two main thoroughfares are S-N *Kingsland Rd*, which becomes the *High St* going N, and E-W *Church St*. While *Kingsland Rd/High St* is rather grey and grotty, with amusement arcades, video shops and takeaways, *Church St* – the high street of the original village, still with many buildings of 18th-century origins – displays all the signs of an area on the up and up, sporting health food shops, delis and a plethora of estate agents. Both streets, however, are good shopping areas for meat, wet fish and vegetables. Further S, *Ridley Rd* market sells all manner of goods at knock-down prices – and has a 24-hour bagel shop. The recent addition of a bookshop on the *High St*, well stocked for kids as well as their parents, is welcome and two smart second-hand furniture shops on *Church St* have gone for '30s to '50s rather than pine, and make for pleasant browsing, as well as purchasing.

Spacious Clissold Park boasts a truly eccentric 'zoo', bowling green, tennis courts and a bandstand for summer sonatas, and has a Victorian swimming pool nearby, while Abney Park Cemetery is the resting place for many eminent Victorians, beneath wonderful gothic tombs. The Geffrye Museum records past local furniture makers in a row of glorious converted almshouses, and the Rio

Cinema serves both West End and local tastes with its increasingly imaginative programming.

The lack of a tube station has perhaps governed the popularity of Stoke Newington in the past, though closeness and convenience for the City – BR's links from Stoke Newington and Rectory Rd are excellent – has pushed up house prices recently. Buses take you there and to the West End: the 73 goes all the way to Harrods via Euston and Oxford St. Nearest tube stations are Finsbury Park, Highbury and Islington or Manor House, a bus or car ride away.

In terms of a bargain Stoke Newington has almost gone – but don't lose heart. You can still find a 'good buy', but it will almost certainly be on the fringes and in poor repair. The area's improvement and desirability looks set to continue.

Lordship Park

The most northerly of Stoke Newington's four neighbourhoods is Lordship Park. This is the area N of *Stoke Newington Church St*, E of *Green Lanes*, S of *Allerton, Fairholt* and *Dunsmure Rds* and W of *Stamford Hill*. Main thoroughfare is *Lordship Park/Manor Rd*, an E-W bus route and general traffic thoroughfare. At the W end are monumental 4-storey buildings, set back from the road making the houses quieter than might be assumed. These give way to smaller 2-storey bay-fronted houses towards E. Most are now flats. N of *Lordship Road* is *Allerton Rd*, one end of which is overshadowed by a bizarre Gothic water tower. Homes on the N side have gardens backing onto the Reservoir, a haven for wildlife. Happily, it may now remain so – at least in part. The Water Board looks like compromising on its plan to develop the reservoir lands: Now the section E of *Green Lanes* may be left for conservation, while that to the W is built on. Check your local authority searches if buying in this area, and ask questions.

Allerton Rd leads into *Queen Elizabeth's Walk*, where prices reach a premium, mainly because at the S end the houses overlook Clissold Park. The back gardens of these are in turn overlooked by council low-rise. Look out for the beautiful double-fronted terraces in the *Walk* – rare beauties. Tree-lined *Fairholt Rd* and shop-studded *Dunsmure Rd* (where many of the shops are open on Sunday since they are run by Orthodox Jews) complete Stoke Newington's northern reaches. Both roads contain generous bay-fronted family houses, some flats, some council. Look here and round about for large houses at lower prices.

Running S, houses tend to be scruffier, and bargains more likely. *Bethune Close, Heathland Rd, St Andrews Grove* and busy *Lordship Rd* are all edged by large Victorian bay-fronted houses where renovation and conversion is taking place. The E-W streets – *Paget, St Kilda's* and *Grangecourt Rds* – are smaller with mainly 2-storey terraces; some very pretty, notably the S side of *Grangecourt* and *St Kilda's* between *Bethune* and *Heathland*. Again much building and renovation.

South of *Manor Rd* the streets are noticeably smarter. Most of the renovation work here has already been done, though the odd patch of run-down Victorian terrace still peeks out from between the glistening paintwork and newly-planted clematis. Here *Bouverie Rd* matches *Queen Elizabeth's Walk* in desirability. At the N end of the road the style is marked by a large detached villa, recently restored. Homes with even numbers back onto

S

the cemetery and there is light industrial at the S end. Odd-numbered houses are either large, 4-storey and flat-fronted or some of the most charming 2-storey terraces in the area. Low odd numbers have small gardens. *Yoakley Rd* has a charming Victorian terrace on the E side, broken now and then by small eccentric detached villas. The whole of the W side is boring council low-rise. Running E-W, *Grayling Rd* has lovely 2-storey bay-fronted houses and *Grazebrook Rd* has a 3-storey terrace on the W side overlooking the edge of a largish modern council development. *Fleetwood St* runs N off *Church St*, a short, one-sided, Victorian terrace running up to the cemetery and home of the local fire station.

Stoke Newington East and borders

This neighbourhood is E of *Stoke Newington Rd*, *High St* and *Stamford Hill* and bordered to the N and E by the busy *Clapton Rd*. The SE border follows *Brooke Rd*, then S again down *Rectory Rd* and *Shacklewell Lane*. The S edge is marked by E-W running *Sandringham Rd*. The further N the larger the houses, interspersed by the large Stamford Hill and Broad Common estates. This big area is split by main E-W through roads: *Cazenove Rd, Northwold Rd, Evering Rd* and *Manse Rd*. Buses tend to stick to these main thoroughfares so accessibility from some roads is poor.

At the N, *Leweston Place* has Victorian terraces on one side of the road and '30s semis on the even side. *Darenth Rd* has large Victorian bay-fronted houses, some with basements. Nearby are *Lynemouth Rd* and *Lampard Grove*, blighted by a ghastly MFI store. Moving a little to the E, *Alkham, Kyverdale, Osbaldeston, Forburg* and charming *Chardmore Rds* have similar large Victorian houses. They are quiet, tree-lined streets and the houses here are generally in poorer condition than further S, and so prices tend to be lower. S of *Cazenove Rd*, where there's an excellent health food shop, much refurbishment has already been done. Many houses have been converted into flats and, although streets seem narrow for the size of buildings, large gardens compensate. E of *Fontaine Rd*, the streets become smaller again, with 2-storey and basement Victorian terraces, bordering the Northwold council estate. *Northwold Rd* has the local shops, and southwards *Alconbury, Geldeston, Narford* and *Reighton Rds* have mostly well-maintained medium sized Victorian houses. But the N ends of *Reighton* and *Narford* Rds are scruffier than the S ends. If the street frontage of these houses look smaller than those further north, the houses themselves often go back a long way and contain a generous number of rooms. Moving W, *Norcott, Maury, Benthal* and *Jenner Rds* are now well maintained and quiet due to an eccentric traffic system. These houses enjoy more generous gardens than you might expect, and the potential of an 'end of terrace' property is exploited by the conservatories built over the porches of two houses at the junctions of *Norcott* and *Brooke Rds*. Odd numbered houses in *Jenner Rd* back onto railway but generally these streets are desirable.

West of *Rectory Rd* but N of *Evering Rd*, the Brooke Road Estate looms, a victim of poor building, bordered on its E side by a beautiful 4-storey flat-fronted terrace overlooking the common. Running S *Darville, Bayston, Leswin*, and (E-W) *Tyssen Rds* have smaller 2-storey houses, some with basements. An area to watch. Some houses have been renovated though there are many more still to go. You are more likely to find a bargain here but a lot of hard searching will be the precursor to any reward. Be careful: the closer to the *High St*, the more plentiful the ugly light industry.

South of *Evering Rd*, curving *Amhurst Rd* returns the would-be purchaser to larger houses, 3-storey with semi basements, some still to be modernised. *Foulden*, *Farleigh* and *Sydner Rds* are narrower, and have smaller houses, some flat-fronted, some bay, and again closer to the *High St* light industry impinges. The S side of *Farleigh* backs onto the Somerford Estate, and the E end is overlooked by The Beckers, a bleak '60s eyesore estate. Further S, the Somerford Estate is bordered by large areas of light indusry. What housing there is is sandwiched between ugly factories and a '30s council block making this whole section less appealing than anywhere further N.

The main N-S road running through Stoke Newington is *Stoke Newington Rd*, which becomes first the *High St* and then *Stamford Hill*. Lined with shops, the flats above are mostly tenanted, though some do come up for sale now and then. Often the backs of these shops are ad hoc workshops/storerooms etc, so they may not provide the most beautiful vistas. The road, it has to be said, is busy all day and most of the night. However, you can't get a location more convenient for all the local consumer amenities, buses or the train, and given that some of buildings are quite large, flats can often be light and spacious.

S

Stoke Newington Central

Stoke Newington Central – the old village of Shacklewell – lies S of *Church St*, W of the *High St*, and has as its southern border a stretch of *Green Lanes*, *Matthias Rd* and *Barrett's Grove*. Whilst the larger houses to the NE of this area have been steadily appreciating in value, it is this central area, with its mix of 2-storey terraces interspersed with streets of larger buildings, which has seen ungentlemanly leaps in price over the past two years.

The area is split in two by *Albion Rd*, a bus route and general N-S thoroughfare. Here 3-storey terraces give way to large Victorian blocks; renovated and already sold once, these are already coming back onto the market. Further S, *Albion Rd* narrows and is lined by 3-storey, bay-fronted Victorian houses. Some still have to be refurbished, others are already converted into flats. To the W of *Albion Rd* lies the section described by one estate agent as the 'North Islington Overspill Quadrant', no less. It's an area yet to have its day and most streets are still quite scruffy but it has, as they say, great potential. *Winston Rd* has small 2-storey houses and off *Winston Rd*, look out for *Redholm Villas* – a wee gem of a cul-de-sac. *Springdale Rd* and *Aden Grove* have larger houses while *Burma Rd's* 3- and 4-storey houses have mostly been renovated, and so look much smarter than neighbouring streets. *Clissold Crescent* has larger houses, some well maintained, some untouched for years.

To the E of *Albion Rd*, N of *Barbauld St* and *Dynevor Rd* is a maze of charming little streets lined mainly with 2-bedroomed houses. Though occasionally turned into tiny flats, for the most part these streets remain relatively unspoilt. Some houses are bigger, having a semi-basement floor as in the N side of *Dumont Rd*; beware of the light industry behind. S of *Barbauld St* and the kink in *Nevill Rd*, the area changes. The new well-designed low rise estate on the E side of *Nevill Rd* faces shops with flats above. From here the horizontal ladder of roads – *Beatty* down to *Barrett's Grove* – hold some larger 3- and 4-storey houses as well as smaller 2-storey homes. *Beatty*, *Walford* and *Brighton Rds* have houses with large gardens on their north sides. These streets still hold the odd unmodernised gem, and many flat conversions. The further S you go, the scruffier the streets become. *Palatine Rd* has smaller 2-storey houses, but the western end of the street finishes with a strange ziggurat configuration of buildings, for long neglected until they were literally falling down. Work has at last started on these, and the wasteland opposite is now a pleasant grassed area. *Prince George Rd* enjoys an open space halfway down with tennis courts. *Belgrade* and *Princess May Rds* and *Barrett's Grove* are a mix of 2- and 3-storey houses, some quite scruffy, all with gardens.

West of *Nevill* and *Wordsworth Rds*, and S of *Barbauld St*, but N of *Allen Rd*, *Milton Grove* and *Shakespeare Walk* are 4-storey terraces, now mainly flats – narrowish streets considering the heights of the buildings but some houses have superb-sized gardens at back. *Londesborough*, *Osterley* and *Clonbrock Rds* have 3-storey houses and many council flats. S of *Allen Rd* the area gives way to a bleak '50s estate, which the council is bravely trying to make more homely with bright paint, trees and turf. It would be a mistake to dismiss the streets surrounding this area out of hand. The local shopkeepers are friendly and offer a wide and interesting range of goods, and the council's genuine attempt to improve the unfortunate architecture they have inherited suggests that these streets around here may well become as sought-after as those a little further north.

Stoke Newington South

This area lies S of *Green Lanes*, *Matthias Rd* and *Barrett's Grove*, and N of the *Balls Pond Rd*. To the W it is bordered by *Wallace* and *Petherton Rds*, and to the E by *Kingsland High St*, and S end of *Stoke Newington Rd*. At the end of *Green Lanes* lies *Newington Green*, its 'green' now a small public garden enclosed by railings and, in effect, a roundabout. Its earlier days are recorded in the form of a small remaining group of Georgian houses and four which, amazingly, are said to have survived from the 1650s.

Starting in the NW corner of the neighbourhood, *Leaconfield Rd* snakes southwards and is edged with 2-storey bay-fronted Victorian houses, with semi-basements. The light industry at the N end is the downside of the coin, while large gardens are the up-side. *Poet's Rd*, similar in size to the *Leaconfield* end, is the first in a ladder of streets: *Ferntower, Pyrland, Beresford Rds* and the E end of *Grosvenor Avenue*. All have large 3- and 4-storey buildings, with good-sized gardens, but the S side of *Grosvenor Avenue* backs on to the railway, as does N side of *Northampton Grove*, where pretty 2-storey cottages are uncomfortably hemmed in by light industry. A corner to watch for conversions, however: one scheme in *Grosvenor Avenue* will provide eleven new flats. *Northampton Park* curves S to join the *Balls Pond Rd* and is a wide tree-lined street, edged with handsome Victorian villas, interspersed with one acceptable low-rise development, and one laughable modern attempt at Victorian proportions.

Crowning this area is wide *St Paul's Place*, where the 4-storey flat-fronted unspoilt terrace has gracious curved windows, and stucco-finished first stories painted uniformly grey. This street has an air of calm superiority unlike anything nearby. Discreet *Bingham St* is lined with lovely double-fronted but modest-sized houses. It joins *Newington Green Rd*, an extension of *Albion Rd*, which runs N-S and takes buses and through traffic. Lined with shops and pubs, it is the place for live music and holds most of the immediate area's amenities.

Some flats available above shops and well-maintained council terrace leads into medium sized high-rise estate, entered by *Mildmay St*, and *Avenue*, and introduces the 'Mildmay' area, where prices are high – sometimes deservedly, sometimes not. Running E-W through the middle of this corner is *Mildmay Grove*, eccentrically not one but two streets, separated along their length by the railway line. The houses stand behind front gardens, and gaze at each other across the walls which separate the grand terraces from the trains. Large gardens at the rear help to hold prices. Busy *Mildmay Park* runs N-S. It is scruffy at the S end, bordered by 4-storey flat-fronted buildings, mostly flats, and some light industry.

Mildmay Rd runs E-W. There are some charming 3- and 4-storey buildings, a featureless '60s block, and homes at the eastern end overlook another bleak council high rise. In between, wide *Wolsey Rd* and *Queen Margaret's Grove* are well worth a look, but there is a lot of council property in the latter. *King Henry's Walk* zigzags N-S and is a hotch-potch of council estate to the N, and Victorian building with shops sandwiched between less arresting structures. Schemes for this corner include one which has both homes and workshops.

Continuing the Tudor theme, *Boleyn Rd* runs N-S with a grim wasteland and run-down buildings at the N end. *Pellerin Rd* runs E and has pretty 2-storey Victorian houses on one side. The southern end of *Boleyn Rd* and the streets running off it is desolate; a place where houses once stood and others, boarded up, now stand, patiently waiting for the renovation which has taken place further north. Movement has begun: Pilot Properties' *Kingsland Green* development is providing 20 studios, flats and maisonettes, with garages/parking.

S

Among those estate agents active in this area are:
- Adam Kennedy
- Holden Matthews
- Michael Naik & Co
- Philip Phillips
- Prudential Property Services
- Winkworth

Streatham

Map ref: p109 (5J)	
Postal districts: SW16	
Boroughs: Lambeth (Lab), Wandsworth (Con)	
Rates: L: 187p in £, W: 130.8p in £	
Constituencies: Streatham (Con)	
Insurance: Scale 1	
Conservation areas: Streatham Village, Ullathorne/Abbotsleigh Rds	
Parking: Free	

Transport	British Rail: Streatham Common, Streatham (Victoria 15 min); Streatham Hill (London Bridge).
Convenient for	Routes to Gatwick Airport and South Coast. Miles from centre: 5.
Schools	ILEA zone 9: Dunraven School, St Martin-in-the-Fields C of E (g).

Flats	S	1b	2b	3b	4b	5b
Average prices	45–60	55–70	65–85	75–95	–	–
Houses	2b	3b	4b	5b	6/7b	8b
Average prices	80–95	85–150	120–170	140–180+	190–250	200–300+

The properties	Terraced Victorian/Edwardian and '20s/'30s semis, plus large blocks of 1900–1940 mansion flats. Some larger houses; Victorian and inter-war. Those overlooking the leafy Common particularly pleasant. Many flat conversions.
The market	Lack of tube lowers prices compared to neighbouring Clapham, Balham. Old-established families plus new-comers seeking larger homes with gardens and good-value flats. Local searches: Lambeth 9–10 weeks, Wandsworth 1 week.

Area Profile

The roots of Streatham go back a long way, but the former village first became popular in the late 17th century as a spa (there was a spring on Streatham Common) and growth was assured by its location on the main road between Croydon and Central London. City merchants built magnificent estates here in the early 1800s, especially on the N side of Streatham Common. Streatham Hill station was opened in 1856 and in the 1870s-80s farmland was sold to speculative property developers eager to capitalise on the success of the railways; as a result many estates were broken up. However, modern Streatham is divided into several neighbourhoods based to a large extent on these same estates.

Although it does not have a tube line yet, Streatham is commuter country with three BR stations (Streatham, Streatham Hill and Streatham Common). Indeed the absence of the tube is considered a positive advantage by some as it has kept house prices down. This will change if the proposed extension of the Victoria tube line down from Brixton goes ahead. However, this is a few years off yet and prices are still stable – and relatively low. On the whole, property is well cared for and the roads are spacious. Streatham has cinemas, restaurants, pubs and wine bars, skating rink and bowling alley – mostly concentrated along the *High Rd*.

Architecture is a mix of Victorian/Edwardian and post-war, the old villas mostly having been demolished. Little new development is planned as spare land is scarce. A fair number of large period properties have been converted into cheaper, smaller units over the years, and this, coupled with the relatively low prices, makes Streatham an affordable area for first and second time buyers. However, Lambeth Borough's conversion policies have been tightened up in an attempt to retain the small family dwelling. An area-based policy is in the pipeline, but currently conversions will not normally be allowed of any house less than 1,000 sq feet, or any 2-storey 3-bed terraced houses. Some developers fear a possible total rejection of all applications for conversion, although this could be professional paranoia as conversions do happen. But one word of warning – planning permission can be a lengthy business in Lambeth. Parts of Streatham are in Wandsworth, where conversion policies are freer – and rates much lower.

S

Furzedown

Furzedown covers the area N of the Tooting-Streatham railway, W of *Mitcham Lane* and *Thrale Rd* and E of *Rectory Lane*. Two thirds is considered part of Streatham – roughly the roads N of *Southcroft Rd* and E of *Freshwater Rd*. The rest is counted as Tooting. Furzedown is a popular family area with comfortably-sized 2-, 3- and 4-bed houses. It consists mainly of Edwardian terraces, the best examples being in *Clairview Rd*, off *Thrale Rd*, with well-maintained large 6-bed properties. The rest of Furzedown has pockets of comfortable Victorian and '30s terraced houses. Catching the 'over-spill' from Tooting, prices are relatively high (between £115-135,000 for terraced 3-bed Edwardian houses, £140-160,000 plus for a 4-bed). Parkside Mews is 11 new 2/3-bed houses in *Westcote Rd*. *Rural Way*, off *Streatham Rd*, has a modern development of smart 3/4-bed houses. These lie just over the borough boundary in Merton. The nearby station and tube line within driving distance add to prices. The large Furzedown School is central to the area.

Streatham Park

Streatham Park is bordered by *Tooting Bec Rd*, *Thrale Rd* and the railway line to the E. This was once the site of the Thrale family's estate. Their close friend, the author Dr Johnson, frequently came to visit, and history is now documented in the road names; *Thrale Rd* and *Dr Johnson Avenue* (across Tooting Bec Common). The main house was demolished in 1863 and the area now holds smart, well-maintained council blocks – notably the GLC's Fayland Estate – most privately owned. There are still some stately period villas from Streatham's 18th century heyday overlooking Tooting Bec Common which are pricy, if a little noisy with the main road opposite, interspersed with modern infill (flats and houses). South of the council blocks, properties are small Edwardian, grand Victorian (with some conversions) and quaint '30s 'whimsy'. The whole area is leafy, quiet and very attractive. Streatham Park also enjoys Wandsworth Borough's favourable rates.

The small neighbourhood to the E of Streatham Park contains real nuggets of local history. Possibly the oldest part in Streatham, it is perhaps better known because of famous resident Cynthia Payne. *Pinkerton Place*, off *Tooting Bec Gardens*, has comfortable early '80s purpose-built flats; small rooms, but well designed (1/2-bed flat c £70,000). Surrounding properties are mainly stately Victorian; road names relating to the Lake District, (*Thirlmere Rd*, *Rydal Rd*, etc) have large 6/7-bed period houses. Tree-lined *Riggindale Rd* has some beautiful conversions of semi-detached Victoriana. The parish church, St Leonards, is on the corner of *Tooting Bec Gardens* overlooking an awesome traffic-blackspot where all the main roads converge.

Central Streatham

Central Streatham contains some truly splendid houses. Well-placed for shops in the *High Rd* and the train stations of Streatham and Streatham Hill, its leafy roads are extremely popular. It comprises roads running E from *Garrad's Rd* to *Streatham High Rd*. Properties are mainly attractive '20s and '30s detached and semi-detached houses in a variety of styles – stucco and bay windows/tile-hung gables/mock Tudor. There are large impressive turn-of-the-century 6-bed houses in *Steep Hill*, *Becmead Avenue*, *Prentis Rd* and *Woodbourne Avenue*. Very few of the houses in this area have been converted and there are only a couple of modern infills – very smart, but rather out of place. Emsworth Court in *Ockley Rd* is flats with a squash club adjoining; and '70s flats in *Tarrington Close*. One noticeable feature of 'Central' is the epidemic of doctors' and dentists' name-plates on the walls. Central is also the renowned red-light district of Streatham and this has tended to depress house prices – not that you'd notice since nothing here is less than £200,000 – but plans are under way to tackle the problem – for example a proposed oneway system.

The roads to the N, running up to Streatham Hill BR, contain period properties in varying states of repair. A number of these large houses have been converted – particularly on the E side of the area near the *High Rd*. Some spacious '20s-'30s houses in *Broadlands Avenue*.

Streatham Hill

Streatham Hill lies N of the BR station and *Leigham Court Rd*, E of *Rastell*

Avenue and *New Park Rd*, S of *Christchurch Rd* and W of *Hillside Rd/Leigham Vale*. It is an increasingly popular area – well located for trains and main roads plus Brixton's Victoria Line tube, a short bus-ride away. The side W of Streatham Hill is mainly attractive period property with purpose-built flats and some flat-conversions, maisonettes and houses. *Killieser Avenue, Criffel Avenue* and *Kirkstall Rd* are particularly popular with charming period terraces and some larger houses. There are also '30s houses in good repair in the area. A few recent 1/2/3-bed flats in *Telford Avenue, Killiese Avenue & Montrell Rd*. The corner between the *South Circular* and *Streatham Hill* holds many conversions. However, until Lambeth's conversion policy is finalised, no further conversions are permitted in *Tierney* and *Montrell Rds*. East of the *High Rd* there is

an OAP and disabled people's enclave in *Barstow Crescent* (off *Palace Rd*) of chalet dwellings round small blocks of flats. *Palace Rd* itself, which is closed off at its junction with the *South Circular*, has a few surviving large 19th century houses and an ex-GLC estate with an attractive grassy setting.

Nearer the station are the popular 'ABCD' roads (*Amesbury, Barcombe, Cricklade and Downton Rds*) which feature late Victorian red brick terraced cottages and maisonettes, built by the philanthropic Artisans & General Dwellings Company in 1889-94 on the site of the old Leigham Court estate: these were the fore-runners of local authority housing. A few conversions (flats to houses ratio is 1:4). Attractive later terraces also in *Cricklade* and *Downton*. Beneath the 'ABCDs' are largely '20s and stately red-brick, eg, the leafy *Mount Nod Rd*, but also note *Hitherfield* – its Victorian cottage terraces lining a steep hill are reminiscent of a Hovis adver-

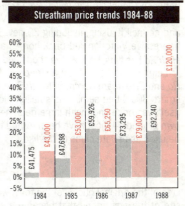

Streatham price trends 1984-88

London average home: percentage rise on previous year, adjusted for inflation.
Typical home in this area, percentage rise on previous year, adjusted for inflation.

Three-bed semi in central Streatham, price change compared to London-wide average home. Value for money seems good here, we commented last year. And in '88 Streatham led the areas plotted in these graphs with a massive increase. Buyers are comparing value here with nearby Tooting and Clapham – and reassessing the virtues of suburbia, perhaps?

tisement. Streatham Hill is a most attractive and popular area. Prices have risen fast over the last couple of years as the Hill picks up the 'overspill' from Clapham – but is generally still good value. The mansion flats along *Streatham hill*, like those along *Streatham High Rd*, remain popular. Gracefield, also known as Culverhouse, lies just beneath the Hill and is a quietly respectable area, popular with local residents, lying E of the *High Rd* and W of the railway line. It has a mix of late Victorian and smart chalet-style '20s/'30s houses. *Pendennis* and *Pinfold Rds* have '30s semis. Turnover of residents is low although demand, especially for the attractive 1930s houses, is high.

Streatham Village

Streatham Village – a name to make the hearts of local historians beat faster –

isn't as old as it sounds. The original nucleii of Streatham around St Leonards Church and Streatham Common date back to mediaeval times, whereas the 'Village' was only started in the mid 1800s. Houses are mixed in style, but rather appealing, especially the charming 3-bed Victorian cottages in *Sunnyhill* and *Wellfield Rds*. There are also larger Victorian villas in red brick and some skillful conversions are available. Also '30s and more modern 2-3 bed units in *Sunnyhill Rd*. *Angles Rd* houses a development of 25 flats and houses, completion this spring. There is heavy demand for the cottage properties in the village, but residents are understandably reluctant to move. Well located for transport between Streatham and Streatham Hill stations, and near to main shopping street, it is a designated conservation area. The streets lying to the S, between *Gleneldon Rd*, *Valley Rd*, *Streatham Common North* and the *High Rd*, contain a real mix of properties from Victorian through to early 20th century and council housing, including 30 new 1/2-bed flats and houses in *Valley Rd*. Impressive Victorian red brick homes are found in *Gleneldon Rd*. The nearby *High Rd* has flats, both above shops and in purpose-built 20th century blocks.

Leigham Court, built on a steep hill, lies between *Leigham Court Rd*, *Valley Rd* and *Streatham Common North Side*. Basically council to the N and largeish, smart '30s 4-bed semis and smaller, older houses to the S. *Leigham Court Rd* itself was once lined with large detached Victorian mansions, standing in their own grounds – most have been turned into flats and the few remaining tend to be used as private clubs or the like.

Streatham Common

One of the original nucleii of the town was centred on Streatham Common, the site of the first spring that became a spa. This area is very popular with the professional classes and filled with excellent Victorian and Edwardian properties with large gardens on the E side of the *High Rd* – pricy, highly desirable being near to the Common, with quiet leafy roads – and cheaper, if smaller and less well-maintained, houses to the W of the *High Rd*. *Lewin* and *Barrow Rds* have many conversions (as does *Gleneagle Rd*, up on the N side of the tracks) and are becoming really popular. Prices reflect this. *Ferrers* and *Natal Rds* have smaller cottages, some of which have been converted to flats and are relatively cheap. Popular roads are *Heybridge Avenue*, *Fontaine Rd* and *Braxted Park* (E of the *High Rd*). Towards W Norwood, in SE27, Canterbury Mews is a handsome new addition to *Canterbury Grove*.

Streatham Vale

The cheapest area in Streatham. Its borders run along the railway lines to the N and W, and along *Greyhound Terrace* and *Hassocks Rd*. Most of the area was built by Wates in the '20s and '30s and consists of row upon row of 2-storey terraced and semi-detached houses. It is a good-value area for first-time buyers and is near to Streatham Common station. There are also some conversions dotted around. Very intensive housing with roads packed tightly together – more like Tooting than Streatham.

Among those estate agents active in this area are:
- Folkard & Hayward
- Hooper & Jackson
- Jackson Property Services
- Winkworths

Tottenham and Finsbury Park

Map ref: p31 (4F)
Postal districts: N22, N18, N17, N15, N4
Boroughs: Haringey (Lab), Islington (Lab), Hackney (Lab)
Rates: Har: 226.83p in £, I: 184.33p, Hac: 229.4p
Constituencies: Tottenham (Lab), Islington North (Lab), Hackney North and Stoke Newington. (Lab)
Insurance: Scale 1
Conservation areas: check town hall
Parking: Free

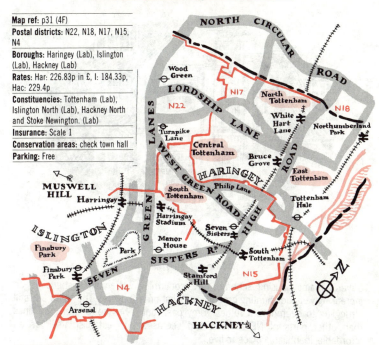

Transport	Tubes: Finsbury Park (zone 2 Piccadilly, Victoria), Arsenal. Manor House, Turnpike Lane, Wood Lane (zones 2/3a Piccadilly), Tottenham Hale, Seven Sisters (zone 3a Victoria). From Seven Sisters: Oxford Circus 20 min, City 25 min (1 change), Heathrow 1 hr (1 change) British Rail: 16 min to Liverpool St. Good buses.

Convenient for North Circular, A10 to Cambridge, Wood Green Shopping City.

Schools Haringey Education Authority, ILEA zones 3/4: The Drayton, Gladesmore Community School, High Cross, Northumberland Park.

Flats	S	1b	2b	3b	4b	5b
Average prices	51–58	56–68	65–80	70–90+	–	–
Houses	2b	3b	4b	5b	6/7b	8b
Average prices	65–90	70–125	90–155	120–170	140–190	–

The properties Terraced houses (2-3 beds) built between 1890-1920 are most common. Fair number of inter-war houses. Flat conversions and council re-sales mean more small houses and 1-2 bed flats.

The market Affordable prices for first-time buyers of flats and original-features terraced houses. N 17 least expensive: far from tube, close to council estates and football. Council encourages newbuild; developers responding. Local searches: Haringey 4 weeks, Islington 2 weeks, Hackney 16 weeks.

Area Profile

Several major housing schemes are confirming Tottenham's status as an increasingly good hunting-ground for first-time buyers. The area is still struggling to overcome a rather grimy past, but it has better transport links than other parts of NE London and seems set to establish itself as an affordable, identifiable place to live.

In broad terms, the Tottenham area is bounded to the N by the *A406* (*North Circular Rd*), to the S by the *A503* (*Seven Sisters Rd*) and the *A107*, to the E by the Lea Valley reservoir complex and to the W by *Wightman Rd* and the northern part of *Green Lanes* (*High Rd*).

Until the last quarter of the 19th century, Tottenham was a small, agricultural village, boasting several fine houses used as country residences by minor titled gentry. Today only one or two of these remain, saved by conversion into public buildings – such as Bruce Castle, which now houses the local history museum. With the advent of the industrial revolution, and because of its proximity to the city, more and more people began to move into Tottenham. By 1881 the population had risen to over 46,000, three times the level in 1861.

Today the area is predominantly residential, composed mainly of 2- and 3-bed terraced houses built between 1890-1920. Although modernised, 50% of these houses have downstairs bathrooms (due to their shape), but estate agents in the area agree that around 30% retain original features, such as fireplaces and cornicing and sash windows. Estate agents also report that houses with one or two original fireplaces are very easy to sell. Of course, original features are much rarer in conversions, though conversion standards have improved greatly over the last year because the council have now implemented much stricter controls. Later residential expansion in Tottenham continued during the inter-war period, particularly in the Dowsett estate region on the eastern side. A programme of council housing development in the '60s resulted in further expansion in the northern area of Tottenham, including the controversial Broadwater Farm Estate. There are some light industrial works and warehouse depots bordering Hackney Marshes, although some of these have tended to fall into disrepair.

Tottenham is served by excellent transport facilities, with quick access by rail and tube to the West End and the City, and by road to the *North Circular Rd*, *M25*, *M1*, and *M11*. Such facilities are a major advantage of living in Tottenham, particularly in the region near Seven Sisters BR and tube stations. Buses are frequent, and particularly good for local travel.

The area is truly cosmopolitan, with a corresponding diversity in the different kinds of shops and cultural activities available to residents. At the same time, the necessary demands of the multi-ethnic community place a heavy burden on education and employment schemes, with high rates as a consequence.

A number of shops – of the 'yuppie' designer tendency – have opened on the High Road, but there is still a dearth of good restaurants in the area. You have to travel to Stoke Newington or Turnpike Lane for a good meal, although Tottenham does boast the famous Empire Tea Rooms on *Broad Lane*.

Property in the area is improving all the time, with prices within the grasp of first-time buyers (of flats, in particular). Despite the notable influx of young professionals seeking manageable mortgages and quick access to work, it remains one of the cheapest parts of N London.

T

South Tottenham (N15)

The area lies S of *West Green Rd* and *Philip Lane*, N of *Seven Sisters Rd* and *Amhurst Park*, W of the *High Rd*, and E of *Green Lanes*. Homes with an N15 postcode tend to be more expensive than equivalent properties in N17, because of their proximity to the Stamford Hill, Stoke Newington and Turnpike Lane regions; the short distance from Seven Sisters tube also helps.

Most homes in this neighbourhood are 2- and 3-bedroomed terraced houses, built during the late 19th and early 20th centuries. Many of the larger houses have been or are currently being converted into flats.

There are good shopping facilities on *West Green Rd*, *Philip Lane* and *Seven Sisters Rd*, including Tesco's at Seven Sisters and Safeway's store at *Stamford Hill*. There are abundant local grocers, butchers and ethnic food shops.

The W side of the *High Rd* from Seven Sisters tube to *Philip Lane* includes (working up from the S) a row of 3-storey terraced houses, built in the 1880s, which have either been converted into flats or are currently undergoing complete modernisation. *Pelham Rd*, which leads directly off the *High Rd* is an attractive, modern Barratts development, with the small terraces of 2-bed properties continuing into *Portland Rd*; good parking space here for residents. Continuing northwards is the Jewish Home and Hospital, the Tottenham College of Technology, the Town Hall (opposite Tottenham Green) and, off *Town Hall Rd*, the site for the new Cultural, Social, and Sports Centre (completion postponed until late this year).

The triangular area formed by *Philip Lane*, *West Green Rd* and the *High Rd* comprises a series of roughly parallel streets of 2- and 3-bed terraced houses (1900s) – broken by the popular *Clyde Circus* and *Clyde Rd*. Similar properties exist S of *W Green Rd* in the rectangle formed with *Green Lanes*, *St Ann's Rd* and *High Rd*, with property in *Seaford*, *Roslyn*, and *Greenfield Rds* still particularly good.

Houses in this section become increasingly expensive towards *Green Lanes* and *Turnpike Lane*, with the houses in *Cranleigh Rd* and *Conway Rd* typical examples of the higher price range of 2- and 3-bed properties.

The region S of *St Ann's Rd* and N of *Seven Sisters Rd* is bisected by *Hermitage Rd* and includes the solid property chain of *Kimberley, Chesterfield,* and *Roseberry Gardens,* which link up to *Warwick Gardens.* These streets tend to serve motorists as short cuts between *St Ann's Rd* and *Grand Parade.* St Ann's General Hospital lies behind *Warwick Gardens,* with the railway running to the S of it.

On the other side of the tracks, this section also includes a major development area, with Harringay Stadium due to be replaced by a large Sainsbury's supermarket. Planning permission has been given to McAlpine for a new housing development next to Sainsburys. It will be called 'St Anne's Village' and will consist of 221 homes, ranging from 1-bed flats to 4-bed houses.

Central Tottenham (N17)

Lying N of *West Green Rd* and *Philip Lane,* S of *Lordship Lane,* W of the *High Rd,* and E of *Westbury Avenue,* this region is served by Bruce Grove BR station. Here there are mainly 2- and 3-bedroomed terraces and the Broadwater Farm Estate, a late '60s concrete block project.

Characteristic mid-range (c £85,000), early 20th century 2- and 3-bed terraced houses cluster in the eastern part of the area – *Napier Rd, Steele Rd, Chester Rd* and *Morrison Rd.* In particular, *Mount Pleasant Rd,* a heavy traffic thoroughfare, is undergoing extensive development, with a fair number of houses being converted into flats. Green spaces come in the form of Lordship Recreation Ground and Downhills Park. The Broadwater Farm council estate still casts a rather depressing shadow over nearby streets (*Higham Rd, The Avenue,* northern end of *Mount Pleasant Rd*).

North Tottenham (N17)

Tottenham's northern reaches stop at a point some half-mile below the *North Circular Rd,* where N17 becomes N18 and the borough boundary also runs. The area is bounded to the S by *Lordship Lane,* on the W by the *A10.* and on the E by the *High Rd.* There are some inter-war semis around *Lordship Lane.* Pleasant post-war council houses lie N of *Lordship Lane* and *Roundway.*

Interesting areas include Tower Gardens, which is enclosed by *Lordship Lane* and *The Roundway* and bisected by *Risley Avenue,* offering attractive property (conservation area); eastwards *Church Lane* has very pleasant 'mews' type houses near the popular Antwerp Arms, and borders Bruce Castle Park (where the Bruce Castle Museum of Local History is situated). Developers Rialto were last winter awaiting planning permission for a major scheme which will bring 200 homes on the old Somerset Upper School site, between *Creighton Rd* and *White Hart Lane.* There will be studios, flats and 3-4-bed townhouses. Selling should start late this spring at prices expected to start at around £58,000.

Further N is Tottenham Cemetary, White Hart Lane BR Station, and the *Great Cambridge Rd,* with purpose-built council houses leading up to the *North Circular.* Prospective buyers in this area should be aware that the widening/ streamlining of the *N Circular* will take around 4 years to complete. Shopping facilities have been improved recently by the Sainsbury's located mid-way up the *High Rd.*

East Tottenham (N15 and N17)

Lies between *High Rd* to the W and Hackney Marshes to the E, and bounded on the N by the *North Circular Rd* and to the S by *Clapton Common Rd. Ferry Lane*, running W-E beneath Tottenham Hale tube station, marks the dividing line between N17 and N15. The easterly section is the light industrial area, currently undergoing development.

The northerly area is characterised by the *Northumberland Park* estate, a development area with generally cheaper house prices because of the proximity to White Hart Lane, Tottenham Hotspur's football stadium. *Park Lane*, in particular, fails to live up to its name. Mainly 2-bedroomed terraced houses here and some conversions into flats.

South of *Lansdowne Rd* is the popular *Dowsett Rd* estate, with *Sherringham*, *Seymour*, and *Thackery Rds* offering reasonable investments. Some inter-war semis here.

In the area enclosed by the *High Rd* and the one-way system (*Chesnut Rd/Broad Lane*) are a strange combination of older, gentrified properties and rather shabby properties behind The Prince of Wales Hospital. *Tynemouth Rd* is still a good first-time buyers' street, with *Talbot Rd* a slightly more up-market version. South of this area, the property tends to decline, but there is room for beneficial development in this region. There is a rumour that there are schemes afoot to build a marina with penthouse flats and shopping centre overlooking the River Lea, on the site where the Gestetner factory used to be. This would obviously benefit properties in S and E Tottenham. And even if the marina scheme doesn't get off the ground, Haringey Council are unlikely to let the land go to waste.

South of *Broad Lane* towards Stamford Hill is the area known as 'Tottenham Village' by residents and local estate agents. Centering on *Wargrave Avenue* and *Grovelands Rd*, prices are higher here.

Tottenham Hale (Victoria Line tube, and BR) provides useful alternative to Seven Sisters tube and rail transport.

T

Border areas

To the S (in Stamford Hill) and to the W (in Harringay and Wood Green) there are more desirable properties, although they are also more costly. 3-bedroomed terraced houses, for example, in the section known as the Harringay Ladder (the series of parallel streets stretching from *Umfreville Rd* up to *Turnpike Lane* on the W side of *Green Lanes*) will sell for between £115,-120,000, particularly in the central section (*Allison Rd, Seymour Rd*). In *Seymour*, an architects' folly, built in 1896, was for sale last winter. The triangular, canalside house is a maze of rooms on different levels, connected by no less than nine short staircases. A fair number of the Ladder's more normal houses have been converted into 1- and 2-bed flats, fetching from £70,000 in streets such as *Frobisher Rd* and *Hewitt Rd*.

However, a recent lorry ban on *Endyminion Rd* may cause increased traffic on the ladder roads as heavy vehicles find alternative routes. Further W, towards Hornsey, beware of the Parkland Walk scheme to build a major dual-carriageway along this railway track-turned-nature reserve. Haringey Council, opposed to these government plans, say it will affect 13,000 houses in the area. It is only one among several proposals for the NE London area. See 'Transport' chapter.

Finsbury Park

Southwards the Haringey borough boundary dips down to take in the green acres of Finsbury Park and some of its surrounding streets – *Stroud Green Rd* marks the border with Islington borough, *Seven Sisters* that with Hackney.

The most significant difference between Finsbury Park and the rest of the Tottenham area is in the size and quality of the houses – there is a much greater number of large, attractive 3- and 4-storey houses, built mainly around the turn of the century. There is also more variety in the style of housing, with more double-fronted, semi-detached, and detached properties.

As a result, many of the streets are more aesthetically pleasing than the streets of smaller, 2-storey terraced houses in the main Tottenham area. The larger houses – originally 5- and 6-bedrooms – are ideal for conversion into flats, something which property developers have exploited to the full. Fortunately, there are still houses available which remain as single properties, though these tend to be run-down and bought by landlords and developers.

The Finsbury Park area is characterised, naturally, by the huge park, which is bordered by *Green Lanes, Seven Sisters Rd, Endymion Rd,* and the BR line running from Harringay Station to Finsbury Park Station.

Recreational facilities within the park include tennis courts, a cricket ground, gardens, and an area set aside for rock concerts, festivals, fairs, and other special events. In a region otherwise largely bereft of greenery, the park represents an important leisure area to the community. There is sometimes a problem when large music festivals are held in the park, not only because of the build-up of traffic, but also because there have in the past been outbreaks of violence. Other recreational facilities in the area include the Michael Sobel Sports Centre on *Tollington Rd.* An exciting and ambitious plan for nearby *Isledon Rd* would result in the transformation of 10 acres of old railway land into 218 new houses, workspace units and garden centre. The Finsbury Park Community Plan's architects, Hunt Thompson, have building society, bank and housing association backing. If the scheme goes ahead, it will have rented homes 'at affordable prices' and could create 500 jobs.

Finsbury Park is difficult to categorise in general terms because it lies in no less than three London boroughs – Haringey, Hackney, and Islington. Consequently house prices, rates and local services vary considerably within the Finsbury Park neighbourhood, depending on the borough you're in.

For example, streets in the borough of Islington tend to be much cleaner than those in the other two boroughs. On the other hand, where Haringey has sometimes sacrificed the quality of housing in favour of its availability (in a bid to assuage the housing shortage), Hackney Council have much stricter planning permission policies, which ensure that rooms have to be of a certain size and quality before they are considered fit for habitation.

Finsbury Park's main advantage is its excellent transport facilities. The area is served by Finsbury Park tube (Piccadilly and Victoria lines) and BR stations (affording quick and easy access to the West End and the City), and by Manor House and Arsenal tubes, and a very good bus service.

The centre of Finsbury Park is marked by the X-shaped road junction formed by *Stroud Green Rd, Blackstock Rd* and *Seven Sisters Rd.* The section of the *Seven Sisters Rd* leading down from Manor House is bordered on its western side by the park and on its eastern side by a series of hotels, most of which serve as DHSS/temporary accommodation. Behind the hotels, in the triangle formed by *Portland Rise, Gloucester Drive,* and *Seven Sisters Rd* are some very attractive homes, including detached 2-storey double-fronted houses, some of which have been converted into flats. Also of interest is the Hammond Roberts development of modern flats, and the Wilberforce Housing Action Area Office, both just off *Seven Sisters Rd*.

The central area of Finsbury Park, at the junction of *Stroud Green Rd*, *Blackstock Rd* and *Seven Sisters Rd* is built around the tube/rail stations, which have been made part of a shopping complex. The one-way traffic system here can be confusing if you're new to the area! The Sir George Robey pub, a short walk from the tube is well known as a live venue for rock bands.

The rectangle formed by *Seven Sisters Rd*, *Queens Drive*, *Blackstock Rd*, and *Brownswood Rd* (incorporating *Wilberforce Rd*) was a red-light district in the '40s, but the roads have been blocked off to prevent curb-crawling, giving rise to relatively quiet, tree-lined streets – the properties are good here, fetching high prices. New residential properties – and possibly a hypermarket – are being built on the site of the old filter beds behind *Queens Drive*. King's Crescent Estate on the S side of *Brownswood Rd* is one of the few large council estates in this area of Finsbury Park. The triangle formed by *Blackstock Rd*, *St. Thomas's Rd*, and *Gillespie Rd* houses large, attractive properties, many of which have again been converted into flats.

The area to the S of *Stroud Green Rd* is made up of attractive streets such as *Charteris Rd*, *Fonthill Rd*, and *Moray Rd*, with many 4-storey houses converted into flats, and also includes the Finsbury Park Trading Estate. Further S is a large council estate in the rectangle formed by *Durham Rd*, *Seven Sisters Rd*, *Birnham Rd/Moray Rd*, and *Hornsey Rd*. SE of here is the Sobell Sports Centre, an excellent modern leisure facility. Check out the properties in the *Corbyn St* area just off the *Hornsey Rd*: they were bombed during the war and there have been some subsidence problems.

In general, then, Finsbury Park is an area with an increasing number of flats and a decreasing number of large single properties. There is little space for new development, but conversions are frequent. Those properties in the borough of Islington will have the cheapest rates and will probably be more 'desirable' since the owner can say 'I live in Islington' rather than in Finsbury Park.

Once again, Finsbury Park is a prime target for the ubiquitous young urban professional – witness the new wine bars, refurbished pubs, new restaurants. There is no restriction on parking, except on main roads and some off-street parking. However, traffic wardens are now making forays into the area. Because of different boroughs, local authority searches may take from 3-6 weeks.

Among those estate agents active in this area are:

Tottenham:
- Adam Kennedy
- Bairstow Eves
- Castles
- Cousins
- Paul Simon
- Talbots
- Winkworths

Finsbury Park:
- Christopher Charles
- Robert Anthony
- Brian Thomas

Totteridge and Whetstone

Map ref: p14 (1C)
Postal districts: N20, N11
Borough: Barnet (Con)
Rates: 189.7p in £
Constituencies: Chipping Barnet (Con). Finchley (Con)
Insurance: Scale 1
Conservation areas: Totteridge and Friern Barnet
Parking: Free

Transport	Tubes: Totteridge & Whetstone (zone 3b, Northern) to Oxford Circus 35 min (1 change), City 35 min, Heathrow 1 hr 30 min (1 change).
Convenient for	North Circular, M1/M25. Miles from centre: 9.
Schools	Barnet Education Authority: Ravenscroft School, Friern Barnet County School. Private: Friern Barnet Grammar.

Flats	S	1b	2b	3b	4b	5b
Average prices	55–65	60–70	70–95	75–150	–	–
Houses	2b	3b	4b	5b	6/7b	8b
Average prices	95–125	125–250+	150–400+	250–650+	→	→2m

The property	Totteridge has grand 6-8+ bedroom houses set in near-countryside. Whetstone has more luxury houses, slightly smaller, and smart p/b flats. Friern Barnet has a range from smaller terraced homes to large detacheds.
The market	People in Totteridge and Whetstone have arrived: show-biz, smart professionals, all with children and attendant ponies and pets. Amenities here can be anything from a nuclear shelter to a sunken recording studio. Friern Barnet is more urban, with scope for less prosperous buyers. Local searches: 4 weeks.

Area Profile

Take Hampstead's Bishop's Avenue, move its mansions to the northern fringes of London and dot them along a meandering country lane, add ponies and paddocks – there you have Totteridge.

This foretaste of open countryside and its attendant areas of Whetstone, with its busy shopping parade and the Northern Line tube, and Friern Barnet, are still London – just. To the N lies Barnet proper, out of the London postal area and suddenly, indefinably, *Greater* London. Southwards lies Finchley, and the metropolis. A sign that these areas are joining London proper is the enhanced interest in them by West End estate agents, who are responding to the growing call for family homes.

Totteridge

Though it has a London postcode (N20), Totteridge is to all intents and purposes a country village – albeit one largely consisting of grand mansions. To the N of *Totteridge Common/Village/Lane* and the roads around lie the golf course and wide open spaces and the village itself is a pretty focal point. Totteridge is not a big place and neighbours tend to know each other. They have met because their children attend the village school or because they are active in the local ratepayer's association or perhaps through one of the local sports clubs – but not, probably, over the garden fence. Houses in the area tend to be set in large, secluded plots of land. On Sundays Totteridge folk drop in to the Orange Tree pub for a drink then take the dogs for a walk and head down to Laurel Farm to feed the ducks and meet their neighbours. The neighbours tend to be professionals or show-business people who relish the privacy that a Totteridge home affords. This is not Hampstead – positively ostentatious by comparison – where people go to be seen; here famous faces go by relatively unremarked.

There are few, if any, small houses in Totteridge which is known for its 6-, 7- and 8-bedroom palaces, complete with tennis court, sauna and good security systems. *Totteridge Lane* and any of the roads that run off it are prime locations, many of the roads are private and have views over the golf course or acres of Green Belt land. Prices are in the £1-2 million range for houses in the best roads, *Totteridge Lane Common*, *Pine Grove*, *Grange Avenue*, and properties in and around *The Green*. The names of *Northcliffe Drive* and *Harmsworth Way* recall the great press baron who lived here. An enclave of new 'executive homes' planned for *Southway* will be the first new development here for nine years. Towards the tube station, roads such as *Hill Crescent*, *Greenway* and *Lynton Mead* are less opulent, though the 4- and 5-bed detached houses still fetch some £280-320,000. Totteridge is not the place to look for flats and agents suggest Woodside Park for luxury purpose-built blocks.

Totteridge lies in the borough of Barnet which means that rates here are comparatively low – another advantage over Hampstead. Schools nearby in Elstree are Haberdashers for boys and girls and Aldenham for boys only, and the *M1* and *M25* motorways are not far away. However, for those without a chauffeur communications are a little more difficult and there is a poor bus service – though the Northern Line does come out to Totteridge and Whetstone. There are no shops to speak of, but last year The Spires, Barnet's new shopping centre, added major stores to the *Whetstone High Rd* selection. *Totteridge Lane* is a long, winding and wooded road, a daunting walk from the

T

tube. Most Totteridge householders seem however to have enough cars to make walking a sport rather than a necessity.

Whetstone

Totteridge becomes Whetstone when *Totteridge Lane* reaches the tube station. The majority of properties in Whetstone are large semi- and detached houses, mostly less expensive than those in Totteridge, and there are also purpose-built flats. Off *High Rd*, Whetstone, there are many favoured streets: *Chandos* and *Buckingham Avenues* offer 5- and 6-bed houses for around £350-400,000. *Church Gate* is a new cul-de-sac of 5-bedroomed houses behind electronic gates off *Church Crescent*: from £375,000. Property along the *High Rd* itself includes many fine houses and purpose-built blocks, but they do have the disadvantage of being set on a busy stretch of road. Heading S along the *High Rd* past the parade of shops is the elegant corner of Oakleigh Park where roads such as *Oakleigh Park North* and *Oakleigh Park South* are quiet, leafy and well-located, as are the surrounding streets. They also have the benefit of Oakleigh Park BR station nearby. The roads offer large houses, a mixture of semi-detached properties with good gardens, and nearby at the beginning of *Oakleigh Rd North* are fine purpose-built blocks. Similar in name, but not stature, the main road from Whetstone to Southgate is *Oakleigh Rd North/Oakleigh Rd South*. It's a mixture of small properties and shops and prices hereabouts tend to be cheaper than elsewhere in Whetstone.

Friern Barnet

Running off *Whetstone High Rd*, *Friern Barnet Lane* leads past the North Middlesex Golf Course to Friern Barnet itself. The great landmark in Friern Barnet is the psychiatric hospital in *Friern Barnet Rd*, but this will be no more in a few years. Once closed, its 37-acre site will be used for housing; the face of Friern Barnet will be changed forever. The area already offers a wide range of properties; a mixture of small terraced homes, some large detached houses in *Friern Barnet Lane* and the surrounding roads, purpose-built flats, and plenty of Victorian and Edwardian properties converted into flats. Conveniently close to the *North Circular* and with a BR line into King's Cross, it is an up-and-coming area and something of a contrast to well-established Whetstone and Totteridge. A good hunting ground for less expensive smaller properties than those of neighbouring areas, it attracts more first-time buyers. Developers are building (mainly flats) here.

There are some fine large semi- and detached houses in and around *Friern Barnet Lane*, probably the prime street, and its location near Friary Park makes it popular. *Friern Barnet Rd*, running towards New Southgate, has much cheaper properties with many solid houses built in the Victorian and Edwardian era. Nearby in *Woodhouse Rd* are 1930s semis and terraces.

There are many larger flats which have been converted from houses, as well as purpose-built ones, and two fairly new purpose-built blocks in *Colney Hatch Lane*, which runs down to the *North Circular* and *Brunswick Park Rd*.

Among those estate agents active in this area are:
- Anscombe & Ringland
- William H Brown
- Hamptons
- Ferrier Tomlin
- Martyn Gerrard
- Michael Lawrence

Wandsworth

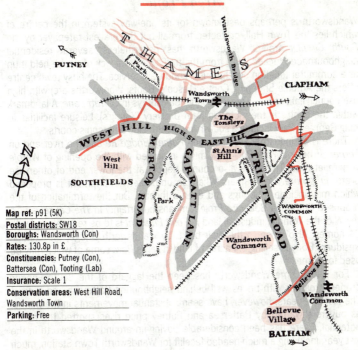

Map ref: p91 (5K)
Postal districts: SW18
Boroughs: Wandsworth (Con)
Rates: 130.8p in £
Constituencies: Putney (Con), Battersea (Con), Tooting (Lab)
Insurance: Scale 1
Conservation areas: West Hill Road, Wandsworth Town
Parking: Free

W

Transport	British Rail: Wandsworth Town (Waterloo 12 min), Wandsworth Common.	
Convenient for	Wandsworth and Clapham Commons, Clapham Junction BR. Miles from centre: 4.	
Schools	ILEA zone 10: Burntwood School (g), John Archer School (b), Southfields. Private: Emanuel (b).	

Flats	S	1b	2b	3b	4b	5b
Average prices	60	65–80	80–120	100–125	–	–
Houses	2b	3b	4b	5b	6/7b	8b
Average prices	95–140	130–170	170–200+	200–225+	300+	–

The properties	Wide range, but main type is Victorian terraced in a range of locations, with cottage-style in the Tonsleys and grander ones near the Common. Despite developers' attentions, still some unmodernised houses to be had. Some '30s and '50s suburban houses in SW of area. Watch, too, for resales of good ex-council. 'Right-to-buy' (and sell) in full swing here.
The market	Some popular corners – Tonsleys, Bellevue, 'Toastrack' (all close to stations) – approach Clapham prices. Putney overspill pushes up prices at W end. Local searches: 1 week.

Area Profile

Wandsworth is perhaps best known for its one-way system in the centre of which lies the Town Hall, protected from all but the bravest ratepayer by the *South Circular* traffic. Wandsworth has nevertheless, several residential neighbourhoods tucked away from the traffic jams. Its lack of a tube held it up as a commuter location but there is a good train service. The busy town centre offers the Arndale Shopping Centre (Tesco's, Boots, Woolworths etc) with high rise council flats above. There is a large Sainsburys in *Garratt Lane*. A landmark within the centre is the Victorian Ram Brewery (Young's). Leisure facilities in King George's Park include a squash and health club and tennis courts.

There is an industrial area between *Putney Bridge Rd* and the river and on *Ferrier St* behind *York Rd* – now much improved with the opening of *Warple Way* relief road. There are also council depots at the lower end of otherwise pretty *Frogmore*. On Feathers Wharf an upmarket development is proposed which may include moorings and even a theatre. But the termination of the proposed Battersea Boatyard Project means uncertainty in *The Causeway*. To the W of the Wandle, industrial land in *Point Pleasant* is to be redeveloped with 24 homes. Also close to the river but E by Wandsworth Bridge, the London Residuary Body is selling 1.4 acres of land in *Jew's Row*, some of which may be used for homes.

For a long time Wandsworth has been the laggard of the South London property market with prices well behind neighbouring Battersea and Putney. The last few years, however, have seen substantial movements in the market as buyers thwarted by Battersea and Putney price rises spotted the area's potential. There has been considerable tidying-up around Wandsworth in the last year, including a much-needed facelift for Wandsworth Town Station, much re-paving and extensive work on council estates.

The Tonsleys

Bordered by *York Rd*, *Trinity Rd*, *East Hill* and *Fairfield St*, this is a quiet enclave of attractive small Victorian cottages (mainly 2- and 3-bed) with some larger 4- and 5-bed houses running up and across the hill which rises out of the Wandle (Wandsworth) basin.

The Tonsleys is within easy reach of Wandsworth Town BR station, (12 minutes to Waterloo via Clapham Junction), and saw some of the biggest property price rises in the borough during 1987/88. The area is popular with Fulham price refugees (easy access to Parsons Green and the White Horse via Wandsworth Bridge).

South of *York Rd* is *Alma Rd* with large 3-storey Victorian houses and a pub at the junction with *Fullerton Rd*. In *Ebner St* (running parallel with *Alma Rd*) a church and C of E primary school are being rebuilt. the development includes an adult education centre and youth club, which may mean that some noise is possible both in *Ebner St* and *Alma Rd*. Especially pretty roads are *Dalby* and *Bramford Rds* which run down the fairly steep hill from *Dighton Rd* to *York Rd*. *York Rd*, until recently a very busy, rather grimy, street, is fast improving following the opening of the by-pass. *Ebner St* and *Tonsley Hill* suffer from some rat-running.

Tonsley Place, leading off *Fairfield St*, has modernised 2-bed cottages from £135,000, 3-bed from £155,000. An unmodernised 2-bed cottage would be around £110,000 – below the record £122,000 reached at the height of buying fever in 1987. Mixed blocks of '30s council and private flats (Fairfield Court) front *Fairfield St* (very heavy traffic) along with four large, semi-detached mid-Victorian houses.

There are larger, 3-storey 4/5-bed houses in *Dempster, Fullerton* and *Birdhurst Rd* N of *East Hill. Birdhurst Rd* overlooks busy *Trinity Rd*, but *Trinity Rd* is in a cutting so traffic noise is no great problem. A new residential development (including a shopping parade) is now completing on *East Hill* backing onto *Fullerton Rd*. The 64 flats and six houses are known as 'Tonsley Heights'. Rialto are the developers. Prices began around £59,000 for a studio and £100,000-plus for a small 2-bed town house; projected prices for the spring in this popular Victorian pastiche are £70-140,000. Next door, more new homes are rumoured for the cricket school site.

St Ann's Hill

South of *East Hill*, between *St Ann's Hill, Allfarthing Lane* and *Wandsworth Common Westside* are mainly well-sized, late Victorian and Edwardian houses with some modern infill developments (including low-rise council flats, many of which are now privately owned). Property prices rise approaching the Common.

W

Popular roads in the area include *Geraldine, Melody* and *Cicada* (although *Geraldine* is slightly less popular due to rat-running). The architectural styles are mixed but most of the houses are large, late Victorian 2- and 3-storey buildings. Good 4-bed houses in *Melody* were running, last autumn, at around £190,000. Four-bed houses in need of modernisation in *Geraldine* were selling at around £145,000. There are still some unmodernised houses available and the area is a prime hunting ground for developers and young families trading up in size. A new Berkeley Homes development of 3-bed/2 bath town houses is under way in *St Ann's Crescent* and will partly overlook the unusual late Georgian 'Pepper Pot' church.

Although *St Ann's Hill* acts as the main through road from *East Hill* to *Allfarthing Lane* and *Earlsfield Rd*, it does not suffer too badly from traffic. Houses on and surrounding *St Ann's Hill* are mainly early Edwardian 3-bed terraces, but there are some '30s-built semi-detached houses on *St Ann's Hill*. Between *St Ann's Hill* and *Garratt Lane* there is a good supply of purpose-built late Victorian maisonettes and flats. A council estate running along the lower end of *Allfarthing Lane* (*Iron Mill Rd, Vermont Rd*) and up to the Wandsworth end of *St Ann's Hill* means big price differentials.

West Hill

Merton Rd joins *West Hill* at the junction with *Wandsworth High St* and *Putney Bridge Rd* and features some good mid- and late-Victorian semi-detached and terraced houses. Many of the houses are set well back from the road with off-street parking so are not affected by the heavy traffic. There is a school at the junction with *Replingham Rd. West Hill Rd*, leading from *Merton Rd* to *West Hill* (A3) now sees prices on a par with Putney. Rat-running is still a problem despite council action. The houses vary in style, there are early, mid and late Victorian and some 1930s and '50s houses. Many of the properties are detached or semi-detached. Expect to pay £220,000 for a 4-bed late Victorian detached house. *Lebanon Rd, Amerland Rd* and *Ringford Rd* all lead off *West*

Hill and are more Putney than Wandsworth. There is a small council infill in *Lebanon Gardens* where a 4-bed ex-council house has made £135,000. Similar period houses nearby were £185,000.

Further E, at the junction with *Broomhill Rd* and *Merton Rd*, Grovewood Homes have built an attractive, simple development of mews-style town houses, some with balconies and garages. Older and larger 2- and 3-storey late Victorian houses follow from this, more quiet, point on *Merton Rd* to the junction with *Buckhold Rd*.

A small council cottage-style estate off *Buckhold Rd* has mainly flat-fronted traditional-style houses. Many have been bought by tenants under Right to Buy who are now selling. Good for first-time buyers. The large gardens of those on the eastern side of *Longstaff Crescent* back on to King George's Park.

Property in central Wandsworth is mainly commercial with some small industrial premises. Exceptionally beautiful Queen Anne houses (now used for commercial and industrial purposes) are to be found in *Wandsworth Plain*. There are four stunning Queen Anne houses on the corner of *Putney Bridge Rd* and *Armoury Way*: one appeared on the market last year, at £350,000. Thereafter are blocks of modernised '30s brick-built council flats which are set well back from the road and are now privately owned. Prices, as these came on the open market, were around £57,000 for 1-bed to £67,000 for 2-beds. They proved popular – reckon now on £70,000 and £80,000 respectively. Behind *Armoury Way* is *Frogmore* with its flat-fronted cottages and a small, modern, private development. *Sudlow Rd* joins *Frogmore* to *North Passage* and offers mid-Victorian cottages.

Huguenot Place is at the junction of *East Hill*, *Wandsworth Common Northside* and *Westside*. The heavy traffic maroons the attractive 18th century Presbytery, church, Book House and Huguenot cemetery. There are some flats and houses, including Huguenot Mansions, which all suffer road noise.

Wandsworth Common

Wandsworth Common Westside is protected from the traffic of *Trinity Rd*, (dual-carriageway at this point) by a section of the Common, which is wide at the junction with *Earlsfield Rd* and narrows to the junction with *East Hill*. The houses and flats on the roads leading off *Wandsworth Common Westside*, from *Jessica Rd* to *East Hill*, are too close for comfort.

Westside offers large 4- and 5-bed mid-Victorian houses, some apparently badly neglected. Especially attractive is the row of ornate Gothic-style houses between *Quarry Rd* and *Heathfield Rd*. Further along *Heathfield Rd* just before the junction with *Earlsfield Rd* is *Heathfield Gardens*, a secret row of enchanting Regency cottages overlooking the common. A double-fronted 4-bed gem here was for sale last winter for £600,000. Across *Earlsfield Rd* and further along *Heathfield Rd* is another Wandsworth landmark: Wandsworth prison. Just opposite is a new 'mews' development called Heathfields, with 2-4-bed houses between £132-197,000. Past the prison lies the pretty early-Victorian flat-fronted cottages of *Alma Terrace* facing land currently let for grazing to a horse owner. Beyond are 1920s and '30s blocks of flats.

Spencer Park, overlooking the Common from the Northern side, offers a stunning variety of large, detached and semi-detached houses built in a variety of styles as show houses for the Great Exhibition. Some have now been converted into flats or are used by institutions, but a number remain as large family homes. They back onto a large private garden. Spencer Court on *Windmill Rd* is a 1930s block of flats overlooking the railway lines and the Victorian Emanuel School beyond.

Wandsworth Common Northside is part of the traffic-plagued South Circular. Many of the houses have been converted into flats, those on the S side of the road are popular for their views over Wandsworth Common. Behind lie *Elsynge Rd* and *Spencer Rd*, where there is a mixture of exceptionally large, fine Victorian houses with large gardens, many remaining in single occupation and smaller late Victorian houses and double fronted 'cottages'.

Approached from an easy-to-miss turning off *Trinity Rd* is Wandsworth's most spectacular building: the Gothic Royal Victoria Patriotic Building. Built to care for orphan daughters of servicemen killed in the Crimean War and later used as an interrogation centre during the Second World War, it now houses a theatre school, design studios and individualistic flats (some in towers and turrets) which are popular with artistic and media types. It is set rather unfortunately between a major railway and an estate of council towers and is perhaps more fun to look at than out of.

The Toastrack, a grid of streets surrounded on three sides by the Common, lies off *Trinity Rd* and takes in *Dorlcote, Nicosia, Baskerville, Henderson* and *Patten Rds*. Here are large, detached or semi-detached 5-6 bed late Victorian houses, some with exceptionally large gardens. Houses on *Dorlcote Rd* overlook the Common from the front, whilst the gardens of houses in *Routh* and *Baskerville* back onto the Common. Prices generally start at around £325,000, rising to well over £500,000 for the best houses in *Routh* and *Baskerville*. After some years of huge popularity all but the best properties are currently proving slow to sell. There is some apprehension about the knock-on effect of the WEIR road plans (see 'Transport' chapter).

W

West of *Trinity Rd* from the Toastrack are some unusually large, often double-fronted houses with good-sized gardens, which currently fetch from £200,000 – and double that for exceptional properties. These are to be found in the roads adjoining *Lyford Rd*, most notably *Herondale Avenue, Loxley Rd, Frewin Rd* and *Westover Rd*. *Lyford Rd* is a no-through road running N-S between *Magdalen Rd* and *Burntwood Lane*. Houses between *Routh Rd* and *Lyford Rd* back onto a wild and overgrown extension of Wandsworth Common, adding to the rural illusion beloved of many of the inhabitants.

Between *Routh Rd* and *Burntwood Lane* are large 3-storey Edwardian and late Edwardian houses (some semi-detached) overlooking the Common. The White House by the junction with *Frewin Rd* was designed by Voysey.

Bellevue Village

The area bordered by *Trinity Rd, St James Drive* and Wandsworth Common offers pretty mid-Victorian cottages, some flat-fronted and larger than they look. The cottages were once inhabited by the working classes but are now occupied by interior designers, junior merchant bankers and divorcees whose alimony payments don't stretch to Fulham. Inhabitants tend to be seriously short tempered owing to the fact that there is no available parking space and each house appears to have 3 cars (Golf GTi etc). *Bellevue Rd* is lined with estate agents, chi-chi delicatessens, wine bars and restaurants which all add to the chaotic parking. None of these existed five years ago: it was a quiet suburban parade of butchers, bakers and junk shops.

St James' Drive has larger mid-Victorian terraced houses, some semi-basement and stuccoed, all suffering road noise. At least with the closure of St James' Hospital the ambulances won't disturb you at night. The future of the site will be decided sometime this year; Wandsworth wants a mixed residential/commercial development, with 'some community use'. Southwest of Bellevue, almost in Tooting, *Broderick*, *Wandle* and *Hendham Rds* have large late-Victorian mainly 3-storey terraced and (just) semi-detached houses, currently suffering rat-running between the ghastly traffic of *Trinity Rd* and fairly awful traffic of *Beechcroft Rd*. They are popular with families offering easy access to Tooting Bec tube, but are really Tooting not Wandsworth (which see). One advantage in this area is Wandsworth Common BR station, which has a good service into Victoria via Clapham Junction.

Among those estate agents active in this area are:
- Bell Son & Co
- Barnard Marcus
- Raymond Bushell
- Friend & Falcke
- John D Wood
- Realm Estates
- William Gyoury
- Rashbrooks
- Roy Brooks

Waterloo to Bermondsey

Map ref: p78 (2C)
Postal districts: SE1, SE17, SE16
Boroughs: Lambeth (Lab), Southwark (Lab)
Rates: L: 187p in £. S: 195.68p in £
Constituencies: Vauxhall (Lab), Southwark & Bermondsey (Lib)
Insurance: Scale 1
Conservation areas: Check town halls.
Parking: Varies

Transport Waterloo, Elephant & Castle (zones 1/2, Northern, Bakerloo); London Bridge, Borough (zone 1, Northern); Lambeth North (zone 1, Bakerloo). From Elephant & Castle to: Oxford Circus 22 min (1 change), City 7 min, Heathrow 1 hr (2 changes). British Rail: Waterloo, London Bridge.

Convenient for City, West End, South Bank, the Thames. Miles from centre: 1.5.

Schools ILEA zones 8/9: London Nautical (b), Bacon's School C of E, Notre Dame High RC (g).

Flats	S	1b	2b	3b	4b	5b
Average prices	55–65	60–75	75–95	80–100	–	–
Houses	2b	3b	4b	5b	6/7b	8b
Average prices	80–140+	95–160	110–190	120–200+	250+	–

The properties Homes for sale scarce and scattered amid commercial and council. Good value small houses in Bermondsey, flats in Borough. Plenty – at a price – along the River and in Surrey Docks: see 'Docklands'.

The market Docklands boom leads adventurous buyers wanting cheap bolt-holes to this very central, very mixed zone where gems and bargains can be found. Hardly a regular market – be prepared to look in odd corners. Many new homes coming at Bricklayers Arms. Ex-council homes: £5–10,000 less. Searches: Lambeth 10 weeks, Southwark 12.

Area Profile

The great sweep of London on the south bank of the Thames, opposite the West End and the City, is considered here as one unit. The area, from Waterloo on the W to Rotherhithe in the E, and spreading S to the Elephant and Castle, contains public and commercial buildings of every kind. There are theatres and railway stations, office blocks and hospitals. There is also quite a lot of council-owned housing in tall and often grim blocks. What there is not a lot of is homes for sale. This is starting to change, as the spillover from Docklands causes developers and buyers to reappraise Bermondsey and the Borough. Now, too, a layer of inexpensive homes is appearing thanks to ex-council resales. For the present, however, anyone wanting to live in this part of town has got quite a search on their hands. This survey is inevitably a patchy one as some homes are well hidden amid acres of commercial property. There can hardly be said to be an organised residential market here, with few estate agents active locally (the Kennington ones tend to cover it). But good-value homes are there for those who look.

The major development taking place in the area, apart from the riverside schemes discussed in the Docklands chapter, is at Bricklayers Arms. This enormous former railway yard has a splendid setting a mile S of Tower Bridge. Its development could spark other housing schemes in the area, whose location is summed up by its detailed views of City towers. For details see below under Bermondsey.

Convenience is this area's greatest asset. It is a lot closer to the heart of London than many a supposedly 'central' residential district. It lacks just about every amenity, however: there is little shopping, less open space. To be able to walk to work or to the South Bank cultural centre is compensation enough for some, however. And the river is always close by.

The curse of South London is the railway line and this bit has more than most and busier ones too. They snake across, at high level, on their way to Charing Cross, Waterloo and London Bridge. The roads are busy, funnelling traffic to the inadequate number of bridges. These problems, plus the concentration of commerce and industry, forces what homes there are into odd pockets. The area has traditionally been one of poverty and overcrowding, and some of the present-day council estates are little improvement on their predecessors. Some areas are so notorious as to be inhabited only by those who can't get a council transfer. The big estate SE of the Elephant & Castle is one such.

Most of the area is in the borough of Southwark, though the W edge is in Lambeth. The Thames-side streets from London Bridge eastwards are in the LDDC zone and the burgeoning housing market there is covered in the Docklands chapter.

Waterloo, South Bank and Borough

County Hall, giant home of the now-defunct Greater London Council, has now been sold to a consortium for a mixed-use scheme. A hotel and offices are planned – and 'possibly some residential' – for its 11 miles of corridors. The South Bank cultural complex lines the river from County Hall round past Waterloo Bridge to the National Theatre, and the land to the S and E is mostly taken up by Waterloo Station. Waterloo will expand to cope with Channel Tunnel traffic and this may affect the vicinity. N of the station, *Theed,*

Whittesley and *Roupell Sts* are quiet streets of little terraced houses on a surprisingly human scale which are popular buys. *Coin St* to the N is the centre of a big and controversial redevelopment scheme, the row in essence pitching commercial interests against community activists supported by Lambeth Council. The activists won, and the redevelopment consequently includes homes for 1,300 people to be let at fair rents, including 56 new stock-brick houses with gardens. Some of the homes are in restored 1829 terraces. *Duchy St* and *Aquinas St* are part of the Duchy of Cornwall Estate (see Kennington). *Aquinas St* has 1911 cottages. Some are being sold freehold as they come vacant. S of Waterloo East station are some '30s council flats in *Wootton St*.

The area around Lambeth North tube is more residential. *Lower Marsh* is a bustling shopping street, with a market. Some flats over shops. Cobbled *Launcelot St*, off *Lower Marsh*, has a handful of cottages. E of *Baylis Rd* is a large council estate with some attractive new houses. Further S, *Mead Row* has some flats run as a housing cooperative. *Hercules St* has a mix of small 19th century cottages and council blocks. *Lambeth Rd* is on the fringe of Kennington and has some similar early 19th century houses.

To the E Southwark borough begins. On the riverside, there is little housing E of the LWT tower except some council homes in *Upper Ground* and some smart riverside flats in part of the King's Reach development. E of Blackfriars Bridge, the enormous brick-built Bankside Power Station is disused and awaits development. It is newly listed, so its future is even more of a puzzle. Close to the bridge are some riverside Southwark Council flats. *Bankside* has one of London's most desirable houses, Cardinal's Wharf. The house was already old when Christopher Wren lived there while building St Paul's. Beautifully restored, it was on the market early in 1988 for £1m. One or two other houses survive alongside, as does the Anchor pub.

East of Southwark Bridge, a renovated dock is the centrepiece of a new range of offices and flats. The dock contains the restored trading schooner Kathleen & May. *Borough High St* meanders S from London Bridge and is the centre of the oldest part of South London. *St Thomas St*, behind London Bridge station, has some Georgian houses. *Snowfields*, behind Guys Hospital, has some good old houses and is a popular location: the doctors provide a ready public for these convenient homes. This is consultants-only territory now: young doctors compete for nearby ex-council 1-bed flats at around £65,000. *Union St* has some working men's cottages built late in the 19th century. Around here is a little neighbourhood of mostly 19th century housing, all built by various philanthropists and public bodies. As such, they are rarely for sale. Further W, *Nelson Square* and nearby streets have council flats, both low-rise and in towers. This continues down towards the S, through *Blackfriars Rd*, like all the main streets in the area, has a few surviving earlier houses, some Georgian. Most of these have, however, become offices. The residential streets S of *St George's Circus* are described under Kennington.

Walworth and The Elephant

The Elephant and Castle has suffered in the transformation from a Victorian pub at a crossroads to a modern 'complex'. Today it is far from being the busy heart of South London it once was, and that the planners intended it would continue to be. It is a vast, bleak double roundabout surrounded by unconvincing '60s buildings and mostly inhabited by pigeons. The shopping

W

centre has failed to generate much bustle, the council housing has a sad reputation.

From the Elephant the *Walworth Rd* runs S towards Camberwell. Once it, like other such streets, was lined with handsome houses, but few survive. *Albany Rd* runs off to the E, forming the boundary between the new Burgess Park, with its boating lake and adventure playground, to the S and the enormous Aylesbury Estate, built to house more than 8,000 people on 64 acres. Pevsner comments: 'an exploration can be recommended only for those who enjoy being stunned by the impersonal megalomaniac creations of the mid 20th-century.' The triangle between *Walworth Rd*, the Elephant and the *New Kent Rd* has little to recommend it, though a few corners of 19th century housing survive amid the council slabs. Some such houses occur in and around *Brandon* and *Chatham Sts*. Many have been converted into flats. *East St* is another place to look, although the area is busy on days when the street market is held. Six new flats have recently been completed in *Fremantle St*, a sign of change in the area. Some purpose-built Edwardian maisonettes can be found in *Aylesbury Rd* and *Wooler St*. A few ex-council flats are beginning to come onto the market, even on these unprepossessing estates. The price differential with private housing still exists: a 3-bed ex-council maisonette in *Darwin St* commands £75,000-80,000, about the same as a nearby 1-bed 'private' flat.

Bermondsey

The most dramatic part of Bermondsey, and that with most housing, is the Thames-side neighbourhood of converted warehouses and new flats developments. These are within the LDDC area and thus dealt with under Docklands. Inland, the Docklands effect has been encouraging interest in the pockets of housing between the river strip and the *Old Kent Rd*. This district has a suprising number of homes, including some of the oldest in London. The Bricklayers Arms site, once a railway yard, is the scene of much activity. Ideal Homes are the major developers of the Bricklayers site; they have retained about half, and the next four years will see some 600 flats and houses, not to mention a new park, appear (first releases this spring). They sold the rest of the land: Wimpey, Declan Kelly and Thameswey have sites. Homes for two housing associations, also homes for rent (a BES scheme) are among the plans for this diverse site. A new road, *Mandela Way* (this is Southwark), leads through the site. Nearby, the Abbey development has some pleasant cottage-style 1-3 bed properties built six years ago. Typical prices are £80-100,000. To the E, the district S of *Southwark Park Rd* has some pleasant streets of Victorian terraced cottages. *Lynton Rd*, *Simms Rd*, *Esmerelda Rd* and *Strathnairn Rd* have flat-fronted cottages which are mostly well-kept and attractive. £85,000 is a typical price. Further S, *Avondale Square* has 3-storey mid-Victorian terraced houses. To the N, *Yalding Rd* has some pretty flat-fronted houses. £75,000 was being asked last autumn for one.

To the W, the area between *Great Dover St* and the Elephant is worth a glance. *Trinity Church Square*, for example, has early 19th-century houses belonging to the Seamens' Widows' Housing Trust. *Bath Terrace* has some Victorian flats in a large block. These seem to offer value at around £75,000 for a 2-bed home. On the other side of *Great Dover St*, *Bermondsey Square* is in truth only a corner of handsome houses overlooking the busy road to Tower

Bridge. One was sold last year for close to £200,000. East of here is *Grange Rd*, the centre of some activity recently as houses have been renovated and buildings converted for homes. Three houses in *Grange Walk* have mediaeval origins, being the last survivors of the great Bermondsey Abbey. One was sold two years ago when the particulars detailed some mouthwatering features including Norman cellars. There are some Victorian houses too. A school in the street has recently been cleverly converted into characterful flats and studio houses; further conversions and newbuild are appearing in this corner. The 165-home Grange Park scheme, between *Grange Rd* and *Rouel Rd*, was completed by Laing last winter. There are 2 and 3-bed houses and 1 and 2-bed flats: a 1-bed flat was £65,000 in November. *Leroy St* has some Victorian flats in a 4-storey terrace. A 1-bed flat was sold in winter '87 for £42,000, another was on sale last winter for £60,000. *Neckinger Cottages* has some neat 2-bed houses, selling when modernized for around £125,000. *Bermondsey St*, which leads back up to London Bridge station, is the old village centre and has some surviving old houses. *Pages Walk* has three new-built 2-bed cottages which came on the market last spring for £135,000.

Rotherhithe

W

Most of Rotherhithe, including all the great peninsula which was once the Surrey Docks, is LDDC country. The old village, described under Docklands, has a pleasant cluster of old buildings gathered peaceably around the parish church. Inland, there is quite a bit of housing, mostly council, in the area W of Southwark Park and on SE towards Deptford. Some of the council estates have their own attractions but, in residential terms, the area is very much in the shadow of the vast Surrey Docks and riverside developments.

Among those estate agents active in this area are:
- Alan Fraser
- Barnard Marcus
- Burnet Ware & Graves
- Daniel Smith
- Jacksons
- Winkworths

West Hampstead

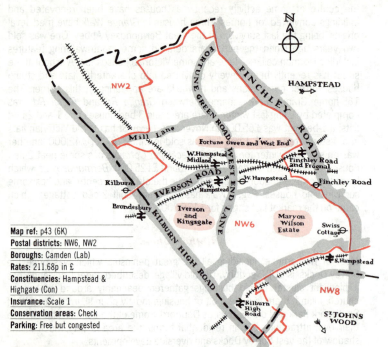

Map ref: p43 (6K)
Postal districts: NW6, NW2
Boroughs: Camden (Lab)
Rates: 211.68p in £
Constituencies: Hampstead & Highgate (Con)
Insurance: Scale 1
Conservation areas: Check
Parking: Free but congested

Transport	Tubes: West Hampstead, Kilburn (zone 2, Jubilee): Finchley Rd (zone 2, Jubilee, Metropolitan). From West Hampstead: Oxford Circus, 15 min (1 change); City, 30 min (1 change); Heathrow, 60 min (1 change). British Rail: West Hampstead (King's Cross 10 min and North London Line).
Convenient for	Hampstead Heath; M1/A1 to the North. Miles from centre: 4.
Schools	ILEA Division 2: St George's RC, Hampstead Comprehensive, Quintin Kynaston Comprehensive

Flats	S	1b	2b	3b	4b	5b
Average prices	60–80	75–95	95–125	140+	170+	–
Houses	2b	3b	4b	5b	6/7b	8b
Average prices	120–150	175–210	210–250	280–450+	→	–

The properties	Victorian terraced homes, 80% of which now converted to flats. Some surviving family houses, plus big mansion flats.
The market	Rapid turnover of flat-buyers, who use area as a staging-post before moving on to family homes. Conversions vary in quality. Mansion flats can be a better bet: but check service charges. Local searches: 12 weeks.

W

Area Profile

West Hampstead is not nearly as old, and certainly nothing like as grand, as its illustrious big sister on the hill, but it has a style and attraction that has proved irresistable to the young professionals who live there until they can afford the inflated prices of Hampstead proper.

The main development of the area took place shortly after the middle of the last century, much of it on the large tracts of land owned by the Maryon Wilson and Eyre estates – which to this day continue to hold the freehold of large areas of leasehold property.

A few of the streets (on the E side) were developed with the relatively well-heeled middle classes in mind, but the bulk of the area was designed to cater for the needs of the Victorian age's growing lower-middle class. The result was large numbers of 2-storey, 2- and 3-bedroom terraced houses and semis. The area was also among the first to see the erection of large blocks of purpose built flats called mansion blocks – the word 'mansion' possibly designed to salve the blighted aspirations of those who could not afford houses. Paradoxically these flats, with their many, spacious and elegant rooms, are among the most sought after properties today.

The change in the area over the last 25 years has been dramatic. Steeply rising prices and the spill-over effect from Hampstead have proved an irresistible temptation to the traditional inhabitants. Properties began to be converted into flats at an almost unprecedented rate – and one agent estimates that as few as 10 per cent of the original houses remain in single occupation. That estimate may be a bit low but nevertheless the rarest beast in West Hampstead is a 4-bedroom family house.

West Hampstead is very much a young person's area, extremely conveniently located between the *Finchley Rd* and *Kilburn High Rd*, both good routes N and S. *West End Lane*, which runs through the centre of West Hampstead, has plenty of restaurants and several trendy pine shops where West Hampstead folk buy their furniture. The Railway Tavern is the place for 'alternative' comedy and live bands and the English National Opera rehearsal rooms are next-door. *West End Lane* leads into *Abbey Rd* and *St John's Wood Rd*; it has the tube and BR stations and also the Acol bridge club.

Rail links from West Hampstead are excellent. In addition to West Hampstead BR and tube there are tube stations at Finchley Rd and Kilburn and BR stations at Finchley Rd and Frognal and Brondesbury nearby. There are scores of bus routes too. Despite excellent public transport services, West Hampstead residents like to have a car. With houses converted into three or four flats – estate agents' boards abound – that means a lot of vehicles and parking in the narrow streets is a nightmare.

Fortune Green and 'West End'

West Hampstead is bisected diagonally by *West End Lane* leading, at the N end, into *Fortune Green Rd* which gives access to a whole group of roads rather marooned from the rest of the suburb by the BR Midland Region Line. These include some uncharacteristically quiet and peaceful enclaves compared with the bustle and congestion of the rest of the area.

Behind the pleasant Fortune Green open space itself is the Hampstead Cemetery which casts a protective shadow over streets like *Gondar Gardens* and *Hillfield Rd*, one of the few corners in the area where the Victorian builders produced family houses of any size. Many have now been converted, but 4- or 5-bedroom houses do still come onto the market. One enormous building, Berridge House in *Hillfield Rd*, was owned by the University of London. They have now sold it, and its 1.7 acre site is likely to be used for family homes 'with private gardens in a secure environment' say the agents.

Also interesting is the group of streets known as 'The Greeks' – not surprisingly since they include *Agamemnon Rd*, *Ajax Rd*, *Ulysses Rd* and *Achilles Rd*. These are still well supplied with modestly sized family houses, and is perhaps the best preserved corner of the entire suburb.

Closer to *Finchley Rd* is the area once known as the West End (of Hampstead, presumably), now dominated by the large mansion blocks in *West End Lane*, *Mill Lane*, *Lyncroft Gardens*, *Cannon Hill* and *Honeybourne Rd*, including Buckingham Mansions, Marlborough Mansions, Cholmley Gardens. Yale Court and Harvard Court. Formerly rented accommodation, they are all now owner-occupied, and the large flats are very popular.

Smartest streets in the area are E of *West End Lane*: *Alvanley Gardens* with its large detached houses grandly overlooking the grounds of Hampstead Cricket Club in *Lymington Rd*, and the attractive semis of *Crediton Hill*.

S of *Mill Lane* (whose wine bar, antique and art deco shops reflect to some extent the new inhabitants of the area) are residential streets such as *Sumatra Rd*, *Broomsleigh St*, *Solent Rd*, *Narcissus Rd* and *Pandora Rd*, all typical of the 2- and 3-storey terraces which West Hampstead has to offer. *Holmdale Rd*, in particular, has a number of new conversions. *Sumatra Rd*, at the E end, is close to the railway. There is also an interesting enclave of streets, including *Menelik Rd*, *Somali Rd* and *Asmara Rd*, in the NW2 corner of the area.

Iverson and Kingsgate

This is the triangle between the Midland Region railway line, *West End Lane* and *Kilburn High Rd*. Towards the N, busy *Iverson Rd* leads past light industrial areas and large new council estates to the slightly run-down areas of *Maygrove*

Rd, *Loveridge Rd* and *Fordwych Rd* where the large number of builders' skips that appeared last year showed that here, too, things are on the move.

Further S, *Sherriff Rd* and *Hemstal Rd* lead from *West End Lane* to the densely packed streets around *Kingsgate Rd*. These are mainly 2-storey small terraced houses, and if there is a less expensive part of the area, this is it. Here the population is less affluent than elsewhere, with a number of council estates and high unemployment levels. There are, however, pleasant corners and significant bargains to be found, both in terms of flats and small houses, and *Lowfield*, *Kylemore*, *Gladys* and *Hilltop Rds* are well worth looking at. Homes in this corner have the advantage of excellent shopping on *Kilburn High Rd*.

The southernmost strip of the area, between a railway line and *Boundary Rd*, is almost completely dominated by very large council blocks, including the Abbey Estate and the extraordinary 1,000 ft long concrete sweep of Camden's Alexandra Road Estate in *Rowley Way*.

The Maryon Wilson estate

The area bounded by *Broadhurst Gardens*, *Finchley Rd*, *Belsize Rd* and *Priory Rd* was built between 1874 and the late 1890s, and contains some of the most attractive, most sought-after and most expensive properties in West Hampstead. They are close not only to the transport and considerable shopping facilities of *West End Lane* but also to the major shopping centre in *Finchley Rd* – with a large Waitrose supermarket and the Habitat furniture and household goods store.

Particularly attractive, in streets such as *Canfield Gardens*, *Compayne Gardens* and *Fairhazel Gardens* are the redbrick mansion blocks, often with attractive turrets on the corner properties, and large communal gardens. Some of the best of these properties are owned by the pioneering Fairhazel Housing Co-operative (the first of its kind), and its flats are not available to the public on the open market. Several refurbishment schemes are planned for '89 in the *Cleve Rd/Compayne Gardens* area.

But there are other elegant roads, including *Broadhurst Gardens*, *Greencroft Gardens*, *Aberdare Gardens* and *Goldhurst Terrace*, where there is a brisk trade in both purpose-built and converted flats, including some luxurious recent conversions. Here and there you might even find the odd large house in single occupation for sale – but you would have to move very fast (and have a very large chequebook) in order to beat the property developers to the purchase. There is talk of making this tract a conservation area.

Among those estate agents active in this area are:

- Allied
- Anscombe & Ringland
- Brian Lack & Co
- Bairstow Eves
- Elliot Ross
- Greene & Co
- Douglas Terry
- London Lets and Sales

W

West Norwood, Norbury and Gipsy Hill

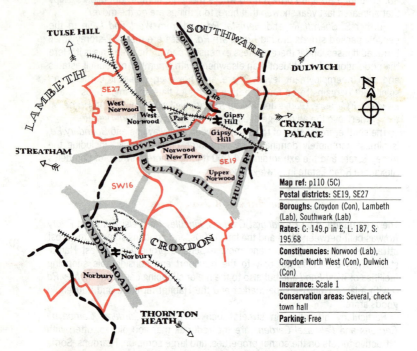

Map ref: p110 (5C)

Postal districts: SE19, SE27

Boroughs: Croydon (Con), Lambeth (Lab), Southwark (Lab)

Rates: C: 149.p in £, L: 187, S: 195.68

Constituencies: Norwood (Lab), Croydon North West (Con), Dulwich (Con)

Insurance: Scale 1

Conservation areas: Several, check town hall

Parking: Free

Transport	British Rail: West Norwood, Gypsy Hill and Norbury to Victoria.
Convenient for	Crystal Palace Park, National Sports Centre. Routes to the south. Miles from centre: 5.5.
Schools	Croydon Education Authority, ILEA zone 9: St Joseph's college RC (b), Norbury Manor (g), Ingram Boys, Sylvan High, Stanley Tech, Selhurst.

Flats	S	1b	2b	3b	4b	5b
Average prices	53–55	55–70	65–80	→	–	–
Houses	2b	3b	4b	5b	6/7b	8b
Average prices	70–90+	80–150	120–170+	140+	150+	200+

The properties Recent developments and conversions mark the interest being shown in this area on the slopes of Crystal Palace. Its larger Victorian terraces have become flats, and there are plenty of family homes with good gardens: Victorian, semis, '60s town houses, '30s Tudor. On Gipsy Hill, mansion and p/b flats take advantage of view.

The market First-time buyers find inexpensive flats, good rail links to town, while families come in search of more home for their money. Both are overspilling from nearby Dulwich and Streatham, and even further afield. Norwood is tipped as good bargain-hunting territory. Local searches: Croydon 2 weeks, Lambeth 10, Southwark 8-12.

Area Profile

The South London suburbs of Norwood and Gipsy Hill lie on the slopes to the W of Crystal Palace. Clues to the area's past are found in its names: Norwood is the old North Wood, which covered the hills to the Thames basin. Tracts survive to this day, most notably the Lawns woodland area and Sydenham Hill woods. Gypsies, who gave Gipsy Hill its name, considered the woods their own until forced out by the 19th century enclosure acts. Margaret Finch was a rather more popular gypsy, a fortune-teller who lived to the age of 108. Local publicans raised funds for her burial in 1740.

Ambitious plans in the early 19th century to establish a Regency-style spa town on *Beulah Hill* never materialized. The spa itself quickly failed as a going concern thanks to a change in fashion, with the promotion of sea water as a new remedy. Later, the arrival of the illustrious Crystal Palace gave the area a taste of prosperity. It was short-lived: 80 years later the towering edifice burnt to the ground, and locals still vividly recall the spectacle of that 1936 night. Today the impressive facilities of the National Sports Centre replace it as the star local attraction.

In recent years, a process of regeneration has been under way, helped by the surge in property prices in surrounding areas. Indeed, many of the new residents form an overspill from nearby Dulwich and Streatham. The area has good potential for improvement, with a wide range of property and fast rail links to Central London. First-time buyers are attracted by the many flat conversions in large Victorian houses. When looking for homes here, it is worth bearing in mind that, along with the choice of roads and types of property comes the choice of rating boroughs – Labour-controlled Lambeth to the N or Conservative Croydon to the S.

W

The high land affords some spectacular views of London and outlying areas – most rewarding at sunrise and dusk. Larger properties are usually found on the higher ground but there are also some sensitive council developments, chiefly on *Central Hill*.

West Norwood is unusual for the combination of church and cemetery at its urban centre. Its outer reaches, towards neighbouring Streatham and Dulwich, are more popular.

Gipsy Hill has some attractive Georgian properties and startling views of the City. Its centre near the *South Croxted Rd* and *Dulwich Wood Park* roundabout has an attractive character largely untypical of the area. The SE19 area as a whole is particularly suitable for families, with good state schools and reasonably priced 3-bedroom houses.

Norwood New Town and Upper Norwood

The N end of *Beulah Hill* starts with an unappealing 1930s parade of shops, a large church and St Joseph's College. Victorian semis occupy the left side, '60s town houses the right. As the road ascends to leafier heights, these give way to large 1930s semis and detached homes, some in mock-Tudor style. Interesting buildings make an appearance like No 71, an 1860 villa and there's opportunity for sweeping views. St-Valery is an impressive Victorian mansion with full-height bay windows. Set away from the road on the left are walled-off '60s town house developments, on the right, Beulah Spa pub. More large, detached '30s Tudor-timber style and Victorian properties complete the road. Some homes here and in *Woodfield Close* have reached around £250,000.

Roads off the left of *Beulah Hill* are mainly 1930s residential. (There's an absence of the shops that go to make a community). *Hermitage Rd* has 1930s semis and council houses, also a small hospital. Larger '30s semis in *Eversley Rd* front a pleasant green. *Ryefield Rd* has recent town houses. The Lawns woodland area marks the site of the now disappeared spa. A cottage-style lodge by Decimus Burton survives, as does a later 1864 one. Early 19th century All Saints, with rural churchyard, stands on the corner with *Church Rd*. By night, the spire – which before the advent of the nearby TV masts dominated the skyline – is illuminated.

Church Rd has some 1930s semis, council blocks and Victorian red-brick mansions and a school. Also a new development: *Old Vicarage Gardens*, a luxury enclave of 1- and 2-bed retirement apartments in garden setting is on the right. Further on No 128, Rockmount, with its elaborate woodwork can look forbidding in semi-darkness. Neighbouring Nos 126 and 124 are early 19th century; the Victorian stucco of the 19th century Queen's Hotel has gained a modern annexe. The road continues into Crystal Palace (which see).

Central Hill has Norwood Park and the imposing Gothic-style Fidelis convent. Further up the hill there's a post-war council estate as well as recent terraced town houses. Also large Victorian houses – multiple occupancy. Roads to the S such as *Essex Grove* and *Gatestone Rd* slope down attractively with Victorian semis. Victorian detached and semis overlook the vast, but carefully crafted, hillside Central Hill estate to the N. Next to the council estate is Gipsy Hill police station.

Gipsy Hill

Proximity to the *Westow Hill* 'Triangle' with its shops and amenities (see Crystal Palace) is a bonus for Gipsy Hill. There's a magnificent view of London with City skyscrapers prominent. Highlights of this busy road are the white stuccoed buildings and red-brick Victorian mansions. Roads leading off such as *Camden Hill* and *Highland Rd* have period houses. Christ Church has been looking like a stump while its restoration is in progress. Past the BR station is a small green.

The Paxton pub, shops, restaurants, and a winebar make an attractive start to *Gipsy Rd*. Some renovation and dereliction characterize this gently rising road of varied Victorian properties, which ends with council estates. Near Kingswood primary school is *Salters Hill* – a road of council homes with occasional Victoriana. It overlooks Norwood Park. *Auckland Hill* is a visually unappealing hotpotch with Victorian, 1930s and modern properties – selling activity here, however. Railway arches mark the junction with *Gipsy Rd*.

Tree-lined *South Croxted Rd* has Victorian semis, '60s town houses and some council estates. There's a shopping area on the junction with *Park Hall Rd*. This neighbourhood has been changing rapidly as developers and new residents move in.

Norwood Rd, also known as *The Broadway*, is Victorian red-brick, able to meet basic shopping needs. The road forks by the striking St Luke's church with its Corinthian six-column portico. There's a modern library next to the 39-acre West Norwood Cemetery of 1836.

In the cosmopolitan streets around West Norwood BR station (Victoria 18 mins) good quality Victorian houses can be found at reasonable prices. *Norwood High St*, frequently congested with traffic, has few shops and is low-rise. *Dunlem Grove* is an attractive, modern cottage-style council estate.

Elder Rd starts off with ugly grey council blocks but improves. There are 1930s semis with nicely tended gardens. *Eylewood Rd* and *Norwood Park Rd* have '30s terraces and semis respectively. There's a concentration of high-rise council blocks up by *Bentons Rise* and *Aubyn Hill*. Facing Norwood Park (tennis courts) is the converted school house for the House of Industry for the Infant Poor. Behind are modern mews houses by Portland Homes in *Elderwood Place*. Next door is Norwood School. *Knights Hill* is Victorian with some dilapidation. Also the modern South London College and a bus station nearby. Opposite the college is a lawn tennis club.

Popular *Lancaster Avenue* has family-owned Victorian houses with pleasant front gardens. Rosemead mixed preparatory school is at the West Dulwich end. *Hawkley Gardens* has town house terraces. *Lavengrove* and *Tulsmere Rds* have 1930s bay-fronted terraces. *Chatsworth Way* is mainly Victorian and has a modern church with a needle-like spire. *Idmiston Rd* has Victorian houses with fancy wrought-iron balconies. The turreted red-brick Barston Towers graces the corner with *Barston Rd*. The road ends modestly with Victorian terraces. *Chancellor Grove* is similar. *Rosendale Rd*, with large Victorian bay-fronted semis, is broad and tree-lined below *Thurlow Park*. A parade of shops and an unattractive council block are other features. Continuing after *Park Hall Rd* are tall bay-fronted balconied Victorian properties, some flat conversions.

W

Tritton Rd has Victorian semis. On the corner with *Martell Rd* is Lambeth Industrial Enterprises. Also in *Martell Rd* is the ugly '30s white Park Hall Road Trading Estate building. There are usually flats to be found in the larger Victorian semis. Park Court (1930s) needs attention on the corner. The high, forbidding wall and cast-iron railings of the cemetery occupy the S of *Robson Rd* to West Norwood. Modest Victorian terraces on the N side.

Council houses and blocks start *York Hill*. *Knollys Rd*, 1930s terraces, Victorian and recent blocks, is undergoing much renovation. *Pyrmont Grove* and *Royal Circus* have quite pleasant Victorian terraces. The entrance to a new Hooper & Jackson development is in Lansdowne Hill. *Broxholm Rd* and *Glennie Rd* are terraced – turn-of-century and '30s. Larger properties are found at the higher points of these hill roads. *Canterbury Grove* has large Victorian and turn-of-century semis, also council, 1930s, Victorian and recent terraces. Thirties semis are found in *Uffington* and *Rockhampton Rds*. *Thurlestone Rd* and *Wolfington Rd* are Victorian/turn-of-century. *St Julian's Farm Rd* goes from 1930s semis and Victorian/turn-of-century to smaller properties lower down.

Quiet pre-war suburbia includes *Lamberhurst Rd* (bay-fronted semis), *Cheviot* and *Greenhurst Rds* (terraces), and *Roxburgh Rd* (semis). Near the *Knights Hill* end, *Lakeview* and *Truslove Rds* are council homes.

Leigham Court Rd has 1930s mansion blocks and private blocks of flats – built high for the sweeping views, also '30s semis. Groveside Homes has built a sympathetic development of luxury studio, 1-bed apartments, and 2-bed town houses. A primary school and Uplands Halls of Residence (ILEA) feature too. Victorian detached houses and imposing red-brick mansions precede a council estate and weathered '30s block before ending at Streatham Common N.

The castellated neo-Jacobean British Home for Incurables is in Crown Lane.

Norbury borders

In Norbury, *London Rd's* dull aspect is emphasized by the Victoriana. Shopping is unexciting, but provides most things necessary for day-to-day living. Large offices, including the headquarters of Wates, signal the approach to Croydon. Most of the area was developed between the wars, and roads such as *Ardfern Avenue* and *Melrose Avenue*, and *Ederline* and *Dunbar* set the tone. Property to the E of *London Rd* is more sought-after than that in the streets towards the Mitcham border. *Gibsons Hill*, *Norbury Hill* and *Virginia Rd* are of the same period. That they look to the wooded areas of Beulah Hill helps to relieve the monotony. *Kensington Avenue* also has a post-war council estate.

Thornton Heath

In this area W of South Norwood, first-time buyers find relatively affordable purpose-built and conversion flats; families are attracted by a range of late-Victorian, early-Edwardian terraces and interwar semis. The market was fairly quiet last winter, but there was still sufficient activity to support the 28 local estate agents. This area has yet, however, to attract much attention from outsiders.

Suburban Thornton Heath is very much a 19-century creation spurred on by the arrival of the railway. Good rail links to town and proximity to Croydon continue as chief attractions. The more expensive properties are found in the upper reaches towards Norbury – in roads such as *Florida, Maryland, Georgia* and *Carolina*. The *Pollards Hill* area is attractive suburbia – neat greens and trimmed hedges. Detached 1930s houses encircle the small common at the summit – views of outer London, the defunct Croydon B Power Station and housing estates.

Agents report little difficulty selling 3-bed properties in and around quiet *Winterbourne Rd* – 1930s bay-fronted terraces. Closeness to local schools and shopping facilities in *London Rd* are advantages. Larger and older properties are found in *Warwick Rd*. Flathunters should concentrate on *Mersham, Moffat, Hythe, St Paul's* and *Liverpool Rds* – mostly 1- or 2-beds – while families may have better luck in the area towards Mitcham. Busy *London Rd* and *Brigstock Rd* are worth investigation – especially for conversions. The Mayday Hospital dominates the lower half of *London Rd*.

The less popular roads south of the *High St* (*Ecclesbourne Rd, Kynaston Avenue, Bensham Lane*) comprise former council houses and older-style terraces – some quite modest. Prudential Property Services is marketing its 1- and 2-bed retirement apartments in *Bensham Lane*.

Roads surrounding the Crystal Palace Football Ground (Also the home of first-division Charlton Athletic) are best avoided. Fans may arrive at any of the three nearby mainline stations virtually every Saturday of the football season. *Whitehorse Lane* is prone to traffic congestion.

Among those estate agents active in this area are:

- Galloways
- Harvey & Wheeler
- Hamptons Levens
- Jackson
- Morgan Gillie
- Home Sellers
- G A Property Services
- Volker & Volker
- Wates
- Winkworth
- John Raymond

Willesden and Brondesbury Park

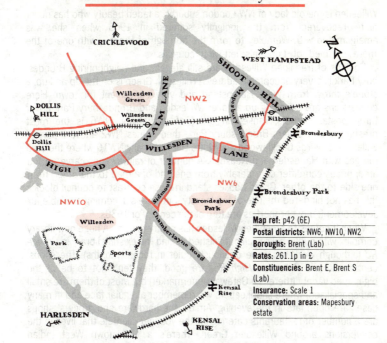

Map ref: p42 (6E)
Postal districts: NW6, NW10, NW2
Boroughs: Brent (Lab)
Rates: 261.1p in £
Constituencies: Brent E, Brent S (Lab)
Insurance: Scale 1
Conservation areas: Mapesbury estate

W

Transport	Tubes: Willesden Green, Kilburn, Dollis Hill (zones 2/3a, Jubilee). From Willesden Green to: Oxford Circus 25 min (1 change), City 35 min (1 change), Heathrow 1 hr 10 min (1 change). British Rail: Brondesbury, Brondesbury Park, Kensal Rise (North London Line).
Convenient for	North Circular and Edgware Roads. Miles from centre: 5.
Schools	Brent Education Authority: Willesden High, Brondesbury & Kilburn High, Aylestone Community School, Cardinal Hinsley RC (b), Convent of Jesus & Mary RC. Private: N W London Jewish.

Flats	S	1b	2b	3b	4b	5b
Average prices	55–68	60–80	68–120	80–130+	100+	–
Houses	2b	3b	4b	5b	6/7b	8b
Average prices	80–100	90–160	100–200+	185–500+	230–700+	→

The properties	Large blocks of flats, late-Victorian villas, plus many streets of terraced homes and later semis. Some larger 20th century homes. Brondesbury Park has some big, imposing late-Victorian houses.
The market	Willesden Green's fast tube attracts young flat buyers as the area revives after a decline since former family inhabitants moved out. Elsewhere still a family neighbourhood – not to mention a celebrity one: £8–950,000 mansions in best roads. Local searches: 3 weeks.

Area Profile

Willesden is the old lady of NW London suburbs, a faded beauty who has never quite recovered from the indignity suffered in 1965 when she was amalgamated with Wembley to form the borough of Brent – with one of the more troubled of London's left-wing councils.

Pockets of tree-lined Willesden are still elegant and neighbouring Brondes-bury Park is a very acceptable address. Willesden Green is on the up-and-up, a stone's throw from West Hampstead and very convenient for town. Here conversions are springing up all over. Willesden and Brondesbury Park cover three postal districts, ranked in order of desirability. NW6 is the most prestigious and covers Brondesbury Park, then comes NW2 and the part of Willesden towards Cricklewood and Dollis Hill and finally NW10 where the area merges with Harlesden and Neasden. A number of railway lines carve up the area; prices can differ considerably from one end of a road to the other, from one side to the other. Grand houses stand in close contrast to council blocks; this has not hindered the rise of the locality. Sites are still coming available for development; most properties are turn of the century or 1930s.

When it comes to amenities Willesden has plenty to offer. A huge new library complex with public halls is all but finished behind the existing library in *Grange Rd* (although work has gone ominously quiet in recent months). The shops, centred around *Willesden High Rd*, are good, they tend not to be of the big-named variety (there is a Gateway supermarket) but most of them are small and specialised, where shopkeepers will remember a regular face and in many cases are open late in the evening. Amidst the hardware and grocers' shops are a number of restaurants catering for the younger clientele that lives in the conversions around Willesden Green. There's a well-known West Indian restaurant near the tube station and several very good Indian eateries. Willesden Sports Centre, fronting *All Souls Avenue*, has swimming pools, an impressive sports ground and open space for the less sporty. The world Hockey Championships were held here a few years ago. Gladstone Park is not too far away in Dollis Hill for tennis, putting and weekend walks.

Willesden

Willesden was given to the Dean and Chapter of St Paul's Cathedral by King Athelstan in 938 – hence names like *Chapter Rd*. A visit to the local Grange Museum will furnish more details. The area is more compact than sprawling Willesden Green; Church End is to the W, *Robson Avenue*, falling between Roundwood Park and Willesden Sports Centre, marks the E divide with Willesden Green, and the Jubilee line is at the top. The New and Jewish Cemeteries cover a fair area. The part of *Willesden High Rd* in the Willesden area is rather shabbier than the section towards Willesden Green, but the small shops are varied.

Willesden Green

Willesden Green used to be a place where well-established Jewish families lived until they moved to suburbs such as Wembley and Stanmore. In recent years the ethnic and religious make-up has broadened and parts have become conversion territory. Houses tend to be larger in Willesden Green than in Willesden. 'Very up and coming', enthuse the estate agents whose boards make Willesden red, yellow and pink as well as Green. The general rule of thumb is that the closer you are to Willesden Green tube station (Jubilee Line), the better, although parts of the best area, the Mapesbury estate, break this rule. The Mapesbury estate consists of the roads in the triangle formed by *Chichele Rd/Walm Lane*, the A5 (known at this point as *Shoot Up Hill*) and *Willesden Lane*. This is the West Hampstead overspill; *Mapesbury, Dartmouth, Teignmouth* and *Chatsworth Rds* are names to look out for if you want a well-located conversion in a stylish Victorian property. Application has been made to build two blocks totalling 32 flats in *Mapesbury Rd* on the site of three houses; at the time of writing, the houses have yet to come down. House prices can be high; a 5-bedroom house in *Coverdale Rd* rates an asking price of £475,000 while another extraordinary 5-bedroom mansion in *Mapesbury Rd*, with staff quarters and swimming pool, hit the market last winter for £895,000.

On the other side of *Walm Lane, St Paul's Avenue* and *Blenheim Gardens* are also popular with flat-hunters. a new development of flats is being built in *Blenheim Gardens*, on the corner with *Station Parade*. In *Melrose Avenue*, towards *Chichele Rd*, Bellway Homes have completed St Gabriels Court, a 1- and 2-bed scheme, all flats now sold. In *Anson Rd* on the Cricklewood borders new penthouses are being added to the three-block Gladstone Court, made possible by the opening of loft space. They should be ready in the spring.

W

Other prestige roads in Willesden Green are found in the Dobree estate: *Dobree, Bryan, Rowdon, Alexander* and *Peter Avenues*, S of *Willesden High Rd*. A 3-bedroom semi-detached house with garage would cost around £160,000, a 4-bedroom £200,000. The starting price for a 4-bedroom detached house is £260,000; £500,000 should get a 5-bedroom house with two bathrooms. The 'royal roads' N of *Willesden High Rd* are also popular and should satisfy a tighter budget; roads like *Sandringham, Balmoral* and *Windsor* fall between Dollis Hill and Willesden Green tube stations.

All Souls Avenue (the Oxford college was a major landowner in the area) runs N-S through Willesden Green and has small semi-detached houses. At the N end lies Clarendon Court, a large '30s block on the corner of *Chamberlayne Rd* and *Sidmouth Rd*. A 3-bed flat here would cost £125-130,000. *Sidmouth Rd* itself is a busy road, home of the South Hampstead club for bowls and tennis. Spreading down towards Kensal Rise, the triangular grid of orderly roads spreading from *All Souls Avenue* to *Chamberlayne Rd* is disturbed by *Chelmsford Square*, a charming oval of semi-detached homes around tennis courts. More modest, pretty streets are to be found in this direction.

Willesden Lane, a main thoroughfare connecting Willesden and Kilburn, has a wide variety of purpose-built blocks, among them Marlow, Belvedere, Beechworth, Bramerton and Hadleigh Courts, the last consisting of 8 flats built in 1987. Down towards *Willesden High Rd* but still on *Willesden Lane*, Paddington Churches Housing Association are building on the former Nissan site. The Willesdenites are spiritual people: a Hindu Temple and a Jewish School are to be found on *Willesden Lane*, while *Walm Lane* has a church, a synagogue and a mosque, and *Chichele Rd* an Islamic youth centre. The Willesden Registry Office in *Willesden Lane* sees a great variety of marriages.

Prices vary a good deal between Willesden Green and Willesden. A 2-bed flat could cost £90,000 on the Mapesbury Estate, while £75-80,000 could buy a 2-bed flat plus garden in *Chapter Rd. Blenheim Gardens* is a good, cheaper alternative to the Mapesbury Estate. Willesden Green becomes Cricklewood to the N and prices go down again.

Brondesbury Park

Brondesbury Park is more exclusive than Willesden Green. Like Willesden Green, the district used to be very Jewish; both areas have witnessed a move away. The population is now very mixed. Houses date from the 1930s or later; the roads are wide and tree-lined and parking is not as problematic as in West Hampstead and Swiss Cottage. Communications are good, the *A5* and Kilburn tube (Jubilee Line) providing access to the West End. *Manor House Drive*, off *Brondesbury Park*, is a beautiful crescent, the best road in the area. Many of its detached houses are double-fronted, all have front and back gardens, many with security gates, a snip, say agents, at around half a million. One of the houses (and certainly not the largest), was on the market for £800,000 last winter. *Manor House Drive* is the expected location for record prices in the area, but the most expensive house on the market in recent months is the 6-bedroom mansion in *Christchurch Avenue*, on the corner with *Aylestone Avenue*. Empty for years but now renovated, the asking price was £950,000. *Christchurch Avenue*, *Cavendish Rd* and *The Avenue* also have very attractive conversions in large Victorian houses. Although such flats are far from cheap there is still room for growth in prices. *Aylestone Avenue* is a wide tree-lined street with both detached and semi-detached family houses.

Brondesbury Park (the road) has seen changes; some of the large detached houses here have been converted into flats and purpose-built blocks have been built. One such is Elstow Grange where a 2-bed flat might cost £100,000. Also in *Brondesbury Prk* is one of the most substantial developments in the area, a Bovis scheme of 40-odd town houses and a leisure complex. Completion is expected in 1989, with marketing in the summer. At the end of the road towards *Willesden High Rd* is another large site: the Heathfield Squash Club, next to a synagogue, is being redeveloped for residential use.

Parts of Brondesbury Park are very expensive, but a house with a garden may still be bought for the sort of money that buys a flat in Maida Vale.

Harlesden

Harlesden was once avoided and the Craven Park estate feared as a blight on re-sell. But things have started to change for the better. Harlesden has some lovely houses, Edwardian and Victorian, most with their original features intact. With an improved Bakerloo Line service, now running every 20 minutes beyond Queens Park to Harrow and Wealdstone with a full service at peak times, the area's potential is becoming evident. The town centre has been improved with funds supplied by Brent and new people are moving in. The better roads are *Springwell Avenue*, *Harlesden Gardens*, *Ancona Rd* and *Cholmondeley Avenue*. Growth in recent years has been rapid; homes which cost £50,000 two years ago could now achieve £80,000. There is still room for further growth; at around £55,000, a studio could be £10,000 cheaper in Harlesden than one in Willesden Green. Fairview Homes have built 22 flats on the *Harrow Rd*, opposite *Scrubs Lane*. The area would see further changes if Willesden Junction were to become the second Channel Tunnel terminal, as suggested.

Among those estate agents active in this area are:
- Buckingham, Ash & Lilley
- Camerons
- Camerons Stiff & Co
- Dutch & Dutch
- Elliot Ross & Co
- Gladstones
- Mendoza
- Prudential
- Winkworths

Wimbledon, Raynes Park, Merton Park

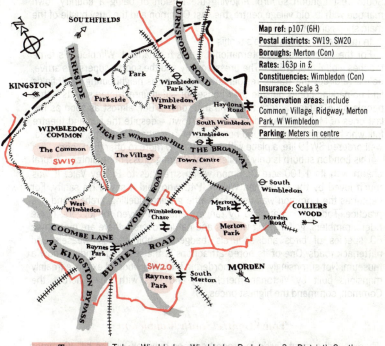

Map ref:	p107 (6H)
Postal districts:	SW19, SW20
Boroughs:	Merton (Con)
Rates:	163p in £
Constituencies:	Wimbledon (Con)
Insurance:	Scale 3
Conservation areas:	include Common, Village, Ridgway, Merton Park, W Wimbledon
Parking:	Meters in centre

Transport Tubes: Wimbledon, Wimbledon Park (zone 3a, District); South Wimbledon (zones 3a/b, Northern). From Wimbledon to: Oxford Circus 35 min (1 change), City 35 min, Heathrow 1 hr (1 change). British Rail: Wimbledon to Waterloo 12 min; others see map.

Convenient for Common, Gatwick Airport (A3/M25),tennis. Miles from centre: 7.

Schools Merton Education Authority: Wimbledon College RC (b), Ursuline Convent School (g), Rutlish School (b). Private: Norwegian School, Wimbledon High (g), Hazelhurst School (g), King's College School (b).

Flats	S	1b	2b	3b	4b	5b
Average prices	60–80	65–100	75–150+	90–220+	200+	–
Houses	2b	3b	4b	5b	6/7b	8b
Average prices	95–200	120–215	160–400	250–700	400+	500–900

The properties Homes (and prices) range from 3-bed terraces near town centre ('down the Hill') via the cottages of the Village to the swimming-pooled mansions near the Common ('up the hill'). Also flats conversions, Edwardian villas, '30s semis, new townhouses, flats. Further Victorian/Edwardian charm in Raynes and Merton Parks.

The market Something for everyone – at a price. High demand, with locals moving within area. Once here, you're hooked, whether heading up to a large house or condensing to a smart flat. Searches: 4–6 weeks.

Area Profile

For 11 months of the year peaceful, leafy Wimbledon is a self-posessed, South-west London suburb, enjoying the illusion of being a country town manqué with its old village centre, the vast Common and the busy bustle of the main shops and station end.

In the twelfth month, there's tennis.

For the duration of the international tennis tournament, Wimbledon's fame reaches global proportions. The press, royalty and the sport's superstars arrive, police re-direct the traffic, residents as far away as neighbouring Southfields find no-parking cones outside their houses or – if in unrestricted streets – that people have parked across their entrance drives. But, almost as soon as the last cries of McEnroe have died away, the town – despite the film and theatre folk who have found year-round homes here – resumes its sedate, well-heeled, well-ordered SW19 life, a place with considerably more to offer than sport.

This London suburb is only 9 miles from Charing Cross, but maintains a rural charm with its 1,100-acre Common which stretches to Putney Vale. It was much loved by the statesman William Pitt, who said it saved his sanity. For centuries the Common was used for cattle grazing, duelling, archery and rifle practice. Today it is patrolled by rangers and is a haven for joggers, horse riders, ramblers, golfers, dog walkers and nature lovers – there are more than 60 species of birds and squirrels, badgers, rabbits, foxes, weasels and natterjack toads. One of its noted attractions is the restored Windmill, now a museum. Not surprisingly, houses bordering this semi-wooded expanse (mainly mansions built by Victorian merchants) and flats with views across the Common, command the highest prices.

Town Centre/South Wimbledon

There is still a great divide in property prices between 'up the hill' (Common and the original Village) and 'down the hill' (the Broadway) which takes in the main shopping centre and station serving BR commuters and the District Line tube. But this 'lower' area, which also includes the Wimbledon Theatre (Victorian) and the famous Polka Children's Theatre, a hotel and several restaurants, is becoming increasingly fashionable.

This 'New' Wimbledon grew up around the railway in the 1850s when housing was built for those working for carriage-folk up the hill. Today, this part of Wimbledon is home to commuters keen to be within walking distance of the station with its fast trains to Waterloo.

The town centre is being redeveloped as a shopping/offices complex and there are plans to convert the Town Hall on the corner of *Queens Rd* into a speciality shopping hall/offices/parking for 770 cars. This long road has mainly solid older-type semis, 3/4-bed, with large rear gardens, and joins *Haydons Rd* to South Wimbledon. A new McCarthy & Stone scheme has 60 retirement flats with resident warden.

Running parallel, *King's Rd* contains 4-bedroomed double-fronted Edwardian houses, some facing South Park Gardens. At the junction of *Trinity Rd* and *South Park Rd, Nairn Court* (Nairn Construction) has 23 new flats with parking spaces in secluded courtyard. And the streets in this corner between *The Broadway* and *Haydons Rd* – including *Evelyn Rd* and *Ashley Rd*, which are typical – have 3-bed, terraced homes with small gardens (popular with young marrieds).

Roads off the busy *Broadway* are quiet, residential, good for first-time buyers (well-heeled ones or two buying together, that is) as many have scope for improvement. In *Pelham Rd*, *The Pelhams* (on the site of the former school playground) now has 64 1/2-bed flats. The red-brick school building itself has been converted (Laing Homes) into luxury apartments.

Across the tracks, going up *Wimbledon Hill Rd* ('The Hill') from the station, *Alwynne Rd* and *Compton Rd*, close to the library in the town centre, have solid '30s semis with gardens. Wimbledon Girls' High School is left, and right are terraced town houses. Higher left is *Draxmont Approach* (luxury balconied flats); right, *Belvedere Drive*, with large houses and the new 'Bluegates' estate.

Wimbledon is, with the various town centre developments, rapidly becoming a major Southwest London shopping and business centre. An asset – but it leads to extra traffic in nearby roads.

Wimbledon Village

The *High St* begins at the top of the Hill and runs through the Village. Quaint Dickensian shops on either side sell high fashion, pretty gifts, exotic foods and the like. There are restaurants and two historic pubs – the Rose and Crown, where the poet Swinburne drank, and the Dog & Fox; the Village riding school is at the rear. Many charming artisan cottages – lovingly renovated, expensive, no room to park – lie off *Church Rd*, *Belvedere Square* and *Lancaster Place*. Opposite, tucked behind new shops, is *Haygarth Place* (24 red-brick 4-bed terraced town houses, underground car park; plus four original cottages, modernised, with car space). Entire courtyard of red pavers. At the approach to Village, in *Belvedere Grove*, are three new 3-bed mews town houses in former car park, fronting on to rear of National Westminster Bank.

W

The Common

At the War Memorial a left turn takes you towards *Southside Common*: pretty Victorian villas facing the Common. *Southside* runs parallel to *The Ridgway* with the Common on the right; on the left, homes in the long tree-lined roads (*Lingfield*, *The Grange*, *Murray*, *Lauriston* and *Clifton*) are a mixture of styles, mostly Victorian; many reverse conversions here, with houses which had been poorly split into flats reverting to single-family homes, often still harbouring many original features.

These roads include expensive houses and cheaper older-type flats, within walking distance of King's College Boys' School. At *Woodhayes Rd* is *Peregrine Way*, left, a spacious modern development of detached Colonial-style 4-bed houses with mature trees. Opposite, across a green, the delightful old Crooked Billet and Hand in Hand pubs, surrounded by former farm labourers' cottages. Turning N towards *North View*, past Chester House (Georgian) come some 1930s houses and a cul-de-sac of council homes (some now owner-occupied). Cannizaro House has recently been converted to a luxury hotel; its famous gardens to the rear are open to public. Two 18th century mansions, The Keir and Stamford House, converted now into flats, both overlook the Common. A nearby mansion, with high walled garden, was on the market last year at around £2m. *North View*, surrounded by common and facing on to the golf course, is distinguished by tall red-brick Victorian houses. Along *Camp Rd*, *Eversley Park* (Octagon Developments) is set in a landscaped garden.

Parkside

Return to *Parkside*, which runs along the E side of the Common and leads, eventually, to Putney. With the common on your left, on the right are the enclave of premier roads (*Marryat Rd, Peek Crescent, Parkside Avenue, Parkside Gardens, Calonne Rd, Somerset Rd, Bathgate Rd* and *Burghley Rd*). To the E of this favoured group, down the hill, is the All England Tennis Club. Parkside Hospital (private) and the residence of the Apostolic Nuncio (the Pope's ambassador's official London home) are also to be found along *Parkside*. Near the Village end, an elegant new conversion of a mansion into 5 flats, with electronic gates and video-screen entrance. *Alfreton Close* is an attractive cul-de-sac of Scandinavian-style family houses in mature woodland. Opposite, in *Windmill Rd* on the site of the Clock House, a former embassy, building has started on ultra-luxurious flats. *Clockhouse Close*, nearby, built on common land, has six luxury detached family houses. On the Putney-Wimbledon border, dominated by the Argyle Estate of high-rise council flats, are Simon Lodge and Radley Lodge, good-value flats for first-time buyers.

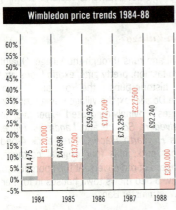

Wimbledon price trends 1984-88

Bars labelled: £41,475 | £120,000 | £47,698 | £137,500 | £59,926 | £172,500 | £73,295 | £227,500 | £92,240 | £230,000

Years: 1984 1985 1986 1987 1988

■ London average home: percentage rise on previous year, adjusted for inflation.
■ Typical home in this area, percentage rise on previous year, adjusted for inflation.

Modern terraced town house in Haygarth Place, price change compared to London-wide average home. After steep rises in '86 and '87, this example's price stood still in '88. Reasons include the stress on flats, and cheaper homes, rather than houses, last year; and perhaps the constant love in this area for older houses.

The Parkside neighbourhood includes an exotic Buddhist Temple (*Calonne Rd*), said to be the finest in Europe. Most of the houses in and around *Parkside* are large (some vast) detached turn-of-the-century family homes, secluded and expensive. These, too, have seen several instances of clumsy flat conversions being removed, and the houses returning to single-family occupation. Off *Somerset Rd* is a modern development, Oakfield Estate: Cedar Court is high density town houses and flats; Burghley House and Somerset House – tower blocks, some flats with views of the Centre Court – have lift, porterage and underground car park. All these roads suffer an annual invasion (30,000 visitors daily) during Tennis Fortnight.

Off *Burghley Rd* is St Mary's parish church (mentioned in the Domesday Book), leading into *Church Rd* and *Welford Place*, and exclusive private development of terraced town houses with indoor swimming complex, sauna and children's play area.

West Wimbledon

The Village is linked to West Wimbledon by *The Ridgway*, Wimbledon's oldest road, running parallel to *Worple Rd* (down the Hill). *Sunnyside*, to the left, has a row of delightful 2-bed cottages with long front gardens but no parking. Then *Ridgway Place*, with a group of houses on both sides built by the Haberdashers Company in 1860. Further along is a 'villagy' area comprising *Denmark Rd*, Thornton Rd and *Hillside*. There is a row of useful small shops, two pubs and livery stables here. *Berkeley Place* and *Ridgway Gardens* are cul-de-sacs with large conversion flats. *Edge Hill*, with its many flats, is popular with Roman Catholics because of nearby Wimbledon College RC Boys' School and Sacred Heart Church and Marie Reparatrice (a newly-built retreat). Work has begun on 14 flats and 2 penthouses with parking spaces on the site of the old chapel. *The Downs* has purpose-built 1930s flats either side. Lower left is *Gordon Court*, eight 2-bed, 2-bath, balconied apartments recently completed. On the site of St Teresa's Hospital, *South Ridge* has 23 4-bedroom town houses (Berkeley Homes). The Ursuline Convent School for Girls and Hazlehurst girls' school are neighbours. On corner of The Downs and *Worple Rd* is *Lantern Court*: 23 flats (garage, video entryphone, 2-bath, open fireplaces in sitting rooms). *Lansdowne Rd*, a cul-de-sac with purpose-built and conversion flats, leads to *Cumberland Close* and *Lansdowne Close*: family town houses, some with roof terraces with spectacular views. And Eve Construction are planning to build 11/12 town houses opposite the new Hospice. *Arterberry Rd* has the Norwegian school and older-type family houses with spacious gardens. There are plans for developing No 34 into flats; and No 40 *Arterberry Rd* on corner of The Ridgway, has been demolished in readiness for new flats.

W

At the Christchurch corner of *Copse Hill* is the West Side Lawn Tennis Club. Behind the club, *Ernle Rd*, *Wool Rd* and *Dunstall Rd* have 4- and 5-bedroom detached houses with big gardens, some backing on to the golf course or woodland. Off *Copse Hill* to the right, is *Rokeby Place*, detached 5-bed family houses (four years old). On the left are two newly converted Victorian mansions, Birch Lodge (10 flats) and Possil House (four maisonettes). *Cedarland Terrace* consists of five 3-storey Georgian-style town houses with wide sweeping drives and landscaped gardens, set well back from the main road. Facing the Atkinson Morley Hospital is *Thurstan Rd*. *Grange Park Place*, with detached family houses backing on to the golf course, is built on site of the old Cottage Hospital. Further on, *Drax Avenue* is a leafy private road of Sussex farmhouse-style and mock-Tudor 5-bed detached houses, some with galleried reception halls and oak staircases. One house in neighbouring *Ellerton Rd* has topped the £1½ million price mark. Leading down to *Coombe Lane*, both sides of *Copse Hill* have solid 1930s 3/4-bed semis with garages, front and rear gardens. A small development (McHawk) of 3-bed 2-bath semis with red pavers is in *Cottenham Park Rd*. From here, turn left for Raynes Park.

Raynes Park

Once, this was little more than an undervalued backwater of Edwardian cottages and purpose-built flats and maisonettes in wide, well-planned tree-lined streets. Today, it still retains a small-town atmosphere and is ripe for improvement. (Note the infallible signs: estate agents now refer to the northern side of the railway as 'West Wimbledon'.)

Worple Rd, a busy main thoroughfare with blocks of new flats and small hotels leads back to Wimbledon town centre. *Elinor Court*, Worple Rd, has 4 architect-designed flats and a penthouse. Roads off to the right have good small semis with price differentials dictated by closeness of the railway: in

Southdown Rd, the side backing on to the elevated railway is considerably cheaper than the other side. On the left, up the hill, are very desirable family houses in roads such as *Thornton Hill*, *Denmark Avenue* and *Spencer Hill*.

Hollymount School (primary, mixed) is in leafy *Cambridge Rd*, together with 3/4-bed family houses. *Amity Grove*, mainly 3-bed Edwardian bay-window cottages. South of the line, off *Kingston Rd*, are 'the apostles': 12 long parallel cul-de-sacs running down to *Bushey Rd*; an inexpensive mix of 2-bed Edwardian terraced and semi-detached, some 1930s, street parking, tiny front gardens. Never on estate agents' books for long! The 'apostles' begin at *Gore Rd* and end at *Bronson Rd*, Wimbledon Chase. Bisecting *Bushey Rd*, *Grand Drive* has inter-war 3/4-bed semi and detached family houses, many with views over Prince George's playing fields; traffic noise (main road to Morden) could be a problem. *Cannon Close*, one of several cul-de-sacs off, has 3-bed '30s semis, with front and rear gardens, street parking, and access to Common.

Wimbledon Park

Merton's main claim to residential fame is the Merton Park Estate, one of the first garden suburbs, developed in the last three decades of the 19th century. John Innes, a millionaire property developer and horticulturalist (you've used the compost) laid out the estate. The area's green appearance survives.

The earliest streets to be built, in the 1870s, were *Dorset*, *Mostyn* and *Kingswood Rds*. Later in the century, larger houses of the Arts and Crafts and other styles were added. The details are reminiscent of Bedford Park, but the styles are more mixed. So too are the scales: Innes decreed that cottages as well as solid villas be built. Development continued into Edwardian times, as the houses in *Melrose* and *Watery Rds* show. Building went on until the '30s, with the opening of the tube at Morden providing a renewed spur. In *Dorset Rd*, property values could be affected by the new relief road.

Merton Park

From Merton Park, take the main road to *Haydons Rd* to connect with Wimbledon Park. Roads N of Wimbledon Park station (District Line), such as *Melrose Avenue*, *Braemar Avenue*, *Normanton Avenue* and *Ashen Grove*, are mainly long terraces of solid 2/3-bed houses with rear gardens and street parking; these are snapped up because they are relatively cheap (bordering Wandsworth) and close to the park (tennis, golf, cricket, lake, fishing, boating and bowling). Around the station are shops and offices; *Arthur Rd*, which leads uphill to the Village, is tree-lined with very large detached houses in secluded grounds; *Camelot Close*, on the left, has 4/5-bed double-fronted Georgian-style detached houses. At *Leopold Rd/Lake Rd* is Ricards Lodge (girls' high school). Also in this corner are two good state schools, Park House middle school and Bishop Gilpin primary, which has a good record for its girls going on to the local high schools. *Vineyard Hill Rd*, *Dora Rd* and *Kenilworth Avenue* have 3/4-bed terraced family houses with street parking, high density but popular.

Among those estate agents active in this area are:
- Aylesfords
- Prudential Property
- Richard Barclay
- Hawes & Co
- Quinton Scott
- Hamptons
- Knight Frank & Rutley
- Townchoice
- G A Property Services

Further Reading

Thousands of books have been written about London, and almost as many on the business of buying and selling a home. Among the most useful are the following:

Elliott, Michael, *Heartbeat London*, Firethorn Press 1986.
A fascinating survey of London's present and future by an *Economist* writer.

Green, Shirley, *Who Owns London?* Weidenfeld & Nicholson 1986.
A contributor to the *London Property Guide*. The definitive account of the great landlords and their holdings today. Complements and updates Simon Jenkins.

Jenkins, Simon, *Landlords to London*, Constable 1975.
Historical account of the rise of the London estates and their role in shaping the city.

Jones, Edward and Woodward, Christopher, *A Guide to the Architecture of London*, Weidenfeld & Nicholson 1983.
Illustrated guide to buildings famous and obscure, with good maps.

London Research Centre, *Annual Abstract of Greater London Statistics* vol 19, 1988.

Pevsner, Nikolaus and Cherry, Bridget, *The Buildings of England*

volumes on South London and the Cities of London & Westminster, Penguin 1983 and 1973.
The 1952 volume on the rest of North London is out of print and a new edition is awaited.

Treanor, Dave, *Buying your home with other people*, Shelter, 1987.

Weinreb, Ben and Hibbert, Christopher, *The London Encyclopaedia*, Macmillan 1983.
Enormous, essential and compulsive alphabetical encyclopedia of London's places, institutions, streets and people.

Weightman, Gavin and Humphries, Steven, *The Making of Modern London*, 3 vols, Sidgwick & Jackson, 1985.
Illustrated history of London from 1815 to the present.

Consumers' Association, *Which? way to buy, sell and move house*, Hodder & Stoughton, 1987.

Wright, Diana, *A Consumer's Guide to Buying & Selling a Home*, Telegraph Publications 1987 (4th edn.).

Useful Addresses

Association of British Insurers
Aldermary House
Queen Street
EC4N 1TU

Tel: 248 4477
A trade association of insurance companies which gives general advice on insurance.

British Association of Removers
279 Grays Inn Road
WC1X 8SY
Tel: 837 3088

British Insurance Brokers' Association
10 Bevis Marks
EC3
Tel: 623 9043

Building Employer's Confederation
82 New Cavendish Street
W1M 8AD
Tel: 580 5588
Operates a guarantee scheme for
building work and will supply list of
local members whose work will be
covered under the scheme.

Building Centre
26 Store Street
WC1E 7BT
Enquiries Tel: Winkfield Row 88 4999
Advice on all aspects of building.

Building Societies Association
3 Saville Row
W1X 1AF
Tel: 437 0655
Advice and information on
mortgages.

Civic Trust
17 Carlton House Terrace
SW1Y 5AW
Tel: 930 0914
An environmental group which
encourages the improvement of the
built environment. Keeps a register of
London's 80 or so local amenity
societies.

Confederation for Registration of Gas
Installers
PO Box 110,
Pinner
Tel: 840 0046

Council for Licensed Conveyancers
Golden Cross House
Duncannon Street
WC2N 4JF
Tel: 210 4604
A statutory body issuing licenses to
conveyancers, upholding standards of
competence and conduct. Issues a
list of licensed conveyancers.

Crown Estate Commissioners
13 Carlton House Terrace
SW1
Tel: 210 3000

Federation of Master Builders
33 John Street
WC1 N2BB
Tel: 242 7583
Keep a register of reputable builders
and give a two-year guarantee on the
work of members on their warranty
register.

First Time Buyers' Advisory Service
18 Seymour Place
W1H 5WH
Tel: 723 6001
A commercial concern that offers a
package deal to first-time buyers.

Georgian Group
37 Spital Square
London E1
Tel: 377 1722
A national society for conserving
Georgian architecture.

Glass and Glazing Federation
44-48 Borough High Street
SE1 1XB
Tel: 403 7177
Gives information on all kinds of
glazing.

Heating and Ventilating Contractors
Association
ESCA House
34 Palace Court
W2 4JG
Tel: 229 2488

Incorporated Society of Valuers and Auctioneers
3 Cadogan Gate
SW1X 0AS
Tel: 235 2282
Members practice as estate agents, surveyors and valuers in the private and public sectors of the housing industry and commerce.

Law Society
113 Chancery Lane
WC2A 1PL
Tel: 242 1222
Advice on solicitors and conveyancing.

London Docklands Development Corporation
West India House
E14
Tel: 515 3000

London Regional Transport
55 Broadway
SW1H 0BD
222 5600
For information call: 222 1234

National Association of Estate Agents
Arbon House
21 Jury St
Warwick CV34 4EH
Tel: (0926) 496800

National Association of Plumbing, Heating and Mechanical Services Contractors
6 Gate Street
WC2A 3HX
Will supply a list of members who provide advice and carry out work.
Tel: 405 2678

National Federation of Roofing Contractors
24 Weymouth St
W1
Tel: 436 0387
Represents contractors dealing in all forms of roof coverings.

National House Building Council
58 Portland Place
W1N 4BU
Tel: Amersham 434477
A consumer protection organisation which sets building specification standards for new homes and offers a 10 year warranty scheme.

National Inspection Council of Electrical Installation Contractors
37 Albert Embankment
SE1 7UJ
Tel: 735 1322
A consumer safety organisation which publishes a roll of approved electrical contractors.

Royal Institute of British Architects
66 Portland Place
W1N 4AD
Tel: 580 5533
RIBA's Clients' Advisory Service will supply information on architects and their services and can list relevant members working in your area.

Royal Institution of Chartered Surveyors
12 Great George Street
Parliament Square
SW1P 3AD
Tel: 222 7000
Members practise as estate agents, surveyors and valuers. They include chartered building surveyors who will advise on all aspects of extensions and improvements.

Town and Country Planning Association
17 Carlton House Terrace
SW1
Tel: 930 8903

Victorian Society
1 Priory Gardens
W4 1TT
Tel: 994 1019
Conservation of Victorian buildings

B

C

C

E

Florence St, Hendon *368*
Florence St, Islington *385*
Florida Rd *600*
Flower Lane *370*
Fontaine Rd *562, 570*
Fontenoy Rd *155*
Fonthill Rd *577*
Forburg Rd *562*
Ford Square *558*
Fordwych Rd *595*
Forest Lane *467*
Forest Drive East *434*
Forest Drive West *434*
Forest Hill East *324*
Forest Rd *434*
Formosa St *438*
Fortis Green *317*
Fortismere Avenue *460*
Fortune Green *594*
Fortune Green Rd *594*
Fouberts Place *529*
Foulden Rd *563*
Foulser Rd *158*
Fountain Mews *388*
Fountain Rd *159*
Fournier St *556*
Fox Hill *271*
Fox Hill Rd *271*
Foxham Rd *411*
Framfield Rd *303*
Francis Chichester Way *168*
Francis Rd *435*
Franciscan Rd *158*
Frank Dixon Way *298*
Free Trade Wharf *282*
Fremantle St *590*
Fremont St *346*
Frere St *172*
Freshwater Rd *158, 567*
Frewin Rd *585*
Friars Lane *516*
Friars Mead *290*
Friary Rd *484, 151*
Friem Barnet *580*
Friend St *256*
Friendly St *429, 463*
Friern Barnet Lane *318, 580*
Friern Barnet Rd *580*
Friern Rd *298, 299*
Frith St *530*
Frobisher Rd *575*
Frogmore *582, 584*
Frognal *357, 359*
Frognal Gardens *357*
Fulham *332*
Fulham Palace Gardens *330*
Fulham Palace Rd *328, 330, 332, 350, 351, 354*
Fulham Park Gardens *332*
Fulham High St *332*
Fulham Rd *228, 231, 328, 331, 332, 535-537, 541, 542*
Fullerton Rd *582, 583*
Fulthorp Rd *342*
Furlong Rd *389*
Furzedown *158, 567*
Gabriel St *324*

Gainsborough Gardens, Golders Green *336*
Gainsborough Gardens, Hampstead *357*
Gainsborough Rd *319, 415*
Gainsford St *284*
Galveston Rd *503*
Galway Rd *254*
Gard St *254*
Garfield Rd *169*
Garford St *496*
Garrad's Rd *568*
Garratt Lane *159, 160, 308-310, 314, 582, 583*
Garratt Terrace *159*
Garrick Close *516*
Garrick St *532*
Garth Rd *262*
Gartmoor Gardens *311*
Gaspar Mews *539*
Gatestone Rd *598*
Gauden Rd *249, 395*
Gawber St *191*
Gayton Rd *357*
Gee St *254*
Geldeston Rd *562*
Genoa Avenue *506, 507*
George St *516*
Georgia Rd *600*
Georgiana St *219*
Gerald Rd *188*
Geraldine Rd *583*
Gerrard St *528*
Gertrude St *231*
Gibson Square *386*
Gibsons Hill *600*
Gilbert Rd *392*
Gilbert St *449*
Gillespie Rd *383, 388, 577*
Gillingham Rd *263*
Gilmore Rd *429*
Gilston Rd *541, 542*
Gipsy Hill *598*
Gipsy Rd *598*
Giraud St *495*
Girdwood Rd *311*
Gladsmuir Rd *375, 412*
Gladstone Park Gardens *294*
Gladstone Park *264*
Gladys Rd *595*
Glasslyn Rd *266*
Glebe Place *227*
Glebe Rd *163*
Gledhow Gardens *539*
Gledstanes Rd *350, 351*
Glenarm Rd *345*
Glenburnie Rd *160*
Gleneagle Rd *570*
Gleneldon Rd *570*
Glenfarg Rd *431*
Glengall Bridge *290*
Glengall Place *288*
Glengall Rd, Kilburn *419*
Glengall Rd, Peckham *484*
Glenilla Rd *360*
Glenloch Rd *360*
Glenmore Rd *360*

Glennie Rd *599*
Glenrosa St *333*
Glenthorne Rd *352*
Glenwood Rd *370*
Globe Rd *191, 556*
Globe Wharf *286*
Globe Rd *556*
Gloucester Avenue *552*
Gloucester Drive *576*
Gloucester Gate *512*
Gloucester Mews *177*
Gloucester Rd *400, 401, 539*
Gloucester Square *180*
Gloucester St *489, 490*
Gloucester Terrace *177, 178*
Gloucester Walk *398*
Gloucester Way *255*
Godfrey St *232*
Godolphin Rd *523*
Golborne *478*
Golborne Rd *473, 478, 479*
Golden Square *529*
Golden Yard *357*
Golders Green *335*
Golders Green Rd *335-337*
Golders Hill Park *335*
Goldhawk Rd *349, 352, 353, 453, 523* **G**
Goldhurst Terrace *595*
Goldsmith Avenue *150*
Gondar Gardens *594*
Goose Green *485, 299*
Gordon Place *398*
Gore Rd, Hackney *346*
Gore Rd, Raynes Park *610*
Gorst Rd *172*
Goswell Rd *252, 254, 255*
Gough St *256*
Gower Mews *197*
Gower St *194, 196*
Gowrie Rd *169*
Graemsdyke Avenue *416*
Grafton Crescent *221, 410*
Grafton Square *247*
Graham Rd *345*
Graham St *189*
Granard Avenue *506*
Grand Avenue *460*
Grand Drive *610*
Grand Parade *574*
Grand Walk *556*
Grange Avenue 579
Grange Grove *386*
Grange Park Place *609*
Grange Rd *602*
Grange, The *607*
Grange Walk *591*
Grangecourt Rd *561*
Grantley St *556*
Grantully Rd *440*
Granville Rd, Cricklewood *262*
Granville Rd, Stroud Green *268*
Granville Rd, Southfields *311, 313*
Grasmere Rd *459*
Gravenel Gardens *159*
Graveney Rd *160*
Gray's Inn Rd *195, 196, 198*

Hatherley Rd *415*
Hatton Garden *258*
Haven Green *304*
Haven Lane *304*
Haverhill *155*
Havering St *557*
Haverstock Hill *359, 360*
Havil St *162*
Hawgood St *202*
Hawgood St *496*
Hawkley Gardens *599*
Hawley Crescent *218*
Hawley Rd *221*
Hay Currie St *495*
Hay Hill *451*
Haycroft Rd *207*
Haydons Rd *606, 610*
Haygarth Place *607*
Hays Mews *451*
Hayter Rd *207*
Hazelbank Rd *431*
Hazeldene Rd *237*
Hazelwood Avenue *455*
Hazlehurst Rd *159*
Hazlewell Rd *506, 507*
Healey St *221, 410*
Heath Close *362*
Heath Drive *358*
Heath Rd *519*
Heath St *357*
Heathfield Rd *309, 584*
Heathfield Terrace *235*
Heathfield Gardens *584*
Heathland Rd *561*
Heathview Gardens *504*
Heathville Rd *267*
Heaver *157*
Hebdon Rd *159*
Helena Rd *305*
Helens Gardens *479*
Helenslea Avenue *336*
Helix Gardens *207*
Helmet Row *254*
Hemstal Rd *595*
Henderson Rd *585*
Hendham Rd *586*
Hendon *368*
Hendon Avenue *320*
Hendon Lane *316, 319*
Hendon Way *260-262,335,336, 367*
Hendon Way *261*
Henniker Gardens *470*
Henrietta St *532*
Henry Jackson Rd *501*
Heralds Place *392*
Herbal Hill *256*
Herbert Crescent *424*
Hercules St *589*
Hereford Rd *176*
Hereford Square *539*
Hereford Mews *176*
Herlwyn Gardens *159*
Hermitage Basin *280*
Hermitage Court *280*
Hermitage Lane *261, 262*
Hermitage Rd, Norwood *598*

Hermitage Rd, Tottenham *574*
Herne Hill *209, 210, 211, 299*
Herne Hill Rd *210*
Heron Quays *290*
Heron Quays *288*
Herondale Avenue *585*
Hertford Avenue *416*
Hertford Rd, Finchley *317*
Hertford Rd, Islington *388*
Hertford St *452*
Hesketh Place *477*
Hessel Rd *304*
Hetley Rd *523*
Hewer St *480*
Hewitt Rd *575*
Heybridge Avenue *570*
Heyward Gardens *506*
High St, Penge *271, 272*
High Rd, North Finchley *316-260*
High Rd, Tottenham *572-575*
High Rd, Wood Green *460*
High St, Acton *149, 150*
High St, Aldgate *557*
High St, Kensington *377, 378, 381, 397, 400-407*
High St, Battersea *172, 173*
High St, Camden *218, 221*
High St, Clapham *246, 248*
High St, Deptford *463*
High St, Ealing *301*
High St, Hampstead *357*
High St, Highgate *373*
High St, Hornsey *267*
High St, Islington *384, 385*
High St, Kingsland *345, 347, 560, 564*
High St, Lewisham *429, 430*
High St, Mill Hill *369*
High St, Mortlake *165*
High St, Northfields *304*
High St, Norwood *598*
High St, Barnes *164*
High St, Peckham *483, 484*
High St, Poplar *494, 495*
High St, Putney *498, 499, 501-435*
High Rd, Whetstone *579, 580*
High St, Shoreditch *191, 192*
High St, St John's Wood *513*
High St, Walthamstow *433*
High Rd, Leytonstone *435, 467*
High St, Wapping *280, 281*
High Holborn *530*
High St, Wimbledon *607*
High Rd, Balham *154-157*
High Rd, Chiswick *184, 234-236, 239*
High Rd, East Finchley *317, 316, 460*
High St, Southgate *546*
High Rd, Kilburn *418*
High Rd, Leyton *434*
High St, Camden *219*
High St, North *470*
High St, Manor Park *468*
High St, Colliers Wood *456*
High St, South *470*
High St, Borough *589*

High St, Manor Park *468*
High St, Streatham *568*
High St, Borough *589*
High St, Thornton Heath *600*
High St, Stoke Newington *562, 563*
Higham Hill *434*
Higham Rd *574*
Highbury *387*
Highbury Crescent *387*
Highbury Grange *388*
Highbury Grove *387*
Highbury Hill *387, 388*
Highbury New Park *388*
Highbury Park *387, 388*
Highbury Place *387*
Highbury Terrace *387*
Highbury Terrace Mews *387*
Highclere St *273*
Highfield Avenue *336*
Highfield Gardens *336*
Highfields Grove *373*
Highgate Rd *409, 410*
Highgate *312*
Highgate Village *373*
Highgate West Hill *372*
Highland Rd *598*
Highlands Heath *498*
Highlever Rd *479, 480*
Highshore Rd *484*
Highway, The *496, 555*
Highway, The, Wapping *282*
Highwood Hill *370*
Hill Crescent *579*
Hill Farm Rd *480*
Hill St, Mayfair *451*
Hill Top *364*
Hillbury Rd *157*
Hillcrest Rd *305*
Hillcross Avenue *454*
Hillfield Avenue *267*
Hillfield Rd *594*
Hillgate Place *398*
HillierRd *171*
Hillmarton Rd *412*
Hillside *609*
Hillside Rd *569*
Hillsleigh Rd *337*
Hilltop Rd *595*
Hindrey Rd *345*
Hippodrome Mews *381, 477*
Hithe Point *287*
Hitherfield *569*
Hobbs Court *285*
Hobday St *495*
Hobury St *231*
Hocroft Avenue *261*
Hocrott Rd *261*
Hodford Rd *335, 336*
Hoe St *433*
Hofland Rd *353*
Hogan Mews *438*
Hogarth Mews *292*
Hogarth Rd *540*
Holborn Circus *258*
Holborn Rd *469*
Holcombe Hill *370*

L

M

R

Southern St *198*
Southfields *310*
Southgate Rd *385*
Southgate St *388*
Southgate Grove *388*
Southgate *545*
Southgate Circus *546*
Southmead Rd *312*
Southover *319*
Southside Common *607*
Southwark Park Rd *590*
Southway, Hampstead *364, 365*
Southway, Totteridge *597*
Southwood Lawn Rd *373*
Sovereign Court *282*
Spanby Rd *202*
Spaniards Rd *357*
Spelman St *558*
Spencer Rd *585*
Spencer St *256*
Spencer Walk *502*
Spencer Hill *610*
Spencer Park *584*
Spencer Close *365*
Spitalfields *243*
Sprimont Place *232*
Spring Hill *347*
Springalls Wharf *285*
Springdale Rd *563*
Springfield Lane *418*
Springwell Avenue *604*
Squires Lane *318*
St Ann's Crescent *583*
St Ann's Gardens *410*
St Ann's Hill, Earlsfield *310*
St Ann's Rd *573, 574*
St Ann's Villas *380, 477*
St Aubyn's Rd *271*
St Augustines Rd *220, 412*
St Charles Square *480*
St Elmo Rd *523*
St Paul's Way *202, 495*
St Ervan's Rd *479*
St George's Rd, Golders Green *337*
St George's Rd, Kennington *392*
St George's Rd, Richmond *517*
St George's Rd, Twickenham *519*
St George's Square *282*
St George's Terrace *553*
St Gerards Close *250*
St Giles Rd *215*
St Helen's Gardens *479, 480*
St Helena Terrace *516*
St Hilda's Wharf *281*
St Mary's Grove, Islington *386*
St James St *433*
St James's *452*
St James's Close *156*
St James's Drive *156*
St James's Gardens *377, 380*
St James's Place *452*
St James's Square *452*
St James's Terrace *513*
St James's Walk *257*
St John St *254-257*
St John's Avenue *504, 507*
St Leonards *416*

St John's Crescent *209*
St John's Gate *204*
St John's Hill *170*
St John's Hill Grove *170*
St John's Lane *257, 258*
St John's Rd *170*
St John's Vale, New Cross *40L*
St John's Way *412*
St John's Wharf *281*
St John's Wood High St *551, 552*
St John's Wood Park *552*
St John's Wood Rd *550, 594*
St Johns *429*
St Johns Rd *337*
St Johns Wood Terrace *551*
St Julian's Farm Rd *599*
St Katharine's Dock *278, 279*
St Lawrence Terrace *481*
St John's Vale, Lewisham *429*
St Leonard's St *202*
St Leonard's Terrace *226*
St Leonards Rd *416*
St Kilda's Rd *561*
St Luke's Avenue *248*
St Luke's Gardens *232*
St Margarets *518*
St Margarets Grove *519*
St Margarets Rd, Ealing *302*
St Margarets Rd, Twick. *518, 519*
St Margarets St *517*
St Luke's Street *232*
St Mark's Crescent *552*
St Mark's Square *513*
St Martin's Close *219*
St James's Rd *157*
St Martin's Rd *395*
St Mary Abbots Terrace *379*
St Mary's Grove, Richmond *517*
St Marks Rd *302*
St Mary's Rd, Ealing *305*
St Mary's Rd, Nunhead *486*
St Maur Rd *332*
St Michael St *178*
St Michael's *395*
St Michael's Gardens *481*
St Olafs Rd *332*
St Mary's Terrace *438*
St Pancras *195*
St Pancras Rd *197*
St Paul's Crescent *220-221*
St George's Square *489*
St Paul's Place *564*
St Paul's St *385*
St Pauls Avenue *603*
St Pancras Way *219, 222*
St Pauls Place *386*
St Pauls Rd *386*
St Peters Rd *519*
St Petersburg Place *176*
St Philip's Square *168*
St Philip's St *168*
St Quintin Avenue *480*
St Peter's Square *352*
St Quintin Estate *479*
St Saviour's Dock *284*
St Simons Avenue *506*
St Ann's Hill, Wandsworth *583*

St Stephens *305*
St Stephens Avenue, Ealing *305*
St Stephens Crescent *179*
St Saviour's Wharf *284*
St Stephens Gardens *179, 518*
St Thomas's Gardens *410*
St Thomas's Rd *577*
St Agnes Place *395*
St Stephens Rd, Ealing *305*
St Alban's Grove *402*
St Albans Avenue *185*
St Andrew's Place *512*
St Stephens Avenue, Shepherds
Bush *523*
St Andrew's Square *476*
St Andrews Grove *561*
St Stephens St *179*
St Andrews Rd *151*
St George's Square Mews *489*
St James's Drive *585, 586*
St George's Square Mews *489*
St Paul's Mews *221*
St Margarets Drive *519*
St Paul's Rd, Thornton Heath *600*
St Paul's Rd, Islington *387*
St Georges Circus *589*
St Thomas St *589*
St Alban's Rd *409*
St Giles's High St *530*
St Thomas St *589*
Stafford Terrace *407*
Stag Lane *367*
Staines Rd *517*
Stamford Hill *561-491, 573*
Stamford Brook Avenue *235*
Stanbridge Rd *501*
Standen Rd *314*
Stanford Rd *402*
Stanhope Avenue *320*
Stanhope Gardens *538*
Stanhope Rd *374*
Stanlake Rd *524*
Stanley Crescent *475*
Stanley Rd *415, 416*
Stanley Grove *168*
Stanmore Gardens *415*
Stannary St *392*
Stanstead Rd *323, 324, 325, 431*
Star Rd *350*
Star St *178*
Starcross St *222*
Station Approach *414, 415*
Station Parade *415, 603*
Station Rd, Barnes *162, 163, 164*
Station Rd, Hendon *369*
Station Rd, Wood Green *460*
Station Terrace *420*
Staveley Rd *237*
Steel Rd *574*
Steeles Rd *360*
Steep Hill *568*
Stephendale Rd *333*
Stepney *556*
Stepney Way *556*
Stepney Green *556*
Stevenage Rd *327,330*
Stillingfleet *163*

S

V